THE

unix

DESK REFERENCE

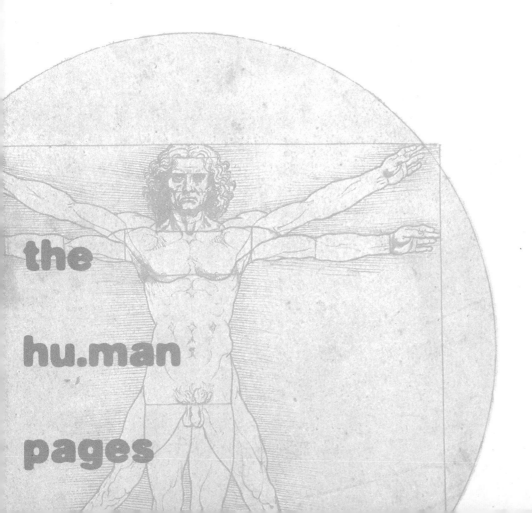

the

hu.man

pages

THE unix DESK REFERENCE

Peter Dyson

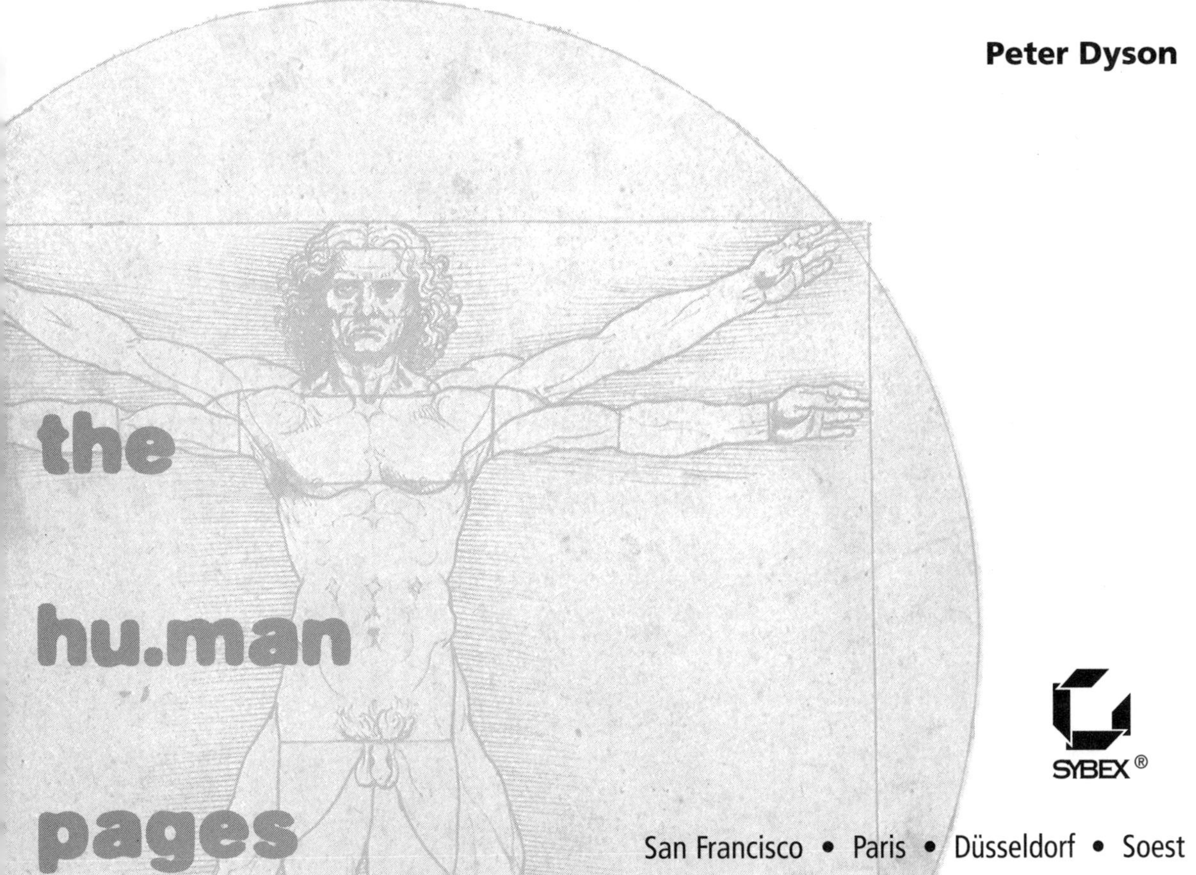

SYBEX®

San Francisco • Paris • Düsseldorf • Soest

Associate Publisher: Gary Masters
Acquisitions Manager: Kristine Plachy
Developmental Editor: John Read
Editor: Nancy Crumpton
Project Editor: Brenda Frink
Technical Editor: Raymond John Felton
Book Designer: Daniel Ziegler
Line Art: Cătălin Dulfu
Desktop Publisher: Ziegler Design
Production Coordinator: Nathan Johanson
Cover Designer: Archer Design

Library of Congress Card Number: 96-67500
ISBN: 0-7821-1658-2

Manufactured in the United States of America

10 9 8 7 6 5 4 3 2 1

For Tom, Unix guru extraordinaire

Acknowledgments

Although this book is already much too long, I must take this opportunity to thank those people without whose help the book would never have been written.

At SYBEX, thanks to Gary Masters, then developmental editor and now associate publisher; John Read, developmental editor; and Kristine Plachy, acquisitions manager, for their help in guiding the book through the early stages.

The editorial team of Nancy Crumpton, copy editor; Ray Felton, technical editor; and Brenda Frink, project editor, brought a wealth of Unix experience to the task and did an outstanding job. The production team of Dan Ziegler and Nathan Johanson rose to the many odd typographical challenges that Unix has to offer. Another thank you to Dan Ziegler and also to Cătălin Dulfu for the sympathetic design of the book.

Thanks to the many people in the Unix community and in the USENET newsgroups who answered my questions or who offered an opinion or an insight into a particularly vexing or controversial element of Unix.

And, as always, thanks to Nancy.

Introduction

Unix is the fastest growing and most universal multiuser operating system in use today. It is found everywhere from desktops to university systems to large corporations. Many hardware and software companies have developed their own versions of Unix. In addition to the main AT&T and Berkeley Unix family members, these versions include Solaris from Sun, IBM's AIX, Open Desktop and UnixWare from SCO, and HP-UX from Hewlett-Packard. You will find versions of Unix running on everything from a workstation all the way up to a Cray supercomputer. There are also several very popular free versions of Unix that run on Intel-based computers, such as FreeBSD and Linux. Unix has a reputation for being difficult to use, for being a programmer's system; this book changes all that by presenting the Unix world in an easy-to-understand reference format.

Who Should Use This Book

This book was written for all the Unix users who want to master the complexities of the operating system—writers and teachers, students and academic researchers, users and administrators in the corporate world—all of whom need a quick but authoritative reference. All sorts of users, from those on large commercial systems to those running Linux on their PCs at home or in their home offices, will find this book to be an essential reference.

Jargon certainly has its place; it is a kind of shorthand, but it can rapidly become incomprehensible, even to the most seasoned Unix user. You don't have to be a Unix guru to understand the definitions in this book, because I have gone out of my way to write the entries in clear, concise, everyday English.

What You Will Find in This Book

This book describes Unix commands, utilities, and concepts in easy-to-understand language. The usual terse Unix programmer's format is not used; entries are written in an approachable and conversational style.

You will find entries in this book that you will not find in the standard Unix books, including information on the X Window system, the Free Software Foundation's GNU project programs, the Internet, and the very popular free (or almost free) versions of Unix such as Linux and FreeBSD. Here's a brief overview of the 2,000 or so topics that this book covers:

- Communications commands
- Comparison commands
- File and directory management commands
- GNU and Free Software Foundation programs
- Internet access programs
- Internet concepts
- Mail and networking terms
- Miscellaneous commands
- Printing commands
- Searching commands
- Security and administrative concepts
- System status commands
- Software development commands
- Text processing and formatting commands
- TCP/IP commands
- Unix concepts
- Unix shells
- Unix slang
- X Window concepts
- X Window programs

This book also contains two appendices. Appendix 1 contains a Unix and DOS Command Comparison for those users migrating to Unix from the DOS world. Appendix 2 contains ASCII tables in the decimal, hexadecimal, and octal numbering systems: essential information you won't find anywhere else.

Two Books for the Price of One

This book is really two books in one: a complete Unix command reference, as well as a dictionary of Unix terms and concepts. It is faster and easier to use than the Unix `man` pages and covers all the major commercial implementations, including System V Release 4.2, BSD, Solaris, UnixWare, AIX, HP-UX, and SCO Open Desktop.

You will also find plenty of information on the free versions of Unix, including FreeBSD, NetBSD, and Linux, and the GNU Project programs from the Free Software Foundation, along with plenty of Internet information to help you access the Internet and use Unix commands quickly and easily.

Some of the entries in the book are short and to the point, while others are longer and broader in scope. I cover all the major Unix utilities from **awk** to **yacc**, as well as important Unix concepts from absolute pathname to Zsh. In taking this dual approach, I have found that I can avoid unnecessary repetition of material by placing information in a separate definition.

There is still disagreement over how certain Unix terms should be presented; is it *i-node* or *inode, path name* or *pathname*? I am not interested in presenting one as the correct nomenclature and the other as an error; I have simply tried to be consistent. In cases in which more than one usage is generally accepted, I have included both in the description. You can decide which one you want to use.

How This Book Is Organized

This book is very easy to use. Entries are in alphabetical order, and characters such as hyphens or leading periods and the / in a directory name are ignored. Symbols with a special meaning in Unix are listed at the beginning of the book in ASCII order, and numerical entries are placed in order as though the numbers were spelled out in full; *10/100* comes after *temporary directories,* and *4.4BSD Lite* comes after *fork.*

Using the Dictionary Entries

For the dictionary entries, you will find information presented in the same consistent way:

- Entry names are presented in alphabetical order, letter by letter.
- Abbreviations and acronyms are given, where appropriate.
- Pronunciation is given in those cases where it isn't obvious.
- Definitions of the terms or expressions are provided.
- Cross-references are given at the end of an entry and are of two types. A *See* reference indicates the entry where you will find the information; this is used for many of the abbreviations. *See also* indicates other entries that provide additional or related information on the topic.

Using the Command-Reference Entries

For the command-reference entries, you will find:

- Command names are presented in alphabetical order, letter by letter.
- A brief introduction to the command is provided.
- The command syntax is shown.
- Details of command arguments and options are included.
- Examples are provided only where it makes sense to give examples; you will not see examples of interactive commands or commands that create system-specific output.
- Notes that draw your attention to peculiarities of the command or any potentially damaging effects of using the command are included.

If a command appears only in one specific version of Unix, this is indicated in the introduction to the command. You will find references to SVR4 (System V Release 4.2), BSD (usually 4.4BSD), SCO (SCO UNIX and Open Desktop), Solaris, SunOS, HP-UX, UnixWare, and AIX, where appropriate.

A Note on the Fonts

Throughout this book you will find information presented in different type styles. Here's a quick look at what the different fonts mean:

`program font`	Used for directories, filenames, commands, options, arguments, and the output from commands.
`bold program font`	Used in examples to indicate text that the user should type.
`italic program font`	Used to indicate generic options and arguments that should be replaced by user-supplied values.
`[ ]`	Square brackets are used to indicate optional elements in a syntax description; you don't type the brackets.
`...`	An ellipsis indicates that the optional element in a syntax description can be repeated as many times as you like. You will find this often applies to commands that accept one or more filenames as their input.

	Any mutually exclusive arguments or options are indicated in the syntax description by a separating vertical bar.
Ctrl-	Starts a control character. To type Ctrl-D, press and hold down the Ctrl key as you also press d or D. Control characters are not case sensitive; you will find that they are shown in uppercase throughout this book for the sake of clarity.

In some cases, a command-line syntax, an Internet URL, or a command example was just too long to fit on one line, and so I have occasionally had to use two lines: the ➥ symbol indicates that the line continues on the following line. This means that you can just type what you see, there are no hyphens to trick you.

And Finally...

Everyone who has worked on the UNIX Desk Reference has tried very hard to make it as complete and as accurate as possible, but if you think we have missed a word or two that you would like to see included in a future edition, please write to this address:

The UNIX Desk Reference
c/o SYBEX, Inc.
2021 Challenger Drive
Alameda, CA 94501
U.S.A.

!

■ *See* **exclamation point.**

!!

■ *See* **history substitution.**

#

■ *See* **pound sign.**

#!

■ *See* **C shell.**

$

■ *See* **dollar sign.**

%

■ *See* **percent sign.**

&

■ *See* **ampersand.**

&&

■ *See* **ampersand.**

`

■ *See* **backquote.**

()

■ *See* **parentheses.**

*

■ *See* **asterisk.**

+

■ *See* **plus sign.**

.

■ *See* **dot.**

..

■ *See* **dot dot.**

/

■ *See* **slash.**

:

■ *See* **colon.**

;

■ *See* **semicolon.**

<

■ *See* **less than symbol.**

>

■ *See* **greater than symbol.**

?

■ *See* **question mark.**

@

■ *See* **at sign.**

[]

■ *See* **square brackets.**

****

■ *See* **backslash.**

^

■ *See* **caret symbol.**

'

■ *See* **single quote.**

|

■ *See* **vertical bar.**

{}

■ *See* **braces.**

~

■ *See* **tilde.**

THE unix DESK REFERENCE

A

ABI

Abbreviation for Application Binary Interface. A specification that aims to ensure binary compatibility between applications running on the same family of processors or CPUs using Unix System V Release 4.

Applications developed using ABI can run on hardware from different manufacturers without the need for recompilation; any system calls needed for specific hardware are maintained in libraries.

The specification was originally developed by AT&T and Sun Microsystems and includes a test and verification suite used to determine if a system complies with the standard.

absolute pathname

A pathname that starts with the root directory (/) and specifies the full name of every directory to the actual file. An absolute pathname locates a file with no reference to the current working directory and always refers to the same file no matter where you are in the filesystem.

■ *See also* **relative pathname.**

access

To use, write to, or read from a file, or to log in to a computer system or network.

access permission

An operating system permission that explicitly controls whether you can execute, read from, or write to a file.

account

On a local area network or multiuser operating system, an account is set up for each user. Before you can use Unix, your *system* administrator must establish an account and a user identifier for you.

Accounts were originally maintained for security or administrative reasons, although in some systems, particularly in online services, they are used as a method of identifying a user for billing purposes.

Your account keeps track of certain system resources, such as disk space.

■ *See also* **user, username.**

acct

An SVR4 command used by the system administrator to turn system accounting on or off.

ACK

Abbreviation for acknowledgment. In communications, a control code, ASCII 06, sent by the receiving computer to indicate that data has been received without error and that the next part of the transmission may be sent.

See also **NAK.**

active window

In a GUI capable of displaying more than one window on the screen at a time, the active window is the window that contains the cursor. Only one window is usually active at any one time.

See also **focus.**

adb

The oldest of the Unix debuggers, `adb` is a general-purpose debugger, used to examine executable files and provide a controlled environment within which the programmer can examine the program as it executes. Extensive discussion of `adb` is beyond the scope of this book; see the `man` pages on your system for more details.

See also **gdb, sdb.**

addftinfo

A command included with 4.4BSD that adds information to `troff` font files for use with `groff`, the Free Software Foundation (FSF) document formatting system.

▶ Syntax

The syntax for `addftinfo` is:

```
addftinfo [-value...] res
➥ unitwidth font
```

`addftinfo` reads a `troff` font file and adds additional information that will be used by `groff`.

▶ Options and Arguments

The `addftinfo` *`res`* and *`unitwidth`* arguments are the same as the corresponding items in the device description file for the printer or output device; *`filename`* is the name of the file describing the font. If the filename ends in I, the font is italic.

The `addftinfo` options are shown in Table A.1.

Table A.1: Options to Use with `addftinfo`

OPTION	DESCRIPTION
x-height	The height of lowercase letters without ascenders.
fig-height	The height of numbers.
asc-height	The height of letters with ascenders.
body-height	The height of characters such as parentheses.
cap-height	The height of uppercase letters.
comma-depth	The depth of a comma.
desc-depth	The depth of characters with descenders.
body-depth	The depth of characters such as parentheses.

adding a new user

One of the essential tasks a system administrator must be able to tackle is that of adding a new user to the system. Some systems, such as SCO and HP-UX, have special applications that automate this process, while on other systems it is more of a manual process using `adduser` or `useradd`. See your `man` pages for more information.

A new user needs more than a login name to be able to access the system. A user must also have the necessary files, directories, and permissions, as well as a password and a home directory.

To add a new user, follow these steps (which must be performed with superuser privileges):

1. Add an entry for the new user in `/etc/passwd`.
2. Create a password for the new account.
3. Create a home directory for the new account with `mkdir`, and change the ownership to that of the new user with `chown`.
4. Add any dot files to the new home directory, and make sure to change the ownership of these files to that of the new account. Users of the C shell will need `.login` and `.cshrc`; Bourne shell users will need `.profile`, and Korn shell users will need `.kshrc`. Default versions of many of these files are usually maintained by the system administrator for this very purpose.

■ *See also* **deleting a user, `passwd`.**

address

- The precise location in memory or on disk where a specific piece of information is stored. Every byte in memory and every sector on a disk has its own unique address.
- To reference or manage a storage location.
- The destination of an e-mail message.
- An IP address as specified in the `/etc/hosts` file.

■ See also **bang path, domain address, e-mail address, Ethernet address, Internet address, IP address, `uucp` network address.**

admin

■ *See* **SCCS.**

afmtodit

A command provided with BSD that creates font files for use with `groff`. `afmtodit` is written in `perl`; you must have `perl` version 3 installed to be able to run this command. Creating a font file is a specialized task that is unfortunately beyond the scope of this book; see the `man` pages for more information.

AFS

Abbreviation for Andrews File System. A protocol developed at Carnegie Mellon University used to share remote files across systems using TCP/IP.

AFS has certain advantages over NFS in that it only allows users to access files linked to AFS rather than giving access to all files, it has a built-in cache that helps to reduce the demands made on the system, and *system administrators* can allocate disk space on the fly as required.

AIX

Acronym for Advanced Interactive Executive. A version of Unix from IBM that runs on its RISC/6000 workstations and on minicomputers and mainframes.

Although AIX is derived from System V Release 3, it contains many of the features available in System V Release 4, is POSIX-compliant, and meets the Trusted Computer Base (TCB) Level C2 security.

One of the major enhancements AIX offers is Visual Systems Management (VSM), a graphical interface into the older System Management Interface Tool (SMIT). VSM contains four main elements: Print Manager, Device Manager, Storage Manager, and Users and Groups Manager.

alias

A built-in command in the Korn and C shells that lets you define new commands. In this way, an alias becomes an alternative name for a script, program, or command.

There are three reasons to use an alias:

- To reduce the amount of typing that you do. If you are in the habit of always using a command with the same options, you can create a one-character alias and use that instead.
- To automate a complex procedure you use only infrequently and find difficult to remember.
- To avoid long path searches. A command starts up more quickly when it is aliased to its full pathname.

The syntax you use for this command depends on which shell you use.

▶ Korn Shell Syntax

In the Korn shell, the syntax is:

```
alias[options]
➥[name[=`command`]]
```

which assigns a shorthand ***name*** to ***command***. If you leave out =`***command***`, you can print the alias for ***name***, and if you leave out ***name***, you can print all the aliases. In the Korn shell, `alias` has two options, as Table A.2 shows.

If you use the `ls` command with the `-alt` options in the Korn shell, you can alias this to a single letter by typing:

```
alias l='ls -alt'
```

Now you can just type **`l`** when you want to see a long directory listing showing all files sorted by the time they were last modified.

▶ C Shell Syntax

The `alias` syntax in the C shell is even easier to remember:

```
alias [name][command]
```

where ***name*** is the shorthand name or alias you want to use with ***command***. As in the Korn shell, if you leave out ***command***, `alias` prints the alias for ***name***, and if you leave out ***name***, `alias` prints all the current aliases. In the C shell, you can define an alias on the command line, but aliases are usually stored in `.cshrc` so that they are available as soon as you log in. To bypass the alias and use the original command name, type `\`***name***.

See also **`unalias`**.

Table A.2: Options to Use with `alias`

OPTION	DESCRIPTION
`-t`	Allows the Korn shell to remember the full pathname for the aliased command, which allows it to be found quickly and to be issued from any directory. Tracked aliases are the same as hashed commands in the Bourne shell.
`-x`	Exports the alias so that you can use it in shell scripts.

alloc

A built-in C shell command that displays information on dynamic memory used by the system. When you provide a memory address (8, or any multiple of 8) with this command, `alloc` displays the status of each memory block as either busy or in use.

alphanumeric

Consisting of letters, numbers, and sometimes special control characters, spaces, and other punctuation symbols.

See also **ASCII, EBCDIC.**

alt newsgroups

A set of USENET newsgroups that contain articles on controversial subjects often considered to be outside of the mainstream.

These newsgroups were originally created to avoid the rigorous process required to create an ordinary USENET newsgroup. Some alt newsgroups contain valuable discussions on subjects that range from agriculture to wolves, others contain sexually explicit material, and others are just for fun. Not all service providers and online services give access to the complete set of alt newsgroups.

See also **CFV, Internet abbreviations, mailing list, moderated newsgroup, unmoderated newsgroup.**

ambiguous file reference

Any reference to a file that does not specify one particular file but can be expanded by the shell to specify a list of filenames.

Special characters representing one character (`?`), zero or more characters (`*`), and character classes (`[ ]`) can all be used in an ambiguous file reference.

See also **regular expressions.**

American National Standards Institute

See **ANSI.**

ampersand

- A character that when added to the end of the command line runs the program in the background.
- A metacharacter used in `vi` or `sed` to repeat a regular expression.
- A C shell numeric variable for a bitwise AND.
- An `awk` AND. Note that two ampersands (`&&`) are needed here.
- The prompt for the `mail` program.
- Two ampersands together have a special meaning for the Bourne and Korn shells. The line:

  `command1 && command2`

  means execute *`command1`* AND *`command2`* or, in other words, execute *`command2`* if *`command1`* succeeds, but if *`command1`* does not succeed, don't do anything.
- A shell symbol used to redirect the standard error.

Because of these special meanings, you should not use an ampersand as a character in a filename.

See also **background processing, child process, standard error.**

angle bracket

The shell uses a less than symbol (<) to redirect standard input to come from a file and a greater than symbol (>) to redirect the standard output.

See also **redirection.**

anonymous ftp

A method used to access an Internet host with `ftp`, which does not require you to have an account on the target computer system. Just log in to the Internet computer with the username "anonymous" and use your e-mail address as your password. This information was originally provided as a courtesy so that system administrators could see who had accessed their systems, but now it is often required to gain access to their systems.

You cannot use anonymous `ftp` with every computer on the Internet; just those that have been set up to offer the service. The system administrator decides which files and directories will be open to public access, and the rest of the system is considered to be off limits and cannot be accessed by anonymous `ftp` users. Some sites only allow you to download files from them; as a security precaution, you are not allowed to upload files to them. All this aside, the world open to anonymous `ftp` users is enormous; you can access tens of thousands of computers, and you can download hundreds of thousands of files.

See also **Archie, archive, `ftp`, `telnet`.**

anonymous posting

In a USENET newsgroup, a public message posted via an anonymous server in order to conceal the identity of the original sender.

anonymous server

A special Internet service that removes from a USENET post all information that could be used to identify the original sender and then forwards the message to its destination. If you ever use an anonymous server, don't forget to remove your signature from the bottom of your post; not all anonymous servers look for and strip off signatures.

ANSI

Acronym for American National Standards Institute, pronounced "an-see." A nonprofit organization of business and industry groups, founded in 1918, devoted to the development of voluntary standards. ANSI represents the U.S. on the International Organization for Standardization (ISO).

ANSI committees have developed many important standards, including the following:

- ANSI C Transition Guide: System V Release 4 guidelines on writing new or upgrading existing C programs so that they conform to the ANSI C standard.
- ANSI X3J11: Standard for the C programming language, including language semantics, syntax, execution environment, and definition of the library and header files.
- ANSI X3J16: Standard for the C++ programming language.
- ANSI X3J3: Definition of the Fortran programming language compiler.
- ANSI X3.131-1986: Definition of the SCSI (Small Computer System Interface) standard. The X3T9.2 standard contains the extensions to SCSI-2.
- ANSI X3T9.5: The working group for the Fiber Distributed Data Interface (FDDI) definition.
- ANSI X3H3.6: The standard for X Window systems.

ANSI C

That version of the C programming language standardized by the ANSI-authorized C Programming Language Committee X3J11 and the ISO-authorized Committee JTC1 SC22 WG14. Sometimes called *Standard C*.

ANSI C is designed to codify existing practices but also adds new features, such as function prototypes to correct deficiencies in the language. The standard resolves the different rules for declaring data objects, and clarifies certain long-standing ambiguous areas.

■ *See also* **C++, K&R, POSIX.**

ansitape

A command provided with BSD that reads and writes files to and from ANSI-standard magnetic tapes.

▶ Syntax

The syntax for `ansitape` is:

```
ansitape [option]
➥[arguments]filenames
```

▶ Options and Arguments

The `ansitape` options are listed in Table A.3.

Once you have chosen an option, you can use one of the *`arguments`* listed in Table A.4 to modify that option.

`ansitape` will not copy certain kinds of files, including directories, character or special block files, or binary executables; if you try, you are rewarded with a warning message, and the file is skipped.

a.out

The default name of the executable file produced by the Unix assembler, link editor, and C compiler.

You can use `a.out` just as you would use other programs by typing its name on the command line, but you should change its name to something more descriptive; otherwise, you may accidentally overwrite it during a later compilation.

To create an executable file with a more meaningful name of your choice, use the compiler's `-o` option and specify the filename you want to use.

■ *See also* **as, cc, gcc, ld.**

Table A.3: Options to Use with ansitape

OPTION	DESCRIPTION
c	Creates a new tape.
r	Files are written to the end of the tape.
t	Lists the specified files each time they occur on tape.
x	Extracts the specified files from the tape.

Table A.4: Arguments to Use with ansitape

ARGUMENT	DESCRIPTION
b	Allows the user to specify the block size to use.
f	Allows the selection of a different tape drive.
F	Creates an ANSI D-type fixed record length tape.
l[*label*]	Creates the specified label on the tape.
n[*filename*]	Uses the specified file as a control file containing the names of the files to store on tape.
v	Turns on verbose mode.

API

Abbreviation for application programming interface. A set of callable functions provided by an operating system or a third-party application that a program can use to perform tasks such as managing files, displaying information, and performing tasks specific to the application area.

An API provides a standard interface along with documentation on how the functions that wake up the interface should be used.

append

- In the C or Bourne shells, to add the standard output from a command to the end of an existing file using the >> redirection symbols.
- In Unix text editors, to place one block of text immediately after an existing block of text.

■ *See also* **greater than symbol.**

append mode

A mode in a text editor or word processor that allows you to add new text to the end of an existing word, line, or block of text.

application layer

The seventh, or highest, layer in the ISO/OSI model, the application layer uses services provided by the lower layers in the model but is completely insulated from the details of the network hardware. It describes how applications interact with the network operating system, including database management, e-mail, and terminal emulation programs.

Application Programming Interface

■ *See* **API.**

application specific integrated circuit

■ *See* **ASIC.**

apply

A command provided with BSD that applies a command to a set of arguments.

▶ Syntax

The syntax for `apply` is:

```
apply [options]command
➥ argument...
```

`apply` runs the *command* against each *argument* in sequence. When character sequences are used in *command* in the form `%d`, where `d` is a number between 1 and 9, the sequence is replaced by the appropriate unused *argument*.

▶ Options and Arguments

Table A.5 shows the two options available with `apply`.

▶ Examples

The following command compares all the "a" files with all the "b" files:

```
apply -2 cmp a1file b1file
➥ a2file b2file a3file b3file
```

Table A.5: Options to Use with apply

OPTION	DESCRIPTION
`-ac`	Substitutes the character specified by *c* for %.
`-n`	Specifies the number of arguments to be passed to *command*. If the number is zero, the *command* is run, without arguments, once for each *argument*. If `%d` appears in *command*, the `-n` option is ignored.

apropro

A command used to look up keywords in the online manual pages.

▶ Syntax

The `apropro` syntax is:

```
apropro [options]keyword...
```

`apropro` shows which manual pages contain any of the keywords in their names or title lines. Each keyword is considered separately, and part words are located; for example, if you search for "edit", you will also find "editor", and if you search for "compile", you will also find "compiler". Case is ignored.

▶ Options and Arguments

`apropro` options are shown in Table A.6.

Table A.6: Options to Use with apropro

OPTION	DESCRIPTION
`-M`	Overrides the standard list of directories and uses *path*. The *path* must be a list of directories separated by colons. This search path may also be set using the environment variable `MANPATH`.
`-m`	Adds a list of colon-separated directories to the beginning of the standard `apropro` path. These directories are searched first.

▶ Examples

To find all the manual pages that have "compile" in their name lines, type:

```
apropro compile
```

and to find all the manual pages with "editor" in their name lines, type:

```
apropro editor
```

▶ Notes

Using `apropro` produces the same result as using `man -k`.

See also **man**, **whatis**.

ar

A command used to create and manage archive libraries, combining several files into one and allowing files to be added to or removed from the archive. `ar` does not compress text, so there are no savings in disk space, although there are savings in file accounting because only one i-node is needed instead of several. The most common use of `ar` is to create and maintain library files used by `ld`, the link editor.

▶ Syntax

The syntax for `ar` is as follows:

```
ar [-V] key [key_modifier]
➥[position]archive[files]
```

Only one *key* letter may be used at a time, but several *key_modifiers* may be combined (with no separating spaces). The *position* argument is a filename used to specify a position within the archive, *archive* is the name of the archive file itself, and *files* represents the names of the files that you want to add or remove. `-V` prints the `ar` version number

▶ Options and Arguments

The *key* argument is one of the characters from Table A.7, combined with one or more of the optional *key_modifiers* listed in Table A.8. The *key* can include a hyphen prefix.

Two other Unix commands are available for archive services; `tar` provides tape-oriented facilities, while `cpio` is oriented toward the directory system and inter-system copying. `ar`, `tar`, and `cpio` all use different archive formats.

Table A.7: Options to Use with ar key

OPTION	DESCRIPTION
d	Deletes the named files from the *archive*.
m	Moves the named file to the end of the *archive*. If one of the *key_modifier* options a, b, or i is specified, the files are placed before or after the *position* file in the archive.
o	In 4.4BSD, sets the access and modification times of all extracted files to the modification time of the file when it was entered into the archive. You must be the owner of the extracted file or be the superuser; otherwise, this option fails.
p	Displays the named files to the standard output.
q	Quickly appends the named files to the end of the *archive* without checking to see if the file has been archived previously. If the *archive* does not exist, it is created.
r	Adds or replaces the named file in the *archive*. New files are written at the end of the *archive* unless the a, b, or i *key_modifier* is used.
t	Displays a table of contents for the *archive*.
x	Extracts the named files into the current directory, or extracts all files if no names are specified. The archive remains unaltered.

Table A.8: Options to Use with `ar key_modifier`

OPTION	DESCRIPTION
`a`	Combine with `r` or `m` to place *`files`* in the *`archive`* after *`position`*.
`b, i`	Use with `r` or `m` to place *`files`* in the *`archive`* before *`position`*.
`c`	Suppresses messages and creates the *`archive`* in silence.
`l`	In System V Release 3 only, places temporary files in the current directory rather than in `/tmp`.
`s`	Forces a regeneration of the archive symbol table. This may become necessary if an *`archive`* has been operated upon by another program.
`T`	In 4.4BSD, limits archived filenames to the first 15 characters; if names are truncated, a warning message is printed to the standard error output.
`u`	When combined with `r`, replaces only files that have been modified since they were last archived.
`v`	Prints a verbose, file-by-file, description. When combined with `t`, it gives a long listing of file information, and when combined with `x`, it displays the name of each extracted file.

▶ Examples

To add `myfile` to the `library.a` archive, type:

`ar -q library.a myfile`

This command adds **`myfile`** to the end of the archive even though the archive may already contain the file. To delete a file from an archive, use:

`ar -d library.a yourfile`

This command removes `yourfile` from the archive `library.a`. To list the contents of the archive file `library.a`, use:

```
ar -t library.a
```

■ *See also* **`ansitape`**.

arbitration

The set of rules used to manage competing demands for a computer resource, such as memory or peripheral devices, made by multiple processes or users.

Archie

A system used on the Internet to locate files available by anonymous `ftp`. Archie was written by students and volunteers at McGill University's School of Computer Science in Montreal, Canada, and is available on Internet servers worldwide.

Once a week, special programs connect to all the known anonymous `ftp` sites on the Internet and collect a complete listing of all the publicly available files. This file listing is kept in an Internet Archive Database, and when you ask Archie to look for a file, this database is searched rather than the whole Internet; you can then use anonymous `ftp` to retrieve the file you are looking for.

To use Archie, you can either use an Archie client on your system, or you can log onto an Archie server using `telnet`; you may even be able to use e-mail with an Archie server.

▶ Using an Archie Client

If you have an Archie client on your system, you can use the `archie` command to perform searches. For example, to use `archie` to search for `myfile`, use:

```
archie -e myfile
```

Table A.9 lists the options you can use with the `archie` command. There is also an X Window Archie client, called `xarchie`, which is even easier to use than `archie`.

▶ Using Archie with telnet

When you log in to an Archie server using `telnet` and the user ID `archie` (you do not need a password), you see the prompt:

```
>archie
```

where you can enter any of the commands listed in Table A.10.

When you set the `pager` variable, Archie displays the output using the paging program `less`, showing you one screenful at a time and then pausing to wait for a command. You can use any of the commands shown in Table A.11 when viewing Archie output. For most of the commands, just press the key; however, for the / and ? commands, you have to press the key and then the Return key.

▶ Using Archie with E-mail

Once you log in to an Archie server with `telnet`, you can use the following archie command to have the result of any search sent to you by e-mail:

```
archie> mail
```

If you want to have the results sent to a different mail address, use the `set mailto` command, as follows:

```
archie> set mailto
➥ pmd@sybex.com
```

and any e-mail sent by the server will go to `pmd@sybex.com`.

Table A.9: Options to Use with Archie

OPTION	DESCRIPTION
`-c`	Searches for sub-strings, case-sensitive.
`-e`	Searches for an exact match. The default setting.
`-h [`*`address`*`]`	Sends Archie server requests to the specified host.
`-l`	Lists one item per line so that you can use the output with another program later if you wish.
`-L`	Displays a list of the Archie servers known to this client.
`-m [`*`number`*`]`	Specifies the maximum number of items to find; `-m10` is a reasonable limit to start with.
`-o [`*`filename`*`]`	Sends output to the specified file.
`-r`	Searches for the following regular expression.
`-s`	Searches for sub-strings.
`-t`	Sorts the output by time and date, from newest to oldest.
`-V`	Turns on verbose mode for comments during a search.

Table A.10: Commands Available on an Archie Server	
COMMAND	DESCRIPTION
Ending an Archie Session	
`quit`	Ends an Archie session and disconnects.
Performing a Search	
`find [`*`pattern`*`]`	Searches the main anonymous `ftp` database.
`prog [`*`pattern`*`]`	Searches the main anonymous `ftp` database. `prog` is the old name for `find`.
`whatis [`*`pattern`*`]`	Searches the Software Description Database for a keyword matching `[`*`pattern`*`]`.
Displaying Information	
`help ?`	Displays a list of Archie commands.
`help [`*`command`*`]`	Displays help for the specified command.
`help set [`*`variable`*`]`	Displays help for the specified variable.
`manpage`	Displays the Archie manual page.
`motd`	Displays the message of the day.
`servers`	Displays a list of Archie servers.
`version`	Displays the Archie software version number.
Displaying Variable Settings	
`show`	Displays the current values for all variables.
`show [`*`variable`*`]`	Displays the value of a specific variable.
Setting General Variables	
`set autologout [`*`minutes`*`]`	Sets the maximum idle time before you are automatically logged off the server.
`set maxhits [`*`number`*`]`	Specifies the maximum number of items for a search.
`set pager`	Displays Archie output using the pager program `less`.
`unset pager`	Does not use `less` to display Archie output.
`set status`	Displays a status line during searches.
`unset status`	Turns off the status line during searches.

Table A.10: Commands Available on an Archie Server (continued)	
COMMAND	DESCRIPTION
Setting Output Preferences	
`set output_format verbose`	Displays output using the long format.
`set output_format terse`	Displays output using the short format.
`set output_format machine`	Displays output using the machine format.
`set sortby none`	Turns off output sorting.
`set sortby filename`	Sorts alphabetically by filename.
`set sortby hostname`	Sorts alphabetically by host name.
`set sortby size`	Sorts by size, largest to smallest.
`set sortby time`	Sorts by time and date, newest to oldest.
`set sortby rfilename`	Sorts by filename into reverse alphabetical order.
`set sortby rhostname`	Sorts by host name into reverse alphabetical order.
`set sortby rsize`	Sorts by size, smallest to largest.
`set sortby rtime`	Sorts by time and date, oldest to newest.
Setting Search Preferences	
`set search exact`	Searches for an exact match.
`set search sub`	Searches for a match that contains the search pattern.
`set search subcase`	Searches for a match that contains the search pattern, but also matches case.
`set search regex`	Searches for a regular expression.
`set search exact_sub`	Searches using the `exact` option, then by the `sub` option.
`set search exact_subcase`	Searches using the `exact` option, then by the `subcase` option.
`set search exac_regex`	Searches using the `exact` option, then by the `regex` option.
Mailing Information	
`set mailto [`*address*`]`	Specifies a mail address for Archie messages.
`mail [`*address*`]`	Mails output of last search to the specified address.

Table A.11: Commands Available When Viewing Archie Output Using `less`

COMMAND	DESCRIPTION
`q`	Quits the program.
Space	Displays the next screenful.
Return	Displays the next line.
[*n*] Return	Displays the next *n* lines.
`b`	Displays the previous screenful.
`y`	Displays the previous line.
[*n*]`y`	Displays the previous *n* lines.
`d`	Displays the next half screenful[l].
`u`	Displays the previous half screenful[l].
`g`	Goes to the first line.
[*n*]	Goes to line *n*.
`G`	Goes to the last line.
`/`[*pattern*]	Searches forward for the specified pattern.
`?`[*pattern*]	Searches backward for the specified pattern.
`n`	Repeats the previous search command.

architecture

The overall design and construction of all or part of a computer system, particularly the processor hardware and the size and ordering sequence of its bytes. Also used to describe the overall design of software.

■ *See also* **big endian, CISC, client/server, little endian, RISC.**

archive

- A collection of related files kept in storage for backup; the files may have been compressed to save hard disk or magnetic tape space.
- To make a copy of a set of files for long-term storage.
- On the Internet, a site containing files available via anonymous `ftp`.

■ *See also* **`ar`, `cpio`, `compact`, `compress`, `compressed file`, `gzip`, `pack`, `tar`.**

argument

Any letter, number, filename, option, or other string that gives additional information to a command at the time the command is used. When a shell script is called, the arguments of the call become available as parameters within the script.

■ *See also* **command-line argument, option.**

argument list

The set of filenames that can be accessed by either the `ex` or the `vi` text editors.

argv

A C shell variable that contains the command-line arguments from the command invoked by the shell. `argv` is used to manipulate positional parameters without requiring a shift mechanism. For example, `argv[0]` contains the name of the calling program, `argv[1]` contains the first command-line argument, and so on. You can change any element of this array with the exception of `argv[0]`, and you can use `argv[*]` to reference all of the arguments together.

A similar variable, `ARGV`, is used in `awk` to get information from the command line. The first element `ARGV[0]` contains the name of the command itself, normally `awk`; the following elements, `ARGV[1]`, `ARGV[2]`, and so on, contain the actual arguments. The related variable, `ARGC`, contains the number of command-line arguments used.

A

arithmetic expression

Any group of numbers, operators, and parentheses that can be evaluated to derive a number. The C shell uses `@` to evaluate an arithmetic expression, the Bourne shell uses the `expr` command, and the Korn shell uses `let`.

array

An ordered collection of data items arranged in one or more dimensions. Each item in an array is known as an *element* or a *member*. Both the C and Korn shells can store and process arrays. For example, the C shell stores its command search path in an array called `path`. The first array element is called `path[1]`, the second `path[2]`, and so on.

article

An e-mail message posted to one of the USENET newsgroups, accessible by anyone with a newsreader and a connection to the Internet.

as

The Unix command that runs the assembler, creating an object file from an assembly language source file.

▶ Syntax

The syntax for `as` is as follows:

`as [`*`options`*`]` *`files`*

Object files have the same name as their source equivalents, except the `.s` suffix is replaced by `.o`.

▶ Options and Arguments

Table A.12 lists the options available with `as`.

■ *See also* **`dis`**.

ASCII

Acronym for American Standard Code for Information Interchange, pronounced "askee." A standard coding scheme that assigns values to letters, numbers, punctuation marks, and control characters, to achieve compatibility between different computers and peripherals.

In ASCII, each character is represented by a unique integer value composed of 7 bits. The values from 0 to 31

Table A.12: Options to Use with as

OPTION	DESCRIPTION
`-m`	Runs the `m4` macroprocessor on *`file`*.
`-n`	Turns off the optimization of long/short addresses.
`-o` *`object-file`*	Places the output in the object file *`object-file`*; the default filename is *`file`*`.o`.
`-Qc`	When *`c`* is set to `y`, places the version number of the assembler in the object file; when *`c`* is set to `n`, does not.
`-R`	Removes *`file`* on completion.
`-V`	Displays the version number of the assembler.
`-Y[`*`key`*`]`*`dir`*	When *`key`* is set to `m`, searches the *`dir`* directory for the `m4` macroprocessor; when set to `d`, searches for a file containing predefined macros. `as` searches for both if *`key`* is omitted.

are used for non-printing control codes, and the range from 32 to 127 is used to represent the letters of the alphabet, numbers, and common punctuation symbols. This set, from 0 to 127, is referred to as the standard ASCII character set and is shown in Table 2.2 in Appendix 2. Alternatively, see the file `/usr/pub/ascii` on your system, or use the `man ascii` command.

All computers that use ASCII can understand the standard ASCII character set. It is used to represent everything from source code to written text and is used when exchanging information between different computers.

Extensions to the ASCII character set that use all eight bits are popular in the PC world; see Table 2.3 in Appendix 2 for a list of the IBM Extended ASCII character set.

■ *See also* **ASCII character set, ASCII file, DBCS, EBCDIC, text file.**

ASCII character set

A character set that consists of the first 128 ASCII characters, shown in Table 2.2 in Appendix 2. The ASCII character set contains uppercase and lowercase letters, numbers, control codes, and some punctuation symbols.

ASCII file

A file that contains only text characters from the seven-bit ASCII character set. An ASCII file contains letters and numbers but does not contain any hidden text-formatting codes. You can print or view an ASCII file using the standard Unix utilities. Because an ASCII file uses only seven bits in a byte but a binary file uses all eight, you must tell programs such as `ftp` which type of file you are transferring. Also known as a *text file* or as an *ASCII text file.*

ASIC

Acronym for application specific integrated circuit. A computer chip developed for a specific purpose, designed by incorporating standard cells from a library, rather than from scratch. ASICs are found in all sorts of appliances, including VCRs, microwave ovens, automobiles, cameras, and security systems.

■ *See also* **RISC.**

assembler

A program that converts assembly language into instructions that a computer can understand. The assembler is a vital part of the source code compilation process, along with the preprocessor, compiler, and link editor.

■ *See also* **`as`, assembly language, interpreter.**

assembly language

A machine-dependent low-level language in which each program statement corresponds to a single machine language instruction that the processor can execute.

Assembly languages are specific to a given microprocessor, or microprocessor family, and as such, are not portable; programs written for one type of processor must be rewritten before they can be used on another type of processor. And assembly language is always hard to maintain.

There are two main reasons for using assembly language in a programming project: to wring as much performance out of the processor as possible (assembly language programs often run faster than their higher level counterparts) and to gain access to specific characteristics of the hardware that might not be accessible from higher level languages.

Unix was originally written in PDP-7 assembly language and later rewritten in C.

■ *See also* **`as`, assembly language, compiler, interpreter.**

asterisk

A metacharacter used as a wildcard in filename expansion that can be used as a substitute for any unknown number of characters, including one or more blank spaces. When you use a wildcard, the shell interprets the pattern and replaces it with the appropriate file names; you must always specify a / (slash), you cannot match it using a wildcard.

For example, when you type:

```
ls q*
```

the shell replaces `q*` with all the filenames that begin with the letter `q`.

This process of using a wildcard to specify filenames is called *filename substitution* in the C shell and in Tcsh; in the Bourne shell and Korn shell, it is known as *filename generation*; and in the Bash shell, it is called *pathname expansion*.

You will hear different terms used to identify the asterisk character: "star," "splat," or even "glob."

The asterisk is used as a metacharacter within regular expressions in the `ed`, `ex`, `vi`, `sed`, `grep`, and `awk` programs.

■ *See also* **globbing, question mark, square brackets.**

asymmetrical multiprocessing

A multiprocessing design in which the programmer matches a specific task to a certain processor at the time of writing the program.

This design makes for a much less flexible system when compared with symmetrical multiprocessing (SMP). SMP allocates tasks to processors as the program starts running on the basis of current system load and available system resources. Needless to say, asymmetrical systems are easier to design, code, and test than SMP systems.

asynchronous communications

A method of data transmission that uses start and stop bits to coordinate the flow of data so that the time intervals between individual elements do not have to be equal. Parity may also be used to check the accuracy of the data received.

■ *See also* **communications parameters, parity.**

asynchronous event

Any event that does not occur regularly or at the same time as another event. In Unix, system signals are asynchronous because they can occur at any time, initiated by any number of different non-regular events.

at

The Unix `at` command takes the list of commands that you type at the keyboard and runs them at the time you specify; you do not have to be logged in to the system at the time the command is scheduled to run. `at` allows you to run certain kinds of jobs unattended when system load is low, for example, printing long documents in the middle of the night.

▶ Syntax

The syntax for `at` is as follows:

```
at options1 time
➥ [date][+increment]commands

at options2[jobs]
```

You can use two sets of options with `at`: *`options1`* controls setting the time and date, and *`options2`* lets you make changes to jobs you have already scheduled.

In *`options1`*, you type the information needed by `at`, followed by the command you want to run, and then terminate the whole sequence by typing Ctrl-D on the following line.

Because `at` takes its input from standard input, you can enter the commands you want to execute from the keyboard, pipe them in from another program, or use input redirection to use an existing file of commands. `at` returns a job ID when it is invoked, and you use this ID number with the second syntax described above.

Many systems restrict the use of `at`. Only those users specified in the file `/usr/lib/cron/at.allow` can schedule jobs; if this file doesn't exist, the file `/usr/lib/cron/at.deny` holds a list of users who cannot use `at`. If this file exists but is empty, everyone can use `at`. If neither file exists, only the *superuser* can use `at`.

When Unix executes commands using `at`, it uses e-mail to send you any output from the resulting process; you can redirect this mail if you want to.

▶ Options and Arguments

In the first line of syntax above, *`time`* is the time of day when you want `at` to run your job, and you can specify *`time`* in one of several different ways:

- A one- or two-digit number specifying the hour.
- A four-digit number specifying the hour and minute.
- Two numbers separated by a colon to specify hours and minutes.
- `noon`, `midnight`, or `now`.

Any of these first three forms can be followed by `am`, `pm`, or `zulu` (for Greenwich mean time) to make the *`time`* specification more precise.

You can specify the *`date`* you want `at` to use as:

- A three-letter month name followed by the day number, an optional comma, and an optional year number.
- A day of the week, abbreviated to the first three letters.
- `today` or `tomorrow`.

If you omit *`date`*, `at` defaults to today if the hour you specify in *`time`* is later than the current time; if not, `at` runs the job at the same time tomorrow.

The final argument, *`increment`*, is a positive number followed by `minutes`, `hours`, `days`, `weeks`, `months`, or `years`, or their singular form. `at` adds this *`increment`* to the *`time`* and *`date`* you specify. In place of *`increment`*, you can use the word `next` to specify `next week`, or `next year`.

In the second line of syntax shown above, *`jobs`* is a list of one or more `at` job numbers.

You can use the options shown in Table A.13 to report or remove jobs.

SCO adds one more option, `q` *`letter`*, which places a job in the queue specified by *`letter`*. Three letters have special significance: `a` (the default) represents the `at` queue, `b` the `batch` queue, and `c`, the `cron` queue.

Table A.13: Options to Use with at

OPTION	DESCRIPTION
Options1	
`-f` *`filename`*	Executes the commands contained in *`filename`*.
`-m`	Sends any mail to the user when the job is complete.
Options2	
`-l[`*`jobs`*`]`	Reports all jobs, or if *`jobs`* is specified, reports on those.
`-r[`*`jobs`*`]`	Removes the specified *`jobs`*. To remove a job, you must be the owner of the job or the superuser.

▶ Examples

To run the `spell` program on a file called `bigfile` at 4 a.m. tomorrow and send any output to a file called `wordout`, use:

```
at 04 tomorrow
spell bigfile > wordout
Ctrl-D

job 424765800.a at Tue Oct 30
➥ 04:00:00 1996
```

The last line above contains the job number and the time `at` will run the job.

■ *See also* **atq**, **atrm**, **batch**.

at sign

- A metacharacter used as the line kill character that deletes all input on the current command line.
- The character in `vi` used to indicate a line has been deleted.

- A character used in e-mail addresses. The at sign (`@`) separates the user ID from the domain name of the computer system used for mail as in `user@host`.
- In the C shell, a command used to assign a value to a numeric variable, as in:

  `@variable = expression`

  If no *`variable`* or *`expression`* is specified, `@` prints the values of all the shell variables.

See also **bang path, `set`.**

AT&T

The parent company of Bell Laboratories, the original developers of Unix. For many years, Bell Labs was one of the two major development centers for Unix (the other being the Computer Systems Research Group at the University of California at Berkeley), but in 1990, AT&T formed Unix Systems Laboratories, or USL, to continue the development. In June 1993, USL was sold to Novell, and in 1995, Novell sold the rights to Unix to SCO.

See also **Baby Bells, BSD, CSRG.**

atq

A command that displays a list of the jobs waiting in the `at` job queue.

▶ Syntax

The syntax for `atq` is as follows:

`atq [`*`options`*`][`*`users`*`]`

Ordinarily, `atq` lists jobs in the order in which they will execute; if *`users`* is specified, those jobs are listed. If you are the superuser, all jobs are listed; otherwise, only those jobs that you own are shown.

▶ Options and Arguments

The options available with `atq` are shown in Table A.14.

See also **`at`, `atrm`.**

Table A.14: Options to Use with `atq`

OPTION	DESCRIPTION
`-c`	Sorts the jobs in the queue by the time that the `at` command was originally given.
`-n`	Displays the total number of jobs in the queue.

atrm

A command used to remove jobs from the `at` job queue.

▶ Syntax

The syntax for `atrm` is as follows:

`atrm [`*`options`*`][`*`jobs`*`][`*`users`*`]`

▶ Options and Arguments

When *`users`* is specified, all *`jobs`* belonging to that user are removed. This argument can be specified only by the superuser.

If a *`jobs`* number is specified, only that job is removed from the queue.

The options available with `atrm` are shown in Table A.15.

See also **`at`, `atq`.**

Table A.15: Options to Use with `atrm`

OPTION	DESCRIPTION
`-a`	Removes all jobs that belong to the current user; the superuser can remove all jobs.
`-f`	Operates quietly. Suppresses all information related to the removal of the specified jobs.
`i`	Prompts for a `y` to remove all *`jobs`*; or for `n`.
`-`	In 4.4BSD, removes all *`jobs`* belonging to the user who invoked `atrm`.

auditing

The process of collecting and reviewing data on system usage and performance to determine if system problems or security violations have occurred.

authentication

The process involved when verifying a user's level of access to a computer system or network.

Authentication usually involves comparing the username and password to a list of authorized users. If an appropriate match is made, the user logs in and can access the system in accordance with the rights and permissions assigned to his or her user account.

■ *See also* **Kerberos.**

autoload

A Korn shell alias used to define or load functions when they are first used. **autoload** is an alias for **typeset -fu**.

■ *See also* **typeset**.

auto-save file

An **emacs** backup file that is maintained automatically and is saved every 300 keystrokes.

This auto-save file has the same name as the file you are editing, except that there is a pound sign (#) at the beginning and end of the filename. For example, if you are working on a file called **myfile**, **emacs** creates an auto-save file called **#myfile#**.

When you save your file, the auto-save file is removed by **emacs**, but if you continue to make changes to your file, **emacs** creates a new auto-save file. This means that in theory, you should never see the auto-save file; however, if your **emacs** session terminates unexpectedly, before you can save your work, the file is preserved. The next time you start to edit that file, **emacs** displays a message similar to the following:

```
Auto-save file is newer;
➥ consider M-x recover-file
```

indicating that **emacs** thinks you should recover the file before continuing. Enter:

```
M-x recover-file
```

When **emacs** displays the name of the file, press Return, and when **emacs** asks if you want to restore the file, answer **yes**.

automounter

A feature in NFS that allows remote resources to be activated as they are needed and unmounted when no longer needed. All this takes place without intervention from the system administrator.

A/UX

A version of Unix developed by Apple Computer that runs on Macintosh computers.

A/UX is based on the System V Release 2 version of Unix and includes a number of Apple features, such as support for the Macintosh toolbox, allowing applications running under A/UX to use the familiar Mac user interface. You need a Macintosh II with a Motorola 68020 and at least 4 MB of memory to use A/UX.

avatar

Another name for the superuser account; an alternative to the name *root*.

awk

A Unix programming language used to manipulate text files. **awk** scans text files for patterns or simple relationships and then performs specified actions on matching lines. **awk** is named after the program creators, Alfred Aho, Peter Weinberger, and Brian Kernighan.

During the 1980s, the authors made several enhancements to **awk** and called this enhanced version **nawk** for new **awk**. This program was released as part of System V Release 3.1 and is still found on many systems. The GNU Project's version of **awk** is known as **gawk**; in the 4.4BSD release, it is installed as **awk**. In most cases, you can assume that **gawk** implements all features of **awk** and **nawk**.

Using a programming language to manipulate text files may sound a bit daunting, but **awk** is straightforward to use; you can even write simple **awk** scripts at the command line. **awk** scans a set of input lines contained in a text file, searching for lines that match a pattern you have specified. For each pattern, you can specify an action; when **awk** recognizes the pattern, the action is performed on each line that matches the pattern. Many of the constructs found in **awk** were taken from the C programming language, including:

- A flexible format
- Regular expressions
- String and numeric variables
- Conditional execution
- Looping statements
- C's `printf` statement

▶ Syntax

awk can be invoked as follows:

awk [*options*]'*script*'
➥ *var=value files*

awk [*options*] -f *program_file*
➥ *var=value files*

You can specify s *script* direct from the command line, or you can store a script in *program_file* and specify it using **-f.** You can assign the variable *var* a value from the command line; the value can be a literal, a shell variable, or a command substitution, but the value is only available after the BEGIN block of the **awk** program has been processed.

▶ Options and Arguments

The options available with **awk** are shown in Table A.16.

▶ Patterns and Procedures

An **awk** program consists of one or more program statements in the form:

`pattern {procedure}`

If *pattern* is missing, then *{procedure}* is performed for all lines in the text file; if *{procedure}* is missing, then the matched line is printed.

A *pattern* can be one of the following:

- A quoted string, number, operator, function, defined variable, or any of the predefined variables listed in Table A.16.
- A regular expression.
- A relational expression using one of the relational operators listed in Table A.17.
- A pattern-matching operator, such as ~ (match) or !~ (don't match).
- The BEGIN pattern lets you specify procedures (such as setting global variables) that take place before the first line of input is processed.
- The END pattern lets you specify what happens after the last line of input has been read.

A *procedure* can be made up of one or more commands or functions, separated by newlines, and contained within curly braces. Commands are of four types:

- Variable or array assignments
- Printing commands
- Flow-control commands
- Built-in **awk** functions

Table A.17 lists all the operators available in **awk**, in order of increasing precedence, Table A.18 lists the predefined functions available in **awk**, and Table A.19 lists the system variables in **awk**, **nawk**, and **gawk**.

Table A.16: Options to Use with awk

OPTION	DESCRIPTION
-F*c*	Sets the field separator character to the single character *c*, rather than the default Space or Tab.
-f*program_file*	Uses the *program_file* rather than command-line instructions.

Table A.17: Operators to Use with awk

OPERATOR	DESCRIPTION
`= += -= *= /= %= ^=`	Assignment.
`?:`	The C programming language conditional expression or the ternary operator.
`||`	Logical OR.
`&&`	Logical AND.
`~ !~`	Match regular expression and negated match.
`< <= > >= != ==`	Relational operators.
`(blank)`	String concatenation.
`+ -`	Addition and subtraction.
`*/ %`	Multiplication, division, and modulus.
`+ - !`	Unary plus, unary minus, and logical negation.
`^`	Exponentiation.
`++ --`	Increment and decrement, either prefix or postfix.
`$`	Field reference.

Of the commands in Table A.18, `atan2`, `close`, `delete`, `do/while`, `function`, `getline`, `gsub`, `match`, `next`, `rand`, `return`, `srand`, `sub`, and `system` are not available in the original `awk` but are available in later versions of `nawk` and `gawk`; `tolower` and `toupper` were not available in `awk` or `nawk` but appeared in `gawk`. All other commands are available in all versions.

▶ Examples

An `awk` program, or script, can be as simple as one command entered at the command line or as complex as any C language program. Here are two simple examples.

```
awk '/waffle/{print FILENAME":
➥ "$0}' myfile
```

This command extracts all lines in the file `myfile` that contain the word "waffle". It then prints the filename and the complete line of text for each line found. You don't need to place a `$` in front of the built-in `awk` variable `FILENAME`, and the `$0` references all fields in the record.

```
awk '{print $1+$2, subtotal
➥ +=$1+$2}' myfile.db
```

This example uses the C language increment operator `+=` to accumulate a subtotal; as this example processes each line in `myfile`, it adds the value of `$1+$2` to `subtotal`.

■ *See also* **icon**, **perl**.

A

Table A.18: Predefined Commands Available in awk	
COMMAND	DESCRIPTION
`atan2(y,x)`	Returns the arctangent of *y/x* in radians.
`break` `close(filename-expr)`	Exits from a `for` or `while` loop.
`close (command-expr)`	Closes a file or pipe using the same expression that opened the file or pipe. Most versions of `awk` let you open up to 10 files and one pipe at a time.
`continue`	Begins the next iteration of a `for` or `while` loop.
`cos(x)`	Returns the cosine of *x* radians.
`delete(array[element])`	Deletes an *element* of *array*.

`Do`
`  body`
`while(expr)`
	Performs a looping statement, executing the statements in *body*, then evaluating *expr*. If *expr* is true, the loop repeats, and *body* executes again.

`exit`	Ignores remaining instructions, does not read more input, but branches directly to the END procedures.
`exp(arg)`	Returns the exponent of *arg*.
`for(i=lower; i<=upper;i++)` `  command`	Performs *command* while *i* is between the values of *lower* and *upper*. If you use a series of *commands*, they must be contained within curly braces ({ }).
`for(item in array)` `  command`	Performs *command* for each *item* in *array*. If you use a series of *commands*, they must be contained within curly braces ({ }).

`function name(parameter-list){`
`statements`
`}`
	Allows you to specify your own user-defined functions.The *parameter-list* is a comma-separated list of variables passed as arguments to the function when the function is called. The body of the function can contain one or more statements and usually contains a `return` statement to pass control back to the point that called the function.

`getline[var][<file]`
or
`command | getline[var]`
	Reads the next line of input. The first syntax reads input from *file*, and the second form reads the output from *command*. Both forms read just one line at a time, which is assigned to `$0` and is parsed into fields setting NF, NR, and FNR.

Table A.18: Predefined Commands Available in awk (continued)

COMMAND	DESCRIPTION
`gsub(r,s,t)`	Substitutes *s* for each match of the regular expression *r* in the string *t*. If *t* is not specified, it is taken to be `$0`. The substitution is made globally. The value returned by `gsub` is the number of substitutions made.

`if(condition)`
`   command`
`[else]`
	If *condition* is true, execute *command*, otherwise execute the *command* in the `else` clause. A series of commands must be enclosed within curly braces (`{ }`).

`index(substr,str)`	Returns the position of the first place within the string *str* where the substring *substr* occurs. If *substr* does not occur within *str*, `index` returns 0.
`int(arg)`	Returns the integer value of *arg*.
`length(str)`	Returns the number of characters in the string *str*; if *str* is not supplied, `S0` is assumed.
`log(x)`	Returns the natural logarithm of *x*.
`match(s,r)`	Tests whether the string *s* contains a match for the regular expression *r*, and returns either the position where the match begins or 0 if no match is found. Sets both `RSTART` and `RLENGTH`.
`next`	Reads the next line of input and starts a new pass through all the pattern/procedure statements in the `awk` program or script.
`print[args][destination]`	Prints *args* on the appropriate output device. Literal strings must be quoted, and successive values separated by commas are separated by the predefined variable `OFS`; successive values separated by spaces are concatenated. You can use redirection with the default output.
`printf[format][, expressions].`	Produces a formatted print following the conventions of the C programming language `printf` statement, including `%s` to print a string, `%d` to print a decimal number, and `%n.mf` to print a floating-point number, where *n* represents the total number of digits and *m* represents the number of digits after the decimal point.

A

Table A.18: Predefined Commands Available in awk (continued)

COMMAND	DESCRIPTION
`rand()`	Returns a random number between 0 and 1. This command returns the same random number each time it is run, unless the random number generator is seeded using `srand()`.
`return[`*`expr`*`]`.	Returns the value *`expr`* at the end of a user-defined function.
`sin(`*`x`*`)`	Returns the sine of *`x`*.
`split(`*`string`*`,`*`array`*`[,`*`sep`*`]`	Splits the string *`string`* into fields using the separator *`sep`* and then puts those fields into the array *`array`*. If *`sep`* is not specified, then `FS` is used.
`sprintf[`*`format`*`[,`*`expression`*`]]`	Returns the value of *`expression`* using the *`format`*. Nothing is actually printed; data is only formatted.
`sqrt(`*`arg`*`)`	Returns the square root of *`arg`*.
`srand(`*`expr`*`)`	Sets a new seed value for the random number generator using *`expr`*. If *`expr`* is not specified, the time of day is used as the default.
`sub(`*`r`*`,`*`s`*`,[`*`t`*`])`	If the string *`t`* is specified, substitute the string *`s`* for the first occurrence of the regular expression *`r`* in *`t`*. If *`t`* is not specified, `$0` is assumed; returns 1 if successful, 0 if not.
`substr(`*`string`*`,`*`m`*`,[`*`n`*`])`	Returns the substring of *`string`* beginning at character number *`m`* and consisting of the next *`n`* characters. If *`n`* is not specified, includes all characters to the end of the string.
`system(`*`command`*`)`	Executes the Unix *`command`* and returns an exit value.
`tolower(`*`str`*`)`	Converts all uppercase characters in *`str`* to lowercase, and returns the new string.
`toupper(`*`str`*`)`	Converts all lowercase characters in *`str`* to uppercase, and returns the new string.
`while(`*`condition`*`)` *`command`*	Executes *`command`* while *`condition`* is true. A series of commands must be contained within curly braces (`{}`).

Table A.19: System Variables to Use with awk, nawk, and gawk	
VARIABLE	DESCRIPTION
awk	
FILENAME	Current filename.
FS	Field separator; the default is a blank.
NF	The number of fields in the current record.
NR	The number of the current record.
OFS	The output field separator; the default is a blank.
ORS	The output record separator; the default is a newline.
RS	The record separator; the default is a newline.
$0	The entire input record.
$*n*	The *n*th field in the current record; the fields are separated by FS.
nawk	
ARGC	The number of arguments on the command line.
ARGV	An array that contains the command-line arguments.
FNR	The input record number in the current input file.
OFMT	The output format for numbers; the default is %.6g.
RSTART	The first position in the string matched by the **match** function, or 0 if no match.
RLENGTH	The length of the string matched by **match**, or -1 if no match.
SUBSEP	The separator character used for multiple subscripts in array elements; the default is \034.
gawk	
ENVIRON	An array containing environment variables.
IGNORECASE	When non-zero, all regular expression matches are made independent of case. The default is 0, so that all regular expression operations are normally case-sensitive.

Baby Bells

A slang term for the Regional Bell Operating Companies, often abbreviated RBOC, formed when AT&T was broken up in 1984. Includes Ameritech, Bell Atlantic, Bell-South, NYNEX, Pacific Telesis, Southwestern Bell, and U.S. West.

■ *See also* **Bell Labs.**

background

A processing environment in which programs or shells operate at a low priority and without input from the user.

In traditional Unix systems, a process spends its entire existence in either the background or the foreground; in newer systems with job control, you can change the processing environment and move a foreground process into the background and vice versa. When a background operation ends, a message appears on the screen.

■ *See also* **ampersand, background processing, bg, fg, foreground processing.**

background processing

A mechanism used to run a program in the background, without input from a terminal or from the user. Also called *detached processing.*

To start a background process, end the command line with the ampersand (&); you do not have to wait for this background process to run to completion before giving additional shell commands.

Both the Bourne shell and the C shell allow background processing, and on Unix systems with job control, the C and Korn shells provide additional commands for manipulating background processing.

If you forget to run a program in the background, you can stop it by typing Ctrl-Z and use the `bg` command to put the program into the background and restart it. You can bring the current background job to the foreground with the `fg` command, and if you have lots of jobs running at the same time, use the `jobs` command to list them by job number.

The best candidates for background processing are programs that do not require input from you and those that do not write to the screen. If a program running in the background needs input from the keyboard, it stops and waits for that input, and it will wait and wait until you finally provide the input. A program that writes to the screen will do so even from the background, and if you are in the middle of doing something else, you may not be able to make sense of the output. With this category of program, you can always redirect the output to a file and look at it later.

When putting several programs separated by semicolons into the background using the Bourne shell, remember to group them using parentheses; the Bourne shell puts the last command on the line into the background but always waits for the first. Use this syntax, and you won't have any problems:

```
(command; command)&
```

Also, any background processes you have running are usually terminated when you log out. Use the `nohup` command to avoid this, or set up the job using `cron` and `at`.

See also **at, cron, foreground processing.**

backing up your system

A backup is an up-to-date copy of the files on your system that your system administrator can use to reload onto your hard disk after an accident. It is an insurance policy against catastrophic loss, but there are several other valid reasons to make a backup:

- Protection against accidental deletion of files. Since it is impossible to recover accidentally deleted files in Unix, reloading them from a recent backup is the only means available.
- A mechanism for moving large numbers of files from one system to another. This is particularly useful if some of the files you want to move are very large.
- An archive at the completion of a project, when a person leaves the team, or at the end of a financial period such as a year-end close.

In the Unix world, very large hard disks are the norm, and the only sensible way to make a backup is to use a tape drive. Many system administrators use `tar` or `cpio` to make backups, while others prefer third-party tape backup utilities instead. Neither `tar` nor `cpio` will back up the special files in `\dev`, but many of the third-party utilities will. Newer Unix systems also provide commands such as `backup`, `restore`, `ufsdump`, and `ufsrestore`.

Deciding when and how often to make a backup depends on how you use your system and how frequently important data on your system changes. Here are some backup tips:

- Keep multiple copies—redundancy should be a part of your backup plan.
- Test your backups to make certain that they are what you think they are.
- Clean the tape drive occasionally, and replace your backup tapes on a regular basis.
- Store the backup tapes in a secure location, preferably off-site. Do not leave them sitting next to the computer because if the computer is damaged by fire or flood, the backup tapes will probably be damaged by the same accident.

It all comes down to one simple rule: back up all the files that you cannot afford to lose. Do it now.

See also **cpio, gzip, tar.**

backquote

The backquote (`), also known as *accent grave* or just *grave*, is not the same as the single quote (').

When you enclose a part of a shell command line in backquotes, that portion is executed as a command, and the output of the command is inserted into the command line. This is also known as command substitution and sounds complex, but it isn't really. Here's an example:

```
now = `date`
```

In this command line, the shell variable `now` is being set to a value. Without backquotes, `now` would be set to the word `date`; with backquotes, `now` is set to the output of the `date` command.

backslash

The backslash (\) is sometimes called the *reverse slash* or *backslant*. This character changes the meaning of the next character in some important way, in the shell, in many standard editors, as well as in `awk`, `sed`, and `grep`.

It is also used to extend a shell command over more than one line. When you reach the end of the line, use the \ to continue the command onto the next line. The \ quotes the newline character that follows it, and the shell does not treat it as a command terminator.

■ *See also* **metacharacter, regular expressions, slash.**

backspace

A key on most keyboards used to move the cursor one space or one column to the left, erasing the character or characters in those spaces or columns.

backup

■ *See* **backing up your system.**

backup table

A table containing information relating to backups, including instructions, timings, lists of files to be backed up, and the storage media to use.

■ *See also* **backing up your system.**

bad sector table

A table containing information about the sectors on a hard disk that should not be used for any kind of storage. If the operating system attempts to write to a bad sector, the write request is forwarded to a known good sector instead.

bandwidth

- In communications, the difference between the highest and the lowest frequencies available for transmission in any given range.
- In networking, the transmission capacity of a computer or a communications channel, stated in megabits per second, or Mbps. For example, Ethernet has a bandwidth of 10 Mbps, and FDDI has a bandwidth of 100 Mbps.

bang

The exclamation point character (`!`), also known as *pling* in the U.K. and other parts of the world.

bang path

An old-style UUCP e-mail address that uses exclamation points to separate the sequence of host computer names to get to the addressee.

Bang paths list the addresses—general to specific—from left to right, which is the reverse of the sequence used by many other addressing schemes.

■ *See also* **DNS, Internet address.**

banner

An SVR4 utility that prints the specified message as very large characters on the standard output. These characters are formed from asterisks (*) or pound signs (#) depending on your system. Each line in the `banner` output can be up to 10 uppercase or lowercase characters for an 80-column display; other hardware can support more characters.

▶ Syntax

Here is the syntax to use:

```
banner string
```

Depending on the capability of your hardware, all characters appear in uppercase; lowercase input characters appear as small uppercase letters. To make all the words stay on the same line, enclose them in quotes.

B

▶ **Examples**

You can use `banner` to create flashy title pages for your reports, signs for birthdays or other celebrations, or page separators for long printouts. This example:

```
banner "NO PARKING" "" "AT
➥ ANY TIME" | lp
```

makes a sign with NO PARKING printed on the first line, then a blank line, followed by the words AT ANY TIME.

■ *See also* **echo.**

banner page

An extra title page added to printouts or listings by most of the print spoolers. The banner page often includes user or account ID information in large character-graphics letters that are formed by rows and columns of letters. (The letter *A*, for example, is formed by rows and columns of *A*s.) Also called a *burst page*, because it indicates the place where fan-folded paper should be separated or burst apart.

■ *See also* **banner.**

basename

The name of a file after the filename extension (the period and anything following the period) has been removed.

■ *See also* **basename, dirname, pathname.**

basename

A utility used to extract a filename from a path statement; the filename is then printed on the standard output. You can also remove the filename extension from the filename using this command.

▶ **Syntax**

The syntax for `basename` is as follows:

```
basename pathname [extension]
```

▶ **Options and Arguments**

Given a *pathname*, this command removes the whole path prefix, leaving just the filename. If you also specify the optional *extension*, it is removed. **basename** is often used with command substitution using backquote characters to generate a filename; this allows the filename to be used rather than simply displayed.

▶ **Examples**

To extract the basename of a file, use:

```
basename /pwd/myfile.txt
```

and the result is `myfile.txt`. You can strip off the filename extension if you use:

```
basename /pwd/myfile.txt.txt
```

This gets you simply `myfile` with no extension.

To assign the basename of a file to a shell variable, use:

```
FILENAME=`basename
➥ /pwd/myfile.txt`
```

If you then execute:

```
echo $FILENAME
```

you will see the result:

```
myfile.txt
```

■ *See also* **dirname, pathname.**

Bash

The Bourne-Again Shell (`bash`), first released in 1989 by Brian Fox and Chet Ramey as part of the Free Software Foundation GNU Project. Bash extends the features found in earlier shells and is a popular addition to systems such as Linux.

Bash provides features found in the Bourne shell, the C shell, the Korn shell, and Tcsh, including Bourne shell syntax, redirection and quoting, C shell command-line editing and tilde expansion, job control, and command history. Bash also includes built-in commands and variables, shell syntax, and aliases from the Korn shell.

When Bash first starts a login shell, commands in `/etc/profile` are executed, followed by commands in `/.bash_profile`, `/.bash_login`, and /.profile, assuming all these files exist on your system. And when you log out, the commands in /.bash_logout are executed.

For more information on Bash, see the bash manual and Info pages or one of the excellent books now available on Bash.

■ *See also* **Bourne shell family, rbash.**

basic regular expressions

■ *See* **regular expressions.**

batch

An SVR4 utility that runs jobs one after the other, as system load allows, even after you log out. The batch utility accepts commands from the standard input and executes these commands, one after the other, waiting for each one to complete before starting the next.

▶ Syntax

To use batch:

```
batch commands
```

and then terminate the sequence with an end-of-file (EOF) character, Ctrl-D. If you prefer, you can use redirection and use a file containing the commands instead of typing them at the command prompt. batch is best for long sequences of commands that do not need much attention from you; you can even log out before they are complete.

Using batch is similar to using the at command, but at executes commands at a specific time; it is also similar to using background processing, except that the job continues after you log out.

▶ Examples

To run a set of commands contained in a file, use:

```
batch < myfile
```

This places all the commands contained in myfile in the job queue.

■ *See also* **at, background, cron, crontab.**

batch queue

A mechanism used to schedule and sequence large jobs. The batch queue receives job requests from users and then schedules the jobs to run one at a time.

SVR4 and Solaris both have a simple batch queue facility similar to the at command, except with batch, you cannot specify the time you want your job to run. To delete jobs from the queue on Solaris systems, use atq and atrm; on SVR4, use at -l, or at -r.

baud

A measurement of data transmission speed. Originally used in measuring the speed of telegraph equipment, it now usually refers to the data transmission speed of a modem or other serial device.

■ *See also* **baud rate.**

baud rate

In communications, a measurement of the number of state changes (from 0 to 1, and vice versa) per second on an asynchronous communications channel.

Baud rate is often assumed to correspond to the number of bits transmitted per second (bps), but baud rate and bits per second are not always the same. In modern high-speed digital communications systems, one state change can be made to represent more than one data bit. A rate of 300 baud is likely to correspond to 300 bps; however, at higher data rates, the number of bits transmitted per second can become higher than the baud rate, and so bits per second is a more accurate statement of modem capacity. For example, 2400 bps can be sent at 1200 baud if each state change represents two bits of information.

In the past, mismatched baud rates were the most common reason for communications failures. These days, modern modems can detect and lock on to the best rate for the prevailing line conditions. Some modems can also change rates in response to changing line conditions during the course of a transmission.

bc

An interactive, programmable scientific calculator that can also be used to convert numbers from one system to another. `bc` is also a language and a compiler quite like the C programming language. Input can be from a file or from the standard input. To exit `bc`, you can type **`quit`**, or press Ctrl-D.

▶ Syntax

To use `bc`:

`bc` *`options filelist`*

where *`filelist`* contains a set of `bc` functions you want to execute. For a complete list of operators and keywords available in `bc`, see Table B.1.

`bc` uses single-character, lowercase identifiers (a, b, c, and so on) as names for variables, arrays, and functions; the same letter may be used for all three simultaneously. The letters *A* through *F* are treated as hexadecimal digits whose values are from 10 to 15. Separate statements one from another with newlines; braces are needed only when grouping multiple statements.

You can choose the base for numerical input and output, and these bases can both be different. This means that you can enter numbers in decimal and display them in binary if you wish. Common bases used in computer-related calculations are base 16 (hexadecimal), base 8 (octal), and base 2 (binary), but `bc` works in any base from base 2 to base 16.

▶ Options and Arguments

Two options are available with `bc`, and they are shown in Table B.2.

▶ Examples

To convert the octal number 20 into decimal:

```
$ bc
ibase=8
20
16
quit
```

To find the square root of 11 to seven decimal places:

```
$ bc
scale=7
sqrt(11)
3.3166247
quit
```

When you enter an expression or number such as `sqrt(11)`, it is evaluated and then printed; assignment statements such as `scale=7` are not printed.

These examples are just a hint of what `bc` can do; you can use it to work up some very complex functions.

■ *See also* **`dc`, `expr`, `xcalc`.**

bcc

■ *See* **blind courtesy copy.**

BCD

Abbreviation for binary coded decimal. A simple system for converting decimal numbers into binary form, in which each decimal digit is converted into binary and then stored as a single character.

In binary, the largest number that can be stored in 8 bits is 255, and this obviously represents a severe limitation to storing larger numbers. BCD is a way around this limitation that stays within the 8-bit storage format. For example, the decimal number 765 can be broken down so that the numbers 7, 6, and 5 are represented by one byte each. In BCD, each decimal digit occupies a byte, so 3 bytes are needed for a 3-digit decimal number.

bdes

A BSD utility used to encrypt and decrypt information using Data Encryption Standard (DES) algorithms.

▶ Syntax

Use this syntax with `bdes`:

`bdes [`*`options`*`]`

`bdes` implements all aspects of the DES as defined in the "Data Encryption Standard," FIPS #46, National

Table B.1: Operators and Keywords Available in bc

OPERATOR	DESCRIPTION
Statement Keywords	
`for (`*`expr1;rel-expr;expr2`*`)` ➥`{`*`statements`*`}`	Repeats one or more *`statements`* as long as *`rel-expr`* is true; similar to `while` with the exception that a `for` statement must contain all three expressions.
`if (`*`rel-expr`*`){`*`statements`*`}`	Executes one or more *`statements`* if *`rel-expr`* is true.
`while(`*`rel-expr`*`){`*`statements`*`}`	Repeats one or more *`statements`* as long as *`rel-expr`* is true; similar to `for`.
Function Keywords	
`auto `*`x,y`*	Establishes *`x`* and *`y`* as variables local to a function definition initialized to zero. *`x`* and *`y`* have no meaning outside the function.
`define `*`j(k)`*`{`	Begins the definition of the function *`j`*, which has a single argument *`k`*. You use additional arguments separated by commas. The statements of the function follow on separate lines, and the whole function is terminated with a closing brace (`}`).
`length(`*`expr`*`)`	Calculates the number of decimals in *`expr`*.
`return(`*`expr`*`)`	Passes the value of *`expr`* back to the program; returns zero if *`expr`* is omitted.
`scale(`*`expr`*`)`	Calculates the number of digits to the right of the decimal in *`expr`*.
`sqrt(`*`expr`*`)`	Calculates the square root of *`expr`*.
Input/Output Keywords	
`ibase=`*`n`*	Sets `bc` to read numbers input in the base *`n`*; the default is base 10. Once `ibase` has been changed to something other than 10, type **`A`** to restore decimal.
`obase=`*`n`*	Sets `bc` to display output in the base *`n`*; the default is base 10. Once `obase` has been changed to something other than 10, type **`A`** to restore decimal.
`scale=`*`n`*	Sets the number of decimal places for calculations; the default is zero, which truncates all results to integers. `scale` has meaning only for calculations performed in decimal; the maximum value of `scale` is 100.

Table B.1: Operators and Keywords Available in bc (continued)

OPERATOR	DESCRIPTION
Math Library Keywords	
`a(n)`	Calculates the arctangent of *n*.
`c(angle)`	Calculates the cosine of *angle*.
`e(expr)`	Calculates e to the power of *expr*.
`l(expr)`	Calculates the natural log of *expr*.
`j(n,x)`	Calculates the Bessel function of integer order *n*.
`s(angle)`	Calculates the sine of *angle*.
Common Operators	
`+`	Addition
`-`	Subtraction
`/`	Division
`*`	Multiplication
`%`	Modulo or remainder after a division
`^`	Exponentiation
`++`	Increment, both prefix and postfix
`--`	Decrement, both prefix and postfix
`=+ =- =* =/ =^ =`	Assignment
`< <= > >= == !=`	Relational
`- ++ --`	Unary
Miscellaneous Symbols	
`/* */`	Encloses comment lines.
`()`	Controls evaluation of precedence.
`{}`	Used to group statements.
`[]`	Used as an array index.
`"text"`	Prints the *text* within the quotes.

OPTION	DESCRIPTION
`-c`	Invokes the compile only option. `bc` is a preprocessor for `dc`, the desk calculator. With this option, `bc` sends the compiled output from `bc` to the standard output instead of `dc`.
`-l`	Loads the math library containing the trigonometric and logarithmic functions.

Table B.2: Options to Use with bc

Bureau of Standards, U.S. Department of Commerce, January 1977. **bdes** reads from the standard input and writes to the standard output. If you don't specify an encryption key on the command line, **bdes** prompts you to enter one.

▶ Options and Arguments

The options shown in Table B.3 are available with **bdes**.

The *key* and the *vector* described in Table B.3 are taken to be ASCII characters that are then mapped onto their bit representations. If either begins with the sequence 0X or 0x, they are assumed to be hexadecimal numbers indicating the bit pattern, and if they begin with 0B or 0b, they are assumed to be a sequence of binary digits indicating the bit pattern. Only the first 64 bits of the *key* and the *vector* are used; if too few bits are supplied, zero bits are added to pad the key out to 64 bits.

■ *See also* **crypt**, **DES**.

bdiff

An SVR4 utility that compares two very long files and reports on the differences. **bdiff** divides the two comparison files into smaller pieces and then runs the **diff** utility on them, thus allowing **diff** to act on files that would normally be too large for it to manage.

▶ Syntax

The syntax for **bdiff** is as follows:

```
bdiff file1 file2 [options]
```

▶ Options and Arguments

bdiff compares *file1* with *file2* and lists every line that is different. If a hyphen (–) is used instead of one of these filenames, **bdiff** reads from the standard input instead.

bdiff takes the two options shown in Table B.4.

▶ Examples

To compare two large files, use:

```
bdiff page1.txt page2.txt
```

■ *See also* **cmp**, **comm**, **diff**, **diff3**, **sdiff**, **split**.

Table B.3: Options to Use with bdes

OPTION	DESCRIPTION
`-a`	Forces both the *key* and the *vector* to ASCII.
`-b`	Uses electronic code book mode.
`-d`	Decrypts the input.
`-Fn`	Uses *n*-bit alternative cipher feedback mode. *n* must be a multiple of 7, between 7 and 56.
`-fn`	Uses *n*-bit cipher feedback mode. *n* must be a multiple of 8, between 8 and 64.
`-k key`	Uses *key* as the encryption key.
`-mn`	Calculates a message authentication code (MAC) of *n* bits on the input; *n* must be a multiple of 8.
`-on`	Uses *n*-bit output feedback mode. *n* must be a multiple of 8, between 8 and 64.
`-p`	Disables resetting the parity bit; only used when the *key* is in ASCII.
`-v vector`	Sets the initialization vector to *vector*.

OPTION	DESCRIPTION
n	Splits each of the comparison files into segments each *n* lines long; the default is 3500 lines. If you use this option, you must use it first.
-s	Suppresses error messages from `bdiff`; does not suppress error messages that come from `diff`.

Table B.4: Options to Use with `bdiff`

Bell Labs

The research arm of AT&T and the birthplace of Unix and the C programming language in the 1970s.

■ *See also* **BSD, CSRG.**

bells and whistles

Features that add complexity to a program or to a piece of hardware but don't necessarily make it more useful to the average user.

benchmark

A specific standard against which some aspect of computer performance can be compared.

A benchmark is a test that attempts to quantify hardware, software, or system performance—usually in terms of speed, reliability, or accuracy.

One of the major problems in determining performance is deciding which of the many benchmarks available actually reflects how you plan to use the system.

■ *See also* **benchmark program.**

benchmark program

A program that attempts to provide a consistent measurement of some aspect of system performance. These programs include Dhrystone (evaluates microprocessor and memory performance), Whetstone (evaluates speed of arithmetic operations), and Khornerstone (evaluates overall system performance, including disk drive access speed, memory access speed, and processor performance).

Some popular benchmark programs have been shown to give wildly overly optimistic results, especially when run outside the environment for which they were originally designed.

The Systems Performance Evaluation Cooperative (SPEC) developed a set of 10 benchmarks to measure performance in actual application environments. The results of these tests are known as *SPECmarks*.

■ *See also* **Dhrystones, SPEC benchmarks, Whetstones.**

Berkeley Unix

■ *See* **BSD.**

bfs

An SVR4 big file scanner that reads a large file into an interactive line editor that uses commands similar to those in `ed`. This command is a holdover from the days when systems were smaller and is not used much these days.

▶ Syntax

The `bfs` syntax is as follows:

```
bfs [option]file
```

`bfs` reads the *`file`* without using a buffer, which can make it more efficient than using `ed`, particularly on small systems.

After starting `bfs`, you can type **`p`** to see a prompt; otherwise, the normal prompt is simply a blank line.

▶ Options and Arguments

`bfs` has a single option; if you use a hyphen (-), it does not print the file size.

■ *See also* **`ed`, `emacs`, `vi`.**

bg

A shell command that resumes a stopped job and runs it in the background. This command runs in all the popular shells with one or two minor differences. It is useful if you forgot to add an ampersand (&) at the end of the command line when you first started the job, or you have since changed your mind and decided to do something else while the current job is running.

In the C shell:

bg %

executes the current job in the background, or:

bg %1

executes job number 1 in the background. To do the same in the Bourne and Korn shells, use:

bg 1

See also **background processing, fg, percent sign.**

bib

A BSD preprocessor for nroff or troff that formats a bibliography from a bibliographic database.

▶ Syntax

The syntax for bib is straightforward:

```
bib [options]
```

The input files are copied to the standard output, except for text between [. and .] pairs, which are assumed to be keywords used in searching the bibliographic database; when a matching reference is found, a citation is created. References are collected, sorted, and written out as specified by the user.

▶ Options and Arguments

The options listed in Table B.5 are available with bib; if you select one of the standard formal styles (see the -t option), you do not usually have to specify any more options for most documents.

You may also encounter other bibliographic-manipulation programs, such as listrefs, bibinc, or bib2tib. The options listed in Table B.5 also work with listrefs.

bib was designed to work with ms macros; to use it with the me macros, you must add a special header to your nroff/troff file.

See also **invert, me macros, ms macros, nroff, troff.**

biff

A BSD utility used to tell the system if you want to be notified when new mail arrives for you during your current session.

biff operates asynchronously and requires that sendmail and lmail are running; for synchronous notification, use the MAIL variable of the Bourne shell or the mail variable of the C shell.

The command:

biff y

enables mail notification, and the command:

biff n

turns it off again. When mail notification is turned on and mail arrives for you, the header and the first few lines of the message are printed on your screen. You will see a message on your screen that looks something like Figure B.1.

It makes sense to include the biff y command in your .login or .profile file, so that the command is run automatically each time you log in.

biff was named for a dog that belonged to a graduate student working at Berkeley during the summer of

Figure B.1: Typical Output from biff

```
New mail for garym@mit.edu has arrived:
----
From: Tom Charlesworth <tom@industry.com>
Continuing our conversation of yesterday about a lunch...

----
```

B

Table B.5: Options to Use with bib

OPTION	DESCRIPTION
-aa	Substitutes initials for authors' first names.
-ar*number*	Reverses the first *number* authors' names, last names appearing first.
-ax	Prints authors' last names in capitals-small capitals format.
-c*string*	Creates citations according to the template *string*.
-d	Changes the default search directory for style files; defaults to /usr/new/lib/bmac.
-ea	Substitutes initials for editors' first names.
-ex	Prints editor's last names in capitals–small capitals format.
-er*number*	Reverses the first *number* editors' names, last names appearing first.
-f	Creates footnote references.
-i*file*	Processes *file*, which may be a file of definitions.
-h	Changes form of three or more references so that 1,2,3,4 becomes 1–4. Used with -o.
-n*string*	Turns off the options indicated by *string*.
-o	Contiguous citations are ordered according to the reference list before they are printed; this is the default.
-p*file*	Searches *file* instead of searching the INDEX file, where *file* is a comma-separated list of indices, created by the invert utility.
-s*string*	Sorts references according to the template *string*.
-t*type*	Uses the standard macros and switch settings indicated by *type* to create citations and references.
-Tib	Use the TiB style macro where the name is enclosed in vertical bars.
-Tibx	Writes a special format file used when converting to TiB-style macros

1980. The story that Biff barked at the mailman is apparently a fiction, although legend has it that Biff once got a B in a compiler class.

■ *See also* **mail, mailx, xbiff.**

big endian

A computer architecture in which the most significant byte has the lowest address and so is stored big end first.

Many processors, including those from Motorola and Sun, certain RISC processors, the PDP-10, and the IBM 3270 series are all big endian. The term comes from Jonathan Swift's *Gulliver's Travels*, in which wars were fought over whether boiled eggs should be opened at the big end or at the little end.

■ *See also* **little endian, holy wars.**

/bin

A Unix root directory used to contain executable software. Many systems have at least two such directories, `/bin` and `/usr/bin`, although you may find many more. The name is derived from the word *binary* because most of the files in `/bin` are binaries.

binaries

A slang term for a group of binary files.

binary

Any scheme that uses two different states, components, conditions, or conclusions.

In mathematics, the binary or base 2 numbering system uses combinations of the digits 0 and 1 to represent all values; the decimal system has a base of 10 (0 to 9).

The first 10 binary numbers and their decimal equivalents are shown below:

0000	0
0001	1
0010	2
0011	3
0100	4
0101	5
0110	6
0111	7
1000	8
1001	9

Unlike computers, most people find binary numbers consisting of long strings of 0s and 1s difficult to read, so many people who work at this level use hexadecimal (base 16) representation instead.

Binary also refers to an executable file containing a program. The names of the standard Unix directories for executable files, `/bin` and `/usr/bin`, are taken from this term.

■ *See also* **ASCII file, binary file, executable file, text file.**

binary coded decimal

■ *See* **BCD.**

binary file

A program or data file that contains binary information in a machine-readable form, rather than in human-readable ASCII form. Because a binary file uses all eight bits in a byte, but an ASCII file only uses seven, you must tell programs such as `ftp` which type of file you are transferring.

binary license

A license granted to a user by a software developer, entitling the user to run a specific software package under well-defined circumstances, using binary files provided by the vendor.

A binary license does not entitle the user to a copy of the source code for the package, although certain limited configuration of the software can be done by the user, and the user does not have the right to modify the software in any way beyond this simple configuration.

A complete operating system released without source code is often referred to as a *binary distribution.*

■ *See also* **source license.**

binary numbers

Numbers stored in binary form. All the values from 0 to 255 can be stored in a single eight-bit byte, while a 16-bit word can store all the values from 0 to 65,535.

■ *See also* **BCD.**

bind

An `emacs` feature that lets you associate a specific key combination with a particular command.

■ *See also* **`emacs`.**

BIND

Abbreviation for Berkeley Internet Name Domain. A BSD client/server program that manages host and Internet Protocol (IP) addresses by matching the hostname with the IP dotted decimal address.

- *See also* **DNS.**

BISON

The Free Software Foundation's version of `yacc` (yet another compiler compiler), a part of the GNU project.

bit

Contraction of binary digit, a bit is the basic unit of information in the binary numbering system, representing either 0 for off or 1 for on. Bits are grouped together to make larger storage units such as the eight-bit byte.

- *See also* **octet.**

bit bucket

An imaginary place where output is sent when you want to throw it away or when your program mysteriously crashes in the middle of an important operation. The Unix system bit bucket is a character special file called `/dev/null`.

bitmapped display

A graphical display in which each pixel (picture element) on the screen is controlled by a bitmap in memory that represents the video image.

bitmapped font

A set of characters in a specific style and size, and each character is defined by a set pattern of dots. You must keep a complete set of bitmaps for every font you use on your system, and these bitmaps can consume large amounts of hard disk space. Also known as *raster fonts.*

bits per inch

- *See* **bpi.**

bits per second

- *See* **bps.**

bitwise operator

An operator that manipulates data as a series of bits. In the C programming language, bitwise operators include bitwise AND (&), inclusive OR (|), exclusive OR (^), shift left (<), shift right (>), and NOT (~).

- *See also* **Boolean.**

blank character

A space or a tab character, also called *whitespace.* In certain contexts, a newline and each of the nonprinting ASCII characters may also be considered blank characters.

blind courtesy copy

Abbreviated bcc. A list of recipients of an e-mail message whose names do not appear in the To: message header so the original recipient does not know that copies have been forwarded to other locations.

blocks

Sections of a disk or tape that are read or written at the same time; units of storage allocation that are transferred as single units.

In some systems a block is 512 bytes, in others it is 1024 bytes, and the BSD fast file system uses 8192-byte blocks. Most block devices always use the same block size when transferring data, although some tape drives can write variable-length blocks on the same tape. The block size may be specified when reading and writing to a device; for example, when you use the `tar -b` option.

- *See also* `tar`.

block device

A peripheral capable of storing a Unix filesystem, in other words a disk or tape drive. A block device is accessed via a block special file and transfers data one block at a time using a specific block size. A block device may also use a cache to speed up reading and writing data.

■ *See also* **character device, device file, raw device.**

block number

In a block device, disk and tape blocks are numbered so that Unix can keep track of data on the tape or disk.

■ *See also* **block size.**

block size

The largest contiguous amount of disk or tape space allocated by the Unix filesystem. If a filesystem's block size is 8192 bytes (or 8 KB), all files of up to this size are always stored in a single block. Files larger than the filesystem's block size may be broken up into smaller fragments when they are stored, with 8 KB sections of the file being stored in different locations across the disk. This division of a file into several pieces is known as "fragmentation," and it can limit system performance in some cases.

The filesystem block size is often different from the disk's physical block size, which is usually 512 bytes.

block special file

A Unix special file that provides an interface to a device that can support a filesystem.

■ *See also* **block device, character special file, device file, special file.**

BNC connector

A small connector with a half-turn locking shell for coaxial cable, used with thin Ethernet and RG-62 cabling.

bookmark

An option that lets you mark your place in an online document so you can return to it quickly and easily. Many Internet-access tools provide bookmarks so that you can identify and return to a favorite site without having to remember exactly how you got there.

■ *See also* **browser, Gopher, Mosaic.**

Boolean

Any variable that can have a logical value of true or false. Boolean is named after George Boole, the developer of a branch of algebra based on the values of true (or 1) and false (or 0), and works with logical rather than numerical relationships.

Boolean operators include AND (logical conjunction), OR (logical inclusion), XOR (exclusive or), and NOT (logical negation), and are sometimes described as logical operators.

■ *See also* **bitwise operators.**

boot

When used as a verb, boot means to start the computer running. The process involves turning the computer on and loading an operating system kernel, usually from a hard disk but occasionally from a floppy disk. This is usually an automatic process begun when you first turn on or reset the computer. The term is supposed to be derived from the saying "pulling yourself up by your own bootstraps."

■ *See also* **bootable disk, booting, bootstrap program.**

/boot

An SVR4 root directory containing files used to load and configure a new operating system installation.

■ *See also* **root filesystem.**

bootable disk

A disk, either a hard disk or a floppy disk, from which you can load an operating system.

An operating system is usually booted from a hard disk, but in single-user mode, it is often useful to boot from a floppy disk. When you first install certain versions of Unix, such as Linux, you must create and load a bootable floppy disk as the first step of the installation process.

booting

The process of loading and running the operating system kernel and associated tasks so that the computer system is ready and available to perform normal operations.

The steps involved in booting a Unix system include the following:

- Turning on all the appropriate hardware
- Loading the bootstrap program
- Loading the kernel and the root filesystem
- Initializing memory
- Running initialization scripts
- Checking the filesystem
- Starting daemons
- Mounting other filesystems
- Running application initialization scripts

You will see a series of system and progress messages on the system console as the operating system is loaded and configured; the content of the messages depends on the system you are loading and your individual hardware configuration.

bootstrap program

The short program loaded after power on or after a system reset that begins the process of booting the computer.

■ *See also* **bootable disk.**

bounce

- The return of an e-mail message to its original sender due to a delivery error. The error may be the result of a spelling mistake in the e-mail address, the recipient's computer system being down, or the recipient no longer having an account on the system. The returned e-mail often contains an indication of why the message bounced.
- The process of taking the system from multiuser state to single user state, usually to solve a particularly difficult problem. A system administrator may bounce the system when trying to kill or clear a hung process.

■ *See also* **state.**

Bourne shell

The oldest Unix shell still in popular use, originally developed by Dr. Steven Bourne of AT&T Bell Labs. The Bourne shell is a command interpreter with a built-in programming language.

The Bourne shell offers the following features:

- A built-in command set for writing shell scripts
- Background execution of commands
- Input and output redirection
- Wildcard or metacharacters for filename abbreviation
- Job control (starting with the Bourne shell in SVR4)
- A set of shell variables to customize your environment
- Exportation of specified variables to a child process

▶ Startup Files

The Bourne shell program, started by the `sh` command, executes the statements in the `/etc/profile` and `$HOME/.profile` files, if they exist. The commands in `/etc/profile` are likely to be general commands applying to all users of the Bourne shell on your system while the commands in `$HOME/.profile` can be modified to suit each user. The normal shell prompt is a dollar sign, and you can log out with Ctrl-D or by typing **`exit`** at this prompt.

▶ Using Commands

The Bourne shell allows you to use and group commands on the command line in several different ways, which are shown in Table B.6.

▶ Filename Metacharacters

You can use any of the patterns shown in Table B.7 to generate filenames.

▶ Redirection

When you execute a command, the shell opens three files known as the standard input, the standard output, and the standard error. By default, the standard input is the keyboard, and the standard output and standard error are the terminal or screen. Redirection is the process of directing input to or output from a different file from that used normally.

In simple redirection, you can change the input source or output destination in any of the ways listed in Table B.8.

The shell assigns a file descriptor to each standard file, using 0 for standard input, 1 for standard output, and 2 for standard error; it may also use higher numbers, starting at 3 for any other files required to complete the process. You can use the file descriptors listed in Table B.9 in redirection.

In multiple redirection, you can use the file descriptors listed in Table B.10.

▶ Quoting

Quoting disables the special meaning of a character and allows you to use it literally. The characters listed in Table B.11 have special meaning in the Bourne shell.

▶ Predefined Variables

The Bourne shell includes a large set of built-in variables as Table B.12 shows; many of these variables are not set by the shell but are used in `.profile` where you can define them to meet your individual needs. You assign value to a variable with the command:

```
$ variable=value
```

If you do not specify values, the Bourne shell applies defaults to certain environment variables, including `PATH`, `PS1`, `PS2`, and `IFS`, and the `HOME` variable is set when you log in to the system.

▶ Built-in Commands

The Bourne shell offers a set of built-in commands as Table B.13 shows; many of these commands are also available in the Korn shell.

Because the Bourne shell was the only significant shell when it was first introduced, you may find that older Unix documentation refers to "the shell" when it really means the Bourne shell; some of these references apply only to the Bourne shell and are not appropriate for newer shells such as the C or Korn shells.

■ *See also* **`csh`, C shell, Bash, Bourne shell family, Korn shell, `ksh`, `sh`, Tcsh, Unix shell, Zsh.**

B

Table B.6: Using Bourne Shell Commands	
COMMAND	DESCRIPTION
cmd &	Executes *cmd* in the background.
cmd1 ; cmd2	Executes *cmd1* and *cmd2* consecutively, with the semicolon acting as a command separator.
(cmd1 ; cmd2)	Creates a subshell to execute *cmd1* and *cmd2* as a group.
cmd1 | *cmd2*	Creates a pipe, and uses the output from *cmd1* as input to *cmd2*.
cmd1 `` `cmd2` ``	Performs command substitution; uses the output from *cmd2* as arguments to *cmd1*.
cmd1 && *cmd2*	Executes *cmd1*, and if *cmd1* completes successfully, then executes *cmd2*.
cmd1 || *cmd2*	Executes either *cmd1*, or if it fails, executes *cmd2*.
{ *cmd1 ; cmd2* }	Executes commands in the current shell.

Table B.7: Bourne Shell Filename Metacharacters	
METACHARACTER	DESCRIPTION
*	Matches any string or zero or more characters; for example, `w*n` matches `wn`, `win`, `won`, `when`, `worn`, and many other filenames.
?	Matches any single character; for example, `myfile.?` matches `myfile._`, `myfile.1`, `myfile.a`, and so on.
[abc...]	Matches any single character from the list, and you can use a hyphen to indicate a range, as in `a-z`,`0-9`, and so on.
[!abc...]	Matches any single character not on the list, and you can use a hyphen to indicate a range.

Table B.8: Simple Redirection in the Bourne Shell	
COMMAND	DESCRIPTION
cmd > *filename*	Sends output from *cmd* to *filename*, overwriting the file if it already exists.
cmd >> *filename*	Appends output from *cmd* to *filename*.
cmd < *filename*	Takes input for *cmd* from *filename*.
cmd << *text*	Reads standard input as far as a line identical to *text*.

Table B.9: Redirection Using File Descriptors in the Bourne Shell	
FILE DESCRIPTOR	**DESCRIPTION**
cmd >&*n*	Sends output from *cmd* to file descriptor *n*.
cmd *m*>&*n*	Same as above, except that output that would normally go to the file descriptor *m* is sent to file descriptor *n* instead.
cmd >&-	Closes standard output.
cmd <&*n*	Takes input for *cmd* from file descriptor *n*.
cmd *m*<&*n*	Same as above, except that output that would normally have come from the file descriptor *m* comes from the file descriptor *n* instead.
cmd <&-	Closes standard input.

<table>
<tr><th colspan="2">Table B.10: Multiple Redirection in the Bourne Shell</th></tr>
<tr><td>FILE DESCRIPTOR</td><td>DESCRIPTION</td></tr>
<tr><td>cmd 2>filename</td><td>Sends standard error to filename while standard output remains the screen.</td></tr>
<tr><td>cmd > filename 2>&1</td><td>Sends both standard error and standard output to filename.</td></tr>
<tr><td>(cmd > filename1)
➥ 2>filename2</td><td>Sends standard output to filename1 and standard error to filename2.</td></tr>
<tr><td>cmd | tee filenames</td><td>Sends output from cmd to standard output and also to filename.</td></tr>
</table>

<table>
<tr><th colspan="2">Table B.11: Quoting in the Bourne Shell</th></tr>
<tr><td>CHARACTER</td><td>DESCRIPTION</td></tr>
<tr><td>;</td><td>Command separator.</td></tr>
<tr><td>&</td><td>Runs a command in the background.</td></tr>
<tr><td>( )</td><td>Command grouping.</td></tr>
<tr><td>|</td><td>Creates a pipe.</td></tr>
<tr><td>*? [ ] !</td><td>Filename metacharacters.</td></tr>
<tr><td>< > & |</td><td>Redirection symbols.</td></tr>
<tr><td>" " ' ' \</td><td>Used when quoting other characters. Anything placed between the double quotes is interpreted symbolically; anything placed between the single quotes is interpreted literally, and the backslash is used to quote a single character.</td></tr>
</table>

Table B.12: Built-in Bourne Shell Variables	
VARIABLE	DESCRIPTION
`$#`	Contains the number of arguments on the command line.
`$?`	Contains the return code for the last command executed.
`$$`	Contains the PID of the current process.
`$!`	Contains the PID of the most recent background process.
`$-`	Displays the options currently in effect for `sh`.
`$0`	The first word on the command line, the command name.
`$`*n*	Individual arguments on the command line; you can reference up to 9, where *n* = 1–9.
`$*`	All the arguments on the command line, quoted as a single string ("`$1 $2 $3...`").
`"$@"`	All the arguments on the command line, quoted as individual strings ("`$1`" "`$2`" "`$3...`").
`CDPATH=`*dirs*	Specifies the search path for the `cd` command, with individual directory names separated by colons.
`HOME=`*dir*	Specifies the home directory; set by `login`. If you use the `cd` command without an argument, the shell makes this directory the current directory.
`IFS='`*chars*`'`	Sets the internal field separator to *chars*; the defaults are space, tab, and newline.
`MAIL=`*filename*	Sets the default name of your mail file; the shell tells you when you receive mail via the `mail` or `mailx` commands.
`MAILCHECK=`*n*	Specifies the frequency *n* with which the shell checks for new mail; the default is 600 seconds, or 10 minutes.
`MAILPATH=`*filename*	Indicates one or more files, separated by a colon, in which to receive mail.
`PATH=`*dir*	Sets one or more pathnames, separated by colons, that the shell should search for commands to execute; the default is `/usr/bin`.
`PS1=`*string*	Specifies the primary shell prompt; the default is `$`.
`PS2=`*string*	Specifies the secondary shell prompt for use in multiline commands; the default is >. The appearance of this prompt indicates that the shell expects more input.
`SHACCT=`*filename*	Specifies the shell accounting file used to log records for all executed shell scripts.

B

Table B.12: Built-in Bourne Shell Variables (continued)

VARIABLE	DESCRIPTION
SHELL=*filename*	Specifies the shell to be used by commands when you escape to a subshell; of special interest to ed and vi.
TERM=*string*	Specifies your terminal type; required by some commands that use the whole screen for output.

Table B.13: Built-in Bourne Shell Commands

COMMAND	DESCRIPTION
:	Null command. The shell performs no action and returns an exit status of 0.
.*filename*	Reads and executes lines in *filename* as part of the current process.
break [*n*]	Exits from *n* levels in a for or while loop; the default is 1.
cd [*directory*]	Changes to the specified *directory*; the default is the home directory.
continue [*n*]	Skips any remaining commands in a for or while loop, resuming with the next iteration of the loop or skipping *n* loops.
echo *args*	Writes *args* to the screen.
eval [*args*]	Executes the specified *args*, allowing evaluation and substitution of shell variables.
exec [*command*]	Executes *command* without starting a new process.
exit [*n*]	Exits from the current shell procedure with an exit status of *n*.
export [*names*]	Exports the value of one or more shell variables, making them global in scope rather than local, which is the default.
getopts *string var* ➥ [*args*]	Checks command options, including *args* if provided, for legal choices.
hash [-r][*commands*]	Establishes a tracked alias for *commands* to speed execution; the -r option clears tracked aliases.
newgrp [-][*group*]	Switches to *group*, or returns to your login group.
pwd	Displays the pathname of the current working directory.
read *var1* [*var2...*]	Reads one line from standard input, and assigns each word to a named variable; all leftovers are assigned to the last variable.

Table B.13: Built-in Bourne Shell Commands (continued)

COMMAND	DESCRIPTION
`readonly [`*`var1`*`...]`	Makes the specified variables read-only so that they cannot be changed.
`return [`*`n`*`]`	Exits from a function with the exit status *`n`*, and returns to the shell.
`set` ➥ `[`*`option arg1 arg2`*`...]`	Without arguments, `set` prints the names and values of all shell variables. *`option`* can be turned on by using a minus sign or turned off with a plus sign, and arguments are assigned in order to the parameters `$1`, `$2`, and so on. The options are listed in Table B.14.
`shift [`*`n`*`]`	Shifts positional arguments *`n`* places (by default 1 place) to the left.
`test`	Tests a condition, and if true, returns a zero exit status.
`times`	Displays cumulative system and user time for all processes run by the shell.
`trap [[`*`commands`*`]` ➥ *`signals`*`]`	Executes *`commands`* if any *`signals`* are received.
`type [`*`names`*`]`	Shows whether *`names`* are Unix commands, built-in commands, or a defined shell function.
`ulimit [-f `*`n`*`]`	Sets a limit of *`n`* hard disk blocks for files created by the shell and child processes. Without *`n`*, displays the current limit.
`umask [`*`nnn`*`]`	Sets the user file creation mask to octal value *`nnn`*; if *`nnn`* is omitted, displays the current user creation mask.
`unset [`*`names`*`]`	Removes definitions of the specified functions or variables in *`names`*.
`wait [`*`n`*`]`	Waits for the process with ID of *`n`* to complete execution in the background and display its exit status.

Table B.14: Options to Use with the set Bourne Shell Command	
OPTION	DESCRIPTION
-/+a	Export/do not export defined or modified variables.
-/+e	Exit/do not exit if a command yields a non-zero exit status.
-/+f	Disable/enable filename metacharacters.
-/+h	Enable/disable quick access to commands.
-/+k	Provide/do not provide all environment variable assignments.
-/+n	Read but do not execute/execute commands.
-/+t	Execute/do not execute one command, and exit.
-/+u	Consider/do not consider unset variables as errors.
-/+v	Show/do not show each shell command line when read.
-/+x	Display/do not display commands and arguments when executed.

Bourne-again shell

See **Bash.**

Bourne shell family

A collective name for the Bourne shell, Korn shell, Bash (the Bourne-again shell), and the Zsh.

The Bourne shell, named after developer Dr. Steven Bourne, is the oldest Unix shell still in popular use; an up-to-date version of the Bourne shell is available on every Unix system. The Bourne shell is a command interpreter with a built-in programming language, started by the `sh` command.

During the mid-1980s, David Korn developed an upward compatible shell named the Korn shell, `ksh`; anything that works in the Bourne shell automatically works in the Korn shell, too. The Korn shell also adds important new features including a history file, command editing, aliasing, and job control.

Next came the Bourne-again shell, or Bash (`bash`), first released in 1989 by Brian Fox and Chet Ramey as part of the Free Software Foundation GNU Project. Bash extends the features found in the Bourne shell in the same way as the Korn shell.

Zsh (pronounced "zee-shell," `zsh`), developed by Paul Falstad in 1990, quickly developed something of a cult following. The design philosophy behind `zsh` was to create a shell capable of doing anything you could think of, and it is packed with advanced features.

See also **C shell family, Unix shell.**

bpi

Abbreviation for bits per inch. bpi is the number of bits (binary digits) that a disk or tape can store per inch of length.

bps

Abbreviation for bits per second. The number of bits (binary digits) transmitted every second during a data transfer. bps is a measurement of the speed of operation of equipment such as a computer's internal data bus or a modem connecting a computer to a communications line.

braces

The two left { and right } characters also known as *curly braces* but never called *brackets*. Braces are used in several different ways:

- In the Bourne shell, they are used to surround commands that you want to execute as a group.
- In the C shell, they are used to surround variable names and also to force the expansion of items in a comma-separated list.
- In the C language, they are used to indicate the beginning and end of blocks of code.

brackets

See **square brackets.**

brain damaged

Any poorly designed program or piece of hardware that does not include those features most users would consider essential. The implication is that the designer should have known better than to leave those features out of the release.

break

A Bourne, C, and Korn shell command that stops or exits from a looping construct such as `for`, `while`, `select`, `until`, or `continue`. In most cases, `break` is combined with some sort of test condition, and execution continues at the next statement following the end of the loop.

breaksw

Abbreviation for break switch. `breaksw` is a C shell command used to indicate the end of a set of commands in a `case` string search.

See also **`case`, `endsw`, `switch`.**

broadcast

In networking, to send a message simultaneously to all users logged on to the network. Also called *multicast.*

See also **`wall`.**

browser

An application used to explore Internet resources. A browser lets you wander from one World Wide Web node to the next, without concern for the technical details of the links between the nodes or the specific methods used to access them, and presents the information—text, graphics, sound, or video—as a document on the screen.

See also **Gopher, Mosaic, Web browser.**

BSD

Abbreviation for Berkeley Software Distribution. One of the two major strains of Unix, the other being Unix from AT&T; also known as Berkeley Unix.

BSD was developed at the University of California at Berkeley by researchers working in the Computer Systems Research Group (CSRG) from the 1970s to 1993, when the group finally closed its doors. BSD added many significant advanced features to Unix, including the C shell, `vi`, `termcap`, virtual memory, TCP/IP networking additions, and the "fast filesystem." Many of these additions were written by Bill Joy, a major influence at Berkeley, who later went on to become a founder of Sun Microsystems.

Because Berkeley was strictly a research effort, BSD was not supported in the normal way; bug fixes were sometimes made available but were never guaranteed. Eventually, a company called Mt. Xinu ("Unix tm" spelled backwards) was formed to support the Berkeley releases. And this is part of the reason that BSD and the AT&T Unix evolved along different paths. Berkeley was not a commercial organization, selling and supporting hardware and software, but an academic group producing state-of-the-art software with no support obligations. For this reason, BSD appealed to the researcher and scientific user, rather than the more conservative commercial user who tended to use Unix from AT&T.

The BSD versions from 4.1 to the last release, 4.4, and the commercial versions developed from them, including Sun Microsystem's SunOS, Ultrix from DEC, and Mt. Xinu, are still very popular and in use in universities and commercial institutions all over the world. System V Release 4 and some earlier System V versions have many BSD features, and it is no longer necessary to advertise that your version of Unix includes Berkeley enhancements; the enhancements are now taken for granted.

The original release from Berkeley—a variation on Unix from AT&T—was known as "the first Berkeley software distribution," and this was soon abbreviated to 1BSD; the next release was called 2BSD, and so on. Here is a brief rundown of the major features available through the various 4.*x*BSD releases. The first number refers to the version number, and the number after the decimal indicates the release number:

- **4BSD**, October 1980. This release contained several performance improvements including virtual memory, job control, more reliable signals, and the Lisp system.
- **4.1BSD**, June 1981. This upgrade added more performance improvements, support for a new VAX system, and autoconfiguration. This release was taken back to AT&T to form the basis for the Eighth Edition Unix.
- **4.2BSD**, September 1983. This major revision added networking support in the form of TCP/IP, a faster filesystem, the C shell, and other improvements.
- **4.3BSD**, June 1986. This release tuned many of the 4.2 improvements and added support for XNS networking and an Internet name server.
- **4.3-Tahoe**, June 1988. This intermediate release was the first release to move off the VAX to Computer Console's Tahoe system and contained improved TCP/IP algorithms, as well as several kernel improvements. Unfortunately, Computer Console's Tahoe turned into a dead end, and the development stopped.
- **BSD Networking Release 1**, November 1988, also known as NET-1. This release was based on 4.3-Tahoe and included source code and documentation for the networking portions of the kernel, C library, and utility programs. Perhaps the most important feature of this release is that it was made available without proof of any prior AT&T or Berkeley license. The source code contained a Berkeley copyright statement, and a statement that permitted redistribution with appropriate attribution.
- **4.3-Reno**, June 1990. This intermediate release added NFS support and ran on several new systems, including Hewlett-Packard's 9000/300 computers based on the Motorola 680*x*0 series of microprocessors.
- **BSD Networking Release 2**, June 1991, also known as NET-2. This release contained a new virtual memory system based on work done on Carnegie Mellon University's Mach system, as well as a port to the Intel 80*x*86 series of microprocessors.
- **4.4BSD**, June 1993. The final release added ISO/OSI networking support, a new virtual filesystem interface, enhancements to support files and filesystems of up to 2^{63} bytes in size, enhanced security and system management support, many kernel changes, as well as the conversion to and addition of many POSIX features. 4.4BSD also runs on SPARC-based SPARCstations 1 and 2, MIPS-based Decstations 3100 and 5000, Sony NEWS, Hewlett-Packard 9000/300, Omron Luna, and Intel 80386 (and later) systems.

For more details on the many different strands of Unix evolution and the many colorful personalities involved, see *A Quarter Century of Unix*, by Peter Salus.

See also **FreeBSD, Hurd, Linux, NetBSD, Unix, Unix history.**

buffer

- An area of memory used as temporary storage, found in either hardware or software.
- Unix uses buffers maintained by the kernel to mediate between running processes and input/output devices; buffers used by disks or block devices are called *block buffers*, and those used by terminals or character devices are called *c-lists*. Several of the Unix editors store text in a buffer or temporary work area as you edit a file; when you are finished, the buffer is copied over and replaces your original file.
- To store information temporarily as it is being sent to or received from a device until it can be used, usually to increase efficiency.
- Buffers are implemented in several different ways, including first-in-first-out (FIFO) used for pipes and last-in-last-out (LILO) used for stacks and circular buffers such as event logs.

See also **ed**, **buffered I/O**, **vi**.

buffered I/O

Any input or output that takes place through a temporary work area or buffer. Buffers are used to increase performance; instead of making lots of small transfers, the system makes one large transfer when the buffer is full. Buffered I/O usually refers to the buffers contained in a program that buffer transactions between the application and the Unix kernel.

building a new kernel

See **rebuilding the kernel.**

built-in command

Any command that is actually a part of the shell and is executed directly by the shell, rather than by forking a new process. This allows built-in commands to execute quickly and lets them affect the environment of the current shell.

Each of the three major shells—the Bourne shell, the C shell, and the Korn shell—have their own distinctive set of commands. Because most of the built-in commands work in the same way as the normal Unix utilities work, you may not always be aware of whether the command is a utility or a built-in command. Table B.15 indicates the number of built-in commands in each of the popular shells.

A built-in command is also known as an *internal command.*

Table B.15: The Number of Built-in Commands in Each Shell

SHELL NAME	NUMBER OF BUILT-IN COMMANDS
Bourne shell	32
Bash	50
C shell	52
Korn shell	43
Tcsh	56
Zsh	73

built-in editor

In the Korn shell, a feature that lets you recall, edit, and re-execute commands from your history file. You can choose one of two built-in editors, which means you can use either **emacs** or **vi**-like commands on your history file.

You indicate which editor you want to use with one of these commands:

```
set -o vi

set -o emacs
```

Once you have settled on a choice, place the appropriate command in your environment file so that your preference is set automatically. You should remember that you are not using the real **vi** or **emacs** editor, but you are using a feature in the shell.

bus

An electronic pathway along which signals are sent from one part of a computer to another. In the PC, several different types are available:

- **ISA:** Industry Standard Architecture
- **EIAS:** Enhanced Industry Standard Architecture
- **VL bus:** Vesa Local bus
- **PCI:** Peripheral Component Interconnect

bus mastering

A technique that allows certain advanced bus architectures to delegate control of data transfers between the central processing unit (CPU) and associated peripheral device to an add-in board. This gives greater system bus access and higher data transfer rates than conventional systems.

In the PC, more modern bus designs, such as MCA, EISA, VL bus, and PCI all support some form of bus mastering, but older designs, such as ISA, do not.

byte

Contraction of binary digit eight. A group of eight bits that in storage terms usually holds a single character, such as a number, letter, or other symbol.

Because bytes represent such a small amount of data storage, they are usually grouped into kilobytes (1024 bytes), megabytes (1,048,576 bytes), or gigabytes (1,073,741,824 bytes) for convenience when describing hard disk capacity or computer memory size.

■ *See also* **ASCII, binary, octet.**

THE **unix** DESK REFERENCE

C

A general-purpose programming language, developed by Dennis Ritchie while at AT&T's Bell Labs in 1972. The language is described in the classic book *The C Programming Language* by Brian Kernighan and Dennis Ritchie, published in 1978. The name *C* derived from an earlier language developed by Ken Thompson called *B*.

C originated as the primary language in the Unix world, and after its standardization by the ANSI X3J11 committee (ANSI C) in the 1980s, it became widely used. It is now the language of choice for programmers developing commercial software on virtually all computer systems.

C is a compiled language with a relatively small set of built-in functions; other functions are available in libraries accessed from C programs, and programmers can create their own libraries of functions as they need them. Although you can call your functions almost anything you like, each program must have one function called `main`, which is the control module of the whole program; program execution always begins with the `main` function. `main` calls other functions, which may call other functions, and so on.

If your program is long and complex, consider dividing it up into several files. A C program can consist of many files, however, each function must be completely contained within one file; a function cannot be split across two files.

You can use C to develop software that ranges from operating systems such as Unix, to complex application programs, to device drivers. It is well-suited to a whole range of tasks; however, it can appear terse and obscure to beginning programmers. Pascal and BASIC were originally developed as teaching languages, but C was developed by and for experienced professional programmers with backgrounds in assembly language programming. Most of the Unix operating system is written in C, and Unix provides an ideal environment for programming in C.

The strengths of C lie in the fact that you can use it to write programs that are fast, powerful, and (perhaps most important of all in the commercial world) easily portable. In other words, you can move a program written for one

computer to a completely different computer with relatively little effort, as long as a C compiler is available for the target machine.

■ *See also* **C++, compiler, compiling a C program, g++, gcc, K&R.**

C++

Pronounced "see-plus-plus." An object-oriented extension of the popular C programming language, developed by Bjarne Stroustrup of AT&T's Bell Labs in the early 1980s. Originally called *C with classes*, C++ combines traditional elements of the C language with object-oriented capability and has been adopted as the in-house programming language by a number of companies including Sun Microsystems.

One of the key benefits to using C++ as a development language is that it allows for greater reuse of code, which in turn provides lower long-term maintenance costs. However, for all but the simplest applications, considerably more design effort may be required in the early development stages of a project. This can be minimized to some extent by the use of established class libraries.

■ *See also* **compiling a C program, g++, gcc, object-oriented programming.**

cache

Pronounced "cash." A set of buffers used to store data from a block device so that the data does not have to be read again when a program asks for it. Caching is particularly efficient when a block interface performs input/output on a filesystem stored on a block device, an operation that affects the performance of most Unix systems

cache controller

Pronounced "cash controller." A special-purpose processor, such as the Intel 82385, whose sole task is to manage cache memory. On newer processors, such as the Intel Pentium, cache management is integrated directly into the processor.

■ *See also* **cache memory.**

cache memory

Pronounced "cash memory." A relatively small section of very fast memory (often static RAM) reserved for the temporary storage of the data or instructions likely to be needed next by the processor. For example, the Intel Pentium has an 8 KB code cache as well as an 8 KB data cache.

■ *See also* **cache controller.**

caddy

The flat plastic container used to load a compact disc into a CD-ROM disc drive.

CAE

Abbreviation for Common Application Environment. A set of standards developed by X/Open for application development, including standards for the operating system, compilers, software development tools, data management, networking, and the graphical user interface (GUI).

cal

A command that prints a simple calendar for the current month on standard out.

▶ Syntax

The syntax for `cal` is straightforward:

```
cal [month][year]
```

▶ Options and Arguments

`cal` prints a 12-month calendar beginning in January for any given *`year`* (ranging from 1 to 9999), in full, as in 1996. If you enter **cal 96**, a calendar for the year 96 is displayed, which is probably not what you want. cal displays a one-month calendar for the specified *month* (ranging from 1 to 12) and *year*.

▶ Examples

To print a calendar for October 1996, use:

```
cal 10 1996
```

This calendar contains more lines than one screen can display, so you might pipe the output through pg and view it one screen at a time:

```
cal 10 1996 | pg
```

And to see a really odd-looking calendar, take a look at the year 1752 when the Gregorian calendar came into being.

■ *See also* **calendar, date.**

calendar

A utility that reads your /home/calendar file and displays all the lines that contain certain dates. You can use this as a to-do list or as a reminder service.

On weekdays, calendar displays items with today's and tomorrow's dates; on Fridays and Saturdays, calendar shows items through Monday; and on Sunday, it displays items for both Sunday and Monday.

▶ Syntax

The syntax for calendar is:

```
calendar [option]
```

In BSD, entries in the calendar text file must contain a reference to a date as the first item; in other systems, the date can appear anywhere on the line. You can enter the date in one of several ways; you can use 05/08, May 8, or 05/08/96. If you use an asterisk (*) in the month position, the associated reminder is posted on that day every month. A day without a month matches that day every week, and a month without a day matches the first day of that month. Your calendar file must be readable by everybody.

▶ Options and Arguments

calendar takes one option, a – in System V and -a in BSD, for superuser use only, which tells calendar to send reminders for today and tomorrow to all users on the system by e-mail.

▶ Examples

You can add entries like these to your calendar file:

```
May 6      Meet VP Eng 2pm
05/08      Buy flowers
```

calendar can be automated by using at or crontab, or by including it in your startup file, .profile, .login, or .cshrc.

On some systems, certain default calendar files are provided, including calendar.birthday, a file of birthdays of famous and infamous people; calendar.computer, a list of important dates in computer history; and calendar .music, a list of musical births, deaths, and other important events.

■ *See also* **cal, cron, date.**

call

In programming, a statement that refers to an independent subroutine or function. A call is turned into a branch instruction by the assembler, compiler or interpreter, and the function that is called is responsible for returning to the original program in an appropriate way.

In most programming languages, it is possible to pass information in the form of arguments to a called function and to receive return values back from the function when it finishes executing. Such function-calling protocols are known as *calling conventions* and allow standardized function calls across object code originating from different languages and different compilers.

■ *See also* **call by reference, call by value.**

call by reference

A feature found in many programming languages that allows you to pass a reference to a variable to a called function. During execution of the function, the value of the referenced variable can change.

■ *See also* **call, call by value.**

call by value

A feature found in many programming languages, including C, that allows you to pass a value to a called function. During execution of the function, the value of the referenced variable can change, but this does not affect the original information.

■ *See also* **call, call by reference.**

calling environment

That list of variables and their values made available to a program; also called the *environment*. In the C shell, you can use the `env` command to display the current environment.

■ *See also* **Bourne shell, environment variables, `export`.**

cancel

An SVR4 utility that cancels a print request made by the `lp` spooler. You can also stop a print job that has already started printing.

▶ Syntax

The syntax for `cancel` is:

```
cancel [options][printer]
```

Unless you are a superuser, you can cancel only the print jobs that you have requested yourself. And if a job is in the middle of printing when you try to cancel it, a message is added to the printout to this effect; the next print job in the queue will start printing.

Table C.1: Options to Use with `cancel`

OPTION	DESCRIPTION
request-id	Cancels print request *request-id*.
printer	Cancels the print request currently printing on *printer*.
-u*user*	Cancels the print request associated with *user*.

▶ Options and Arguments

`cancel` has three options shown in Table C.1.

▶ Examples

To cancel print request number 10 on the default printer, use:

```
cancel 10
```

To find out the *request-id* or the name of the *printer* to cancel, use the `lpstat` command. Each *request-id* contains the name of the printer, followed by a hyphen, followed by a sequence number.

To cancel two jobs at once, use:

```
cancel laser-10 laser-15
```

cancelbot

An application that automatically detects cross posting in USENET newsgroups and then issues Cancel replies that delete the original messages.

■ *See also* **knowbot.**

canonical

The usual or standard Unix way of doing something. This term has a more precise meaning in mathematics, where rules dictate the way that formulas are written, but in Unix it tends to mean "according to ancient or religious law."

■ *See also* **holy wars, vanilla.**

caret symbol

- A metacharacter with many meanings and uses within Unix. Do not use a caret in a filename, because to access the file you will always have to turn off the special meaning of this character—more trouble than it is worth.
- One representation of a control character; for example, Ctrl-D can also be written as `^D`.
- A metacharacter used in regular expressions in the `awk`, `ed`, `egrep`, `ex`, `grep`, `sed`, and `vi` programs. The caret matches character strings located only at the beginning of a line. It is also used to invert a match; for example, the sequence `^[^a]` means select all lines not starting with `a`.
- An indicator in the C shell that shows a command substitution has been made in command-line input. To replace some of the characters in the previous command, type ^, followed by those characters you want to replace, then another ^, followed by the new characters.

See also **history, history substitution, regular expressions.**

carriage return

A control character (Ctrl-J) that signals the print head or display cursor to return to the first position of the current line.

See also **ASCII, EBCDIC, linefeed, newline.**

Carrier Sense Multiple Access/Collision Detection

See **CSMA/CD.**

case

- A conditional statement in the Bourne and Korn shells; each alternative in the case statement begins with a `case` label.
- A C shell keyword used to mark each label in a `switch` statement; this usage is the same as that found in the C programming language.

See also **`esac`, `if`, `switch`.**

C

case-insensitive

Any situation that ignores the case of letters and accepts input in both uppercase and lowercase letters. DOS is an example of an operating system that is case-insensitive.

case-sensitive

Any situation in which the case of letters is important. Unix is case-sensitive in most areas, and the C programming language is always case-sensitive. For example, unless you set the `ignorecase` parameter, `vi` always performs case-sensitive searches; similarly, unless you use the `-i` option with `grep`, searches are always case-sensitive.

cat

A common Unix command used to concatenate (join end-to-end) and display files on the standard output.

▶ Syntax

The syntax for `cat` is:

```
cat [options][-][filename...]
```

The `cat` utility reads the specified files in sequence, writing them to standard out; the single hyphen represents standard input.

▶ Options and Arguments

The options available with `cat` are shown in Table C.2.

Table C.2: Options to Use with cat

OPTION	DESCRIPTION
-b	In the BSD version, implies the -n option but does not number the lines.
-e	Prints a $ at the end of each line; must be used with the -v option.
-n	In the BSD version, numbers all output lines, starting at 1.
-s	Suppresses messages when cat cannot find nonexistent files. In the BSD version, this option squeezes out multiple adjacent lines, making output single spaced.
-t	Displays each tab as Ctrl-I and each formfeed as Ctrl-L; must be used with the -v option.
-u	Prints the output as unbuffered; the default mode is buffered in blocks or screen lines.
-v	Displays control characters and other nonprinting characters found in binary files. Control characters are displayed as ^*n* where *n* is the corresponding octal character in the range octal 100 to octal 137; see Appendix 1 for more on octal numbers. The del character is shown as ^? .

▶ Examples

To display the contents of a file use:

```
cat /etc/passwd
```

You can use cat to create short text files without bothering to open an editor. To send input from the keyboard to a file, use the following redirection instruction:

```
cat > myfile.txt
```

In this mode, you can use the basic editing keys on the keyboard, but you cannot rework an existing line. Use Ctrl-D on a line by itself to end your input and return to the shell.

If you want to empty a file, but leave the file in place, use:

```
cat /dev/null > myfile.txt
```

The /dev/null file is a system file 0 bytes long used to consume unwanted output; you can also use cp with /dev/null to create a new, empty file.

▶ Notes

Because of the way the shell language mechanism works when performing redirection, the command:

```
cat filename1 filename2 >
➥ filename1
```

overwrites and destroys the original data in *filename1*. If you are using the C shell or the Korn shell, you can prevent this kind of problem by setting the noclobber variable.

■ *See also* **cp, echo, od, pg, pr.**

catenate

To join end-to-end or sequentially. The Unix cat utility catenates files—it displays them one after the other.

■ *See also* **concatenate.**

cb

The C programming language beautifier; a utility that formats C language source code files using proper C programming structure, making the content of the files look neat and more readable.

■ *See also* **cc, gcc, C compiler.**

cbreak mode

An operational mode of the BSD terminal handler that allows a terminal to receive each character as it is typed, but still lets you use the interrupt and quit characters as you normally would. cbreak mode is a compromise between cooked mode and raw mode.

cc

The Unix C programming language compiler. The compiler processes a source-code file through the four stages of preprocessing, compiling, assembling, and linking. This entry describes the SVR4 compiler with notes on Solaris and SCO implementations. BSD includes the GNU C compiler, **gcc**, which is also used on many other systems including Linux; see the **gcc** entry for more details on **gcc**.

▶ Syntax

You can invoke the C compiler using:

`cc [`*`options`*`][`*`filename...`*`]`

This command runs the ANSI C compiler; to use the compiler for Kernighan and Ritchie's C, use:

`/usr/bin/cc`

▶ Options and Arguments

You can use the options listed in Table C.3 with **cc**. Table C.3 describes options available for use with the SVR4 C compiler and includes comments specific to the Solaris compiler. Options for use with the SCO C compiler are given in Table C.4.

▶ Examples

To compile the source file **myprog.c** into an executable file called **skinny**, use:

`cc -o skinny myprog.c`

See also **C, C++, cb, C compiler, C libraries, compiling a C program, gcc, makefile.**

Table C.3: Options for Use with cc

OPTION	DESCRIPTION
-#	A Solaris-only option that indicates when each separate compiler stage is invoked.
-A *name*[*tokens*]	Supplies an assert directive, assigning ***name*** with any optional ***tokens*** as parameters.
-A-	Ignores predefined assertions and macros.
-B *mode*	When ***mode*** is **dynamic**, libraries are shared, and library files ending in both **.so** and **.a** are searched. When ***mode*** is **static**, only **.a** files are searched.
-c	Creates a linkable object file for each file compiled, but does not call the link editor.
-C	Keeps comments during preprocessing.
-d*c*	Tells the link editor to link dynamically when ***c*** is **y** (the default), or to link statically when ***c*** is **n**.
-D *name*[=*def*]	Supplies a **define** directive, specifying ***name*** to be ***def***, or if no ***def*** is given, the value of 1.
-dalign	Produces double load/store instructions to improve performance—Solaris only.

Table C.3: Options for Use with cc (continued)

OPTION	DESCRIPTION
-E	Runs just the macro processor, sending the output to standard out.
-fast	A Solaris-only option that uses the cc options that give the fastest compilation.
-flags	A Solaris-only option that briefly describes the available options.
-fnonstd	Produces a special Solaris format.
-fsingle	A Solaris-only option that evaluates float expressions as single-precision.
-g	Generates extra symbol table information for the dbx and sdb debuggers.
-G	Produces a shared object file instead of a linked executable.
-H	Lists the pathnames of the header files on standard out.
-I *dir*	Searches for include files in the specified *dir*. You must use a separate -I option for each new *dir* you want searched.
-K *word*	When *word* is PIC, produces position-independent code; when *word* is minabi, cc compiles with minimum dynamic linking to keep ABI compliance.
-keeptmp	A Solaris-only option that preserves temporary files.
-L *dir*	Searches for library archive files in the specified *dir*. You must use a separate -L option for each new *dir* you want searched.
-o *filename*	Creates an object file with the name of *filename* rather than the default a.out.
-O	Makes the compiler optimize the object code.
-p	Generates profile information that counts each time a routine is called. Results are stored in the file mon.out, and you can use the profiler prof to analyze the results and create an execution profile.
-P	Runs just the preprocessor, and stores the result in the file *filename*.i.
-Q*c*	When *c* is y, lists information about the compilation tools invoked; when *c* is n, no list is created.
-ql	Produces code to count the number of times each source line is executed. Use lprof to list the counts.
-qp	Same as -p.

Table C.3: Options for Use with cc (continued)

OPTION	DESCRIPTION
`-S`	Compiles only (and optimizes if `-O` is supplied), but does not assemble or link.
`-U` *`name`*	Removes the definition of *`name`* as in an `#undef` directive.
`-v`	Checks C language semantics strictly.
`-V`	Prints the version numbers of the compiler tools.
`-W[p0abl]`*`arg1`* ➥`[,`*`arg2...`*`]`	Sends a particular `cc` option *`arg1`*, *`arg2...`* to a specific compiler tool. The `p` or `0` specifies the compiler, `2` the optimizer, `b` the basic block analyzer, and `l` specifies the link editor.
`-X`*`c`*	Specifies *`c`* as the level of ANSI C compliance. When *`c`* is set to `a`, specifies ANSI compliance; to `c`, specifies conformance, which is stricter than ANSI; to `t`, specifies pre-ANSI features; and the Solaris-only `s` setting is for a Sun C setting.
`-xpg`	A Solaris-only option used like `-p` to create a file `gmon.out` for analysis by `gprof`.
`-xsb`	A Solaris-only option that creates symbol-table data for the Solaris Source Code Browser.
`-xsbfast`	A Solaris-only option, the same as `xsb` but does not compile.
`-xstconst`	A Solaris-only option that adds string literals to the text segment rather than to the data segment.
`-Y`*`c`*`,`*`dir`*	Specifies that item *`c`* is searched in *`dir`*, where *`c`* can be `p, 0, 2, a, b`, or `l` as in `-W` above. With this option, *`c`* can also be `I` (see `-I`), `P` (see `-L`), or `S` for startup object files.

C

Table C.4: Options for Use with the SCO UNIX C Compiler

OPTION	DESCRIPTION
`-ansi`	Enforces full ANSI compliance.
`-B1` *path/filename*	Defines alternate first pass for compiler.
`-B2` *path/filename*	Defines alternate second pass for compiler.
`-B3` *path/filename*	Defines alternate third pass for compiler.
`-c`	Creates a linkable object file for each file compiled, but does not call the link editor.
`-C`	Keeps comments during preprocessing.
`-compat`	Creates an executable file that is binary-compatible across 386 UNIX System V Release 3.2, UNIX-286 System V, UNIX-386 System V, UNIX-286 3.0, and UNIX-8086 System V. Uses XENIX libraries, and creates OMF object files.
`-CSON, -CSOFF`	Enables or disables common subexpression optimization when the `-O` option is specified.
`-d`	Displays compiler passes and their arguments before execution.
`-dos`	Creates a DOS executable.
`-D`*name*`[=`*string*`}`	Defines *name* to the preprocessor in the same way as a `#define` statement in the source file.
`-E`	Preprocesses each source file as described for `-P`, sending the results to standard out.
`-EP`	Preprocesses each source file as described for `-P`, sending the results to standard out and to a file.
`-F`*number*	Sets the stack size to *number* in hexadecimal.
`-Fa, -Fa`*filename*	Creates a `masm` assembly source listing in `source.asm` or in *filename*.
`-Fc, -Fc`*filename*	Creates a merged assembly and C source listing in `source.L` or in *filename*.
`-Fe`*filename*	Creates an executable file *filename*.
`-Fl, -Fl`*filename*	Creates a listing file in `source.L` or *filename* with assembly source and object code.
`-Fm, -Fm`*filename*	Creates a map file called `a.map` or *filename*.

Table C.4: Options for Use with the SCO UNIX C Compiler (continued)	
OPTION	DESCRIPTION
`-Fo`*`object-filename`*	Creates an object file called *`object-filename`*.
`-FPa, -FPc, -FPc87, -FPi, -FPi87`	These options are used with `-dos` or `-os2` to specify the type of floating-point code generated and the library support to use.
`-g`	Generates symbol table information needed by the `sdb`, `dbxtra`, and Code View debuggers.
`-Gc`	Specifies calling sequences and naming conventions used with System V 386 Pascal and Fortran.
`-Gs`	Removes stack probe routines. This option can make the binary file smaller and can increase execution speed somewhat.
`-H`*`length`*	Sets the maximum length of internal symbols to *`length`*.
`-help, -HELP`	Prints a help menu.
`-i`	Creates separate code and data spaces for small model programs in 8086/186/286 compilations only.
`-I` *`dir`*	Searches for include files in the specified *`dir`*. You must use a separate `-I` option for each new *`dir`* you want searched.
`-iBCS2`	Enforces strict Intel Binary Compatibility Standard 2 compliance.
`-J`	Changes the default `char` mode from signed to unsigned.
`-K`	Removes the stack probes from a program.
`-L`	Creates an assembler listing that contains assembled code and assembly source code in the file `source.L`.
`-l` *`name`*	Searches library *`name`*`.a` for unresolved function references.
`-LARGE`	Invokes the compiler's large model mode.
`-link`	Passes all options that follow this option directly to the link editor.
`-m` *`filename`*	Creates a map file called *`filename`*.
`-M` *`string`*	Sets program configuration to *`string`*, where *`string`* can be any of those listed in Table C.5.
`-n`	Sets pure text model.
`-nl` *`length`*	Sets maximum length of external symbols to *`length`*.

Table C.4: Options for Use with the SCO UNIX C Compiler (continued)

OPTION	DESCRIPTION
`-nointl`	Creates an executable file without international functions.
`-ND` *`name`*	Sets the data segment for each assembled or compiled source file to *`name`*.
`-NM` *`name`*	Sets the module name for each assembled or compiled source file to *`name`*.
`-NT` *`name`*	Sets the text segment name for each assembled or compiled source file to *`name`*.
`-O`	Makes the compiler optimize the object code.
`-o` *`filename`*	Creates an object file with the name of *`filename`* rather than the default `a.out`.
`-O` *`string`*	Invokes the object code optimizer; *`string`* can contain one or more of the items listed in Table C.6.
`-os2`	Creates an OS/2 executable, using OS/2 libraries.
`-p`	Generates profile information that counts each time a routine is called. Results are stored in the file `mon.out`, and you can use the profiler `prof` to analyze the results and create an execution profile.
`-P`	Runs just the preprocessor, and stores the result in the file *`filename`*`.i`.
`-pack`	Packs structures.
`-posix`	Enforces strict POSIX compliance.
`-ql`	Invokes the basic block analyzer to count the number of times each source line is executed. Use `lprof` to list counts.
`-qp`	Same as `-p`.
`-quiet`	Turns off echoing of source filenames during compilation.
`-r`	Performs an incremental link.
`-s`	Tells the linker to remove symbol table information from the executable file.
`-S`	Creates an assembly listing in `masm` format.
`-Sl` *`linewidth`*	Specifies the maximum characters per line for the source file.
`-Sp` *`pagelength`*	Specifies the number of lines per page in the source file.
`-Ss` *`string`*, `-St` *`string`*	Sets the subtitle (`-Ss` *`string`*) and title (`-St` *`string`*) for source listings, and bypasses `cc`'s linking operation.
`-strict`	Restricts language to ANSI C.
`-svid`	Enforces SVID compliance.

Table C.4: Options for Use with the SCO UNIX C Compiler (continued)

OPTION	DESCRIPTION
`-Tc` *filename*	Tells `cc` that *`filename`* is a C source file.
`-u`	Removes all manifest defines.
`-U` *definition*	Removes or undefines the *`definition`* manifest define.
`-unix`	Generates Unix COFF files, the default mode.
`-V` *string*	Places *`string`* in the object file.
`-w`	Suppresses compiler error messages.
`-W` *number*	Sets the level for compiler error messages, from 0 (no warnings issued) to 3 (all warning messages are issued).
`-WX`	Turns all errors into fatal errors.
`-xenix`	Creates a XENIX program using XENIX libraries and `#include` files.
`-x2.3`	Same as `-xenix`, but adds extended functions available with XENIX System V 386 Release 2.3.
`-xout`	Same as `-x2.3`, but adds functions from SCO UNIX 3.2.
`-xpg3`	Enforces XPG3 compliance.
`-xpg3plus`	Enforces XPG3 compliance with SCO added value.
`-X`	Removes standard directories from list of directories to search for `#include` files.
`-z`	Displays compiler passes and arguments, but does not execute them.
`-Za`	Confines language to ANSI specifications.
`-Zd`	Includes line numbers in the object file.
`-Ze`	Enables `near`, `far`, `huge`, `pascal`, and `fortran` keywords.
`-Zg`	Generates function declarations from function definitions and writes declarations to standard out.
`-Zi`	Includes information for the `sdb`, `dbxtra`, and Code View debuggers.
`-Zl`	Removes the default library information from the object file.
`-Zp`*n*	Packs structure members in memory. *n* can be 1 for the 8086 processor, 2 for the 80286 processor, or 4 for the 80386 processor.
`-Zs`	Performs only a syntax check.

Table C.5: Values to Use with the -M Option in the SCO Unix C Compiler

VALUE	DESCRIPTION
0	8086 code generation.
1	80186 code generation.
2	80286 code generation.
3	80386 code generation.
b	Reverses word order for `long` data types.
c	Creates a compact model program for 80186/80286 compilations only.
d	Tells `cc` not to assume register SS equates to register DS.
e	Enables `near`, `far`, `huge`, `pascal` and `fortran` keywords.
f	Enables software floating point.
h	Creates a huge model program for 80186/80286 compilations only.
l	Creates a large model program for 8086/80186/80286 compilations only.
m	Creates a medium model program for 8086/80186/80286 compilations only.
s	Creates a small model program; the default setting.
t *number*	Sets largest size of a data item to *number*; default is 32,767.

Table C.6: Values to Use with the -O Option in the SCO Unix C Compiler

VALUE	DESCRIPTION
3	Disables pass 3 optimization.
a	Relaxes alias checking.
c	Enables default local common expressions.
d	Turns off all the following optimization options; `a`, `c`, `e`, `g`, `i`, `l`, `s`, `t`.
e	Enables global register allocation.
g	Enables global optimization.
h	Optimizes code for functions returning `short` or `char`.
i	Generates intrinsics.
l	Performs loop optimizations.
n	Disables unsafe loop optimizations.
p	Improves floating-point calculations.
r	Disables inline returns from functions.
s	Optimizes code for size.
t	Optimizes code for speed, the default setting.
x	Performs maximum optimization.
z	Enables maximum loop- and global-register allocation.

ccat

A BSD shell script used to cat files compressed by the `compact` command.

▶ Syntax

The syntax to use with `ccat` is:

```
ccat [-v][filename...]
```

The `compact` command compresses the specified *`filename`* using adaptive Huffman coding into a file called *`filename`*`.C`, and you can use `ccat` to cat the file without uncompressing it first. If you use the `-v` option, `ccat` provides the names of the compressed files.

■ *See also* **`compact`**, **`compress`**, **`makefile`**, **`pack`**, **`uncompact`**.

C compiler

A program that translates high-level programming language statements written in C into a machine language program capable of execution.

A compiler translates the entire program into machine language at the same time, checking syntax and posting error messages or warnings as appropriate. Only when this process is complete can the program execute. This is in contrast to an interpreter, which translates and then executes one line at a time.

The process of compiling a C program is more complex than this, of course, and requires that several programs work together to create an executable program. Here is a closer look at the steps involved.

1. Create the source code for the program using an editor such as `vi`. Add `.c` as an extension to the source code filename because the C compiler expects C source code filenames to end with this extension; C++ source code filenames should end with `.C` or `.cc`.
2. You can use `cb`, the C beautifier, to impose a standard layout on your source code if you wish.
3. Invoke the C compiler, which in turn calls the C preprocessor, the C compiler, the assembler, and the linker or link editor.

   The C preprocessor expands macro definitions and also includes header files.

   The compiler creates assembly language statements that correspond to the instructions in your source code and then creates machine-readable object code. One object file is created for each source file; the object file has the same name as the source code file, except that the `.c` extension is changed into `.o`.
4. Finally, the linker searches specified C libraries for functions needed by your program and combines object modules for these functions with your program's object modules, creating an executable file called `a.out`, which you can use just like other executable programs or shell scripts. It makes sense to rename this file to a more meaningful name, because it will be overwritten by the file created the next time you use the compiler.

The C compiler usually has a default mode that does a good job of compiling most programs; however, it also has a number of options you can use for special circumstances, such as optimizing your code to run as efficiently as possible.

■ *See also* **`as`**, **assembler**, **`cc`**, **compiling a C program**, **`dbx`**, **`g++`**, **`gcc`**, **`imake`**, **`lint`**, **`make`**.

C

cd

A built-in shell command used to change from one working directory to another. When used without arguments, `cd` changes directories to your home directory1; otherwise, it changes to the specified directory. If the specified directory is a relative pathname, the `CDPATH` (Bourne and Korn shells) or `cdpath` (C shell) variable is searched.

In the Korn shell, you can also use:

```
cd -
```

where – indicates the name of the previous directory, or:

```
cd [old-dir new-dir]
```

where the shell replaces the string *`old-dir`* with *`new-dir`* and changes to the resulting directory.

See also **cdpath, CDPATH, chdir, pwd.**

cdc

See **SCCS.**

CDDI

Abbreviation for Copper Distributed Data Interface. A version of the FDDI standard designed to run on shielded and unshielded twisted pair cable rather than fiber optic cable. CDDI is capable of 100 Mbps data transfer rates.

CDE

Abbreviation for Common Desktop Environment. A set of specifications developed by the Common Open Software Environment (COSE) that define an API for a common Unix graphical user interface (GUI). The specifications cover the interoperability of applications across different hardware platforms, multimedia and networking operations, as well as object-oriented technology and system administration issues.

cdpath

A C shell variable used to specify the paths to be checked when the `cd` or `chdir` commands are used. If this variable is not set, you can execute a file only by specifying its complete pathname.

CDPATH

A Bourne and Korn shell variable used to specify the paths to be checked when the `cd` or `chdir` commands are used.

This variable is usually defined in your `.profile` file and contains shorthand names for commonly used directories. If this variable is not set, you can execute a file only by specifying its complete pathname.

CD-R

Abbreviation for CD Recordable. A type of CD device that brings CD-ROM publishing into the realm of the small business or home office. From a functional point of view, a CD-R and a CD-ROM are identical; you can read CD-R discs using almost any CD-ROM drive, although the processes that create the discs are slightly different. Low-cost CD-R drives are available from many manufacturers, including Kao, Kodak, Mitsui, Phillips, Ricoh, Sony, TDK, 3M, and Verbatim, and will soon challenge tape as the archive or backup media of choice.

See also **erasable CD.**

CD-ROM

Acronym for compact disc-read only memory, pronounced "see-dee-rom." A high-capacity, optical storage device that uses compact disc technology to store large amounts of information, up to 650 MB (the equivalent of approximately 300,000 pages of text), on a single 4.72" disc.

CD-ROMs are important components of multimedia PCs and are used to store encyclopedias, dictionaries and other large reference works. They also store libraries of fonts and clip art for desktop publishing. Increasingly they are used as the distribution mechanism for large software packages: instead of shuffling 20 or 30 floppy disks, you can load the whole package (or operating system) from a single compact disc.

A CD-ROM uses the constant linear velocity encoding scheme to store information in a single, spiral track divided into many equal-length segments. To read data, the CD-ROM drive must increase the rotational speed as the read head gets closer to the center of the disc, and decrease as the head moves back out. Typical CD-ROM data access times are in the range of 0.3 to 1.5 seconds; much slower than a hard disk.

CD-ROMs are usually considered to be WORM (write once, read many) devices, but several vendors are working toward a format that will allow users to add information to an existing multisession compact disc.

■ *See also* **CD-R, SCSI.**

CD-ROM drive

A disk device that uses compact disc technology to store large amounts of information. Many CD-ROM drives also have headphone jacks, external speaker jacks, and volume controls.

CD-ROM drives designed for computer use are more expensive than audio CD players because CD-ROM drives are manufactured to much higher tolerances. If a CD player misreads a small amount of data, the human ear probably will not detect the difference; if a CD-ROM drive misreads a few bytes of a program, the program will not run.

CD-ROM drives are available with the following data transfer rates:

- **Single-speed** drives transfer data at up to 150 Kbps (kilobytes per second). The earliest available drives were single speed.
- **Double-speed** drives transfer data at up to 300 Kbps.
- **Quad-speed** drives have a data transfer rate of 600 Kbps.
- **6X speed** drives have a data transfer rate of 900 Kbps and a disk access time of only 140 milliseconds.

The two most popular CD-ROM drive interface cards are SCSI and ATAPI (AT Attachment Packet Interface). ATAPI is part of the Enhanced IDE specification introduced by Western Digital in 1994 and lets you plug an IDE CD-ROM directly into an IDE controller on the system's motherboard. Other CD-ROM drives may use the computer's parallel port or a PCMCIA connection.

■ *See also* **CD-ROM, SCSI.**

CD-ROM Extended Architecture

Abbreviated CD-ROM/XA. An extension to the CD-ROM format, developed by Microsoft, Phillips, and Sony, that allows for the storage of audio and visual information on compact disc, so that you can play the audio at the same time you view the visual data.

CD-ROM/XA is compatible with the High Sierra specification, also known as ISO standard 9660.

CD-ROM/XA

■ *See* **CD-ROM Extended Architecture.**

central processing unit

■ *See* **CPU.**

CERN

Abbreviation for European Laboratory for Particle Physics, located in Geneva, Switzerland, which used to be called Conseil Europeen pour la Recherche Nucleaire.

CERN is known as the birthplace of the World Wide Web, which was originally intended as a research tool for the scientific community but quickly became the standard way of accessing Internet resources. In 1994, CERN joined with MIT to develop standards for commercial use of the Web, for security, and for privacy.

You can use a Web browser to access the CERN home page with the following URL:

```
http://info.cern.ch
```

■ *See also* **browser.**

CFV

Abbreviation for Call for Votes. A USENET posting to the newsgroup `news.announce.newsgroups` soliciting votes for the creation of a proposed new newsgroup. Voters have from 21 to 31 days to vote using e-mail; to pass, a proposed newsgroup must attract a two-thirds majority of votes, with at least 100 more yes votes than no votes. If the proposal fails, the proposer must wait at least six months before trying again. These rules do not apply to alt newsgroups; anyone can create an alt newsgroup without any kind of vote.

■ *See also* **RFD.**

character

A symbol that corresponds to a key on the keyboard. A character can be a letter, number, punctuation, or special symbol and is usually stored in a single byte. A collection of related characters is known as a *character set*, and the most common character set on Unix systems is the ASCII character set. EBCDIC is still used on some IBM systems. In an attempt to rationalize the many international character sets in use these days, some systems use more than one byte to store a character.

■ *See also* **ASCII, DBCS, extended ASCII character set.**

character class

A group of characters in a regular expression, usually surrounded by square brackets, that define which characters can occupy a single character position. For example, the character class defined by:

```
[abcd]
```

represents a single character that can by occupied by an `a`, a `b`, a `c`, or a `d`.

■ *See also* **caret symbol, regular expressions.**

character device

A device that displays, processes, or stores one character at a time, such as a terminal, a printer, and certain types of communications links. Character devices are accessed via a character special file.

■ *See also* **block device, raw device.**

character I/O

Abbreviation for character input/output. Any communication with a peripheral or remote device that takes place one character or one byte at a time with no buffering.

■ *See also* **caret symbol, character device, regular expressions.**

character set

A standard group of letters, numbers, and other control and punctuation symbols used by a computer. Common character sets include ASCII, the extended ASCII character set, and EBCDIC.

character special file

A Unix special file that provides an interface definition to a character device such as a terminal or printer. This interface is used with devices that cannot support a filesystem and as an alternative interface for those devices that can.

You can find these files in the `/dev` directory; some of the more important are `/dev/console`, the system console; `/dev/tty`, your terminal; and `/dev/null`, the null device.

■ *See also* **block device, character special file, device file, special file.**

character terminal

Any terminal that can only display characters such as letters, numbers, and punctuation marks.

■ *See also* **dumb terminal, X terminal.**

characters per inch

See **CPI.**

characters per second

See **CPS.**

chat

See **IRC.**

chdir

A built-in C shell command used to change the current working directory. The `cd` command is a much more popular way of achieving the same end, but `chdir` can be useful if you want to redefine `cd`.

checking/repairing a filesystem

The system administrator has to check a filesystem for errors and for consistency from time to time and make any necessary repairs. Filesystem errors can be caused by a system crash or a power outage that prevents the kernel from synchronizing the filesystem cache with the information on the hard disk. These errors are usually fairly minor, but if you were interrupted while writing a very large file, those lost blocks may be marked as in use when no file entry corresponds to them. The system administrator can use the `fsck` program to check for and then repair these problems.

Some systems execute `fsck` at boot time, mounting the `root` filesystem initially as read-only, running `fsck`, and then remounting the filesystem with new parameters so that it is mounted read-write. Any further discussion of `fsck` is beyond the scope of this book; see the `man` pages for more details, or talk to your system administrator.

checkmail

An SCO command that reports on the status of mail you have sent but has not yet been delivered.

▶ Syntax

The syntax for `checkmail` is:

```
checkmail [options]
```

▶ Options and Arguments

If you use `checkmail` without arguments, the `Subject:` of each message is displayed along with a list of addressees who have yet to receive this message. The `checkmail` options are listed in Table C.7.

If mail consistently remains in the queue, it may mean that a host computer is down somewhere in the network.

See also **CRC, mail, Mail, mailx.**

Table C.7: Options for Use with checkmail

OPTION	DESCRIPTION
`-a`	Shows all addresses, both delivered and undelivered.
`-f`	Suppresses display of the `Subject:` line.
`-m`	Checks all the mail in the mail queue; not just your mail.

checknr

A BSD command that checks `nroff` or `troff` input files for certain types of errors and unknown commands.

▶ Syntax

The syntax for `checknr` is:

```
checknr [options] filename
```

If no files are specified, `checknr` checks standard input.

▶ **Options and Arguments**

You can use the options listed in Table C.8 with `checknr`.

`checknr` is intended for use on files prepared with `checknr` originally in mind, and expects certain document style standards; `checknr` also understands the `me` and `ms` macro packages.

■ *See also* **me macros, ms macros, `nroff`, `troff`.**

checksum

A method of providing information for error detection, usually calculated by summing a set of values.

The checksum is usually appended to the data that it is calculated from, so that data and checksum can be compared. Some checksum algorithms are simple, aimed at detecting major errors, while others are much more subtle. It is important to remember that the value of the checksum must depend only on the file or data being checked, rather than on the hardware or the individual implementation.

Xmodem, the popular file transfer protocol, uses a 1-byte checksum calculated by adding all the ASCII values for all 128 data bytes and ignoring any numerical overflow. The checksum is added to the end of the Xmodem data packet. This kind of checksum does not always detect all errors and, in later versions of the Xmodem protocol, was replaced by a cyclical redundancy check (CRC) for more rigorous error control.

■ *See also* **CRC, `sum`.**

chflags

A BSD command used to change file flags.

▶ **Syntax**

The syntax for `chflags` is as follows:

```
chflags [-R[-H|-L]-P]
➥ flags filename...
```

`flags` represents a comma-separated list of keywords, which are listed in Table C.9.

To turn a flag off, add `no` before an option, so that `dump` becomes `nodump`, for example.

▶ **Options and Arguments**

The options for `chflags` are listed in Table C.10.

chgrp

A command that changes the group associated with a file or a set of files. You must be the superuser or the owner of a file before you can change the group association of a file; if you are the owner, you must also belong to the specified group.

▶ **Syntax**

The syntax for `chgrp` is as follows:

```
chgrp [options] group
➥ filenames
```

where *`group`* is the name or numeric ID of the new group, and *`filenames`* represents the file or files whose group association you want to change.

Table C.8: Options for Use with `checknr`

OPTION	DESCRIPTION
`-a.`*`x1.y1...xn.yn`*	Adds additional pairs of macros to the list of known macros. This option must take the form of a period, the first macro name, another period, and the second macro name. For example, to define the macros .BS and .BT, use `-a.BS.BT`.
`-c.`*`x1.x2...xn`*	Adds new command definitions.
`-f`	Ignores `\f` font changes.
`-s`	Ignores `\s` size changes.

Table C.9: Keywords for Use with `chflags`

KEYWORD	DESCRIPTION
`dump`	Sets the dump flag.
`sappnd`	Sets the system append-only flag; superuser only.
`schg`	Sets the system-immutable flag; superuser only.
`uappnd`	Sets the user append-only flag; owner or superuser only.
`uchg`	Sets the user-immutable flag; owner or superuser only.

Table C.10: Options for Use with `chflags`

OPTION	DESCRIPTION
`-H`	When the **`-R`** option is used, symbolic links on the command line are followed.
`-L`	When the **`-R`** option is used, all symbolic links are followed.
`-P`	When the **`-R`** option is used, no symbolic links are followed.
`-R`	Changes the file flags for the file hierarchies rooted in the files, instead of just the files themselves.

▶ Options and Arguments

Table C.11 lists the options that are available with this command.

SCO supports no options for this command, SVR4 supports the **`-R`** option, while BSD supports several more, as shown in Table C.11; see the **`man`** pages for more information about the options available on your system.

Table C.11: Options to Use with `chgrp`

OPTION	DESCRIPTION
`-f`	Invokes force option that ignores errors.
`-h`	Changes a symbolic link, not the file referenced by a symbolic link. This option is not available on all systems.
`-H`	When the **`-R`** option is used, symbolic links on the command line are followed.
`-L`	When the **`-R`** option is used, all symbolic links are followed.
`-P`	When the **`-R`** option is used, no symbolic links are followed.
`-R`	Changes the group ID for files, subdirectories, and symbolic links.

▶ Examples

To change the group that the file `myfile.doc` is associated with to that of `pub`, use:

```
chgrp pub myfile.doc
```

■ *See also* **chmod, chown.**

child process

Also known as a *subprocess,* a child process is any process that was created by another process, the parent process.

Processes in Unix have a hierarchical structure just like the filesystem; a process has a parent, children, and even a root. When a Unix system starts running, one of the first things to happen is that it starts a single process with the process ID (PID) of 1. This process has the same position in the process structure that the root directory does in the filesystem; it is the ancestor of all other processes.

A parent process forks or spawns (these terms are interchangeable) a child process. The child process inherits information from the parent, including user and group ID, but the child is assigned a new process ID.

When you run a shell command, the shell spawns a child process to run the command you requested. Built-in commands such as `cd` do not create child processes.

chip

A small semiconductor circuit that contains many electronic components. Also known as an integrated circuit, which may be abbreviated IC.

chkey

A BSD command used to change your encryption key. `chkey` first prompts you for your login password and then uses your password to encrypt a new encryption key for storage in the public key database.

See also **`keylogin`**.

chmod

A command that changes the access mode of one or more files. Only the owner of the file or the superuser can change the access mode, or permissions, of a file.

The mode of a file controls the access permissions associated with that file. There are three levels of security: ownership, group access, and everyone else; and within these levels there are three permissions: read, write, and execute. Read permission means that you can look at the contents of the file, write permission means that you can change the file, and execute permission means that you can execute the file; the permissions for directories behave only slightly differently. You can use the `ls -l` command to display these file access privileges.

▶ Syntax

The syntax for `chmod` is as follows:

```
chmod [options] mode filename
```

You can specify the new access mode either absolutely, by specifying an octal number representing the mode, or symbolically, by specifying individual modes. The latter is a more incremental method because you can add and remove permissions.

▶ Options and Arguments

The *mode* argument can contain either:

- **An absolute mode:** An octal number that sets all the permissions for this file for all levels. Each number sets the appropriate bit in the file's mode field.
- **A symbolic mode:** A set of arguments that specify the class of user, the operation to be performed, and the access permission you want to change.

Absolute modes are listed in Table C.12. Build up the number you need by ORing the values from the table together; this is equivalent to adding them together. Some of the more common modes are listed in Table C.13 for your convenience; for example, 0644 is combined from 0400 (owner-read) plus 0200 (owner-write) plus 0040 (group-read) plus 0004 (all other-read).

To use a symbolic mode, you must select a class of user, an operation, and the access permission you want to change or modify from each part of Table C.14. These three elements are then combined into a string that is applied to the file or files you are working with.

▶ Examples

All three examples in this section assign read-only permission to everyone for the file `myfile.doc`:

```
chmod 444 myfile.doc
```

```
chmod =r myfile.doc
```

```
chmod a-wx,a+r myfile.doc
```

The symbolic mode is more useful when you want to tweak individual modes, while the absolute mode method is better if you want to set all permissions at the same time.

See also **`ls`**.

Table C.12: Absolute Modes Used with chmod

OCTAL NUMBER	DESCRIPTION
4000	Sets user ID when the program executes.
2000	Sets group ID when the program executes.
1000	Sets the "sticky bit"; superuser only.
0400	Allows the owner to read the file.
0200	Allows the owner to write to the file.
0100	Allows the owner to execute the file.
0040	Allows the group to read the file.
0020	Allows the group to write to the file.
0010	Allows the group to execute the file.
0004	Allows others to read the file.
0002	Allows others to write to the file.
0001	Allows others to execute the file.

Table C.13: Common Absolute Modes Used with chmod

OCTAL NUMBER	DESCRIPTION
0777	Allows the owner, group, and public to read, write, and execute the file.
0755	Lets the owner read, write, and execute the file; lets the group and public read and execute the file.
0711	Lets the owner read, write, and execute the file; allows the group and public to execute the file.
0644	Lets the owner read and write the file; lets the group and public read the file.

Table C.14: Symbolic Modes Used with chmod

SYMBOLIC MODE	DESCRIPTION
Select a Class of User	
`u`	Selects user or owner of a file.
`g`	Selects group to which the owner belongs.
`o`	Selects all other users.
`a`	Selects all users, which is the default. This option can be used in place of `u`, `g`, and `o` listed above.
Select an Operation	
+	Adds permission for the specified class of user.
-	Removes permission from the specified class of user.
=	Sets the permission for the specified user, and resets all other unspecified permissions for that user class.
Select an Access Permission	
`r`	Sets read permission.
`w`	Sets write permission.
`x`	Sets execute permission.
`s`	Sets user ID or group ID to that of the owner of the file while the file is being executed.
`t`	Sets the sticky bit; superuser only.

C

choosing a password

A password is a security method used to identify a specific authorized user of the system by a unique string of characters. You must type these characters correctly to gain access to the system.

In general, passwords should be a mixture of letters and numbers and longer than six characters. Here are some guidelines on what not to use:

- Your user ID
- Your own first or last name or the name of a relative or friend
- Your phone number, social security number, or birthdate
- A real word, however obscure, from a dictionary, even from a foreign language

Never write your password down because someone will inevitably find it, and remember to change your password regularly.

People who break into computers spend long hours compiling lists of words from "Star Trek," movie actors' names, book and movie titles to attempt to guess your password.

■ *See also* **cracker.**

chown

A command that changes the ownership of a file or files.

Syntax

The syntax for `chown` is:

`chown [`*`option`*`]` *`owner filename`*

▶ Options and Arguments

The *`owner`* is the name or the numeric user ID of the new owner, and *`filename`* is a list of files whose ownership you want to change. Some systems are configured so that only the superuser can change file ownerships.

▶ Examples

To change the ownership of the file `myfile/chapter1.doc` to that of Brenda, use:

`chown brenda`
➥ `myfile/chapter1.doc`

■ *See also* **`chgrp`.**

chpass

A BSD command used to change user database information.

▶ Syntax

Syntax for `chpass` is as follows:

`chpass [-a` *`list`*`]`
`➥[-s` *`newshell`*`][`*`username`*`]`

`chpass` allows you to edit information contained in the user database associated with your username; the information is formatted and supplied to `vi` for changes unless you specify a different editor.

▶ Options and Arguments

Two options are available with `chpass`, as shown in Table C.15.

Possible display items are taken from the list in Table C.16.

■ *See also* **`finger`, `login`, `passwd`.**

Table C.15: Options Available with chpass

OPTION	DESCRIPTION
`-a` *`list`*	As superuser, you can specify items directly to the database without using an editor. *`list`* must be a colon-separated list of all the user database fields, although some fields may be left empty.
`-s` *`newshell`*	Changes the user's shell to *`newshell`*.

Table C.16: Display Items for Use with chpass

ITEM	DESCRIPTION
Login:	User's login name.
Password:	User's login password in encrypted form.
Uid:	The number associated with the user's login field.
Gid:	The number associated with the user's login group.
Change:	The date by which the password must be changed.
Expire:	The date on which the account expires.
Class:	Unused.
Home Directory:	The absolute pathname where the user will be placed at login.
Shell:	The name of the user's shell; if this field is empty, the Bourne shell is assumed.
Full Name:	User's full name.
Location:	User's office location.
Home Phone:	User's home phone number.
Office Phone:	User's office phone number.

`ci`

■ *See* **RCS.**

CISC

Acronym for complex instruction set computing; pronounced "sisk." A processor that can recognize and execute well over 100 different assembly language instructions. CISC processors can be very powerful, but there is a price for that power in terms of the number of clock cycles these instructions take to execute.

This is in contrast to reduced instruction set computing processors, in which the number of available instructions has been cut to a minimum. RISC processors are common in workstations and can be designed to run up to 70 percent faster than CISC processors.

C-Kermit

A fully featured Unix data communications program that evolved from earlier implementations of Kermit from the University of Columbia.

C-Kermit offers:

- Support for serial port communications
- Support for X.25 and TCP/IP data links
- File transfers for ASCII and binary files
- Terminal emulation services featuring all the most popular emulations
- `telnet` services
- Modem configuration services
- Support for and translations between multiple character sets

C-Kermit is not part of any standard Unix distribution, not even of Linux, but can be obtained by anonymous `ftp` from `/kermit/columbia.edu`; look for the compressed `tar` package in `/kermit/archives/cku190.tar.Z`. It is also available at other sites, or by post from:

Kermit Distribution, Dept CI
Center for Computing Activities
Columbia University
612 W. 115th Street
New York, NY 10025
U.S.A.
212-854-3703

■ *See also* **RZSZ, Xmodem, Ymodem, Zmodem.**

C

cksum

A BSD command that displays a file's checksum cyclic redundancy check, size of the file, and the filename.

▶ Syntax

The syntax for `cksum` is:

```
cksum [-o[1|2]][filename ...]
```

where the `-o` option specifies a different checksum calculation be used rather than the default. Algorithm 1 is the algorithm traditionally used by BSD `sum` and by AT&T System V `sum -r`. Algorithm 2 is that used by the default `sum` algorithm.

ClariNet newsgroups

Moderated ClariNet newsgroups containing current news stories from the national and international wire services, including Newsbytes (computer industry news) and Techwire (technical, scientific, and industrial news), as well as syndicated columns. To subscribe to ClariNet, you must pay a fee and agree to sign a license. Apart from `clari.news.talk`, all ClariNet newsgroups are moderated and only accept posts from qualified news organizations. All articles are copyrighted, so if you subscribe to ClariNet, you can't repost articles without explicit permission.

class

In object-oriented programming, a type of data structure that is instantiated to create a real-world object of that type. A class is used in a program to define a set of services or characteristics available to other parts of the program. The definition of a class in object-oriented programming is similar to the definition of types in languages such as Pascal or C, but differs from a Pascal or C data structure in that it also contains the program code for operating on that data.

■ *See also* **C++, encapsulation.**

clear

An SVR4 command that clears the terminal screen and leaves the prompt in the upper left corner of the screen. This command has no options.

C library

A collection of standard functions available to C programmers. Several different libraries have been developed to support programming in the C language. Many of the libraries access basic operating system services using Unix system calls, while others serve special purposes such as the math library functions.

When you use a library function in your program, it is automatically added to your code by the linker as your source code is compiled into an executable.

There are two main kinds of libraries:

- Static libraries contain the actual code of the function you used in your program, such as the `printf()` function, and this code is added to your executable.
- Shared libraries do not contain the actual code for the function but contain stub code that tells the program loader where on disk it will find the library code needed at runtime.

Because many programs use the same functions from the C libraries, it does not always make sense for every program to contain its own copy of the library code. Shared libraries contain all the common function code in a single library file on disk and allow the compiler executables to be smaller than they would be with static libraries.

The type of library used is of particular relevance when an application is delivered to another user on a different system. Any dynamic libraries required by the application should also be included in the package, unless they are system libraries. This is a common source of problems, and library compatibility should be considered when developing new programs.

■ *See also* **`curses`.**

click

To press and release a mouse button quickly; often used when making a selection.

■ *See also* **double-click.**

`click`

A SunOS command used to control the keyboard click. `click` with no arguments turns off the key click. To turn it on again, use `click -y`.

client

A device or application program that makes use of the services provided by a server.

A client may be a PC or a workstation on a network using services provided from the network file server, or may be that part of an application program that runs on the workstation, supported by additional software running on the server. There are numerous examples of this kind of software in the Unix world; anonymous `ftp`, Gopher, and World Wide Web browsers are all clients running on your system using services provided by other software running on remote servers.

■ *See also* **client/server, server, X Window.**

client/server

A computing architecture that distributes processing between clients and servers on a network.

In the past, traditional computing has used a hierarchical architecture based on nonprogrammable dumb terminals connected to a mainframe computer. In this scheme, the database was on the same computer that was running the application. A client/server approach replaces this structure by dividing the application into two separate parts: a front-end client and a back-end server, usually referred to as a *client* and a *server.* The client component provides the user with the power to run the data-entry part of the application, and this part of the client is usually optimized for user interaction with the system. The server component, which can be either local or remote, provides the data management, administration, and system security features and manages information sharing with the rest of the network. In other words, clients request information from the servers, while the servers store data and programs and provide networkwide services to clients.

Client/server architecture can sustain several levels of organizational complexity, including:

- Standalone (non-networked) client application programs, such as local word processors.
- Applications that run on the client but request data from the server, such as spreadsheets.
- Programs that use server capabilities to share information between network users, such as e-mail systems.
- Programs such as databases in which the physical search of the records in the database takes place on the server, while a much smaller program running on the client handles all user interface functions and the database application.

Client/server computing lightens the processing load for the client workstation but increases the load on the server. For this reason, server computers tend to have larger and faster hard disk drives and much more memory installed than conventional file servers. The server may also be a minicomputer or a mainframe.

Typically, a client/server approach reduces network traffic, because relatively small amounts of data are moved over the network. This is in sharp contrast to the typical network, in which entire files are constantly being transmitted between the workstation and the file server.

Database applications were some of the first to embrace the client/server concept, particularly with Structured Query Language (SQL, pronounced "sequel"). SQL has grown into an industry standard database language; it is relatively easy to implement, robust, powerful, and easy for users to learn to use.

■ *See also* **client, server, X Window.**

clock speed

Also known as *clock rate*. The internal speed of a computer or processor, normally expressed in megahertz (MHz).

The faster the clock speed, the faster the processor can perform a specific operation; and you normally see this translated into greater system performance, assuming the other components in the system, such as memory, peripherals, and disk drives, can keep up with the increased speed.

The Intel 8088 processor used in the original IBM PC had a clock speed of 4.77 MHz. The current Pentium chips from Intel are available in a range of several different speeds from 60 MHz up to 180 MHz, and in the future, processors will run even faster.

Certain chips use a technique known as *clock doubling* or *clock multiplying* to allow the chip to process data and instructions at a different speed from that used by the rest of the system. For example, the Intel 80486 DX2 operates at 50 MHz internally but at 25 MHz when communicating with other system components, which is known as *clock doubling.* The Intel DX4 chip uses clock-tripling technology, and the PowerPC 601 can run at one, two, three, or four times the speed of the bus.

cmchk

An SCO command that reports hard disk block size.

cmdedit

A special version of the C shell written by Digital Equipment Corporation (DEC), which includes command-line editing.

cmp

A command used to compare two files. `cmp` is often used to identify copies of files so that duplicates can be removed.

▶ Syntax

The syntax for `cmp` is as follows:

```
cmp [options] file1 file2
```

`cmp` reports the first difference between *`file1`* and *`file2`* but reports nothing if the two files are identical.

If you replace *`file1`* with a hyphen (-), `cmp` uses standard input instead.

▶ Options and Arguments

The `cmp` options let you list differences between the files or suppress all output. This can be useful if you use `cmp` in a shell script in which you are interested only in the exit value returned by `cmp` rather than any other output. Options are listed in Table C.17. Bytes and line numbers are numbered beginning at 1.

▶ Examples

The two files `brenda` and `brenda1` can be compared using:

```
cmp brenda brenda1
```

```
brenda brenda1 differ:
➥ char  20, line 1
```

This output shows that the first difference between the two files is at the 20th byte or character in the first line. If you are performing some file housekeeping, you can use the shell's `&&` AND operator to delete a file once a comparison is complete:

```
cmp -s brenda brenda1 && rm
➥ brenda1
```

If `cmp` finds that the two files are identical, the `rm` command is used to delete the second file. If the two files are not identical, the `&&` operator cannot pass control to the `rm` command. The `-s` options runs `cmp` in quiet mode.

■ *See also* **comm**, **`diff`**, **`diff3`**.

co

■ *See* **RCS.**

Table C.17: Options to Use with cmp

OPTION	DESCRIPTION
`-l`	For each difference found, prints the byte number (in decimal) and the values of the differing bytes (in octal).
`-s`	Suppresses all output and works silently. This is the form to use in your shell scripts; returns the following exit codes: 0 files are identical; 1 files are different; 2 files are missing or inaccessible.

coaxial cable

Abbreviated coax, pronounced "co-ax." A high-capacity cable used in networking that contains a solid inner copper core surrounded by plastic insulation and an outer braided foil shield.

Coaxial cable is used for broadband and baseband communications networks, as well as for cable television and closed-circuit video, because the cable is usually free from external interference and permits high transmission rates over relatively long distances.

■ *See also* **fiber optic cable, thick Ethernet, thin Ethernet.**

cof2elf

An SVR4 command that converts one or more COFF files to ELF format, overwriting the originals in the process.

▶ Syntax

The command-line syntax for `cof2elf` is:

`cof2elf [`*`options`*`][`*`filename`*`]`

Input files can be object files or archives.

▶ Options and Arguments

You can use the options listed in Table C.18 with `cof2elf`.

Table C.18: Options for Use with cof2elf

OPTION	DESCRIPTION
`-i`	Ignores any unrecognized data, and continues with the conversion.
`-q`	Runs in quiet mode; suppresses all output.
`-Q`*`c`*	Prints information when *`c`* is set to `y`, and prints nothing when *`c`* is set to `n`, the default.
`-s`*`dir`*	Saves the original file into the existing directory specified by *`dir`*.
`-V`	Prints the version number of `cof2elf` on standard error.

COFF

Abbreviation for common object file format. A revision to the format of executable and object files to provide support for dynamically linked libraries. The COFF definition was replaced by the Executable and Link Format (ELF) in System V Release 4.

■ *See also* **ELF.**

col

A command that filters out reverse linefeeds and escape characters so that output from `nroff` and `tbl` can be shown on the screen; these characters cannot be displayed on an ordinary terminal or printer.

▶ Syntax

The syntax to use with `col` is straightforward:

`col [`*`options`*`]`

`col` reads from the standard input and writes to the standard output; this means that you use redirection to examine a file or create a new output file.

▶ Options and Arguments

The options listed in Table C.19 are available when using `col`.

C

Table C.19: Options for Use with col

OPTION	DESCRIPTION
-b	Ignores backspace characters; useful when printing **man** pages.
-f	Print forward half linefeeds on the following line.
-l*number*	In BSD, buffers *number* of lines in memory; the default is to buffer 128 lines.
-p	In SVR4, prints any unknown escape characters as regular characters; this can garble the output and is not usually recommended.
-x	Replaces tabs with spaces.

▶ Examples

To display a file on your terminal that contains reverse linefeeds, use:

col < document1

If you then decide you want to print this file, pipe the output from col to your printer like this:

col < document1 | lp

■ *See also* **colcrt, expand, nroff, tbl.**

colcrt

A BSD command that filters out reverse linefeeds and underline characters so that output from nroff and tbl can be shown on the screen. These characters cannot usually be displayed on an ordinary terminal or printer.

▶ Syntax

Syntax for use with colcrt is:

colcrt [-][-2][*filename...*]

Half linefeeds and underlines are placed on new lines, and underlines are converted to hyphens.

▶ Options and Arguments

Two options are available for use with colcrt, and they are shown in Table C.20.

▶ Examples

colcrt reads from standard in and writes to standard out, so you can use input redirection or pipes to control the input and output to this command. For example, to pipe output from an nroff file called jenny.doc to the screen, you can use:

nroff jenny.doc|colcrt| more

The more filter sends output to the screen one page at a time.

■ *See also* **col, nroff, tbl, troff, ul.**

Table C.20: Options for Use with colcrt

OPTION	DESCRIPTION
-	Suppresses all underlining; this can be useful when looking at output from tbl.
-2	Prints all half lines, effectively double-spacing the screen output.

collision

In networking or communications, an attempt by two nodes to send a message at exactly the same moment on the same channel.

■ *See also* **CSMA/CD, demand priority.**

colon

The null shell command; sometimes used as the first character in a file to signify a Bourne shell script. In the Korn shell, you can place shell variables after the **:** to expand them to their values.

colrm

A BSD command that removes specified columns from the lines in a text file.

▶ Syntax

The syntax to use with `colrm` is:

```
colrm [start[stop]]
```

`colrm` reads from the standard input and writes to the standard output, so you can use pipes or input redirection with this command.

▶ Options and Arguments

A column is defined as a single character in a file, and columns can be removed beginning with *`start`* and continuing as far as *`stop`*.

Columns are numbered from 1, not from 0, and a tab character increments the counter to the next multiple of eight, while a backspace character decreases the count by one.

▶ Examples

To extract all the characters from the file `tyler.doc` between columns 10 and 30 and then display these characters on the screen page by page, use:

```
colrm 10 30 tyler.doc | more
```

■ *See also* **cat**, **less**, **more**, **pg**.

column

A BSD command that forms its input into multiple columns.

▶ Syntax

The syntax to use with `column` is:

```
column [-tx][-c columns]
➥[-s sep][filename...]
```

Input comes from *`filename`* or from standard input, and empty lines are ignored.

▶ Options and Arguments

The `column` options are shown in Table C.21.

Table C.21: Options for Use with column

OPTION	DESCRIPTION
`-c`	Formats output in a display *`columns`* wide.
`-s`	Specifies a set of characters to be used as delimiters with the `-t` option.
`-t`	Creates a table from the input.
`-x`	Fills columns before filling rows.

▶ Examples

To form a small table from the output of the `ls` command, use:

```
ls -l | column -t
```

■ *See also* **colrm**, **paste**, **sort**.

comb

■ *See* **SCCS**.

comm

A command that finds common lines in sorted files.

▶ Syntax

The syntax to use with this command is:

```
comm [options]file1 file2
```

`comm` creates a three-column output, consisting of lines unique to *`file1`*, lines unique to *`file2`*, and lines that are common to both files. Lines in the second column are preceded by a tab character, while lines in the third column are preceded by two tabs.

▶ Options and Arguments

`comm` compares *`file1`* and *`file2`*; you can use a hypen in place of either one (but not both) to make `comm` use standard input instead.

The options available with `comm` are listed in Table C.22.

Table C.22: Options for Use with comm

OPTION	DESCRIPTION
-1	Suppresses display of column 1; suppresses the lines it finds only in *file1*.
-2	Suppresses display of column 2; suppresses the lines it finds only in *file2*.
-3	Suppresses display of column 3; suppresses the lines it finds in both files.
-12	Displays only the lines common to both files; column 3.
-13	Displays only the lines unique to *file2*; column 2.
-23	Displays only the lines unique to *file1*; column 1.

▶ **Examples**

If you want to extract the lines common to both files and store the results in a third file called `newlist`, use:

```
comm -12 list.one list.two >
➥ newlist
```

■ *See also* **cmp**, **diff**, **diff3**, **dircmp**, **sdiff**, **sort**, **uniq**.

command

- An instruction given to the operating system to perform a specific operation. Most commands are executed by the shell, either by a built-in command, running a shell script, or running a separate program.
- In Unix, utilities that exist as separate programs are often referred to as *commands*.
- In an application, you control the execution of the program by using the appropriate commands. These commands may be typed at a prompt or given via a menuing system.

■ *See also* **command line.**

command directories

That collection of directories in Unix that contain commands, including `/bin`, `/usr/bin`, `/etc`, and `/usr/lib`. You may also find that other directories are specifically configured for your system by your system administrator.

command file

An ordinary text file containing a list of executable commands, usually shell commands. Also known as a *shell program* or, more commonly, a *shell script*. These files exist throughout the Unix system and are responsible for many of the system functions.

command interpreter

A program that reads your input from the keyboard and passes it on to the operating system for execution. In Unix, the command interpreter is known as the *shell;* it displays a shell command prompt on the screen, interprets and executes all the commands and filenames that you enter, and displays error messages when appropriate.

The command interpreter also contains the environment, an area that holds values for important system defaults; these values can be changed by the user.

■ *See also* **Bash, Bourne shell, C shell, Korn shell, Unix shell.**

command line

The commands you enter at the shell command prompt; a line of instructions and related command-line arguments used to execute a shell command or Unix utility. In Unix, a command line may have more than one command joined by operators such as semicolons (`;`), pipes (`|`), or ampersands (`&`).

Usually, the elements found on the command line are the command name, followed by any appropriate command-line arguments you want to use with the command. You can also use options, usually preceded by a hyphen, to modify the operation of the command itself.

In the `vi` editor, the command line is the bottom line of the screen, where certain commands are echoed as you type them.

command-line argument

When you type a command at a shell prompt, the first word you type is the name of the command; anything that follows is considered to be an argument to that command.

Arguments provide more information to the command and are often filenames, directory names, options, or parameters. Options come right after the command name and consist of a hyphen (-) and one or more letters, while parameters follow the command name and provide additional information to the command.

command mode

A mode in many applications that allows you to enter commands. In the `vi` editor, command mode interprets anything you type as a command to act upon the text rather than new text to be added to the buffer.

■ *See also* **input mode.**

command substitution

A feature of the shell in which the output of one command is passed to another command, which is then executed.

A command substitution is always enclosed in backquotes (`), and the shell replaces the command, and the backquotes, with the output from the command. Here is an example:

```
now = `date`
```

In this example, the shell variable `now` is being set to a value. Without backquotes, `now` is set to the word `date`; with backquotes, `now` is set to the output of the `date` command—in other words, the actual calendar date.

Command substitution is often used within shell scripts. For example, you can add a timestamp to a specific operation such as backing up a file, as in this next example:

```
echo $0 utility used `date`
➥ >> transaction.log
```

If this line is in a shell script called `backit`, the variable `$0` contains the name of the shell script and so is set to `backit`. Then, the `echo` command creates the message:

```
backit utility used
➥ Wed May 8 1996 02:22:25 PST
```

and appends this message to the end of a file called `transaction.log`.

If you use the Korn shell, these examples will work, but you can use another syntax. Rather than enclosing the command in backquotes, you can use a dollar sign followed by the command in parentheses, as in this example:

```
print The time is $(date)
```

In the Korn shell, the `print` command usually replaces the `echo` command.

comment

Any part of a program or shell script that is intended to convey information to the user but should be ignored by the language compiler or interpreter. Comments are useful to annotate complex or seldom-used operations or to add other information of use to the user. In the C programming language, comments must be enclosed between `/* */` pairs; in C++, comments start with `//`, and in the C shell, a comment must start with the pound sign (#).

comment out

To remove a certain portion of code from a program by temporarily converting the program code to comments, usually for testing or debugging purposes. Once the test is complete, the commented-out code can be returned to its original status once again. Programmers use this technique to avoid having to delete and then retype sections of code; an operation that may itself lead to the accidental introduction of more errors.

Common Application Environment

See **CAE.**

Common Desktop Environment

See **CDE.**

common object file format

See **COFF.**

Common Open Software Environment

See **COSE.**

communications parameters

Any one of several settings required to allow computers to communicate successfully.

In asynchronous transmissions, commonly used in modem communications, the settings for baud rate, number of data bits, number of stop bits, and the parity setting must all be correct.

communications protocol

A standard way of communicating between computers or between computers and terminals.

Communications protocols can vary in complexity from a simple file-transfer protocol, such as Xmodem, used to transfer files from one computer to another, to the seven-layer International Standards Organization's Open Systems Interconnection (ISO/OSI) model for computer-to-computer communications used as the theoretical basis for many large complex computer networks. Communications protocols can also refer to hardware interface standards such as the serial communications RS-232-C standard.

See also **ISO/OSI model, TCP/IP.**

compact

A BSD command used to compress files so that they occupy less hard disk space.

▶ Syntax

The syntax to use with `compact` is:

```
compact [-v][filename...]
```

`compact` compresses the specified *filename* using adaptive Huffman coding; if no filenames are supplied, the standard input is compacted to the standard output. Files are compacted to a file called *filename*`.C`. Usually `compact` does its job in silence, but if you use the `-v` option, `compact` reports the compression percentage for each file. Typical compression values for text are 38 percent; Pascal source code, 43 percent; C source code, 36 percent; and binary files, 19 percent; however, the `compress` and `pack` commands can both achieve better compression ratios than this and take less time to compute.

See also **ccat, compress, gzip, pack, uncompact, uncompress, unpack, zcat.**

compact disc

Abbreviated CD. A nonmagnetic, polished, optical disk used to store large amounts of digital information. A CD can store approximately 650 MB of information, equivalent to over 1700 low-density floppy disks. This translates into approximately 300,000 pages of text or 72 minutes of music, all on a single 4.72" disc.

Digital information is stored on the compact disc as a series of microscopic pits and smooth areas that have different reflective properties. A beam of laser light shines on the disc so that the reflections can be detected and converted into digital data.

See also **CD-R, CD-ROM, CD-ROM Extended Architecture.**

compile

The process of converting a set of program language source code statements into a machine-readable form suitable for execution by a computer.

■ *See also* **compiler.**

compiler

A program that converts a set of program language source code statements into a machine-readable form suitable for execution by a computer.

Most compilers do much more than this, however; they translate the entire program into machine language, while at the same time they check your source code syntax for errors and post messages or warnings as appropriate.

In the Unix world, the machine language output from the compiler is known as an *object file,* which must be linked with other files by the link editor before it can execute. The compiler usually invokes the link editor automatically.

■ *See also* **C compiler, compile.**

compiler compiler

A program capable of transforming a tabular description of a compiler, including all the syntax rules, into an actual compiler. The Unix system's compiler compiler is called `yacc`, for "yet another compiler compiler."

compiling a C program

The process of compiling a C program requires that several programs work together; here is a closer look at the steps involved.

1. Create the source code for the program using an editor such as `vi`. Add `.c` as an extension to the source code filename because the C compiler expects C source code files to end with this extension; C++ source code filenames should end with `.C` or `.cc`.
2. You can use `cb`, the C beautifier, to impose a standard layout on your source code if you wish.
3. Invoke the `cc` utility, which in turn calls the C preprocessor, the C compiler, the assembler, and the linker or link editor. These major elements in the compilation process are shown in Figure C.1.

   The C preprocessor expands macro definitions, and also includes header files or include files.

   The compiler creates assembly language statements that correspond to the instructions in your source code and then creates machine-readable object code. One object file is created for each source file; the object file has the same name as the source code file, except that the `.c` extension is changed into `.o`.
4. Finally, the linker searches specified C libraries for functions needed by your program and combines object modules for these functions with your program's object modules into an executable file called `a.out`, which you can use just like other executable programs or shell scripts. It makes sense to rename this file to a more meaningful name because `a.out` will be overwritten by the file created the next time you use the compiler.

The C compiler usually has a default mode that will do a good job of compiling most programs; however, it also has a number of options you can use for special

Figure C.1: Major Elements of the Compilation Process

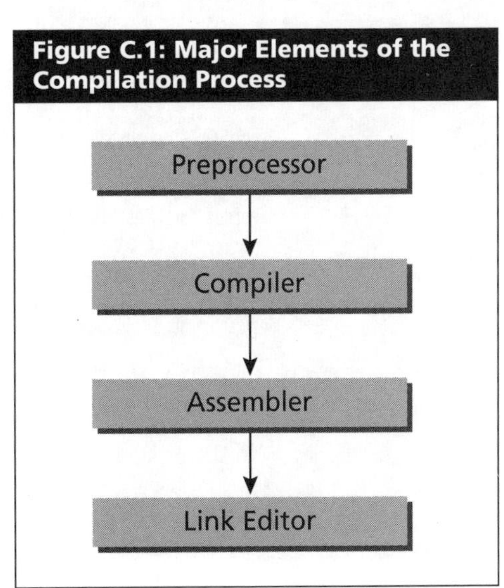

circumstances such as optimizing your code to run as efficiently as possible.

See also **as, assembler, cc, dbx, g++, gcc, imake, lint, make.**

complex instruction set computing

See **CISC.**

compress

A command used to compress files so that they occupy less hard disk space.

▶ Syntax

The syntax to use with `compress` is:

```
compress [options]
➥[filename...]
```

`compress` uses adaptive Lempel-Ziv coding to compress *filename* to *filename*.Z, but if compression would not decrease the size of *filename*, then *filename* is simply ignored.

▶ Options and Arguments

Several options are available for use with `compress`, as Table C.23 shows. SVR4 and BSD provide a basic set of options, while other systems add more.

One of the options lets you force compression, so if you are creating an archive, you can use this option to be sure that all files in the archive are in the same format.

Compression ratios of up to 50 to 60 percent can be achieved when compressing text files or C source code files with `compress`. The `compress` utility consistently outperforms both the `pack` and `compact` commands in this respect.

Table C.23: Options for Use with compress

OPTION	DESCRIPTION
-b*n*	Limits the number of bits in coding to *n*, where *n* is between 9 and 16, with 16 as the default. Making *n* smaller produces a larger, less compact file.
-c	Writes compressed files to standard out, leaving the original files unchanged.
-d	On SCO and UnixWare, decompresses a compressed file.
-F	On SCO and UnixWare, forces compression of *filename* even if the size of the file won't be reduced.
-f	Forces compression of *filename* even if the size of the file won't be reduced, and overwrites files without prompting for confirmation.
-H	On SCO and UnixWare, uses a slightly different compression algorithm to achieve approximately 20 percent greater compression.
-P *fd*	On SCO and UnixWare, reads a list of filenames from a pipe associated with the file descriptor *fd*.
-q	On SCO and UnixWare, runs in quiet mode, suppressing all messages except error messages.
-v	Shows the percentage reduction for each *filename*.

▶ Examples

To compress the file `lonestar.doc` and display the compression percentage, use the following command:

```
compress -v lonestar.doc

lonestar.doc: Compression:
➥ 52.44% - replaced with
➥ lonestar.Z
```

To compress all the files in the current directory, use:

```
compress *
```

■ *See also* **ccat, compact, gzip, pack, uncompact, uncompress, unpack, zcat.**

compressed file

A file that has been processed by a special utility program so that it occupies as little hard disk space as possible. When the file is needed, a program decompresses the file back into its original form so that it can be read by the computer.

Common compression techniques include schemes that replace commonly occurring sequences of letters by tokens that take up less space. The `pack` and `compact` utilities use Huffman coding to shrink a file, and the `compress` utility uses adaptive Lempel-Ziv coding.

■ *See also* **ccat, compact, compress, gzexe, gzip, tar, uncompact, uncompress, unpack, zcat.**

compressing a file

Most files can be compressed so that they take up less space on disk or take less time to transmit over a communications link.

Compressing a file involves running a utility on the file so that it takes up the smallest possible amount of hard disk space. Savings can be in the order of 30 to 70 percent, depending on the file type, and compressed files are always binary files, even if they started out as text files; this means that you can't read compressed files without uncompressing them first.

Several file compression programs are available in the Unix world; one program compresses the file, while another uncompresses the file when you want to use it again. Sometimes a third program is available that can both catalog and uncompress a compressed file at the same time. For example, in BSD, `compress` reduces the size of files, storing them as *`filename`*`.Z`, `uncompress` restores them to their original form, and `zcat` catalogs files as they are uncompressed. `compact` (which stores compressed files as *`filename`*`.C`), `uncompact`, and `ccat` perform similar functions. In System V, you can use `pack` (which stores compressed files as *`filename`*`.z`), `unpack`, and `pcat`. And from the GNU Project comes `gzip` (which stores files as *`filename`*`.gz`) and `gunzip`, an excellent way to solve your file compression needs. `gunzip` can uncompress the files created by `compress`, as well as those created by `gzip`, and has been widely adopted by many users, especially Linux users.

■ *See also* **ar, filename extension, Internet file types, tar.**

computation bound

A condition in which the speed of operation of the processor actually limits the speed of program execution. The processor is limited by the number of arithmetic operations it must perform.

■ *See also* **input/output bound.**

concatenate

To combine two or more sets of characters or files into one single sequence. The `cat` program serves this function; it concatenates two or more input files. If you concatenate the character strings "Hello" and " world", the result is one string containing "Hello world".

■ *See also* **catenate.**

C

concurrent

When two or more programs have access to the processor at the same time and must share the system resources, they are said to be running concurrently. Because a computer can perform operations so quickly, they seem to be occurring at the same time, when in reality they are not.

See also **task, thread.**

conditional compilation

The process of selectively compiling certain parts of a program source code, based on specific logical conditions. For example, C programs may contain preprocessor macros such as `#define` and `#endif` to selectively isolate part of a program.

conditional execution

A state in which the start of one program depends on the successful completion of another.

conditional statement

A programming language element in which a condition, such as `A = B` or `X > Y`, is tested, and its truth or falsehood determines whether the program performs an operation (or which of several operations to perform). A simple example is the `IF` statement. When the condition is true, the following command is executed, but if it is false, that command is skipped, and program execution continues elsewhere.

See also **`case`, `while`.**

/config

An SVR4 root file system directory that contains the files used to create a new operating system.

configuration files

Those files needed to configure a Unix system. In SVR4, the main configuration files are kept in the `/etc` directory, and in BSD, they are located in the `/sys` directory.

console

In the past, the console was the main system terminal used by the system administrator or superuser. In more modern systems, the console is not a specific terminal but is just the `tty` the system was booted from. The normal name for the character special file that provides access to the console is `/dev/console`.

continue

- In the Bourne and Korn shells, the `continue` command resumes the next iteration of the loop containing the `continue` statement; this may be a `while`, `for`, or `until` statement.
- In the C shell, the `continue` statement resumes the next iteration only when used with the `while` and `foreach` statements.

control character

A nonprinting character with a special meaning. Control characters, such as carriage return, linefeed, and the bell, perform a specific operation on a terminal, printer, or communications line. Control characters are represented by the ASCII codes below 32 decimal; see Table 2.1 in Appendix 2 for details.

You can type a control character from the keyboard by pressing and holding the Ctrl key while simultaneously pressing another key. For example, if you press and hold the Ctrl key and then press D, you create Ctrl-D, an end-of-file character used to tell a program that it has reached the end of its input. Control characters are sometimes represented by the caret symbol; you may find that Ctrl-D is written as ^D. By convention, control key combinations are always shown with capital letters as they are easier to read; compare Ctrl-L with Ctrl-l, for example.

See also **`stty`.**

control flow commands

Any of the commands that change the order of execution of commands in a program or a shell script. All the popular Unix shells provide control structures, such as

if and **while**, as well as other commands used to change the order of execution.

See also **control structure.**

control key

See **Ctrl key.**

control structure

A statement that changes the order of execution of statements in a program or shell script. Control structures are among those commands known as *control flow commands.*

cooked mode

Any system mode that performs extensive preprocessing before presenting data to a program.

More specifically, cooked mode refers to the hardware-independent input mode of the Unix `tty` handler, in which the input is passed to a program one line at a time, rather than one character at a time. No input is available to the program until the entire line, including the carriage return, has been received. This is the reason that the shell commands do not work until after you press the Enter key; the shell cannot see these commands until you do.

See also **`cbreak` mode, raw mode, `stty`.**

copy

An SCO command used to copy the contents of one directory to another directory.

▶ Syntax

The syntax for the `copy` command is as follows:

```
copy [options] source
➥ destination
```

▶ Options and Arguments

`source` may be an existing file, a special file, or a directory, and *`destination`* must be a filename or directory different from *`source`*. If the *`destination`* files or directories do not exist, they are created with the same owner and permissions as their source equivalents; if they already exist, the owner and permissions are not changed. You can use several options with `copy`; they are listed in Table C.24.

▶ Examples

To copy all the files in the current directory to the `/usr/recipe` directory, use:

```
copy -v * /usr/recipe
```

If the current directory contains subdirectories you also want to copy, remember to use the `-r` option:

```
copy -r * /usr/recipe
```

See also **`cp`.**

copyleft

The copyright statement or General Public License of the Free Software Foundation (FSF), which states that any of the software developed using free software from the FSF must be distributed to others without charge.

core dump

A long listing produced by the Unix kernel under certain error-related circumstances that details the contents of memory, as well as other aspects of the state of the computer; also called a *core file* or *core image.*

This information is stored in a file called `core`, located in the faulty program's working directory. Your system administrator can use the contents of `core` when attempting to debug the problem.

Unix provides a variety of debuggers, including `adb`, `sdb`, and `dbx`; the GNU Project debugger found on Linux and other systems is called `gdb`. The most frequent cause of a core dump is a memory violation; in other words, your program tries to read and write to an area of memory that it does not have access to.

The use of the word *core* is a bit quaint and derives from the times when computer memory still consisted of a magnetic core.

See also **crash, Ctrl-\, panic.**

C

Table C.24: Options for Use with copy

OPTION	DESCRIPTION
`-a`	Asks permission before starting a copy. A response starting with `y` is assumed to be a yes; anything else is assumed to be no.
`-ad`	Asks you if the `-r` option applies (recursively copies directories) when `copy` encounters a directory; if the answer does not begin with `y`, the directory is ignored and not copied.
`-l`	Uses links when possible; otherwise, a copy is made. If links are possible, this makes for a very fast copy because no data is actually copied; this option cannot be used with directories.
`-m`	Sets modification time and access time to be same as the source. Without this option, modification time is set to the time of the copy.
`-n`	Creates a new destination file; if the destination file already exists, no copy is made. This option applies only to files, not to directories.
`-o`	Sets the owner and group to be the same as the source. Without this option, the owner is set to the user who invoked.
`copy-r`	Recursively examines directories as they are located, copying each file and directory as they are encountered. When this option is not set, directories are ignored.
`-v`	Verbose mode. When used with `-a`, messages are not displayed.

COSE

Acronym for Common Open Software Environment, pronounced "cosy." An industry group consisting of almost 100 members, organized to develop a standard graphical user interface (GUI) for Unix, known as the Common Desktop Environment, or CDE. Original members included Hewlett-Packard, IBM, SCO, Sun, and the UNIX Systems Group.

cp

A command used to copy one or more files to another file, a list of files, or a directory.

▶ Syntax

There are two forms of the `cp` command:

```
cp [options] source
➥ destination
```

```
cp [options] source directory
```

In the first case, *`source`* is copied to *`destination`*, and in the second, the files contained in *`source`* are all copied to *`directory`* using the same names. If the destination is an existing file, the file is overwritten, so take care; if the destination is an existing directory, the file or files are copied into the directory. You cannot use the `cp` command to copy a file onto itself.

▶ Options and Arguments

You can use several different options with `cp`, depending on the version of Unix you use. Table C.25 lists the options available with SVR4 and BSD.

▶ Examples

To copy one file to another, use:

```
cp lonestar texas
```

This command copies the contents of `lonestar` to `texas`. If `texas` does not exist, it is created; if it does exist, the original contents are overwritten and lost.

Table C.25: Options Available with cp	
OPTION	DESCRIPTION
`-f`	In BSD, forces `cp` to overwrite existing files without asking for confirmation, regardless of the existing permissions. This option also ignores the `-i` option, if specified.
`-H`	In BSD, when the `-R` option is specified, symbolic links are allowed on the command line.
`-i`	Asks for confirmation before overwriting an existing file.
`-L`	In BSD, when the `-R` option is specified, all symbolic links are followed.
`-p`	Preserves the modification time and as many of the file permissions as possible. Without this option, `cp` provides the permissions of the user who invoked `cp`.
`-P`	In BSD, when the `-R` option is specified, no symbolic links are followed.
`-r`	Copies directories, files, and subdirectories to ***directory***.
`-R`	In BSD, if ***source*** is a directory, `cp` copies that directory and all subdirectories, duplicating the original form of the directory tree.

To copy complete directories, across different filesystems if necessary, use:

```
cp -pR /usr/tom /usr/peter
```

The `-p` option preserves the modification time and permissions of the original files, and the `-R` option makes `cp` copy symbolic links, block and character device files, as well as regular data files.

See also **copy**, **ln**, **mv**, **rcp**, **rm**.

CPI

Abbreviation for characters per inch. The number of characters of a given font that fit into an inch.

cpio

A command used to copy files and directories into and out of archive files; `cpio` is also useful when you want to move files around the filesystem.

▶ Syntax

There are three major forms of syntax for `cpio`; they are as follows:

```
cpio -i [options][pattern]
```

The `-i` or copy in mode extracts specified files whose names match ***pattern*** from an archive of files and places the copies in the current directory. A ***pattern*** can include filename metacharacters and should be quoted or escaped so that they are interpreted by `cpio` rather than the shell. If you don't use a ***pattern***, all files are copied in. During extraction, existing files are not overwritten by older versions in the archive, unless you use the `-u` option.

```
cpio -o [options]
```

The `-o` or copy out mode copies a specified list of files from a directory into an archive file.

```
cpio -p [options] directory
```

Finally, the `-p` or pass mode copies files from one directory tree to another without creating an archive.

▶ Options and Arguments

The `cpio` command can use many different options in each of the three modes as Table C.26 illustrates; the hyphen in front of each option has been omitted from this table for the sake of clarity.

The options themselves are listed in Table C.27. Some of these options may be used in slightly different ways in different versions of `cpio`; check the `man` pages on your system for details.

C

Table C.26: Comparison of `cpio` Options

`cpio` MODE	VALID OPTIONS
`-i`	`6 b B c C d E f H I k m M r R s S t u v V`
`-o`	`a A B c C H L M O v V`
`-p`	`a d l L m R u v V`

▶ Examples

To copy all the files in the current working directory to the tape mounted on `/dev/rmt/1`, use:

```
ls | cpio -o > /dev/rmt/1
14 blocks
```

This command does not copy any subdirectories since `ls` does not list them. When `cpio` finishes, the number of 512-byte blocks used is displayed.

To restore all `txt` files from a tape archive and place them in the current directory on the hard disk, use:

```
cpio -iv "*.txt" </dev/rmt/1
```

The `-v` option tells `cpio` to list all the files as they are restored.

▶ Notes

Archives created by `cpio` are not compatible with those made by `tar` or `ar`.

■ *See also* **ar, find, ls, tar.**

cpp

A command used to invoke the GNU C compiler preprocessor; sometimes `cccp` is used instead. You automatically invoke the preprocessor as part of a C program compilation cycle, but there might be an occasion when it is appropriate to call the preprocessor individually. For a complete description of the GNU C preprocessor and the available options, see the file `cpp.info` or the manual *The C Preprocessor* created from the documentation source file called `cpp.texinfo`, which accompanied the preprocessor.

■ *See also* **cc, C compiler, compiling a C program.**

CPS

Abbreviation for characters per second. The number of characters, or bytes, transmitted every second during a data transfer. A measurement of the speed of operation of equipment such as serial printers and terminals.

CPU

Abbreviation for central processing unit. The computing and control part of the computer. The CPU in a mainframe computer may be contained on many printed circuit boards; the CPU in a minicomputer may be contained on several boards; and the CPU in a PC is contained in a single, extremely powerful microprocessor.

cracker

An unauthorized person who breaks into a computer system planning to do harm or damage, or with criminal intent. Often mislabeled as a *hacker* in the popular press. A hacker is a person who enjoys discovering and sharing arcane system information, who likes programming to the point of an obsession, and knows how to squeeze that last drop of system performance out of the system. A cracker, on the other hand, is a criminal. The popular press sometimes portrays crackers as programmers with extraordinary talents, but the truth is much more mundane; crackers use a well worn set of tricks to exploit common security weaknesses in the systems they target.

■ *See also* **intruder, SATAN, security.**

Table C.27: Options to Use with `cpio`	
OPTION	DESCRIPTION
`-a`	Resets the access times of input files to those values before `cpio` was used; by default, the access times are updated. Appends files to an existing archive; must be used with `-O`.
`-b`	Swaps bytes and half-words; this option assumes 4-byte words.
`-B`	Uses 5120-byte blocks; used only with files representing character devices such as raw tape drives. The default is 512-byte blocks.
`-c`	Reads or writes header information as ASCII for increased portability between different systems.
`-C`*n*	Specifies a block size of any positive integer, *n*, in multiples of 1024 bytes or 1 KB.
`-d`	Creates directories as needed; this is useful if you are copying a mixture of files and directories.
`-E` *filename*	Extracts the files listed in *filename* from an archive.
`-f`	Reverses the sense of the `cpio` syntax by copying all those files except those that match *pattern*.
`-H` *format*	Reads or writes header information according to *format*, which can be `crc` (ASCII header containing expanded device numbers), `odc` (ASCII header information containing small device numbers), `ustar` (IEEE/P1003 Data Interchange Standard header), or `tar` (`tar` header). Solaris adds another type, `bar` (`bar` header and format). Not available in SCO.
`-I` *filename*	Reads *filename* as input.
`-k`	Skips corrupted file headers, ignores input/output errors, and extracts as much good information as possible. You should use this option only when you know that an archive has been damaged by a disk or tape error and would otherwise be unreadable.
`-K`*volume-size*	Specifies *volume-size* as the size of the media volume; only available in SCO.
`-l`	Links files instead of copying them.
`-L`	Follows symbolic links.
`-m`	Keeps the previous file modification time; does not apply to directories.
`-M` *message*	Prints *message* when switching between media. You can use `%d` in your message to indicate the number of the next tape or disk. This option can be used only with `-O` and `-I`.
`-O` *filename*	Directs output to *filename*.

Table C.27: Options to Use with cpio (continued)

OPTION	DESCRIPTION
`-r`	Allows you to rename files interactively. When `cpio` copies a file, it prompts you with the old filename and waits for you to enter a new one. If you press Enter (or Return), the file will be skipped. If you type a period (`.`), the original path and filename will be used.
`-R` *`ID`*	Reassigns file ownership and group information to the user's login *`ID`*; available to the superuser only.
`-s`	Swaps bytes within each half-word; assumes four bytes per word.
`-S`	Swaps half-words within each word; assumes four bytes per word.
`-t`	Prints a table of contents of the input but creates no files. When used with the `-v` option, this list includes file-access permissions, ownership, and access time, along with the name of each file. Looks like output from `ls -l`.
`-u`	Copies unconditionally and allows old files to overwrite newer ones with the same name; without this option, `cpio` does not overwrite these newer files.
`-v`	Prints a list of filenames.
`-V`	Indicates that `cpio` is working by printing a dot on the screen for every file read or written.
`-6`	Processes a file in the old Unix Sixth Edition archive file format. Not available in Solaris.

crash

An unexpected system halt. Also refers to an application program error that is so severe that the program cannot continue running.

■ *See also* **core dump.**

CRC

Abbreviation for Cyclic Redundancy Check. A complex calculation method used to check the accuracy of a digital transmission over a communications link or to ensure the integrity of a file stored on disk.

The sending computer calculates a 1- or 2-byte CRC from the bits contained in the data, and this field is appended to the message before it is sent. The receiving computer performs the same calculation on the same data and compares this result with the received CRC. If the two CRCs do not match, indicating a transmission error, the receiving computer asks the sending computer to retransmit the data. This procedure is known as a redundancy check because each transmission includes extra or redundant error-checking values as well as the data itself.

As a security check, a CRC may be used to compare the current size of an executable file against the original size of the file to determine if the file has been tampered with or changed in some way.

■ *See also* **checksum, C-Kermit, Kermit, RZSZ, Xmodem, Ymodem, Zmodem.**

creation mask

A three-digit octal code that sets file-access permissions when a file is first created.

Use the `umask` command to set the file creation mask when you first create a file, or use the `chmod` command to change it later.

cron

A Unix background program or daemon that runs continuously, starting other programs at specified times. These programs are identified and scheduled by `crontab`.

`cron` is normally started automatically, so you never have to type this command.

crontab

A utility that specifies jobs to be run at regularly scheduled times.

▶ Syntax

The syntax for `crontab` takes two forms as follows:

`crontab [`*`filename`*`]`

`crontab [`*`options`*`][`*`username`*`]`

`crontab` lets you specify a list of jobs that the system will run for you at the times you choose. This information is stored in a file known as a `crontab` file; the system daemon `cron` reads this file and executes the commands it contains at the appropriate times.

▶ Options and Arguments

In the first line of syntax shown above, *`filename`* is the name of a `crontab` file; if you don't specify a filename, you can enter commands at the command prompt, terminating them with Ctrl-D.

Each `crontab` entry starts with five fields that specify the time when the command should run, followed by the command itself. An entry must be in the form:

`M H D m d command`

where:

M	Minute, from 0 to 59
H	Hour, from 0 to 23
D	Day of the month, from 1 to 31
m	Month, from 1 to 12
d	Day of the week, starting with 0 for Sunday
`command`	The command you want to execute at the specified time

If you place an asterisk (*) in one of these fields instead of a number, `crontab` interprets that as a wildcard for all possible values. Use a comma to separate multiple values and a hyphen to indicate a range; you can also include comments by preceding them with the pound (#) character.

In the second line of example syntax, *`username`* can be specified only by the superuser to change the contents of a specific user's `crontab` file.

Table C.28 lists the options available with `crontab`.

▶ Examples

To set up your `crontab` file, use:

`crontab mytodo_file`

With this command you copy the contents of the `mytodo_file` into your `crontab` file; you can have only one `crontab` file at a time.

▶ Notes

On some systems, not all users can use `crontab`. The `cron.allow` file in the `/etc/cron.d` directory (or `/usr/lib/cron` on some systems) lists the login names of users who can use `crontab`, and a file called `cron.deny` lists those users not allowed to use `crontab`.

See also **at, batch.**

Table C.28: Options to Use with crontab

OPTION	DESCRIPTION
`-e`	Opens an editor on your `crontab` file so you can create, add, delete, or change entries.
`-l`	Lists the contents of your `crontab` file.
`-r`	Removes your `crontab` file.

C

cross compiler

A program language compiler that runs on one operating system but prepares executable files to run on a different system. By using a cross compiler, programmers can take advantage of the software development tools available in Unix, which may not be available on the target system. Unix is often used to develop software that will eventually run on robots, industrial embedded systems, and other computers that do not have any kind of software development environment.

cross posting

In USENET, to post the same article to more than one newsgroup. Sometimes it may make sense to post the same message to more than one newsgroup, but in general, the practice is frowned upon as it wastes network resources.

■ *See also* **followup, posting.**

C runtime library

■ *See* **C library.**

crypt

A utility used to encrypt and decrypt a file.

▶ Syntax

The syntax for `crypt` is as follows:

```
crypt [password]
```

`crypt` uses the same *`password`* to encrypt and decrypt a file; if you don't provide a password, `crypt` asks you to supply one. `crypt` uses a one-rotor encryption machine similar to the German Enigma but with a 256-element rotor.

▶ Examples

`crypt` reads from the standard input and writes to standard output, so you must use redirection, as in this example of file encryption:

```
crypt megalith < secrets.txt
➥ > secrets.enc
```

which uses the password `megalith` to encrypt the file `secrets.txt`; the encrypted file is named `secrets.enc`.

▶ Notes

Although this utility is documented in many Unix systems, it is available only in the United States due to export restrictions. `crypt` generates files compatible with the Unix editors `ed`, `edit`, `ex`, and `vi` when in encryption mode.

■ *See also* **bdes, DES.**

cscope

An SVR4 interactive utility that builds a symbol cross-reference from one or more C, `lex`, or `yacc` source files and then lets you search for functions, macros, variables, and so on.

csh

A command used to invoke the C shell or interactive command interpreter.

▶ Syntax

The syntax to use with `csh` is:

```
csh [options][arguments]
```

`csh` uses syntax that resembles the *C* programming language and can execute commands from the keyboard or from a file.

▶ Options and Arguments

The C shell is usually available on all Unix systems; you may find some small differences in options between these different systems, but in general, usage is very consistent.

Table C.29 lists the options available with `csh`.

▶ Examples

If you want to launch a new shell temporarily, use:

```
csh
```

This command works no matter which shell you were using. When you exit from the C shell, you are returned to your previous working environment.

OPTION	DESCRIPTION
`-b`	Allows the remaining command-line options to be interpreted as options to a command, rather than as options to **csh**. Not available in SCO.
`-c`	Executes commands or scripts contained in the first *filename* argument.
`-e`	Exits the shell if a command produces an error or a non-zero exit status.
`-f`	Starts **csh** without searching for or executing commands found in the file **.cshrc** or **.login**.
`-i`	Invokes interactive shell.
`-l`	Makes the shell a login shell when only the **-l** option is specified. Available in BSD only.
`-n`	Parses and checks commands, but does not execute them. You can use this mode to check your shell scripts.
`-s`	Reads commands from standard input.
`-t`	Exits from **csh** after executing just one command; you can use a \ to escape the newline at the end of this line and continue on to the next.
`-v`	Sets verbose mode, which displays commands before executing them.
`-V`	Same as **-v**, but sets verbose mode before executing **.cshrc**. This means that the contents of **.cshrc** are displayed.
`-x`	Displays commands before executing them, and expands all substitutions; often used with **-v**. This option has the same effect as setting the C shell **echo** variable.
`-X`	Same as **-x**, but sets the mode before executing **.cshrc**. This means that the contents of **.cshrc** are displayed.

Table C.29: Options Available with csh, the C Shell

To execute a command or shell script contained in a file, use:

```
csh -c mystuff.txt
```

This is a good way of ensuring that a C shell script is executed properly.

See also **Bourne shell, C shell, Korn shell, ksh, sh, Unix shells.**

C shell

Pronounced "sea shell." The C shell has been the favorite shell of many users since it was developed by Bill Joy at the University of California at Berkeley between 1979 and 1981 as part of the BSD development and an alternative to the Bourne shell. It was first included in standard System V with SVR4, although several manufacturers included it in their own earlier implementations, and is the standard shell on many Unix systems, particularly those derived from BSD.

The C shell offers the following features, which are also found in the Bourne shell:

- Input and output redirection
- Wildcard or metacharacters for filename abbreviation
- A set of shell variables to customize your environment

The C shell adds the following new features:

- Integer arithmetic
- A history mechanism allowing you to recall previous commands in whole or in part
- Aliasing for abbreviating frequently used commands without using a shell script
- More flexible forms of command substitution
- Job control—the ability to switch between several processes and control their progress
- A built-in set of operators based on the C programming language for writing shell scripts

▶ Startup Files

The C shell program, started by the `csh` command, first executes the statements in the file `.cshrc` in your home directory; if you invoked `csh` as your login shell, the C shell then executes the contents of `.login` and also executes the commands contained in `.logout` when it terminates. Every time you start a new shell or run a shell script, the commands in `.cshrc` are executed; the commands in `.login` are executed only once, when you log in.

The normal prompt in the C shell is the percent symbol (`%`), and you can use `exit` or `logout` at any prompt to leave the C shell.

▶ Using Commands

The C shell allows you to use and group commands on the command line in several different ways. Table C.30 lists the ways you can use C shell commands.

▶ Filename Metacharacters

You can use any of the patterns shown in Table C.31 to generate filenames.

You can also combine these metacharacters into more complex expressions.

▶ Redirection

When you execute a command, the shell opens three files known as the standard input, the standard output, and the standard error. By default, the standard input is the keyboard, and the standard output and standard error are the terminal or screen. Redirection is the process of directing input to or output from a different file from that used ordinarily.

In simple redirection, you can change the input source or output destination in any of the ways shown in Table C.32.

In more complex multiple redirection, you can use any of the ways shown in Table C.33.

Table C.30: Using C Shell Commands

COMMAND	DESCRIPTION
cmd &	Executes *cmd* in the background.
cmd1 ; *cmd2*	Executes *cmd1* and *cmd2* consecutively, with the semicolon acting as a command separator.
(*cmd1* ; *cmd2*)	Creates a subshell to execute *cmd1* and *cmd2* as a group.
cmd1	*cmd2*	Creates a pipe and uses the output from *cmd1* as input to *cmd2*.
cmd1 \`*cmd2*\`	Performs command substitution; uses the output from *cmd2* as arguments to *cmd1*.
cmd1 && *cmd2*	Executes *cmd1*, and if *cmd1* completes successfully, then executes *cmd2*.
cmd1 || *cmd2*	Executes either *cmd1*, or if it fails, executes *cmd2*.

Table C.31: C Shell Filename Metacharacters

META-CHARACTER	DESCRIPTION
*	Matches any string or zero or more characters; for example, `w*n` matches `wn`, `win`, `won`, `when`, `worn`, and many other filenames.
?	Matches any single character; for example, `myfile.?` matches `myfile._`, `myfile.1`, `myfile.a`, and so on.
[*abc...*]	Matches any single character from the list, and you can use a hyphen to indicate a range, as in `a-z,0-9`, and so on.
~	Current user's home directory.
~ *name*	Home directory for user *name*.

▶ Quoting

Quoting disables the special meaning of a character, and allows you to use it literally. These characters, listed in Table C.34, have special meaning in the C shell.

Also, the newline, space, and tab are used as word separators.

▶ Predefined Variables

The C shell includes a large set of predefined variables, as shown in Table C.35. You can set a variable in one of two ways:

`set` *`variable=value`*

or by simply turning them on:

`set` *`variable`*

The C shell automatically sets the `argv`, `cwd`, `home`, `path`, `prompt`, `shell`, `status`, `term`, and `user` variables.

▶ Environment Variables

The C shell also maintains a set of environment variables, which are distinct from shell variables and are not really part of the C shell. Shell variables only have meaning within the current shell, but environment variables are exported automatically, making them act globally, which means that they can be accessed by mail systems, your favorite editor, and your shell scripts. These environment variables are listed in Table C.36.

In the cases where the shell variable and the environment variable have the same name (the shell variable in lowercase and the environment variable in uppercase letters), you can change the value of the shell variable and the appropriate environment variable value will also change automatically. This is a one-way street, however; changing the environment variable does not change the shell variable.

▶ Built-in Commands

The C shell offers a rich set of built-in commands, as shown in Table C.37. Built-in shell commands are executed as part of the current shell process; there is no need to fork or spawn a new process to execute them.

The C shell is a huge, complex topic and has been the subject of many excellent books and articles over the years. To make sure you get the best out of the C shell, consult the reference material that comes with your system, or seek out a book that deals exclusively with `csh`.

■ *See also* **Bash, Bourne shell, Bourne shell family, `csh`, C shell family, Korn shell, `ksh`, `sh`, Tcsh, Unix shell, Zsh.**

Table C.32: Simple Redirection in the C Shell	
COMMAND	DESCRIPTION
cmd > *filename*	Sends output from *cmd* to *filename*, overwriting the file if it already exists.
cmd >! *filename*	Same as above, even if the **noclobber** shell variable is set; see the section "Predefined Variables" for more information.
cmd >> *filename*	Adds or appends output from *cmd* to the end of *filename*.
cmd >>! *filename*	Same as above, even if the **noclobber** shell variable is set.
cmd < *filename*	Takes input for *cmd* from *filename*.
cmd << *text*	Reads standard input as far as a line identical to *text*.
<&-	Closes the standard input.
>&-	Closes the standard output.

Table C.33: Multiple Redirection in the C Shell	
FILE DESCRIPTOR	DESCRIPTION
cmd >& *filename*	Sends both standard output and standard error to *filename*.
cmd >&! *filename*	Same as above, even if **noclobber** is set.
cmd >>& *filename*	Appends both standard output and standard error to the end of *filename*.
cmd >>&! *filename*	Same as above, but creates *filename* even if **noclobber** is set.
cmd1 |& *cmd2*	Pipes standard error together with standard output.
(*cmd* > *filename1*) ➥ >& *filename2*	Sends standard output to *filename1* and standard error to *filename2*.
cmd | tee *filename*	Sends the output from **cmd** to standard output and to *filename* by creating a tee.

Table C.34: Quoting in the C Shell

CHARACTER	DESCRIPTION
;	Separates commands.
&	Runs commands in the background.
( )	Groups commands.
|	Creates a pipe.
*? [ ] ~	Filename metacharacters.
{ }	String expansion characters; they don't usually require quoting.
< > & !	Redirection symbols.
! ^	Characters used for history substitution and quick substitution.
" " ' ' \	Used when quoting other characters. Anything placed between double quotes is interpreted symbolically; anything placed between single quotes is interpreted literally, and the backslash is used to quote a single character.
`	Command substitution.
$	Variable substitution.

Table C.35: C Shell Variables

VARIABLE	DESCRIPTION
0	The name of the current shell script.
`?`*`variable`*	Contains 1 if the *`variable`* is set; zero if it is not set.
$	Contains the PID of the current process.
`argv=`*`arguments`*	List of arguments passed to the current command.
`cdpath=`*`directories`*	Contains the list of directories to search when locating arguments for `cd`, `popd`, or `pushd`.
`cwd=`*`directory`*	Contains the complete pathname of the current directory.
`echo`	Redisplays each command before executing it; same as using `csh -x`.
`fignore=`*`characters`*	Contains a list of filename suffixes to ignore during filename completion.
`filec`	Enables filename completion, using two special key combinations: Ctrl-D displays filenames that begin with the string you just entered, and Esc replaces the string you just entered with the longest possible extension.
`hardpaths`	Forces the `dirs` C shell command to display the actual pathnames of directories without their symbolic links.

Table C.35: C Shell Variables (continued)

VARIABLE	DESCRIPTION
`histchars=`*`ab`*	Specifies the two-character string to use in history substitution (`!`) and quick substitution (`^`); this makes the default `!^`.
`history=`*`n`*	Specifies the number of commands you want to save in the history list—typically between 100 and 200.
`home=`*`directory`*	Contains the name of your home directory, initialized from the environment variable `HOME`; the ~ character is shorthand for this directory.
`ignoreeof`	Ignores end-of-file (EOF) Ctrl-D characters when typed at the keyboard to avoid accidental logouts.
`mail=`*`n filename`*	Contains a list of mail files checked for new mail every five minutes; if the list begins with a number, this specifies a check every *`n`* seconds.
`nobeep`	Turns off the ambiguous filename completion beep.
`noclobber`	Does not allow redirection to an existing file; prevents accidental overwriting of files.
`noglob`	Turns off filename expansion; this is sometimes a good idea in shell scripts.
`nonomatch`	Treats filename metacharacters as normal characters, and does not generate an error if the filename expansion does not match anything.
`notify`	Forces the shell to tell you as soon as a job has completed, rather than waiting for the next prompt.
`path=`*`directories`*	Lists the pathnames to search for commands to execute prompt=`'`*`string`*`'`.
`savehist=`*`n`*	Specifies the number of commands you want to save in the `.history` file when you log out; the higher this number gets, the longer the C shell takes to log you in next time.
`shell=`*`filename`*	Specifies the name of the shell you are currently using; the default is `/bin/csh`.
`status=`*`n`*	Contains the exit status of the last command; built-in commands return 0 indicating success or 1 indicating failure.
`term=`*`ID`*	Contains a terminal type, initialized to `/etc/ttytype`.
`time='n %`*`c`*`'`	If a command execution takes longer than *`n`* CPU seconds, reports user time, elapsed time, system time, and CPU percentage.
`user=`*`name`*	Contains your login name; initialized from `USER`.
`verbose`.	Displays commands after history substitution; same as invoking `csh -v`.

Table C.36: C Shell Environment Variables

VARIABLE	DESCRIPTION
`EXINIT`	Contains a string of startup commands for `ex` or `vi`; similar to `.exrc`.
`HOME`	Home directory, same as `home`.
`LOGNAME`	Contains your username; another name for the `USER` variable.
`MAIL`	Specifies the file that holds mail; this is not the same as the C shell `mail` variable, which only checks for mail.
`PATH`	Contains the search path used when executing commands.
`PWD`	Contains the name of the current directory; initialized from `cwd`.
`SHELL`	Contains the pathname of the shell in current use.
`TERM`	Contains your terminal type; same as `term`.
`TERMCAP`	Contains the filename that holds the cursor-positioning codes for use with your terminal.
`USER`	Contains your username, same as `user`.

Table C.37: Built-in C Shell Commands

OPTION	DESCRIPTION
#	The comment character in a C shell script; any script that begins with this character is interpreted as a C shell script.
`#!`*`shell`*	Often used as the first line in a shell script to invoke the named *`shell`*.
`:`	Null command; returns an exit status of zero.
`@` *`variable`* `=` *`expression`*	Assigns the value of *`variable`* to *`expression`*; if none is specified, prints the values of all the shell variables
`alias [`*`name`*`[`*`command`*`]]`	Assigns *`name`* as the shorthand name for *`command`*.
`alloc`	Displays a report on the amount of used and free memory.
`bg [`*`jobIDs`*`]`	Places the current or the specified job in the background.
`break`	Skips to the next `end` command from the enclosing `while` or `foreach` statement.
`breaksw`	Breaks from a `switch` statement, and continues execution after the `endsw` statement.

Table C.37: Built-in C Shell Commands (continued)	
OPTION	**DESCRIPTION**
`case [pattern]`	Identifies a `pattern` in a `switch` statement.
`cd [directory]`	Changes to the specified directory; the default directory is your home directory.
`chdir`	Same as `cd`.
`continue`	Resumes execution of the enclosing `while` or `foreach` statement.
`default:`	Labels the default case, usually the final case in a `switch` statement.
`dirs [-l]`	Prints the directory stack, with the current directory first; use `-l` to expand the ~ symbol to the complete home directory name.
`echo [-n] string`	Writes the specified `string` to the standard output; specify `-n` to remove the newline character from the end of the `string`. This command, unlike the Unix and the Bourne shell `echo`, does not accept escape sequences.
`end`	Terminates a `foreach` or `while` statement.
`endif`	Terminates an `if` statement.
`eval arguments`	Scans and evaluates the command line; often used in shell scripts.
`exec command`	Executes `command` in the place of the current shell, terminating the current shell, rather than creating a new process.
`exit [expr]`	Exits a shell script with the status provided by `expr`.
`fg [jobIDs]`	Moves the current or specified job into the foreground.
`foreach name (wordlist)` `commands`	Assigns `name` to each value in `wordlist`, and executes the `commands`.
`glob wordlist`	Similar to `echo`, but does not display spaces between its arguments and does not place a newline at the end.
`goto string`	Skips to the line labeled `string` followed by a colon, and continues execution there.

C

Table C.37: Built-in C Shell Commands (continued)	
OPTION	DESCRIPTION
`hashstat`	Displays statistics on the C shell's `hash` mechanism; `hash` speeds up the process of searching through the directories in your search path.
`history [`*`options`*`]`	Displays the history list of commands. Options are listed in Table C.38.
`if`	Begins a conditional statement.
`jobs [-l]`	Lists all running or stopped jobs; use the `-l` option to display PIDs.
`kill [`*`options`*`]` *`ID`*	Terminates the specified process; use the `-l` option to list all the signal names, and use *`-signal`* for the signal number or name.
`limit [-h][`*`resource`*`[`*`limit`*`]]`	Limits the number of resources that can be used by the current process and by any processes it creates. By default, the current limits are listed; use the `-h` option to set a hard limit.
`login [`*`user`*`| -p]`	Logs in a user; `-p` preserves the environment variables.
`nice[+/-`*`n`*`]`*`commands`*	Changes the execution priority for *`command`*, or if none are given, changes the priority of the current shell. This is a useful command if you want to run a job that makes large demands on the system, but you can wait a while for the final output. Priority range for *`n`* is from +20 to -20, with a default of 4; -20 gives the highest priority.
`nohup [`*`command`*`]`	Lets you log off without terminating background processes; some systems are set up to do this automatically.
`notify [`*`jobID`*`]`	Reports any change in job status to you immediately.
`popd [+`*`n`*`]`	Removes a directory from the directory stack, or removes the *`n`*th entry.
`pushd [`*`name`*`]`	Changes the working directory to *`name`* and adds it to the directory stack.
`rehash`	Forces the shell to recreate its internal hash tables. You should always use `rehash` if you add or create a new command during the current session; otherwise, the shell may not be able to find it.

Table C.37: Built-in C Shell Commands (continued)	
OPTION	DESCRIPTION
`repeat` *n command*	Executes the *command n* times.
`set`	Sets, initializes, and displays the values of local variables.
`setenv [`*name*`[`*value*`]]`	Sets, initializes, and displays the values of environment variables; assigns the *value* to the variable *name*.
`shift [`*variable*`]`	When *variable* is specified, shifts the elements in an array; without *variable*, shifts the command-line arguments. Often used in a `while` loop.
`source [-h]` *script*	Reads and executes the commands in a C shell *script*; with `-h`, the commands are added to the history list but are not executed.
`stop [`*jobIDs*`]`	Stops the specified background job.
`suspend`	Suspends the current foreground job.
`switch`	Runs specified commands depending on the value of a variable, which is useful when you have to manage more than three choices.
`time` *command*	Executes the specified *command*, and displays how much time it uses.
`umask [`*nnn*`]`	Displays the file creation mask, or sets the file creation mask to the octal number *nnn*.
`unalias` *name*	Removes *name* from the alias list.
`unhash`	Turns off the hash mechanism.
`unlimit [`*resources*`]`	Removes the imposed limits on *resources*.
`unset` *variables*	Removes a variable declaration.
`unsetenv` *variable*	Removes an environment variable.
`wait`	Makes the shell wait for all child processes to complete.
`while (`*expression*`)` *commands*	As long as *expression* is true, executes *commands*.

Table C.38: Options to Use with the history C Shell Command

OPTION	DESCRIPTION
`-h`	Prints history list without event numbers.
`-r`	Prints history list in reverse order.
n	Prints the last *n* history commands, rather than the number specified by the `history` variable.

C shell family

A collective name for the C shell (pronounced "sea shell"), written by Bill Joy while at the University of California, Berkeley, as part of the BSD development, and Tcsh ("pronounced tee sea shell"), developed by Ken Greer, Paul Placeway, and several others.

The C shell is an advanced command interpreter that also offers a C-like programming language. The C shell has many advantages over the original Unix shell, the Bourne shell, including history, aliasing, and job control. The C shell is very popular with many Unix users and is the default shell on many systems.

Tcsh is an enhanced C shell, offering many advanced features. The "T" in the name refers to Tenex, an operating system used on the old DEC PDP-10 computers; the original work on this shell was done on Tenex. To learn more about Tcsh, take a look at the `man` pages for `tcsh`.

■ *See also* **Bourne shell family, Unix shell.**

.cshrc

A file in your home directory that the C shell reads and executes each time you invoke a new copy of the C shell. You can customize your environment by setting variables and aliases that you define in this file.

CSMA/CD

Abbreviation for Carrier Sense Multiple Access/Collision Detection. A baseband communications protocol with a built-in collision-detection technique. Each node on the network listens first and transmits only when the line is free. If two nodes transmit at exactly the same time and a collision occurs, both nodes stop transmitting. Then, to avoid a subsequent collision, each of the two nodes waits for a different random length of time before attempting to transmit again. Ethernet uses CSMA/CD access methods.

■ *See also* **demand priority, Fast Ethernet, 100VG-AnyLAN.**

csplit

A utility used to separate a file into smaller pieces, breaking each file at a point specified by the user.

▶ Syntax

The syntax used with `csplit` is as follows:

`csplit [`*`options`*`]` *`filename`*
➥ *`arguments`*

This utility splits a named file into smaller files called `xx00` through `xxnnn`, where *`nnn`* is less than 100, breaking the original file at locations specified by *`arguments`*.

▶ Options and Arguments

`arguments` can be any one or any combination of those listed in Table C.39.

Several options are also available for use with `csplit`; see Table C.40 for details.

▶ Examples

To divide a file into sections, each 200 lines long, use:

```
csplit myreport 200 {50}
```

The argument `200` specifies each file will be 200 lines in length, while the `{50}` repeats this argument 50 times. Any lines remaining will appear in the last file.

■ *See also* **`split`**.

Table C.39: Arguments for Use with csplit

ARGUMENT	DESCRIPTION
/expression/	Creates a file f to the line containing the regular expression *expression*. You can also use an optional suffix +*n* or −*n*, where *n* specifies a number of lines above or below *expression*.
%*expression*	Same as the previous argument, except that no file is created for lines before the line containing *expression*.
number	Creates a file from the current line up to the line number specified by *number*.
{*n*}	Repeats any of the above arguments *n* times.

Table C.40: Options for Use with csplit

OPTION	DESCRIPTION
-f *filename*	Names the new files *filename*00 through *filenamennn* (where *nnn* must be less than 100) rather than using the default filenames.
-k	Keeps any newly created files, even in the case of an error that would normally cause them to be destroyed.
-s	Suppresses all character counts.

CSRG

Abbreviation for Computer Systems Research Group. The University of California, Berkeley, group responsible for the development of the Berkeley Software Distribution (BSD).

CSRG was home to some remarkable programmers over the years and introduced into Unix many fundamental features that we now take for granted. The last BSD release, 4.4BSD, was made during 1993, and the group was disbanded shortly afterward.

ct

An SCO utility that dials a phone number and issues a login prompt on a terminal accessed by modems and a telephone line.

▶ Syntax

The syntax for ct is as follows:

```
ct [options] number
```

ct actually works by spawning a getty to a remote terminal.

▶ Options and Arguments

You can use the following to specify the telephone number *number* to use; 0–9, – (one-second delays), = (secondary dial tones), *, and #. There are also several important communications parameters you must set using the options listed in Table C.41 before you can use ct.

▶ Examples

To dial out on a 9600-baud modem to the number 111-1212, waiting one minute for a dial tone, use:

```
ct -s9600 -w1 111-1212
```

■ *See also* **cu, stty, uucp**.

Table C.41: Communications Options for Use with ct

OPTION	DESCRIPTION
-h	Prevents a hangup.
-s*speed*	Sets the modem baud rate; the default is 1200.
-v	Sends comments and error messages to standard error; useful for debugging difficult or new connections.
-w*minutes*	Specifies the number of minutes to wait for a dial tone before hanging up.
-x*n*	Sends a detailed copy of program comments and error messages to standard error; useful for debugging difficult or new connections.

ctags

A Unix software development command that creates a list of macro and function names from the specified C, Pascal, Fortran, `yacc`, or `lex` source file. This list contains three sets of entries: `name`, which represents the macro or function name, `filename`, which represents the name of the source file containing `name`, and `context`, which shows the line of code containing `name`.

ctrace

A Unix software development command used to debug a C language program. This command reads the C source file and sends a modified version (depending on the options you choose) to standard output.

Ctrl-\

The control character used as the quit key. This key combination sends a quit signal to your program to halt it immediately and also generates a core dump of memory at that instant. Mostly used by programmers testing software, Ctrl-\ is not intended for casual use.

Ctrl-C

The default control character used to interrupt a running program; on some systems, you can use Del or Delete instead. Also known as the *break key*.

Ctrl-D

The default control character used to indicate an end-of-file character. Control-C is used to tell a program that it has come to the end of its input. You can also use Ctrl-D in response to a Bourne or Korn shell prompt to log out from your system.

Ctrl-H

The default control character used on some systems to indicate backspace or erase. On Sun systems, use the Delete key (the one on top).

Ctrl key

A key on the keyboard that, when pressed in conjunction with another key, generates a nonprinting control character. On some keyboards, the key is labeled Control rather than Ctrl; both perform the same function.

- *See also* **`stty`**.

Ctrl-L

The default control character used to redraw the screen in `vi` and other full-screen display applications.

Ctrl-Q

The control character used to restart screen output after it has been paused temporarily.

- *See also* **Ctrl-S**.

Ctrl-R

An alternative control character used to redraw the screen in `vi`.

■ *See also* **Ctrl-L.**

Ctrl-S

The control character used to pause screen output temporarily.

■ *See also* **Ctrl-Q.**

Ctrl-U

The control character used to erase the entire line of input. On some systems, Ctrl-X performs this function.

Ctrl-W

The control character used to erase the last word you typed from the input.

Ctrl-X

The control character used to erase the entire line of input. On some systems, Ctrl-U performs this function.

Ctrl-Z

The control character used to suspend, but not kill, the currently active process.

cu

A command used to call up a remote Unix system or terminal using a direct line or a modem.

▶ Syntax

The syntax for `cu` is:

`cu [`*`options`*`][`*`destination`*`]`

`cu` connects you to a remote system. Since you have to log in to be able to use the system, it makes sense to use `cu` to call systems on which you have an account.

The `cu` command actually runs as two separate processes; a transmit process reads lines from your keyboard (standard input) and transmits them to the remote system; any lines that begin with a tilde (~) are treated as local commands rather than information that should be transmitted to the remote system. A receive process takes input from the remote system and passes it to your screen (standard output). These tilde commands are listed in Table C.42.

▶ Options and Arguments

The arguments for `cu` are listed in Table C.43.

There are several options you can use with `cu`, as shown in Table C.44.

▶ Examples

To connect to the system called `sausage`, use:

```
cu sausage
```

To connect to the phone number 111-1212 at 9600 baud, use:

```
cu -s9600 111-1212
```

■ *See also* **anonymous `ftp`, `ftp`, `telnet`, `tn3270`, `uucp`, `uux`.**

current working directory

The directory in which you are now working, with immediate access to all the files and directories that it contains.

When you first log in, your current working directory is set to your home directory. Unix always keeps track of which directory you are working in currently and lets you access a file in that directory by using just its basename, rather than requiring you to enter a fully qualified absolute pathname.

■ *See also* **absolute pathname, directory tree, pathname.**

Table C.42: Tilde Commands Used with cu	
COMMAND	DESCRIPTION
`~.`	Terminates the connection.
`~!`	Escapes to the shell on the local system.
`~!`*command*	Runs *command* on the local system.
`~$`*command*	Runs *command* on the local system, and sends output to the remote system as a command to be run there.
`~+`*command*	Runs *command* on the local system, but takes input from the remote system. Available on SCO only.
`~%cd`	Changes directory on the local system.
`~%take` *filename* ➥ [*target*]	Copies *filename* from the remote system to *target* on the local system. If you omit *target*, *filename* is used, or in other words, the new file will have the same name as the original.
`~%put` *filename* ➥ [*target*]	Copies *filename* from the local system to *target* on the remote system. If you omit *target*, *filename* is used, or in other words, the new file will have the same name as the original.
`~~`*line*	Allows you to pass a *line* that begins with a tilde to a remote system, so that you can issue commands to more than one system in a chain; you need to enter a tilde for every system you want the command to pass through.
`~%b`	Sends a Break sequence to the remote system. This command may appear as `~%break` on some systems.
`~%d`	Toggles debug mode on or off.
`~t`	Prints information for the local terminal.
`~l`	Prints information about the communications line.
`~%ifc`	Toggles between XON/XOFF flow control and no flow control.
`~%ofc`	Toggles output flow control.
`~%divert`	Toggles diversions not specified by `~%take`.
`~%old`	Toggles old-style syntax for diversions received.
`~%nostop`	Toggles between XON/XOFF flow control and no flow control.

Table C.43: Arguments Used with cu	
ARGUMENT	DESCRIPTION
number	The telephone number of the modem you want to connect to.
system	The name of the system to call.
address	The address of the system to call.

curses

A C library of screen-handling routines written by Mark Horton, which allows you to control the location of the cursor on the screen. `curses` can interact with either SVR4's `termcap` or BSD's `terminfo` files so that the software can run on any terminal, even creating windows on simple ASCII terminals.

cut

A command that extracts a list of columns or fields from one or more files.

▶ Syntax

The syntax for `cut` is:

```
cut options [filename]
```

You can use `cut` to print certain columns from a table or to select certain fields from a data file. Fields may be defined by specific integer character positions, or relatively, by using a comma as a field separator, or by using a hyphen to specify a range. You can also combine all three methods if you wish. The notation `23-` specifies from column 23 to the end of the line.

▶ Options and Arguments

Several options are available for use with `cut`; see Table C.45. However, you must specify either `-c` or `-f`, as they are mutually exclusive.

▶ Examples

To extract the user ID and names from the password file, use:

```
cut -f1,5 -d: /etc/passwd
```

Table C.44: Options for Use with cu	
OPTION	DESCRIPTION
`-b`*n*	Sets the character size in bits, where *n* is either 7 or 8.
`-c`*name*	Searches UUCP's `devices` file for a system called *name*.
`-d`	Prints diagnostics.
`-e`	Uses even parity; this option is the opposite of `-o`.
`-h`	Emulates a local echo to support connections to remote systems that expect to see half-duplex terminals.
`-l`*device*	Communicates using *device*, e.g., `/dev/tty002`; not used when *destination* is set to *address*.
`-n`	Prompts you to enter a phone number to call.
`-o`	Uses odd parity; this option is the opposite of `-e`.
`-s`*number*	Sets the transmission rate to *number*; not used when *destination* is set to *address*.
`t`	Dials an ASCII terminal that has auto-answer set. Carriage return is mapped to carriage return/linefeed. Used only when *destination* is set to *number*.

The `/etc/passwd` file uses a colon to separate fields, and the `-d:` option makes the colon the field delimiter.

■ *See also* **join**, **newform**, **paste**.

Table C.45: Options for Use with cut

OPTION	DESCRIPTION
`-clist`	Cuts the column positions specified by *list*.
`-dchar`	Specifies the field separator character as *char*; use with the `-f` option. The default is a tab; if you plan to use a special character such as a space, make sure that it is quoted.
`-flist`	Cuts the fields specified in *list*.
`-s`	Suppresses lines without delimiters; use with the `-f` option.

cut

To remove a marked portion of a document into a temporary storage area. This material can then be pasted into a different place in the original document or even into an entirely different document. Cutting moves the marked text, it does not copy the marked text.

■ *See also* **cut-and-paste.**

cut-and-paste

To remove a marked portion of a document into temporary storage and then insert it into either a different document or a new place in the original document.

Cut-and-paste allows compatible application programs to share text and graphics.

■ *See also* **cut.**

cxref

A Unix software development command that builds a cross-reference table for each C language source code file. The table lists all symbols, giving the name, associated function, filename, and line number.

cyclic redundancy check

■ *See* **CRC.**

daemon

Pronounced "dee-mon," sometimes "daymon." A Unix program that runs unattended and is usually invisible to the user, providing important system services.

Daemons manage all sorts of tasks, including mail management, networking, Internet services, `ftp` sessions, and NFS services. Some daemons are triggered automatically by events to perform their work; others operate at set time intervals. Because they spend most of their time inactive, waiting for something to do, daemons do not consume large amounts of system resources. Table D.1 lists some of the common daemons and their areas of responsibility, although some of their names may differ on different versions of Unix.

■ *See also* **`cron`, `init`, kernel.**

Table D.1: Common Unix Daemons

DAEMON	DESCRIPTION
`ftpd`	File transfer protocol daemon
`inetd`	Internet daemon
`lockd`	Network lock daemon
`lpd`	Printer lock daemon
`named`	Internet domain name server daemon
`nfsd`	NFS daemon
`pppd`	Point-to-point protocol daemon
`uucpd`	UUCP daemon

DARPA

Abbreviation for Defense Advanced Research Projects Agency, a U.S. military research funding agency that funded the ARPANET, the predecessor to the Internet.

DAT

Abbreviation for Digital Audio Tape. A method of recording information in digital form on a small tape cassette, originally developed by Hewlett-Packard. Over three gigabytes of uncompressed information can be recorded

on a single cassette, so a DAT can be used as a backup medium. Like all tape devices, however, DATs are relatively slow.

data bits

In asynchronous transmissions, the bits that actually make up the data; usually seven or eight data bits are in a single data word.

■ *See also* **communications parameters, parity.**

data block

One of the elements of a filesystem, along with the boot block, superblock, and i-nodes. Data blocks store all the information contained within directories or files.

■ *See also* **blocks, free blocks.**

data compression

Any one of several popular methods of encoding data so that it occupies less space than in its original form.

Many different mathematical techniques are used, but the overall purpose is to compress the data so that it can be stored, transmitted, and retrieved more efficiently.

■ *See also* **`compact`, `compress`, compressed file, `gzip`, lossless compression, lossy compression, `pack`.**

Data Encryption Standard

■ *See* **DES.**

data processing

■ *See* **DP.**

data stream

A continuous flow of serial data resulting from an input or output operation.

■ *See also* **`sed`, stream, stream editor.**

datagram

In communications, a message unit that contains source and destination address information, as well as the data itself, which is routed through a packet-switching network.

A datagram sent over the Internet is usually known as an IP datagram.

data-link layer

The second of the seven layers of the ISO/OSI model for computer-to-computer communications.

The data-link layer validates the integrity of the flow of data from one node to another by synchronizing blocks of data and controlling the flow of data.

date

A command that displays the system time and date. Only the superuser can use it to change the date.

▶ Syntax

The syntax for `date` is:

```
date [options][+format]
```

```
date [options] string
```

When used without arguments, `date` displays the current system time and date in the form:

```
Sun Oct 30 16:18:20 PDT 1996
```

▶ Options and Arguments

When the superuser specifies a new date in the form of *`string`*, it must have the following form:

`nnddhhmm[cc[yy]]`

where *`nn`* is the number of the month (from 1 to 12), *`dd`* is the day of the month (from 1 to 31), *`hh`* is the hour (from 00 to 23), and *`mm`* is the minutes (from 00 to 59). The final four digits are optional and are only used when changing the year; *`cc`* specifies the first two digits of the year and *`yy`* the last two.

If you specify *`+format`*, a string normally enclosed in single quotes, you can specify the format of `date` output by using field descriptors preceded by percent signs. Anything in the string that is not a field descriptor or a percent sign is copied directly to the output, and you can use this feature to add text or punctuation to the date. Table D.2 lists some of the common field descriptors used with **date**.

The options for use with **date** are shown in Table D.3.

Table D.2: Common date Field Descriptors

FIELD DESCRIPTOR	DESCRIPTION
%a	The abbreviated weekday name, Sun to Sat
%A	The full weekday name, Sunday to Saturday
%b	The abbreviated month name, Jan to Dec
%B	The full month name, January to December
%c	The time and date representation
%C	The century
%d	Day of the month, 01 to 31
%D	Date in mm/dd/ty format
%h	The abbreviated month name, Jan to Dec; same as %b
%H	Hour in 24-hour format, 00 to 23
%I	Hour in 12-hour format, 01 to 12
%j	Julian day of the year, 001 to 366
%m	Month of the year, 01 to 12
%M	Minutes, 00 to 59
%n	Inserts a newline character
%p	String to indicate a.m. or p.m.; the default is AM or PM
%r	Uses AM/PM notation, the default
%R	Time in HH:MM format
%S	Seconds, 00 to 61; 61 permits up to two leap seconds
%t	Inserts a tab character
%T	Time in HH:MM:SS format, 24-hour clock
%U	Week number, starting on Sunday, 0 to 53
%w	Day of the week, 0 (Sunday) to 6
%W	Week number, starting on Monday, 0 to 53
%x	Country-specific date format
%X	Same as %x
%y	Last two digits of the year, 00 to 99
%Y	Four-digit year
%Z	The time zone name

▶ Examples

To set the date to 3:46 p.m. on 30th October, 1996, use:

```
date 10301546
```

```
Wed Oct 30 15:46 PDT 1996
```

If you use the following command:

```
date `+%h %d, 19%y`
```

the date is displayed as:

```
Oct 30, 1996
```

■ *See also* **time**.

D

Table D.3: Options Used with `date`

OPTION	DESCRIPTION
`-a s.f`	Allows the superuser to adjust the current time by *s* seconds in increments of *f* fractional seconds; this lets the clock be adjusted slowly while the system is still running. By default, time increases; use `-s.f` to slow the clock down.
`-r`	In 4.4BSD, use this option to print time in elapsed seconds since the beginning of Unix time at 00:00:00 GMT, January 1st, 1970.
`-u`	Displays or sets time in GMT (Greenwich mean time).

DBCS

Abbreviation for double-byte character set. A method that uses two bytes to hold the definition of a character rather than the single character used in ASCII. By utilizing two bytes instead of one, the many international character sets in use these days can be managed much more easily.

■ *See also* **ASCII, ASCII character set, character, EBCDIC, extended ASCII character set, unicode.**

dbx

A Solaris source code debugger for programs written in C, C++, Fortran, or Pascal. `dbx` offers a large number of commands, and you can store these commands in a file called `.dbxinit` in your home directory. This file is read and the commands executed just before the symbol table is read. See the `dbx man` pages for more information.

■ *See also* **adb, sdb.**

dc

A command that starts an interactive desk calculator that uses reverse polish, or postfix, notation. You don't normally run `dc` directly because it is usually called automatically when you start `bc`.

Because `dc` uses reverse polish notation, you enter operators and commands after the numbers they apply to; if you are not comfortable in reverse polish, just use `bc` instead.

■ *See also* **xcalc.**

DCE

Abbreviation for Distributed Computing Environment, the Open Software Foundation's (OSF) architecture for developing applications software for use on different networks.

dd

A command used to copy and convert files. `dd` is different from the normal Unix copy command `cp` in that `dd` can access the raw devices, such as floppy disks. You can also use `dd` to convert files from one format to another so that you can swap them between different computer systems.

▶ Syntax

The syntax for `dd` is as follows:

```
dd [option=value]
```

You can use any number of options with `dd`, but `if` and `of` are two very common options and are often specified first; `if` lets you specify an input filename, while `of` lets you specify the name of an output file.

▶ Options and Arguments

All the options available with `dd` are listed in Table D.4.

You can multiply the size values indicated by *n* in Table D.4 by a factor of 2, 512, or 1024 by appending the letter `w`, `b`, or `k`. If you separate these arguments with an `x` indicating multiplication, the product of the numbers is used as the argument.

You can also string the conversion types together, separated by a comma, although `ascii`, `ebcdic`, `ibm`, `block`, and `unblock` are all mutually exclusive.

Table D.4: Options for Use with dd

OPTION	DESCRIPTION
`bs=`*n*	Sets the input and output block size to *n*, superseding the `ibs` and `obs` options.
`cbs=`*n*	Sets the conversion record size to *n* bytes; used only when the conversion *type* is `ascii`, `ebcdic`, `ibm`, `block`, or `unblock`.
`conv=`*type*	Converts the input according to one or more of the *types* listed in Table D.5.
`count=`*n*	Copies only *n* input blocks before terminating.
`files=`*n*	Copies only *n* files before terminating.
`ibs=`*n*	Sets the input block size to *n* bytes, the default is 512 bytes.
`if=`*filename*	Reads input from *filename* rather than from the standard input.
`obs=`*n*	Sets the output block size to *n* bytes, the default is 512 bytes.
`of=`*filename*	Writes output to *filename* rather than to the standard output.
`iseek=`*n*	Seeks *n* blocks from the start of the input file.
`oseek=`*n*	Seeks *n* blocks from the start of the output file.
`seek=`*n*	Seeks *n* blocks from the start of the output file before copying; same as `oseek` and retained for compatibility.
`skip=`*n*	Skips the first *n* input blocks before copying.

▶ Examples

The `dd swap` option lets you swap each byte as it is processed, which is useful when moving from a big-endian system to a little-endian system. You can also use `dd` to convert from ASCII to EBCDIC and back again:

```
dd if=myfile.ascii
➥ of=mtfile.ebcdic conv=ebcdic
```

This command converts the ASCII file `myfile.ascii` into the EBCDIC file `myfile.ebsdic` using the conversion `ebcdic`.

To read from a tape using one block size and output to a file using a different block size, use a command like this:

```
dd if=/dev/rmt02
➥ of=/usr/myfiles/wally
➥ ibs=1024 obs=512
```

This command reads input from a tape with 1024-byte blocks and writes this data into a file called `wally` that is written with 512-byte blocks.

■ *See also* **cp**, **cpio**, **copy**, **hd**, **mt**, **tar**, **tr**.

DDI

Abbreviation for Device Driver Interface, an SVR4 definition for device drivers and hardware interfaces intended to improve system compatibility.

DDRM

Abbreviation for Device Driver Interface/Driver Kernel Interface Reference Manual. An SVR4 system document aimed at programmers who create or maintain device drivers.

Table D.5: Conversion Types Available with the `conv=type` Option in `dd`	
TYPE	DESCRIPTION
`ascii`	From EBCDIC to ASCII
`block`	From variable-length records to fixed-length records
`ebcdic`	From ASCII to EBCDIC
`ibm`	From ASCII to EBCDIC with IBM conventions
`lcase`	From uppercase to lowercase, multibyte characters are not converted
`noerror`	Continues processing after an input error
`swab`	Swaps all pairs of bytes
`sync`	Pads the input blocks to the size specified by **`ibs`**
`unblock`	From fixed-length records to variable-length records
`ucase`	From lowercase to uppercase, multibyte characters are not converted

deadlock

An error condition or stalemate that occurs when two programs or devices are each waiting for a signal from the other before they can continue. The term *deadlock* is in common use in the U.S.

■ *See also* **deadly embrace.**

deadly embrace

An error condition or stalemate that occurs when two programs or devices are each waiting for a signal from the other before they can continue. The term *deadly embrace* is in common use in the United Kingdom and Europe.

■ *See also* **deadlock.**

debug

The process of finding, locating, and removing logical or syntactical errors from a computer program. This can range from simply checking the results of calculations to locating obscure errors that only occur under very specific conditions.

■ *See also* **debugger.**

debugger

A software development tool that helps a programmer to find and correct errors in a program.

Simple syntax errors are usually caught by the language compiler before the program is ever run, but errors in arithmetic or logic are not. A debugger lets the programmer step through a program, look at the contents of the data structures, and check program logic.

■ *See also* **`adb`, `dbx`, debug, `gdb`, `sdb`.**

decapsulation

A process used in networking in which the receiving system looks at the header of an arriving message to determine if the message contains data. If the message does contain data, the header is removed and the data decoded.

■ *See also* **encapsulation.**

decimal

The base ten numbering system; also known as the *base ten radix* or the *decimal radix.*

See also **binary, hexadecimal, octal.**

declaration

A specification of the type and name of a variable to be used in a C program.

Declarations are not needed in shell scripts because the shell creates variables dynamically, as they are needed, and they are all of the type called text.

decryption

The process of converting encrypted data back into its original form.

See also **`crypt`, encryption.**

default

A standard value or action that is used if you do not explicitly choose a different option.

A default is usually a relatively safe course of action to try first; many programs provide defaults you can use until you know enough about the program to specify your own settings. For example, `ls` lists the files in the working directory by default when you use it without arguments.

`default`

A C shell programming command used to label the default case in a `switch` statement; the default usually follows all the `case` labels.

delayed execution

Any mechanism used to delay or reschedule a job for a time when the system is less busy, including:

- The `at` command lets you submit a job at a specific time and date.
- The `batch` command provides a simple batch queuing system.
- The `crontab` utility lets you schedule jobs on a periodic basis.
- The `sleep` command lets you slow things down just a little.

delete

To remove an item, such as a file or directory, or to remove an element of a file, such as a word or line in a document file or a record in a database file.

The Unix editors and word processors all have commands to delete text ranging from a single character to large blocks of text.

The Unix command that deletes files is the `rm` command, and some systems have a similar command, `rmdir`, that is used for deleting directories.

deleting a user

Deleting a user account is often simpler than creating the account in the first place. Remove the user's entry in `/etc/passwd`, remove any references to the user in `/etc/group`, and then delete the user's home directory and any other additional files you can find. The following command removes Brenda's account, her home directory (the `-r` option forces removal of the home directory), and all her files:

```
userdel -r brenda
```

See also **adding a new user.**

delimiter

A special symbol used to separate one element from another; the Unix command line uses space characters as delimiters between words.

In a C program, comments are delimited by `/* */` pairs; in a tab-delimited file, data items are separated by tabs, and in a comma-delimited file, the comma is the separator.

`delta`

See **SCCS.**

D

demand paging

A common form of virtual memory management in which pages of information are read into memory from disk only when they are required.

■ *See also* **swapping.**

demand priority

A technique used in 100VG-AnyLAN to arbitrate access to the network and avoid collisions. Demand priority replaces CSMA/CD, which is used in slower Ethernet networks.

deroff

A command used to remove all `nroff`/`troff` dot requests, macros, escape sequences, and `eqn` and `tbl` formatting commands from a file.

▶ Syntax

The syntax used with `deroff` is as follows:

```
deroff [options][filename]
```

If you don't specify an input *`filename`*, `deroff` reads from the standard input.

▶ Options and Arguments

There are several options you can use with `deroff`, and they are listed in Table D.6. In BSD, only the `-w` option is available.

▶ Examples

To remove all `nroff`/`troff` formatting and macro commands from the file `myfile.doc` and write the resulting text into a file called `burke.txt`, use a command like the following:

```
deroff -mm myfile.doc >
➥ burke.txt
```

■ *See also* **`eqn`, `nroff`, `tbl`, `troff`.**

Table D.6: Options for Use with `deroff`

OPTION	DESCRIPTION
`-mm`	Suppresses any text that appears on macro lines; paragraphs will print, but the headings may have been stripped away.
`-ml`	Same as **`-mm`**, but also removes lines created by **`mm`** macros.
`-w`	Outputs the text as a list with one word on each line.

DES

The abbreviation for Data Encryption Standard. A standard method of data encryption and decryption developed by the United States National Bureau of Standards.

DES works by a combination of transposition and substitution and is used by the federal government and most banks and money-transfer systems to protect all sensitive transactions.

■ *See* **Pretty Good Privacy.**

des

A Solaris command used to encrypt and decrypt a file according to the DES. Some Sun SPARCstations have an encryption chip installed, and you can direct `des` to use it; encryption using software only is about 50 times slower.

descriptor table

A list created for every process running on a system that identifies all input and output functions.

DeskSet

A collection of graphical desktop applications included as part of Solaris. DeskSet includes a file manager with options for copying, moving, renaming, and deleting files, a terminal emulator, text editor, calculator, clock, and a calendar, as well as special programs and utilities.

destination host

A computer system on a network that is the final destination for a file transfer or for e-mail.

detached processing

■ *See* **background processing.**

/dev

A root directory that contains the files needed to manage device drivers for terminals, printers, and other hardware devices used on the system. Table D.7 lists some of the entries you can find in `/dev` and explains what they are.

In SVR4, the `/dev` directory is divided into subdirectories named after the type of device it supports; `dsk` and `rdsk` for disks accessed in block mode and raw mode, `term` for terminals, and `pts` and `ptc` for pseudo-terminals.

■ *See also* **major device number, minor device number.**

devconfig

A file in SVR4 Basic Network Utilities used in streams-based communications.

■ *See also* **stream.**

device

Any peripheral hardware attached to a Unix system, including disk drives, tapes, printers, and terminals. Unix treats all peripherals as though they were files, and each device is represented by a special file located in the `/dev` directory. When your Unix system displays information on your terminal, it is actually writing to the special file that represents your terminal.

This treatment of a peripheral as a file is one of the fundamental Unix features, along with redirection and pipes.

■ *See also* **block special file, character special file, device driver.**

device-dependent

Any software system designed to run only with specific input or output hardware. Device-dependent software is

Table D.7: Typical /dev Entries

ENTRY	DESCRIPTION
`/dev/console`	The character special file for the system console.
`/dev/null`	The null device; any output sent here is discarded, and any attempt to read from `/dev/null` produces an immediate end-of-file. Also known as the bit bucket.
`/dev/tty`	Files used to manage the generic terminal management, such as the handling of erase and kill characters, tabs, and so on. You will also find files used to access specific communications lines or terminals, which might be called `/dev/tty10` for the tenth serial port. These numbers are specific to each Unix installation.
`/dev/mem`	A device that corresponds to the system's memory, through which certain authorized programs can read or modify virtual memory; used only for debugging. A similar device, `/dev/kmem`, is used to read or modify the kernel's memory.

often very difficult to port, or move, to another computer system due to this reliance on specific hardware.

■ *See also* **device-independent, hardware-dependent, hardware-independent.**

device driver

The part of the Unix kernel that controls a specific hardware device such as a tape drive, printer, or terminal. Selecting the appropriate device drivers is one of the main tasks for the system administrator during Unix system generation.

■ *See also* **`/dev`, major device number, minor device number.**

device driver calls

A set of standard calls used with device drivers, including those listed in Table D.8.

Table D.8: Device Driver Calls

CALL	DESCRIPTION
`close`	Indicates the end of a transmission of data, and terminates the connection to the device.
`ioctl`	Establishes input/output control for the device.
`open`	Readies the device to receive commands.
`read`	Requests data from a device.
`write`	Transmits data or control information to the device.

device file

A file in the `/dev` directory that represents a device; also known as a *special file.* There are two types of device files: character special files and block special files. Many versions of Unix also support named pipes and sockets. Device files identify the type and location of a particular piece of hardware so that information can be sent to or received from that device.

■ *See also* **major device number, minor device number.**

device filename

The pathname of a device file. Device files are usually found in the `/dev` directory.

device-independent

Any software system designed to run without requiring the presence of specific input or output hardware but can run on a range of hardware systems.

■ *See also* **device-dependent, hardware-dependent, hardware-independent.**

device number

An address or path used to access a particular device.

■ *See also* **major device number, minor device number.**

df

A command that reports the amount of free disk space on a mounted device.

▶ Syntax

The syntax for `df` is:

`df [`*`options`*`][`*`name`*`]`

If you use `df` with no arguments, it reports the amount of free disk space on all of the currently mounted devices; otherwise, it reports on *`name`*, where *`name`* can be a device name, the directory name of a file-system mounting point, a directory, or an RFS or NFS resource name.

▶ Options and Arguments

The `df` command has a wide range of different options on different versions of Unix. Apart from those listed in Table D.9, many additional options relate specifically to different types of filesystems; see your `man` pages for more details.

▶ Examples

To see how full each mounted filesystem is and to print that information on the default printer, you can use;

```
df -t | lpr
```

You will see a listing of all the mounted filesystems and the number of free blocks and i-nodes.

▶ Notes

In the BSD version of `df`, the `-n` and `-t` options are ignored when you specify a filename or filesystem name as *`name`* in the syntax given above.

See also **dfspace**.

DFS

Abbreviation for Distributed File System. A standard set of commands used with NFS and RFS to manage a distributed network environment and provide users with

Table D.9: Options for Use with df

OPTION	DESCRIPTION
`-b`	Reports the amount of free disk space in kilobytes.
`-e`	Reports only the number of free files.
`-f`	An SVR3 option that reports the number of free blocks but not the free i-nodes.
`-F` *`type`*	Reports on the unmounted filesystem *`type`*. A list of the available *`types`* is in `/etc/vfstab`.
`-g`	Reports the amount of occupied and free disk space, type of filesystem and the filesystem ID, filename length, block size, and fragment size.
`-i`	In BSD and SCO, this option includes statistics on the number of used and free i-nodes.
`-k`	Reports the allocation in kilobytes. In some versions of Unix, this option reports the amount of occupied and free space in kilobytes, as well as the percentage of used disk capacity.
`-l`	Reports only on the local filesystem.
`-n`	Prints the filesystem *`type`* name. When you use this option by itself, it lists the types for all mounted file systems. On BSD systems, this option prints out statistics obtained previously, to avoid a potentially long delay in reporting. Some of this information may be out-of-date by the time you see it.
`-o` *`suboptions`*	Lets you specify a comma-separated list of options specific to *`type`*.
`-t`	Reports the total allocated space as well as the amount of free space.
`-v`	On some systems, including SCO, this option reports the free percentage of blocks and number of free and used blocks.
`-V`	Echoes the command line but does not run the command.

easy and transparent access to all files they have the appropriate permissions to use.

■ *See also* **mount.**

dfspace

An SCO shell script similar to the `df` command that reports free disk space. When used with no arguments, `dfspace` reports the total amount and percentage of disk space used, and the space available on each mounted filesystem.

■ *See also* **`df`.**

/dgn

An SVR4 root directory that contains the programs used for system diagnostics.

DG/UX

A version of Unix developed for Data General Corporation's computer systems.

Dhrystones

Pronounced "dry-stones." A standard public-domain benchmark program used to quantify and compare the performance of different computers.

The program reports system performance as the number of times that the program can operate per second and emphasizes string operations, integer arithmetic, and general-purpose instructions rather than floating point operations.

■ *See also* **SPEC benchmark, Whetstones.**

diagnostics

Any program or set of programs designed to test a specific part of a computer system to determine if a problem exists and, if possible, to locate and identify the nature of the problem.

Diagnostics are usually run only by the system administrator or by maintenance personnel.

diction

A BSD command used to find poorly written or unnecessarily wordy text.

▶ Syntax

The syntax for `diction` is as follows:

```
diction [options] filename
```

The `diction` command prints all sentences in a document containing phrases that are either frequently misused or are unnecessarily wordy. The document is compared against a database containing several hundred phrases; you can provide your own version of this file if you prefer.

`diction` uses the `deroff` command to prepare the text for comparison; use the `-ml` option if your document contains many lists of items that you want `diction` to skip.

▶ Options and Arguments

Table D.10 lists the options you can use with `diction`.

Table D.10: Options Used with `diction`

OPTION	DESCRIPTION
`-f` *`filename`*	Uses *`filename`* in addition to the default pattern file; this option lets you add your own phrases to those used by `diction`.
`-ml`	Makes `deroff` skip all lists; use this option if your document contains many lists that do not consist of sentences.
`-mm`	Overrides the default `-ms` macro package.
`-n`	Turns off usage of the default pattern file.

▶ Examples

To check the text contained in **myfile.doc**, use:

```
diction myfile.txt | lpr
```

All the errors that **diction** finds are displayed in square brackets; in this example, the file is piped to the default printer.

See also **deroff, explain, style.**

diff

A command that displays the differences between two text files, line by line.

▶ Syntax

The syntax for **diff** can take several forms, as follows:

```
diff [options] file1 file2

diff [options] file1
➥ directory

diff [options] directory
➥ file2

diff [options] directory1
➥ directory2
```

You can use **diff** to find the differences between two files; if one of the filenames is replaced by a hyphen (**-**), **diff** uses the standard input. By carefully choosing options, you can also use **diff** to create an **ed** script you can use to re-create the second file from the first.

In the Unix tradition, no output is created if the two files are identical.

▶ Options and Arguments

When you use two filenames as arguments to **diff**, the files are compared. If you use *directory* rather than *file1*, **diff** looks for a file in *directory* with the same name as *file2*, and if you use *directory* rather than *file2*, **diff** looks for a file in *directory* with the same name as *file1*. When two directory arguments are used, **diff** sorts the contents of each directory by name and then compares all files in *directory1* with files in *directory2* that have the same filenames. Binary files, common subdirectories, and files that appear in only one of the directories are noted.

In Table D.11, the options you can use with **diff** are arranged under three headings: Output Options, Comparison Options, and Directory Comparison Options.

diff always assumes that you want to change *file1* into *file2*, and when you use it without any options, the output is a series of lines containing add (**a**), delete (**d**), or change (**c**) instructions. Each of these lines is followed by the lines from the file that you need to modify. A less than symbol (<) precedes lines from *file1*, and a greater than symbol (>) precedes lines from *file2*. If you want to know how to change *file2* into *file1*, just run **diff** again, but this time reverse the order of the file arguments.

▶ Examples

You can create an **ed** script that converts **document1.doc** into **document2.doc** by using:

```
diff -e document1.doc
➥ document2.doc >
➥ edscript.doc
```

Redirection captures the output from this comparison in the file called **edscript.doc**.

▶ Notes

The Unix commands **comm**, **diff** (and **diff3**), and **cmp** all compare files; **comm** is limited to sorted text files, and **diff** to text files. You can use **cmp** with both text and non-text files, including binary files, but the output is rather less informative.

See also **bdiff, cmp, comm, diff3, ed, RCS, sdiff.**

D

Table D.11: Options Available with `diff`

OPTION	DESCRIPTION
Output Options	
`-cn`	Presents three lines of content, although you can optionally specify *n* lines of context.
`-Dstring`	Merges the two files into one file containing conditional C preprocessor statements so that compiling while defining *string* yields *file2* and compiling without defining *string* yields *file1*.
`-e`	Creates output in a form suitable as input to `ed`, which can then be used to convert *file1* into *file2*.
`-f`	Produces output reversed from that produced by the `-e` option; this output cannot be used with `ed`.
`-h`	Uses a different comparison algorithm capable of managing very long files. The algorithm requires that changes are well defined and brief; otherwise, it gets confused.
`-n`	Produces similar output to the `-f` option, but counts the changed lines. This option is useful with the RCS command `rcsdiff`.
Comparison Options	
`-b`	Causes leading and trailing blanks and tabs to be ignored.
`-i`	Ignores uppercase and lowercase distinctions.
`-t`	Expands tabs in output lines.
`-w`	Similar to `-b`, but ignores all blanks and tabs.
Directory Comparison Options	
`-l`	Produces a long output format; each file compared is passed through `pr` so that it is paginated, and other differences are summarized at the end.
`-r`	Runs `diff` recursively through common subdirectories.
`-s`	Reports on identical files, which would otherwise receive no report.
`-Sfilename`	Restarts a directory `diff` beginning with *filename*. This option skips all files whose names begin with letters before the first letter of *filename*.

diff3

A command that compares three versions of a file and reports the differences to the standard output.

▶ Syntax

The syntax for **diff3** is:

```
diff3 [options] filename1
➥ filename2 filename3
```

Differences are reported using the following indicators:

====	Lines below this indicator are different in all three files.
====1	*filename1* is different.
====2	*filename2* is different.
====3	*filename3* is different.

Changes are described in terms of the **ed** commands, add (**a**), delete (**d**), or change (**c**), needed to create the target from the different versions.

▶ Options and Arguments

You can use several options with **diff3**, as Table D.12 shows, allowing you to merge the different versions into a new file.

■ *See also* **bdiff**, **cmp**, **comm**, **diff**, **ed**, RCS, **sdiff**.

diffmk

A command used to compare revisions or changes made between drafts of a document.

▶ Syntax

The syntax for **diffmk** is as follows:

```
diffmk oldfile newfile
➥ changes
```

▶ Options and Arguments

The **diffmk** command compares the two versions of the document contained in *oldfile* and *newfile* and creates a third file, *changes*, that contains **troff** change mark requests.

When you format *changes* using either **nroff** or **troff**, differences between the two files are marked in the margin, even if the changes are trivial, such as extra spaces or different line lengths. A | marks changed lines and a * marks deleted lines.

■ *See also* **bdiff**, **cmp**, **comm**, **diff**, **sdiff**.

D

Table D.12: Options Available with diff3

OPTION	DESCRIPTION
-e	Creates output suitable as input to **ed** to add to *file1* all the differences between *file2* and *file3*.
-E	Same as option **-e**, but lines that differ between all three files are marked with a line of <<<<<< and >>>>>> symbols.
-x	Creates an **ed** script that incorporates into *file1* all differences among all three files.
-X	Same as **-x**, but lines that differ between all three files are marked with a line of <<<<<< and >>>>>> symbols.
-3	Creates an **ed** script that incorporates into *file1* any differences between *file1* and *file3*.

dig

A BSD command used to query DNS name servers.

▶ Syntax

The syntax for use with `dig` is:

```
dig @server domain query-type
➥ query-class
```

`dig` is an abbreviation for domain information groper, which is used to collect information from the DNS servers.

▶ Options and Arguments

In the syntax given above, *`server`* can be either the name or the dotted decimal IP address; if your system does not support DNS, you have to use the dotted decimal address. *`domain`* is the domain name you are requesting information about. *`query-type`* is the type of information or DNS query type you are requesting; if you leave it out, the default is `a` for network address. *`query-class`* is the network class requested by the query; if you omit this argument, the default is `in` for Internet class domain. Several other very complex options are available with this command; see the `man` pages on your system for more information.

■ *See also* **nslookup**.

digest

A collection of Internet mailing list posts collected together and sent out as a single large message rather than a number of smaller messages. Using a digest is a good way to cut down on the number of noncritical e-mail messages you receive.

■ *See also* **listserver.**

digital

Describes any device that represents values in the form of binary digits or bits.

dircmp

An SVR4 command that compares the contents of two directories, listing the files unique to each directory.

▶ Syntax

The syntax to use with `dircmp` is:

```
dircmp [options] directory1
➥ directory2
```

▶ Options and Arguments

The `dircmp` command compares the contents of *`directory1`* and *`directory2`* and lists information on the files unique to each directory. This list is made up of two columns, with the word `same` before all files that are the same in both directories. A period (`.`) indicates that one of the directories for comparison is the current directory.

You can use the options listed in Table D.13 with the `dircmp` command.

■ *See also* **cmp, diff.**

Table D.13: Options Available with dircmp

OPTION	DESCRIPTION
`-d`	Runs `diff` on files with the same name.
`-s`	Suppresses all messages about identical filenames.
`-w`*`width`*	Sets the width of the output to *`width`*; the default is 72 characters.

direct memory access

■ *See* **DMA.**

directory

An abbreviation for directory file. In Unix a directory is considered to be a special kind of file that lists the filenames and corresponding i-nodes for all the files and directories it contains. A directory may be empty, it may contain a number of other files, or it may contain other directories.

Unix uses a hierarchical system of directories to organize the thousands of files required by a typical installation, beginning at the root directory (`/`). Other directories branch from the root, including `/dev`, `/usr`, `/etc`, and `/bin`, for example, and other directories (often called subdirectories) branch in turn from these directories.

See also **`cd`, current working directory, dot, dot dot, file type, home directory, `ls`, ordinary file, `pwd`, special file.**

directory abbreviations

Unix uses symbols when referring to the current directory and to the parent directory of the current directory.

The name of the current directory is referred to by a period usually referred to as a *dot,* and the name of the parent of the current directory is referred to by two periods (*dot dot*). These two entries are found in every Unix directory, and they cannot be removed by the `rm` command.

The Unix shells use other abbreviations to access specific directories; for example, the tilde character (~) represents the name of the user's home directory in the Korn shell, the C shell, Bash, Tcsh, and Zsh but not in the Bourne shell. In the Korn shell, you can also use `~+` as a shortcut for the name of the current directory and `~-` as a shortcut for the name of the previous directory. In the C shell, you can use `~name` to represent the home directory of the user specified by *`name`*.

See also **Bourne shell, home directory, Korn shell.**

directory access mode

The bit pattern that defines the access permissions available for a file or directory.

Directories support the three operations of reading, writing, and executing, and these can be allowed or denied to the owner, the group, and all others, as you would expect. For a directory, the execute permission means that you can use the directory name as a part of a pathname; you cannot `cd` to a directory whose execute permission is denied, nor can you access any of the files within that directory.

directory commands

That group of Unix commands related to directory operations, including `cd`, `chgrp`, `chmod`, `cpio`, `dircmp`, `dirname`, `find`, `ls`, `mkdir`, `mv`, `pwd`, `rm`, `rmdir`, and `tar`.

directory file

See **directory.**

directory tree

The Unix directory structure is arranged as an inverted tree-like structure, beginning with the root directory (`/`) as the starting point from which all other directories must branch, either directly or indirectly. All the other directories except the root directory can be added to or removed from the system. Also known as a *hierarchical file structure.*

dirname

An SVR4 command used to extract a directory name from a complete pathname.

▶ Syntax

Here is the syntax to use for `dirname`:

`dirname` *`pathname`*

This command removes a filename from a pathname and sends the resulting directory name to the standard output. `dirname` is often used in shell scripts that create a new file in a specific directory. There are no options for `dirname`.

▶ Examples

When you provide this command with a complete pathname, it returns the pathname without the final component:

```
dirname /usr/pmd/wally
/usr/pmd
```

See also **`basename`.**

D

Table D.14: Options for Use with `dis`

OPTION	DESCRIPTION
`-d` *section*	Disassembles the specified *section* of data, printing the offset.
`-D` *section*	Same as `-d`, but also prints the data's actual address.
`-F` *function*	Disassembles the specified *function*; repeat the option for additional functions.
`-l` *string*	Disassembles the library file *string*.
`-L`	Looks for C source labels in files compiled using `cc -g`.
`-o`	Prints the output in octal rather than the default hexadecimal.
`-t` *section*	Same as `-d`, but prints text output.
`-V`	Prints the `dis` version number on the standard output.

dirs

A C shell command that lists the current working directory. When in your home directory, this command lists the tilde (~), and you can use `dirs -l` to expand this symbol to the actual name of your home directory.

■ *See also* **popd**, **pushd**.

dis

The Unix software development command that runs the disassembler on an executable, object, or archive file.

▶ Syntax

The disassembler is a programmer's tool used to look at executable or object files in hexadecimal machine instructions. Here's the syntax:

```
dis [options] filename
```

▶ Options and Arguments

`dis` disassembles the executable or object file specified by *filename*. Several options are available with this command, and they are listed in Table D.14.

■ *See also* **as**.

disable

To turn a function off or prevent something from happening.

■ *See also* **enable.**

disable

A command that temporarily turns off terminals or printers.

▶ Syntax

Here's the syntax for `disable`:

```
disable tty...
disable [options] printer
```

The `disable` command is often used when clearing up paper jams in printers or when swapping out printers or terminals for maintenance.

When you disable a printer, the current print job stops; when you enable the printer once again, this print job starts from the beginning unless you use the `-c` option described in the next section.

▶ Options and Arguments

In the first line of syntax shown above, `disable` will not allow logins on *tty*, and in the second line, `disable` stops print jobs from being sent to the

OPTION	DESCRIPTION
`-c`	Cancels the print job currently printing.
`-r[reason]`	Associates *reason* with the specified *printer*. This *reason* is reported by `lpstat`. To use more than one word in *reason*, be sure to enclose the text in double quotes (as in `"a message"`).
`-W`	Waits for the current print job to complete before disabling *printer*.

Table D.15: Options Available with `disable`

named *printer*. Table D.15 lists the options you can use with `disable`.

▶ Examples

To prevent logins on the tenth terminal on your system, use:

```
disable tty10
```

To let everyone know that you are clearing out a paper jam on the department printer, use a message such as:

```
disable -c -r"Paper Jam!
➥ Printer back up in 5
➥ minutes." deptptr
```

■ *See also* **cancel**, **enable**, **lp**, **lpstat**.

disabled command

A command that is turned off by default. For example, in `emacs`, certain advanced commands are disabled and so cannot be executed until you explicitly turn them on. This is often done to protect new users from potentially dangerous commands.

disassembler

A software development tool used to convert a machine language program back into the assembly language source code from which it was originally created.

■ *See also* **assembler**, **dis**.

disk cache

Pronounced "disk cash." An area of computer memory where data is temporarily stored on its way to or from a disk.

When an application asks for information from the hard disk, the cache program first checks to see if that data is already in the cache memory. If it is, the disk cache program loads the information from the cache memory rather than from the hard disk. If the information is not in memory, the cache program reads the data from the disk, copies it into the cache memory for future reference, and then passes the data to the requesting application.

disk commands

That group of Unix commands related to disk operations, including `dd`, `df`, `diskcmp`, `diskcp`, `du`, `fsck`, `mount`, and `umount`.

disk striping

The technique of combining a set of disk partitions located on different hard disks into a single volume, creating a virtual stripe across the partitions that the operating system recognizes as a single drive; see Figure D.1. Disk striping allows multiple concurrent disk accesses and can improve performance considerably.

■ *See also* **disk striping with parity**, **RAID**.

Figure D.1: Disk Striping Can Improve System Performance.

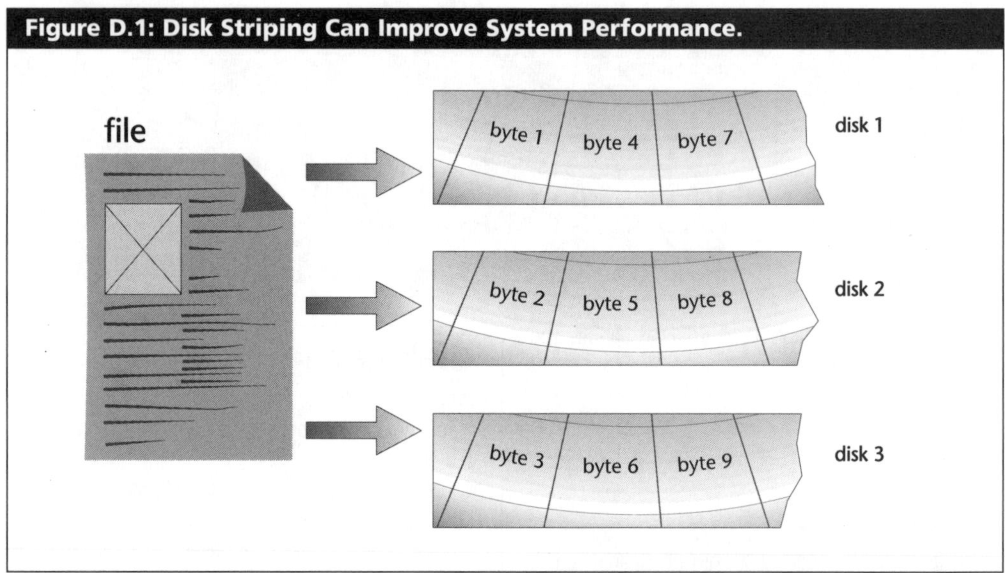

disk striping with parity

The addition of parity information across a disk stripe so that if a disk partition fails, the data on that disk can be recreated from the information stored across the remaining partitions in the disk stripe.

■ *See also* **disk striping, RAID.**

diskcmp

An SCO command that compares the contents of two floppy disks, using the **cmp** utility.

▶ Syntax

Here's the syntax for **diskcmp**:

```
diskcmp [options]
```

The **diskcmp** command presents self-explanatory prompts for its use.

▶ Options and Arguments

Most of the options available with the **diskcmp** command are used to specify the type of floppy disk for the comparison, as Table D.16 shows.

■ *See also* **diskcp**.

Table D.16: Options to Use with diskcmp

OPTION	DESCRIPTION
-d	Specifies your computer has two floppy disk drives; ordinarily the contents of the source floppy disk are copied to the hard disk, and then the comparison is made.
-s	Runs a checksum to verify the accuracy of the comparison.
-48ds9	Specifies a 360 KB floppy.
-96ds9	Specifies a 720 KB 5¼ floppy.
-96ds15	Specifies a 1.2 MB 5¼ floppy.
-135ds9	Specifies a 720 KB 3½ floppy.
-135ds18	Specifies a 1.44 MB 3½ floppy.

diskcp

An SCO command that copies floppy disks.

▶ Syntax

Here's the syntax for `diskcp`:

```
diskcp [options]
```

The `diskcp` command presents self-explanatory prompts for its use, telling you when to insert and remove the source and target floppy disks.

▶ Options and Arguments

Most of the options available with the `diskcp` command are used to specify the type of floppy disk for the comparison, as Table D.17 shows.

■ *See also* **diskcmp.**

Table D.17: Options to Use with diskcp

OPTION	DESCRIPTION
-d	Specifies your computer has two floppy disk drives; ordinarily the contents of the source floppy disk are copied to the hard disk, and then the comparison is made.
-f	Formats the target floppy disk before starting the copy.
-r	Uses the second floppy disk drive as the source drive.
-s	Runs a checksum to verify the accuracy of the comparison.
-u	Prints out a usage message.
-48ds9	Specifies a 360 KB floppy.
-96ds9	Specifies a 720 KB 5¼ floppy.
-96ds15	Specifies a 1.2 MB 5¼ floppy.
-135ds9	Specifies a 720 KB 3½ floppy.
-135ds18	Specifies a 1.44 MB 3½ floppy.

diskless workstation

A networked computer that does not have any local disk storage capability. The computer boots and loads all its programs from the network file server. Diskless workstations are particularly valuable when sensitive information is processed; information cannot be copied from the file server onto a local disk, because the workstation does not have one.

■ *See also* **security.**

display editor

■ *See* **visual editor.**

display manager

An X Window program that manages the login process, and also automatically starts X Window and a window manager.

distributed computing

■ *See* **distributed processing/computing.**

Distributed Computing Environment

■ *See* **DCE.**

distributed file system

Any filesystem in which user files and programs are located on more than one computer system or server. Users can access files and programs as though they were stored on a single local system.

■ *See also* **NFS, RFS.**

Distributed File System

■ *See* **DFS.**

distributed processing/computing

A computer system in which processing is performed by several separate computers linked by a communications network. The term often refers to any computer system supported by a network, but more properly refers to a system in which each computer is chosen to handle a specific workload and the network supports the system as a whole. Each computer contributes to the completion of a common task by completing one or more subtasks independently of its peers, and then reports the results from these subtasks when they are complete. All of this is totally transparent to the user; all he or she sees is the results of the process.

■ *See also* **client/server.**

distribution

- A Unix software package ready to be installed using the standard Unix tools.
- Any topic-specific mailing list or USENET newsgroup with multiple recipients.

distribution medium

The type of data storage device used to distribute original software or updates.

Tapes used to be the favorite distribution medium, but compact discs are rapidly gaining in popularity.

■ *See also* **distribution.**

`ditroff`

A version of the `troff` command, known as the *device-independent* `troff`. The original version of `troff` was designed to run with one specific typesetter, and so the program was modified by Brian Kernighan to be hardware independent and run with a variety of typesetters, terminals, and printers. Most modern versions of `troff` are really `ditroff`.

■ *See also* **`nroff`**, **`troff`**.

DKI

Abbreviation for driver kernel interface; an SVR4 standard for the interface between device drivers and the kernel.

DLL

Abbreviation for dynamic link library. A program module that contains executable code and data that can be used by applications, or even by other DLLs, in performing a specific task.

The DLL is linked to the application only when the program runs, and it is unloaded again when no longer needed. If two DLL applications are running at the same time and both perform a particular function, only one copy of the code for that function is loaded, for more efficient use of limited memory. Another benefit of using dynamic linking is that the .EXE files are not as large because frequently used routines can be put into a DLL rather than repeated in each .EXE file that uses them. Smaller .EXE files mean saved disk space and faster program loading.

DMA

Abbreviation for Direct Memory Access. A method of transferring large blocks of information directly to or from a mass-storage device, such as a hard disk, into memory without the information passing through the processor. Because the processor is not involved in the transfer, DMA is usually very fast.

DNS

Abbreviation for Domain Name Service. A distributed addressing system that resolves the domain name (such as `pd.sybex.com`) into the IP address (such as 194.65.87.3). DNS is used in the Internet, Bitnet, and other networks.

do

A Bourne and Korn shell programming command that indicates the beginning of a block of commands following a `for`, `while`, `select`, or `until` loop.

document instance

In SGML (Standard Generalized Markup Language), the text component of a document as distinct from the structure of the document.

See also **DTD.**

document type definition

See **DTD.**

dollar sign

- The default system prompt used in the Bourne shell.
- A metacharacter used to match characters at the end of a line by `vi`, `ed`, `ex`, `sed`, `grep`, and `awk`.
- A character used when accessing shell variables in both the Bourne shell and the Korn shell.

See also **regular expression.**

domain

A unique name that identifies a computer system. The most common high-level domains on the Internet include:

.com: a commercial organization

.edu: an educational establishment such as a university

.gov: a branch of the U.S. government

.int: an international organization

.mil: a branch of the U.S. military

.net: a network

.org: a nonprofit organization

Most countries also have unique domains based on their international abbreviations—for example, .uk for the United Kingdom and .ca for Canada.

domain address

A unique name that identifies a computer within a network. For example, `wally.my.iberia` defines a computer called `wally` within the subdomain `my`, which in turn is part of the larger `iberia` domain.

domain member list

A file maintained by the primary name server in an RFS system that contains a list of all hosts within the domain and their passwords.

domain name

In DNS, a unique name that identifies an Internet host.

See also **domain address.**

domain name server

A host computer in an RFS system acting as the network's primary name server, maintaining and monitoring the network's file-sharing environment.

Domain Name Service

See **DNS.**

domainname

A Solaris command that sets or displays the name of the current Network Information Service (NIS) domain.

▶ Syntax

The syntax for `domainname` is:

```
domainname name
```

Only the superuser can set the domain name, and this is usually done during system installation. Using the `domainname` command without arguments displays the current domain name. There are no options for this command.

done

A Bourne and Korn shell programming command that indicates the end of a `for`, `while`, `select`, or `until` statement.

DOS

Acronym for disk operating system. An operating system originally developed by Microsoft for the IBM PC.

DOS exists in two similar versions: MS-DOS, developed and marketed by Microsoft for use with IBM-compatible computers, and PC-DOS, supported and sold by IBM for use on computers manufactured by IBM.

Many important Unix concepts have been copied in DOS, including the hierarchical file structure, redirection, pipes, and filters, but DOS remains a poorly featured operating system when compared to Unix.

Several DOS emulators are available for the Unix world so that you can run DOS and Windows applications on Unix workstations. SCO and UnixWare both use Merge from Locus Computing Corporation, and Linux uses a program called **dosemu** or an X Window version called **xdos**. A Windows emulation package for Linux is under development.

■ *See also* **DOS commands.**

DOS commands

Certain versions of Unix include a set of commands you can use to access files and disks created by the DOS filesystem to run your DOS and Microsoft Windows applications. SCO and UnixWare both use an emulation package called Merge from Locus Computing Corporation. Linux uses a program called **dosemu** or an X Window version called **xdos**.

These programs create a DOS environment within Unix, and let you run as many DOS and Windows sessions as your computer's memory allows. Table D.18 lists the common commands used when accessing DOS disks and files from Unix.

Unfortunately, DOS and Unix use very different file-naming conventions, and so Merge changes Unix filenames that do not conform to the DOS rules. These changed names are only for display purposes; the actual filenames on disk are not changed. When you use a DOS application or a Merge command, you see the changed name; at all other times, you see the full Unix name.

Table D.18: Commands Used to Access DOS Disks and Files

COMMAND	DESCRIPTION
`doscat`	Displays a DOS file by copying it to the standard output.
`doscp`	Copies files between a DOS disk and the Unix filesystem.
`dosdir`	Lists DOS files in the DOS-style directory listing.
`dosformat`	Formats a DOS floppy disk; cannot be used to format a hard disk.
`dosls`	Lists DOS files in a Unix format.
`dosmkdir`	Creates a directory on a DOS disk.
`dosrm`	Deletes files from a DOS disk.
`dosrmdir`	Deletes directories from a DOS disk.

The UnixWare desktop contains commands you can use to convert DOS files to Unix format, and vice versa.

■ *See also* **dtox**, **xtod**.

dosemu

A DOS emulation program often used with Linux. **dosemu** requires that you own a licensed copy of DOS and creates a virtual machine allowing you to run DOS and DOS applications in real mode. The virtual machine emulates the BIOS, XMS, and EMS memory, keyboard, serial ports, printer, and disk services ordinarily found on a PC.

The **dosemu** package is still in development, but you can obtain a copy of the source code from the anonymous `ftp` sites `tsx-11.mit.edu` or dspsun.eas.asu.edu. The files are in the /pub/linux/ALPHA/dosemu directory; the ALPHA in the pathname refers to the status of the software release, not to the microprocessor.

■ *See also* **xdos.**

dot

A synonym for the name of the current directory. The Unix **mkdir** command places this entry in every directory, but it is usually invisible because its name begins with a period. If you use the **ls -i** command (the **-i** option shows i-node numbers), you see that the name is a link to the same i-node as the directory's name in the parent directory.

■ *See also* **dot dot, dot file.**

dot command

A Bourne shell and Korn shell command that reads a file and executes its contents as though they were input from the command line.

dot dot

A synonym for the name of the parent directory of the current directory. The Unix **mkdir** command places this entry in every directory, but it is usually invisible because its name begins with a period.

■ *See also* **dot, dot file.**

dot file

A file whose name begins with a period and so is not usually displayed in an ordinary directory listing. Also known as a *hidden file*.

Many programs, including the Unix shells, use one or more dot files to store configuration information; you can customize your environment by creating the appropriate dot file in the current directory or in your home directory.

Table D.19 contains a list of common dot files and their uses.

dot requests

Formatting commands in the **nroff** family of text-processing programs. Each command that begins with a dot (or period) tells the program to format the document in a specific way; for example, the **.bp** (for break page) command produces a new page.

dots per inch

■ *See* **DPI.**

dotted decimal

A method of representing an IP address as four decimal numbers separated by dots or periods; for example, 194.65.87.3.

double-click

To press and release a mouse button rapidly, twice in quick succession, without moving the mouse. The way that double-clicking is used can vary from application to application.

■ *See also* **click.**

double quote

The " character; used to enclose that part of the command line in which you want the shell to perform command and variable substitution and, in the C shell, history substitution. Double quotes allow specific characters, the dollar sign ($), the backquote (`), and the backslash (\) to keep their special meanings.

■ *See also* **single quote.**

download

- In communications, to transfer a file or files from one computer to another over a network or by using a modem.
- To send information such as font information or a PostScript file from a computer to a printer.

Table D.19: Common Dot Files and Their Uses	
FILENAME	CONTENTS
.bash_logout	Bash logout commands
.bash_profile	Bash login initialization commands
.bashrc	Bash initialization commands
.cshrc	C shell initialization commands
.elm	Directory of elm configuration files
.emacs	emacs editor initialization commands
.exrc	vi editor initialization commands
.gopherrc	Gopher initialization commands
.history	History file
.login	C shell login commands
.logout	C shell logout commands
.netrc	ftp autologin information
.newsrc	List of USENET newsgroups you can access
.mailrc	List of mail initialization commands
.pinerc	Pine configuration information
.plan	Information displayed by finger
.project	Additional finger information
.profile	Bourne shell initialization commands
.rcrc	rc shell initialization commands
.signature	Signature file used in postings to USENET newsgroups
.tcshrc	Tcsh shell initialization commands
.xsession	X Window start-up commands
.xinitrc	X Window initialization commands
.zshenv	Zsh shell initialization commands
.zshrc	Zsh shell initialization commands
.zlogin	Zsh shell login initialization commands
.zlogout	Zsh shell logout initialization commands
.zprofile	Zsh shell login initialization commands

download

An SVR4 command that adds a font to the beginning of a PostScript file.

▶ Syntax

The syntax for `download` is:

```
download [options][filename]
```

You can use this command to make additional fonts available when printing a PostScript file; fonts are added as PostScript comments that begin with the string:

```
%%DocumentFonts:
```

followed by a list of PostScript font names. The `download` command loads the fonts listed in a special table that links PostScript names with the font definition files.

▶ Options and Arguments

Table D.20 lists the options you can use with `download`.

If you do not specify *`filename`*, `download` reads from the standard input.

■ *See also* **`lp`**, **`lpr`**.

DP

Abbreviation for data processing. Also called *electronic data processing (EDP)*. A term used to describe work done by minicomputers and mainframe computers in a data center or business environment.

DPI

Abbreviation for dots per inch. A measure of resolution expressed as the number of dots that a device can display or print in an inch. Laser printers can print at 300 to 600 dpi, while Linotronic laser imagesetters can print at resolutions of between 1270 and 2450 dpi.

dpost

A postprocessor command used to translate `troff`-formatted files into PostScript for printing.

▶ Syntax

The syntax for `dpost` follows:

```
dpost [options][filename]
```

▶ Options and Arguments

If you do not specify *`filename`*, `dpost` reads from the standard input. Table D.21 lists the options available with this command.

▶ Examples

If you want to print five copies of each page of the file `trevor.eon` to the default printer, use:

```
dpost -c5 trevor.eon | lpr
```

■ *See also* **`lp`**, **`lpr`**, **`nroff`**, **`troff`**.

drag

In a graphical user interface (GUI), to move a selected object using just the mouse.

■ *See also* **drag-and-drop.**

Table D.20: Options to Use with download

OPTION	DESCRIPTION
`-f`	Searches the entire PostScript file rather than just the header.
`-H` *`fontdirectory`*	Specifies *`fontdirectory`* as the directory to search for font files; the default directory is `/usr/lib/postscript`.
`-m` *`table`*	Uses the map table specified by *`table`*.
`-p` *`printer`*	Checks the location specified by *`printer`* for font files.

Table D.21: Options Available with dpost	
OPTION	DESCRIPTION
`-c n`	Prints *n* copies of each page; the default is one copy.
`-e n`	Sets text encoding to *n*, where *n* can be 0 (the default), 1, or 2; higher numbers speed processing and reduce output size but may be less reliable.
`-F directory`	Specifies *directory* as the font directory; the default is `/usr/lib/font`.
`-H directory`	Sets the host-resident font directory to *directory*. Files contained in *directory* must describe PostScript fonts and must have filenames corresponding to a two-letter `troff` font.
`-L filename`	Specifies *filename* as the PostScript prolog; the default is `/usr/lib/postscript/dpost.ps`.
`-m scale`	Increases the size of each logical page by a factor of *scale*; the default is 1.0.
`-n n`	Prints *n* pages of output on each page; the default is 1.
`-o list`	Prints the pages specified in the comma-separated *list*.
`-O`	Removes PostScript pictures from the output.
`-p layout`	Sets *layout* to `p` for portrait or `l` for landscape.
`-w n`	Draws `troff` graphics (`pic` or `tbl`) using a line *n* points wide; the default is 0.3.
`-x n`	Offsets the x coordinate of the origin *n* inches to the right when *n* is a positive number—otherwise, to the left when *n* is negative.
`-y n`	Offsets the y coordinate of the origin *n* inches down when *n* is a positive number—otherwise, to the left when *n* is negative.

drag-and-drop

In a graphical user interface (GUI), to use the cursor to move a selected object onto another object to initiate a process. For example, if you drag a document icon and drop it onto a word processor's icon, the program runs and opens the document. To print a file, you can drag the file to the printer icon using the mouse and then release the mouse button. You can also use drag-and-drop to copy a file from one disk to another or to move a marked block of text to a new location inside a word-processed document.

■ *See also* **drag.**

DRAM

Abbreviation for dynamic RAM, pronounced "dee-ram." A common type of computer memory that uses capacitors and transistors storing electrical charges to represent memory states. These capacitors lose their electrical charge, so they need to be refreshed every millisecond, during which time they cannot be read by the processor.

DRAM chips are small, simple, cheap, easy to make, and hold approximately four times as much information as a static RAM (SRAM) chip of similar complexity. However, they are slower than SRAM. Processors operating at clock speeds of 25 megahertz (MHz) or more need DRAM with access times of faster than 80 nanoseconds, while SRAM chips can be read in as little as 10 to 20 nanoseconds.

driver

Jargon for device driver.

driver kernel interface

See **DKI.**

DTD

Abbreviation for document type definition. In SGML (Standard Generalized Markup Language), the structural component of a document as distinct from the actual data or text contained in the document.

See also **document instance.**

dtox

A command that converts a DOS text file into a Unix text file.

▶ Syntax

The syntax for `dtox` is:

```
dtox filename >
➥ output-filename
```

Unix uses a single newline character to indicate the end of a line, while DOS uses two characters, a linefeed followed by a carriage return. DOS also uses Ctrl-Z as an end-of-file marker. `dtox` removes the carriage return and the Ctrl-Z characters so that Unix can read the file successfully.

▶ Options and Arguments

The *`filename`* argument contains the name of the DOS file you want to convert; if you leave it out, `dtox` reads from standard input. Because `dtox` always writes to standard output, you must use redirection to capture the converted output in a file *`output-filename`*.

▶ Examples

To convert the DOS file `norman.dos` into a Unix file called `norman.unix`, use:

```
dtox norman.dos > norman.unix
```

See also **DOS commands, `xtod`.**

dtype

An SCO command used to determine the type of a floppy disk, print a report to the standard output, and then exit with an exit code related to the disk type.

▶ Syntax

Here's the syntax for `dtype`:

```
dtype [options] devices
```

▶ Options and Arguments

The `dtype` command has just one option, `-s`, which suppresses the report to standard output. With this option, `dtype` will return only the exit code, and the exit code will refer only to the last disk specified by *`devices`*. Table D.22 lists all the `dtype` exit codes.

▶ Examples

To create a report on the high-density drive:

```
dtype /dev/rfd096 > lpr
```

▶ Notes

This command is reliable only when used with floppy disks; it may not recognize `tar` or `cpio` formats created on a foreign system.

Table D.22: dtype Exit Codes

EXIT CODE	DESCRIPTION
60	Error
61	Unrecognized data or empty disk
70	Backup format
71	`tar` format
72	`cpio` format
73	`cpio` character format
80	DOS 1.*x*; 8 sectors/track, single-sided
81	DOS 1.*x*; 8 sectors/track, double-sided
90	DOS 2.*x*; 8 sectors/track, single-sided
91	DOS 2.*x*; 8 sectors/track, double-sided
92	DOS 2.*x*; 9 sectors/track, single-sided
93	DOS 2.*x*; 9 sectors/track, double-sided
94	DOS 2.*x*; hard disk
100–103	DOS data disk
110	DOS 3.*x*; 9 or 15 sectors/track, double-sided
111	DOS 3.*x*; 18 sectors/track, double-sided
112	DOS 3.*x*; 8 sectors/track, single-sided
113	DOS 3.*x*; 8 sectors/track, double-sided
120	XENIX 2.*x* filesystem
130	XENIX 3.*x* filesystem
140	Unix 1K filesystem

du

A command that reports on the amount of disk space used by a specific directory and its subdirectories; the information is reported as a number of 512-byte blocks. Partial blocks are rounded up.

▶ Syntax

Here's the syntax for the `du` command:

```
du [options] [directories]
```

If no *`directories`* are specified, the **`du`** command reports on the current directory and all of its subdirectories and files.

▶ Options and Arguments

This command has different options on different versions of Unix; check the **`man`** pages on your system for more details. Table D.23 lists the major options you can use with the **`du`** command.

▶ Examples

To find out the total number of blocks used by the `trainspotter` directory, its files, and subdirectories, use:

```
du -s /trainspotter
3462 ./trainspotter
```

■ *See also* **df**, **dfspace**.

dumb terminal

A combination of keyboard and screen that has no local computing power, used to input information to a large, remote computer, often a minicomputer or a mainframe. The remote computer provides all the processing power for the system.

dump

A complete listing, often in hexadecimal or octal, of the contents of a file or a portion of system memory, used in troubleshooting. The memory listing shows the state of the system at the time of the failure

■ *See also* **core dump**, **od**.

Table D.23: Options to Use with du

OPTION	DESCRIPTION
`-a`	Displays totals for all files and subdirectories.
`-f`	Displays totals for files and directories in the current filesystem only; other filesystems are ignored. Not available on all Unix systems.
`-k`	On Solaris, reports totals in kilobytes.
`-L`	In BSD, all symbolic links are followed.
`-P`	In BSD, no symbolic links are followed.
`-r`	Displays the message "`cannot open`" for directories it cannot access and files it cannot read; normally `du` does not report the information.
`-s`	Displays a summary total for each specified filename and directory name.
`-u`	Ignores files with more than one link. Not available on all Unix systems.
`-x`	In BSD, displays totals for files and directories in the current filesystem only; other filesystems are ignored.

duplex

In asynchronous transmissions, the ability to transmit and receive on the same channel at the same time; also referred to as *full duplex*. Half-duplex channels can transmit only or receive only.

■ *See also* **communications parameters.**

duplicate block

Any block that is being accessed by two or more i-nodes.

dynamic RAM

■ *See* **DRAM.**

dynamic file system

Any filesystem structure that can be modified while the operating system is running; also known as a *scalable filesystem*.

dynamic linking

The process of binding C language library functions at runtime rather than at compile or link time. Dynamic linking tends to produce smaller executable files and has the additional advantage that bugs can be fixed in the libraries without requiring a complete recompile and relink of the whole application.

dynamic link library

■ *See* **DLL.**

e

- A system-level alias for the Unix editor `ed`, a line editor included with almost all Unix systems.
- On AIX systems, the `e` command starts the INed editor, a multiwindow editor with a built-in file manager.

E

See **exa-.**

EB

See **exabyte.**

eb

Abbreviation for error bells; a variable in the `ex` and `vi` editors that sounds the bell to alert you to an impending error message.

EBCDIC

Acronym for Extended Binary Coded Decimal Interchange Code, pronounced "eb-se-dic." EBCDIC is the character set commonly used on large IBM mainframe computers, most IBM minicomputers, and computers from many other manufacturers. It is an 8-bit code, allowing 256 different characters. Unlike with ASCII, the placement of the letters of the alphabet in EBCDIC is discontinuous. Also, there is no direct character-to-character match when converting from EBCDIC to ASCII; some characters exist in one set but not in the other, and several slightly different versions exist.

echo

The ability of the Unix tty driver to display typed characters on the screen. Characters may come from a program or may be typed on the keyboard.

See also **echoing.**

echo

A command that writes arguments to the standard output. `echo` is also a built-in command in the C shell and Bourne shell.

▶ Syntax

The syntax for `echo` is:

```
echo [-n] [string]
```

`echo` is particularly useful in shell scripts to prompt the user for input or report on the status of a process.

▶ Options and Arguments

The `echo` command normally follows any output with a newline character; the `-n` option turns the newline off. *`string`* represents any characters that you want `echo` to output; enclose them in quotes. The sequences listed in Table E.1 create special effects when you include them in *`string`*.

Table E.1: Special echo Sequences

SEQUENCE	DESCRIPTION
`\b`	Backspace
`\c`	Suppress final newline, same as `-n` option
`\f`	Formfeed
`\n`	Newline
`\r`	Carriage return
`\t`	Tab
`\v`	Vertical tab
`\\`	Backslash
`\0n`	An octal number, specified by *n*

▶ Examples

To display the current setting of the `path` variable, use:

```
echo $PATH
```

To prompt the user for a yes or no answer without a newline, use:

```
echo "Please enter Y or N \c"
```

You would then use the `read` command to obtain the user's input, followed by an `if` statement to decode the input.

You can also use `echo` in creative ways. The `spell` command accepts input only from a file, not from the command line, so you can use:

```
echo trainsptter | spell
```

to pipe a single word into `spell`. If the word is misspelled, `spell` redisplays the word; if you just get the command prompt back, you know the word was spelled correctly.

■ *See also* **cat, sh.**

echo area

The bottom line on the screen in `emacs`, used to echo the commands that you type and to display error messages. The echo area shares this screen line with the minibuffer.

■ *See also* **emacs.**

echoing

Displaying characters on a screen as a result of input from the user and keyboard, or from a program. Echoing may be turned off occasionally, for example, when you enter your password.

■ *See also* **echo.**

ed

Pronounced "ee-dee." The oldest and the simplest of the Unix text editors; `ed` is a line editor.

▶ Syntax

The syntax for `ed` is:

```
ed [options] filename
```

`ed` is not much used these days; it has been superseded by more capable and easier to use screen editors such as `ex`, `vi`, and `emacs`. Some of the older commands, such as `diff` continue to use `ed`.

▶ Options and Arguments

If the specified *filename* does not exist, **ed** creates it; if it does exist, **ed** opens the file for editing. The options you can use with **ed** are listed in Table E.2.

See also **emacs, ex, sed, vi.**

Table E.2: Options for Use with ed

OPTION	DESCRIPTION
-p *string*	Specifies *string* as the ed command prompt; there is no default ed prompt.
-s	Suppresses the ed character count and other explanatory messages.
-v	In 4.4BSD, displays the ed mode, either BSD or POSIX.
-x	Specifies a key to encrypt or decrypt *filename* using the crypt command; crypt encryption is available only in the U.S. because it is illegal to export certain encryption schemes.

edit

To change the information in a file; often refers to modifying a text file with one of the Unix editors.

edit

A simplified version of the **ed** line editor, often used by people new to Unix text processing.

See also **ed.**

edit buffer

The area of temporary storage used by an editor. A replica of the file you are editing is held in the edit buffer, and when you have finished work, the contents of this buffer are written to disk, replacing and overwriting the original file. The term may also refer to a local area of memory used to hold sections of text between commands, such as, for example, the yank buffer in **vi**.

editing commands

That group of Unix commands related to text editing, including **addftinfo**, **afmtodit**, **awk**, **bib**, **colcrt**, **cscope**, **cxref**, **deroff**, **dpost**, **ed**, **eqn**, **ex**, **emacs**, **lookbib**, **nroff**, **sed**, **troff**, and **vi**.

editing macros

See **emacs.**

edit mode

An editor mode that allows you to enter, display, change, or delete text.

editor

An application used to perform text processing functions; also known as a *text editor.* Unix includes several different editors, including **ex**, **ed**, **vi**, and **emacs**.

Unix provides three different types of editors:

- Line editors such as **ed** let you work on one line at a time and treat all the other text relative to the current line.
- Screen editors are much easier to use than line editors because they display much more of the surrounding text; **ex**, **vi**, and **emacs** are all screen editors.
- Stream editors such as **sed** are different from both line and screen editors because they can act as a filter and can be used to make changes to very large files.

See also **.exc.**

EDITOR

- A Korn shell environment variable used to identify the default editor you want to use.
- An e-mail variable used to identify the default editor to use when creating e-mail messages.

See also **.mailrc.**

E

egrep

A command that searches one or more files for text strings that match a specified regular expression. This command, along with the related `fgrep` command, is considered to be obsolete.

■ *See also* **grep**.

eject

A Solaris command used to eject a disk from a drive without an eject button.

▶ **Syntax**

Here is the syntax to use with `eject`:

```
eject [options][device]
```

▶ **Options and Arguments**

You can specify *device* as a name, but if no *device* is specified, `eject` uses the default device `/dev/rdiskette`. The `eject` command automatically checks for any mounted filesystems on the device and attempts to `umount` them before ejecting them. The options for `eject` are listed in Table E.3.

Table E.3: Options for Use with eject

OPTION	DESCRIPTION
-d	Displays the name of the default drive.
-f	Forces an eject, even if the device contains a currently mounted partition.
-n	Displays the system nickname for the device.
-q	Checks if media is present in the drive.

▶ **Examples**

Use this command on a Sun system to eject a floppy disk from the default disk drive:

```
eject /dev/fd0
```

You can use this command to eject a CD from a CD-ROM drive:

```
eject /dev/sr0
```

■ *See also* **fdformat**, **mount**.

elif

A Bourne and Korn shell programming command used to mark the beginning of the `else` part of an `if then else` construct. If the commands that follow the `if` statement fail, the commands that follow the `elif` statement are executed.

■ *See also* **else**, **fi**, **if**, **then**.

elm

A screen-oriented mailer written by Dave Taylor, and now in the public domain.

Like other modern e-mail programs, `elm` lets you reply to or forward a message, delete messages, and create aliases for groups of addresses that you use frequently. `elm` is easy to use and simple to learn.

The `elm` mailer is bundled with some versions of Unix, including Linux, or you can `ftp` to `ftp.dsi.com` and retrieve `elm` from the `/pub/elm` directory yourself. You can get a list of other sites where `elm` is available by sending the message:

```
send elm elm.ftp
```

to `archive-server@dsi.com`. You can also consult the USENET newsgroup `comp.mail.elm`. The `elm` distribution contains several useful documents, including a reference guide and a user's guide.

■ *See also* **mail**, **mailx**, **mush**, **Pine**.

else

A Bourne and Korn shell programming command that is part of an `if then else` conditional statement.

■ *See also* **elif**, **fi**, **if**, **then**.

emacs

A popular Unix screen editor, written by Richard Stallman, founder of the Free Software Foundation (FSF) and author of much of the GNU software. **emacs** is a contraction of "editing macros." There are many versions of **emacs**; this entry covers GNU **emacs**.

emacs is much more than a simple text editor, however, and includes extensions for all sorts of tasks, ranging from compiling and debugging programs, to reading and sending e-mail, to X Window system support, and more. You can even extend **emacs** yourself because the editing commands are written in the Lisp programming language.

▶ Syntax

The syntax for **emacs** is as follows:

```
emacs [options][filename]
```

You can also simply specify ***filename*** on the command line, and **emacs** will open the file for editing.

▶ Options and Arguments

You can use several options with **emacs**, and they are listed in Table E.4.

You can also use a large number of X Window configuration switches when you start **emacs**; see the *GNU Emacs Manual* from the FSF for more details.

▶ Major and Minor Modes

The **emacs** editor has a large number of major and minor modes you can choose between. Your editing needs when entering C source code are different from those when you are working with straightforward text, and **emacs** has a major mode to suit everyone, as Table E.5 shows. Major modes are mutually exclusive;

Table E.4: emacs Options

OPTION	DESCRIPTION
`+n filename`	Goes to the line number specified by *n* in ***filename***.
`-batch command-file`	Opens **emacs** in batch mode using the commands in ***command-file***; the text is not displayed. If you use this option, it must be the first argument on the command line; usually combined with `-f` or `-l`.
`-f function`	Executes the Lisp function without arguments.
`-kill`	Performs all initialization operations, then exits from **emacs** batch mode.
`-l filename`	Loads the Lisp code contained in ***filename***.
`-q`	Does not load the **.emacs** initialization file from your home directory.
`-t filename`	Uses ***filename*** as the terminal rather than standard in and standard out; if you use this option, it must be the first argument on the command line.
`-u user-name`	Loads the specified user's **.emacs** initialization file.

Table E.5: Major and Minor Modes	
MODE	DESCRIPTION
Major Modes	
asm-mode	Assembly language programming
awk-mode	awk scripts
bibtex-mode	BibTEX files
c++-mode	C++ programming
c-mode	C programming
change-log-mode	For working with change logs
command-history-mode	For working with command history files
completion-list-mode	For working with lists of possible completions
edit-abbrevs-mode	For working with abbreviation definitions
emacs-lisp-mode	emacs Lisp programming
forms-mode	For working with field-structured data using a form
fortran-mode	Fortran programming
fundamental-mode	Unspecialized, nonspecific mode (when in doubt, use this mode)
hexl-mode	For working with hexadecimal and ASCII data
indented-text-mode	For working with indented paragraphs
latex-mode	For working with LATEX formatted files
lisp-interaction-mode	For evaluating and entering Lisp forms
lisp-mode	Non-emacs Lisp programming
mail-mode	For sending outgoing mail messages
makefile-mode	Used with make
mh-letter-mode	For managing MH mail messages
nroff-mode	For working with nroff and troff-formatted text files
outline-mode	For working with outlines and a selective display
pascal-mode	For Pascal programming

Table E.5: Major and Minor Modes (continued)

MODE	DESCRIPTION
`perl-mode`	For Perl programming
`picture-mode`	For working with text-based drawings
`plain-tex-mode`	For working with $\TeX$-formatted files
`prolog-mode`	Prolog programming
`rmail-mode`	For managing mail with **`rmail`**
`scheme-mode`	Scheme programming
`scribe-mode`	For working with Scribe-formatted text files
`sgml-mode`	For working with Standard Generalized Markup Language files
`slitex-mode`	For working with SliTEX-formatted files
`tcl-mode`	For working with Tool Command Language files
`tex-mode`	For working with $\TeX$, $\LaTeX$, or SliTEX-formatted files
`texinfo-mode`	For working with TEXinfo files
`text-mode`	Used with normal text
`tpu-edt-mode`	TPU/EDT emulation of a DEC-style editor
`vi-mode`	Makes **`emacs`** work like **`vi`**
`wordstar-mode`	Makes **`emacs`** use WordStar keystrokes
Minor Modes	
`abbrev-mode`	For working with abbreviations
`auto-fill-mode`	Uses automatic filling
`auto-save-mode`	Uses automatic saving
`binary-overwrite-mode`	For editing and overwriting binary files
`compilation-minor-mode`	For compiling programs
`delete-selection-mode`	Replaces typed text with selected text
`double-mode`	Makes certain keys work differently when you press them twice
`font-lock-mode`	Shows text in the selected font as you enter it

Table E.5: Major and Minor Modes (continued)	
MODE	**DESCRIPTION**
`hide-ifdef-mode`	C programming, hides certain constructs
`indent-according-to-mode`	Indents for the major mode
`iso-accents-mode`	Uses ISO accents
`ledit-mode`	Lisp programming
`outline-minor-mode`	Variation on the major outline mode
`overwrite-mode`	Overwrites/inserts text
`pending-delete-mode`	Same as `delete-selection-mode`
`resize-minibuffer-mode`	Dynamically changes the mini-buffer
`tpu-edt-mode`	TPU/edt emulation
`toggle-read-mode`	Opens `emacs` in read-only mode
`transient-mark-mode`	Highlights defined regions
`vip-mode`	VIP emulation of `vi`
`vt100-wide-mode`	Uses 132 columns for a VT100 terminal

only one can be active at any time. Minor modes add variations that you can turn on or off as you wish; minor modes are independent of each other.

If you are in doubt about which of these modes you should use, try `fundamental-mode`, it is fairly safe.

▶ Key Combinations in emacs

The `emacs` editor does not use modes like the `vi` editor; anything you type in `emacs` appears as text, unless you use special key combinations to indicate you are invoking a command rather than entering text.

There are a lot of key combinations in `emacs`, and most of them use either the Ctrl key or the Meta key:

- **Ctrl key**. The Ctrl key is used as you would expect; hold down the Ctrl key and press another key, but some commands consist of more than one Ctrl combination in a row, or a Ctrl combination followed by another letter. To quit `emacs`, you press Ctrl-X Ctrl-C—that is, Ctrl-X immediately followed by Ctrl-C. And to open the `emacs` tutorial, you press Ctrl-H `t`—Ctrl-H followed by `t`. In `emacs`, the Ctrl key is often represented by a letter *C* followed by a lowercase letter, so instead of writing *Ctrl-X*, you would write *C-x* or *C-h t*.
- **Meta key**. The Meta key is used in the same way as the Ctrl key; you hold it down while you press another key. The Meta key is a virtual key; a key that acts as the Meta key. Sun workstations often use the keys with the small diamonds close to the spacebar; PCs often use the Alt keys, and Macintoshes use the Command or Option keys. You may also be able to use the Escape (Esc) key as the Meta key; however, don't hold it down, press it, release it, and then press the appropriate letter. The Meta key is abbreviated as `M`, and key combinations are written as `M-f`, for example.

Other important keys include the Delete (Del) key and the Enter (or Return) key. To display information about all the key combinations used in **emacs**, you have to know how to use the built-in help system.

▶ How to Get Help

Unlike many other Unix programs, a great deal of excellent help material is built right into **emacs**; you just have to know how to get to it. Table E.6 lists the most common ways you can access **emacs** help information.

▶ Using Point, Cursor, Mark, and Region

Point, cursor, mark and region are basic **emacs** concepts:

- **Point:** Point (just "point", never "the point") is the place between two characters where the editing commands actually take effect. Point can also be at the very beginning or end of the buffer.
- **Cursor:** The cursor is always on the character to the right of point. Even though you may have several **emacs** windows open at the same time, there is always only one cursor.
- **Mark:** The mark is a location in the buffer, which, like point, is either at the beginning or the end of the buffer or between two characters. The mark stays in one place until you explicitly move it to a new location.
- **Region:** The region is the area between point and the mark. Many **emacs** commands operate on the region.

▶ Yanking Killed Text or Cutting and Pasting

When you delete (or kill in **emacs** terminology) text in **emacs**, it is not deleted immediately but is kept in a special area called the *kill ring*, which can hold the last 30 deletions. And you can retrieve (or yank) text from the kill ring back into your editing buffer. So in **emacs**, killing and yanking are roughly the same as cutting and pasting in other applications, and you can use them to move and to copy text in much the same way.

▶ Editing Commands

The heart of any editor is that set of commands used to manipulate text. The most common editing commands are listed in Table E.7 under several important subheadings. For more information, see the help system.

In Table E.7, commands are shown as Ctrl-x Ctrl-y, which means press Ctrl-x followed by Ctrl-y, or as Ctrl-x y, which means press and release Ctrl-x and then press y. You can use the Escape key or the Alt key as the Meta key depending on your configuration.

Table E.6: Help Commands in emacs

COMMAND	DESCRIPTION
Ctrl-H ?	Displays a summary of all the help options.
Ctrl-H a	Prompts you for a string, then lists all the commands that contain the string.
Ctrl-H b	Displays a very long list of all the key combinations.
Ctrl-H c	You specify a key, and **emacs** briefly tells you what it does.
Ctrl-H f	Prompts you for the name of a function, then tells you what that function does.
Ctrl-H i	Starts the Info documentation browser.
Ctrl-H k	You specify a key, and **emacs** tells you its function.
Ctrl-H m	Describes the current major mode.
Ctrl-H t	Starts the **emacs** tutorial.
Ctrl-H v	Prompts you for a Lisp variable name, and then displays the documentation for that function.
Ctrl-H w	Prompts you for a command name, and shows you the key combination for that command.

E

Table E.7: Editing Commands

COMMAND	DESCRIPTION
Working with Files	
Ctrl-X Ctrl-F	Prompts you for a filename you want to create or open for editing.
Ctrl-X I	Inserts a file at the current point in the buffer.
Ctrl-X Ctrl-W	Saves the file, and allows you to specify a new filename.
Ctrl-X Ctrl-S	Saves the file to the original filename.
Ctrl-X Ctrl-C	Terminates `emacs`, and gives you a chance to save your file.
Moving the Cursor	
Ctrl-F	Moves the cursor one character to the right.
Ctrl-B	Moves the cursor one character to the left.
Meta-f	Moves the cursor forward one word.
Meta-b	Moves the cursor backward one word.
Ctrl-A	Moves the cursor to the beginning of the line.
Ctrl-E	Moves the cursor to the end of the line.
Ctrl-P	Moves the cursor up to the previous line.
Ctrl-N	Moves the cursor down to the next line.
Meta-{	Moves the cursor to the previous paragraph.
Meta-}	Moves the cursor to the next paragraph.
Ctrl-X {	Moves to the previous page.
Ctrl-X }	Moves to the next page.
Ctrl-V	Moves one screen forward.
Meta-V	Moves one screen backward.
Meta->	Moves the cursor to the end of the buffer.
Meta-<	Moves the cursor to the beginning of the buffer.
Ctrl-L	Clears and redraws the screen with the current line placed in the center of the screen.
Editing Text	
Del	Deletes the character to the left of the cursor.
Ctrl-D	Deletes the character under the cursor.

Table E.7: Editing Commands (continued)

COMMAND	DESCRIPTION
Meta-d	Deletes from the cursor to the end of the word.
Meta-Del	Deletes from the cursor backward to the beginning of the previous word.
Meta-k	Deletes to the end of the sentence.
Ctrl-X Del	Deletes to the beginning of the sentence.
Ctrl-K	Deletes to the end of the line.
Ctrl-@	Sets the mark to the current location of point.
Meta-@	Sets the mark after the next word without moving point.
Ctrl-X Ctrl-X	Swaps the locations of the mark and point.
Meta-h	Places a region around the current paragraph.
Ctrl-X h	Places a region around the entire buffer.
Ctrl-W	Deletes (or "kills") a marked region.
Ctrl-Y	Restores (or "yanks") the most recently deleted region at point; sets the mark at the beginning of this text, and sets the cursor and point at the end.
Meta-w	Copies the region to the kill ring without deleting text from the buffer.
Ctrl-X Ctrl-U	Converts the region to uppercase.
Ctrl-X Ctrl-L	Converts the region to lowercase.
Ctrl-G	Aborts the current command.
Working with Buffers and Windows	
Ctrl-X Ctrl-B	Displays the buffers you are using in a new window.
Ctrl-X b	Prompts you for a buffer name, and then changes to that buffer.
Ctrl-X k	Prompts you for a buffer name, and then deletes the buffer.
Ctrl-X o	Selects the other window.
Ctrl-X 0	Deletes the current window.
Ctrl-X 1	Deletes all windows except the current window.
Ctrl-X 2	Splits the current window into two, vertically.
Ctrl-X 3	Splits the current window into two, horizontally; in older versions of `emacs`, this command was Ctrl-X 5.

COMMAND	DESCRIPTION
Ctrl-X }	Widens the current window.
Ctrl-X {	Narrows the current window.
Ctrl-X ^	Enlarges the current window.
Searching	
Ctrl-S	Incrementally prompts for a string; as soon as you type the first character, immediately starts searching forward. Type Meta-P or Meta-N to cycle through previous search strings. Enter terminates the search; mark is set to point, which is at the end of the matched string.
Ctrl-R	Incrementally prompts for a string; as soon as you type the first character, immediately starts searching backward. Type Meta-P or Meta-N to cycle through previous search strings. Enter terminates the search; mark is set to point, which is at the end of the matched string.
Ctrl-S Enter	Prompts you for a string, and searches forward for that string.
Ctrl-R Enter	Prompts you for a string, and searches backward for that string.
Ctrl-S Enter Ctrl-W	Prompts you to enter a word, and searches forward for that word.
Ctrl-R Enter Ctrl-W	Prompts you to enter a word, and searches backward for that word.
Meta Ctrl-S	Searches incrementally forward for a regular expression.
Meta Ctrl-R	Searches incrementally backward for a regular expression.

Table E.7: Editing Commands (continued)

▶ **Notes**

You can get GNU **emacs** from the Free Software Foundation at:

675 Massachusetts Ave.
Cambridge MA 02139, U.S.A.
617-876-3296

or by anonymous **ftp** from **prep.ai.mit.edu** in the **/gnu/emacs** directory; **emacs** is free, although there may be a small charge for the distribution media.

An excellent **emacs** FAQ file can be found in the USENET newsgroups **gnu.emacs.help**, **comp.emacs**, and **news.answers**. The FAQ contains answers to over 100 common **emacs** questions.

There is no doubt that **emacs** is a broad subject. As well as the extensive online help and the printed **emacs** manual, several good books have been written on how to get the most out of **emacs**; if you want to know more, check out one of them.

■ *See also* **vi**.

e-mail

The use of a network to transmit text messages, memos, and reports; also called *electronic mail* or *messaging* and sometimes just *mail*.

Users can send a message to one or more individuals, to a predefined group, or all users on the system. When you receive a message, you can read, print, forward, answer, or delete it. E-mail is by far the most popular Internet application, with well over 80 percent of Internet users taking advantage of the service.

E-mail has several advantages over conventional mail systems, including:

- E-mail is fast; very fast when compared to conventional mail.
- If something exists on your computer as a file—text, graphical images, even program files and video segments— you can usually send it as e-mail.

The problems associated with e-mail are similar to those associated with online communications in general, such as security, privacy (always assume that your e-mail is not private), and the legal status of documents exchanged electronically.

See also **`elm`, `mail`, mailbox, mailer, `mailx`, MIME, `talk`, `wall`, `write`.**

e-mail address

The addressing information required for an e-mail message to reach the correct recipient.

See also **bang path, mailbox.**

embedded command

An `nroff` or `troff` dot command placed in a text file and used in formatting the document. For example, the command `.c3` is used to center text, and the `.pl` command sets the page length.

See also **`nroff`, `troff`.**

emoticon

A set of text characters often used in e-mail and posts to USENET newsgroups to signify emotions.

An emoticon can be as simple as including <g> or <grin> in your text, indicating that the writer is joking, to some of the more complex smiley faces, which are all designed to be read sideways, such as the wink ;-) or the frown :-(.

emulator

A device built to work exactly like another device—hardware, software, or a combination of both. For example, a terminal emulation program lets a workstation or PC pretend to be a terminal attached to a mainframe computer or to an online service by providing the control codes that the remote system expects to receive.

enable

To turn a function on or allow something to happen. In a graphical user interface (GUI), enabled menu commands are often shown in black and disabled menu commands in gray.

See also **disable.**

`enable`

An SCO UNIX command that enables terminals and printers.

▶ Syntax

The syntax for `enable` is:

```
enable name
```

where *`name`* is a particular terminal or printer. `enable` allows logins from the specified terminal and lets the specified printer process print requests made by `lp`.

No command-line options are available with `enable`.

See also **`disable`.**

encapsulated PostScript

Abbreviated EPS. The file format of the PostScript page-description language. The EPS standard is device independent, so that images can easily be transferred between different applications, and they can be sized and output to different printers without any loss of image quality or distortion.

The EPS file contains the PostScript commands needed to recreate the image, but the image itself cannot be displayed on a monitor unless the file also

contains an optional preview image stored in either TIFF or PICT format.

The EPS file can be printed only on a PostScript-compatible laser printer, and the printer itself determines the final printing resolution; a laser printer might be capable of 300 dots per inch (dpi), whereas a Linotronic printer is capable of 2450 dpi.

encapsulation

- In object-oriented programming, the definition of a data structure of attributes and a group of member functions as a single unit known as an *object*. The goal is to isolate the internal workings of a particular object class so that it can be changed and improved by the programmer without causing any dangerous side effects anywhere else in the system.
- The process of inserting the header and data from a higher-level protocol into the data frame of a lower-level protocol.

■ *See also* **inheritance, polymorphism.**

enclosure

A term for a file—text, fax, binary, or image—sent as a part of an e-mail message.

■ *See also* **MIME.**

encryption

The process of encoding information in an attempt to make it secure from unauthorized access. The reverse of this process is known as *decryption*.

Two main encryption schemes are in common use:

- **Private (Symmetrical) Key Schemes**: An encryption algorithm based on a private encryption key known to both the sender and the recipient of the information. The encrypted message is unreadable and can be transmitted over non-secure systems.
- **Public (Asymmetrical) Key Schemes**: An encryption scheme based on using the two halves of a long bit sequence as encryption keys. Either half of the bit sequence can be used to encrypt the data, but the other half is required to decrypt the data.

■ *See also* **`crypt`, `des`, DES, Pretty Good Privacy, rot13.**

end

A C shell programming command used to terminate a `foreach` or `switch` statement; `end` must always appear on a line by itself.

end-of-file character

Abbreviated EOF. A special code placed after the last byte in a file that indicates to the operating system that no more data follows. An end-of-file code is needed because disk space is assigned to a file in blocks, and the file may not always terminate at the end of a block. In the ASCII system, an EOF is represented by the decimal value 4 or by the Ctrl-D control character.

You can also type Ctrl-D to signal the end of data entry from the keyboard.

end-of-text character

Abbreviated ETX. A character used in computer communications to indicate the end of a text file. In the ASCII system, an ETX is represented by the decimal value 3 or by the Ctrl-C control character. A different symbol, end-of-transmission (EOT, ASCII 4 or Ctrl-D), is used to indicate the end of a complete transmission.

end-of-transmission

Abbreviated EOT. A character used in computer communications to indicate the end of a transmission. In the ASCII system, an EOT is represented by the decimal value 4 or by the Ctrl-D control character.

endif

A C shell programming command used to terminate an `if` statement.

■ *See also* **`fi`, `if`.**

endsw

A C shell programming command used to terminate a `switch` statement.

enhanced C shell

See also *See* **Tsch.**

Enter key

Also known as the *Return key*, short for *carriage return*. The key that indicates the end of a command or the end of user input from the keyboard.

enterprise

A term used to encompass an entire business group, organization, or corporation, including all local, remote, and satellite offices.

env

A command that displays or changes environment variables.

▶ Syntax

The syntax for the `env` command is as follows:

```
env [option]
➥ [variable=value ...]
➥ [command]
```

When used without options or arguments, the `env` command displays all the global environment variables.

▶ Options and Arguments

The `env` command has a single option, hyphen (-), which instructs it to ignore the current environment and restricts the environment for *`command`* to just those variables specified by *`variable=value`*. The *`variable=value`* argument sets the specified *`variable`* to *`value`* and adds it to the environment before executing *`command`*.

▶ Examples

To display your current environment, enter:

```
env
```

To change your home directory before starting a subshell, use:

```
env HOME=/usr/user/pmd bash
```

See also **`printenv`, `set`, `setenv`.**

ENV

A Korn shell environment variable that sets the path to the environment file you want to execute when you start the shell. This environment file is used to establish user variables, aliases, and other configuration options.

environment

The set of environment variables that are passed to a program when it is started by the shell.

environment file

A Korn shell file used along with the `.profile` file to set up and run your environment. These initialization commands are executed every time you start a new copy of the shell.

environment variables

In the Unix shell, a variable accessible to any program. Environment variables are exported so that they are available to any command executed by the shell. A Unix process automatically gets its own copy of its parent's environment, and any changes it makes to those variables it keeps to itself; a process cannot change its parent's environment.

The C shell has three commands for managing environment variables: `setenv` marks a variable for export, `unsetenv` removes a variable from the environment, and `printenv` prints the environment variables.

In the Korn shell, environment variables are often called *shell variables*.

See also **child process.**

EOF

See **end-of-file character.**

EOT

See **end-of-transmission.**

epoch

The date used as the beginning of time in Unix.

In most Unix systems, the epoch is 00:00:00 GMT (Greenwich mean time), January 1, 1970, and system time is measured in seconds (or ticks) past the epoch. This means that a Unix day is 86,400 seconds long.

See also **date, Julian date, time.**

e protocol

One of the three common UUCP protocols, along with the g and the G protocols.

The e protocol is a simple protocol that assumes data is being transferred without errors; it does no error checking or flow control and is most often used over TCP/IP links. It should not be used over serial lines or modem connections.

The protocol sends an initial packet containing details of the file to be transferred, including size information, and then sends the rest of the file in 4096-byte packets until everything has been sent.

See also **f protocol, g protocol, G protocol, t protocol, x protocol.**

EPS

See **encapsulated PostScript.**

eqn

A preprocessor for troff designed to manage the typesetting of mathematical formulas and equations.

▶ Syntax

The syntax for eqn is:

```
eqn [options][filename]
```

eqn reads a troff file that contains pairs of special codes: .EQ starts special typesetting, and .EN ends special typesetting. The mathematical formula for typesetting is located between these two directives. The output from eqn is a troff input file in which this mathematical formula has been replaced by troff instructions for creating the formula on the printed page, normally on a line by itself, although you can force a formula within a line by using special delimiters.

eqn manages:

- Special mathematical symbols and Greek letters
- Superscripts and subscripts
- Summations, products, integrals, and limits
- Fractions, matrices, and arrays
- Specialized commands for spacing parts of formulas

▶ Options and Arguments

The options you can use with eqn are listed in Table E.8.

▶ Notes

The eqn command is often used in a pipeline containing several commands to format a file:

```
myfile.doc | eqn | troff | lpr
```

In this example, myfile.doc is piped into eqn, and output from that command is passed to troff for final output to the default printer.

See also **groff, LaTeX, nroff, pic,** tbl, **TeX, troff.**

Table E.8: Options Available with eqn

OPTION	DESCRIPTION
-d*xy*	Uses *x* and *y* as start and stop delimiters.
-f*n*	Changes the font to the font specified by *n*.
-p*n*	Reduces the superscript and subscript size by *n* points.
-s*n*	Reduces the point size by *n* points.
-T*name*	Formats the output to the device specified by *name*.

erasable CD

A standard format that allows users to store and revise large amounts of data on an ordinary compact disc. The standard is supported by Sony, Phillips, IBM, Hewlett-Packard, and other leading companies. One of the major advantages of this new standard is that it is completely compatible with existing compact discs, and makers of CD-ROM drives only have to make minor manufacturing changes to existing drives to meet the standard.

See also **archive, backup, CD-R, CD-ROM.**

erase

A key on the keyboard that lets you move the cursor back one character, erasing that character in the process. The erase key is normally Ctrl-H but can be defined by the user.

See also **backspace, erase character.**

erase character

The character on the keyboard that, when typed, erases the previous character. Usually Ctrl-H or backspace, the erase character can be defined by the user.

error

The difference between the expected and the actual. The way that the operating system reports unexpected, unusual, impossible, or illegal events is by displaying an error number or error message. Errors range from trivial, such as an attempt to write a file to a disk drive that does not contain a disk, to fatal, such as when a serious operating system bug renders the system useless.

In communications, errors are often caused by line noise and signal distortion. Parity or cyclical redundancy check (CRC) information is often added as overhead to the data stream, and techniques such as error detection and correction are employed to detect and correct as many errors as possible.

See also **error handling, error message, error rate.**

`error`

A BSD software development command that analyzes the diagnostic error messages produced by several of the Unix language compilers and software development tools, including `as`, `cc`, `cpp`, `f77`, `ld`, `lint`, and `make`.

error detection and correction

Abbreviated EDAC. A mechanism used to determine whether transmission errors have occurred and, if so, to correct those errors. Some programs or transmission protocols simply request a retransmission of the affected block of data if an error is detected. More complex protocols attempt to both detect and determine at the receiving end what the correct transmission should have been.

error handling

The way that a program copes with errors that occur as the program is running. Good error handling manages unexpected events or wrongly entered data gracefully, usually by prompting the user to take the appropriate action or enter the correct information. Badly written programs may simply stop running when the wrong data is entered or when an unanticipated disk error occurs.

error message

A message from the program or the operating system that contains information about a condition that requires some human intervention to solve.

Error messages can indicate relatively trivial problems, such as a disk drive that does not contain a disk, as well as fatal problems, such as when a serious operating system bug renders the system useless and requires a system restart.

error rate

In communications, the ratio between the number of bits received incorrectly and the total number of bits in the transmission, also known as *bit error rate (BEA)*. Some methods for determining error rate use larger or logical units, such as blocks, packets, or frames. In these cases, the measurement of error rate is expressed in terms of the number of units found to be in error out of the total number of units transmitted.

esac

A Bourne and Korn shell programming command that ends a `case` statement (`esac` is `case` spelled backwards). Leaving out the `esac` statement is a very common shell programming error.

■ *See also* **`case`.**

escape

- A feature of the shell that lets you suspend an operation, start a new copy of the shell, and run commands.
  For example, many interactive programs let you temporarily leave the program to enter shell commands by entering the `!` command.
- To disable the special meaning that certain characters have for the shell, for example, the asterisk (`*`) or question mark (`?`). This is done by preceding the special character by a backslash (`\`) or by enclosing the character inside single or double quotes. Sometimes called *quoting*.

■ *See also* **escape key, escaped character.**

escape character

A character that tells the shell to ignore the special meaning of the following character or characters and to use the literal meaning instead. Escape characters vary from application to application; in the shell, an escape character is preceded by a backslash (`\`) or enclosed inside single or double quotes.

■ *See also* **escape key, escaped character.**

escape commands

A command used in the `mailx` program when in input mode. The `mailx` program distinguishes between ordinary text input and commands by requiring that you type a tilde (~) to signal that what follows is a command rather than message text.

■ *See also* **tilde escape commands.**

escaped character

A character that follows an escape character. The escape character removes any special meaning that the character may have had.

Escape key

The key on the keyboard labeled Esc. This key is often used in Unix applications; for example, the `vi` editor uses the Escape key to switch between insert mode and command mode. The Escape key generates an ASCII ESC code, which is 033 in octal and 027 in decimal.

■ *See also* **escape sequence.**

escape sequence

A sequence of characters, beginning with Escape (ASCII 027 in decimal, 033 in octal) and followed by one or more other characters, that performs a specific function. Escape sequences are often used to control printers or monitors, which treat them as commands and act upon them rather than process them as characters that should be printed or displayed.

/etc

The root directory where the system administration and configuration commands are located. Table E.9 lists some of the files and directories you might expect to find in `/etc`.

You may also find some administrative commands in the `/usr/etc` directory on some systems.

Table E.9: Files and Directories Located in /etc	
ENTRY	DESCRIPTION
/etc/bkup	Files used to backup and restore the system.
/etc/checklist	Filesystems to be mounted.
/etc/cron.d	File used to manage the cron daemon.
/etc/default	Contains default parameter values for many commands.
/etc/dfs	Contains system files for DFS.
/etc/ethers	Database used to match Ethernet addresses with computer host names.
/etc/ff	Command that displays filenames and filesystem statistics.
/etc/ffstat	Command that displays filesystem statistics.
/etc/fstypes	Command that displays filesystem type.
/etc/fuser	Command that displays processes using a file.
/etc/gettydefs	SVR4 file used to control serial interfaces, equivalent to 4.4BSD /etc/gettytab.
/etc/gettytab	4.4BSD file used to control serial interfaces, equivalent to /etc/gettydefs in SVR4.
/etc/group	Lists all the groups on the system along with which users belong to which group.
/etc/hosts	Lists Internet hosts, including host names, addresses, and aliases.
/etc/hosts.equiv	Lists trusted hosts; checked by the system for access authorization when a rsh or rlogin attempt occurs.
/etc/inetd.conf	Lists hosts available once the inetd Internet daemon is started.
/etc/init.d	File used during system state changes.
/etc/inittab	SVR4 file used to initialize serial interfaces; equivalent to 4.4BSD /ect/ttys.
/etc/login	Login file read by the C shell.
/etc/lp	Contains printer configuration information.
/etc/mail	Contains files for the mail system.
/etc/mnttab	Contains currently mounted local and remote filesystems.

E

Table E.9: Files and Directories Located in /etc (continued)	
ENTRY	DESCRIPTION
`/etc/motd`	Contains the message of the day; often used by administrators as a way of posting important information to users as they log in.
`/etc/netmasks`	Contains configuration information for the Internet Protocol.
`/etc/passwd`	Lists login information for each user on the system. Each line gives information for one user, including encrypted password, login name, full name, user ID, group ID, home directory, and the name of the login shell.
`/etc/profile`	Contains the profile file read by the Bourne and Korn shells.
`/etc/shadow`	Contains secure password information.
`/etc/shutdown`	Contains the system shutdown command.
`/etc/ttys`	Contains the 4.4BSD file used to initialize serial interfaces; equivalent to `/etc/inittab` in SVR4.
`/etc/uucp`	Contains UUCP configuration information.
`/etc/vfstab`	Contains default parameters for DFS.

Ethernet

A popular network protocol and cabling scheme with a transfer rate of 10 megabits per second, originally developed by Xerox in 1976. Ethernet uses a bus topology and network nodes are connected by thick or thin coaxial cable, fiber optic cable, or twisted pair cabling.

Ethernet uses CSMA/CD (Carrier Sense Multiple Access/Collision Detection) to prevent network failures or collisions when two devices try to access the network at exactly the same time.

The original DIX (Digital Equipment, Intel, Xerox), or Blue Book, standard has evolved into the slightly more complex IEEE 802.3 standard and the ISO's 8802.3 specification.

The advantages of Ethernet include:

- Easy to install at a moderate cost.
- Technology is available from many sources and is very well known.
- Offers a variety of cabling options.
- Works very well in networks with only occasional heavy traffic.

And the disadvantages include:

- Heavy traffic can slow down the network.
- A break in the main cable can bring down large parts of the network, and troubleshooting a bus topology can prove difficult.

See also **CDDI, demand priority, Fast Ethernet, FDDI, 100VG-AnyLAN.**

Ethernet address

The address assigned to a network interface card by the original manufacturer or, if the card is configurable, by the network administrator.

This address identifies the local device address to the rest of the network and allows messages to find the correct destination. Also known as the media access control (MAC) address or hardware address.

Ethernet packet

A variable-length unit in which information is transmitted on an Ethernet network. An Ethernet packet consists of a synchronization preamble, a destination address, a source address, a type code indicator, a data field that can vary from 46 to 1500 bytes, and a cyclic redundancy check (CRC) that provides a statistically derived value used to confirm the accuracy of the data.

ETX

■ *See* **end-of-text character.**

euid

Abbreviation for Effective User Identifier. A part of the Unix system security, the `euid` is used to identify the user who owns a program. This `euid` is then checked for the appropriate permissions before the program can access specific files and directories.

eval

A Bourne and Korn shell command used to evaluate shell variables and then run the output as arguments to other shell variables.

ex

The line editor, found on almost all Unix systems, was written by Bill Joy while at UC Berkeley. The `ex` or extended editor was so called because it extended the original `ed` editor.

▶ Syntax

The syntax used with `ex` is as follows:

`ex [`*`options`*`]` *`filename`*

The file you are editing is kept in a buffer, and a typical editing sequence would be to read the file into the buffer, make the required editing changes, and then write the buffer back out to the same file.

▶ Options and Arguments

The options available for use with `ex` are listed in Table E.10

▶ Line Addressing in ex

Most of the `ex` commands operate on a line or on a range of lines, and so you must know how to specify a particular line. The most useful methods of specifying a line or range are listed in Table E.11.

▶ Useful ex Commands

`ex` uses about 50 commands, many of which you will never need; the commands used most often are listed in Table E.12.

▶ Notes

Encryption options are only available in the U.S.

■ *See also* **`ed`, `emacs`, `.exrc`, regular expressions, `vi`.**

Table E.10: Options for Use with ex

OPTION	DESCRIPTION
`-c`*`command`*	Starts an editing session by executing the specified `ex` *`commands`*.
`-C`	Same as `-c` but assumes that *`filename`* was in encrypted form.
`-L`	Lists filenames that were saved due to an editor or system crash.
`-r`*`filename`*	Recovers *`filename`* after an editor or system crash.
`-R`	Sets read-only mode to prevent accidental editing.
`-s`	Turns off error messages; used when running an `ex` script.
`-t` *`tag`*	Edits the file containing *`tag`*.
`-v`	Invokes the `vi` editor.
`-x`	Requires a key to encrypt or decrypt *`filename`*.

Table E.11: Line Addressing in ex

COMMAND	DESCRIPTION
0	Adds a line before the first line.
.	Specifies the current line.
`1,$`	Specifies all lines in the file.
$	Specifies the last line of the file.
n	Specifies the `n`th line in the file.
-n	Specifies *n* lines previous.
-	Specifies the previous line.
+n	Specifies *n* lines ahead.
`'l`	Specifies the line marked by the letter `l`.
`''`	Specifies the previous mark.
/pattern/	Specifies the next line matching regular expression *pattern*.
?pattern?	Specifies the previous line matching regular expression *pattern*.

exa-

Abbreviated E. A prefix meaning one quintillion or 10^{18}. In computing, 1,152,921,504,606,846,976, or the power of 2 closest to one quintillion (10^{60}).

exabyte

Abbreviated EB. 1 quadrillion kilobytes, or 1,152,921,504,606,846,976 bytes.

exclamation point

The **!** character, often called *bang* or *pling*.

- In UUCP, a character used as a host name delimiter, as in: `yoursystem!mysystem!myname`.
- In the C shell, repeats a command. For example, `!!` repeats the last command you entered, and `!3` means repeat the third command.
- The exclamation point is used in some interactive programs to execute a shell command; when using `ftp`, you can use `!date` to run the `date` command without leaving your `ftp` session. When `date` exits, you return to the `ftp` prompt once again.
- An exclamation point is sometimes used to override an automatic check. For example, if you set the `noclobber` variable, the shell will not let you overwrite an existing file when redirecting the standard output. To override this, you can use `>!` instead.

See also **bang path, shell escape.**

exec

A Unix system call that replaces the current process with another using the same process ID number (PID) as the original process. This means that you cannot return to the original program when the new one has done its job, but it saves the overhead of creating a new process space.

See also **fork, spawn.**

exec

A built-in Bourne and C shell command that causes the current shell to be replaced by another program.

executable file

Any file that can be executed by the operating system. Some executable files contain binary instructions, while others are text files containing commands or shell scripts. In Unix, files may be executed only when the execute permission is set.

Table E.12: Useful ex Commands

COMMAND	ABBREVIATION	DESCRIPTION
`append`	[*address*]a *text*	Appends the specified *text* at *address*.
`change`	[*address*]c *text*	Replaces the specified lines with *text*.
`copy`	[*address*]co *destination*	Copies the lines in *address* to *destination*.
`delete`	[*address*]d [*buffer*]	Deletes the specified lines; if *buffer* is specified, saves the text to the buffer.
`global`	[*address*]g/*pattern*/ ➥[*commands*]	Executes *commands* on all lines containing *pattern* or, if *address* is specified, on the lines in that range.
`insert`	[*address*]i *text*	Inserts *text* before the specified address.
`move`	[*address*]m *destination*	Moves the specified lines to *destination*.
`print`	[*address*]p *count*	Prints the lines given by *address*; *count* specifies the number of lines to print, beginning with *address*.
`quit`	q	Ends the current editing session.
`read`	[*address*]r *filename*	Copies in the text from *filename* to the line after *address*.
`source`	so *filename*	Reads and executes the `ex` commands contained in *filename*.
`substitute`	[*address*]s ➥[/*pattern*/*replacement*/]	Replaces each instance of *pattern* with *replacement*.
`write`	[*address*]w[*filename*]	Writes the lines specified by *address* to *filename*.

E

execute

- To run a program, command, or shell script.
- One of the permissions on a file or directory, the others being read permission and write permission. You can execute a file or command only when the execute permission is turned on.

execute permission

An access permission on a file or directory that gives you permission to execute the file or access the contents of the directory.

You cannot change to a directory or include that directory in your path unless you have execute permission in that directory. When you use the `ls -l` command to make a long file and directory listing, an `x` indicates you have execute permission for that file or directory; `r` indicates read permission, and `w` indicates write permission.

executing remote commands

Several Unix commands allow you to access a remote system. These commands include `rcmd` in SCO UNIX and `rsh` in Solaris and UnixWare, both used over a TCP/IP link. You can also use the UUCP command `uux` in a UUCP communications session or `telnet` over a modem and telephone line.

See also **ftp**, **rlogin**, **telnet**.

exit

- A built-in shell command that terminates the current process and returns control to the previous shell.
- A shell programming command that terminates the current shell script.
- In an X Window system, a command that closes an `xterm` window.
- A command used to exit the shell and log out of the system; same as pressing Ctrl-D.

exit status

Sometimes called *exit value* or *return value*. A value returned by a process or command that indicates a successful (usually 0) or unsuccessful (usually 1) conclusion.

In a Bourne shell script, the exit status of the previous command is stored in the built-in `$?` variable, and in the C shell the exit status of the previous command is stored in the `$status` variable.

A few commands such as `grep` return a different non-zero exit value for different kinds of problems; see the `grep man` pages for more details.

expand

A command that converts tab characters to spaces or blanks.

▶ Syntax

The syntax to use with `expand` is:

```
expand [-tabstop][-tab1,
➥ tab2,...]filename
```

`expand` processes the specified *`filename`*, or the standard input, writing the results to the standard output, and all tab characters are converted to space characters.

▶ Options and Arguments

If you use a single *`tabstop`* argument, tabs are set at *`tabstop`* spaces apart, the default being eight spaces. If you specify several *`tab`* settings, these are used instead to set tabs. The `expand` command has no options.

▶ Examples

To convert the tabs in a file called `myphonelist` to 4 spaces, use:

```
expand -4 myphonelist >
➥ myphonelist.notabs
```

See also **unexpand**.

explain

A BSD interactive program that looks up words in a thesaurus file and displays synonyms you can use instead. You can also use `explain` with the output from the `diction` program.

■ *See also* **diction**.

export

A Bourne and Korn shell command that gives global meaning to one or more shell variables. For example, a variable defined in one shell script must be exported before it can be used by another program called by the script.

■ *See also* **global variable, local variable.**

/export

An SVR4 root directory used by the NFS as the root of the export filesystem tree.

exportfs

An NFS command used to make resources on a computer available to all users on the network.

expr

A command that evaluates its arguments as an arithmetic expression and prints the results.

▶ Syntax

Here's the syntax to use with `expr`:

`expr` *`arg1 operator arg2`* `...`

All *`args`* and *`operators`* must be separated by spaces on the command line. `expr` accepts three kinds of operators: arithmetic, comparison, and logical, and they are listed in Table E.13.

Several of the symbols in Table E.13 have special meaning to the shell and so must be escaped before they can be used. Always escape the symbols `*`, `(`, `)`, >, <, |, and `&`.

The `expr` command provides three different exit status values: 0 indicates that the expression is non-zero and non-null, 1 indicates that the expression is 0 or null, and 2 indicates that the expression is invalid.

Table E.13: Operators Used with `expr`

OPERATOR	DESCRIPTION
Arithmetic Operators	
+	Adds the arguments.
–	Subtracts *`arg2`* from *`arg1`*.
`*`	Multiplies the arguments.
/	Divides *`arg1`* by *`arg2`*.
`%`	Modulus when *`arg1`* is divided by *`arg2`*.
Comparison Operators	
=	Is *`arg1`* equal to *`arg2`*?
`!=`	Is *`arg1`* not equal to *`arg2`*?
>	Is *`arg1`* greater than *`arg2`*?
>=	Is *`arg1`* greater than or equal to *`arg2`*?
<	Is *`arg1`* less than *`arg2`*?
<=	Is *`arg1`* less than or equal to *`arg2`*?
Logical Operators	
|	Logical OR.
&	Logical AND.
`:`	Matching operator.

E

▶ **Examples**

To use `expr` in a shell script as a loop counter, use:

```
i=`expr $i + 1`
```

The spaces before and after the addition operator are required.

You can also use `expr` as a fast integer calculator from the command line. To add two numbers, use:

```
expr 20 + 277
```

▶ **Notes**

The `expr` command cannot manipulate floating point numbers, just integers; decimals are truncated so that an answer of 9.3 appears as 9.

See also **bc, dc.**

expressions

See **regular expressions.**

.exrc

An initialization file located in the user's home directory for the `ed`, `ex`, and `vi` editors. When you start one of these editors, the configuration commands contained in `.exrc` are executed first, so you can automatically initialize your own custom environment.

exstr

A software development command used to extract strings from C language source code. These strings are stored in a database and retrieved by a Unix system call when the compiled application program is run. This process is often used when preparing an application for international use.

See also **mkmsgs, mkstr, srchtxt.**

ext2fs

Abbreviation for Second Extended Filesystem; a popular Linux filesystem that allows filenames of up to 256 characters and filesystems of up to 4 terabytes in size.

extended ASCII character set

The second group of characters, from 128 to 255, in the ASCII character set.

The extended ASCII character set is assigned variable sets of characters by computer hardware manufacturers and software developers, and it is not necessarily compatible among different computers. The IBM extended character set used on the PC (see Table 2.3 in Appendix 2) includes mathematical symbols and characters from the PC line drawing set.

See also **ASCII, ASCII file, EBCDIC.**

eyacc

Another version of `yacc` (yet another compiler compiler), called *extended* `yacc`. `eyacc` is based on the original `yacc` but provides rather better error recovery.

See also **yacc.**

F

f

A frequently used system alias for the **finger** command.

■ *See also* **finger, w, who**.

face

The command that starts the Framed Access Command Environment (FACE), a window and menu-based user interface released with SVR4.

▶ Syntax

The syntax to use with **face** is as follows:

```
face [options][filenames]
```

This command invokes FACE and opens *filename*. Each *filename* must have the form menu.*string*, or text.*string*, or form.*string*, depending on the kind of object you are opening.

If no *filenames* are specified, this command opens the FACE menu and default objects as specified by the environment variable LOGINWIN.

▶ Options and Arguments

You can use three configuration-related options with **face**, as shown in Table F.1.

■ *See also* **curses**.

Table F.1: Options to Use with face

OPTION	DESCRIPTION
-a *afilename*	Loads the list of pathname aliases from *afilename*. Entries in this file have the form *alias=pathname*.
-c *cfilename*	Loads the list of command aliases from *cfilename*.
-i *ifilename*	Loads *ifilename*, which specifies startup features.

FACE

Abbreviation for Framed Access Command Environment, a window and menu-based graphical user interface (GUI) released with SVR4. FACE gives ASCII terminals the capability of displaying windows and pop-up menus. You can also use function keys and menus in certain system administration and file and printer management tasks.

`factor`

A command used to produce the prime factors of a specified number. If you don't specify a number on the command line, `factor` waits for input and then factors the number you enter.

`false`

- A null shell programming command used to return an unsuccessful (non-zero) exit status from a shell script. Often used in Bourne shell scripts.
- A Korn shell alias for `let 0`.

See also **`true`**.

FAQ

Abbreviation for frequently asked questions, pronounced "fack." A USENET document that contains answers to questions that new users often ask when they first subscribe to a newsgroup. The FAQ contains answers to common questions that the seasoned users have grown tired of answering. New users should look for and read the FAQ before posting their questions, just in case the FAQ contains the answers.

FAQs are posted to the newsgroup on a regular basis, weekly or monthly, and some grow so large that they are divided into sections; the designation "1/4" indicates that the section being viewed is the first of a total of four sections.

Fast Ethernet

A term applied to the IEEE 802.3 Higher Speed Ethernet Study Group proposals, which were originally developed by Grand Junction Networks, 3Com, SynOptics, Intel, and others. Also known as *100BaseT.*

Fast Ethernet modifies the existing Ethernet standard of 10 Mbps, to allow speeds of 10 or 100Mbps, or both, and uses the CSMA/CD access method.

The official standard defines three physical layer specifications for different cabling types:

- **100BaseTX** for two pair Category 5 unshielded twisted pair cable.
- **100BaseT4** for four pair Category 3, 4, or 5 unshielded twisted pair.
- **100BaseFX** for fiber optic cable.

See also **100VG-AnyLAN.**

fault tolerance

A design method that ensures continued system operation in the event of individual failures by providing redundant elements. At the component level, the design includes redundant chips and circuits and the capability to bypass faults automatically. At the computer system level, any elements that are likely to fail, such as processors and large disk drives, are replicated.

Fault-tolerant operations often require backup or UPS (uninterruptible power supply) power systems in the event of a main power failure. In some cases, the entire computer system is duplicated in a remote location to protect against vandalism, acts of war, or natural disaster.

See also **RAID.**

`fc`

A Korn shell command used to display or edit the command history list.

▶ Syntax

There are two ways to use the `fc` command:

```
fc [options][first[last]]
```

```
fc -e -[old=new][command]
```

▶ Options and Arguments

In the first form above, *first* and *last* are numbers or strings used to specify the range of commands you want to display or edit; use *first* alone if you just want to work with a single command. If you leave out both these arguments, `fc` edits the last command or edits the last 16 commands.

In the second form above, `fc` replaces the string *old* with the string *new* in *command* and then executes the modified command. If you don't specify these strings, *command* is re-executed, and if you leave out *command*, the previous command is re-executed.

Table F.2 lists the options you can use with the `fc` command.

Table F.2: Options for Use with fc

OPTION	DESCRIPTION
`-e [editor]`	Opens the specified *editor* to edit the history commands; the default name is specified by the `FCEDIT` shell variable.
`-e -`	Executes a history command.
`-l[n]`	Lists the specified command *n*, the range of commands, or the last 16 commands if *n* is not specified.
`-n`	Turns off command numbering from the `-l` listing.
`-r`	Reverses the order of the `-l` listing.

▶ Examples

To list commands 25 through 35, use:

```
fc -l 25 35
```

To list the last command beginning with ls:

```
fc -l ls
```

If you want to edit a series of commands, say commands 5 through 25 inclusive, with **emacs**, use:

```
fc -e emacs 5 25
```

■ *See also* **history**, **r**.

FCEDIT

A Korn shell environment variable that contains the name of the default text editor, usually either `emacs` or `vi`. This information is used by the built-in command `fc` unless overridden by the `-e` option.

FDDI

Abbreviation for Fiber Distributed Data Interface. The ANSI X3T9.5 specification for fiber optic networks transmitting at a speed of up to 100 Mbps over a dual, counter rotating, token ring topology.

FDDI's 100 Mbps speed is close to the internal speed of most computers, which makes it a good choice to serve as a super backbone linking two or more LANs, or as a fiber optic bus connecting high-performance engineering workstations.

FDDI is suited to systems that require the transfer of large amounts of information, such as medical imaging, three-dimensional seismic processing, and oil reservoir simulation. The FDDI-II version of the standard is designed for networks transmitting real-time full-motion video (or other information that cannot tolerate any delays) and requires that all nodes on the network use FDDI-II; otherwise, the network automatically reverts to FDDI.

An FDDI network using multimode fiber optic cable can include as many as five hundred stations up to 2 kilometers (1.25 miles) apart; with single mode fiber, run length increases up to 60 kilometers (37.2 miles) between stations. This type of network can also run over shielded and unshielded twisted pair cabling (when it is known as CDDI, or Copper Distributed Data Interface) for shorter distances.

fdformat

A Solaris command used to format a floppy disk.

▶ Syntax

The syntax for `fdformat` is as follows:

```
fdformat [options]
```

The `fdformat` command formats and verifies all the tracks on the floppy disk and terminates if it finds any bad sectors. Any previous data on the floppy is destroyed during the formatting process. You can also use `fdformat` to create a DOS-compatible disk.

▶ Options and Arguments

Table F.3 lists the options for use with `fdformat`.

Table F.3: Options Available with `fdformat`

OPTION	DESCRIPTION
`-d`	Installs a DOS filesystem and boot sector on the disk once formatting is complete.
`-D`	Formats a 720 KB disk under Solaris 2 for x86.
`-e`	Ejects the disk when the formatting is complete. This option only works with disk drives without manual eject buttons.
`-f`	Starts formatting immediately without asking you to confirm the format operation.
`-l`	Formats a 720 KB disk on a Sun workstation.
`-m`	Formats a 1.2 MB disk.
`-v`	Verifies the disk when the formatting is complete.
`-b` *`label`*	Writes the DOS *`label`* on the disk when formatting is complete; use only with the `-d` option.

▶ Examples

If you want to format a 1.44 MB floppy disk for use with a Unix filesystem, use:

```
fdformat /dev/rfd0c
```

To format a floppy disk using a DOS-compatible format, and to install a DOS filesystem and boot sector, use:

```
fdformat -d /dev/rfd0c
```

■ *See also* **DOS commands.**

fg

A Korn shell and C shell command used to bring the current or specified job to the foreground.

■ *See also* **background processing, `bg`, job control, percent sign.**

fgrep

A command that searches one or more files for text strings that match a specified regular expression. This command, along with the related `egrep` command, is considered to be obsolete.

■ *See also* **`grep`.**

fi

A Bourne and Korn shell programming command used to terminate an `if` statement.

■ *See also* **`if`.**

fiber-optic cable

A transmission technology that sends pulses of light along specially manufactured optical fibers. Each fiber consists of a core, thinner than a human hair, surrounded by a sheath with a much lower refractive index. Light signals introduced at one end of the cable are conducted along the cable as the signals are reflected from the sheath.

Fiber optic cable is lighter and smaller than traditional copper cable, is immune to electrical interference, offers better security, and has better signal-transmitting qualities. However, it is more expensive than traditional cable and is more difficult to repair. Fiber optic cable is often used for high-speed backbones, but as prices drop, we may even see fiber-optic cable running to the desktop.

FIFO file

Abbreviation for first in first out file. In SVR4, a named pipe.

A special type of temporary file that exists independently of any process and allows unrelated processes to exchange information; normal pipes work only between related processes. Any number of processes can read or write to a FIFO file.

■ *See* **mkfifo**, **mknod**.

fignore

A C shell predefined variable that contains a list of filename suffixes. The C shell ignores the specified suffixes when it performs filename completion.

file

A collection of related information, usually referred to by a single filename. The Unix operating system also views peripheral devices as files, so a program can read or write to a device, just as it can to a hard disk file.

In Unix, files are collected together in directories for convenience.

■ *See also* **block special file, character special file, FIFO, file type.**

file

A command that determines file type and then lists each filename followed by a brief description.

▶ Syntax

Here's the syntax for the `file` command:

```
file [options]filename
```

This command can recognize whether a file is a 286 executable, 386 executable, ASCII text file, C source code, and so on. Many of the Unix commands are shell scripts, and you can use this command to tell those files apart from the utilities that are executable files.

▶ Options and Arguments

The `file` command looks in the so-called magic file, `/etc/magic` (or another file that you specify), for information on how to determine a specific file's type. `file` looks at the first part of a file, looking for keywords and special numbers placed there by the link editor and other software development programs. `file` also looks at the file permissions associated with the file.

The options you can use with `file` are listed in Table F.4.

Table F.4: Options to Use with file

OPTION	DESCRIPTION
`-c`	Checks the format of the magic file.
`-flist`	Runs `file` on the filenames contained in *list*.
`-h`	Does not follow symbolic links.
`-mfilename`	Specifies *filename* instead of `/etc/magic`.

▶ Examples

To determine the type of a file, use:

```
file myfile.doc
```

```
myfile.doc        ascii text
```

F

The `file` classifications include the following:

```
ascii text
commands text
c program text
c-shell commands
data
English text
empty
executable
iAPX 386 executable
directory
sccs
shell commands
symbolic link to
```

▶ **Notes**

Because of all the possible combinations of file types, the results from `file` are not always correct.

file attributes

A collection of general information concerning a file, including the type of file, its i-node, its size, the name of the device the file is on, and information about the owner of the file.

file commands

That group of Unix commands related to file operations, including `cat`, `cp`, `ln`, `ls`, `mv`, `rm`, `touch`, and `umask`.

file comparison commands

That group of Unix commands used when making comparisons between files, including `bdiff`, `cmp`, `dd`, `diff`, `diff3`, `diffmk`, `dircmp`, `sccsdiff`, `sdiff`, and `uniq`.

file compression program

A utility that compresses files so that they take up less space on the disk or take less time to transmit over a communications link.

■ *See also* **`compact`, `compress`, `gzip`, `pack`, `uncompact`, `uncompress`.**

file consistency check

The process of checking a filesystem for consistency and correctness or hardware errors. A system administrator often uses the `fsck` program for this purpose.

file creation mask

■ *See* **creation mask.**

file description

A record containing information on how a file has been accessed by a program or a group of programs.

■ *See also* **file descriptor.**

file descriptor

Information provided by the kernel that allows a program to refer to a file. Each file descriptor has a number, and by convention in Unix, file descriptors 1, 2, and 3 refer to a program's standard input, standard output, and standard error, respectively.

■ *See also* **file description.**

file handle

An NFS term that describes a key sent by the server to a client to manage requests between the two.

file locking

A method of controlling file access in a multiuser environment, in which there is always a possibility that two users may attempt to update the same file at the same time but with different information. The first user to access the file locks out all the other users, preventing them from opening the file. After the file is updated and closed again, the next user can gain access.

File locking is a simple way to prevent simultaneous updates, but it can seriously degrade system performance if many users attempt to access the same files time after time. To prevent this slowdown, many database management systems use record locking instead. Record locking limits access to individual records within the database file.

file permissions

A special binary number associated with a file that specifies who can access the file and in what way.

There are three independent permissions: read, write, and execute.

- Read permission lets you read the file.
- Write permission lets you write to the file and change it if you wish.
- Execute permission means that you can execute the file.

You can set and change the file permissions for your own files, and the main reasons for doing this are to prevent others from accessing your files and to protect yourself against accidental changes or deletions to important files.

Directories also have these three same permissions, but they work in a slightly different way:

- Read permission lets you read the filenames in the directory.
- Write permission lets you make changes to the directory; you can create, rename, move, or delete files.
- Execute permission means that you can search the directory; to include a directory in your path, you must have execute permission for that directory.

There are also three sets of file permissions: one set for the user or owner of a file, one set for the group of the file, and another set for everyone else.

■ *See also* **`chmod`, `ls`, `umask`.**

file server

A networked computer used to store files for access by other client computers on the network. This allows computers without local storage to access filesystems from the server.

■ *See also* **NFS, RFS, server.**

file type

There are several types of files in the Unix system, including:

- **Ordinary files** hold user data and programs; most files are of this type. An ordinary file may be a text file or a binary file. Sometimes known as *regular files.*
- **Directories** hold files or other directories.
- **Block special files** represent a specific kind of device driver that communicates with the hardware in units known as *blocks.*
- **Character special files** represent a specific kind of device driver that communicates with the hardware character by character.
- **FIFO special files** allow unrelated programs to exchange information; sometimes called *named pipes.*
- **Sockets** allow unrelated programs on the same or different computers to exchange information.
- **Symbolic links** let you link files that are in different filesystems.

The type of each file is displayed in the first column of the long format `ls` listing.

■ *See also* **Internet file types.**

`filec`

A C shell environment variable that allows filename completion. When this variable is set, an input line followed by Ctrl-D prints all the filenames that begin with the contents of the input line. You can also enter an input line followed by an Escape keystroke to replace the line with the longest non-ambiguous filename extension.

filename

The name of a file within a directory; sometimes written as two words, *file name.*

In some cases, filename refers to the full absolute pathname for a file; in others, just to the filename itself.

Within a directory, filenames must be unique, although files with the same name may exist in different directories.

You can use almost any character you like in a Unix filename. Table F.5 lists some of the characters you should avoid because they have a special meaning in Unix.

Table F.5: Characters to Avoid in Unix Filenames

CHARACTER	DESCRIPTION
!	Exclamation point
#	Pound sign
&	Ampersand
( )	Parentheses
'	Single quote
"	Double quote
`	Backquote
;	Semicolon
< >	Redirection symbols
\	Backslash
@	At sign
$	Dollar sign
^	Caret
{ }	Braces
~	Tilde
?	Question mark

You should also avoid the space, backspace, and tab characters, and you cannot create a file named `.` (dot) or `..` (dot dot) because these two names are reserved for the names of the current and the parent directories.

■ *See also* **filename extension.**

filename completion

The automatic completion of filenames and usernames after you specify a unique prefix.

■ *See also* **filename substitution.**

filename expansion

The process that the shell uses to convert the contents of the command line, including any metacharacters, into real filenames.

■ *See also* **asterisk, filename substitution.**

filename extension

That part of a filename that follows a period. Unix, unlike DOS, doesn't have any rules about filename extensions; the period has no special significance as a separating character, and extensions can be any length.

Table F.6: Common Unix Filename Extensions

EXTENSION	DESCRIPTION
`.a`	Archived file or assembler code
`.au`	Audio file
`.c`	C language source code
`.csh`	C shell script
`.enc`	Encrypted file
`.f`	Fortran source code
`.F`	Fortran source code before preprocessing
`.gif`	Graphics Interchange Format file

Table F.6: Common Unix Filename Extensions (continued)	
EXTENSION	DESCRIPTION
`.gl`	Animation file
`.gz`	File compressed with the `gzip` command
`.h`	C program header file
`.jpg` or `jpeg`	Joint Photographic Experts Group format still image
`.mm`	Text file containing `troff mm` macros
`.mpg` or `.mpeg`	Motion Picture Experts Group format video file
`.ms`	Text file containing `troff ms` macros
`.o`	Object file
`.ps`	PostScript source file
`.s`	Assembly language source code
`.sh`	Bourne shell script
`.shar`	Shell archive
`.tar`	`tar` archive file
`.tex`	Text file formatted with TEX commands
`.txt`	ASCII text file
`.uu`	A `uuencode` file
`.xx`	Text file formatted with LATEX commands
`.z`	File compressed by the `pack` command
`.Z`	File compressed by the `compress` command
`.1` to `.8`	Online manual source files

Some Unix software development programs, such as the C compiler, do use specific one-character extensions such as .c for a C language source file, while others use extensions as indicators of their contents, such as `.txt` to indicate a text file. Table F.6 lists common Unix filename extensions and their associations.

■ *See also* **Internet file types.**

filename generation

A term used in the Bourne shell, Korn shell, and Zsh as a synonym for *filename substitution*.

filename substitution

In the C shell, replacing a pattern that is a part of a command with all the filenames that match that pattern. The pattern may also contain metacharacters or wildcards with special meanings.

■ *See also* **asterisk.**

filesystem

A complex collection of files, directories, and management information, usually located on a hard disk or other mass storage device such as a compact disc. Sometimes written as two words, *file system*.

All Unix systems have at least a root filesystem, with additional filesystems, as requirements dictate. Each filesystem is controlled by a superblock containing information about the filesystem and consists of i-nodes, which contain information about individual files, and data blocks, which contain the information in the files.

■ *See also* **`/etc`, NFS, RFS, standard directories.**

filter

A Unix command that can take its input from the standard input, perform some sort of operation on the data, and then send the result to the standard output. A filter usually just does one operation on the data but does it well. Table F.7 contains a list of useful Unix filters.

F

Table F.7: A List of Useful Unix Filters

FILTER NAME	DESCRIPTION
`cat`	Copies standard input to standard output; combines files.
`colrm`	Removes the specified columns from each line.
`crypt`	Encrypts or decrypts data using a specified key.
`cut`	Extracts specified columns from each line.
`fmt`	Formats text.
`grep`	Extracts lines that contain a specified pattern.
`head`	Displays the first few lines of data.
`less`	Displays data one screen at a time.
`look`	Extracts lines that begin with a specified pattern.
`more`	Displays data one screen at a time.
`nl`	Creates line numbers.
`paste`	Combines columns of data.
`pg`	Displays data one screen at a time.
`pr`	Formats data for printing.
`rev`	Reverses the order of the characters in each line.
`sort`	Sorts data.
`spell`	Checks for spelling errors.
`tail`	Displays the last few lines of data.
`tr`	Translates selected characters.
`uniq`	Locates repeated lines.
`wc`	Counts characters, words, or lines.

An important aspect of filters is that they can be used with redirection and with pipes. This means that you can combine filters with input from a file or from the keyboard or with the output of another command.

find

A command that searches for files meeting certain specified criteria, descending the Unix directory tree as it goes.

▶ Syntax

The syntax to use with `find` is as follows:

`find` *`pathname expression`*

Files can be matched according to name, size, creation date, modification time, and several other criteria.

You can also execute a command on the files each time a match is found.

▶ Options and Arguments

The `find` command is an extremely useful, adaptable, and powerful tool; it may seem difficult to master, but it is well worth the effort. `find` searches *`pathname`*, a space-separated list of directory names that you want to search for a file or files, and *`expression`* contains the matching specification or description of the files that you want to find. *`expression`* may also contain a list of actions to be taken on each match.

The *`expression`* list is evaluated from left to right, and as long as the test in *`expression`* evaluates to true, the next test is performed; the expression is evaluated as though connected by a logical AND. If the test is not met, processing on the current file ends, and the next file is checked. You can group conditions by enclosing them in escaped parentheses `\(`*`expression`*`\)`, negate them by `!`*`expression`* (you must use `\!`*`expression`* in the C shell), or separate alternatives with *`expression`* `-o` *`expression`* (this acts as a logical OR).

Table F.8 lists the options that you can use with the `find` command. You can also use a + or – with any of the *`n`* arguments in Table F.8 to indicate either more than or less than, respectively.

The most useful options are `-print`, which you must use if you want to see any output from `find`,

Table F.8: Options for Use with `find`	
OPTION	DESCRIPTION
`-atime` *`n`*	Finds files accessed more than, less than, or exactly *`n`* days ago.
`-cpio` *`dev`*	An SVR3 option that writes matching filenames on the device *`dev`*.
`-ctime` *`n`*	Finds files that were changed more than, less than, or exactly *`n`* days ago; includes files whose permissions have changed.
`-depth`	This option indicates an action to follow rather than a check that must be made, and so is always true. Makes `find` act on entries within a directory before acting on the directory itself; often used with `cpio`.
`-exec` *`command`*`{}\;`	Runs *`command`* on each matched file. The specified *`command`* must be followed by an escaped semicolon (`\;`), and when the *`command`* runs, the `{}` argument substitutes the name of the current file.
`-follow`	Follows symbolic links.
`-fstype` *`type`*	Finds files on filesystem *`type`*.
`-group` *`groupname`*	Finds files belonging to *`groupname`*.
`-inum` *`n`*	Finds files with the i-node number *`n`*.
`-links` *`n`*	Finds files with *`n`* links.
`-local`	Finds files on the local filesystem.
`-mount`	Searches for files on the same filesystem as specified by *`pathname`*.
`-mtime` *`n`*	Finds files modified or written to more than, less than, or exactly *`n`* days ago.
`-name` *`pattern`*	Finds files whose names match *`pattern`*; you can use an `*`, `?`, or `[` and `]`, but they must be escaped within quotes or preceded by a backslash.
`-newer` *`filename`*	Finds files modified more recently than *`filename`*.
`-nogroup`	Finds files that belong to a group not found in `/etc/passwd`.
`-nouser`	Finds files that belong to a user not found in `/etc/passwd`.
`-ok` *`command`*`{}/;`	Same as `-exec`, but you must respond (with a `y`) before *`command`* is executed.
`-perm` *`nnn`*	Finds files whose permissions match the octal number *`nnn`*.

F

Table F.8: Options for Use with find (continued)	
OPTION	DESCRIPTION
`-print`	Prints matching filenames, along with their full pathnames; this option is always true because it is an option to perform rather than a check to be made.
`-prune`	This option is always true because it is an option to perform rather than a check to be made. Makes `find` skip unwanted directory searches.
`-size` *n*	Finds files of *n* 512-byte blocks; if *n* is followed by a `c`, the size is in characters not in blocks.
`-type` *c*	Finds files of type *c*, where *c* can be one of the types listed in Table F.9.
`-user` *username*	Finds files belonging to *username*; you can use a numeric user ID.

`-name`, and `-type`. More advanced users will want to experiment with `-exec` and `-size`, too. Most of the others are best left to system administrators.

▶ **Examples**

To list all filenames and directories, starting in the current directory and continuing through all subdirectories, use:

```
find . -print
```

To print the names of all the files in the current directory whose names end in `.txt`, use:

```
find . -name \*.txt -print
```

Table F.9: File Types Converted by the -type Option in find	
FILE TYPE	DESCRIPTION
b	block special file
c	character special file
d	directory
f	ordinary file
l	symbolic link
p	named pipe
s	socket

To find all files accessed more recently than 10 days ago, use:

```
find / -atime +10 -print
```

To find those files not accessed in the last 10 days, substitute `-atime -10` instead.

If you want to delete all files that you have not accessed within the last 30 days, use:

```
find . -type f -size +1000c
➥ -atime +30 -ok rm {} \;
```

This command finds ordinary files of larger than 1000 characters that have not been accessed within the last 30 days and then asks if you want to delete them. It actually uses the `rm` utility to perform the deletion.

▶ **Notes**

The `find` command changes the access time of directories provided as *pathname*; this may be important if you plan on repeating several *find* commands.

■ *See also* **chgrp, chmod, ln, ls.**

finger

A command that displays information about users logged on to the system.

▶ **Syntax**

To use `finger`, here's the syntax you need:

finger [*options*]*username*

If you don't specify a *username*, `finger` displays information about each user logged on to the system, including:

- Login name
- Full name
- Terminal name (You will see a * by the name if write permission is denied.)
- Idle time—time since the user typed a key
- Login time
- Location, taken from the comment field in `/etc/ttytab`.

When you specify a *username* as a first name, last name, or login name, `finger` also displays:

- User's home directory and login shell
- Time the user logged in
- Terminal information from `/etc/ttytab`
- Time the user received and read mail
- Contents of the user's `.plan` file, if it exists, from his or her home directory
- Contents of the user's `.profile` file, if it exists, from his or her home directory

▶ Options and Arguments

The options you can use with `finger` are listed in Table F.10.

If you work in a networked environment or have access to the Internet, `finger` also recognizes *username* in the form:

user@host

▶ Examples

Several Internet users use `finger` in a rather novel way. The University of Wisconsin has a computerized soft drink vending machine. To buy a drink, you log in to a terminal next to the machine and use the appropriate commands; you must pay in advance to have credit in your account. The command:

```
finger coke@cs.wisc.edu
```

displays the instructions for the system.

Other non-traditional uses include the baseball scores displayed by:

```
finger jtchern@sandstorm
➥.berkeley.edu
```

or the recent earthquake activity displayed by:

```
finger quake@geophys
➥.washington.edu
```

■ *See also* **finger entry, w, who.**

Table F.10: Options for Use with `finger`

OPTION	DESCRIPTION
`-b`	Omits user's home directory and shell from the display.
`-f`	When used with `-s`, removes display heading.
`-h`	Does not display contents of `.profile`.
`-i`	Displays information in a condensed format.
`-l`	Outputs a long format. This option is the only option you can use over a network link.
`-m`	Matches only the username.
`-p`	Does not display contents of `.plan`.
`-q`	Displays the shortest format.
`-s`	Displays the short format.
`-w`	When used with `-s`, omits the user's full name.

finger entry

Information contained in the `/etc/passwd` file that identifies the user and location to the `finger` command.

■ *See also* **`finger`**.

F

firewall

A computer that sits between a trusted in-house network and the Internet to protect the internal network against unauthorized access by restricting the type of information that can pass between them.

A firewall provides controlled access to authorized users and should be configured to block all services by default, except those that you specifically intend to allow.

■ *See also* **hacker.**

flame

A deliberately insulting e-mail message or post to a USENET newsgroup, often containing a personal attack on the writer of an earlier post.

If a writer is about to post what might be considered to be an inflammatory message, you may see the expression "flame on" at the beginning of the offending message, followed by "flame off" at the end.

■ *See also* **flame bait, flame war.**

flame bait

An insulting or outrageous e-mail post to a USENET newsgroup specifically designed to provoke other users into flaming the originator.

■ *See also* **flame, flame war.**

flame war

In a USENET newsgroup, a prolonged series of flames that may have begun as a creative exchange of views but quickly descended into personal attacks and crude name calling.

■ *See also* **flame bait.**

flavor

A slang expression meaning type or kind, as in "Unix comes in a variety of different flavors."

■ *See also* **vanilla.**

`flex`

The GNU version of the `lex` software development tool, often available on Linux and other systems.

FMLI

Abbreviation for Forms and Menu Language Interpreter. An SVR4 addition to aid programmers in writing windowed applications.

■ *See also* **FACE, `fmli`.**

`fmli`

A command used to invoke the Form and Menu Language Interpreter (FMLI).

▶ Syntax

The syntax to use with `fmli` is as follows:

`fmli [`*`options`*`][`*`filenames`*`]`

This command invokes FMLI and opens *`filename`*. Each *`filename`* must have the form `menu.`*`string`*, `text.`*`string`*, or `form.`*`string`*, depending on the kind of object you are opening.

▶ Options and Arguments

You can use three configuration-related options with `fmli` as Table F.11 shows.

Table F.11: Options for Use with `fmli`

OPTION	DESCRIPTION
`-a` *`afilename`*	Loads the list of pathname aliases from *`afilename`*. Entries in this file have the form *`alias=pathname`*.
`-c` *`cfilename`*	Loads the list of command aliases from *`cfilename`*.
`-i` *`ifilename`*	Loads *`ifilename`*, which specifies startup features.

fmt

A command that starts a simple text formatter.

▶ Syntax

The usual syntax for `fmt` is:

`fmt [options][filenames]`

`fmt` breaks long lines of text into lines of roughly the same length; lines are not justified, and blank lines or lines starting with a period are ignored.

In 4.4BSD, the `fmt` command is slightly different:

`fmt [goal[maximum]]filename`

where *goal* is the required line length, and *maximum* is the longest allowable line length. Spacing at the beginning of lines is preserved, as are blank lines.

▶ Options and Arguments

The SVR4 `fmt` command has the three options shown in Table F.12.

Table F.12: Command Options to Use with fmt

OPTION	DESCRIPTION
`-c`	Leave the first two lines in a paragraph alone; used when paragraphs have a hanging indent.
`-s`	Splits long lines but leaves short lines intact.
`-w n`	Creates lines of up to *n* characters long; the default is 72 characters.

▶ Examples

In the `emacs` editor, you can use Esc-q to join paragraphs, but in `vi` the following command reformats a paragraph, evening up the lines:

```
!]fmt
```

This next command shortens long lines to 80 characters but leaves short lines intact. When the formatting is complete, the resulting text is written to a new file:

```
fmt -w 80 -s myfile.txt
➥ > myfile80.txt
```

■ *See also* **fold**, **nroff**.

fmtmsg

An SVR4 command used in shell scripts to print messages.

▶ Syntax

The syntax to use with `fmtmsg` is as follows:

`fmtmsg [options] text`

The text is printed on standard error as part of a formatted error message and must be quoted as a single argument.

▶ Options and Arguments

You will find the options available with `fmtmsg` listed in Table F.13.

Table F.13: Options for Use with fmtmsg

OPTION	DESCRIPTION
`-a action`	A string describing the action to be taken; preceded by the words `TO FIX` when output.
`-c source`	The source of the problem; can be `hard`, `soft`, or `firm`, for hardware, software, or firmware.
`-l label`	A string used to identify the source of the message.
`-s severity`	An indication of importance; one of `halt`, `error`, `warn`, or `info`.
`-t tag`	An additional string identifier for the message.

F

Table F.13: Options for Use with fmtmsg (continued)

OPTION	DESCRIPTION
`-u` *types*	Message type. Can be one of `appl` (application), `util` (utility), or `opsys` (operating system), either `recov` or `nrecov` (recovery is possible or not possible), `print` (message displays on standard error), or `console` (the message displays on the system console).

▶ Examples

Messages display in this format:

```
label:     severity:    text
TO FIX:    action       tag
```

focus

In an X Window environment, a term used to describe which window is active. Once the right window has the focus, anything you type at the keyboard is used as input for the program running within that window.

fold

A command that breaks long lines in text files into shorter segments.

▶ Syntax

The syntax for `fold` is:

```
fold [option]filename
```

▶ Options and Arguments

The `fold` command has one option, `-w` width, that specifies the length of the lines in characters; the default is 80 characters. If the file contains tabs, make `width` a multiple of 8 or use the `expand` command on the file before you use `fold`.

▶ Examples

To reformat `myfile80.txt` so that lines are 30 characters or less in length, use:

```
fold -w 30 myfile80.txt
➥ > myfile30.txt
```

■ *See also* **fmt**, **nroff**.

followup

A reply to a post in a USENET newsgroup. Also known as *followup post.*

A followup may quote the original post so that readers are reminded of the discussion so far, and this quoted part of the post is usually indicated by greater than symbols (>). If you do quote from a previous post, make sure that you only quote the minimum amount to get your point across; never quote the whole post because this is considered a waste of Internet resources and may result in a flame.

The initial post and the followup form the beginning of a thread, a series of posts on (more or less) the same subject.

foo

A generic name; also foobar. Used as a name for absolutely anything in any kind of syntax to illustrate a general point.

For example, when describing how a program works, you might hear a programmer say, "And then the foo function returns an integer," or "Then the program opens the file `foo.test` and writes the result into that file."

for

A Bourne shell and Korn shell keyword used to start a loop or repetitive process. A typical example might look like this:

```
for n [in list]
do
        commands
done
```

In other words, for the variable *n* in the optional `list` of values, execute all the `commands`.

■ *See also* **do, done, foreach.**

foreach

A C shell keyword used to start a loop or repetitive process. An example might look like this:

```
foreach name (wordlist)
     commands
end
```

In other words, assign the variable `name` to each of the values in `wordlist`, and execute all the `commands`.

■ *See also* **do, done, for.**

foreground

A processing environment in which one program or shell is directly controlled by input from a terminal.

In traditional Unix systems, a process spends its whole existence in either the background or the foreground; in newer systems with job control, you can change the processing environment and move a foreground process into the background, and vice versa.

■ *See also* **ampersand, background processing, bg, fg, foreground processing.**

foreground processing

A mechanism used to run a program in the foreground, with direct input from a terminal or from the user.

When you enter a command to run a program in the foreground, the shell waits for the program to finish before displaying the system prompt so you can enter the next command.

If your Unix system has job control, you can move a foreground process to the background, and vice versa.

■ *See also* **background processing.**

fork

To create a new process. When a process starts another identical process by making a copy of itself, it is said to fork the process.

■ *See also* **child process, exec.**

format

An SCO UNIX command that formats floppy disks for use with Unix.

▶ Syntax

The syntax to use with `format` is:

```
format [options]device
➥[-i interleave]
```

The `format` command formats floppy disks for use with Unix (not with DOS) and can be used interactively or as a command-line utility.

▶ Options and Arguments

The name of the floppy disk drive to use is specified by `device`; the default device is specified in `/etc/default/format`. The available options are listed in Table F.14.

■ *See also* **DOS commands, fdformat.**

formfeed

Abbreviated FF. A command that advances the paper in a printer by one whole page. In the ASCII character set, a linefeed has the decimal value of 12.

■ *See also* **linefeed, newline.**

4.4BSD Lite

A version of the 4.4BSD source code from which all the AT&T code has been removed in an attempt to avoid licensing conflicts. It is not possible to compile and then run 4.4BSD Lite without a pre-existing system because several important files (including several utilities and some important files from the operating system) are missing from the distribution.

4.4BSD Lite has served as the basis for several other important Unix implementations, including FreeBSD and NetBSD.

Table F.14: Options to Use with `format`	
OPTION	DESCRIPTION
`-f`	Forces `format` into command-line mode.
`-i` *`interleave`*	Specifies the interleave factor to use while formatting. This option should be placed after the *`device`* argument.
`-n`	Turns off disk verification.
`-q`	Turns off track and head display; combine with `-f` to suppress all output.
`-v`	Verifies the floppy disk once formatting is complete.

FPATH

A Korn shell environment variable that specifies search paths for function definitions; these paths are searched after those specified by the `PATH` variable.

fpr

A BSD filter that translates a Fortran file into a file formatted according to the normal Unix conventions.

f protocol

One of the UUCP protocols, developed for use on X.25 communications links as part of the Berkeley Software Distribution (BSD). Not available in all versions of Unix.

The `f` protocol is a simple protocol that assumes data is being transferred without errors; it has one checksum for the entire file.

■ *See also* **e protocol, g protocol, G protocol, t protocol, x protocol.**

fragment

A small part, usually one quarter, of a filesystem data block. Originally developed as a feature in the Berkeley Software Distribution (BSD) filesystems.

If the last part of a file doesn't completely occupy all of the last disk block, the filesystem can allocate that space to another file; fragments allow the BSD filesystem to use large block sizes without the inefficiency of too much unusable empty space. Do not confuse fragments with fragmentation.

fragmentation

The storage of files in small pieces scattered on a disk. As files grow on a hard disk, they can be divided into several small pieces. By fragmenting files, the operating system makes reasonable use of the disk space available. The problem with file fragmentation is that the disk heads must move to different locations on the disk to read or write to a fragmented file. This process takes more time than reading the file as a single piece. Do not confuse fragmentation with fragments, a useful feature of the BSD filesystem.

free blocks

Unused data blocks on a disk, which are available for use by a file.

Free Software Foundation

■ *See* **FSF.**

FreeBSD

A free implementation of Unix for the Intel series of microprocessors, derived from the 4.4BSD Lite releases. The distribution is free, but there may be a small charge to cover the distribution media and packaging. FreeBSD also includes XFree86, a port of the X Window system to the Intel architecture, which supports a large number of graphics adapters.

A complete distribution is available over the Internet from `ftp.FreeBSD.org`, and information is available from `info@FreeBSD.org`.

Most of FreeBSD is covered by a license that allows redistribution as long as the code acknowledges the copyright of the Regents of the University of California and the FreeBSD Project. Those parts of FreeBSD that include GNU software, the C compiler, **emacs**, and so on, are all covered separately by the FSF license.

See also **Linux, NetBSD.**

freeware

A form of software distribution in which the author retains copyright of the software but makes the program available to others at no cost.

See also **copyleft.**

frequently asked questions

See **FAQ.**

fried

A slang expression for burnt-out hardware, especially hardware that has suffered from a power surge. Sometimes applied to people, as in "My brain is fried today; I haven't slept since the weekend."

from

A BSD command that prints the names of those who have sent mail to you.

▶ Syntax

The syntax to use with `from` is:

`from [`*`options`*`][`*`username`*`]`

The `from` command prints out the mail headers from your mailbox.

▶ Options and Arguments

You can use two options with the `from` command, as Table F.15 shows.

Table F.15: Options to Use with from

OPTION	DESCRIPTION
`-f` *`filename`*	Examines *`filename`* instead of the mailbox; if you use this option, do not use the *`username`* argument.
`-s` *`sender`*	Examines mail from mail addresses specified in the string *`sender`*.

If you specify *`username`*, that user's mailbox is examined, but you must have the appropriate privileges and permissions.

See also **`biff`**, **`mail`**.

fsck

The Unix filesystem check command, pronounced "fisk." `fsck` is used by a system administrator logged in as the superuser to check for and repair hard disk related problems.

When `fsck` is run on a filesystem, the filesystem must not be mounted; often the best way of running `fsck` is to bring the system into single-user mode, check the filesystem, and then reboot and restore normal operations.

For each problem `fsck` finds, it asks whether you want to try to fix the problem or to ignore it. If you choose to repair the problem, which is usually the most reasonable approach, you may lose some data. The best insurance against data loss is not `fsck` but is a comprehensive backup program.

See also **`/lost+found`**.

f77

A Fortran 77 compiler supplied with many Unix systems. This version of Fortran is popular among scientists and engineers for technical programming.

FSF

Abbreviation for Free Software Foundation, an organization founded by Richard Stallman that develops the freely available GNU software.

The FSF philosophy is that all software should be free for everyone to use, and source code should accompany the software. That way, if you make a modification to or fix an error in the software, that change can be sent out to all the other users, saving everyone time and preventing duplication of effort. Also, any software developed under the FSF General Public License (GPL) must also be covered by the same terms of the GPL.

Their address is:

675 Massachusetts Avenue
Cambridge, MA 02139, U.S.A.

See also **copyleft.**

fsplit

A 4.4BSD software development command used to split a multiroutine Fortran source code file into files containing individual routines.

fstat

A BSD command that identifies and reports on open files. Because `fstat` takes a snapshot of the system, the results it reports are valid only for a very short period of time. This command is of most interest to system administrators.

ftp

A command used to transfer files to and from remote hosts using the File Transfer Protocol (FTP). You can use `ftp` to log in to an Internet computer and transfer ASCII or binary files during your Internet connection.

▶ Syntax

The syntax to use with `ftp` is as follows:

`ftp [`*`options`*`] [`*`hostname`*`]`

When you use `ftp`, you start a client program on your computer that connects to a server program running on the remote host. The commands that you give to `ftp` are translated into instructions that the server program executes for you.

▶ Options and Arguments

You can use the options listed in Table F.16 on the command line when you start `ftp`. *`hostname`* can be either a domain address or an IP address. Many computers, not just Unix systems, support the File Transfer Protocol (FTP) and allow file transfers using `ftp`.

▶ Using the `ftp` Interpreter

If you do not specify any command-line arguments, `ftp` starts its command interpreter and waits for you to enter commands. The normal prompt is `ftp>`. Table F.17 lists the commands commonly used during an `ftp` session. On most systems other commands are available, but they are mostly concerned with troubleshooting transfers; see the `man` pages if you want to know more.

Once you have made a connection using `ftp` and found your way to the right directory on the remote

Table F.16: Options to Use with `ftp`

OPTION	DESCRIPTION
`-d`	Enables debugging.
`-g`	Turns off filename expansion so that filenames are read literally.
`-i`	Turns off interactive prompting during multifile transfers.
`-n`	Does not try to log in to the remote system automatically on initial connection; unless you specify this option, `ftp` assumes that your login name of the remote system is the same as on your local system.
`-v`	Displays all responses from the remote host and all file transfer statistics.

system, you need only a few commands to move files across the Internet to your own computer. You can become an `ftp` expert with just five commands: `ascii`, `binary`, `get`, `put`, and `quit`.

Depending on the level of security in place on the remote computer, you may find that you are not allowed to use many of those `ftp` commands that create or delete files and directories, and you may find that your ability to transfer files to a remote computer is also limited.

▶ Examples

To transfer a text file called `faq` from the `/pub` directory on the remote computer and rename the file `faq.txt` on the local computer, the `ftp` dialog might look like this:

```
ftp> cd pub
250 CWD command successful.
ftp> ascii
ftp> get faq faq.txt
200 PORT command successful.
150 Opening ASCII mode data
➥ connection for faq
➥ (50007 bytes)
226 Transfer complete.
ftp>
```

The original `ftp` program started as a Unix utility, but versions are now available for all popular operating systems. The traditional `ftp` program starts a text-based command processor; the newer versions use a graphical user interface (GUI) with pull-down menus. The consensus seems to be that the GUI versions may be easier to use, but once you get the hang of things, the text-based versions, while not as pretty, are usually faster.

■ *See also* **anonymous `ftp`, `ftpmail`, `telnet`**.

FTP

Abbreviation for File Transfer Protocol, the TCP/IP Internet protocol used when transferring single or multiple files from one computer system to another.

FTP uses a client/server model, in which a small client program runs on your computer and accesses a larger FTP server running on the Internet host. FTP provides all the tools needed to look at directories and files, change to other directories, and transfer ASCII or binary files from one computer to the other.

■ *See also* **`ftp`**.

ftpmail

A service that allows you to obtain files from FTP archive sites using Internet e-mail. `ftpmail` can be very slow and can sometimes overload your e-mail spooler.

full regular expressions

■ *See* **regular expressions.**

full-screen editor

Any text editor capable of using the whole screen.

■ *See also* **`emacs`, line editor, `vi`**.

fvwm

An X Window window manager specifically developed for use with Linux.

Table F.17: ftp Commands

COMMAND	DESCRIPTION
Basic Commands	
`?`	Displays a list of the `ftp` interpreter commands.
`?` *command*	Displays information on *command*.
`!`	Pauses `ftp`, and starts a shell on the local computer.
`!` *command*	Executes the specified *command* on the local computer.
`bye`	Terminates `ftp`.
`help`	Displays a list of the `ftp` interpreter commands.
`quit`	Closes the connection to the remote computer, and terminates `ftp`.
Connecting Commands	
`account` [*passwd*]	Supplies a password required by the remote system.
`open` [*hostname*]	Establishes a connection to the specified remote computer.
`close` [*hostname*]	Terminates the connection to the specified remote computer, but continues to execute `ftp`.
`disconnect`	Same as `close`.
`user` [*name*[*password*]]	Identifies the user to the remote computer.
Directory Commands	
`cd` [*directory*]	Changes to *directory* on the remote computer.
`cdup`	Changes the current directory on the remote computer to its parent directory.
`delete` [*remote_filename*]	Deletes the specified file from the remote system.
`dir` [*directory*]	Displays a listing of *directory* on the remote computer.
`lcd` [*directory*]	Changes the current directory on the local computer to *directory*.
`ls`	Displays a listing of the current directory on the remote computer.
`mkdir` [*directory*]	Creates the specified directory on the remote computer.

Table F.17: ftp Commands (continued)

COMMAND	DESCRIPTION
`pwd`	Displays the name of the current directory on the remote computer.
`rmdir [`*`directory`*`]`	Deletes the specified directory on the remote computer.
File Transfer Commands	
`append [`*`local_filename`*`] ➥[`*`remote_filename`*`] cr`	Toggles stripping of Return characters during the transfer of an ASCII file. Appends a local file to a file on the remote system.
`get [`*`remote_filename`* `➥[`*`local_filename`*`]]`	Transfers *`remote_filename`* from the remote computer and renames the file *`local_filename`* on the local computer.
`mget [`*`remote_filenames`*`]`	Transfers the specified files from the remote computer.
`mput [`*`local_filenames`*`]`	Transfers the specified files to the remote computer.
`put [`*`local_filename`* `➥[`*`remote_filename`*`]]`	Transfers the file specified by *`local_filename`* to the remote computer, and renames the file *`remote_filename`*.
Option Setting Commands	
`ascii`	Sets the file transfer type to ASCII.
`bell`	Sounds the terminal bell after each command is complete; a very irritating option and rarely used.
`binary`	Sets the file transfer type to binary.
`hash`	Toggles printing of a pound sign (#) for each block of data transferred. This can be a useful indicator that the transfer is continuing as you expect, especially when transferring large files.
`prompt`	Toggles interactive prompting.
`status`	Shows the current status of `ftp`.

F

G

Abbreviation for giga-, meaning 1 billion, or 10^9.

■ *See also* **gigabyte.**

g++

A shell script to be used instead of the **gcc** command when compiling C++ code with the GNU C language compiler from the Free Software Foundation (FSF).

■ *See also* **gcc.**

gadgets

In the X Window system programming toolkit, a graphical object, not directly associated with a window, used to create graphical applications.

■ *See also* **widget.**

gateway

A shared connection between two local area networks, or LANs, and a larger system, such as a mainframe computer or a large packet-switching network, whose communications protocols are different. A gateway is a combination of hardware and software with its own processor and memory used to route messages and perform protocol conversions.

gawk

The GNU version of the **awk** command, available from the Free Software Foundation (FSF) and standard on some Unix systems.

■ *See also* **awk, nawk, perl.**

GB

■ *See* **gigabyte.**

gcc

The GNU C compiler available from the Free Software Foundation (FSF) and standard on some Unix systems, including 4.4BSD and Linux. **gcc** also compiles C++ source code, as well as source code written in other dialects of the C language.

▶ Syntax

The syntax for use with `gcc` is as follows:

```
gcc [options] filename
```

▶ Options and Arguments

Many of the options you can use with `gcc` are very complex and have to do with subtle distinctions between different versions of the C language and machine-dependent options; they are not discussed in this book. See the `man` pages or the `Info` files for complete details. Table G.1 lists some of the general-purpose options used when compiling either C or C++ source code with `gcc`.

■ *See also* **adb, as, cc, cpp, dbx, g++, gdb, ld, sdb.**

gcore

A troubleshooting command used to obtain a core image of a running process. The core image can then be examined using a debugger such as `gdb` or `sdb`.

gdb

The GNU debugger, available from the Free Software Foundation (FSF) and standard on some Unix systems, including 4.4BSD. You can use `gdb` to debug a running program or to examine the cause of a program crash with a core dump.

▶ Syntax

To use `gdb`, here's the syntax:

```
gdb [options]
➥[program[core|PID]]
```

Table G.1: Options for Use with gcc

OPTION	DESCRIPTION
`-c`	Compiles source code, but does not link.
`-E`	Stops when the preprocessor is complete, but does not compile the source code.
`-g`	Turns on debugging information.
`-I` *`directory`*	Appends *`directory`* to the list of directories searched for include files.
`-l` *`library`*	Uses the specified *`library`* when linking.
`-L` *`directory`*	Adds the specified *`directory`* to the list to be searched for libraries used for linking.
`-O`	Turns on optimization; the compiler attempts to reduce code size and execution time.
`-o` *`filename`*	Names the compiler output *`filename`*. If this option is not specified, output is placed in the file `a.out`.
`-S`	Halts after compiling, does not assemble.
`-traditional`	Attempts to support aspects of traditional C compilers.
`-v`	Prints the commands executed to run the various stages of compilation.
`-w`	Turns off all warning messages.

You can use **gdb** in four main ways to help locate programming errors:

- Start the program with **gdb** specifying anything that might affect its behavior.
- Make your program stop on certain specified conditions.
- Examine a stopped program.
- Make changes to a stopped program and continue execution.

You can use **gdb** to debug programs written in C, C++, and Modula-2; Fortran support is expected when a GNU Fortran compiler becomes available.

You can start **gdb** with a specified ***program*** name, with both a ***program*** and a core file, or with a ***program*** name and a process ID (PID) number.

▶ Options and Arguments

The options available for use with **gdb** are listed in Table G.2.

Table G.3 lists some of the common **gdb** commands you might use during the course of a debugging session.

See also **adb, sdb.**

GDS

Abbreviation for Global Directory Service, an implementation of the X.500 directory service for managing remote users and addresses.

Table G.2: Options for Use with gdb

OPTION	DESCRIPTION
-b *bps*	Sets the baud rate of a serial connection used for remote debugging to *bps*.
-batch	Runs **gdb** in batch mode.
-c *filename*	Uses the specified file as a core dump to examine.
-cd *directory*	Uses the specified *directory*, rather than the current directory.
-command *filename*	Executes the **gdb** commands contained in *filename*.
-d *directory*	Adds *directory* to the path to search for source files.
-e *filename*	Specifies *filename* as an executable file.
-f	Set by **emacs** when it runs **gdb** as a subprocess.
-h	Lists help information.
-n, -nx	Does not execute commands from the **.gdbibit** file.
-q	Turns off initial copyright messages.
-s *filename*	Reads the symbol table from *filename*.
-se *filename*	Reads the symbol table from *filename*, and uses it as the executable file.
-tty=*device*	Specifies *device* as your program's standard input and standard output.
-x *filename*	Executes the **gdb** commands contained in *filename*.

Table G.3: Common gdb Commands

COMMAND	DESCRIPTION
`break [`*`filename`*`:]`*`function`*	Sets a breakpoint at *`function`* within *`filename`*.
`bt`	Backtrace; displays the program stack.
`c`	Continues execution after a breakpoint.
`help`	Displays help information.
`help` *`command`*	Displays help information for *`command`*.
`next`	Executes the next program line, stepping over any function calls in the line.
`print` *`expression`*	Displays the value of *`expression`*.
`quit`	Terminates `gdb`.
`step`	Executes the next program line, executing any function calls in the line.

gencat

A command used to append or merge message files into a message file database.

The syntax to use for `gencat` is:

`gencat [`*`option`*`]` *`database`*
➥ *`messagefile`*

This command merges or appends one (or more) *`messagefile`* into the formatted *`database`* file; if the file does not exist, it is created. Every message in *`messagefile`* is numbered, and you can add comment lines by placing a dollar sign at the beginning of a line, followed by a space or a tab.

`gencat` has only one option, `-n`, used to ensure that the `database` is compatible with previous versions of the command.

get

■ *See* **SCCS.**

getoptcvt

An SCO command used to convert old-style shell scripts that use the obsolete `getopt` command into scripts that use `getopts` instead. `getoptcvt` reads the shell script, converts it to use `getopts`, and writes the result to the standard output. A single option, `-b`, ensures that the results of `getoptcvt` are portable to earlier UNIX releases.

getopts

A built-in Bourne shell command used to parse command-line options and check for legal options. `getopts` is often used in shell script loops to ensure a standard syntax for command-line options.

The syntax to use for `getopts` is as follows:

`getopts` *`string name`*
➥ `[`*`arguments`*`]`

`string` contains the option letters to be recognized by `getopts`, which are processed in turn and then placed in *`name`*.

The `getopts` command is also available in SCO UNIX as an ordinary utility and is available to many non-Bourne shell users as `/usr/bin/getopts`.

gettxt

An SVR4 command used to manage message files. The syntax to use for **gettxt** is:

```
gettxt messagefile:n[default]
```

Extracts the message identified by *n* from the *messagefile*. If the command fails, it displays the contents of the *default* string, or if the string is not specified, it displays "Message not found!!"

■ *See also* **exstr**, **mkmsgs**, **srchtxt**.

Ghostview

A GNU application for viewing PostScript files on the X Window system. The document is displayed with a vertical scrollbar on the right side of the screen and a horizontal scrollbar across the bottom; menu options are shown on the left side of the window.

GID

■ *See* **group ID.**

giga-

A prefix meaning 1 billion, or 10^9.

■ *See also* **gigabyte.**

gigabyte

Abbreviated GB. Strictly speaking, one billion bytes; however, in computing, in which bytes are most often counted in powers of 2, a gigabyte becomes 2^{30}, or 1,073,741,824 bytes.

glob

A built-in C shell command often used in shell scripts to set a value so that it remains constant for the rest of the script.

The syntax is:

```
glob wordlist
```

and the command performs filename, variable, and history substitution on *wordlist*.

■ *See also* **global variable, local variable.**

global variable

Any variable whose value is available to the shell and to any other programs that you run. In the C shell, a global variable is known as an environment variable; in the Korn shell, a global variable is often called a *shell variable*.

■ *See also* **export**.

globbing

In the shell, the process of performing filename substitution. The shell globs when it replaces a pattern in a command with all the filenames that match that pattern.

■ *See also* **wildcard.**

GNU

Pronounced "ga-noo." A Free Software Foundation (FSF) project devoted to developing a complete, freely available Unix system that contains no AT&T code. The name GNU is a recursive acronym standing for "GNU's not Unix!"

Many of the tools designed for this project have been released and are very popular with users of 4.4BSD, Linux, and many other systems.

■ *See also* **Hurd.**

Gopher

A popular client/server application that presents Internet resources as a series of menus, shielding the user from the underlying mechanical details of IP addresses and different kinds of access methods.

Gopher menus may contain documents you can view or download, searches you can perform, or additional menu selections. When you choose one of these items, Gopher does whatever is necessary to obtain the resource you requested, either by downloading a document or by

jumping to the selected Gopher server and presenting its top-level menu.

Gopher clients are available for most popular operating systems, including the Macintosh, DOS, Windows, and OS/2.

See also **Gopherspace.**

Gopherspace

A collective term used to describe all the Internet resources accessible using Gopher. Gopher is so good at hiding the mechanical details of the Internet that this term was coined to represent all the resources reachable using Gopher.

GOSIP

Acronym for Government Open System Interconnection Profile. A suite of standards intended for use in government projects and based on the Open Systems Interconnection (OSI) reference model. Some measure of GOSIP compliance is required for government computer and networking purchases. GOSIPs exist both in the United States and the United Kingdom.

goto

A C shell keyword used to change the flow in a shell script. `goto` skips to a line in the script labeled by a string ending in a colon (`:`). This string cannot be located within a `foreach` or `while` construct.

gprof

A BSD and Solaris software development tool used to create an execution profile of a C, Pascal, or Fortran program.

See also **`lprof`, `prof`.**

g protocol

The original UUCP protocol, designed to provide good performance over 1200 baud modems. The protocol uses 64-byte packets for 8-bit transfers over modems and telephone lines, with a checksum calculated for each packet. Superseded by the G protocol.

See also **`e` protocol, `f` protocol, `t` protocol, `x` protocol.**

G protocol

An enhanced version of the UUCP `g` protocol, released with SVR4, which increased the packet size from 64 bytes to 256 bytes. A clear 8-bit channel between the two ends of the connection is required.

See also **`e` protocol, `f` protocol, `t` protocol, `x` protocol.**

graph

A BSD and SCO command that draws a graph.

▶ Syntax

The syntax is:

```
graph [options]
```

`graph` takes pairs of numbers from the standard input as abscissas and ordinates of the graph, and entered data points are connected by straight lines.

If the coordinates of a point are followed by a non-numeric string, the string is printed as a label at that point.

▶ Options and Arguments

The options you can use with `graph` are listed in Table G.4.

graphical user interface

See **GUI.**

grave

See **backquote.**

greater than symbol

The greater than symbol (>) is used in redirection of the standard output from a command to a file or to another device. If the file already exists, it is overwritten by this operation.

Table G.4: : Options for Use with graph	
OPTION	DESCRIPTION
-a	Supplies abscissa automatically; spacing is given by the next argument, and the default is 1.
-b	Disconnects the graph following each label in the input.
-c	Specifies the character string given by the next argument as the default label for each data point.
-g	Specifies grid style; 0 for no grid, 1 for a frame with no ticks, 2 (the default) for a full grid.
-h	Specifies a fraction of space for height.
-l	Specifies a graph label.
-m	Specifies line style; 0 for disconnected data points, 1 (the default) for connected points.
-r	Specifies a fraction of space to the right.
-s	Saves the screen.
-t	Swaps horizontal and vertical axes.
-u	Specifies a fraction of space up.
-w	Specifies a fraction of space for width.
-x [*1*]	If *1* is specified, the x axis is logarithmic; the next two arguments specify the lower and upper axis limits, and the third argument specifies the grid spacing.
-y [*1*]	If *1* is specified, the y axis is logarithmic; the next two arguments specify the lower and upper axis limits, and the third argument specifies the grid spacing.

By using two greater than symbols together (>>), the output from the command is added or appended to the end of an existing file.

Some command interpreters, including programs such as `ftp`, use the greater than symbol as part of their command prompt.

■ *See also* **less than symbol.**

greek

An SCO command that selects a terminal filter. `greek` translates the extended character set, including reverse and half-line commands, of a 128-character Teletype Model 37 terminal.

grep

A command used to search for patterns in files.

▶ Syntax

The syntax to use with `grep` is:

`grep [`*`options`*`]`*`pattern`*`[`*`filename`*`]`

`grep` searches one or more files, line by line, for a *`pattern`*, which can be a simple string or a regular expression, and then takes various actions, specified by the command-line options, on each line that contains a match for *`pattern`*.

If you use `grep` to search a file for the word `moth`, it will also find `mother` and `motherhood`; to restrict the search to `moth`, surround `moth` in single

quotes, ' moth ' with spaces at the start and end of the word. Use the caret (^) to specify the beginning of a line and a dollar sign ($) for the end. To specify any of several characters, enclose them in square brackets; [Ee]vis matches elvis or Elvis, and [A-Z]lvis matches any uppercase letter followed by lvis.

Use a period to match any single character, and in a range enclosed in square brackets, a caret indicates any character except those in the brackets, so [^0-9] matches any non-numeric character.

If you have to specify any of the special Unix characters, escape it with a backslash.

▶ Options and Arguments

The grep utility takes input from the standard input or from *filename* specified on the command line. The options available for use with grep are listed in Table G.5.

grep's exit status is 0 if any lines in the file match the specified *pattern*, 1 if none match, and 2 if a syntax error occurred or the file is unreadable.

▶ Examples

To list all files in the current directory that contain the word SYBEX, use:

```
grep SYBEX *
```

To search for lines in files in the current directory that contain numbers, use:

```
grep '[0-9]' *
```

▶ Notes

The grep command is a very useful Unix tool, and there have been many variations on this theme:

- Extended grep, or egrep, handles extended regular expressions.
- Fast grep, or fgrep, is not particularly fast but can be used to find expressions containing

Table G.5: Options Available with grep

OPTION	DESCRIPTION
-b	Preceeds each line with its hard disk block number.
-c	Counts the matched lines found in each file.
-h	Prints matched lines but omits filenames; the reverse of the -l option.
-i	Ignores any distinctions between uppercase and lowercase letters. A good option to use when searching for a word that sometimes begins a sentence and other times occurs in the middle of a sentence.
-l	Prints filenames but omits matched lines; the reverse of the -h option. Lists each filename once only, even if the file contains more than one match.
-n	Precedes each matched line with its line number, even if the file does not contain line numbers.
-o	In 4.4BSD grep, always prints filename headers with output lines.
-s	Turns off error messages for nonexistent or unreadable files. In 4.4BSD, this option turns everything off except error messages.
-v	Inverts the search; prints all the lines that don't match *pattern*.
-w	In 4.4BSD, limits the search to whole words.

Table G.6: Options for Use with groff	
OPTION	DESCRIPTION
`-e`	Uses `eqn` as preprocessor.
`-h`	Prints help information.
`-l`	Sends the output to a printer.
`-L` *`argument`*	Passes *`argument`* to the spooler.
`-p`	Uses `pic` as preprocessor.
`-P` *`argument`*	Passes *`argument`* to the postprocessor.
`-R`	Uses `refer` as preprocessor.
`-s`	Uses `soelim` as preprocessor.
`-t`	Uses `tbl` as preprocessor.
`-T` *`device`*	Prepares output for *`device`*.
`-v`	Forces the programs run by `groff` to print their version numbers.
`-z`	Suppresses `troff` output; only error messages are printed.
`-Z`	Does not use `troff` as the postprocessor.

literal backslashes, asterisks, and other characters that you ordinarily have to escape.

- Approximate `grep`, or `agrep`, a public domain `grep` that locates lines that more or less match your specified search string.
- The Free Software Foundation's fast version of `grep`, called `egrep`.
- A version of `grep` called `rcsgrep`, which is used to search through Revision Control System (RCS) files.

grodvi

See **groff**.

groff

The Free Software Foundation's implementation of the Unix text processing commands `nroff` and `troff`. `groff` is distributed with many systems, including 4.4BSD and Linux.

▶ Syntax

The syntax to use is:

`groff [`*`options`*`][`*`filename...`*`]`

The `groff` command is the front end to the `groff` document formatting system, and it normally runs `troff` followed by the appropriate postprocessor.

▶ Options and Arguments

If you omit *`filename`* and use – instead, `groff` reads from the standard input. The options for use with `groff` are listed in Table G.6.

▶ Notes

You might encounter several other members of the `groff` family, including:

- `grodvi` converts `groff` output into TEX format.
- `grog` guesses the correct options to use with `groff`.
- `grops` is a PostScript driver for `groff`.
- `grotty` is a `tty` driver for `groff`.

See also **eqn, LATEX, nroff, pic, soelim, tbl, TEX, Texinfo, troff.**

grog

See **groff.**

grops

See **groff.**

grotty

See **groff.**

group

A collection of users; the basis for establishing file permissions.

Each file in the filesystem has a group identifier associated with it, and members of the group are given permissions to use the file, which are not available to other users. Group access permissions for files are displayed as the middle three characters of the nine-character access mode in a long `ls` listing.

In most Unix systems, you can belong to several different groups simultaneously; on older systems, you could only belong to one group at any time.

See also **chgrp, chmod, groups, newgrp.**

group ID

A number defined in the password database when a user is assigned a group number. Each group is identified by a number that defines the permissions assigned to members of the group. Sometimes abbreviated as group GID.

See also **chgrp, newgrp.**

groups

A command that lists all groups to which a user belongs. The syntax is:

```
groups [username]
```

Groups are listed in `/etc/passwd` and `/etc/groups`. With no arguments, this command lists the groups that the current user belongs to; with a *`username`*, the command lists the groups to which the *`username`* belongs.

See also **chgrp, newgrp.**

groupware

Network software designed for use by a group of people all working on the same project or using the same data.

Groupware can range from relatively simple programs designed to do one thing well, to enhanced e-mail products (such as WordPerfect Office or Banyan Intelligent Messaging Service), all the way to total operating environments, offering applications program development capabilities (such as Lotus Notes or DEC TeamLink).

See also **workflow software, workgroup.**

GUI

Abbreviation for graphical user interface, pronounced "gooey." A graphics-based interface that allows users to select files, programs, or commands by pointing to pictorial representations or icons on the screen rather than by typing long, complex commands from a command prompt.

Applications execute in windows, using a consistent set of pull-down menus, dialog boxes, and other graphical elements, such as scroll bars and icons. This consistency among interface elements is a major benefit for the user, because as soon as you learn how to use the interface in one program, you can use it in all other programs running in the same environment. You can have several windows open all at the same time, although only one window can have the focus or be active at a time.

The GUI gained popularity in the Apple Macintosh interface, which in turn was based on work done at the Xerox Palo Alto Research Center in the early 1970s. In the Unix world, the X Window system has been the basis for GUI development, leading to popular products for SCO, UnixWare, HP-UX, and other versions of Unix.

See also **Motif, Open Look, window manager, XFree86.**

gunzip

See **gzip**.

guru

A Unix expert with a reputation for being helpful to other, less knowledgeable Unix users.

See also **magic.**

gwm

The name of the X Window system generic window manager; a very flexible window manager able to emulate either the Open Look or the Motif window managers.

gzexe

A BSD command that compresses executable files in place and then automatically uncompresses them when you run them. There is a performance penalty for this convenience, and `gzexe` is most often used on systems with small hard disks.

The syntax is:

```
gzexe filename...
```

The only option is `-d`, used when you want to decompress the executable without running it.

See also **gzip**.

gzip

A set of file compression utilities from the Free Software Foundation's GNU Project, available with many systems, including 4.4BSD and Linux.

The `gzip` family has three members; `gzip` compresses the file, `gunzip` uncompresses the file, and `zcat` cats the file.

▶ Syntax

The syntax to use is:

```
gzip [options] filename...
```

The `gzip` command compresses the specified *`filename`* using a Lempel-Zif compression method, keeping the original filename and timestamp, and adds the filename extension `.gz` whenever possible, while preserving ownership modes, modification times, and so on. The original uncompressed file is removed when `gzip` completes the compression process; it is very difficult to delete files accidentally using `gzip`.

The `gunzip` command uncompresses files that were compressed using `gzip`, `zip`, `compress`, or `pack`. The compressed file is removed once the decompression process is complete.

Using `zcat` is identical to using `gunzip -c`.

▶ Options and Arguments

The options available with these utilities are listed in Table G.7.

You can use all of these options with `gzip` and `gunzip`; you can only use `-f`, `-h`, `-L`, and `-V` with `zcat`.

▶ Examples

To compress the file `allmine.doc`, use:

```
gzip allmine.doc
```

The file will be replaced by a compressed file called `allmine.doc.gz`.

To decompress this file, use:

```
gunzip allmine.doc.gz
```

The file is decompressed and restored to its former name of `allmine.doc`.

▶ Notes

The `gzip` command uses the same Lempel-Zif method used in the other familiar file-compression programs `zip` and PKZIP. The amount of compression you see depends on the original file type; ASCII text files and program source code files may show a 60 to 70 percent reduction in size. If the file is already in a compressed form, such as JPEG files, `gzip` will have little or no effect.

■ *See also* **compress, gzexe, pack**.

Table G.7: Options Available with gzip, gunzip, and zcat

OPTION	DESCRIPTION
`-a`	ASCII mode, supported on some non-Unix systems. For DOS, carriage return–linefeed pairs are converted to linefeeds when compressing a file, and the reverse translation is performed when decompressing a file.
`-c`	Leaves the original files intact, and writes the output to the standard output.
`-d`	Decompresses the specified file.
`-f`	Forces a compression or decompression even if the file has multiple links or a corresponding file already exists.
`-h`	Displays help information.
`-l`	Lists information on compressed files, including compressed size, uncompressed size, compression ratio percentage, and name of the original file.
`-L`	Displays license information and terminates.
`-n`	When compressing, saves the original filename and timestamp; when decompressing, restores the original name and timestamp.
`-q`	Turns off all warnings.
`-r`	Compresses (or uncompresses) files in the specified directories.
`-S.`*`suffix`*	Uses `.`*`suffix`*, rather than `.gz`.
`-t`	Tests the compressed file's integrity.
`-v`	Displays the version number and then terminates.
`-`*`n`*	Specifies the speed of compression, where `-1` indicates the fastest method with the least compression, and `-9` indicates the slowest compression with the most compression; the default is `-6`. This option is not available with `gunzip`.

hack

Originally, an expedient, although short-term, solution to a programming problem. The solution often bypasses some of the more traditional software-development processes. Now hack is often used to describe a well-crafted piece of work that produces just what is needed; it does not imply malicious intent to break into other people's systems for gain.

■ *See also* **hacker, kluge.**

hacker

A person who pursues knowledge of computer systems for its own sake, someone willing to "hack through" the steps of putting together a working program. More recently, in popular culture at large, the term has come to mean a person who breaks into other people's computers with malicious intent (whom programmers call a *cracker*). Many countries now treat convicted crackers in the same way that they treat conventional breaking-and-entering criminals.

■ *See also* **firewall, intruder.**

handshake

The exchange of control codes or particular characters to maintain and coordinate data flow between two devices, so that data is only transmitted when the receiving device is ready to accept the data.

Handshaking can be implemented in either hardware or software, and it occurs between a variety of devices. For example, the data flow might be from one computer to another computer or from a computer to a peripheral device, such as a modem or printer.

hang

- When a program waits for an event that never occurs, as in "the program hangs waiting for a character from the keyboard."
- Jargon used when attaching a new piece of hardware to a system, usually an external device attached by one or more cables, as in "I'm going to hang a new tape drive on the server this afternoon."

■ *See also* **deadlock, deadly embrace.**

hard-coded

A description of software written in a way that does not allow for flexibility or future expansion. For example, when program variables are placed directly in the code rather than supplied as input from the user, the entire program must be recompiled to change the value, an obvious waste of resources.

See also **hard-wired.**

hard link

A directory entry containing the filename and i-node for a file. The i-node identifies the location of the file's control information, which, in turn, defines the location of the file's contents on the hard disk. Hard links are always confined to the same filesystem; they cannot cross into another filesystem, and you cannot create a hard link to a directory.

See also **link, soft link, symbolic links.**

hard reset

A system reset made by pressing the computer's reset button or by turning the power off and then on again. A hard reset is used only when the system has crashed so badly that software solutions do not work.

See also **hang.**

hardware

All the physical electronic components of a computer system, including peripheral devices, printed circuit boards, displays, and printers. If you can stub your toe on it, it must be hardware.

hardware-dependent

The requirement that a specific hardware component be present for a program to work. Hardware-dependent software is often difficult to move or port to another computer system. Also known as *machine-dependent.*

See also **hardware-independent.**

hardware-independent

The ability to produce similar results in a wide variety of environments, without requiring the presence of specific hardware. The PostScript page description language is an example of hardware independence; PostScript is used by many printer manufacturers. Also known as machine-independent.

See also **hardware-dependent.**

hardware interrupt

An interrupt or request for service generated by a hardware device, such as a keystroke from the keyboard or a tick from the clock. Because the processor may receive several such signals simultaneously, hardware interrupts are usually assigned a priority level and processed according to that priority.

See also **interrupt handler.**

hard-wired

Describes a system designed in a way that does not allow for flexibility or future expansion. May also refer to a device that is connected directly to an individual computer system, such as a printer.

See also **hard-coded.**

hash

A built-in Bourne shell command that reports the path associated with the previous command or with commands running in the background.

Used with no arguments, `hash` displays `hits` (the number of times that the shell has previously run the command) and `cost` (a relative indicator of the amount of work needed to find the command); the output looks like this:

```
hash
hits        cost        command
0           1            /bin/eric
```

hashing

The process of creating or rebuilding a hash table by recalculating the search index code assigned to each piece of data in the table.

In the C shell, hashing involves creating a table of commands in your path and then searching that table (rather than the full path) when you ask for a command to be executed. Without hashing, every directory specified in your path must be searched on every new command.

hash table

A method of representing data so that it can be found again very quickly.

A hash table assigns a special index code to each piece of data, and specially designed software uses this code to locate the data, rather than repeating what might be a lengthy search each time the data is requested.

The C shell uses a hash table to locate commands quickly, and the `rehash` command is used to rebuild this hash table after you add a new command. Hash tables are also used by many database products.

hashstat

A built-in C shell command that displays statistics indicating the hash tables' success rate at locating commands via the `path` variable.

hd

An SCO command used to display files in character, decimal, hexadecimal, and octal formats.

▶ Syntax

The syntax for this command is:

hd [-*format*][*options*]
➥[*filename*]

▶ Options and Arguments

The -format argument specifies what information is displayed and in what form. This information is provided in Table H.1.

The default is `-abx -A`, for addresses and bytes displayed in hexadecimal. The default also specifies that characters are printed.

If no *filename* is specified, `hd` reads from the standard input. The options listed in Table H.2 are available with the `hd` command.

Table H.1: hd *format* Flags

FLAGS	DESCRIPTION
acbwlA	Specifiers for addresses, characters, bytes, words (2 bytes), long words (4 bytes), and ASCII.
xdo	Specifiers for hexadecimal, decimal, or octal.
t	Specifies that the text file be printed with each line numbered.

Table H.2: Options Available with hd

OPTION	DESCRIPTION
-n *count*	Specifies the number of bytes to process.
-s *offset*	Specifies the offset from the beginning of the file where you want printing to start, as a decimal number, a hexadecimal number (prefaced by `0x`), or an octal number (prefaced by `0`). *offset* can be followed by an optional multiplier: `w` for words (2 bytes), `l` for long words (4 bytes), `b` for half kilobytes (512 bytes), or `k` for kilobytes (1024 bytes).

▶ Examples

To list the contents of the file `allmine.txt` in octal, starting 100 bytes (in decimal) into the file, use:

```
hd -Ao -s 100 allmine.txt
```

■ *See also* **cat, hexdump, more, od, pg.**

HDB

■ *See* **HoneyDanBer UUCP.**

head

A command that prints the first few lines of one or more text files.

The `head` command sends the beginning of a file (or the standard input) to the screen (or to the standard output). The syntax to use is:

```
head -n filename...
```

where `-n` specifies the number of lines of the file you want to display; if you don't specify a value, `head` prints the first 10 lines.

If you specify multiple files, each file is separated by the header:

```
==> filename <==
```

where *`filename`* is the name of the file.

There are no options for the `head` command.

■ *See also* **cat, less, more, pg, tail.**

header

Information placed at the beginning of a file. In an e-mail message, the header contains information about the message, including the sender and recipient, and the route the message took as it was being delivered. In an archive file, the header is a block that contains information describing the contents of the archive.

header file

A source code file that contains definitions of macros and variables. C language header files traditionally have the filename extension `.h`. Also known as an *include file.*

heartbeat

An Ethernet signal quality test function. This signal proves that a component is working and is capable of detecting collisions. Also known as *signal quality error* or *SQE.*

hello

An SCO command that sends a message to a terminal.

The syntax is:

```
hello user [tty]
```

When you first start `hello`, the following message is displayed:

```
Message from sending-system!
➥ sender's-name sender's-tty
```

Communication continues between the two terminals until one user terminates the session with Ctrl-C or Del, and `hello` outputs:

```
(end of message)
```

help

■ *See* **SCCS.**

hexadecimal

Abbreviated hex. The base 16 numbering system that uses the digits 0 to 9, followed by the letters A to F, which are equivalent to the decimal numbers 10 through 15.

Hex is a convenient way to represent the binary numbers computers use internally, because it fits neatly into the 8-bit byte. All the sixteen hex digits 0 to F can be represented in four bits, and two hex digits (one digit for each set of four bits) can be stored in a single byte. This means that one byte can contain any one of 256 different hex numbers, from 0 through FF.

■ *See also* **binary, decimal, octal.**

Table H.3: Options to Use with hexdump	
OPTION	DESCRIPTION
`-b`	Displays the input offset in hexadecimal, followed by the data displayed in one-byte octal.
`-c`	Displays the input offset in hexadecimal, followed by the data displayed in hexadecimal.
`-d`	Displays the input offset in hexadecimal, followed by the data displayed in unsigned decimal.
`-e` *`format-string`*	Specifies a *`format-string`* for displaying the data.
`-f` *`format-file`*	Specifies a *`format-file`* for displaying the data.
`-n` *`length`*	Displays only *`length`* bytes of data from the file.
`-o`	Displays the input offset in hexadecimal, followed by the data displayed in two-byte octal.
`-s` *`offset`*	Skips *`offset`* from the beginning of the file; by default a decimal number, a leading `0x` is interpreted as a hexadecimal number, and a leading `0` as an octal number. You can also specify *`offset`* as `b` (multiples of 512 bytes), `k` (multiples of 1024 bytes), or `m` (multiples of 1,048,576 bytes).
`-v`	Forces the display of all data.
`-x`	Displays the input offset in hexadecimal, followed by the data displayed in two-byte hexadecimal.

hexdump

A BSD filter command that displays a file in a specified format—as ASCII, decimal, hexadecimal, or octal.

▶ Syntax

The syntax for `hexdump` is as follows:

`hexdump [`*`options`*`]`*`filename...`*

The `hexdump` command reads from the specified file or files, or if none are specified, it reads from the standard input.

▶ Options and Arguments

Several options are available with `hexdump`, as Table H.3 shows.

■ *See also* **`cat`, `hd`, `more`, `od`, `pg`.**

hidden character

Any nonprinting character that performs a special function, such as backspace or erase.

hidden file

■ *See* **dot file.**

hierarchical file structure

The organizational system used by Unix to keep track of files and directories on a disk.

The Unix file structure resembles an inverted tree, with the root directory (/) as the starting point. Files and directories are contained within directories that branch off from the root. A directory is usually devoted to files relating to a specific subject or purpose and may or may not contain subdirectories.

One of the strengths of the Unix filesystem is its ability to adapt to the needs of different users. In a standard Unix system, users start with one directory, and within this directory, they can make as many subdirectories as they like, expanding the structure to any level according to their own needs. This hierarchical structure has been adopted in many other operating systems, including the Macintosh, DOS, Windows, and OS/2.

■ *See also* **current working directory, directory tree, home directory.**

`histchars`

A C shell environment variable that contains the two characters used to replace `!` and ^, respectively, in history substitution commands.

history

A mechanism found in the C and Korn shells, which allows you to modify and re-execute recent commands without having to retype them.

All your previously executed commands are stored in the history file, even your mistakes, and the shell lets you access this list so that you can repeat commands or re-issue them in a modified form. Each command is assigned a number, beginning with 1, so you can refer to command number 5 or command number 20, and so on.

By default, the shell saves the last 128 commands; if you want to save more, increase the value of the `HISTSIZE` variable in the Korn shell or the `history` variable in the C shell.

■ *See also* **`fc`, `history`, history substitution.**

`history`

A built-in C shell command that lists recent keyboard commands. The syntax is:

```
history [options]
```

The options available with this command are listed in Table H.4.

`history` also is a Korn shell command that lists the last 16 commands; `history` is a Korn shell alias for `fc -l`.

■ *See also* **`fc`, history, `.history`, history file.**

Table H.4: Options to Use with `history`

OPTION	DESCRIPTION
`-h`	Prints the history list without event numbers.
`-r`	Prints the history list in reverse order, oldest commands first.
n	Displays only the last *n* commands, rather than the number set by the shell variable.

`.history`

The name of the history file, which is the file that holds all the commands entered by a user while that user was logged on to the system; the file is deleted or cleared when the user logs off at the end of a session.

■ *See also* **history.**

history file

A file that holds all the commands entered by a user while that user was logged on to the system; the file is deleted or cleared when the user logs off at the end of the session. The history file is called `.history`.

■ *See also* **history.**

history substitution

A feature of the shell that lets you edit and then re-issue commands from the history file without having to retype them every time. For example, in the C shell, you can select historical commands using `!n`, where *n* is the number of the command; you can also use `!!` to select the last command.

HISTSIZE

A Korn shell environment variable that specifies how many past commands are accessible; the default is 128 commands.

■ *See also* **history.**

holy wars

In the Unix community, a fundamentally unresolvable computer-related argument in which the participants spend most of their time trying to establish often wildly personal choices as carefully thought out and deeply considered technical evaluations. Examples might include AT&T Unix versus BSD, the C programming language against Pascal (or any other programming language), the `emacs` editor versus `vi`, big endian systems versus little endian systems, and so on.

home

The initial cursor location at the top left corner of the screen.

home

A C shell variable containing the full path of your home directory. The ~ character is a shorthand notation for the name of your home directory.

■ *See also* **HOME.**

HOME

A Bourne shell and Korn shell variable containing the full path of your home directory. The tilde character (~) is a shorthand notation for the name of your home directory.

/home

An SVR4 root directory that contains user home directories and files.

home directory

A directory that contains the files for a specific user ID. The name of your home directory is kept in the `passwd` file, and when you log in, your current directory is always set to be your home directory. The home directory is usually the starting point for your own directory structure, which you can make as austere or as complex as you like.

As a shortcut, you can use the tilde character (~) as a symbol for the name of your home directory. The complete path for your home directory is stored in the `home` or `HOME` variable, depending on which shell you use.

■ *See also* **cd, pwd.**

home page

On the Internet World Wide Web, an initial starting page. A home page may be prepared by an individual, a nonprofit group, or a corporation and is a convenient jumping-off point to other Web pages or Internet resources.

■ *See also* **HTML, HTTP, SGML, URL.**

HoneyDanBer UUCP

A version of UUCP developed by Peter Honeyman, David Nowitz, and Brian D. Redman, which replaced the original AT&T version. Also known as the *Basic Networking Utilities*, sometimes abbreviated *BNU*.

hop

A single link between two computer systems that a mail message must cross on its way to its destination. A message may have to pass over many hops to reach its ultimate destination; if it must pass between five computer systems, then it is said to have taken four hops to reach its destination.

horizontal application

Any application software that is broad in scope and not designed for use in one specific industry or setting. Word processing software falls into this category, while software specifically designed to manage a medical practice does not.

■ *See also* **vertical application.**

host

The central or controlling computer in a networked or distributed processing environment, providing services that other computers or terminals can access via the network.

A large system accessible on the Internet is also known as a host. Sometimes known as a *host system* or a *host computer.*

hostid

A command that prints the hexadecimal ID number for the host system. The command is found in `/usr/uch/hostid`.

■ *See also* **`hostname`.**

hostname

A command that sets or prints the name of the current host. The syntax is:

```
hostname [newhost]
```

where ***`newhost`*** is the new name to use for the host; you must be the superuser to change this name.

■ *See also* **`hostid`.**

HotJava

An interactive Internet World Wide Web browser from Sun Microsystems.

HotJava is the player for programs written in Java, a programming language designed to create small executable programs that can be downloaded quickly and can run in a small amount of memory.

Using Java, you can create interactive World Wide Web sites that can download programs to other computers. These programs can display animation or video and perform other tasks; they can also cooperate with other programs on the Web. You can find out more by pointing your Web browser at `http://java.sun.com`.

■ *See also* **HTML, HTTP, Java, SGML.**

hp

An SCO command that handles special functions found on Hewlett-Packard's 2640 series of terminals so that accurate `nroff` output can be displayed on them.

HP-UX

A version of Unix for Hewlett-Packard that runs on HP computers. HP-UX includes BSD extensions, including the networking commands, the Korn shell, and a version of **`emacs`**. VUE (Visual User Environment) is HP's GUI, with individual workspaces for different tasks, drag-and-drop functions, a text editor, color icon editor, as well as other productivity tools.

HP-UX also includes SAM (System Administration Manager) for common administration tasks, such as adding new users, installing and configuring peripherals, managing processes and scheduling jobs. Diskless computers, either clients or servers, can boot from the server and can support locally mounted filesystems, so that each client has access to its own data files as well as being able to share files with others.

HTML

Abbreviation for Hypertext Markup Language. A standard hypertext language used to create World Wide Web pages and other hypertext documents.

When you access an HTML document, you see a mixture of text, graphics, and links to other documents or to other Internet resources. When you select a link, the related document opens automatically, no matter where that document is located. Hypertext documents often have the filename extension `.html` or `.html`.

HTML has been vital in the development of the World Wide Web; however, the functions that it can provide via the Web browser are becoming restrictive. This has led to other developments such as Java, which can provide 3D interactive applications.

See also **home page, HTTP, SGML, URL.**

HTTP

Abbreviation for Hypertext Transfer Protocol. The protocol used to manage the links between one hypertext document and another.

HTTP is the mechanism that opens the related document when you select a hypertext link, no matter where that related document happens to be.

See also **home page, HTML, SGML, URL.**

100VG-AnyLAN

A term applied to the IEEE 802.12 standard, originally developed by Hewlett-Packard and supported by Novell, Microsoft, AT&T, and others.

100VG-AnyLAN modifies the existing Ethernet standard to allow speeds of 10 or 100 megabits per second (Mbps) and uses the demand priority access method.

100VG-AnyLAN runs over four-pair Category 3, 4, and 5 unshielded twisted pair wiring, and up to five repeaters are allowed between end nodes.

See also **Fast Ethernet, 10/100.**

Hurd

A project from the Free Software Foundation (FSF) to develop and distribute a free version of Unix for many different hardware platforms. Still in the early stages of development, Hurd (or sometimes HURD) is considered to be a collection of all the GNU software, compilers, editors, utilities, as well as the operating system.

hwconfig

An SCO command that lists configuration information contained in `/usr/adm/hwconfig`.

▶ Syntax

The syntax for this command is:

```
hwconfig [options]
```

Information is displayed in the following columns:

- `magic_char`
- `device_name`
- `base+finish`
- `vec`
- `dma`
- `rest`

where `magic_char` is a percent sign (`%`), `device_name` is the name of the device driver, `base+finish` are the starting and ending addresses of the driver working space, `vec` is the interrupt vector number (in decimal), `dma` is the number of the DMA channel, and `rest` is a list of *`parameter=value`* pairs. `rest` may also be empty.

▶ Options and Arguments

Options for use with `hwconfig` are listed in Table H.5.

H

Table H.5: Options for Use with hwconfig	
Option	**Description**
`-c`	Checks for device conflicts.
`-f` *`filename`*	Uses information from *`filename`* rather than from `/usr/adm/hwconfig`.
`-h`	Uses long format with headers.
`-l`	Uses long format, the default setting.
`-n`	Forces the output of the device name.
`param`	Shows values for *`param`*. Valid system *`param`* include `name`, `base`, `offset`, `vec`, `dma`, `unit`, `type`, `nports`, `hds`, `cyls`, `secs`, and `drvr`.
`param=value`	Shows information from the entry where *`param`* is equal to *`value`*.
`-q`	Quiet mode; when used with `-c` displays conflicts only.

hypermedia

A term used to describe nonsequential applications that have interactive hypertext linkages between different multimedia elements of graphics, sound, text, animation, and video.

If an application relies heavily on text-based information, it is known as hypertext; however, if full-motion video, animation, graphics, and sound are used, it is considered to be hypermedia.

hypertext

A method of presenting information so that it can be viewed by the user in a non-sequential way, regardless of how the topics were originally organized.

Hypertext was designed to make a computer respond to the nonlinear way that humans think and access information—by association, rather than the linear organization of film, books, and speech.

In a hypertext application such as the World Wide Web, you can browse through the information with considerable flexibility, choosing to follow a new path each time you access the information. When you click on a highlighted word, you activate a link to another hypertext document, which may be located on the same Internet host or can be on a completely different system thousands of miles away. These links depend on the care that the document originator used when assembling the document; unfortunately, many links turn into dead ends.

■ *See also* **home page, HTML, HTTP, SGML.**

Hypertext Markup Language

■ *See* **HTML.**

Hypertext Transfer Protocol

■ *See* **HTTP.**

IAB

Abbreviation for Internet Architecture Board, the coordinating committee for the management of the Internet.

Astonishing as it sounds, no single person runs the Internet, no single organization pays all the costs, and there is no Internet Company or Internet Corporation. The development and determination of the direction of the Internet is performed by the IAB and two subcommittees:

- **Internet Engineering Task Force (IETF):** Specifies protocols and recommends standards.
- **Internet Research Task Force (IRTF):** Researches new technologies and makes subsequent recommendations to the IETF.

Previously, the abbreviation IAB stood for Internet Activities Board.

See also **RFC.**

icon

In a graphical user interface (GUI), a small screen image representing a specific element that the user can manipulate in some way. You select the icon by clicking a mouse or other pointing device.

An icon may represent an application program, a document, a hard disk drive, or several programs collected together in a group icon. Some well-designed icons are very easy to understand, but in programs that use icons to represent every function, they can get more than a little obscure.

See also **X Window.**

Icon

A general-purpose high-level language with a large number of string-processing functions, developed by Ralph Griswold at the University of Arizona. Icon has a C-like syntax and is available as an interpreter and also as a compiler.

You can get Icon by anonymous `ftp` from `ftp.cs.arizona.edu`; look in the directory `/icon`. You can send your Icon-related questions to `icon-projects@cs.arizona.edu`.

See also **`perl`**.

I

iconv

A command used to convert a file from one character set into another. The syntax is:

```
iconv -f char-set1
➥ -t char-set2 filename
```

where *filename* is converted from *char-set1* to *char-set2*; if there is no equivalent for a character in *char-set2*, that character is translated into an underscore (_). You will find supported conversions listed in `/usr/lib/conv`.

id

A command that displays a user's login name, ID, and group ID. When used with the `-a` option, the `id` command lists all the groups to which you belong.

■ *See also* **finger**, **users**, **w**, **who**.

ident

■ *See* **RCS.**

if

A shell programming command used to provide a conditional branching statement.

An `if` statement in the C shell is used in a different way from an `if` statement in the Bourne and Korn shells:

- In the C shell, you don't need brackets around the test part of the statement.
- The C shell uses == for an equality statement rather than a single = as in the Bourne and Korn shells.
- In the C shell, a semicolon must follow `then`.
- The C shell uses `endif` to terminate the `if` statement rather than `fi`.

■ *See also* **elif**, **else**.

IFS

A Bourne and Korn shell variable used to specify the characters used as the shell's default field separators, which are the space, tab, and newline.

ignoreeof

A C shell environment variable that ignores end-of-file (EOF) characters typed from the keyboard and so prevents an accidental logout.

image copy

A term used to describe an exact, byte-for-byte copy of a file.

imake

An extension to the `make` software development command used when compiling source files into an application.

Creating makefiles by hand can be a long complex process; `imake` automates the process from a template of `cpp` macro functions, reading an input file called `Imakefile` and then converting the two into a makefile. `imake` provides an excellent solution to the long-standing problem of how to maintain a set of hierarchical makefiles when an application's source files exist in several different directories.

inactive window

In an interface capable of displaying multiple windows on the screen, all open windows except the currently active window, the window that contains the cursor. If you click on an inactive window with the cursor, it becomes the active window.

include file

A source code file that contains code needed by several different program modules. Also called a *header file*. These files are normally given characteristic filename extensions such as `.h`, `.hpp`, `.hxx`, and so on.

incremental backup

A backup of a hard disk that consists of only those files created or modified since the last backup was performed.

incremental search

In **emacs**, a search that starts as soon as you type the first letter of the search string and is modified as you enter subsequent letters.

indent

A BSD software development command used to reformat C language source code. This a complex utility, with more options than the **ls** command; there are in fact over 50 different options.

■ *See also* **cb, cc.**

index node

■ *See* **i-node.**

indxbib

A command used to create an inverted index file for bibliographic databases.

▶ Syntax

The syntax for this command is:

indxbib [*options*][*filename...*]

If you don't specify an output filename, the index file is stored as /usr/share/dict/papers/Ind.i.

▶ Options and Arguments

The options available with **indxbib** are listed in Table I.1.

■ *See also* **invert, lkbib, lookbib, refer.**

Table I.1: Options Available with indxbib

OPTION	DESCRIPTION
-c*filename*	Reads a list of common words from *filename*.
-d*directory*	Specifies that the index is stored in *directory*.
-f*filename*	Reads *filename* as the input file.
-h*n*	Specifies the size of the hash table; the default is 997.
-i*string*	Doesn't index the fields specified in *string*.
-k*n*	Uses *n* keys per input record; the default is 100.
-l*n*	Throws away keys shorter than *n*; the default is 3.
-n*n*	Throws away the *n* most common words; the default is 100.
-o*basename*	Specifies the base filename for the output file.
-t*n*	Truncates key to *n*; the default is 6.
-v	Prints the program version number.
-w	Indexes entire files; each file is a separate record.

`info`

The command used to start the InfoExplorer application on an IBM Unix system. InfoExplorer is a large hypertext help system with both an ASCII terminal and an X Window system interface.

inheritance

In object-oriented programming, the ability of one class of objects to pass on properties to another, lower class. Inheritance can even include features of the parent's environment, such as open files; and multiple inheritance lets you create a new class with properties of more than one previously defined class.

See also **encapsulation, polymorphism.**

`init`

The first process created by the Unix kernel as the system boots up; an abbreviation for initialize. The `init` process always has the process ID number (PID) of 1. `init` creates all subsequent processes and additional `init` processes for new users as they log on to the system. `init` also controls the level or state in which Unix runs, as Table I.2 shows.

On BSD systems, `init` starts the system but then relies on instructions generated by the `kill` command to change run levels or to shut down the system.

Table I.2: Unix System States

STATE	DESCRIPTION
0	Shutdown state; used before turning the computer off.
1	Administrative state; starts Unix so that the filesystem is available to the system administrator but not to other users. Used when troubleshooting corrupted files or changing hardware configuration information.
2	Multiuser state; the normal operating mode, in which filesystems are mounted and available to all users.
3	Remote File Sharing (RFS) state; used to start the RFS, and to mount and share resources over the network.
5	Firmware state; used to run special commands and system diagnostics.
6	Stop and reboot state; used to restart in the mode specified by the `initdefault` entry in `/etc/inittab`.
S or s	Single-user state; used by the system administrator for maintenance. Only a limited number of kernel processes are running, and only the root filesystem is available.

initialization file

A file executed by a program as it starts running, before it begins its main purpose. Most initialization files are found in your home directory, and so you can customize them to your exact needs. For example, the `emacs` editor loads the contents of the `.emacs` file as it starts up; `vi` loads `.exrc`, and so on.

See also **dot file.**

initialization string

A string of characters sent to your terminal as you log on to configure it to your specific needs.

i-node

Pronounced "eye-node"; the abbreviation for information node, sometimes written *inode*. A data structure on the disk that describes a file. Each directory entry associates a filename with an i-node; although a single file may have several filenames (one for each link), a file has only one i-node. Within a filesystem, the number of i-nodes (and therefore the number of files) is defined when the filesystem is first initialized.

An i-node contains all the information Unix needs to be able to access the file, including the file's length, the times that the file was last accessed and modified, the time that the i-node was last modified, owner and group ID information, access permissions, the number of links to the file, the type of the file, and the disk addresses of the data blocks that contain the actual file itself.

■ *See also* **i-number.**

i-node table

A list of all the i-nodes in a filesystem. Within the i-node table, each i-node is known by a number, the i-number or index number. If a file is defined by i-node #300, it is said to have an i-number of 300.

input

Any information that is sent to a program from the keyboard, a file, another process, or from a hardware device.

■ *See also* **standard input.**

input mode

A mode in which a program expects its input to be ASCII characters or text, rather than commands.

■ *See also* **command mode.**

input redirection

The process of reassigning the shell's standard input to a file rather than a terminal. To change the standard input to a file, use the less than symbol (<) on the command line, as in the following example, which sends a message to three users of the `mail` program:

```
mail tim al jill < message
```

■ *See also* **redirection, standard error, standard output.**

input/output

Abbreviated I/O. The transfer of data between the computer and its peripheral devices, disk drives, terminals, and printers.

input/output bound

Abbreviated I/O bound. A condition in which the speed of operation of the input/output port limits the speed of program execution. Getting the data into and out of the computer is more time-consuming than actually processing that same data.

■ *See also* **computation bound.**

`install`

A utility often used in makefiles to update files and install binaries.

`/install`

An SVR4 root directory containing the utilities for installing or removing binary software packages. These utilities are only available to the system administrator.

installing a hard disk

Installing an additional hard disk is a task for the system administrator and requires the following steps:

1. Physically installing the hard disk in the computer.
2. If the disk is not preformatted, you must format the disk using a command such as `format` in Solaris or `fmthard` in SVR4.

3. Make sure that the disk contains the appropriate system files. These files specify the major and minor device numbers of the device, giving the kernel both the device location and a pointer to the device driver. Systems such as SCO UNIX automate these steps; Solaris users can use the **makedev** script.
4. Create a filesystem for the disk using the SVR4 and Linux **mkfs** command or the Solaris and BSD command **newfs**.

These steps get extremely Unix system–specific, and it is very difficult to provide more precise information than the general steps outlined above; see your system documentation for more information.

On computers based on Intel microprocessors, **fdisk** is the program used to create or modify hard disk partitions, and you can usually create a partition with one system's **fdisk** that can be accessed by a different operating system. As an example, the Linux **fdisk** command can create a DOS partition, and Linux itself can use a partition made by DOS.

Several PC operating systems also provide system programs known as boot managers that act as hard disk traffic cops; when you first turn on the computer, the boot manager asks you to choose which of several operating systems installed on the hard disk you want to boot today. This sounds good in theory, but in practice, it can be very difficult to get the process to work smoothly.

instruction set

The set of machine-language instructions that a processor recognizes and can execute.

An instruction set for a reduced instruction set computer (RISC) may only contain a few dozen instructions, while a complex instruction set computer (CISC) may be able to recognize several hundred instructions.

integer

A built-in Bourne shell and Korn shell command used to specify integer variables.

interactive

Any program that allows a dialog with the user to take place; most modern programs are interactive.

Interactive UNIX

A version of Unix from Sun Microsystems based on AT&T's System V Release 3.2 kernel.

■ *See also* **Solaris.**

interface

That point where a connection is made between two different parts of a system, such as between two hardware devices, between a user and a program or operating system, or between two application programs.

In hardware, an interface describes the logical and physical connections used, as in the serial interface standard RS-232-C, and is often considered to be synonymous with the term *port.*

A user interface consists of all the means by which a program communicates with the user, including a command line, menus, dialog boxes, online help systems, and so on. User interfaces can be classified as character-based, menu-driven, or graphical.

Software interfaces are application programming interfaces (APIs); the codes and messages used by programs to communicate behind the scenes.

■ *See also* **GUI, interface standard, X Window.**

interface standard

Any standard way of connecting two devices or elements that have different functions. Many different interface standards are used for personal computers. These include SCSI, Integrated Drive Electronics (IDE), the Enhanced Small Device Interface (ESDI) for hard disks, RS-232-C and the Centronics parallel interface for serial devices and parallel printers, and the ISO/OSI model for local area network (LAN) communications over a network.

internals

A slang expression used to describe the essential elements of a subject. If a job advertisement asks for "knowledge of Unix internals," the advertiser wants a kernel expert, rather than an applications programmer.

International Organization for Standardization

■ *See* **ISO.**

internet

Abbreviation for internetwork. Two or more networks using different networking protocols, usually connected by means of a router. Users on an internetwork can access the resources of all the connected networks as though they were all local.

Internet

The world's largest computer network, consisting of more than two million computers supporting over twenty million users in hundreds of different countries. The Internet is growing at a phenomenal rate—between 10 and 15 percent per month—so any size estimates are quickly out-of-date.

The Internet was originally established to meet the research needs of the U.S. defense industry, but it has grown into a huge global network serving universities, academic researchers, commercial interests, and government agencies, both in the U.S. and overseas. The Internet uses TCP/IP protocols, and many of the Internet hosts run Unix.

Internet use falls into several major areas, including:

- **E-mail:** Well over 80 percent of the people who use the Internet on a regular basis use it for e-mail. You can send e-mail to recipients in over 150 countries on the Internet, as well as to subscribers of the commercial online services such as America Online, CompuServe, Delphi, GEnie, and Prodigy.
- **IRC chat:** A service that connects large numbers of users in real-time group discussions.
- **Mailing lists:** Private discussion groups accessed by e-mail.
- **USENET newsgroups:** Larger public discussion groups that focus on a specific subject. Posts and threads in USENET newsgroups are accessed with a newsreader.
- **Gopher:** A modern menu-based system used to browse Internet resources that hides the underlying mechanical aspects of the Internet.
- **World Wide Web:** A hypertext-based system used for finding and accessing Internet resources, the World Wide Web is one of the fastest growing and most exciting of all the Internet applications.
- **`ftp`:** A client/server application used to transfer files to and from Internet host computers. FTP is also the name of the file transfer protocol used to accomplish this task.
- **`telnet`:** A client/server application used to log in to Internet computers and run applications. A version of this program called tn3270 is used to access IBM rather than Unix Internet host computers.

The sheer volume of information available through the Internet is staggering; however, due to the fact that the Internet is a casual grouping of many networks, there is often no easy way to determine the location of specific information. Other problem areas include network security, privacy, copyright protection, and authentication.

Internet access can be via a permanent network connection or by dial-up through one of the many service providers.

■ *See also* **Gopherspace, IAB, Internet address, `ftp`, PPP, SLIP, `telnet`, USENET.**

Internet abbreviations and acronyms

Like any culture, the Internet world has developed a whole language of abbreviations, acronyms, and slang terms. Table I.3 lists some of the common terms you are likely to encounter in USENET newsgroups or in your e-mail.

■ *See also* **emoticons, newbie, smiley.**

Table I.3: Internet Abbreviations and Acronyms

ABBREVIATION/ ACRONYM	DESCRIPTION
aTdHvAaNkCsE	thanks in advance
AWTTW	a word to the wise
BRB	be right back
BTW	by the way
CU	see you
FAQ	frequently asked question
FAQL	frequently asked question list
FOAF	friend of a friend
F2F	face to face
FWIW	for what it's worth
FYI	for your information
GR&D	grinning, running, and ducking
IMHO	in my (often not very) humble opinion; used to indicate a genuine opinion and to imply sarcasm
IWBNI	it would be nice if
IYFEG	insert your favorite ethnic group
LOL	laughing out loud
MEGO	my eyes glaze over
MOTAS	member of the appropriate sex
MOTOS	member of the opposite sex
MOSS	member of the same sex
MUD	multiuser dungeon, a group of role-playing games based on "Dungeon and Dragons"
Ob-	obligatory, as in ob-joke
OTOH	on the other hand
PD	public domain
PITA	pain in the ass
PMFJI	pardon me for jumping in
RL	real life
ROTFL	rolling on the floor laughing
RTFM	read the (expletive deleted) manual
SO	significant other
TIA	thanks in advance
TTFN	ta ta for now
WRT	with respect to
YMMV	your mileage may vary
$0.02	my two cents worth

Internet address

An absolute address on the Internet. An Internet address takes the form `someone@abc.def.xyz`, where `someone` is a user's account name or part of his or her name, `@abc` is the network computer of the user, and `def` is the name of the host organization. The last three letters `xyz` denote the kind of institution the user belongs to: in the U.S. you will find **edu** for educational, `com` for commercial, `gov` for a branch of the government, `mil` for the military, `org` for non-profit organizations, and `net` for Internet administrative organizations. In other countries, other identifiers are used, and outside the U.S., you will also find an identifier for the specific country. For example, `ca` for Canada or `uk` for Great Britain.

▪ *See also* **bang path, domain, domain address, dotted decimal, IP address.**

Internet file types

The Internet offers many opportunities for downloading files from a huge number of Internet hosts. These files may have been generated on different computer systems, and so before you download a file, it is important that you understand the type of file you are dealing with. Many files are compressed to minimize the time the file takes to download. Table I.4 lists many of the common file types you may encounter on your Internet travels.

▪ *See also* **compress, gzip, pack, tar, uudecode, uuencode.**

Internet Worm

A well-known incident in November 1988 in which a worm or self-propagating program spread through the Internet, severely loading the system and crashing thousands of Internet host computers.

The creator of the program, Robert Morris, was the first person tried under the Federal Computer Fraud and Abuses Act of 1986 and was sentenced to three year's probation, 400 hours of community service, and a $10,000 fine. The sentence was appealed to the U.S. Supreme Court, which upheld the conviction in 1991.

▪ *See also* **cracker, hacker, intruder.**

interpreter

A programming language translator that converts high-level program source code into machine language statements one line at a time.

Unlike a compiler, which must translate the whole program before execution can start, an interpreter translates and then executes each line one at a time; this usually means that an interpreted program runs more slowly than a compiled program.

BASIC was often an interpreted language, although recent releases of the language have used a compiler instead, and C, C++, and Pascal are always compiled.

▪ *See also* **command interpreter.**

interprocess communications

Abbreviated IPC. A term that describes all the methods used to pass information between two programs running on the same computer or between two programs running on a network, including pipes, shared memory, message queues, sockets, and semaphores.

▪ *See also* **ipcrm, ipcs.**

interrupt

A signal to the processor generated by a device under its control (such as the system clock) or by software, which interrupts normal processing.

An interrupt indicates that an event requiring the processor's attention has occurred, causing the processor to suspend and save its current activity, block out any lower priority interrupts, and then branch to an interrupt handler or service routine. This service routine processes the interrupt, whether it was generated by the system clock, a keystroke, or a mouse click; and when it's complete, returns control to the original suspended process.

Table I.4: Internet and Unix File Types

FILENAME EXTENSION	DESCRIPTION
`tar`	A tape archive file created by the `tar` utility.
`Z`	A file created by the `compress` utility. You must use the `uncompress` utility to restore the file before you can use it.
`tar.Z`	A compressed tape archive file.
`z`	A compressed file created using `pack`. You must use `unpack` to restore the file before you can use it.
`ls-lR.Z`	A file listing sorted by time, showing the most recent files first. The file is also compressed.
`ls-ltR.Z`	A file listing sorted into alphabetical order; the file is also compressed.
`ZIP`	A compressed file created using PKZIP that must be uncompressed with PKUNZIP before you can use it.
`gz`	A Unix file compressed by the GNU `gzip` utility. This file must be decompressed before you can use it.
`HQX`	A compressed Macintosh file.
`SIT`	A Macintosh file compressed by StuffIt.
`TIF` or `TIFF`	A graphics file in TIFF format.
`GIF`	A graphics file in GIF format.
`JPG` or `JPEG`	A graphics file in JPEG format.
`MPG` or `MPEG`	A video file in MPEG format.
`TXT`	A text file.
`1`	An `nroff` source file.
`ps`	A PostScript file ready for printing on a PostScript printer.
`uue`	A `uuencoded` file. You must use `uudecode` before you can use the file.
`uue.z`	Compressed `uuencoded` file.
`shar`	A USENET newsgroup archive file created by the `shar` program.
`shar.Z`	Compressed shar file.

interrupt handler

Software in the Unix kernel that manages and processes system interrupts. The actual task performed by the interrupt handler depends on the nature of the interrupt itself. Also known as an *interrupt service routine*.

intruder

An unauthorized user of a computer system, usually a person with malicious intent.

■ *See also* **cracker, firewall, hacker, sniffer.**

i-number

Contraction of index number. A number used to identify an i-node; part of the file control information that Unix keeps in an i-node. Sometimes written as *inumber*.

■ *See also* **i-node table.**

invert

A BSD command that creates an inverted index intended for use with `bib`.

▶ Syntax

The syntax for this command is:

```
invert [options]filename...
```

▶ Options and Arguments

Table I.5 lists the options you can use with `invert`.

■ *See also* **`bib`, `lookup`.**

Table I.5: Options to Use with `invert`

OPTION	DESCRIPTION
`-c` *`filename`*	Specifies that the words listed in *`filename`* will not be used as keys.
`-k` *`i`*	Specifies the maximum number of keys per record; the default is 100.
`-l` *`i`*	Specifies the maximum length of keys; the default is 6.
`-p` *`filename`*	Specifies *`filename`* as the name of the output file.
`-s`	Turns off statistics, silent mode.
`-%`*`string`*	Ignores lines that begin with % followed by any characters defined in *`string`*.

invisible character

Any nonprinting character such as backspace, erase, or any of the control characters.

invisible file

Any file whose name begins with a period. Such files are known as invisible files because the `ls` command does not list them in the normal file and directory display, although you can see them when you use the `-a` option.

It is also worth noting that the shell will not expand an asterisk (*) to match the names of invisible files.

■ *See also* **dot file.**

IP

Abbreviation for Internet Protocol. The TCP/IP session-layer protocol that regulates packet forwarding by tracking Internet addresses, routing outgoing messages, and recognizing incoming messages.

■ *See also* **TCP, UDP.**

IP address

A unique 32-bit number used to identify an Internet host. An IP address is usually written (in decimal) as 190.45.122.88 and can be divided into two parts. The network address is made up from the higher-order bits of the address, and the host address comprises the rest.

In the example above, 190.45 is the network address and 122.88 is the host address; or to put it another way, host number 122.88 is on the network 190.45. In addition, the host part of the address can be divided further to allow for a subnetwork address. In the example, host 45 is on subnetwork 190 of network 122.88.

■ *See also* **dotted decimal, Internet address.**

ipcrm

A command used by the system administrator to clean up after a program has failed to de-allocate space for message queues, semaphores, or shared memory.

▶ Syntax

The syntax for the `ipcrm` command is as follows:

```
ipcrm [options]
```

▶ Options and Arguments

Table I.6 lists the options you can use with `ipcrm`.

■ *See also* **`ipcs`**.

ipcs

A command that prints interprocess communications (IPC) information.

▶ Syntax

The syntax to use with this command is:

```
ipcs [options]
```

This command provides information on waiting processes, shared memory segments, and message queues.

▶ Options and Arguments

You can use the options listed in Table I.7 with the `ipcs` command. When you use the `-m`, `-q`, or `-s` options, only information about the specific interprocess communications facility is given; otherwise, information is displayed about all three.

The default display produced when you use this command with no options lists the IPC type, associated ID, key, mode, owner, and group.

■ *See also* **`ipcrm`**.

IPX

Abbreviation for Internet Packet Exchange. Part of Novell NetWare's protocol stack, used to transfer data between the server and workstations on the network. IPX packets are encapsulated and carried by the packets used in Ethernet and the frames used in Token Ring networks.

■ *See also* **SPX.**

IRC

Abbreviation for Internet Relay Chat. An Internet client/server application that allows large groups of users to communicate with each other interactively, developed by Jarkko Oikarinen in Finland. Specific channels are devoted to one particular topic, from the sacred to the profane, and topics come and go regularly as interest levels change. Each channel has its own name, usually prefaced by the pound sign (#), as in #hottub.

When you join a channel, you can see what others have already typed; when you type a line and press the Enter key, your text is seen by everyone else. Table I.8 lists a summary of basic IRC commands.

Most but not all the conversations are in English. If somebody asks you for your password during an IRC session, don't be tempted to give it; somebody is trying to trick you into giving away important information about your system that he or she might be able to use against it.

Table I.6: Options to Use with icprm

OPTION	DESCRIPTION
`-m` *shmemid*	Removes the shared memory identifier *shmemid*.
`-M` *shmemkey*	Removes the shared memory identifier created with the key *shmemkey*.
`-q` *msgqid*	Removes the message queue identifier *msgqid*.
`-Q` *msgkey*	Removes the message queue identifier created with the key *msgkey*.
`-s` *semid*	Removes the semaphore identifier *semid*.
`-S` *semkey*	Removes the semaphore identifier created with the key *semkey*.

Table I.7: Options for Use with ipcs

OPTION	DESCRIPTION
`-a`	Combines all the display options; equivalent to `-bcopt`.
`-b`	Displays the maximum number of message bytes, segment sizes, and number of semaphores allowed.
`-c`	Displays login name and group.
`-C` *filename*	Reads status from the specified *filename*, rather than from `/dev/kmem`.
`-m`	Reports only on active shared memory segments.
`-N` *list*	Uses the arguments contained in *list*.
`-o`	Displays outstanding usage.
`-p`	Displays process numbers.
`-q`	Reports only on active message queues.
`-s`	Reports only on semaphores.
`-t`	Displays time information.

Table I.8: Summary of Basic IRC Commands

COMMAND	DESCRIPTION
`/flush`	Discards remaining output for the current command.
`/help`	Displays a list of all IRC commands.
`/help` *`command`*	Displays help information about the specified *`command`*.
`/help intro`	Displays an introduction to IRC.
`/help newuser`	Displays information for new users.
`/join` *`channel`*	Lets you join the specified *`channel`*.
`/leave` *`channel`*	Lets you leave the specified *`channel`*.
`/list`	Lists information about all channels.
`/list` *`channel`*	Lists information about a specific *`channel`*.
`/mode * +pi`	Makes the current channel completely private.
`/msg` *`nicknames text`*	Sends a private message, *`text`*, to *`nicknames`*.
`/msg ,` *`text`*	Sends a message back to the last person who sent a message to you.
`/msg .` *`text`*	Sends a message to the last person you sent a message to.
`/nick`	Displays your own nickname.
`/nick` *`nickname`*	Changes your current nickname to *`nickname`*.
`/query`	Stops sending private messages.
`/set novice off`	Allows more advanced options, such as joining multiple channels.
`/who` *`channel`*	Shows who is on the specified *`channel`*.
`/who` *`nickname`*	Displays information about the specified person.
`/who *`	Shows who is joined to the current channel.
`/whois` *`nickname`*	Displays complete information about the person.
`/whois *`	Displays all information about everyone.

ismpx

An SVR4 command that tests whether the standard input is running under layers software. Output is either `yes` (exit status 0) if the terminal is running under layers, or `no` (exit status 1) if it is not. The main use for this command is in shell scripts that use a windowing terminal or require a certain screen size.

■ *See also* **`jterm`**.

ISO

Abbreviation for International Organization for Standardization. An international standard-making body, based in Geneva, that establishes global standards for communications and information exchange. ANSI is the United States member of ISO.

The seven-layer International Organization for Standardization's Open Systems Interconnection (ISO/OSI) model for computer-to-computer communications is one of the ISO's most widely accepted recommendations.

■ *See also* **ISO/OSI model.**

ISO/OSI model

Abbreviation for International Organization for Standardization/Open System Interconnection model. A networking reference model defined by the ISO that divides computer-to-computer communications into seven connected layers. Such layers are known as a protocol stack.

Each successively higher layer builds on the functions of the layers below, as follows:

- **Application layer 7:** The highest level of the model. It defines the way that applications interact with the network, including database management, e-mail, and terminal-emulation programs.
- **Presentation layer 6:** Defines the way that data is formatted, presented, converted, and encoded.
- **Session layer 5:** Coordinates communications and maintains the session for as long as it is needed, performing security, logging, and administrative functions.
- **Transport layer 4:** Defines protocols for structuring messages and supervises the validity of the transmission by performing some error checking.
- **Network layer 3:** Defines protocols for data routing to ensure that the information arrives at the correct destination node.
- **Data-link layer 2:** Validates the integrity of the flow of data from one node to another by synchronizing blocks of data and controlling the flow of data.
- **Physical layer 1:** Defines the mechanism for communicating with the transmission medium and interface hardware.

isochronous

A communications mode used to transmit real-time data over a preallocated bandwidth, allowing time-synchronized transmissions with very little delay.

Isochronous service is needed for real-time data such as synchronized voice and video and multimedia presentations, in which delays in delivery would be unacceptable and very easy to detect with the human eye or ear.

ISV

Abbreviation for Independent Software Vendor. A company that develops and sells computer software but is completely independent from the makers of the hardware on which the software runs.

jabber

A continuous and meaningless transmission generated by a network device, often the result of a user error or a hardware malfunction on a network interface card.

Jargon File

Originally a collection of hacker jargon available on USENET and other networks. First published on paper in *CoEvolution Quarterly* in 1981, the contents of the Jargon File were revised by Guy Steele and others and published by Harper & Row in book form as *The Hacker's Dictionary* in 1983. This book, now out of print, is often referred to as *Steele-1983*.

In 1993, the Jargon File was revised and updated by Eric Raymond with assistance from Guy Steele, and published by MIT Press as *The New Hacker's Dictionary*.

This book contains definitions such as "plokta" (press lots of keys to abort) and "wave a dead chicken" (to look for a problem in one place when you really know it is elsewhere). Very funny indeed.

Java

A programming language developed by Sun Microsystems, designed specifically for use with interactive World Wide Web applications. Java technology has been licensed by Microsoft, IBM, Abode Systems, Oracle, Borland, and many other companies developing World Wide Web applications.

■ *See also* **HotJava, World Wide Web.**

job

A command or group of commands that exists as a single unit. A job can be moved from the foreground to the background (and vice versa) on any Unix system with job control. It is easy to use the terms *process*, *program*, and *job* as though they are interchangeable, but strictly speaking, *job* refers to one command line. That command line may be very complex and consists of several processes (for example, you can use pipes and redirection to link several processes together on a single command line), but as far as Unix is concerned, it is still just one job.

Table J.1: Bourne and Korn Shell Job Control Commands	
COMMAND	DESCRIPTION
`bg`	Places a job in the background.
`fg`	Places a job in the foreground.
`jobs`	Lists all the active jobs.
`kill`	Terminates a job.
`stop`	Suspends a background job.
`stty tostop`	Stops a background job if it attempts to write to the terminal.
`suspend`	Suspends a foreground job.
`wait`	Waits for a background job to finish.
`Ctrl-Z`	Suspends a foreground job.

job control

A Unix mechanism that manages jobs, allowing them to be started, stopped, killed, and moved between the background and foreground. Job control lets you run several jobs at the same time, with different priorities, and was first included in the 4.0BSD Unix releases from the University of California, Berkeley.

The Bourne shell and Korn shell provide several commands for job control as Table J.1 shows.

There are other ways in Unix that you can run several jobs at a time. The X Window system allows you to run multiple processes, running each one in its own window. Certain versions of Unix, such as Linux and UnixWare, support virtual terminals that you can switch between, each acting as an independent connection to your computer but sharing the same physical keyboard and screen.

See also **ampersand, bg, Ctrl-Z, `fg`, `jobs`, `jsh`, `kill`.**

job number

Those shells with job control assign a number to every command that is stopped or is running in the background.

Job numbers are easier to use than PIDs, if only because they are smaller, usually between 1 and 10, and you can use them with several Unix utilities such as `at` and `atrm`.

See also **ampersand, bg, Ctrl-Z, `fg`, `jobs`, `kill`.**

`jobs`

- A built-in C shell command that lists all running or stopped jobs that were started with the current instance of the C shell. If you use the `-l` option (the only option available), this command also includes the process IDs (PIDs).
- A built-in Korn shell command that lists all running and stopped jobs or lists those jobs specified by the *`jobID`* command-line argument. This command recognizes three options: `-l`, which lists the process IDs (PIDs); `-n,` which displays jobs that

have stopped or whose status has changed in some way; and `-p`, which lists just the process group IDs.

■ *See also* **bg**, **fg**, **kill**, **ps**.

joe

A text editor based on `emacs`.

■ *See also* **jove**, **pico**.

join

A command that extracts common lines from two sorted files.

▶ Syntax

The syntax for the `join` command is as follows:

```
join [options] filename1
➥ filename2
```

Table J.2: Options to Use with join

OPTION	DESCRIPTION
`-a` *n*	Lists unmatched lines from file *n* or from both if *n* is omitted.
`-e` *string*	Replaces any empty field with *string*.
`-j`*n m*	Joins the two files on the *m*th field of file *n*; if *n* is not specified, the files are joined on the *m*th field of both files.
`-o`*n*.*m*	Specifies the fields to output from each file for each line with matching join fields, where *n* specifies the file number and *m* specifies the field number.
`-t`*char*	Uses character *char* as a field separator for input and output.

One line of output is created for each line in the two files that match, based on the information you specify.

▶ Options and Arguments

This command joins the common lines found in *filename1* and *filename2*; if you don't specify *filename1*, `join` reads from the standard input. You can use the options listed in Table J.2 with `join`.

In the options shown in Table J.2, the argument *n* can be either 1 or 2, referring to *filename1* or to *filename2*. In `join`, all field numbering starts at 1 rather than at zero.

■ *See also* **comm**, **sort**, **uniq**.

Joint Photographic Expert Group

■ *See* **JPEG**.

jot

A BSD command used to print sequential or random data, usually numbers, one per line.

▶ Syntax

The syntax for this command is:

```
jot [options][repetitions
➥[begin[end[increment]]]]
```

`jot` is used to print increasing, decreasing, or random numbers, or specific words, a specified number of times.

▶ Options and Arguments

In the syntax given above, *repetitions* defines the number of data items; *begin*, the starting point or lower bound; *end*, the ending point or upper bound; and *increment*, the step size, or for random data, the seed. The default values are 100, 1, 100, and 1, respectively, and when random numbers are used, the seed is based on the time of day. You can also use the options listed in Table J.3 with `jot`.

J

Table J.3: Options Available with `jot`

OPTION	DESCRIPTION
-b *word*	Prints *word*.
-c	Prints character data.
-n	Suppresses newlines.
-p *precision*	Specifies how many digits of data to print.
-r	Specifies random data.
-s *string*	Separates data by *string*.
-w *word*	Prints *word* with the generated data appended to it. You can specify octal, hexadecimal, exponential, ASCII, zero padded, or right justified formats by using the appropriate C language `printf` convention inside *word*.

jove

A popular text editor, based on `emacs` written by Jonathon Payne. The name is an abbreviation for Jonathon's Own Version of `emacs`.

JPEG

Abbreviated JPEG, pronounced "jay-peg." An image-compression standard and file format developed as a joint effort of CCITT and ISO.

Since image files can often be very large, JPEG was developed to define a set of compression methods for high-quality still images such as photographs, single video frames, or scanned pictures; compressed images occupy much less memory or disk space. JPEG does not work very well when compressing line art, text documents, or vector graphics.

JPEG uses lossy compression methods that result in some loss of original data; when you decompress the image, you don't get exactly the same image you originally compressed, although JPEG was specifically designed to discard information not easily perceived by the human eye. We can detect small changes in brightness much easier than we can see small changes in color. JPEG can store 24-bit color images in up to 16 million colors; by comparison, files in GIF (Graphics Interchange Format) format can only store up to 256 colors. JPEG can achieve a compression ratio as high as 20 to 1, and files usually have the filename extension `.jpg` or `.jpeg`.

■ *See also* **data compression, lossless compression, MPEG.**

jsh

In some versions of SVR4 you can use the Bourne shell with job control features by executing `jsh` rather than `sh`. The job control features are similar to those found in the C shell and Korn shell. Jobs are tracked by number, starting at 1 for the first job.

■ *See also* **bg, fg, kill.**

jterm

A command that resets a windowing terminal after a program changes the attributes of the layer. This command is only used with `layers`.

■ *See also* **ismpx, jwin.**

Jughead

An Internet search mechanism used to construct an index of high-level Gopher menus. Once a search is complete, you interact with the Jughead-built menu in the same way that you use a Gopher menu.

Jughead was written by Rhett Jones at the University of Utah and released in 1993. The program is designed to search a relatively limited area of Gopherspace, rather than all Gopher servers on the Internet. To use Jughead, someone must already have set up a Jughead server that maintains a database of menu items within the area of Gopherspace that you are interested in searching.

■ *See also* **Veronica.**

jukebox

A high-capacity storage device that uses an autochanger mechanism to mount or dismount optical disks automatically. A jukebox typically contains one to four disks and a mechanism that picks up disks from a bay and loads them into the drives as they are needed.

Julian date

A method of representing the date often used in computer systems. The first digit, from 0 to 9, represents the year, and the remaining three digits represent the day of the year, counting from January 1st. In some systems, two digits are used to represent the year, from 00 to 99.

■ *See also* **epoch.**

`jwin`

A command used with `layers` that prints the size of the current window, in bytes.

■ *See also* **`ismpx`**, **`jterm`**.

K

■ *See* **kilo-**.

K&R

A reference to the hugely influential book, *The C Programming Language*, written by Brian Kernighan and Dennis Ritchie and published in 1978. The book is sometimes referred to as *Kernighan & Ritchie* or *The C Bible* or, simply, *The White Book* because of the white cover used on the original edition. Dennis Ritchie was the original designer of the C language, and the version of the C language described in an appendix to this book is often called *K&R C*.

Kb

■ *See* **kilobit.**

KB

■ *See* **kilobyte.**

Kbit

■ *See* **kilobit.**

Kbps

■ *See* **kilobits per second.**

Kbyte

■ *See* **kilobyte.**

`kdestroy`

A BSD command that destroys Kerberos tickets by writing zeros to the file that contains them and then removing the file. If `kdestroy` cannot wipe out the ticket file, it beeps your terminal.

This command has two options; `-f` runs `kdestroy` without displaying any status messages, and `-q` turns off terminal beeping.

■ *See also* **Kerberos**, **`kinit`**, **`klist`**, **`register`**.

Table K.1: Options for Use with kdump	
OPTION	DESCRIPTION
`-d`	Displays all information in decimal.
`-f filename`	Displays *filename* rather than the default file, `ktrace.out`.
`-l`	Loops trace reading.
`-m maxdata`	Displays up to *maxdata* when decoding input/output.
`-n`	Turns off certain translations.
`-R`	Displays relative timestamp.
`-T`	Displays absolute timestamp.
`-t cnis`	Sets tracepoints; *c* traces system calls, *n* traces namei translations, *i* traces input/output, *s* traces signal processing.

kdump

A BSD command that displays kernel trace information in the file `ktrace.out`. This file is created by `ktrace`.

▶ Syntax

The syntax to use for this command is:

```
kdump [options]
```

▶ Options and Arguments

You can use the options listed in Table K.1 with `kdump`.

■ *See also* **ktrace**.

Kerberos

A network security system developed as part of Project Athena at MIT. Kerberos is used to authenticate a user who is asking to use a particular network service.

Kerberos can be used to control the initial connection to a server or can be used to authenticate every single request and message passed between the client and the server. It grants tickets to a client to allow the use of a specific service and is secure even on a non-secure network.

Kerberos takes the following precautions:

- Passwords are never sent unencrypted over the network. This means that network snoopers cannot capture passwords easily.
- All Kerberos messages are timestamped so that they cannot be captured and then replayed later; Kerberos does not accept old messages.
- When you request access to a service—to access a file server, for example—Kerberos gives you a "ticket," which is valid for access to the file server but not valid for any other service. When you try to connect to the server, you send your ticket with the request. Once the server knows who you are, the server decides whether to grant you access. Tickets also expire, and if your session lasts longer than the predefined time limit, you will have to re-authenticate yourself to Kerberos to get a new ticket.

Kerberos is named after the three-headed dog Cerberus, who guards the gates of the underworld in Greek mythology.

You can obtain the files for Kerberos by anonymous `ftp` from `athena-dist.mit.edu`, and you can get the source code, documentation, and articles on Kerberos from MIT Software Center:

W32-300
20 Carlton Street
Cambridge, MA 02139 U.S.A.

See also **kdestroy, kinit, klist, ksrvtgt, register.**

Kermit

A file transfer protocol developed at Columbia University in 1980 by Frank das Cruz and placed in the public domain, Kermit is used to transfer files between PCs and mainframe computers over standard telephone lines.

Data is transmitted in variable-length blocks up to 96 characters long, and each block is checked for transmission errors. Kermit detects transmission errors and initiates repeat transmissions automatically.

See also **C-Kermit, RZSZ, Xmodem, Ymodem, Zmodem.**

kernel

The central, memory resident part of the Unix operating system that allocates resources, manages memory, and controls processes.

The design strategy behind Unix has always been to keep the kernel as small as possible (when compared to other similar operating systems) and to add functions as small, separate utility programs.

See also **Mach, rebuilding the kernel, shell, system call.**

kernel address space

That part of memory used to store data and programs that can only be accessed by the kernel.

key binding

In `emacs`, the connection between a specific key on the keyboard and the command that it invokes.

kernel description file

A standard file describing devices attached to the system and the different kernel settings. Only the superuser can look at or change this information.

keylogin

A command that prompts the user for a login password and then uses it to decrypt the user's secret key. This key can then be used by secure network services. If the user is always prompted for a password when he or she logs in to the system, there is no need for this command to be used.

See also **chkey, keylogout.**

keylogout

A command that revokes the secret key used in secure network services. If used with the `-f` option, `keylogout` can remove the root key that, if invoked on a file server, can compromise network security.

See also **chkey, keylogin.**

keyword

Those words in a programming language that have a special reserved meaning and so cannot be used as variable names.

Most languages have keywords for conditional statements (`if`, `while`), for defining data and functions (`int`, `float`, `static`, `extern`), and for input and output (`scanf`, `printf`, `putchar`, `getchar`). Some specialized languages also have keywords relating to their particular function.

Table K.2: Common Unix Signals

SIGNAL	DESCRIPTION
`-1`	Hangup, sent when you log out or hang up the modem
`-2`	Interrupt, sent when you type Ctrl-C
`-3`	Quit, sent when you type Ctrl-\
`-4`	Illegal instruction
`-5`	Trace trap
`-6`	IOT instruction
`-7`	EMT instruction
`-8`	Floating point exception
`-9`	Kill, stops the process immediately
`-10`	Bus error
`-11`	Segment violation, indicates you have tried to access memory illegally
`-12`	Bad argument to a system call
`-13`	Write to a pipe, but no reading process
`-14`	Alarm clock
`-15`	Default software termination
`-16` and `-17`	User-defined
`-18`	Child process died
`-19`	Restart after a power failure

kill

A command used to terminate one or more process IDs (PIDs). This command is similar to the `kill` command built into the C and Korn shells.

▶ Syntax

The syntax for the `kill` command is:

`kill [`*`options`*`]`*`IDs`*

The `kill` command terminates a process, as defined by its PID, by sending it a signal. A signal is a kind of message, and `kill` usually sends a signal `-15` to a process to request that the process shut down; if the process is harder to terminate, a `-9` may be needed instead. A process may ignore a `-15`, but it cannot ignore a `-9`. Some of the more commonly used signals are listed in Table K.2.

▶ Options and Arguments

You can use two options with `kill`; both are listed in Table K.3.

Table K.3: Options for Use with `kill`

OPTION	DESCRIPTION
`-l`	Lists all the signal names.
`-signal`	Specifies either the signal number (determined by `ps -f`) or the signal name (from `kill -l`).

Only the superuser can kill other users' processes. To determine the appropriate PID number, use the `ps` command first.

▶ Examples

To kill process ID 100, use:

`kill 100`

The default signal is `-15`. If this doesn't work, try:

`kill -1 100`

As a last resort, use:

`kill -9 100`

Although a `-9` is a sure bet, it is always better to try `-15` or `-1` first. These signals are caught by the application and give it a chance to halt in an orderly fashion, closing files as it does so. When you use `-9`, the application must terminate immediately, and you will inevitably be left with some cleaning up to do.

▶ Notes

If you are logged on as the superuser and you execute the command:

```
kill -9 0
```

you will bring down the system.

■ *See also* **ps**.

kill character

A character that when typed, deletes the contents of the current line so you can retype your command or entry. The default is Ctrl-U or the at sign (`@`) but can be changed by the user. Also called the *line erase* character. This character has nothing to do with, and should not be confused with, sending a kill signal to a process.

kill file

A file maintained by your USENET newsreader that excludes articles that match certain criteria, such as subject, author, or other header lines. The articles identified in this way are abandoned and not presented for reading in the normal way; it is as though they are not there at all. They do not appear in thread or subject lists.

Using a kill file is the proper defense against those subjects or people that you find give offense, and many newsreaders let you kill at two different levels, one within a particular newsgroup, and one for all newsgroups. This means that you can ignore one person in a specific newsgroup and one subject in all newsgroups.

■ *See also* **flame, flame war.**

kill signal

A signal sent to a process to terminate it immediately.

Unlike other Unix signals, a kill signal (number 9, also known as SIGKILL) cannot be intercepted or ignored.

Sending a kill signal to a process should only be used as a last resort when all else fails; because the process cannot ignore the signal, it cannot close open files and terminate in a tidy fashion, and there is a very good chance that you will lose data.

■ *See also* **kill**.

kilo-

A prefix indicating 1000 in the metric system. Because computing is based on powers of 2, kilo usually means 2^{10}, or 1024. To differentiate between these two uses, a lowercase *k* indicates 1000 (as in kHz), and an uppercase *K* indicates 1024 (as in KB).

■ *See also* **mega-.**

kilobit

Abbreviated Kb or Kbit. 1024 bits (binary digits).

■ *See also* **gigabit, megabit.**

kilobits per second

Abbreviated Kbps. The number of bits, or binary digits, transmitted every second, measured in multiples of 1024 bits per second. Used as an indicator of communications transmission rates.

■ *See also* **megabits per second.**

kilobyte

Abbreviated K, KB, or Kbyte. 1024 bytes.

■ *See also* **exabyte, gigabyte, megabyte, petabyte, terabyte.**

kinit

A BSD command used to log in to the Kerberos authentication and authorization system.

▶ Syntax

The syntax for this command is:

```
kinit [options]
```

You only need to use **kinit** after your initial Kerberos tickets have expired.

▶ Options and Arguments

When you use **kinit** without options, you are prompted for your username and Kerberos password, and **kinit** then attempts to authenticate your login with the Kerberos server. You can use the options listed in Table K.4 with **kinit**.

■ *See also* **Kerberos, kdestroy, klist, ksrvtgt, register.**

Table K.4: Options for Use with kinit

OPTION	DESCRIPTION
`-i`	Prompts for a Kerberos instance.
`-l`	Prompts for a ticket lifetime in minutes; this value must be between 5 and 1275 minutes.
`-r`	Prompts for the name of a Kerberos realm; not fully implemented.
`-v`	Prints the name of the ticket file used, along with various status messages.

klist

A BSD command that lists currently held Kerberos tickets.

▶ Syntax

The syntax for this command is as follows:

```
klist [options]
```

klist prints the name of the tickets file, as well as the principal names of all the Kerberos tickets held by the user along with the issue and expiration dates for each authenticator.

▶ Options and Arguments

You can use the options listed in Table K.5 with **klist**.

■ *See also* **Kerberos, kdestroy, kinit, ksrvtgt, register.**

Table K.5: Options to Use with klist

OPTION	DESCRIPTION
`-t`	Checks for unexpired tickets in the ticket file. The exit status is set to 0 if one is present; otherwise, the exit status is 1. No other output is displayed.
`-file` *name*	Specifies *name* as the ticket file.
`-srvtab`	The ticket file is treated as a key file, and the names of the keys it contains are printed.

kluge

Pronounced "klooj." A program that doesn't work as well as it should, is not carefully designed, and is not well written. A kluge may also be a program that works but for all the wrong reasons, and only under very specific, highly unrealistic conditions.

■ *See also* **hack.**

knowbot

On the Internet, an experimental software robotic librarian or independent information retrieval tool.

As the knowbot roams the Internet performing its designated tasks, it sends reports back to the user, and then, when its task is complete, the program pauses to wait for new instructions or automatically deletes itself.

Korn shell

Pronounced "corn shell." The Korn shell is a very popular upward-compatible extension of the original Unix shell (the Bourne shell), written by David Korn of AT&T Bell Labs and first released as part of System V in 1982. Major improvements were made in 1986, 1988, and 1993. The Korn shell is the default shell on many Unix systems, particularly those based on System V, including UnixWare and many others.

Because the Korn shell is an upward-compatible extension of the Bourne shell, everything that works with the Bourne shell also works in the Korn shell; however, the Korn shell can do a lot more, and adds:

- Interactive editing of the command line with either `emacs` or `vi`.
- Better function definitions providing local variables and the ability to create recursive functions.
- Extensive pattern matching for filenames, similar to regular expressions.

Several features were also adapted from the C shell, including:

- Command history for retrieval and reuse of previously typed commands.
- Job control, and the mechanism for moving jobs between the background and the foreground.
- Aliases for abbreviated command names.
- The tilde (~) used as shorthand for the name of the home directory.

▶ Startup Files

The Korn shell program, started by the `ksh` command, first executes the statements in the environment file `.kshrc` in your home directory. If you invoked `ksh` as your login shell, then the commands found in `/etc/profile` and `/HOME/.profile` are executed first, when you log in, just before the environment file is processed.

The default prompt for the Korn shell is the dollar sign (**$**).

▶ Using Commands

The Korn shell allows you to use and group commands on the command line in several different ways, which are shown in Table K.6.

▶ Filename Metacharacters

You can use any of the patterns listed in Table K.7 to generate filenames.

▶ Redirection

When you execute a command, the shell opens three files known as the standard input, the standard output, and the standard error. By default, standard input is the keyboard, and standard output and standard error are the terminal or screen. Redirection is the process of directing input to or output from a different file from that used normally.

In simple redirection, you can change the input source or output destination in any of the ways listed in Table K.8.

The shell assigns a file descriptor to each standard file, using 0 for standard input, 1 for standard output, and 2 for standard error; it may also use higher numbers, starting at 3 for any other files required to complete the process. You can use the file descriptors listed in Table K.9 in redirection.

In multiple redirection, you can use the file descriptors listed in Table K.10.

Don't use a space between the redirection symbol and a file descriptor; in the other cases, spacing is less strict, and you can space characters as you wish.

▶ Quoting

Quoting disables the special meaning of a character and allows you to use it literally. The characters listed in Table K.11 have special meaning in the Korn shell.

▶ Korn Shell Options

You can customize your shell with the shell options listed in Table K.12. These options are like on/off switches; when you use the `set` command to turn on an option, you tell it to act in a certain way, and when you unset an option, it stops. To display all current shell options and their settings, use:

```
set -o
```

To turn an option on, use:

```
set -o option
```

and to turn an option off, use:

```
set +o option
```

Not all of the options listed in Table K.12 are available in all versions of the Korn shell; your list may be slightly different.

▶ Built-in Shell Variables

The Korn shell automatically sets built-in variables, and they are often used in shell scripts. In Table K.13, which lists the built-in shell variables, the dollar sign character (`$`) is not part of the variable name, although the variable is always referred to in this way.

▶ Other Shell Variables

The shell variables described in this section are not set by the shell but are usually set by commands in your `.profile` file, where you can configure them to your exact needs. Use the following form to set them:

```
$ variable=value
```

Table K.14 lists the Korn shell variables.

▶ Built-in Commands

The Korn shell offers a rich set of built-in commands, as shown in Table K.15.

▶ Command History

The Korn shell lets you change and re-enter previous commands without having to retype them, even commands from a previous session. The shell saves everything you type (including your mistakes) into the history file, giving each command a number starting at 1; this means that you can refer to command 6 or command 126, using this number. By default the shell stores the last 128 commands you typed, but by changing the value of the `HISTSIZE` variable, you can change that number if you wish. The Korn shell also stores all lines of a

Table K.6: Using Korn Shell Commands

COMMAND	DESCRIPTION
cmd &	Executes *cmd* in the background.
cmd1 ; *cmd2*	Executes *cmd1* and *cmd2* consecutively, with the semicolon acting as a command separator.
(*cmd1* ; *cmd2*)	Creates a subshell to execute *cmd1* and *cmd2* as a group.
cmd1 | *cmd2*	Creates a pipe and uses the output from *cmd1* as input to *cmd2*.
cmd1 \`*cmd2*\`	Performs command substitution; uses the output from *cmd2* as arguments to *cmd1*.
cmd1 $(*cmd2*)	Command substitution; nesting of commands is allowed.
cmd1 && *cmd2*	Executes *cmd1*, and if *cmd1* completes successfully, then executes *cmd2*.
cmd1 || *cmd2*	Executes either *cmd1* or if it fails, executes *cmd2*.
{ *cmd1* ; *cmd2* }	Executes commands in the current shell.

Table K.7: Korn Shell Filename Metacharacters	
METACHARACTER	DESCRIPTION
`*`	Matches any string or zero or more characters; for example, `w*n` matches `wn`, `win`, `won`, `when`, `worn`, and many other filenames.
`?`	Matches any single character; for example, `myfile.?` matches `myfile._`, `myfile.1`, `myfile.a`, and so on.
`[abc...]`	Matches any single character from the list, and you can use a hyphen to indicate a range, as in `a-z,0-9`, and so on.
`[!abc...]`	Matches any single character not on the list, and you can use a hyphen to indicate a range.
`?(pattern)`	Matches zero or one instance of *pattern*.
`*(pattern)`	Matches zero or more instance of *pattern*.
`+(pattern)`	Matches one or more instance of *pattern*.
`@(pattern)`	Matches just one instance of *pattern*.
`!(pattern)`	Matches strings that don't contain *pattern*.
`~`	Home directory of the current user.
`~name`	Home directory of the user specified by *name*.
`~+`	Current working directory.
`~-`	Previous working directory.

Table K.8: Simple Redirection in the Korn Shell	
COMMAND	DESCRIPTION
cmd > *filename*	Sends output from *cmd* to *filename*, overwriting the file if it already exists.
cmd >> *filename*	Appends output from *cmd* to *filename*.
cmd < *filename*	Takes input for *cmd* from *filename*.
cmd << *text*	Reads standard input as far as a line identical to *text*.

Table K.9: Redirection Using File Descriptors in the Bourne Shell	
FILE DESCRIPTOR	DESCRIPTION
cmd >&*n*	Sends output from *cmd* to file descriptor *n*.
cmd *m*>&*n*	Same as above, except that output that would normally go to the file descriptor *m* is sent to file descriptor *n* instead.
cmd >&-	Closes standard output.
cmd <&*n*	Takes input for *cmd* from file descriptor *n*.
cmd *m*<&*n*	Same as above, except that output that would normally have come from the file descriptor *m* comes from the file descriptor *n* instead.
cmd <&-	Closes standard input.

Table K.10: Multiple Redirection in the Korn Shell	
FILE DESCRIPTOR	DESCRIPTION
cmd 2>*filename*	Sends standard error to *filename* while standard out remains the screen.
cmd > *filename* 2>&1	Sends both standard error and standard output to *filename*.
(*cmd* > *filename1*) 2>*filename2*	Sends standard output to *filename1* and standard error to *filename2*.
cmd | tee *filenames*	Sends output from *cmd* to standard output and also to *filenames*.

Table K.11: Quoting in the Korn Shell	
CHARACTER	DESCRIPTION
;	Command separator.
&	Runs a command in the background.
( )	Command grouping.
|	Creates a pipe.
*? [ ] !	Filename metacharacters.
< > & |	Redirection symbols.
" " ' ' \	Used when quoting other characters. Anything placed between the double quotes is interpreted symbolically; anything placed between the single quotes is interpreted literally, and the backslash is used to quote a single character.

Table K.12: Korn Shell Options

OPTION	DESCRIPTION
allexport	Sets the export attribute for each shell variable as it is assigned a value.
bgnice	Runs all background jobs at a lower priority.
emacs	Uses the emacs built-in editor for command-line and history editing.
errexit	Executes the ERR trap after a command fails with a non-zero exit status.
gmacs	Uses the gmacs built-in editor for command-line and history editing.
ignoreeof	Does not exit when you type an EOF (Ctrl-D); when this option is set, you must use exit.
keyword	Uses Bourne shell syntax for assignments on the command line.
markdirs	Adds a / character to directory names created using wildcard expansion.
monitor	Runs background jobs in a separate process group; the default on all systems with job control.
noclobber	Does not allow redirection to overwrite an existing file.
noexec	Reads commands and checks their syntax, but does not execute them.
noglob	Turns off expansion of filenames.
nolog	Does not store function definitions in the history file.
nounset	Treats unset variable names as errors.
physical	Makes the built-in cd and pwd commands use physical mode; they will not track symbolic links.
privileged	Disables $HOME/.profile, and uses /etc/suid_profile instead.
protected	The old version of the privileged setting.
trackall	Tracks all aliases.
verbose	Displays each command before running it.
vi	Uses the vi built-in editor for command-line and history editing.
viraw	Like vi but uses character input rather than line input.
xtrace	Turns on trace debugging.

K

Table K.13: Built-in Shell Variables	
VARIABLE	DESCRIPTION
`$#`	Contains the number of arguments on the command line.
`$?`	Contains the return code for the last command executed.
`$$`	Contains the PID of the current process.
`$!`	Contains the PID of the most recent background process.
`$-`	Displays the options currently in effect for `sh`.
`$0`	The first word on the command line; the command name.
`${n}`	Individual positional parameters on the command line specified by *n*.
`$*`	All the arguments on the command line, quoted as a single string ("`$1 $2 $3`…").
`"$@"`	All the arguments on the command line, quoted as individual strings ("`$1`" "`$2`" "`$3`…").
`$_`	A temporary variable; stores the pathname of the script being executed, the last argument of the previous command, or the name of the `MAIL` file during `mail` checks.
`$ERRNO`	Error number of the most recent system call, listed in `/etc/include/sys/errno.h`.
`$LINENO`	Current line number in the current shell script or function.
`$OLDPWD`	The name of the previous working directory, the directory before the most recent `cd` command.
`$OPTARG`	The name of the last option processed by `getopts`.
`$OPTIND`	The numerical index of the option that `getopts` processes next, the index of `$OPTARG`.
`$PPID`	The PID number of this shell's parent.
`$PWD`	The current working directory.
`$RANDOM[=n]`	Generates a new random number with each reference, beginning with *n*, if specified.
`$REPLY`	The default reply used by `select` and `read`.
`$SECONDS[=n]`	The number of elapsed seconds since this shell was started; if *n* is specified, number of seconds since the shell started plus the value *n*.

multiline command, whereas the C shell does not; it only stores the first line.

You can modify commands in your history file by using one of the two built-in editors, `emacs` or `vi`, or by using the `fc` command. When you use one of the editors, you use the normal editing commands to find and then revise a command from the history file, you then press Return to execute the command. The `vi` editor starts in input mode; remember to press the Escape key before you type a `vi` command.

Two options in the `fc` command are very handy; use `fc -l` to list commands and `fc -e` to edit them. You can also use the `r` command (really an alias for `fc -e-`) to re-execute the previous command.

▶ Arrays and Arithmetic Expressions

The Korn shell supports a wide range of arithmetic expressions, including integer arithmetic and array manipulation. Some later versions of the Korn shell also support floating point as well as integer arithmetic.

The arithmetic operators used in the Korn shell are those used by the C programming language, and they are most often used in combination with the `let` command.

▶ Coprocesses

The Korn shell supports a feature called a *coprocess*, which lets you start a process in the background that can communicate directly with the parent shell. You invoke a coprocess by ending the command line with `|&`.

There are restrictions on coprocesses; they must be filters and must process their input line by line, rather than processing several lines at the same time. When you start a coprocess, it is connected to the current shell by a two-way pipe. You can use `read -p` to read its standard input or `print -p` to write to its standard output. You can also use *`command`* `<&p` to take input for *`command`* from the coprocess and *`command`* `>&p` to send the output from *`command`* to a coprocess.

▶ Notes

The Korn shell is a huge, complex topic and has been the subject of many excellent books and articles over the years. To make sure you get the best out of the Korn shell, consult the reference material that comes with your system or seek out a book that deals exclusively with `ksh`.

■ *See also* **`csh`, C shell family, Bash, Bourne shell, Bourne shell family, `ksh`, `sh`, Tcsh, Unix shell, Unix shells, Zsh.**

Table K.14: Korn Shell Variables

VARIABLE	DESCRIPTION
`CDPATH=`*`dirs`*	Specifies the search path for the `cd` command, with individual directory names separated by colons (`:`).
`COLUMNS=`*`n`*	Specifies the number of columns or characters across your screen or window; the default is 80.
`EDITOR=`*`filename`*	Specifies the editor to use, usually `emacs` or `vi`; used when `VISUAL` is not set.
`ENV=`*`filename`*	Name of the shell script to execute at startup, usually `$HOME/.ksrc`.
`FCEDIT=`*`filename`*	Editor used by the `fc` command; the default is `/bin/ed`.
`FPATH=`*`directories`*	Directories to search for function definitions.

Table K.14: Korn Shell Variables (continued)	
VARIABLE	DESCRIPTION
HISTFILE=*filename*	Name of the file used to store command history; the default is `$HOME/.sh_history`.
HISTORY=*n*	Number of lines to keep in the history file; the default is 128.
HOME=*directory*	Specifies the home directory; set by `login`. If you use the `cd` command without an argument, the shell makes this directory the current directory.
IFS='chars'	Sets the internal field separator to *chars*; the defaults are space, tab, and newline.
LANG=*directory*	Directory to use for certain language-dependent functions.
LINES=*n*	Specifies the number of rows or characters down your screen or window.
MAIL=*filename*	Sets the default name of your mail file; the shell tells you when you receive mail via the `mail` or `mailx` commands.
MAILCHECK=*n*	Specifies the frequency *n* with which the shell checks for new mail; the default is 600 seconds, or 10 minutes.
MAILPATH=*filename*	Specifies one or more files, separated by a colon, in which to receive mail.
PATH=*dir*	Sets one or more pathnames, separated by colons, that the shell should search for commands to execute; the default is `/usr/bin`.
PS1=*string*	Specifies the primary shell prompt; the default is `$`.
PS2=*string*	Specifies the secondary shell prompt for use in multiline commands; the default is >. The appearance of this prompt indicates that the shell expects more input.
PS3=*string*	The prompt used by the `select` command; the default is `#?`.
PS4=*string*	The prompt used with the trace option; the default is +.
SHELL=*filename*	Specifies the shell to be used by commands when you escape to a subshell; of special interest to `ed` and `vi`.
TERM=*string*	Specifies your terminal type; required by some commands that use the whole screen for output.
TMOUT=*n*	Specifies the timeout to wait after the last command before logging you out automatically.
VISUAL=*filename*	Sets the name of the default editor to use, `emacs` or `vi`; overrides the `EDITOR` variable.

Table K.15: Built-in Korn Shell Commands

COMMAND	DESCRIPTION
`:`	Null command. The shell performs no action and returns an exit status of 0.
`.`*`filename`*	Reads and executes lines in *`filename`* as part of the current process.
`alias[`*`options`*`]` ➥`[`*`name`*`[=`` ` ``*`cmd`*`` ` ``]]`	Establishes the shorthand *`name`* as an alias for *`cmd`*. If `=`` ` ``*`cmd`*`` ` `` is omitted, prints the alias for *`name`*, and if *`name`* is also omitted, prints all aliases.
`autoload`	Korn shell alias for `typeset -fu`.
`bg [`*`JobIDs`*`]`	Places the current job or the jobs specified by *`JobIDs`* into the background.
`break [`*`n`*`]`	Exits from *`n`* levels in a `for` or `while` loop; default is 1.
`case`	Starts a case statement.
`cd [`*`directory`*`]`	Changes to the specified *`directory`*; the default is the home directory. You can also use `cd -`, where – stands for the name of the previous directory, or `cd` *`old new`*, which replaces the string *`old`* with the string *`new`* and changes to the resulting directory.
`continue [`*`n`*`]`	Skips any remaining commands in a `for` or `while` loop, resuming with the next iteration of the loop, or skipping *`n`* loops.
`do`	Keyword used in a `for`, `while`, `until`, or `select` statement.
`echo` *`args`*	Writes *`args`* to the screen.
`esac`	Keyword that ends a `case` statement.
`eval [`*`args`*`]`	Executes the specified *`args`*, allowing evaluation and substitution of shell variables.
`exec [`*`command`*`]`	Executes *`command`* without starting a new process.
`exit [`*`n`*`]`	Exits from the current shell procedure with an exit status of *`n`*.
`export [`*`names`*`]`	Exports the value of one or more shell variables, making them global in scope rather than local, which is the default.
`fg [`*`JobIDs`*`]`	Places the current job or the jobs specified by *`JobIDs`* into the foreground.
`fi`	Keyword that ends an `if` statement.
`for`	Keyword used in a looping construct.

Table K.15: Built-in Korn Shell Commands (continued)

COMMAND	DESCRIPTION
`function` *name* ➥ {*commands*;}	Korn shell alias for `typeset -f`.
`getopts` *string* ➥ *var* [*args*]	Checks command options, including *args* if provided, for legal choices.
`hash`	Korn shell alias for `alias -t`; creates a tracked alias for the named command.
`history`	Displays the last 16 commands; a Korn shell alias for `fc -l`.
`if`	Keyword used in an `if/then/else/fi` conditional statement.
`integer`	Korn shell alias for `typeset -i`.
`jobs` [*options*][*jobIDs*]	Lists all running or stopped jobs, or lists those specified by *jobIDs*.
`kill` [*options*] *IDs*	Terminates the specified process; to do this you must be either the owner of the process or the superuser.
`let` *expressions*	Keyword that performs the arithmetic specified by one or more expressions.
`newgrp` [*group*]	Switches to *group*, or returns to your login group.
`nohup`	Prevents termination of a command after the owner logs out.
`print` [*options*] ➥[*string*]	Prints the specified *string* on the standard output; used instead of `echo` on most systems.
`pwd`	Displays the pathname of the current working directory.
`r`	Korn shell alias for `fc -e-`; repeats the previous command.
`read` *var1* [*var2...*]	Reads one line from standard in, and assigns each word to a named variable; all leftovers are assigned to the last variable.
`readonly` [*var1...*]	Makes the specified variables read-only so that they cannot be changed.
`return` [*n*]	Exits *{*t*}* from a function with the exit status *n*, and returns to the shell.
`select` *x* [`in` *list*]	Displays a list of menu items on the standard output in the order specified in *list*.

Table K.15: Built-in Korn Shell Commands (continued)

COMMAND	DESCRIPTION
`set` ➥ [*option arg1 arg2...*]	Without arguments, `set` prints the names and values of all shell variables. *option* can be turned on by using a minus sign or turned off with a plus sign, and arguments are assigned in order to the parameters `$1`, `$2`, and so on. The options are listed in Table K.16.
`shift` [*n*]	Shifts positional arguments *n* places (by default 1 place) to the left.
`test`	Tests a condition and, if true, returns a zero exit status.
`time` *command*	Executes *command* and prints the total number of elapsed seconds.
`times`	Displays cumulative system and user time for all processes run by the shell.
`trap` ➥ [[*commands*] *signals*]	Executes *commands* if any of *signals* are received.
`type` [*names*]	Shows whether *names* are Unix commands, built-in commands, or a defined shell function; an alias for `whence -v`.
`typeset`[*options*] ➥[*variable*[=*value...*]]	Assigns a type (function, integer, flush-left, or flush-right string) to each variable and an optional value.
`ulimit` [*options*][*n*]	Prints the value of one or more resource limits, or when *n* is specified, sets the limit to *n*.
`umask` [*nnn*]	Sets the user file creation mask to octal value *nnn*; if *nnn* is omitted, displays the current user creation mask.
`unalias` *names*	Removes the specified aliases.
`unset` [-f]*names*	Removes definitions of the specified functions or variables in *names*.
`until`	Starts an `until/do/done` construct.
`wait` [*n*]	Waits for the process with ID of *n* to complete execution in the background and display its exit status.
`whence` ➥ [*options*]*commands*	Shows whether a command is a Unix command, a built-in shell command, an alias, or a defined shell function.
`while`	Starts a `while/do/done` construct.

K

Table K.16: Options to Use with the `set` Korn Shell Command	
OPTION	**DESCRIPTION**
`-/+a`	Export/do not export defined or modified variables.
`-/+A`*`name`*	Assign the remaining arguments as elements of the array *`name`*.
`-/+e`	Exit/do not exit if a command yields a non-zero exit status.
`-/+f`	Disable/enable filename metacharacters.
`-/+h`	Enable/disable quick access to commands.
`-/+k`	Provide/do not provide all environment variable assignments.
`-/+m`	Enable/disable job control; **`-m`** is usually set automatically.
`-/+n`	Read but do not execute/execute commands.
`-/+o` *`options`*	Turn on/off the Korn shell options listed in Table K.12.
`-/+p`	Start up as a privileged user, don't process `$HOME/.profile`.
`-/+s`	Sort/do not sort the positional parameters.
`-/+t`	Execute/do not execute one command and exit.
`-/+u`	Consider/do not consider unset variables as errors.
`-/+v`	Show/do not show each shell command line when read.
`-/+x`	Display/do not display commands and arguments when executed.

ksh

Command used to invoke the Korn shell or interactive command interpreter.

▶ Syntax

When starting the Korn shell, the syntax to use is:

```
ksh [options][arguments]
```

If you use **ksh** without options or arguments, you will start a new instance of the Korn shell, even if you are already running the C shell or the Bourne shell.

▶ Options and Arguments

ksh can execute commands from a terminal when the **-i** option is specified, from a file when the first argument on the command line is a shell script filename, or from the keyboard (standard input) if you specify the **-s** options. All the options you can use with **ksh** are listed in Table K.17.

■ *See also* **Bash, csh, sh, Tcsh, Zsh.**

Table K.17: Options for Use with ksh

OPTION	DESCRIPTION
-c *string*	Reads commands from *string*.
-i	Starts an interactive shell that prompts for input.
-p	Starts the shell without executing the commands in /$HOME/.profile.
-r	Starts a restricted shell; same as executing rksh or rsh.
-s	Reads commands from the standard input.

.kshrc

The Korn shell environment file, executed each time a new instance of the shell is started. The **.kshrc** file defines shell-specific information and is usually located in your home directory. You can set **ENV=$HOME/.kshrc** in your **.profile** file and then create a **.kshrc** file in your home directory for these commands.

ksrvtgt

A BSD Kerberos utility that retrieves and stores a ticket-granting ticket using a service key. The syntax to use is:

```
ksrvtgt name.instance
➥ [[realm[srvtab]]
```

This command retrieves a ticket-granting ticket valid for five minutes for the principal who can be identified as *name.instance@realm*, decrypts the response with the service key *srvtab*, and stores the ticket in the standard ticket cache.

■ *See also* **Kerberos, kdestroy, kinit, klist, register.**

ktrace

A BSD command that turns on kernel process tracing.

▶ Syntax

Here's the syntax:

```
ktrace [options]
```

Kernel trace data is written into the file **ktrace.out**, and you must use the **kdump** command to examine the contents of the file.

▶ Options and Arguments

You can use the options listed in Table K.18 with the **ktrace** command.

The **-g**, **-p**, and *command* options are all mutually exclusive.

■ *See also* **kdump.**

K

Table K.18: Options to Use with `ktrace`

OPTION	DESCRIPTION
`command`	Executes *`command`* with the specified trace options.
`-a`	Appends output to the `ktrace.out` file.
`-c`	Clears all trace points.
`-C`	Disables all tracing.
`-d`	Performs the trace operation on all children of the specified process.
`-f` *`filename`*	Specifies *`filename`* as the log file rather than `ktrace.out`.
`-g` *`pgid`*	Enables or disables tracing on all processes in the process group.
`-i`	Uses the trace options on all future children of the specified process.
`-p` *`pid`*	Enables or disables tracing on the specified process.
`-t` *`cnis`*	Sets tracepoints; *`c`* trace system calls, *`n`* trace namei translations, *`i`* trace input/output, and *`s`* trace signal processing.

l

A common alias for the `ls` command, used to list files and directories.

■ *See also* **ls**.

lam

A BSD command that copies files side by side onto the standard output.

▶ Syntax

The syntax for this command is:

```
lam [options]filename...
```

The `lam` command can also read from the standard input if you use –.

▶ Options and Arguments

Each option usually affects the following filename, unless the option letter is an uppercase letter; then the option affects all files until the option is respecified as a lowercase letter. Table L.1 lists the options available.

▶ Examples

To join four files together along each line, use:

```
lam file.a file.b file.c
➥ file.d > file.out
```

■ *See also* **join**, **pr**.

LAN

Abbreviation for local area network. A group of computers and peripheral devices connected by a communications channel, capable of sharing files and other resources between several users. Usually restricted to a relatively small area, a single company or campus department.

last

A Solaris and BSD command that reports the last logins by a user or a terminal.

▶ Syntax

The syntax for this command is:

```
last [options] user...
```

This command is useful as a fast accounting log of which users are accessing which systems.

▶ Options and Arguments

This command has several options, as Table L.2 shows.

▶ Examples

To see a list of the last 10 logins, use:

```
last -n 10
```

On some systems, this can be expressed as:

```
last -10
```

To see the names of everyone who has logged in to the system console, use:

```
last console
```

See also **lastcomm**, **login**.

lastcomm

A BSD command that displays information on previously executed commands. Commands are listed in reverse order. The syntax is:

```
lastcomm
➥ [option][command...]
➥[username...][terminal...]
```

When used with no arguments, `lastcomm` displays information on all commands stored in the current accounting file. When you use the `-f` *`filename`* option, information is read from *`filename`* rather than from the default accounting file. And when you specify an argument, only those commands with a matching *`command`* name, *`username`*, or *`terminal`* name are displayed. For each entry in the file, this command displays the command name, the name of the user executing the command, the associated terminal port, the execution time of the command, and the date and time the command was executed.

See also **last**.

Table L.1: Options Available with `lam`

OPTION	DESCRIPTION
`-f` *`min.max`*	Prints lines according to the format *`min.max`* where *`min`* is the minimum field width and *`max`* is the maximum field width.
`-p` *`min.max`*	Pads the file when the end-of-file is reached and other files are still active.
`-s` *`separator`*	Prints *`separator`* before printing information from the next file.
`-t` *`char`*	Terminates lines with *`char`* rather than with a newline.

Table L.2: Options for Use with `last`

OPTION	DESCRIPTION
`-f` *`filename`*	Reads the specified file instead of the default `/var/log/wtmp` (on BSD systems), `/etc/wtmp` (on SCO systems), or `/var/adm/wtmp`.
`-h` *`host`*	Specifies the name *`host`*, which can be either a name or a number.
`-n` *`n`*	Limits the display to *`n`* entries.
`-t` *`tty`*	Specifies the *`tty`*.

LATEX

A set of extensions to TEX, the text processing system developed by Leslie Lamport of DEC. LATEX commands are really TEX macros, and they greatly simplify the use of TEX, hiding almost all the low-level functions from the view of the writer.

For more details, see *LATEX; A Document Preparation System* by Leslie Lamport, published in 1994.

A large collection of public domain LATEX (and TEX) material is available from the Comprehensive TEX Archive Network (CTAN) via anonymous `ftp` from `ftp.shsu.edu`, or from `ftp.tex.ac.uk`, or `ftp.dante.de`. You will also find a useful collection of TEX-related material developed by Karl Berry via anonymous `ftp` from `ftp.cs.umb.edu` in the `pub/tex` directory.

layers

The command used to start the ASCII windowing system in SVR4.

▶ Syntax

The syntax for this command is:

```
layers [options][program]
```

▶ Options and Arguments

`program` is the name of a file containing configuration information that `layers` downloads to the terminal as it starts running.

Table L.3 lists the options available with this command.

■ *See also* **ismpx, jterm, jwin.**

Table L.3: Options to Use with layers

OPTION	DESCRIPTION
-d	Prints information on the downloaded file on standard error.
-D	Prints debugging information on standard error.
-f *filename*	Loads *filename* as a configuration file.
-h *list*	Supplies *list* of modules for layers.
-m *size*	Sets the data packet size; range is 32 to 252.
-p	Prints downloading statistics on the standard error.
-s	Exits layers and creates a protocol statistics report on the standard error.
-t	Exits layers and then creates a trace dump on the standard error.

LBX

Abbreviation for low-bandwidth X. A protocol included in the X11 Release 6 (X11R6) X Window system designed to improve the performance of X Window terminals operating at 9600 baud or less over dial-up connections. The performance boost is achieved by removing a certain amount of the X Window system handshaking and information swapping usually found on networks.

ld

The Unix command that starts the link editor. The link editor is a software development tool used to combine several object files into a single executable. Ordinarily, you invoke the link editor automatically as part of a C program compilation cycle, but there might be an occasion when it is appropriate to call the linker individually. For a complete description of the link editor and the many options available, see the `man` pages on your system.

■ *See also* **cc, C compiler, cpp, compiling a C program.**

ldd

A utility that lists any dynamic dependencies or shared objects that would be loaded if the specified file were executed; if the file has no such shared objects, the utility does not display any output. The syntax is:

```
ldd [options]filename
```

The command has two options. The `-d` option checks references to data objects, and the `-r` option checks references to both data objects and functions.

■ *See also* **lorder**, **lprof**.

leaf

In an hierarchical filesystem, the last node on the end of a branch. In Unix, a file that is not a directory is considered to be a leaf.

■ *See also* **node.**

learn

A BSD command that starts a computer aided instruction course on the use of Unix and several important subjects, including the C programming language, files, and the `vi` editor.

When you first start `learn`, the program asks you questions to decide what subject to begin with; you can specify a `subject` or even a `lesson` to bypass some of these questions. If you are restarting a previous session, `learn` uses information stored in `$HOME/.learnrc` to start at the place you left off last time. To end a session, type **bye**.

leave

A BSD command that reminds you when it is time to go home.

▶ Syntax

The syntax for this command is:

```
leave [+[hhmm]]
```

▶ Options and Arguments

If you use `leave` with no arguments, you see the prompt:

```
When do you have to leave?
```

You can enter the appropriate time; if you press Enter, `leave` exits. You can also specify a time on the command line in the form of *hhmm*. If you precede the time with a + sign, `leave` sets the alarm for that many hours and minutes from the current time.

`leave` reminds you 5 minutes and 1 minute before the designated time, at the time, and then every minute afterward. When you log off to go home, `leave` terminates.

■ *See also* **calendar**.

less

A popular and flexible pager utility generally available as part of the GNU package. `less` contains all the features found in `more`, and adds backwards scrolling, bookmarks, searching, and many other useful features.

▶ Syntax

Here's the syntax to use with `less`:

```
less [options][filename...]
```

▶ Options and Arguments

You can use the command-line options listed in Table L.4 with `less`.

`less` displays the contents of the file you specify one screenful at a time. After each screen, you see a prompt at the bottom left corner of your screen, where you can enter any of the commands listed in Table L.5.

▶ Examples

The simplest way to use `less` is with a single file:

```
less letter
```

This command displays the file, one screen at a time, with a prompt in the bottom left corner of your screen.

▶ Notes

You can get `less` by anonymous `ftp` from `prep.ai.mit.edu` in the `/pub/gnu` directory or from any other site that carries GNU software.

■ *See also* **more, pager, pg.**

Table L.4: Options to Use with less

OPTION	DESCRIPTION
`-c`	Displays new information from the top of the screen down.
`-C`	Clears the screen before displaying new information.
`-e`	Exits from `less` at the end of the file.
`-f`*`filename`*	Opens the specified binary file.
`-h`*`n`*	Scroll backwards *n* lines.
`-i`	Ignores case when searching through a file.
`-m`	Displays the percentage of the file that has been displayed.
`-M`	Displays the name of the file being viewed, the current line number, and the percentage of the file that has been displayed.
`-N`	Adds line numbers to the display.
`-s`	Replaces multiple blank lines with a single blank.
`-S`	Turns off word wrap.

less than symbol

The less than symbol (<) is used in redirection of the standard input to a command from a file rather than input from a terminal; in other words, the shell reads the input from the file instead of the keyboard.

■ *See also* **greater than symbol.**

Table L.5: Commands Available to Use with less

COMMAND	DESCRIPTION
`q`	Quits the program.
Space	Displays the next screenful.
Return	Displays the next line.
`[`*`n`*`]`Return	Displays the next *n* lines.
`b`	Displays previous screenful.
`y`	Displays previous line.
`[n]y`	Displays previous *n* lines.
`d`	Displays next half screenful.
`u`	Displays previous half screenful.
`g`	Goes to the first line.
`n``g`	Goes to line *n*.
`G`	Goes to the last line.
`/[`*`pattern`*`]`	Searches forward for the specified pattern.
`?[`*`pattern`*`]`	Searches backward for the specified pattern.
`n`	Repeats the previous search command.

let

A Korn shell keyword used when performing arithmetic or conversions between different number bases.

■ *See also* **expr**.

lex

A command that generates a lexical analysis program created from regular expressions and C language statements contained in specified source files. The lexical analyzer searches for strings and expressions and then executes the C routines when they are found. You can use `lex` to create classic Unix filters that read from the standard input, perform a function on the data, and send the results to the standard output.

■ *See also* **flex**, **yacc**.

lexical analysis

Any analysis of programs or commands to find patterns of symbols, such as numbers, operators, keywords, and variable names.

■ *See also* **flex**, **lex**, **parse**.

/lib

A root directory that contains program libraries.

■ *See also* **library**.

library

A collection of routines stored in executable files available for use by several different programs. Using libraries saves programmers time and effort (as well as minimizing the potential for making mistakes) as they don't have to rewrite common routines every time they are needed.

Libraries can include standard routines for a particular programming language (such as the Unix `stdio` library or a math library) or can consist of custom routines prepared by the programmer.

■ *See also* **ar**, **archive**, **makefile**.

library function

In programming, a routine or collection of routines stored in a library that can be used by any program that can link into the library.

■ *See also* **system call**.

LILO

- Abbreviation for Linux loader, a general-purpose boot manager program used to load Linux. You can use LILO to boot Linux in the usual way from your hard disk, or you can also use it to boot from a floppy disk.
- LILO is also an abbreviation for "last in last out," an alternative to the FIFO data management method.

limit

A built-in C shell command used to display or set limits on system resources used by the current process.

The syntax is:

```
limit [-h][resource[value]]
```

If you don't specify a *`value`*, the current value is displayed, and if you don't specify a *`resource`*, all `values` are printed. When you use the `-h` option, a hard limit is set that can only be changed by the superuser. Table L.6 lists the resources you can control with this command.

You can specify the *`value`* as a number followed by an optional units specifier. For `cputime`, use *`n`*`h` for hours, *`n`*`m` for minutes, or *`mm`*`:`*`ss`* for minutes and seconds, and for the other resources, use *`n`*`k` for kilobytes (the default) or *`n`*`m` for megabytes.

■ *See also* **ulimit**.

limited regular expressions

■ *See* **regular expressions**.

Table L.6: Resource Names to Use with `limit`

RESOURCE	DESCRIPTION
`cputime`	Maximum number of processor seconds.
`filesize`	Maximum size of any file.
`datasize`	Maximum size of data, includes the stack.
`stacksize`	Maximum size of the stack.
`coredumpsize`	Maximum size of a core dump file.

`line`

A command that reads a line from the standard input and writes that same line to the standard output. This command is often used in shell scripts that read input from the terminal.

line editor

A text editor that displays and manipulates just one line of text at a time. The Unix editors `ed` and `ex` are both line editors.

■ *See also* **screen editor.**

linefeed

Abbreviated LF. A command that advances the cursor on a terminal or the paper in a printer by one line. In the ASCII character set, a linefeed has the decimal value of 10.

■ *See also* **formfeed, newline.**

line printer

Any high-volume printer that prints a complete line at a time, rather than printing one character at a time (as a dot matrix or daisy wheel printer does) or one page at a time (as a laser printer does). Line printers are very high-speed printers and are common in the corporate environment where they are used with mainframe computers, minicomputers, and networked systems.

`LINENO`

A Korn shell variable that contains the line number of the command currently executing in a shell script.

lines per minute

Abbreviated lpm. A measurement of line printer speed; the number of lines of characters that the printer can produce in one minute. Dot-matrix printer speed is usually measured in characters per second, and laser printer speed in pages per minute.

link

- The last stage in creating a program—the process of combining object files into a single executable.
- A connection between a filename and the corresponding i-node. There are two kinds of links—hard links and symbolic links. A hard link associates a filename with the place on the hard disk where the contents of the file are located. A symbolic link associates the filename with the pathname of a hard link to a file.

■ *See also* **`ln`.**

link editor

A software development tool used to combine separately compiled source programs into a single executable program.

The Unix link editor is called `ld`.

linker

See **link editor.**

`lint`

A software development tool that carefully checks C source code for syntax errors, portability problems, and fragments of code that are never used or are unreachable, even though the source code may have compiled correctly. Use `lint` before you use the C compiler, and you will avoid all sorts of problems.

See also **`cb`, `cc`.**

Linux

A free Unix-compatible operating system for Intel-based PCs developed by Linus Torvalds at the University of Helsinki in Finland.

Strictly speaking, Linux is the name of the operating system kernel, the central part of the system that manages the basic operating system services, but many people use the name to refer to a complete operating system package, including utilities, editor and compilers, and games. Many of these important elements are actually part of the GNU Project, particularly the C compiler and other software development tools, while others have been written and released by volunteers.

Linux is a complete Unix clone and supports the X Window system, TCP/IP (including PPP, SLIP, support for many Ethernet cards, `ftp`, and `telnet`), `emacs`, UUCP, `mail`, newsreaders, NFS, a DOS emulation, and a complete set of GNU software development tools.

Linux is available free, although there may be a charge for the distribution media and additional printed documentation. You can get Linux on CD from Yggdrasil or from Slackware at:

Walnut Creek CDROM
4041 Pike Ln Suite D-386
Concord, CA 94520

or by calling 1-800-786-9907.

It is even bundled with several books, including Dan Tauber's *The Complete Linux Kit* from SYBEX. A huge number of Linux and Linux-related documents are available from many sites by anonymous `ftp`, and you can reach the Linux documentation home page at `http://sunsite.unc.edu/pub/Linux`. And as you might imagine, there are Linux newsgroups on USENET, too, including:

- `comp.os.linux.admin`
  Linux system administration topics.
- `comp.os.linux.advocacy`
  Merits and demerits of various operating systems.
- `comp.os.linux.announce`
  New announcements for Linux users, moderated.
- `comp.os.linux.answers`
  Linux HOWTO documents, moderated.
- `comp.os.linux.development`
  Discussions on kernel development.
- `comp.os.linux.development.apps`
  Information on porting applications to Linux.
- `comp.os.linux.development.system`
  Discussions on software development tools.
- `comp.os.linux.hardware`
  Supported hardware.
- `comp.os.linux.help`
  General questions and answers on running Linux.
- `comp.os.linux.misc`
  Other Linux topics.
- `comp.os.linux.networking`
  Networking with Linux.
- `comp.os.linux.setup`
  Discussions on setup problems.
- `comp.os.linux.x`
  X Window and X Window applications and Linux.

You can also subscribe to the *Linux Journal*, published by Specialized System Consultants, at:

SSC
7723 24th NW
Seattle, WA 98117 U.S.A.

See also **`dosemu`, XFree86.**

listserver

An automatic mailing system available on the Internet.

Rather than sending e-mail on a particular topic to a long list of people, you send it instead to a special e-mail address, where a program automatically distributes the e-mail to all the people who subscribe to the mailing list.

Several programs have been written to automate a mailing list; the most common is called `listserv`, but you may also encounter **`mailserv`**, **`majordomo`**, or `almanac`. Table L.7 summarizes the most important `listserv` commands. To issue one of these commands, send an e-mail to the listserver address, leaving the subject line blank, and include one command as the body of the message; do not add a signature file. For example, if I wanted to subscribe to the `listserv` mailing list called `writers`, my e-mail message would look like this:

`subscribe writers peter dyson`

Many listservers require your real name; they will not let you sign up otherwise. And finally, remember that almost all these mailing list services are run by volunteers in their spare time; be nice to them.

Mailing lists are usually devoted to a very specific subject, such as training dogs or wearing panty hose, rather than for general interest communications.

See also **digest, distribution, newsgroup, USENET.**

Table L.7: Summary of Important `listserv` Commands

COMMAND	DESCRIPTION
`help`	Sends back a summary of basic commands.
`info ?`	Sends back a list of available topics.
`info` *`topic`*	Sends back information on the specified *`topic`*.
`review` *`list`*	Sends back information about the specified *`list`*.
`set` *`list`* `ack`	Sends a confirmation message for the specified *`list`*.
`set` *`list`* `noack`	Does not send a confirmation message for the specified *`list`*.
`set` *`list`* `mail`	Begins mail deliveries from *`list`*.
`set` *`list`* `nomail`	Stops mail deliveries from *`list`*.
`set` *`list`* `repro`	Sends copies of your own messages.
`set` *`list`* `norepro`	Does not send copies of your own messages.
`subscribe` *`list your-name`*	Opens a subscription to *`list`*.
`signup` *`list your-name`*	Opens a subscription to *`list`*.
`unsubscribe` *`list your-name`*	Cancels a subscription to *`list`*.
`signoff` *`list`*	Cancels a subscription to *`list`*.

listusers

A command found on UnixWare and some other systems that displays a list of usernames and IDs. This command has two options; the `-g` *`groupname`* option lists members of *`groupname`*, and the `-l` *`login`* lists the users with the name *`login`*.

little endian

A computer architecture in which the least significant byte has the lowest address and so is stored little end first.

Many processors, including those from Intel, the PDP-11, and the VAX family of computers, are all little endian. The term comes from Swift's *Gulliver's Travels*, in which wars were fought over whether boiled eggs should be opened at the big end or at the little end.

See also **big endian, holy wars.**

lkbib

A BSD command used to search bibliographic databases.

▶ Syntax

Here's the syntax to use with `lkbib`:

```
lkbib [options] key...
```

Table L.8: Options for Use with `lkbib`

OPTION	DESCRIPTION
`-i` *`string`*	If no index exists for the search file, ignore any fields whose names appear in *`string`*.
`-p` *`filename`*	Searches *`filename`*.
`-t`*`n`*	Requires only the first *n* characters of a *`key`*; the default is 6.
`-v`	Prints the version number.

▶ Options and Arguments

The `lkbib` command searches bibliographic databases for references containing *`key`* and prints matching references to the standard output. This command has the options listed in Table L.8.

See also **`bib`, `indxbib`, `lookbib`, `refer`.**

ln

A command that creates hard links, allowing a file to have more than one name.

▶ Syntax

There are two syntax forms you can use with the `ln` command:

```
ln [options] filename1
➥ filename2
```

```
ln [options] filenames
➥ directory
```

In the first form above, *`filename1`* is linked to *`filename2`*, which is usually a new name; if *`filename2`* exists, it is overwritten.

In the second form, `ln` creates a link in *`directory`* to *`filenames`*. The new links will have the same filenames as the originals but different full pathnames.

▶ Options and Arguments

You can use the options listed in Table L.9 with the `ln` command.

▶ Examples

If you and a coworker insist on using different names for the same file, `ln` can solve the dilemma. To create a link, use something like this:

```
ln little large
```

which creates a link to `little` called `large`.

▶ Notes

A hard link to a file behaves just like the original filename; you can use the original filename or the name

Table L.9: Options for the `ln` Command

OPTION	DESCRIPTION
`-f`	Forces the link to be created without asking for overwrite permission.
`-n`	Does not overwrite existing files.
`-s`	Creates a symbolic link rather than a hard link.

assigned by the `ln` command, and the result is always the same. All hard links to a file must be in the same filesystem as the original file.

There is a very important difference between creating a link with `ln` and simply copying the file to another location. With linked files, when one copy is updated, all the links to that file are also updated simultaneously and automatically. With a copy, you must update each copy individually.

■ *See also* **`cp`, link, `rm`, symbolic links.**

load average

One measurement of how much work the central processing unit (CPU) is doing, defined as the average number of jobs in the run queue plus the number of jobs that are blocked while waiting for a disk access. This measurement is usually taken at 1, 5, and 15 minute intervals during a 24-hour period to give useful statistics.

■ *See also* **uptime.**

load balancing

A technique that distributes network traffic along parallel paths to make the most efficient use of the available bandwidth while providing redundancy at the same time. Load balancing automatically moves a user's job from a heavily loaded network resource to a less loaded resource.

locale

A set of components, such as language character sets, currency symbols, decimal point symbols, and date and time formats, used to customize an application for a specific nationality.

local variable

A variable in a program or in the shell, which is not visible or available to any other program.

■ *See also* **`exec`, global variable, `typeset`.**

`locate`

A BSD command that finds files by searching a database for all pathnames that match the specified pattern; `locate` *`pattern`*. The database, located in the file `locate.database`, is updated from time to time and contains the pathnames of all publicly accessible files.

■ *See also* **find.**

`lock`

A BSD and SCO command that locks a terminal. The `lock` command asks the user to enter and then verify a password and then locks the terminal until the password is re-entered.

In BSD, the `-p` option does not ask for a password but uses the user's current login password, and the `-t` *`timeout`* option changes the default 15 minute time out to the value specified by *`timeout`*.

In the SCO version, the `-`*`timeout`* option does not have an initial `-t`, and the `-v` option sets verbose mode.

`logger`

A BSD command that provides a shell command interface to the `syslog` system log module and creates entries in the system log; see the `man` pages for more details.

logging in

The process of establishing a connection to a Unix system by responding appropriately to the `login:` and `Password:` prompts. Sometimes written as *log in* or *login*.

logging off

The process of terminating a Unix session. Sometimes written *log off* or *log out.*

login

A command used to identify yourself and gain access to the system. By requiring users to log in, the system can be customized for each user, and the system itself can be protected against unwelcome intruders.

■ *See also* **exit, logout, passwd.**

.login

A C shell initialization file executed when you first log in. You can use `.login` to set environment variables and to run any commands that you want to execute at the beginning of each new login session.

■ *See also* **.cshrc, .logout.**

;login

The name of the newsletter provided to all members of the USENIX Association, containing articles and technical papers.

login name

The name that you type in response to the `login:` prompt on a Unix system. Every login name has a corresponding user ID number, and both are established in the password database or `/etc/passwd` file.

login shell

The shell that is available immediately when you log in to a Unix system. The login shell can fork other processes to run a different shell, utilities, or other programs. The name of your login shell is kept in the `/etc/passwd` file.

logname

A command that displays your login name. There are no arguments or options available for use with this command.

■ *See also* **login, who, whoami.**

logout

A built-in C shell command that terminates the current login shell.

.logout

A C shell file executed when you logout from the system. You can place commands in `.logout` that you want to execute automatically every time that you logout from the system.

■ *See also* **.cshrc, .login.**

long filename

The ability of a filesystem to take advantage of multiple-character filenames.

Unix filesystems can all manage long filenames, even those containing spaces, more than one period, and mixed upper- and lowercase letters.

look

A Solaris and BSD command that finds words in the system dictionary (`/usr/dict/words` or `/usr/share/dict/words`) or lines in a sorted file that start with a specified string.

▶ Syntax

The syntax to use with `look` is as follows:

look [*options*]*string filename*

▶ Options and Arguments

The `look` command displays the lines in *`filename`* that contain *`string`* as the first word. If you don't specify *`filename`*, the system dictionary is used instead, the case of letters is ignored, and only alphanumeric characters are compared. You can use the options listed in Table L.10 with `look`.

■ *See also* **grep**, **sort**.

Table L.10: Options for Use with `look`

OPTION	DESCRIPTION
`-d`	Compares only alphanumeric characters.
`-f`	Ignores case.
`-t` *`termchar`*	Specifies a string termination character *`termchar`*; only the characters in *`string`* up to and including *`termchar`* are compared.

lookbib

A BSD command that searches a bibliographic database for a specified keyword.

▶ Syntax

The syntax for this command is as follows:

```
lookbib [options]
➥ filename ...
```

▶ Options and Arguments

The `lookbib` command displays a prompt and reads a line from the standard input containing a set of keywords. `lookbib` searches the specified *`filename`* for references containing those keywords and prints the matches it finds on the standard output. You can use the options in Table L.11 with this command.

■ *See also* **bib**, **indxbib**, **lkbib**.

Table L.11: Options for Use with `lookbib`

OPTION	DESCRIPTION
`-i` *`string`*	When searching files for which no index exists, ignore those fields whose names are specified in *`string`*.
`-t`*`n`*	Requires only the first *`n`* characters of a key; the default is 6.
`-v`	Prints the program version number.

lorder

A utility that lists dependencies for a group of object files specified on the command line. Output from `lorder` is usually used with `tsort` when a library is created to determine the optimum ordering of the object modules so that the loader can resolve all references in a single pass.

■ *See also* **ldd**, **lprof**.

lossless compression

Any data compression method that compresses a file by rearranging or recoding the data that it contains in a more compact fashion. With lossless compression, none of the original data is lost when the file is decompressed again. Lossless compression methods must be used on program files and images such as medical X-rays, in which data loss cannot be tolerated.

Many lossless compression programs use a method known as the Lempel-Ziv (LZ) algorithm, which searches a file for redundant strings of data and converts them to smaller tokens; when the compressed file is decompressed, this process is reversed.

■ *See also* **JPEG**, **lossy compression**, **MPEG**.

lossy compression

Any data compression method that compresses a file by throwing away any data that the compression mechanism decides is unnecessary. Original data is lost when the file is decompressed again. Lossy compression methods may be used for shrinking audio or image files in which absolute accuracy is not required and the loss of data will never be noticed, but it is unsuitable for more critical applications in which data loss cannot be tolerated, such as medical images or program files.

■ *See also* **JPEG, lossless compression, MPEG.**

/lost+found

A root directory found in most filesystems, which is used as a collection point for damaged files identified by the `fsck` command. Once the files have been copied into this directory, the system administrator can decide on an appropriate fate for the files.

■ *See also* **`fsck`**.

low-bandwidth X

■ *See* **LBX.**

lp

An SVR4 command that sends files to the print queue for printing.

▶ Syntax

The syntax used with the `lp` command is:

```
lp [options][files]
```

The `lp` command also allows you to print several files, one after the other.

▶ Options and Arguments

The *`files`* argument specifies one or more pathnames of ordinary text files that you want `lp` to print. Specify – if you want to use the standard input rather than a file. The options available with this command are listed in Table L.12; check with your system administrator for details on the many printer-dependent options available with this command.

▶ Examples

To print a text file to the default printer, use:

```
lp text.file
```

▶ Notes

In BSD systems, the `lpr` command is equivalent to SVR4's `lp` command.

■ *See also* **`cancel`, `lpstat`, `pr`**.

lpm

■ *See* **lines per minute.**

lpq

A BSD command that displays the printer queue status.

▶ Syntax

Here's the syntax to use with the `lpq` command:

```
lpq [options][jobID...]
➥[user...]
```

For each print job, `lpq` displays the username, rank in the queue, filenames, the job ID, and the total size in bytes.

▶ Options and Arguments

When you use `lpq` with no arguments, the command reports on all jobs currently in the queue. You can request information by specifying a *`jobID`* or *`user`*. The options for `lpq` are listed in Table L.13.

▶ Notes

In SVR4 systems, the `lpstat` command is equivalent to BSD's `lpq` command.

■ *See also* **`lpr`, `lprm`, `lpstat`**.

Table L.12: Options Available with lp

OPTION	DESCRIPTION
`-c`	Copies the files before printing so that they cannot be changed. If you don't use this option, any changes you make to the file after the print request is made but before it is completed will be reflected in the printed output.
`-d` *`destination`*	Specifies *`destination`* as the printer; may be the name of an individual printer or a class of printers.
`-m`	Sends you a mail message to let you know that the files have been printed.
`-n` *`number`*	Prints the specified *`number`* of copies.
`-o` *`option`*	Specifies printer-dependent options; see your system administrator for details.
`-P` *`list`*	Prints only the pages specified in *`list`*.
`-q` *`priority`*	Assigns this print request the specified *`priority`*. Values for *`priority`* range from 0, the highest priority, to 39, the lowest.
`-s`	Suppresses messages including the request ID message you would otherwise see on submitting a print job.
`-w`	Displays a message on your terminal when all the files have been printed. If you have logged off, you will get a mail message instead.

Table L.13: Options for Use with lpq

OPTION	DESCRIPTION
`-l`	Displays all available information; ordinarily, only one line is displayed for each print job.
`-P` *`printer`*	Specifies a particular *`printer`*.

lpr

A BSD command that sends text files to the print queue for printing.

▶ Syntax

The syntax to use with `lpr` is as follows:

```
lpr [options]filename...
```

The `lpr` command also allows you to print several files, one after the other.

▶ Options and Arguments

The `lpr` command uses the print spooler to output the print jobs to the printer; if no *`filename`* is specified, `lpr` prints from the standard input. Table L.14 lists the options available with this command.

▶ Examples

To print three copies of the text files `my.txt` and `your.txt`, use:

```
lpr -#3 my.txt your.txt
```

▶ Notes

In SVR4, the `lp` command is equivalent to BSD's `lpr command`. On some systems, such as SCO, the `lpr` command is a link to the `lp` command, and so the two names can be used interchangeably.

■ *See also* **`lpq`**, **`lprm`**, **`pr`**.

Table L.14: Options Available with `lpr`	
OPTION	DESCRIPTION
Print Job Options	
`-h`	Does not print a burst page.
`-m`	Sends the user a `mail` message when the print job is complete.
`-P` *`printer`*	Specifies a particular *`printer`*.
`-r`	Removes the file when printing is complete.
`-s`	Uses symbolic links rather than copying files; used to save disk space when printing very large files.
Printing Options	
`-#` *`number`*	Prints the specified *`number`* of copies of each file.
`-i` *`font`*	Specifies a particular font.
`-C` *`class`*	Prints the job classification on the burst page.
`-J` *`job`*	Prints the job name on the burst page, usually the filename.
`-T` *`title`*	Prints the *`title`* rather than the filename on the burst page.
`-U` *`user`*	Prints the username on the burst page.
`-i` *`columns`*	Sets the number of leading blank characters, usually 8.
`-w` *`number`*	Specifies the page width.
Filter Options	
`-c`	File was created by `cifplot`.
`-d`	File contains TEX data.
`-f`	File contains Fortran source code.
`-g`	File contains `plot` data.
`-l`	File contains control characters.
`-n`	File contains `ditroff` data.
`-p`	Use `pr` to print the file.
`-t`	File contains `troff` data.
`-v`	File contains raster data.

lprint

An SCO command that prints a text file on a local printer rather than using the print spooler and the default system printer. The syntax is:

```
lprint [option] filename...
```

The only option you can use with this command is a hyphen (–), which prints from the standard input rather than from a file.

lprm

A BSD command that removes jobs from the print spooler.

▶ Syntax

The syntax to use with `lprm` is:

```
lprm [options][jobID...]
➥[user...]
```

Since the spooling directory is protected from users, this command is the only way to remove a job from the print spooler.

▶ Options and Arguments

You can remove a print job by specifying the appropriate *jobID* (obtained from the `lpq` command), and the superuser can remove a print job belonging to a specified *user*. The other two options are listed in Table L.15.

▶ Notes

In SVR4, the `cancel` command is equivalent to BSD's `lprm` command.

■ *See also* **lpq**, **lpr**, **pr**.

lprof

A command that displays a program's profile data, line by line. Information displayed includes a list of the source code files, each source code line, and the number of times each line executes.

■ *See also* **gprof**, **ldd**, **lorder**, **prof**.

Table L.15: Options for Use with lprm

OPTION	DESCRIPTION
–	Removes all jobs owned by the current user; if this option is invoked by the superuser, the print queue is emptied completely.
-P *printer*	Selects the print queue associated with a particular *printer*.

lpstat

A command used to display status information for the `lp` print spooler.

▶ Syntax

Here's the syntax to use with `lpstat`:

```
lpstat [options]
```

For each of the jobs in the queue, `lpstat` displays the name of the user requesting the print job, the job's current location in the queue, the name of the file being printed, the print request number (the number you need to remove the job from the queue), and the size of the print job in bytes.

▶ Options and Arguments

Table L.16 lists the options you can use with `lpstat`.

Some of the options in Table L.16 take a *list* argument, and if you leave out the *list*, all the information available for that option is displayed. Items in *list* can be separated by commas or, if enclosed in double quotes, by spaces.

If you specify the print request number, `lpstat` reports on just that print job; if you specify a *userID*, `lpstat` reports on all jobs associated with that user.

▶ Notes

In BSD systems, the `lpq` command is equivalent to SVR4's `lpstat` command.

■ *See also* **cancel**, **lp**.

Table L.16: Options Available with `lpstat`

OPTION	DESCRIPTION
`-a` *`list`*	Shows whether the printers specified in *`list`* are accepting print requests.
`-c` *`list`*	Displays class names for the printers specified in *`list`*.
`-d`	Reports the default system printer.
`-D`	Used with `-p` to display a short printer description.
`-f` *`list`*	Verifies that the *`list`* of forms are defined by the `lp` spooler.
`-l`	Used with `-f` to display the available forms; after `-p` to show printer configuration and after `-S` to display print wheel information.
`-o` *`list`*	Reports the status of all output requests, including printer names and print request ID numbers.
`-p` *`list`*	Reports the status of printers in *`list`*; used to see if the printer is enabled, and if not, why not.
`-r`	Indicates whether the print spooler is on or off; if the spooler is not running, no print jobs can be scheduled, and no printing can take place.
`-R`	Displays the job's position in the print queue.
`-s`	Displays a status summary of the spooler, including whether the spooler is running, the default printer, and the printer names and the devices associated with them.
`-S` *`list`*	Verifies that the *`list`* of print wheels and character sets is known to `lp`.
`-t`	Displays all information; equivalent to using `-acdusr`. If you have several printers on your system, this option provides more information than will fit on one screen; use `more` to prevent the information from scrolling off your screen.
`-u` *`list`*	Similar to `-o` but for *`list`* of users.
`-v` *`list`*	Displays a list of printers and the devices associated with them.

lptest

A command that sends a ripple test to the standard output. Originally developed to test printers, the ripple test outputs all 96 printable ASCII characters in all positions, taking 96 lines to complete the test. The syntax is:

`lptest [length][count]`

where *length* specifies the line length (the default is 79 characters), and *count* sets the number of lines to output (the default is 200 lines). This test is also used with terminals.

ls

The command is used to list the contents of a directory.

▶ Syntax

The syntax to use with this command is:

`ls [options] pathname ...`

The `ls` command lists the files and subdirectories in a directory, sorted in alphabetical order, and adds additional information about each file, depending on the options you choose. If you do not specify *pathname*, the contents of the current directory are displayed.

▶ Options and Arguments

The `ls` command has a large number of options that determine the type of information that `ls` displays; see Table L.17 for details. If you use `ls` without an option, you see a short listing that contains just filenames.

▶ Using the Long Option

The `ls -l` command produces a long listing of information, as Figure L.1 shows.

▶ Examples

To display a list of all the files in the current directory and its subdirectories, sorted by their modification time, enter:

`ls -altR`

■ *See also* **chmod, file permissions.**

Table L.17: Options for Use with `ls`

OPTION	DESCRIPTION
`-1`	Lists one file per line.
`-a`	Lists all files, including those whose names begin with a dot.
`-A`	Lists entries, including those whose names begin with a dot, except for `.` and `..` (BSD only).
`-b`	Displays nonprinting characters in octal (SVR4 only).
`-c`	Lists files sorted by creation/modification time.
`-C`	Lists files in columns, sorted down each column.
`-d`	Lists only directory names, not their contents.
`-f`	Lists the files within directories, but not the directories themselves.
`-F`	Places / after listed directories, * after executable files, and @ after symbolic links.
`-g`	Lists files in the `-l` long format, but without owner names (SVR4 only).
`-i`	Displays the i-node for each file.

Table L.17: Options for Use with `ls` (continued)

OPTION	DESCRIPTION
`-l`	Lists files in the long format; see the section "Using the Long Option" in this entry for more details.
`-L`	Lists the file or directory referenced by a symbolic link rather than the link itself.
`-m`	Lists the files separated by commas (SVR4 only).
`-n`	Lists files in the `-l` long format, with user and group numbers rather than names (SVR4 only).
`-o`	Lists files in the `-l` long format, but without group name.
`-p`	Places a / after directory names (SVR4 only).
`-q`	Displays nonprinting characters as `?`.
`-r`	Lists files in reverse order.
`-R`	Lists subdirectories recursively.
`-s`	Displays the file size in blocks.
`-t`	Lists files according to modification time, with the newest first.
`-T`	Displays complete time information, including year, month, day, hour, minute, and second (BSD only).
`-u`	Lists files according to file access time.
`-x`	Displays files sorted in rows across the screen (SVR4 only).

Figure L.1: Output from the `ls-l` Command

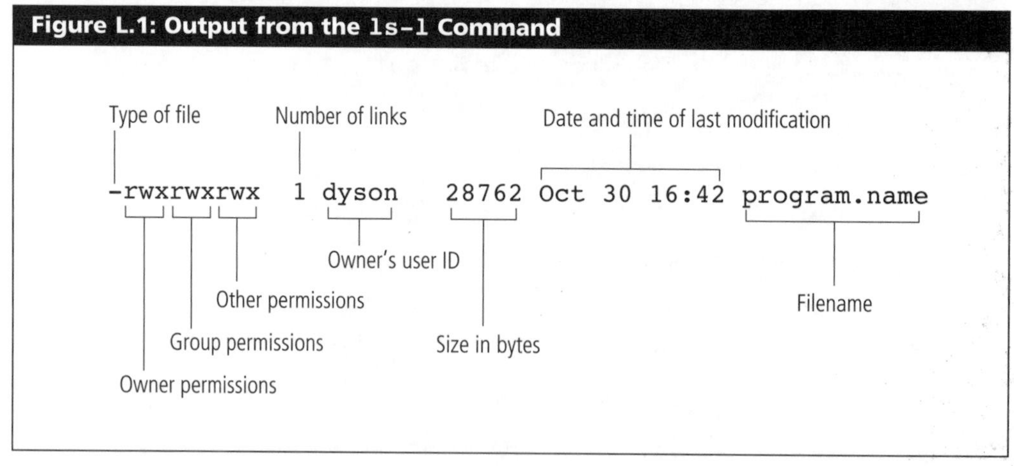

lurking

The practice of reading an Internet mailing list or USENET newsgroup without posting anything yourself. In the online world, lurking is not considered to be particularly antisocial; in fact, it is a good idea to lurk for a while when you first subscribe so you can get a feel for the tone of the discussions in the group and come up to speed on recent history.

See also **FAQ, newbie.**

Lynx

A text-based World Wide Web browser for VT100 terminals, developed by Lou Montoulli of the University of Kansas. Lynx is very easy to use and is available on a variety of different Unix systems. Lynx includes keyword searches and also stores a history list of the sites you have visited.

LZ

Abbreviation for Lempel-Ziv, an algorithm used in data compression developed by Abraham Lempel and Jacob Ziv in the late 1970s.

m

■ *See* **milli-**.

M

■ *See* **mega-**.

Mach

An operating system created from scratch at Carnegie Mellon University, designed to support advanced features such as multiprocessing and multitasking.

Mach has its roots in the Unix world and was originally based on BSD 4.2; however, its most notable feature is that it employs a relatively small microkernel rather than a conventional monolithic kernel.

The microkernel is designed to manage only the most fundamental operating system operations, including interrupts, task scheduling, messaging, and virtual memory; other modules can be added as necessary for file management, network support, and other tasks.

The NeXT operating system and OSF/1 are both based on Mach.

machid

An SCO command that determines the type of Intel microprocessor on which the system is running. The `machid` command is used with one of the following options, and returns a true value if the machine is of this type: `i286`, `iAPX286`, `i386`, `i486`.

On certain other systems this command is replaced by the `mach` or the `machine` command.

machine collating sequence

The sequence in which the computer orders characters. As most systems use ASCII, except large IBM systems that use EBCDIC, the machine collating sequence is based on the ordering of characters in the ASCII character set (see Appendix 2 for details). As a result, a `sort` command run on a system using ASCII produces different results from those produced on a system based on EBCDIC.

machine language

The native binary language used internally by the computer; also known as *machine code*. Machine language is difficult for humans to read and understand. Programmers create applications using high-level languages, which are translated into a form that the computer can understand by an assembler, a compiler, or an interpreter. Whichever method is used, the result is machine language.

See also **C, compiling a C program.**

macro

A stored group of keystrokes or instructions that can automate a complex or repetitive sequence of commands. Many of the major editor, mail, and text processing programs let users create and edit macros to speed up or simplify complex operations. Some macros can incorporate control structures such as do...while loops and if...then branching statements.

Some of the most often used macros in Unix are those used with `nroff` and `troff`—the `mm` macros, `me` macros, and `ms` macros. The C compiler also recognizes macros, which may be defined by a `#define` instruction to the preprocessor.

See also **compiling a C program, shell script.**

magic

A substance that is sprinkled or a phrase that is chanted by gurus to make something work.

In `vi` and `ex`, `magic` is a toggled variable that treats special characters as such during a search; to turn `magic` off again, use `nomagic`.

A magic character is one with special, often hard to understand capabilities, used at every opportunity by gurus demonstrating their prowess.

A magic number is a number that represents a particular condition, but whose value is unusual, given the conditions, and which certainly would never be guessed by anyone who is not a guru. Many Unix files have magic numbers at the beginnings of the files to help identify what types of files they are.

mail

In the Unix world, when someone talks about mail, they mean e-mail, rather than the U.S. Postal Service. Unix has supported some form of e-mail since the very beginning, and perhaps as a result, there are several different kinds of mail programs. You may find that more than one of them is available on your system. Some programs developed from the AT&T branch of Unix, others from BSD, and then there are some programs that are in the public domain. Here's a look at the more popular mail programs:

- `mail`: The original, rather primitive, AT&T e-mail program.
- `Mail`: A much enhanced BSD version of `mail`.
- `mailx`: An SVR4 version of `Mail` known as extended `mail`, hence `mailx`.
- `MH`: The `MH` (Message Handling) system is different from the standard mail programs, in that it consists of a large set of commands rather than one single large program. `MH` was originally developed at the Rand Corporation and then adopted as part of the BSD releases; it is now in the public domain. An X Window interface to `MH` called `xmh` is also available.
- `elm`: `elm` is a menu-driven program designed as a replacement for the `mail` program. `elm` combines power and ease of use with advanced features you can use to create your own customized mail-handling system.
- Pine: An easy-to-use program well suited to new or occasional users, Pine comes with its own built-in editor called `pico` for creating messages and a paging program used to read messages.
- `mush`: An abbreviation for mail user's shell. A public domain program with two modes; you can use it with a line-oriented interface or with a full-screen interface.
- `emacs`: The `emacs` editor includes a large number of commands for handling e-mail. `emacs` uses its own mail format, called Rmail format for mail files, which is not compatible with the standard Unix mail-file format but does provide commands for converting between the two formats.

Both `mailx` and `Mail` are upwardly compatible with `mail` and are quite similar to each other. Nowadays, most systems are set up so that when you type the word `mail`, either `mailx` or `Mail` starts, whichever is appropriate on your system. Also, many versions of Unix include graphical mailers as a part of their desktop environment; these mailers are often very easy to use and extremely powerful.

The mail programs that you work with as a user are known as mail user agents, and most of them use other mailers to manage the actual transmission of your message. These mailers are known as *mail transport agents*, and it is unlikely that you will ever have to deal with them directly; `delivermail`, `sendmail`, and `rmail` are all mail transport agents.

mail

The original Unix e-mail program; also used on many systems as an alias to one of the modern mail programs, either `mailx` or `Mail`.

▶ Syntax

The syntax to use with `mail` is as follows:

```
mail [options][users]
```

▶ Options and Arguments

The `mail` command reads incoming e-mail or sends mail to one or more *`users`*. The options for use with `mail` are listed in Table M.1; you can also type a question mark to see a summary of commands.

See also **`elm`, mail, `Mail`, `mailx`, MH, `mush`, Pine.**

Table M.1: Options for Use with `mail`

OPTION	DESCRIPTION
Options for Sending Mail	
`-m` *`type`*	Prints `Message-type:`*`type`* in the message header.
`-t`	Prints `To:` in the message header, listing the names of the recipients.
`-w`	Forces mail to be sent.
Options for Retrieving Mail	
`-e`	Test to see if mail exists without displaying anything; the exit status is zero if mail exists, 1 if there is no mail.
`-f` *`filename`*	Reads mail from the mailbox specified by *`filename`*.
`-F` *`Names`*	Forwards all incoming mail to *`Names`*.
`-h`	Displays several messages.
`-p`	Prints all messages.
`-P`	Prints all messages and all message headers.
`-q`	Terminates on an interrupt.
`-r`	Reverses the message order and prints the oldest messages first.

Mail

The BSD e-mail program; sometimes called `mail`.

▶ Syntax

The syntax to use with `Mail` is:

`Mail [`*`options`*`]`*`address`*

Used without options, `Mail` checks for new mail, then displays a one-line header for each message found. You can move up and down through the message list using `+` and `-`, and you can print messages using the `print` command, often abbreviated to simply `p`.

To send a message, use `Mail` with the appropriate *`address`*, then type the message, and press Ctrl-D.

When you have read all your mail, you can delete or reply to individual messages, and then end your session by pressing either `e` for exit or `q` for quit.

The section "Command Summary" below lists the commands you can use in your `Mail` session.

▶ Options and Arguments

You can use the options listed in Table M.2 when you first start `Mail`.

▶ Command Summary

The `Mail` program also has a large number of commands, each typed on a line by itself, followed by any appropriate arguments. You don't have to type many of these commands in full; they can be abbreviated. In Table M.3, which lists these commands, the abbreviation is shown in the left column before the full command name.

When you are in input mode composing your message, you can use tilde (~) escape commands to perform special functions; the tilde is only recognized when it is the first character on a line.

■ *See also* **`biff`, `elm`, mail, `MAILCHECK`, `mail.rc`, `.mailrc`, `mailx`, MH, `mush`, Pine, tilde escape commands, `xbiff`.**

Table M.2: Options for Use with `Mail`

OPTION	DESCRIPTION
`-b` *`list`*	Sends blind carbon copies to *`list`* of users.
`-c` *`list`*	Sends carbon copies to *`list`* of users.
`-f` *`filename`*	Reads mail from the mailbox specified by *`filename`*.
`-i`	Ignores interrupts.
`-I`	Forces interactive mode.
`-n`	Prevents reading `mail.rc` on startup.
`-N`	Turns off initial display of message headers.
`-s` *`subject`*	Specifies *`subject`*.
`-u` *`username`*	Reads mail from the mailbox specified by *`username`*.
`-v`	Displays delivery details.

mailalias

An SVR4 command that displays the e-mail address associated with one or more *`names`*. The syntax is:

`mailalias [`*`options`*`]`*`names`*

This command takes two options; `-s` displays the address associated with *`names`*, and `-v` turns on debug mode.

mail bomb

To send thousands of long e-mail messages on random subjects to the same e-mail address as an indication of your disgust with something that the e-mail address owner said online or in a USENET newsgroup.

Table M.3: `Mail` Command Summary	
COMMAND	**DESCRIPTION**
`-`	Displays the previous message.
`?`	Displays a summary of commands.
`!` *`command`*	Executes the shell *`command`*.
`a` or `alias`	Displays, creates, or changes an alias.
`alt` or `alternate`	Avoids message duplication if you have accounts on several different systems.
`c` or `chdir`	Changes the directory.
`co` or `copy`	Saves the message file.
`d` or `delete`	Deletes a message.
`dp` or `dt`	Deletes the current message and prints the next message.
`e` or `edit`	Edits the message.
`ex`, `x`, `xit` or `exit`	Exits immediately, without making any changes.
`fi` or `file`	Lists all files.
`fo` or `folder`	Changes to a new mail folder.
`folders`	Lists all your folders.
`f` or `from`	Prints the message headers from a list of messages.
`h` or `headers`	Lists headers in groups of 18 messages.
`help`	Displays a summary of commands.
`ho` or `hold`	Saves messages in the user's system mailbox; opposite of `mbox`.
`ignore`	Adds header fields to your ignore list, a list of fields that are not displayed when you look at a message.
`m` or `mail`	Sends mail to the specified names.
`mbox`	Saves messages in `mbox` in your home directory; opposite of `hold`.
`n` or `next`	Displays the next or the next matching message.
`pre` or `preserve`	Saves messages in the user's system mailbox; opposite of `mbox`.
`p` or `print`	Displays messages on your terminal without `ignore` fields.
`P` or `Print`	Displays messages on your terminal including `ignore` fields.

M

Table M.3: Mail Command Summary (continued)	
COMMAND	DESCRIPTION
q or quit	Quits after saving all unsaved messages in mbox.
r or reply	Replies to the sender and all recipients of a message.
R or Reply	Replies only to the sender of a message.
respond	Replies to the sender and all recipients of a message.
retain	Adds header fields to your retain list, a list of fields that are displayed when you look at a message.
s or save	Saves the message in the specified file.
se or set	With no options, prints all variable values; otherwise, sets variables.
saveignore	When saving messages, does not save ignored list fields.
saveretain	When saving messages, saves ignored list fields.
sh or shell	Invokes an interactive version of the shell.
size	Displays the size of each message.
top	Displays the first few lines of each message.
t or type	Same as print.
T or Type	Same as Print.
unalias	Removes aliases.
u or undelete	Recovers a deleted message.
U or unread	Marks a message you have read as unread.
unset	Discards variable values; reverse of set.
v or visual	Opens the editor on each message.
w or write	Saves just the message text without the header information.

mailbox

In e-mail systems, an area of hard disk space used to store e-mail messages until users can access them. An on-screen message often tells users that they have mail.

■ *See also* **mailer, primary mailbox.**

MAILCHECK

An environment variable that specifies how often you want the shell to check for the arrival of new e-mail; if you set MAILCHECK to 0, the shell checks after every command you execute.

■ *See also* **biff, mail, MAILPATH, mailx, notify, xbiff.**

mailer

A program used for sending and receiving e-mail.

■ *See also* **mail, mailx, MH.**

mailing list

On the Internet, a group of people who share a common interest and automatically receive all the mail posted to the listserver, or mailing list manager program.

Contributions are sent as e-mail to the listserver and then distributed to all subscribers. Most listserver programs include a command that sends you a complete list of all the subscribers' e-mail addresses by return e-mail.

■ *See also* **moderated newsgroup.**

MAILPATH

The environment variable used to inform you that new mail has arrived. It consists of a set of filenames, separated by colons; when one of these files is updated with new mail, you are informed by the shell.

■ *See also* **biff, mail, MAILCHECK, mailx, notify, xbiff.**

mailq

A BSD command that prints a short summary of the messages waiting for delivery in the mail queue. A single option, `-v` prints extra information, including the priority of the message.

mail.rc

A file located in the `/usr/lib/mailx` directory that establishes the system-wide e-mail variables.

■ *See also* **.mailrc, mailx.**

.mailrc

A file used to establish your own e-mail configuration, containing commands that configure the mail system to your own liking and establish groups of mail recipients as aliases. This file is located in your home directory.

■ *See also* **mail.rc.**

mail reflector

On the Internet, a program that manages a mailing list.

■ *See also* **listserver.**

mail transport agent

A program that manages the transportation and delivery of e-mail. The mail transport agent accepts messages from a mail user agent, performs any translations required, and then routes the messages to the appropriate mail transport agent.

■ *See also* **SMTP.**

mail user agent

A program that provides a user interface for sending and receiving e-mail, as well as those other features required in any mail application, including creating, reading, forwarding, and deleting messages.

■ *See also* **mail transport agent, SMTP.**

mailx

The SVR4 e-mail program; sometimes called `mail`.

▶ Syntax

The syntax for the `mailx` command is as follows:

```
mailx [options][users]
```

▶ Options and Arguments

The command-line options you can use with `mailx` are listed in Table M.4.

▶ Command Summary

The `mailx` program also has a large number of commands, each typed on a line by itself, followed by any appropriate arguments. You don't have to type many of these commands in full; they can be abbreviated. In Table M.5, which lists these commands, the abbreviation is shown in the left column before the full command name.

When you are in input mode composing your message, you can use tilde (~) escape commands to perform

Table M.4 Options for Use with `mailx`	
OPTION	DESCRIPTION
Options for Sending Mail	
`-F`	Saves messages in a file named after the first recipient.
`-i`	Ignores interrupts.
`-n`	Prevents reading `mail.rc` on startup.
`-s` *`string`*	Sets the message subject to *`string`*.
Options for Retrieving Mail	
`-e`	Tests for presence of mail without printing anything.
`-f` *`filename`*	Reads mail from *`filename`* rather than `mbox`.
`-h` *`n`*	Stops sending after *`n`* network hops.
`-H`	Displays only message headers.
`-I`	Assumes the first newsgroup in the `Newsgroups` field is the sender; use only with the `-f` option.
`-N`	Don't display initial header summary.
`-r` *`address`*	Passes the *`address`* to network delivery software.
`-T` *`filename`*	Saves the list of `article-id` fields in *`filename`*.
`-u` *`user`*	Reads mail from *`user`* mailbox.
`-U`	Converts UUCP addresses into Internet addresses.

special functions; the tilde is only recognized when it is the first character on a line.

■ *See also* **biff**, **elm**, mail, **Mail**, **MAILCHECK**, **mail.rc**, **.mailrc**, **MH**, **mush**, Pine, **xbiff**.

mailx.rc

A file used to establish the system-wide e-mail configuration, containing commands that should be appropriate for all users. It is named either `/usr/lib/mailx/mailx.rc` or `/usr/lib/Mail.rc` depending on your system.

■ *See also* **.mailrc**.

main

In a C program, the name of the first user-written routine to run when the program starts. `main` often calls other functions from a library to complete its task.

maintenance release

A software upgrade that corrects minor bugs or adds a few minor features, distinguished from a major release by an increase in only the decimal portion of the version number. For example, a maintenance release might increase the version number from 3.0 to 3.1, while a major new release might increase it from 3.1 to 4.0.

Table M.5: mailx Command Summary

COMMAND	DESCRIPTION
n	Displays message number *n*.
–	Displays the previous message.
. or =	Displays the current message number.
#	Treats the rest of the line as a comment.
?	Displays a summary of commands.
! *command*	Executes the shell *command*.
a or alias	Displays, creates, or changes an alias.
alt or alternate	Avoids message duplication if you have accounts on several different systems.
cd	Changes to the specified directory.
ch or chdir	Changes the directory.
c or copy	Saves the message file.
C or Copy	Saves each message in a file named for the message's author.
d or delete	Deletes a message.
di or discard	Does not display the specified header fields when displaying messages.
dp or dt	Deletes the current message and prints the next message.
ec or echo	Echoes the specified string.
e or edit	Edits the message.
ex, x, xit, or exit	Exits immediately, without making any changes.
fi or file	Lists all files.
fold or folder	Changes to a new mail folder.
folders	Lists all your folders.
fo or followup	Replies to a message, and stores the reply in a file named for the message's author.
F or Followup	Replies to the first specified message, and sends the reply to all the originators of the list of messages.
f or from	Prints the message headers from a list of messages.
g or group	Creates a group alias.

Table M.5: mailx Command Summary (continued)

COMMAND	DESCRIPTION
h or headers	Lists headers in groups of 18 messages.
help	Displays a summary of commands.
ho or hold	Saves messages in the user's system mailbox; opposite of mbox.
ignore	Adds header fields to your ignore list, a list of fields that are not displayed when you look at a message.
l or list	Lists available commands without explanations.
m or mail	Sends mail to the specified names.
M or Mail	Sends mail to the specified name, and stores the message in a file named for the recipient.
mb or mbox	Saves messages in mbox in your home directory; opposite of hold.
n or next	Displays the next or the next matching message.
pi or pipe	Passes the specified messages to a command.
pre or preserve	Saves messages in the user's system mailbox; opposite of mbox.
p or print	Displays messages on your terminal without ignore fields.
P or Print	Displays messages on your terminal including ignore fields.
q or quit	Quits after saving all unsaved messages in mbox.
r or reply	Replies to the sender and all recipients of a message.
R or Reply	Replies only to the sender of a message.
respond	Replies to the sender and all recipients of a message.
s or save	Saves the message in the specified file.
se or set	With no options, prints all variable values; otherwise, sets variables.
sh or shell	Invokes an interactive version of the shell.
size	Displays the size of each message.
source	Reads and executes commands from a specified file.
top	Displays the first few lines of each message.
tou or touch	"Touches" each message so it appears to have been read.
t or type	Same as print.

COMMAND	DESCRIPTION
T or Type	Same as Print.
u or undelete	Recovers a deleted message.
unset	Discards variable values; reverse of set.
ve or version	Displays the version number and release date of mailx.
v or visual	Opens the editor on each message.
w or write	Saves just the message text without the header information.
z or z+	Scrolls the header summary one screen forward.
z-	Scrolls the header summary one screen backward.

Table M.5: mailx Command Summary (continued)

major device number

A number assigned to a class of devices such as disk drives, tape drives, printers, or terminals.

If you use the ls -l command to list the contents of the /dev directory, you will see the major and minor device numbers, separated by commas, listed where you would expect to see the file sizes in bytes in a normal listing. The rest of the information is the same as that shown by any ls -l listing.

■ *See also* **special file.**

major mode

Within emacs, one of many modes in which aspects of emacs operation are tailored to suit the needs of a particular common type of text processing. Major modes include those specially designed for C programming, normal text processing, awk scripts, nroff and troff-formatted files, and so on.

■ *See also* **minor mode.**

make

A software development utility used to maintain a set of source code file dependencies so that changes to these files can be managed with the minimum of effort, and the resulting executables can be kept up-to-date.

The time dependency rules used by make utilities can be used on any project in which dependencies between files must be explicitly controlled.

Almost every commercially offered compiler and assembler includes some form of make utility these days.

■ *See also* **imake, makefile, RCS, SCCS.**

makefile

A file, created by the make utility, that lists the source code files, object files, and their dependencies for a specific software development project. Using information from this makefile, make keeps track of the sequences needed to create certain files and can perform updating tasks automatically for the programmer. This means that when a program is changed in some way, make can recreate the proper files with the minimum of input from the programmer.

■ *See also* **SCCS.**

makekey

A utility that creates a complex encryption key; due to export restrictions, makekey is only available in the U.S.

man

A utility that displays the Unix online reference manuals.

▶ Syntax

Here's the syntax to use with `man`:

```
man [options]
➥[[section]subject]
```

▶ Options and Arguments

The `man` command displays information from the Unix online reference manual, where *subject* is normally the name of a command or system call and *section* is a section number between 1 and 8. Some of the online reference material is terse and difficult to understand, but it does contain a wealth of information that it is difficult to find elsewhere. See Table M.6 for a list of the command-line options you can use with `man`.

Because the command-line options for `man` differ from system to system, check the `man` pages on your system for details by entering:

```
man man
```

▶ Examples

To display the manual page for the `vi` editor, use:

```
man vi
```

If you want to know if a particular word occurs in a specific manual page but don't want to read through the page yourself, you can use `grep` with the `man`

Table M.6: Options for Use with man

OPTION	DESCRIPTION
-a	Displays all specified *section* and *name* combinations.
-c	Copies the specified page to the standard output rather than using the `more` command to break it up into pages (4.4BSD only).
-C *filename*	Uses the specified *filename* rather than the default configuration file `man.conf` (4.4BSD only).
-d	Enters debug mode (Solaris only).
-f *filenames*	Displays a one-line summary of one or more reference *filenames*.
-h	Displays just the "SYNOPSIS" section of the page (4.4BSD only).
-k *keywords*	Displays any header line containing the specified *keywords*.
-l	Displays all page references for the specified *section* and *name* combinations (Solaris only).
-m *pathname*	Adds *pathname* to the list of directories searched by `man`; *pathname* contains a comma-separated list of directory names.
-M *pathname*	Replaces the standard list of directories with *pathname*, which contains a comma-separated list of directory names.
-t	Formats the pages with `troff`.
-T *macro*	Displays information using the specified *macro* package.
-w	Lists the pathnames for the specified *section* and *name* combinations.

command. For example, to see if the word `alias` appears in the `csh` page, use:

```
man csh | grep alias
```

See also **apropos, man pages, whatis, whereis, xman.**

man pages

The `man` (`manual`) utility displays pages from the system documentation stored on disk on your terminal screen. Type the `man` command, followed by the name of the command that you want information about, and Unix displays the documentation for that command.

The Unix system manual is divided into eight sections, as follows:

1. User Commands
2. System Calls
3. C Library Functions
4. Devices and Network Interfaces in BSD; Administrative Files in SVR4
5. File Formats in BSD; Miscellaneous Information in SVR4
6. Games and Demos
7. Environments, Tables, and Macros in BSD; I/O and Special Files in SVR4
8. System Maintenance Commands

Most users find everything they want to know (and more) in sections 1 and 6; system administrators and programmers may have to consult the other sections. On some versions of Unix, you will find that these major categories have been further subdivided into even more categories; for example, UnixWare includes networking commands in Section 1C and X Window commands in Section 1X.

A command name followed by a number in parentheses—`ls (1)`, for example— means that information on the `ls` command is in Section 1 of the online manual. You can use this form of the `man` command to look at that entry:

```
man 1 ls
```

Each `man` page treats a single topic; some are short, while others are much longer, but they are all organized according to a standard format using the headings described in Table M.7.

Not all `man` pages have all of these headings, and some versions of Unix use slightly different names for these headings.

Figure M.1 shows the information you get when you ask the `man` command to display information on the `man` command; in other words, Figure M.1 is what you see when you enter:

```
man man
```

Table M.7: Organization of man Pages

HEADING	DESCRIPTION
NAME:	The name and main purpose of the command.
SYNOPSIS:	The syntax to use with the command.
DESCRIPTION:	A complete description of the command; in some cases, such as the C shell (`man csh`), this description is very long.
FILES:	A list of the important files related to this command.
SEE ALSO:	Places to look for related information.
DIAGNOSTICS:	A list of warning and error messages.
BUGS:	Details of programming errors, and shortcomings of the command.

Figure M.1: The man page for the man Command

```
MAN(1)                        USER  COMMANDS              MAN(1)
NAME
     man - display reference manual pages; find reference pages
by keyword
SYNOPSIS
     man[-] [section] title ...
     man -k keyword ...
     man -f filename ...
DESCRIPTION
     Man is a program which gives information from the programmers manual.
     It can be asked for one-line descriptions of commands specified by
     name, or for all commands whose description contains any of a set of
     keywords. It can also provide on-line access to the sections of the
     printed manual.
     When given the option -k and a set of keywords, man prints out a one
     line synopsis of each manual section whose listing in the table of
     contents contains one of those keywords.
     When given the option -f and a list of names, man attempts to locate
     manual sections related to those files, printing out the table of
     contents lines for those sections.
     When neither -k or -f is specified, man formats a specified set of
     manual pages. If a section specifier is given man looks in that
     section of the manual for the given titles. Section is either an
     Arabic section number (3 for instance), or one of the words "new",
     "local", "old", or "public". A section number may be followed by a
     single letter classifier (for instance, lg, indicating a graphics
     program in section 1). If section is omitted, man searches all
     sections of the manual, giving preference to commands over
     subroutines in system libraries, and printing the first section it
     finds, if any.
     If the standard output is a teletype, or if the flag - is given, man
     pipes its output through more (1) with the option -s to crush out
     useless blank lines and to stop after each page on the screen. Hit a
     space to continue, a control-D to scroll 11 more lines when the
     output stops.
FILES
     /usr/man          standard manual area
     /usr/man/man?/*   directories containing source for manuals
     /usr/man/cat?/*   directories containing preformatted pages
     /usr/man/whatis   keyword database
SEE ALSO
     apropos(1), more(1), whatis(1), whereis(1), catman(8)
BUGS
     The manual is supposed to be reproducible either on a
     photo-typesetter or on an ASCII terminal. However, a on terminal
```

managing processes

Every process running under Unix has several important pieces of information associated with it, including:

- The process ID (PID) is a number assigned when a process starts; no two processes can have the same PID at the same time.
- The user ID tells Unix to whom the process belongs and so determines the files and directories that the process is allowed to read from and write to.
- The group ID tells Unix to which group the process belongs.
- The environment is a list of variables and their values, often customized for each user.

■ *See also* **background processing, `bg`, `fg`, foreground processing, job control, `kill`, `nice`, `ps`.**

mandatory argument

An argument that you must provide to a command so that the command can work as expected. For example, the `mkdir` command, used to create a new directory, cannot work unless you provide the name of the directory you want to create.

manual pages

■ *See* **`man` pages.**

map

- An NFS term describing a file containing the mount points and their resources.
- The process of relating a piece of data, for example, a network address, with a physical location such as a network interface card (NIC).
- In `vi`, a command used to create a macro.

MAPI

Abbreviation for Messaging API. An application interface used to add messaging capabilities to any Microsoft Windows application. MAPI handles the details of message storage, forwarding, and directory services.

mask

A binary number, usually written in octal, which is used to remove bits from another binary number. Masks are often used when manipulating file permissions.

■ *See also* **`chmod`, creation mask, `umask`.**

master map

A file that contains the names and configurations of systems using the NFS.

MB

■ *See* **megabyte.**

Mb

■ *See* **megabit.**

MBONE

Acronym for Multicast Backbone. An experimental method of transmitting digital video over the Internet in real time.

The TCP/IP protocols used for Internet transmissions are unsuitable for real-time audio or video; they were designed to deliver text and other files reliably but with some delay. MBONE requires the creation of another backbone service with special hardware and software to accommodate video and audio transmissions; the existing Internet hardware cannot manage time-critical transmissions.

mbox

A default system file that contains e-mail messages from other users that have been read and saved.

Mbps

■ *See* **megabits per second.**

mcs

An SVR4 command used to add to, delete from, compress, or print one or more comments sections from an ELF object file.

▶ Syntax

The syntax for `mcs` is:

```
mcs [options]filenames
```

▶ Options and Arguments

Table M.8 lists the options you can use with this command; at least one option must be specified. The name of the default comments section is `.comment`.

■ *See also* **face**, **FACE**, **fmli**.

meg

Slang commonly used for megabyte; often heard in casual conversation.

Table M.8: Options to Use with mcs

OPTION	DESCRIPTION
-a *string*	Appends *string* to the comment area of *filenames*.
-c	Compresses the comment section of *filenames*.
-d	Deletes the comments section from *filenames*.
-n *name*	Specifies *name* as the comments section rather than .comment.
-p	Prints the comments on the standard output.
-V	Displays the version number of mcs on the standard output.

mega-

Abbreviated M. A prefix meaning one million in the metric system. Because computing is based on powers of 2, in this context, mega usually means 220 or 1,048,576; the power of 2 closest to one million.

megabit

Abbreviated Mbit. Usually 1,048,576 binary digits or bits of data. Often used as equivalent to 1 million bits.

■ *See also* **megabits per second.**

megabits per second

Abbreviated Mbps. A measurement of the amount of information moving across a network or communications link in one second, measured in multiples of 1,048,576 bits.

megabyte

Abbreviated MB. Usually 1,048,576 bytes. Megabytes are a common way of representing computer memory or hard disk capacity.

megahertz

Abbreviated MHz. One million cycles per second. A microprocessor's clock speed is often expressed in MHz. The original IBM PC operated an Intel 8088 running at 4.77 MHz; the more modern Pentium Pro processor runs at speeds in excess of 200 MHz.

me macros

A set of over 80 `nroff` and `troff` macros distributed with BSD systems, originally created by Eric Allman while at Berkeley. The **me** macro package is equivalent to the **ms** and **mm** macro packages on SVR4 systems and supports all common preprocessors such as `eqn`, `tbl`, and `refer`. Macros are used to provide complex formatting options such as automatic numbering of lists, running head control, and font changes.

■ *See also* **mm macros, ms macros.**

menu

A list of the commands or options available in the program displayed on the screen.

You select a menu item by typing a letter or number corresponding to the item, by clicking it with the mouse, or by highlighting it and pressing the Enter key.

Merge

A DOS emulator from Locus Computing Corporation that runs DOS and Microsoft Windows 3.1 applications under Unix. Merge provides a complete DOS environment, which acts as though your system is running just DOS. Merge is available on UnixWare, SCO, and other systems, and provides:

- Support for DOS and Windows applications via an X terminal or X-based workstation
- A shared DOS and Unix filesystem
- Shared peripherals
- Support for extended and expanded memory

■ *See also* **DOS commands, `dosemu`, VP/ix.**

merge

An operation that combines two ordered lists or files in such a way that the resulting list is still in order.

■ *See also* **`merge`, `sort`.**

`merge`

A BSD command that combines separate sets of changes from two files into one.

Syntax

Here's the syntax for `merge`:

```
merge [options] filename1
➥ filename2 filename3
```

▶ Options and Arguments

The `merge` command is very useful for combining the separate sets of changes into one file. For example, if *`filename2`* contains the original text, and *`filename1`* and *`filename3`* include modifications, you can use `merge` to create one file that contains all the modifications.

To send the results of the merge to the standard output rather than to *`filename1`*, use the `-p` option, and to suppress all messages, use the `-q` option.

■ *See also* **`diff3`.**

`merge`

■ *See* **RCS.**

`mesg`

A command used to control message posting on your terminal. To stop other users from sending you messages with the `write` command, use:

```
mesg -n
```

and use

```
mesg -y
```

when you are ready to start receiving messages once again.

■ *See also* **`write`, `talk`.**

message buffer

An area of memory that stores all the messages sent to the console.

message channel

A form of interprocess communication that allows two programs running in the same computer to share information.

■ *See also* **pipe, queue, semaphore.**

message of the day

■ *See* **motd.**

metacharacter

A character with a special meaning in certain specific situations. Metacharacters are used in ambiguous file references in the shell and in regular expressions in other programs. You must always quote a metacharacter with

a backslash (\) or single quotes if you want to use the ordinary meaning of the character. Sometimes called a *wild card*.

See also **asterisk, question mark, regular character.**

metafile

A file that contains both data and output control information. For example, a graphics metafile contains not only a graphical image of some kind but also information on how the image should be displayed. This allows one single version of a file to be output to a variety of different display devices.

Meta key

A key used extensively in `emacs`. Some keyboards have a Meta key, while others map the function of this key onto the Alt or other suitable key on the keyboard. The Meta key is used in the same way as the Ctrl key, in combination with other keys to create unique commands.

m4

A macro language preprocessor for Ratfor (a version of Fortran), Pascal, or other languages that do not have a built-in macro processing feature.

MH

A message handling system, originally developed by the Rand Corporation and now in the public domain; sometimes written as `mh`.

`MH` is different from `Mail` or `mailx` in that it consists of a large set of individual commands rather than one single program; this makes it easy to combine mail-handling tasks with other chores, and you can combine `MH` commands with shell features such as pipes, redirection, aliases, and command history if you wish.

`MH` stores each message as a separate file with a numerical name, and you can use all the usual Unix file-management commands with these files. Table M.9 lists the `MH` commands.

You can get `MH` from a variety of sites including `ftp.ics.uci.edu` in `mh/mh-6.8tar.Z`; consult the USENET newsgroup `comp.mail.mh` for more information.

See also **mail, `Mail`, `mailx`, `xmh`.**

microcode

Very low-level instructions that define how a particular microprocessor works by specifying what the processor does when it executes a machine-language instruction.

microkernel

An alternative kernel design developed by researchers at Carnegie Mellon University and implemented in the Mach operating system.

Traditionally, the kernel has been a monolithic piece of the operating system, resident in memory at all times, taking care of operations as varied as virtual memory management, file input/output, and task scheduling. The microkernel, on the other hand, is a kernel stripped down to the essentials in that it is concerned only with loading, running, and scheduling tasks. All other operating system functions (virtual memory management, disk input/output, and so on) are implemented and managed as tasks running on top of the microkernel.

microprocessor

Also referred to as the *processor*. Usually described as a CPU on one single chip. The first microprocessor was developed by Intel in 1969. Common microprocessors include the Motorola 680x0 series used in the Apple Macintosh computers, the Intel 80x86 family used in IBM and IBM-compatible computers, the PowerPC, and the DEC Alpha.

Table M.9: MH Commands

COMMAND	DESCRIPTION
`ali`	Lists mail aliases.
`anno`	Annotates a message.
`bbc`	Checks on electronic bulletin boards (BBSs), a form of newsgroup.
`burst`	Separates a digest into individual messages.
`comp`	Creates a message.
`dist`	Distributes a message to additional recipients.
`folder`	Sets the current folder or directory.
`folders`	Lists all folders or directories.
`forw`	Forwards a message.
`inc`	Incorporates new mail.
`mark`	Marks a message.
`mhl`	Creates formatted listings of messages.
`mhmail`	Sends or receives mail.
`mhn`	Manages multimedia mail, including audio and video.
`mhook`	Runs a program automatically when you receive mail.
`mhparam`	Prints MH parameters.
`mhpath`	Displays all MH folder pathnames.
`msgchk`	Checks for mail.
`msh`	Invokes the `msh` shell on a file in `packf` format, a program that combines the most often used MH commands into one single program.
`next`	Displays the next message.
`packf`	Compresses a folder into a single file.
`pick`	Selects a message by content.
`prev`	Displays the previous message.
`prompter`	Opens an editor so you can create a new message.
`rcvstore`	Stores a message entered at the keyboard (standard input) into a message file.

Table M.9: MH Commands (continued)	
COMMAND	DESCRIPTION
refile	Files messages in other folders.
repl	Replies to a message.
rmf	Removes a folder.
rmm	Removes a message.
scan	Creates a one-line summary of each message.
send	Sends a message.
show	Lists messages.
slocal	Creates a message for special local mail delivery.
sortm	Sorts messages.
vmh	Opens an **MH** windowing interface.
whatnow	Prompts for **send** information.
whom	Expands a message header.

middleware

A category of software that shields an application program from the underlying mechanics of a network, so that the developers of the application do not have to know which network and communications protocols will be used. Middleware is often implemented in a client/server environment, in which different protocols are used.

■ *See also* **RPC.**

milli-

Abbreviated m. A prefix meaning one thousandth in the metric system, often expressed as 10^{-3}.

millisecond

Abbreviated ms or msec. A unit of measurement equal to one thousandth of a second. In computing, hard disk and CD-ROM drive access times are often described in terms of milliseconds; the higher the number, the slower the disk system.

MIME

Abbreviation for Multipurpose Internet Mail Extensions. A set of extensions that allows Internet e-mail users to add non-ASCII or binary elements such as graphics, PostScript files, audio, or video to their e-mail. Most of the common e-mail client programs such as **elm**, Z-mail, and **MH** include MIME capabilities. (**mail**, however, does not support MIME.)

You can obtain **metamail**, a public domain MIME implementation from **thumper.bellcore.com** in **/pub/nsb/mm.2.6.tar.Z**. For more information on MIME, consult the USENET newsgroup **comp.mail.mime** or the FAQs posted in **news.answers**.

■ *See also* **uudecode, uuencode.**

minibuffer

In emacs, the line at the bottom of the screen, used to ask you questions and to display your replies. The minibuffer shares this screen line with the echo area.

minor device number

A number assigned to a specific device within a class of devices.

If you use the `ls -l` command to list the contents of the /dev directory, you see the major and minor device numbers, separated by commas, listed where you would expect to see the file sizes in bytes in an ordinary listing. The rest of the information is the same as that shown by any `ls -l` listing.

■ *See also* **major device number, special file.**

minor mode

Within emacs, an optional feature that you can turn on or off as you work, including inset mode or overstrike mode, automatic file saving, automatic indenting, and so on.

■ *See also* **major mode.**

mkdep

A BSD software development command that creates a makefile dependency list.

■ *See also* **make.**

mkdir

A command that creates one or more new directories in the filesystem.

▶ Syntax

Here's the syntax for mkdir:

```
mkdir [options]directory ...
```

You must have write permission in the parent directory to be able to create a new directory.

▶ Options and Arguments

The mkdir command has two options, as shown in Table M.10. The *directory* argument contains the name or names of the directories that you want to create, and mkdir automatically includes the two invisible entries . (representing the directory itself) and .. (representing the parent directory) in the newly created directory.

▶ Examples

To create a new directory called accounts in the current directory, use:

```
mkdir accounts
```

To create a directory as a subdirectory of another directory, use:

```
mkdir -p
➥ /home/julia/cookbook/part1
```

■ *See also* **cd, chdir, chmod, rm, rmdir, umask.**

Table M.10: Options to Use with mkdir

OPTION	DESCRIPTION
-m *mode*	Specifies the access mode for the new directories; see the chmod entry for details.
-p	Creates the specified intermediate directories if they do not exist.

mkfifo

A BSD and SCO command that creates a FIFO file. The syntax is:

```
mkfifo name ...
```

The FIFO is created with access mode 0777 in BSD and 0666 in SCO; you must have write permission in the parent directory before you can create a FIFO.

■ *See also* **mknod.**

mklocale

A BSD command that reads a LC_CTYPE source file from the standard input and creates a binary file on the standard output suitable for use in `/usr/share/locale/LC_CTYPE`.

mkmsgs

An SVR4 command that converts a list of text strings contained in *`string_file`* into a message file *`message_file`* in a format readable by several other commands. The syntax is:

```
mkmsgs [options] string_file
➥ message_file
```

The `-i` option creates the *`message_file`* in the specified directory, and the `-o` option lets you overwrite an existing *`message_file`*.

mknod

An SCO command that creates a directory entry and an i-node for a special file.

▶ Syntax

The syntax for `mknod` is:

```
mknod name [options]
➥ major minor
```

▶ Options and Arguments

In the syntax line above, *`name`* specifies the name of the entry, *`major`* specifies the major device number, and *`minor`* the minor device number.

Only the superuser can use all the options listed in Table M.11; ordinary users can use only `-p`.

■ *See also* **`mkdep`**.

mksrt

A BSD command that creates an error message file from C source code.

■ *See also* **`xstr`**.

mm macros

Abbreviation for manuscript macros. A set of almost 100 `nroff` and `troff` macros distributed with SVR4 systems. The **mm** macro package is equivalent to the **me** macro package on BSD systems. Macros are used to provide complex formatting options such as automatic numbering of lists, running head control, and font changes. The **mm** macros also support the `eqn` and `tbl` preprocessors.

■ *See also* **me macros, ms macros.**

Table M.11: Options to Use with `mknod`

OPTION	DESCRIPTION
`-b` *`major minor`*	Indicates that the special file is a block special file with specified *`major`* and *`minor`* device numbers.
`-c` *`major minor`*	Indicates that the special file is a character special file with specified *`major`* and *`minor`* device numbers.
`-m`	Creates shared memory.
`-p`	Creates a pipe.
`-s`	Creates a semaphore.

mnemonic

Pronounced "nee-monic." A name or abbreviation used to help you remember a long or complex instruction. Programming languages use many different mnemonics to represent complex instructions.

/mnt

An SVR4 root directory often used as the mount point where filesystems are mounted.

mode

An octal number that specifies what access a file's owner, group, and others have to the file.

■ *See also* **chmod, file permissions, mkdir.**

mode line

In `emacs`, a line at the bottom of each window in which `emacs` displays information about the contents of the window.

■ *See also* **echo area, minibuffer.**

moderated newsgroup

On the Internet, a USENET newsgroup or mailing list that is managed by one or more people in an attempt to maintain standards for the newsgroup. All posts to the newsgroup are reviewed by the moderator to make sure that they meet the standards the newsgroup has set for subject and commercial content before being passed on to the whole group. Moderation is not censorship but an attempt to avoid some of the more extreme antics of those who enjoy flaming and flame wars.

■ *See also* **listserver.**

moderator

A person or small committee of people who review the contents of all posts to a USENET newsgroup or mailing list in an attempt to ensure that the postings meet the standards set by the group. Moderators are almost always volunteers, so be nice to them.

■ *See also* **moderated newsgroup.**

motd

Abbreviation for message of the day; a message sent to all users as they log in to the system. The motd may be a trenchant remark about life and the pursuit of happiness or may be a rather more prosaic message from the system administrator concerning the status of the system.

modulo

The remainder after an integer division; sometimes called *modulus* or *mod*.

You may also find that modulo is used in expressions such as "modulo wildcards," which just means "everything but wildcards."

more

A Unix filter program that displays the contents of a text file one screenful at a time.

▶ Syntax

Here's the syntax to use with `more`:

`more [`*`options`*`]` *`filenames`*

The command displays the contents of *`filenames`* and waits for you to press the Return key to view the next line, or the spacebar to see the next screenful.

When the `more` command pauses, it interprets several keystrokes as commands; you can press **`h`** for help information, **`q`** to quit, even **/** followed by a regular expression to search. Table M.12 lists the most common `more` commands.

▶ Options and Arguments

You can use the options listed in Table M.13 with the `more` command.

▶ Examples

To look at the contents of your `.profile` file, use:

```
more .profile
```

M

Table M.12: Commands to Use with more

COMMAND	DESCRIPTION
=	Displays the current line number.
`/pattern`	Searches for the next occurrence of *`pattern`*.
`h`	Displays help information.
`n``b`	Skips back *`n`* screenfuls; `b` alone skips back one screenful.
`n``f`	Skips forward *`n`* screenfuls; `f` alone skips forward one screenful.
`n``s`	Skips *`n`* lines and displays the next screenful; `s` alone skips one line.
`q` or `Q`	Quits the **`more`** command.
`v`	Starts the `vi` editor on the current file at the current line.

You can also use **`more`** with a pipe on the command line; this is a good way to slow down the display of a long listing so that you can read it before it flashes past:

```
ls -R | more
```

This command displays all files in all directories and so can be a very long listing. Using **`more`** lets you read each screenful; press the spacebar to see the next screenful, and press `q` when you are ready to quit.

See also **cat, `less`, MORE, pg, `pr`.**

MORE

An environment variable used by the **`more`** command to determine the line options available to the user. Users of the Bourne shell and Korn shell set `MORE` in their `.profile` files, while C shell users set it in their `.cshrc` files.

See also **`more`.**

Table M.13: Options to Use with more

OPTION	DESCRIPTION
`-c`	Clears the screen before displaying the file's contents.
`-d`	Displays the prompt `Press space to continue, 'q' to quit`.
`-f`	Counts logical lines rather than screen lines; useful when a file contains very long lines.
`-l`	Ignores formfeed characters.
`-r`	Displays control characters as `^`*`x`*.
`-s`	Displays multiple blank lines as one blank.
`-u`	Turns off display of backspace and underline.
`-w`	Waits for a keystroke before exiting **`more`**.
`-`*`n`*	Sets the display window to *`n`* lines; the default is to use the whole screen.
`+`*`number`*	Starts the display at line *`number`*.
`+/`*`pattern`*	Starts the display two lines before *`pattern`*.

Mosaic

A World Wide Web client program, originally written by the National Center for Supercomputing Applications (NCSA) at the University of Illinois.

Mosaic uses a graphical user interface (GUI) to provide access to Internet resources and allows users to navigate through hypertext documents quickly and easily using a mouse.

Mosaic is available for most operating systems and requires a direct connection to the Internet and that TCP/IP be installed on the client computer. You can obtain Mosaic binaries for most versions of Unix by anonymous `ftp` from `ftp.ncsa.uiuc.edu` in the `/Mosaic` directory.

See also **Lynx, URL, Web browser.**

Motif

A widely adopted X Window-based graphical user interface (GUI) developed by the Open Software Foundation (OSF). The first version was released in 1989, along with a style guide and a plan for application certification—two important elements for a consistent user interface.

See also **mwm, Open Look.**

Motion Picture Experts Group

See **MPEG.**

mount

- To make a filesystem available to other users. A filesystem must first be mounted before you can read or write to the files that it contains.
- To physically place a tape on a tape drive.

See also **mounting a filesystem, mount point.**

`mount`

An NFS command that mounts or adds a filesystem. Only the superuser can use this command. Using `mount` you can add filesystems contained on floppy disks, CD-ROMs, or hard disks.

To track filesystems, `mount` keeps a table in `/etc/mtab` on BSD systems or in `/etc/mnttab` on SVR4 systems; you may also find additional filesystem information in `/etc/fstab` (BSD) or `/etc/vfstab` (SVR4). The list of filesystems that can be mounted is defined in `/etc/mnttab`, while the list of filesystems that are actually physically mounted is maintained in `/etc/vfstab`.

See also **mounting a filesystem, mount point, `umount`.**

mounting a filesystem

To be able to access any filesystem under Unix, you must first `mount` it on a certain directory known as the mount point. This directory must already exist, and it becomes the root directory of the newly mounted filesystem. Once this is done, the files in the filesystem appear to be located in the mount point directory, and you can read and write to them just like any other files on the system. If the mount point directory contained files or directories prior to the new filesystem being mounted, they are hidden until the file system is unmounted again.

The reverse of this process is known as "unmounting" a filesystem and is done with the `umount` command. Unmounting a filesystem does two things: first, it synchronizes the system buffers with the filesystem on the disk, and second, it makes the filesystem inaccessible from its mount point. You are now free to mount a different file system on that mount point.

See also **`mount`, `umount`.**

mount point

Any directory in which a filesystem is mounted. You can mount a filesystem on any directory you like; it does not have to be directly off the root directory.

See also **mounting a filesystem.**

mouse

A small input device with one or more buttons used for pointing or drawing.

As you move the mouse in any direction, an on-screen mouse cursor follows the mouse movements; all movements are relative. Once the mouse pointer is in the correct position on the screen, you can press one of the mouse buttons to initiate an action or operation;

different user interfaces and programs interpret mouse clicks in different ways.

A mouse has been standard equipment on the Macintosh family of computers for a long time, and with the inclusion of a windowing environment in every new Unix system, it will continue to gain in popularity.

MPEG

Pronounced "em-peg." Abbreviation for Motion Picture Experts Group. An image-compression standard and file format that defines a compression method for moving images such as desktop audio, animation, and video.

MPEG hardware compares each successive image in a video sequence with its predecessor. If parts of the image have not changed, MPEG notes and stores this information. MPEG is a lossy compression method that results in some loss of original data; when you decompress the image, you don't get exactly the same image you originally compressed. You should avoid repeated cycles of compression and decompression because this can lead to noticeably degraded image quality. MPEG can achieve a compression ratio of up to 200 to 1.

■ *See also* **data compression, JPEG, lossless compression.**

ms

■ *See* **millisecond.**

MS-DOS

■ *See* **DOS.**

mscreen

An SCO command, normally invoked from your `.profile` or `.login` file, that allows a terminal to have multiple login screens.

msec

■ *See* **millisecond.**

mset

A BSD command used with IBM 3270 systems that retrieves an ASCII-to-3270 keyboard map.

■ *See also* **`tn3270`.**

msgs

A BSD command used to read system messages.

▶ Syntax

The syntax for `msgs` is as follows:

```
msgs [options]number
```

This command is used to read short system messages that you only need to read once. It is normally invoked from your `.login` or `.profile` file.

▶ Options and Arguments

You can specify a message *`number`* from the command line, or if you use *`-number`*, you can start *`number`* messages back from the current message; you can also use the options listed in Table M.14 with the `msgs` command.

■ *See also* **`mail`, `more`.**

Table M.14: Options to Use with `msgs`

OPTION	DESCRIPTION
`-c` *`days`*	Removes all messages over *`days`* old; the default is 21 days.
`-f`	Turns off `No new messages` display.
`-h`	Prints just the first part of each message.
`-l`	Displays only local messages.
`-q`	Checks for new messages; `msgs -q` is often used in login scripts.
`-s`	Enables posting of messages.

ms macros

Consists of the original set of approximately fifty `nroff` and `troff` macros. The `ms` macro package is no longer supported but is often found on many systems. Macros are used to provide complex formatting options such as automatic numbering of lists, controlling running heads, and changing fonts.

■ *See also* **me macros, mm macros.**

mt

A BSD utility used to manipulate a magnetic tape drive.

▶ Syntax

The syntax for `mt` is:

```
mt [tape_name]command[count]
```

▶ Options and Arguments

The *`tape_name`* argument refers to a raw device. The commands you can use with `mt` are listed in Table M.15; you have to enter only enough characters to make the command unique; you don't have to type them all. You can repeat the command by specifying a *`count`*.

MUD

Acronym for Multiuser Dungeon. A role-playing fantasy or adventure game on the Internet that allows many people to participate in the game at the same time. MUDs are text-oriented; when you enter a new room, you see a description of that room, and when you type the `WHO` command, you receive a list of the characters present in the room.

Players can also change the game as they play it, and if the game is an object-oriented MUD known as a MOO (MUD, object oriented), they can manipulate objects using the game's command language.

MULTICS

Acronym for Multiplexed Information and Computing Service, pronounced "mul-tix." A 1960s timesharing operating system designed by a consortium of MIT, GE, and Bell Labs. MULTICS introduced several notable innovations, including the concept of treating all devices as files, an idea that was also implemented in Unix. Use of MULTICS, and the breakup of the consortium, led Dennis Ritchie and Ken Thompson, who were both working for Bell Labs, to develop Unix.

■ *See also* **Unix history.**

Table M.15: Commands to Use with `mt`

COMMAND	DESCRIPTION
`eof` *`count`* or `weof` *`count`*	Writes *`count`* end-of-file marks at the current location on tape.
`fsf` *`count`*	Forward space for *`count`* files.
`fsr` *`count`*	Forward space for *`count`* records.
`bsf` *`count`*	Backward space for *`count`* files.
`bsr` *`count`*	Backward space for *`count`* records.
`offline` or `rewoffl`	Rewinds the tape, and places the unit offline.
`rewind`	Rewinds the tape.
`status`	Displays tape drive status information.

multiprocessing

The ability of an operating system to use more than one central processing unit (CPU) in a single computer.

Symmetrical multiprocessing refers to the operating system's ability to assign tasks dynamically to the next available processor. Asymmetrical multiprocessing requires that the original program designer choose the processor to use for a given task when writing the program.

Multipurpose Internet Mail Extensions

See **MIME.**

multitasking

The simultaneous execution of two or more programs in one computer.

multithreading

The concurrent processing of several tasks or threads inside the same program. Because several tasks can be processed in parallel, one task does not have to wait for another to finish before starting.

multiuser system

Describes a computer system that supports more than one simultaneous user.

DOS, OS/2, and Windows are all single-user operating systems; Unix and its derivatives are all multiuser systems.

mush

Abbreviation for mail user's shell. A public-domain e-mail program with two modes: you can use it with a line-oriented interface (rather like `mail`) or with a full-screen interface (such as Pine or `elm`).

You can get `mush` by anonymous `ftp` from many sites, including `ftp.uu.net` in `/usenet/comp.sources.misc`, and `ftp.waseda.ac.jp` in `/pub/archives/comp.sources.misc`. For more information, you can read the postings in the USENET newsgroup `comp.mail.mush`.

An enhanced version of `mush` is commercially available as Z-mail.

See also **`elm`, mail, `Mail`, `mailx`, MH, Pine.**

mv

A command used to rename or move files.

▶ Syntax

Here's the `mv` syntax:

```
mv [options] source target
```

There are three ways you can use `mv`:

- To change the name of a file.
- To change the name of a directory.
- To move a file or directory to a different directory.

Remember, when moving a file, `mv` copies the file to its new location and then deletes the original.

▶ Options and Arguments

The `mv` command moves or renames the files or directories specified in *`source`* to *`target`*; if the *`target`* directory does not exist, `mv` creates it for you. Table M.16 lists the two mutually exclusive options for this command.

If you use `mv` with no arguments, you will only see a usage message.

Table M.16: Options to Use with `mv`

OPTION	DESCRIPTION
`-f`	Forces removal, even if the file and directory permissions do not allow it.
`-i`	Asks for confirmation before replacing an existing file or directory.

▶ Examples

To move all the files from the current directory to the `/home/pmd/new` directory, use:

```
mv -i * /home/pmd/new
```

The `-i` option tells **mv** not to overwrite any existing files without asking for confirmation.

The **mv** command just returns to the system prompt if the command completed without problems, and with new users, this lack of communication may lead to accidentally deleted files. It is a good idea to use `mv -i` until you are sure about the results of your **mv** commands.

▶ Notes

You cannot use **mv** to move directories across NFS filesystems.

Because **mv** first removes the *target* file, if one exists, before completing the move, any links on the *target* file are lost. To preserve those links, you should copy the file to the *target* name and then remove the original file.

See also **chmod, copy, cp, cpio, rm, rmdir, tar, umask.**

---

mwm

Abbreviation for Motif window manager, a window manager developed by the Open Software Foundation.

\n

■ *See* **newline.**

NAK

Acronym for negative acknowledgment. In communications, a control character, ASCII 21, sent by the receiving computer to indicate that the data was not properly received and should be sent again.

■ *See also* **ACK.**

named pipe

A special type of temporary file that exists independently of any process and allows unrelated processes to exchange information; ordinary pipes only work between related processes. Any number of processes can read or write to a named pipe. Also known as a *FIFO* (first in, first out) *special file.*

■ *See also* **interprocess communications.**

nawk

Acronym for new `awk`, an updated version of the `awk` pattern-matching language, used to scan text files for patterns or simple relationships and then perform specified actions on matching lines.

The original `awk` is named after the program creators, Alfred Aho, Peter Weinberger, and Brian Kernighan. During the 1980s, they made several enhancements to `awk` and called this enhanced version `nawk` for new `awk`. This program was released as part of System V Release 3.1 and is still found on many systems.

▶ Syntax

The syntax for `nawk` is as follows:

```
nawk [options]['program']
➥[files][var=value]
```

You can specify a script direct from the command line, or you can store a script in *`program`* and specify it using `-f`. You can assign the variable *`var`* a value from the command line; the value can be a literal, a shell

N

variable, or a command substitution, but the value is only available after the BEGIN block of the **awk** program has been processed.

▶ Options and Arguments

Table N.1 lists the options you can use with **nawk**.

Table N.2 lists the predefined commands available in **nawk**; some of these commands are available in **awk**, but many are new in **nawk**.

■ *See also* **awk, gawk, icon, perl**.

Table N.1: Options to Use with nawk

OPTION	DESCRIPTION
-f *filename*	Reads instructions from *filename* instead of providing instructions on the command line.
-F *regular-expression*	Separates fields using *regular-expression*.
-v *variable=value*	Assigns *value* to *variable* before starting '*program*'.

Table N.2: Predefined Commands Available in nawk

OPTION	DESCRIPTION
atan2(*y*,*x*)	Returns the arctangent of *y*/*x* in radians.
break	Exits from a for or while loop.
close(*filename-expr*) close (*command-expr*)	Closes a file or pipe using the same expression that opened the file or pipe.
continue	Begins the next iteration of a for or while loop.
cos(*x*)	Returns the cosine of *x* radians.
delete(*array*[*element*])	Deletes an *element* of *array*.
do *body* while(*expr*)	Performs a looping statement, executing the statements in *body*, then evaluating *expr*. If *expr* is true, the loop repeats, and *body* executes again.
exit	Ignores remaining instructions, does not read more input, but branches directly to the END procedures.
exp(*arg*)	Returns the exponent of *arg*.
for(*i=lower*; *i<=upper*;*i*++) *command*	Performs *command* while *i* is between the values of *lower* and *upper*. If you use a series of *commands*, they must be contained within curly braces ({ }).

Table N.2: Predefined Commands Available in nawk (continued)	
OPTION	DESCRIPTION
`for(item in array)` `  command`	Performs *command* for each *item* in *array*. If you use a series of *commands*, they must be contained within curly braces ({ }).

`function`
`➥ name(parameter-list){`
`  statements`
`}`
	Allows you to specify your own user-defined functions. The *parameter-list* is a comma-separated list of variables passed as arguments to the function when the function is called. The body of the function can contain one or more statements and usually contains a `return` statement to pass control back to the point that called the function.

`getline[var][<file]`
or
`command | getline[var]`
	Reads the next line of input. The first syntax reads input from *file*, and the second form reads the output from *command*. Both forms read just one line at a time, which is assigned to `$0` and is parsed into fields setting `NF`, `NR`, and `FNR`.

`gsub(r,s,t)`	Substitutes *s* for each match of the regular expression *r* in the string *t*. If *t* is not specified, it is taken to be `$0`. The substitution is made globally. The value returned by `gsub` is the number of substitutions made.

`if(condition)`
`  command`
`[else]`
`  [command]`
	If *condition* is true, execute *command*; otherwise, execute the *command* in the `else` clause. A series of commands must be enclosed within curly braces ({ }).

`index(substr,str)`	Returns the position of the first place within the string *str* where the substring *substr* occurs. If *substr* does not occur within *str*, `index` returns 0.
`int(arg)`	Returns the integer value of *arg*.
`length(str)`	Returns the number of characters in the string *str*; if *str* is not supplied, `S0` is assumed.
`log(x)`	Returns the natural logarithm of *x*.
`match(s,r)`	Tests whether the string *s* contains a match for the regular expression *r*, and returns either the position where the match begins or 0 if no match is found. Sets both `RSTART` and `RLENGTH`.

Table N.2: Predefined Commands Available in nawk (continued)	
OPTION	DESCRIPTION
`next`	Reads the next line of input and starts a new pass through all the pattern/procedure statements in the **nawk** program or script.
`print[`*args*`][`*destination*`]`	Prints *args* on the appropriate output device. Literal strings must be quoted, and successive values separated by commas are separated by the predefined variable OFS; successive values separated by spaces are concatenated. You can use redirection with the default output.
`printf[`*format*`]` ➥`[, `*expressions*`]`	Produces a formatted print following the conventions of the C programming language `printf` statement, including `%s` to print a string, `%d` to print a decimal number, and `%`*n*`.`*m*`f` to print a floating point number, where *n* represents the total number of digits and *m* represents the number of digits after the decimal point.
`rand()`	Returns a random number between 0 and 1. This command returns the same random number each time it is run, unless the random number generator is seeded using `srand()`.
`return[`*expr*`]`	Returns the value *expr* at the end of a user-defined function.
`sin(`*x*`)`	Returns the sine of *x*.
`split(`*string*`,`*array*`[,`*sep*`]`	Splits the string *string* into fields using the separator *sep*, and then puts those fields into the array *array*. If *sep* is not specified, then `FS` is used.
`sprintf` ➥`[`*format*`[,`*expression*`]]`	Returns the value of *expression* using the *format*. Nothing is actually printed; data is only formatted.
`sqrt(`*arg*`)`	Returns the square root of *arg*.
`srand(`*expr*`)`	Sets a new seed value for the random number generator using *expr*. If *expr* is not specified, the time of day is used as the default.
`sub(`*r*`,`*s*`,[`*t*`])`	If the string *t* is specified, substitute the string *s* for the first occurrence of the regular expression *r* in *t*. If *t* is not specified, `$0` is assumed; returns 1 if successful, 0 if not.

Table N.2: Predefined Commands Available in nawk (continued)

OPTION	DESCRIPTION
`substr(`*`string,m,`*`[`*`n`*`])`	Returns the substring of *string* beginning at character number *m* and consisting of the next *n* characters. If *n* is not specified, includes all characters to the end of the string.
`system(`*`command`*`)`	Executes the Unix *command*, and returns an exit value.
`tolower(`*`str`*`)`	Converts all uppercase characters in *str* to lowercase and returns the new string.
`toupper(`*`str`*`)`	Converts all lowercase characters in *str* to uppercase and returns the new string.
`while(`*`condition`*`)` *`command`*	Executes *command* while *condition* is true. A series of commands must be contained within curly braces (`{ }`).

NCSA

Abbreviation for National Computer Security Association, based in Washington, D.C., which performs research on issues relating to computer security.

NCSA Mosaic

■ *See* **Mosaic.**

NCSC

Abbreviation for National Computer Security Center, based in Fort Meade, Maryland, part of the National Security Agency. Publishes requirements for and certifies security levels in computer systems for the federal government.

neqn

A version of `eqn` used with `nroff` to format text containing mathematical symbols and equations.

■ *See also* **`eqn`, `nroff`.**

NetBEUI

Abbreviation for NetBIOS Extended User Interface, pronounced "net-boo-ee." A network device driver for the transport layer supplied with Microsoft's LAN Manager, Windows for Workgroups, and Windows NT. NetBEUI communicates with the network interface card via the NDIS (Network Driver Interface Specification).

■ *See also* **NetBIOS.**

NetBIOS

Acronym for network basic input/output system, pronounced "net-bye-os." A session layer network protocol, originally developed in 1984 by IBM and Sytek, to manage data exchange and network access.

NetBIOS provides an API with a consistent set of commands for requesting lower level network services to transmit information from node to node, thus separating applications from the underlying network operating system. Many vendors provide either their own versions of NetBIOS or emulations of its communications services in their products.

NetBSD

A free implementation of Unix derived from the BSD series of releases, designed to run on Intel microprocessors. The distribution is usually free but there may be a small charge to cover the distribution media and the packaging.

NetBSD emphasizes multiple platform support, and so has been ported to several non-Intel systems. You can get the system from `ftp.netbsd.org`.

See also **FreeBSD, Linux.**

netiquette

A contraction of network etiquette. The set of unwritten rules governing the use of e-mail to USENET newsgroups.

Like any culture, the USENET world has its own rules and conventions, and if you understand and observe these conventions, you can take your place in the online community without problems. Here are a few tips:

- Remember that the people reading your post are human, too; if you wouldn't say it to their faces, don't post it in your e-mail.
- Lurk before you leap. Spend a few days reading the postings in any group you are interested in joining before you post anything of your own.
- If you use a signature file to close your e-mail, remember to keep it short; people don't want to read lots of cute stuff.
- Don't post messages in uppercase because it is the online equivalent of YELLING; to add emphasis, place an asterisk before and after a word.
- Don't flame or mount personal attacks on other users.
- Check your grammar and spelling before you post.
- Don't be shy; if you are an expert, share your knowledge with others.

See also **cross posting, flame war.**

`.netrc`

A file located in your home directory that contains the configuration information required to make an FTP connection to a remote computer system or to the Internet.

See also **anonymous `ftp`.**

network

A group of computers and associated peripheral devices connected by a communications channel, capable of sharing files and other resources among several users. A network can range from a peer-to-peer network connecting a small number of users in an office or department, to a local area network (LAN) connecting many users over permanently installed cables and dial-up lines, to a metropolitan area network (MAN) or wide area network (WAN) connecting users on several different networks spread over a wide geographic area.

See also **TCP/IP.**

network administration commands

That group of commands used by the system administrator to manage users, security, and network operations. These commands often differ from Unix system to Unix system, and in modern systems, network administration functions are often collected into a single menu-driven application, such as `sysadmsh` found on SCO systems.

network architecture

The design of a network, including the hardware, software, access methods, and the protocols in use. Several well-accepted network architectures have been defined by standards committees and major vendors. For example, the International Standards Organization (ISO) developed the seven-layer ISO/OSI model for computer-to-computer communications, and IBM designed SNA (Systems Network Architecture). Both of these architectures organize network functions into layers of hardware and software, with each layer building on the functions provided by the previous layer.

The ultimate goal is to allow different computers to exchange information freely in as transparent a fashion as possible.

network filesystem

See **NFS.**

network interface card

See **NIC.**

network layer

The third of seven layers of the ISO/OSI model for computer-to-computer communications. The network layer defines protocols for data routing to ensure that the information arrives at the correct destination node and manages communications errors.

newalias

A command used to recreate the database for the mail alias file `/etc/aliases`. This command must be run each time the file changes so that the changes take effect. There are no options or arguments used with this command.

newbie

A newcomer to the world of the Internet.

- *See also* **netiquette.**

newform

An SVR4 command that acts as a text file formatter.

▶ Syntax

The syntax to use with `newform` is as follows:

`newform [`*`options`*`]`*`filename`*

▶ Options and Arguments

The `newform` command formats the specified *`filename`* according to the options listed in Table N.3.

You can combine options with this command, and you can intersperse them (with the exception of `-s`, which must always appear first), between different filenames on the command line.

Table N.3: Options to Use with `newform`

OPTION	DESCRIPTION
`-a`*`n`*	Appends *n* characters to the end of each line; if you don't specify *n*, each line is expanded to the length specified by `-l`.
`-b`*`n`*	Deletes *n* characters from the beginning of each line; if you don't specify *n*, each line is shortened to the length specified by `-l`.
`-c`*`m`*	Uses the character specified by *m* when padding lines with `-a` or `-p`; `-c` must appear before `-a` or `-p`.
`-e`*`n`*	Deletes *n* characters from the end of each line; if you don't specify *n*, each line is shortened to the length specified by `-l`.
`-f`	Displays the `tabspec` format used by the last `-o` option used.
`-i '`*`tabspec`*`'`	Expands tabs to spaces using `tabspec`.
`-l`*`n`*	Sets the line length to *n*; the default is 72 characters. This option usually appears before any other options that modify the line length.
`-o '`*`tabspec`*`'`	Converts spaces into tabs using `tabspec`.
`-p`	Appends *n* characters to the beginning of each line; if you don't specify *n*, each line is expanded to the length specified by `-l`.
`-s`	Strips the leading characters from each line up to and including the first tab.

▶ **Examples**

To convert all tabs in a file to eight spaces, set the output to 80 characters wide, and truncate any lines longer than 80 characters, use:

```
newform -i -l80 -e september.
➥sales >> yearly.sales
```

This example also appends the results of processing the file `september.sales` to the end of the file `yearly.sales` using redirection.

■ *See also* **cut, paste.**

newgrp

A Unix command as well as a built-in Bourne and Korn shell command that changes your current group so that you can work with the new group's files. Only the group ID is changed; you are still a member of your previous group. If you don't specify a new group name (and this new group must already exist), your original group as specified in `/etc/passwd` is reinstated. The `newgrp` command has no options.

■ *See also* **chgrp, chmod, chown, id, passwd.**

newline

The character that by convention marks the end of a line of text in most Unix files; a combination of a carriage return and a linefeed, represented by `\n`.

news

A command used to read the news items posted in `/usr/news` (`/var/news` on certain systems). This command is for a local network news system and is not a USENET newsreader.

▶ **Syntax**

The syntax for this command is:

`news [`*`options`*`][`*`filenames`*`]`

`news` reads simple text files placed in the publicly accessible `/usr/news` (or `/var/news`) directory by other users. To create a news item, you just copy a text file into this directory.

▶ **Options and Arguments**

With no arguments, the `news` command displays all the current *`filenames`* in `/usr/news`. You can use the options listed in Table N.4 with `news`.

Table N.4: Options for Use with news

OPTION	DESCRIPTION
`-a`	Displays all *`filenames`*, current or not.
`-n`	Displays the names of news items, but not the contents.
`-s`	Reports the number of news items.

▶ **Examples**

Some news items are long so it makes sense to pipe them through a pager such as `more`, like this:

```
news -a | more
```

▶ **Notes**

The `news` command places a zero-length file called `.news_time` in your home directory and compares the time and date from this file to the articles in the `/usr/news` directory to determine if you have read an article.

■ *See also* **Mail, mailx, motd, write.**

newsfeed

A USENET server that provides articles to another server; sometimes called a *feed*.

newsgroup

A USENET e-mail group devoted to the discussion of a single topic. Subscribers post articles to the newsgroup, which can then be read by all the other subscribers. Newsgroups do not usually contain hard news items.

■ *See also* **alt newsgroups, newsreader.**

newsgroup categories

USENET newsgroup names fit into a formal structure in which each component of the group name is separated from the next by a period. The left-most part of the name represents the recreational category of newsgroup, and the name gets more specific from left to right. The seven major top-level newsgroup categories are:

- **comp:** Computer science and related topics, including information about operating systems and hardware, as well as more advanced topics such as artificial intelligence and graphics
- **misc:** Anything that doesn't fit into the other six categories
- **news:** Information on USENET and newsgroups
- **rec:** Recreational activities such as hobbies, the arts, movies, and books
- **sci:** Discussion groups on scientific topics, including math, physics, biology
- **soc:** Groups that address social issues and different cultures
- **talk:** Groups that concentrate on controversial subjects such as gun control, abortion, religion, and politics

■ *See also* **alt newsgroups, newsreader.**

.newsrc

A file in your home directory maintained by your USENET newsreader that contains a list of all newsgroups, which ones you subscribe to, and which articles you have read. All the newsreaders use this file, and fortunately, there is only one format.

Your newsreader makes changes to this file when you read an article, and whenever you subscribe to a new newsgroup or unsubscribe from an old one. In addition, if new newsgroups become available, this file is updated automatically with the details.

newsreader

An application used to read the articles posted to USENET newsgroups.

Newsreaders are of two kinds; threaded newsreaders group the newsgroup posts into threads of related articles, while unthreaded newsreaders just present the articles in their original order of posting. Of the two types, threaded newsreaders are much more convenient to use.

■ *See also* **`.newsrc`, `nn`, `rn`, `tin`, `trn`.**

NFS

Abbreviation for network filesystem. A distributed file-sharing system developed almost a decade ago by Sun Microsystems. NFS allows a computer on a network to use the files and peripheral devices of another networked computer as if they were local, subject to certain security restrictions. The physical location of files is usually unimportant to you; all of the standard Unix utilities work with NFS files in just the same way that they work with local files stored on your computer. Using NFS, you can share files on your system with other computers running DOS, the Macintosh operating system, Unix, VMS, or many other operating systems.

NFS is platform-independent and runs on mainframes, minicomputers, RISC-based workstations, diskless workstations, and personal computers. NFS has been licensed and implemented by more than three hundred vendors.

■ *See also* **RFS, RPC.**

NIC

Abbreviation for network interface card. In networking, the PC expansion board that plugs into a personal computer or server and works with the network operating system to control the flow of information over the network. The network interface card is connected to the network media (twisted pair, coaxial, or fiber optic cable), which in turn connects all the network interface cards in the network.

nice

A command that lowers a process's scheduling priority. `nice` is also a built-in C shell command.

The syntax for this command is:

```
nice [-n]command
```

The `-n` argument tells `nice` just how nice to be; the larger the number, the lower the priority that *command* gets and the slower it runs. You can use a number in the range of 1 (highest priority) to 19 (lowest priority), with the default being 10. On certain BSD systems, this range is 0 to 39, with a default of 20.

Only the superuser can increase the priority; entering `-n` as a negative number such as -10 increases the scheduling priority of the command.

When using the C shell's `nice` command, a plus sign followed by a number decreases the priority (this means that you are being nice to other users by taking fewer system resources for your command); the range is from -20 (highest priority) to +20 (lowest priority), with a default of 4.

nine-track tape

A tape storage format that uses nine parallel tracks on 1/2-inch, reel-to-reel magnetic tape. Eight tracks are used for data and one track is used for parity information. These tapes often serve as backup systems on minicomputer and mainframe systems; digital audio tapes (DATs) are more common on networks.

See also **QIC.**

NIS

Abbreviation for Network Information Service, formerly known as the *Yellow Pages* or *YP*; a part of NFS.

A program used to manage password and group files, host address information, access permissions, and data for a system running NFS. NIS makes configuration information consistent across all the systems using NFS by locating a master database on one system, and making this database available to all the other computers on the network, so avoiding the problem of inconsistent updating.

See also **RPC.**

nl

A command that adds line numbers to a text file.

▶ Syntax

Here's the syntax to use:

```
nl [options][filename]
```

The `nl` command is a filter, reading input from the standard input if you do not specify a *filename*, and writing output to the standard output. `nl` adds numbers to each line in a text file, with numbering reset to 1 at the top of each page. A page consists of three elements:

- Header: defined by one line containing only `\:\:\:`
- Body: defined by one line containing only `\:\:`
- Footer: defined by one line containing only `\:`

Different line-numbering options are available within each section.

▶ Options and Arguments

You can use the options listed in Table N.5 with the `nl` command.

▶ Examples

To number all the lines in a file called `first-draft` and send the results to the printer, use:

```
nl first-draft | lp
```

If you want to number those lines that contain text and display the results on your terminal, one screenful at a time, use:

```
nl -bt first-draft | more
```

See also **pr, wc.**

Table N.5: Options to Use with `nl`

OPTION	DESCRIPTION	
`-b` *`type`*	Numbers the lines in the file according to *`type`*, where *`type`* is one of the following:	
	`a`	All lines
	`n`	No numbering
	`p` *`string`*	Only those lines containing *`string`*
	`t`	Printable text, the default
`-d` *`xy`*	Specifies the characters *`xy`* as logical page delimiters; the default is `\:`.	
`-f` *`type`*	Same as `-b`, but controls numbering for the file footer. Numbers the lines in the file according to *`type`*; the default *`type`* is `n`.	
`-h` *`type`*	Same as `-b`, but controls numbering for the file header. Numbers the lines in the file according to *`type`*; the default *`type`* is `n`.	
`-i` *`n`*	Increments the line count by *`n`*; the default is 1.	
`-l`*`n`*	Counts *`n`* consecutive blank lines as one line.	
`-n` *`format`*	Sets the format for the line numbers; *`format`* is one of the following:	
	`ln`	Left justified with no leading zero
	`rn`	Right justified with no leading zero, the default
	`rz`	Right justified
`-p`	Continues line numbering across page breaks without a reset.	
`-s`*`c`*	Specifies the character *`c`* used as a separator between the line number and the text.	
`-v`*`n`*	Starts the numbering on each page at *`n`*; the default is 1.	
`-w`*`n`*	Uses *`n`* columns to show line numbers; the default is 6.	

nm

A software development command that prints the symbol table from one or more object files in alphabetical order.

The output includes each symbol's name, value, type, size, and so on. The `nm` command is most often used with `ELF` or `COFF` files; see the `man` pages on your system for more details.

nn

A newsreader application designed to simplify locating and reading posts in USENET newsgroups; it was originally written by Kim Storm of Texas Instruments in Denmark and released in 1989.

`nn` is a threaded newsreader that automatically groups USENET posts by subject, or thread, which makes it much easier to follow continuing discussions.

Once you select a newsgroup, **nn** displays a list of articles you have not yet read, you mark just those articles that you want to read, and **nn** displays them for you. As you go through the articles, you can save the article in a file, mail a copy of an article to another person, develop a kill file for articles with a certain subject, or decode an article encoded with rot-13. You can also reply directly to the author of an article or post your reply to the newsgroup for others to read.

The **nn** program actually consists of several programs, and their names and functions are listed in Table N.6.

Table N.7 lists the common **nn** commands by function. **nn** works in cbreak mode, which means that you don't have to press the Enter or Return key after a single-letter command; **nn** responds as soon as you type the command letter.

Table N.6: The nn Programs

PROGRAM	DESCRIPTION
nn	Starts the **nn** newsreader.
nncheck	Checks for unread articles in the newsgroups that you subscribe to.
nngoback	Marks a specific day's articles as unread.
nngrab	Finds all the articles whose subject contains a specific pattern.
nngrep	Finds all the newsgroups whose name contains a specific pattern.
nnpost	Posts articles to a specific newsgroup.
nntidy	Cleans up your .newsrc file.
nnusage	Displays **nn** usage statistics.

One aspect of **nn** operation that is easy to remember is that pressing the spacebar selects the default choice at any point, and **nn** has been designed so that the default is often a very good choice.

■ *See also* **.newsrc, rn, tin, trn.**

noclobber

A C shell environment variable that is used for safer redirection processing by preventing accidental destruction of existing files. When set, **noclobber** allows redirection (>) to be used only to create new files, not to overwrite existing files, and appending (>>) can be used only with existing files.

node

- In the Unix hierarchical filesystem, a directory is considered to be a node, the end of a branch capable of supporting other branches.
- Any device attached to the network capable of communicating with other network devices.

■ *See also* **leaf.**

noglob

A C shell environment variable that disables filename expansion.

nohup

A command that lets you continue to execute a command in the background after you log out. Normally, when you log out, Unix kills all the processes that you started during your session.

The syntax for this command is:

```
nohup command [arguments...] &
```

If you don't redirect the output from a process you execute with **nohup**, both the standard output and the standard error are sent to a file called **nohup.out** in the current directory; if you don't have write permission in the current directory, the file is created in your home directory instead.

The **nohup** command is built into the C shell.

Table N.7: Common nn Commands

COMMAND	DESCRIPTION
Basic Commands	
`Ctrl-G`	Cancels the current command.
`Space`	Accepts the default action, usually a good choice to make under most circumstances.
`!`	Pauses `nn`, and starts a new shell.
`!` *`command`*	Executes the specified Unix *`command`*.
`?`	Displays a summary of commands.
`:help`	Shows help information.
`:man`	Displays the `nn man` pages.
`:post`	Posts a new article.
`Q`	Quits `nn`.
Selecting/Unselecting Articles	
`id`	Selects/unselects the specified article.
`id-id`	Selects/unselects the specified range of articles.
`id*`	Selects/unselects articles with the same subject as *`id`*.
`,`	Moves down one line.
`.`	Selects/unselects the current article, then moves down.
`/`	Moves up one line.
`*`	Selects/unselects articles with the same subject as the current article.
`@`	Reverses the selections on the current page.
`=. Return`	Selects all articles in the newsgroup.
`~~`	Unselects all articles in the newsgroup.
Displaying A Selection List	
`Space`	Goes to next page; selected articles are flagged as read.
`>`	Goes to next page.
`<`	Goes to previous page.

Table N.7: Common nn Commands (continued)	
COMMAND	DESCRIPTION
^	Goes to first page.
$	Goes to last page.
Reading Articles	
Space	Starts displaying articles.
X	Starts displaying articles; goes to next newsgroup when all articles have been read.
Z	Starts displaying articles; stays in the current newsgroup when all articles have been read.
Saving Articles	
O	Saves article and a shortened header to a file.
S	Saves article and complete header to a file.
W	Saves article without header to a file.
Responding to Articles	
F	Creates a followup post in the current newsgroup.
K	Creates a kill file to screen articles with a specific subject or articles from a specific author.
M	Mails a copy of the current article to a specific recipient.
R	Replies by mail to the originator of the current article.
Managing Newsgroups	
A	Changes to the next newsgroup in sequence.
B	Changes to the previous newsgroup in sequence.
G	Goes to a specific newsgroup.
N	Changes to the next subscribed newsgroup.
P	Changes back to the last newsgroup that you looked at.
U	Unsubscribes/subscribes to the current newsgroup.
Y	Displays list of newsgroups containing unread articles.

nomagic

A toggle in the `ex` and `vi` editors that turns off the `magic` variable.

■ *See also* **magic.**

no news is good news

A fundamental Unix principle employed in many commands and utilities. If the operation you are attempting completes without any problems, Unix stays silent and says nothing; if you make an error, or some sort of nonstandard result occurs, Unix sends you a message.

nonfatal error

Any error from which the system can recover easily, such as attempting to delete a nonexistent file.

nonprinting character

Any character that cannot be printed or does not have a graphical equivalent, such as a space, a tab, or one of the control characters.

■ *See also* **printable character.**

nonomatch

A C shell environment variable that treats metacharacters as literal characters without any special meaning.

notify

A command that tells you when any new mail arrives.

▶ Syntax

The syntax for this command is:

```
notify [options]
```

▶ Options and Arguments

If you use `notify` without options, the command displays the current state (on or off) of automatic mail notification. The options you can use with this command are listed in Table N.8.

Table N.8: Options for Use with `notify`

OPTION	DESCRIPTION
`-m` *`filename`*	Saves mail in the specified *`filename`* rather than the default file.
`-n`	Turns off automatic mail notification; this option must be used by itself.
`-y`	Turns on automatic mail notification.

▶ Notes

`notify` is also a built-in C shell command that immediately informs users about completed jobs instead of waiting for the next prompt.

The syntax is:

```
notify jobID
```

If you don't specify a *`jobID`*, the current background job is assumed.

■ *See also* **`biff`**, **`xbiff`**.

novice

An environment variable in the `vi` editor that displays the name of the current editor mode at the bottom of the screen.

nroff

A text-processing program that creates a file suitable for output to a line printer; an acronym for New Runoff, `nroff` is pronounced "en-roff."

Unix often includes two programs for text processing, `nroff` and `troff`. The `nroff` program is used when you want to output formatted text to a line printer or to a line-oriented display, and `troff` is used when you want to send text to a laser printer, bitmapped display, or to a typesetter.

An input file for `nroff` contains lines of text interspersed with lines that begin with a period and contain

one- or two-letter commands. `nroff` also allows you to define a macro as a series of input lines, and three major macro packages are available that automate complex formatting functions.

The main benefit to using `nroff` and `troff` rather than a commercial word processor is that their input files are simple text files. This allows you to use many other Unix utilities (`grep`, `diff`, and so on) with your files, which is something you can't do with the proprietary formats used by word processors.

See also **eqn, LATEX, groff, me macros, mm macros, ms macros, pic, soelim, tbl, TEX, TEXinfo, troff.**

nslookup

A TCP/IP command that provides the IP address of any domain, as well as other information of interest to network administrators.

Used with no arguments, `nslookup` enters interactive mode, in which you can query name servers for information on hosts or print a list of the hosts in a domain. When you specify the name of a host as the first argument on the command line, `nslookup` prints the name and the requested information about a host or a domain.

null

Something that is empty, has zero length, and contains no characters.

See also **null string.**

null argument

A command-line argument that has no value but is needed so that arguments are interpreted in their correct position. When you use explicit options, null arguments are not necessary.

null character

A special value used to indicate the end of a character string, the end of a file, or an empty pointer. By convention, the character is represented by all zeros.

null device

The Unix null device, also known as the *bit bucket*, is `/dev/null`. When you send output to the null device, it is discarded.

null string

A string that contains no characters; a string of zero length.

numbered buffer

In the `vi` editor, one of nine storage areas used to store text that has been deleted from a file; when the tenth deletion is made, the first buffer is overwritten.

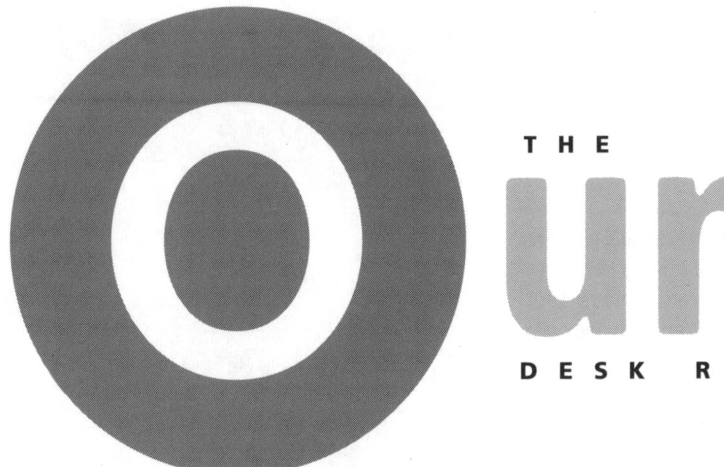

object

- Any distinct entity. Program objects can represent applications such as word processors, spreadsheets, and so on. Folder objects can represent a directory and contain a group of files, a group of programs, or a group of other folders. Data file objects can include information such as text, memos, letters, spreadsheets, video, and sound. Device objects can be printers, fax modems, plotters, servers, and CD-ROMS.
- In object-oriented programming, a program consists of a set of related but self-contained objects that can contain both code and data.

object file

A file created by compiling source code. The file contains machine language instructions and can be linked with other object files to form an executable program that can be loaded into memory and run.

■ *See also* **`as`, `a.out`, compiling a C program.**

object-oriented

A term that can be applied to any computer system, operating system, programming language, application, or graphical user interface that supports the use of objects.

object-oriented programming

Abbreviated OOP. A programming model that views a program as a set of self-contained objects that interact with other objects by passing messages between them. Object-oriented programming also lets you create procedures that work with objects whose exact type may not be known until the program actually runs.

In object-oriented programming, each object contains both data and code. Also, each object is completely self-contained. The program incorporates an object by making it part of a layered hierarchy. Object-oriented programming did not just appear overnight but is the result of many years of theoretical development. It is

seen by many to be the current extension of the theory behind modular programming.

See also **class, encapsulation, inheritance, polymorphism.**

octal

The base 8 numbering system that uses the digits 0 to 7, inclusive. The octal system is used in programming as a compact way of representing binary numbers. Each octal digit consists of three bits; for example, the octal number 14 is equivalent to the decimal number 12. Octal numbers are used throughout Unix, but they are considered to be something of an anachronism.

See also **decimal, hexadecimal.**

octet

The Internet's own term for eight bits or a byte. Some computer systems attached to the Internet have used a byte with more than eight bits, hence the need for this term.

od

A command used to make an octal, decimal, hexadecimal, or ASCII dump of a file.

▶ Syntax

Here's the syntax to use with `od`:

```
od [options][filename]offset
```

▶ Options and Arguments

The `od` command makes a dump of the specified *`filename`* in octal unless one of the options is used. The file is dumped starting at the beginning unless you specify an *`offset`*, which is normally in octal bytes; use a **.** if you want to specify the *`offset`* in decimal, or `b` to specify that the *`offset`* represents blocks of 512 bytes. Table O.1 lists the options you can use with `od`.

See also **`bc`, `dd`, `hexdump`, `more`.**

Table O.1: Options to use with od

OPTION	DESCRIPTION
`-a`	ASCII, text
`-b`	Octal, byte
`-B`	Short, octal
`-c`	ASCII, byte
`-C`	Extended ASCII
`-d`	Unsigned short, decimal
`-D`	Unsigned long, decimal
`-e`	Double-precision floating point
`-f`	Single-precision floating point
`-F`	Double-precision floating point; same as `-e`
`-h`	Short, hexadecimal
`-H`	Long, hexadecimal
`-i`	Short, signed decimal
`-I`	Long, signed decimal
`-p`	Even parity
`-P`	Odd parity
`-s`	Accepts a string
`-v`	Displays all data

offline reader

An application that lets you read postings to USENET newsgroups without having to stay connected to the Internet.

The program downloads all the newsgroup postings you have not read and then disconnects from your service provider. This means that you can read the postings at your convenience without incurring online charges or tying up your telephone line. If you reply to any of these postings, the program automatically uploads your reply to the right newsgroup the next time you connect to your service provider.

olwm

The name of the Open Look window manager, developed by Sun Microsystems.

■ *See also* **mwm, Open Look.**

onintr

A C shell keyword used to manage interrupts in a shell script. You can use `onintr` in three different ways: the command `onintr` *`label`* works like a `goto` and branches to the line beginning with *`label`*; the command `onintr -` allows the script to ignore interrupts; and the command `onintr` without arguments turns interrupt processing back on again.

Open Desktop

A graphical user interface (GUI) from SCO that provides access to system utility functions, SCO, and DOS on the desktop. Files, directories, and programs are represented by icons and displayed in windows.

■ *See also* **OpenServer.**

open file

Any file currently in use is said to be open or open for use.

OpenGL

Acronym for Open Graphics Library; a set of graphics libraries originally developed by Silicon Graphics and now supported by IBM, Intel, Microsoft, and many other companies.

OpenGL lets developers create 3D graphical applications for workstations running the Programmer's Hierarchical Interactive Graphics System (PHiGS) extensions to the X Window system.

■ *See also* **X Consortium, X Window.**

Open Look

An X Window-based graphical user interface (GUI) developed by AT&T and Sun Microsystems. Open Look is used as the standard window manager on Sun's workstations, but it has not been adopted as widely as OSF's Motif.

■ *See also* **olwm, push pin.**

OpenServer

A scalable set of Unix-based products from SCO, including the Desktop System, Host System, and Enterprise System, based on SVR3.2 but containing many significant SVR4 enhancements. The Desktop System is a single-user multitasking system that includes DOS emulation, Microsoft Windows 3.1 support, TCP/IP connectivity, a built-in World Wide Web browser, a graphical newsreader, and e-mail support.

The Enterprise and Host systems provide high-performance scalable servers for Intel-based platforms, supporting over 8,000 applications, with extensive networking support, UPS, and advanced power management support.

■ *See also* **SCOadmin, sysadmsh.**

open system

A term used to describe hardware and software that is not dependent on any specific vendor's proprietary systems but which follows well-known public standards.

openwin

A command used to start the X Window system and the OpenWindows window manager on a system running Solaris.

▶ Syntax

The syntax for this command is:

```
openwin [options]
```

▶ Options and Arguments

Table O.2 lists the options you can use with the `openwin` command.

■ *See also* **xrdb.**

O

Table O.2: Options Used with openwin

OPTION	DESCRIPTION
-banner	Displays the OpenWindows startup banner.
-noauth	Lowers the security level.
-includedemo	Adds the demo directory to your path.
-nobanner	Disables the OpenWindows startup banner making startup slightly faster.

OpenWindows

A graphical user interface available with Solaris, based on Open Look. OpenWindows includes a set of applications, called DeskSet, used to perform common day-to-day tasks.

■ *See also* **olwm.**

operand

Any data upon which a mathematical function or computer operation is being performed. An operand can be actual data contained in a variable or the memory or disk location where the data is stored.

operating system

Abbreviated OS. The software responsible for allocating system resources, including memory, processor time, disk space, and peripheral devices such as printers, modems, and monitors. All application programs use the operating system to gain access to these system resources as they are needed. The operating system is the first program loaded into the computer as it boots, and it remains in memory at all times thereafter.

■ *See also* **kernel, microkernel.**

/opt

A root directory often used to contain additional application programs.

■ *See also* **/bin.**

OPTARG

An environment variable that contains the last option argument processed by the getopts command.

■ *See also* **OPTIND.**

OPTIND

An environment variable that contains the index of the last option argument processed by the getopts command.

■ *See also* **OPTARG.**

option

A command-line argument that modifies the effect of a command. Sometimes called *switches*, options are usually preceded by a dash or hyphen on the command line (as in ls -l), and they can sometimes be grouped together following a single hyphen (as in ls -la), depending on the specific command. The hyphen is usually pronounced "minus," as in "ls minus l" for ls -l. Many options consist of a single letter, but some are groups of letters or, in some cases, even short words.

There is little consistency in the use of option letters between commands; do not expect that the -l option for one command will perform a similar function in a different command.

■ *See also* **optional argument.**

optional argument

A command-line argument that is not required for a command to be able to function but changes the way in which the command works. For example, the `ls` command lists the contents of a directory and has approximately 20 different options you can use to specify the exact details of the command's output.

■ *See also* **option.**

Orange Book

Jargon for the *Trusted Computer System Evaluation Criteria*, published in August 1983 by the U.S. Department of Defense; so-called because of its orange cover.

This publication details standards for security levels used to control access to computer systems from Class A1, the highest verifiable security level, to Class D, the lowest, which has no security.

Class C2 is the security level most appropriate to the business world; higher levels of security tend to intrude too much into normal work patterns. C2 security requires that the operating system provide individual logins with separate accounts and a verifiable audit trail. Some software vendors have layered additional security features on top of Unix to conform to the C2 level of security required by certain users.

■ *See also* **security.**

ordinary file

A file that contains text or other user data accessible by a person or an application program. An ordinary file is what most users think of as a file and has no specific structure required by the system.

■ *See also* **binary file, block special file, character special file, directory, FIFO file, socket, text file.**

orphaned file

A file whose name has been lost but whose contents remain, usually as a result of damage to the filesystem. Such files are usually placed in the `/lost+found` directory by the `fsck` utility. Sometimes called an *unreferenced file.*

orphan process

A process whose parent has died.

■ *See also* **child process, parent process, zombie.**

OSF

Abbreviation for Open Software Foundation. A nonprofit organization engaged in research into standards for computers and networked systems. Originally formed in 1984 to develop an operating system to compete against SVR4, founding members included IBM, DEC, Hewlett-Packard, and others.

■ *See also* **OSF/1.**

OSF/1

An operating system from the Open Software Foundation, released in 1990 and based on the Mach kernel developed by Carnegie Mellon University.

■ *See also* **POSIX.**

OSIRM

■ *See* **ISO/OSI model.**

OSx

A version of Unix from Pyramid Technology that includes elements of both AT&T and BSD systems.

output

Any information that a program sends to a terminal, printer, or another file.

■ *See also* **standard output.**

output redirection

The mechanism used to send output to a file or to an alternative device rather than to the standard output, usually a terminal.

To redirect the standard output, use the greater than symbol (>) on the command line, as in the following example, which sends the output from the `ls` command to a file called `directory.list`:

```
ls > directory.list
```

You can then use the `cat` command to look at the contents of `directory.list`. If the file `directory.list` already exists, this command overwrites it; to add (or append) the `ls` listing to the end of a file, use two greater than symbols together like this:

```
ls >> directory.list
```

■ *See also* **ampersand, input redirection, less than symbol, standard input, standard error.**

owner

The Unix user who creates a file and controls the file's access modes and permissions.

The long version of the `ls` command (`ls -l`) used to list the contents of a directory also lists the names of file owners.

■ *See also* **chown**.

THE unix DESK REFERENCE

P

P

See **peta-**.

pack

An SVR4 command used to compress files so that they occupy less hard disk space. The syntax is:

```
pack [options]filename...
```

The `pack` command compacts files and replaces them with compressed files with `.z` appended to the original filename. To restore the files to their original states, use the `unpack` command. The *`filename`* argument can be a single filename or a space-separated list of filenames for compression. File permissions and the modification date of the original file remain unchanged.

When you specify the – option, `pack` displays statistical information about the packing of files, and the `-f` option forces the file to be packed even though no space is saved. This option is useful when preparing a project archive and you have to pack all the project files.

See also **`cat`, `compress`, `gzip`, `uncompact`, `uncompress`, `unpack`, `zcat`.**

packet

Any block of data sent over a network. Each packet contains sender, receiver, and error control information, in addition to the actual message. Packets may be fixed-length or variable-length, and they are reassembled, if necessary, when they reach their destinations. The actual format of a packet depends on the protocol that creates the packet; in addition to data packets, some protocols use special packets to control communications functions.

See also **Ethernet, `ping`.**

page

A system level alias for the `more` command.

pager

Any program that breaks a file into screen-sized chunks and sends these chunks, one by one, to your terminal for display.

■ *See also* **head, less, more, pg.**

pagesize

A BSD command that displays the page size of system memory in bytes. This command has no options.

paging

A mechanism, originally developed as part of the BSD releases and similar to swapping, that is used to manage scarce memory resources. When memory is full, pages, or sections, of programs are first moved to a memory buffer known as the *dirty page list*, and then when that is full, pages are moved out to disk. When a certain page is needed, the operating system looks for it in the dirty page list first and then on the hard disk. Because smaller sections of programs are managed in this way, the total impact on performance is less overall than with swapping in which complete processes are written out to disk.

■ *See also* **virtual memory.**

panic

Unix jargon for a special kind of crash. A panic occurs when Unix detects that the kernel cannot continue to run and so shuts down the system before any damage can be done. As it shuts down, Unix prints a "panic" message on the console.

parallel processing

A computing method that can be performed by systems containing two or more processors operating simultaneously. Parallel processing uses several processors, all working on different aspects of the same program at the same time or running separate programs in parallel, in order to share the computational load.

Parallel processing computers can achieve incredible speeds; the Cray T3E peaks at one teraflop using from 16 to 2,048 extremely powerful processors, while parallel-hypercube systems, first marketed by Intel, can exceed 65,536 processors with speeds of up to 262 billion floating point operations per second (262 GFLOP).

In all but the most trivial parallel processing applications, the programmer or the operating system must assign appropriate CPU loads; otherwise, it is possible for nonoptimized applications to fail to take advantage of the power available and, in the worst case, run more slowly than on single-processor systems.

All this speed is used for applications such as weather forecasting, in which the predictive programs can take as long to run as the weather actually takes to arrive, 3D seismic modeling, groundwater and toxic flow studies, and modeling full-motion dinosaur images used in movies.

■ *See also* **asymmetrical multiprocessing, symmetrical multiprocessing.**

parameter

In programming, a variable that is passed to a program or function from the host environment and holds a constant value. A parameter can be a number, a date, a filename, or simple text—anything that customizes program operation.

■ *See also* **argument, option, variable.**

parameter substitution

The mechanism used by the shell to replace a reference to a parameter by its value; sometimes called *variable substitution.*

parent directory

The directory immediately above the current directory in the filesystem; only the root directory has no parent. Two periods .. (dot dot) are shorthand for the name of the parent directory, and you can use:

```
cd ..
```

to change to the parent directory without having to type (or even remember) its name.

parentheses

Either of the characters **(** or **)** that are often used for grouping.

parent PID

See **PPID.**

parent process

A process that forks other processes. Every process can identify its parent because the PPID number is stored in the process' user table.

See also **child process, exec, fork, spawn.**

parity

In communications, a simple form of error checking that uses an extra, or redundant bit, after the data bits but before the stop bits.

Parity may be set to odd, even, mark, space, or none. Odd parity indicates that the sum of all the 1 bits in the byte plus the parity bit must be odd. If the total is already odd, the parity bit is set to zero; if it is even, the parity bit is set to 1.

In even parity, if the sum of all the 1 bits is even, the parity bit must be set to 0; if it is odd, the parity bit must be set to 1.

In mark parity, the parity bit is always set to 1 and is used as the eighth bit.

In space parity, the parity bit is set to 0 and used as the eighth bit.

If parity is set to none, there is no parity bit, and no parity checking is performed.

The parity setting on your computer must match the setting on the remote computer for successful communications.

See also **asynchronous communications.**

parse

A mechanism used by assemblers, compilers, interpreters, and the shell, which breaks a string of characters into its component elements and then interprets each separate piece.

See also **lexical analysis.**

P

passwd

A command used to maintain users' login passwords.

Syntax

The syntax to use with `passwd` is simple:

```
passwd
```

The `passwd` command prompts you for your old password, then for the new password you want to use instead, and then asks you to confirm the new password a second time. Only your system administrator can change your password without knowing your current password.

This command has several options, which are not shown here because they can be used only by the superuser. Many modern Unix systems provide a system administrator's shell for password management; if yours does, you should use it because it is indeed the most convenient way to manage passwords and changes to passwords.

Notes

Many systems use NIS to share information. The original name for NIS was the Sun Yellow Pages, and so the `yppasswd` command is used to maintain the network-wide password database.

Some BSD systems use the Kerberos security system, which stores passwords in an authentication database; on these systems, use the `kpasswd` command to change passwords.

See also **password, password file.**

password

A secret sequence of characters that you type to verify your identity when you log in to the system.

In general, passwords should be a mixture of uppercase and lowercase letters and numbers and

should be longer than six characters. Here are some general guidelines:

- Passwords should be kept secret and changed frequently. The worst passwords are the obvious ones: people's names or initials, place names, names of pets, TV characters, or anyone associated with "Star Trek," phone numbers, birth dates, groups of the same letter or simple patterns of keys such as "qwerty," or complete English words. There are a limited number of words in the English language, and it is easy for a computer to try them all relatively quickly.
- Change all passwords at least every 90 days, and change those associated with high-security privileges every month.
- Some systems provide default passwords, such as MANAGER, SERVICE, or GUEST, as part of the installation process. These default passwords should be changed immediately.
- Limit concurrent sessions to one per system.
- Do not allow more than two or three invalid password attempts before disconnecting.
- Do not allow generic accounts.
- Promptly remove the accounts of transferred or terminated employees, as well as all unused accounts.
- Review the security log files periodically.

See also **NCSC, security.**

password encryption

In Unix, passwords are not stored as ordinary text but are encrypted. When you type your password as you log in to the system, it is encrypted, and the result is compared against the encrypted password stored in `/etc/passwd`. If they match, the login continues, and you can use the system; if not, you return to the `Password:` prompt.

password file

A file containing passwords and other information about users on the system. In Unix, the file is called `/etc/passwd` and contains the information in the seven fields listed in Table P.1.

See also **`passwd`**.

Table P.1: Contents of `/etc/passwd`

FILENAME	DESCRIPTION
`userID`	Your username as defined by the system administrator, usually all in lowercase letters.
`password`	Your encrypted password.
`userID number`	Numeric value for your user ID.
`groupID number`	Numeric value for your group ID, indicating the groups you belong to. The names of the groups are in `/etc/group`.
`text field`	Sometimes called the GECOS field, after an ancient General Electric operating system. Traditionally, this entry has four comma-separated fields for your full name, your office number, your office phone number, and your home phone number.
`users home directory`	The name of your home directory.
`shell`	The name of the shell that automatically starts when you log in to the system.

paste

A command used to create columnar output from one or more files, each file contributing one column. Output is to the standard output.

▶ Syntax

The syntax for `paste` is as follows:

```
paste [options]files
```

The `paste` command merges corresponding lines in several files; each file is considered to represent one column, and the columns are joined horizontally. The newline character at the end of the first line is replaced by a tab, then the second file is pasted to the first, and so on.

▶ Options and Arguments

In the syntax shown above, *`files`* specifies the list of files you want to paste together; if this argument is missing, you can use `-` to indicate that the standard input be used instead. The options available with `paste` are listed in Table P.2.

■ *See also* **cat, cut, join, newform, pr.**

Table P.2: Options to Use with paste

OPTION	DESCRIPTION
-d *delim*	Specifies the character to use when delimiting columns; tab is the default.
-s	Merges lines serially from one file, combining them into one long line; if you use this option with more than one input file, you will get confused and meaningless results.

patch

A BSD command used along with the `diff` command to update a text file to a later version.

▶ Syntax

The syntax to use with `patch` is as follows:

```
patch [options] filename
```

The guardian of a file first uses `diff` to create a set of differences between two files; these differences are the patches. Another person who has a copy of the same original file can use the `patch` command to apply the differences and produce a patched copy that reflects the new version of the file.

By default, the patched file takes the place of the unpatched original, and the original is renamed *`filename`*`.orig`.

▶ Options and Arguments

In the above syntax, *`filename`* represents the file you want to patch. The patches are read from the standard input unless a different file *`pfile`* is specified with the `-i` option; see Table P.3 for a complete listing of options available with `patch`.

■ *See also* **diff, diff3.**

path

In the C shell, a variable that contains a list of directories separated by spaces and updated by the `set` command, as follows:

```
set path = ( /usr/bin /
➥usr/bin/myprograms . )
```

The spacing also applies to the name of the current directory, represented here by the `.` (dot).

■ *See also* **PATH.**

PATH

In the Bourne shell and Korn Shell, an environment variable that defines the system path for the shell, used to locate executable files or commands. Each time you ask the shell to execute a command, it searches each directory in this variable to find the command. Directory names in the `PATH` statement are separated by colons.

The best place to customize your path is in `$HOME/.profile`.

■ *See also* **path, pathname.**

Table P.3: Options for patch	
OPTION	DESCRIPTION
-b *extension*	Saves the original file in *filename.extension* rather than in *filename*.orig.
-c	Assumes that the patches were generated by diff -c.
-d *directory*	Changes to the specified *directory* before starting work.
-D	Makes patch use the C language #ifdef...#endif construct to mark changes.
-e	Assumes that the patches were generated by diff -e.
-f	Turns off prompts for user input.
-F *n*	Sets the fuzz factor to *n*.
-i *pfile*	Reads patches from the specified *pfile*.
-l	Treats groups of spaces as equivalent.
-n	Assumes that the patches were generated by diff with no options.
-N	Ignores patches already applied.
-o *filename*	Writes the patched output to *filename*.
-p *n*	Deletes *n* pathname elements from the name of the file to be patched. This is useful if you keep your files in different directories than the person who sent you the patch.
-r *rfile*	Sends rejected patches to *rfile*.
-R	Reverses the patch.
-s	Sets silent working mode.

pathname

A list of directory names separated by slashes (/) that ends with the name of a file. The pathname is used to follow through a directory structure to locate a specific file. Sometimes written as pathname, and sometimes called *search path*.

■ *See also* **absolute pathname, basename, relative pathname.**

pathname expansion

A term used in the Bash shell as a synonym for *filename expansion*.

■ *See also* **asterisk, filename substitution.**

pattern matching

The process of searching for a character or string of characters.

■ *See also* **grep, regular expressions.**

P

PB

■ *See* **petabyte.**

pcat

A command used to display the contents of one or more packed files. The `pcat` command has no options.

■ *See also* **`compress`, `pack`, `unpack`, `zcat`.**

PDP-11

A 16-bit computer released by DEC in 1970 that was important in the early days of Unix development. Eventually, over 250,000 PDP-11s were sold in a wide variety of configurations; the base unit cost $10,800.

■ *See also* **Unix history.**

PEM

Abbreviation for Privacy Enhanced Mail, a proposed addition to SMTP designed to ensure the privacy of e-mail by letting users encrypt e-mail so that only the recipient can decode and read the message.

percent sign

The `%` character, which is the default command prompt for the C shell. Also the modulo operator, used to determine the remainder after an integer division.

■ *See also* **dollar sign.**

period

The `.` character, pronounced "dot."

- A symbol used to indicate the current directory in a pathname.
- A built-in Bourne shell and Korn shell command that reads a file and executes its contents as though you had typed them at the command prompt.
- A metacharacter used to match any single character in a regular expression.

■ *See also* **dot, dot dot, dot file.**

perl

`perl`, an acronym formed from Practical Extraction and Report Language (also known as Pathologically Eclectic Rubbish Lister), is an interpreted language developed by Larry Ward, used to manipulate text, files, and processes and to print reports based on extracted information. It works something like a combination of `awk`, `sed`, the C language, and the C shell.

`perl` is rapidly becoming the system administrator's answer to all those problems that a C program does not seem to fit, and `perl` is well suited to perform other kinds of tasks. It does not have those arbitrary limitations that plague other commands—lines can be of any length, arrays can be of any size, variable names can be as long as you care to make them, and binary data does not cause problems.

You can get `perl` by anonymous `ftp` from `prep.ai.mit.edu` in the `/pub/gnu` directory. The file is called `perl`*`ver`*`.tar.gz`, where *`ver`* represents the current version number. You can also get it from the `comp.sources.unix` archive. `perl` is public domain software, and several excellent books are available as both introductions to `perl` and advanced `perl` programming tutorials. You might also check the USENET newsgroup `comp.lang.perl`.

■ *See also* **`awk`, `sed`.**

permission bits

A special binary number associated with a file that specifies who can access the file and in what way.

There are three independent permissions—read, write, and execute:

- Read permission lets you read the file.
- Write permission lets you write to the file and change it if you wish.
- Execute permission means that you can execute the file.

You can set and change the file permissions for your own files; the main reasons for doing this are to prevent others from accessing your files and to protect yourself against accidental changes or deletions to important files.

Figure P.1: An Example of the Permuted Index

exec:overlay shell with specified	command	chs(1)
time: time	command	csh(1)
grog: guess options for groff	command	grog(1)
routines for returning a stream to a remote	command. rcmd,rresvport,rusero:	rcmd(3)
rexec: return stream to a remote	command	rexec(3)
nice: execute a	command at a low scheduling priority . . .	nice(1)
switch: multiway	command branch	csh(1)
time: time	command execution	time(1)
uux: unix to unix	command execution	uux(1)
rehash:recompute	command hash table	csh(1)

The permissions are divided into three sets of three: one set (rwx) for the user or owner of a file, one set (rwx) for the group owner, and another set (rwx) for everyone else.

See also **chmod, ls, umask.**

permissions

See **file permissions.**

permuted index

A special kind of index used in several of the Unix system manuals. Many of the Unix manuals treat each command on a separate page, and the pages are not numbered continuously, they are only numbered within each command. This makes it easy to add or remove pages as the system changes but can make it difficult to find specific information. The permuted index is a solution to this problem.

The permuted index has three columns as the example in Figure P.1 shows; the middle column is in alphabetical order and that is where you start your search. The column to the right lists the command that performs the function and the section number of the manual (or the **man** pages) where you can find a detailed description, and the column to the left contains additional keywords to help confirm you have found the correct entry.

See also **apropos, man, man pages, ptx.**

peta-

Abbreviated P. A prefix for one quadrillion, or 10^{15}. In computing, based on the binary system, peta has the value of 1,125,899,906,842,624 or the power of 2 (2^{50}) closest to one quadrillion.

petabyte

Abbreviated PB. Usually 1,125,899,906,842,624 bytes (2^{50}) but may also refer to one quadrillion bytes (10^{15}).

pfbtops

A BSD command that translates a PostScript font file in `.pfb` format into ASCII, which can then be used with `groff`.

pg

A Unix filter that displays the contents of a text file on the screen, one screenful at a time.

▶ Syntax

Here's the syntax to use with `pg`:

`pg [`*`options`*`]` *`filenames`*

The command displays the contents of *`filenames`* and waits for you to press the Return key to view the next screenful.

When the `pg` command pauses, it interprets several keystrokes as commands; you can press `h` for help information, `q` to quit, even `/` followed by a regular expression to search. Table P.4 lists the most common commands.

▶ Options and Arguments

You can use the options listed in Table P.5 with the `pg` command.

▶ Examples

To look at the contents of your `.profile` file, use:

`pg .profile`

You can also use `pg` with a pipe on the command line; this is a good way to slow down the display of a long listing so that you can read it before it flashes past:

`ls -R | pg`

This command displays all files in all directories, and so can be a very long listing. Using `pg` lets you read each screenful; press the Return key to see the next screenful, and press `q` when you are ready to quit.

See also **`cat`**, **`less`**, **`more`**, **`MORE`**, **`pr`**.

Table P.4: pg Commands

COMMAND	DESCRIPTION
`!` *`command`*	Executes *`command`*.
/pattern/	Searches forward for the next occurrence of *`pattern`*.
`?`*`pattern`*`?` or `^`*`pattern`*`^`	Searches backward for the next occurrence of *`pattern`*.
`.` or `Ctrl-l`	Redisplays the current page.
`d`	Displays the next half page.
`f`	Skips to the next page forward.
`h`	Displays help information.
`l`	Displays the next line.
`n`	Displays the next file.
`p`	Displays the previous file.
`q` or `Q`	Quits the `more` command.
`n``w`	Sets the window size to *`n`* lines and displays the next page.
`$`	Displays the last page.

Table P.5: Options to Use with pg	
OPTION	DESCRIPTION
`-c`	Clears the screen before displaying the file's contents.
`-e`	Does not pause between files.
`-f`	Does not split lines longer than the screen width.
`-n`	Issues a `pg` command without waiting for you to press Return.
`-p` *`string`*	Uses *`string`* as the command prompt; the default prompt is a colon (`:`).
`-s`	Displays messages in inverse video.
`-`*`n`*	Sets the display window to *`n`* lines; the default is to use the whole screen.
`+`*`number`*	Starts the display at line *`number`*.
`+/`*`pattern`*`/`	Starts the display at the line containing *`pattern`*.

PGP

See **Pretty Good Privacy.**

physical device

A piece of hardware, such as a disk drive or a tape drive, that is physically separate from other devices.

physical layer

The first and lowest of the seven layers in the ISO/OSI model for computer-to-computer communications. The physical layer defines the physical, electrical, mechanical, and functional procedures used to connect the equipment.

pic

A preprocessor for the `troff` text-processing system capable of translating a graphics language into simple pictures.

▶ Syntax

The syntax for `pic` is:

pic [*options*][*filename*]

`pic` reads a `troff` file that contains pairs of special codes; `.PS` starts special typesetting, and `.PE` ends special typesetting. The graphic for typesetting is located between these two directives. Because `pic` requires full typesetting capabilities, you cannot use `pic` with `nroff`.

`pic` provides facilities for:

- Drawing boxes, circles, arcs, arrows, and lines
- Placing text inside graphical elements
- Joining objects with various kinds of line types
- Exact placing of graphical objects in relation to other objects

▶ Options and Arguments

The options you can use with `pic` are listed in Table P.6.

▶ Notes

The `pic` command is often used in a pipeline containing several commands to format a file:

```
myfile.doc  |pic|troff|lpr
```

In this example, `myfile.doc` is piped into `pic`, and output from that command is passed to `troff` for final output to the default printer.

See also **eqn, groff, nroff, tbl, troff.**

OPTION	DESCRIPTION
-c	Enables tpic compatability.
-C	Recognizes .PS and .PE, even when they are followed by a character other than a space or a newline.
-D	Draws lines using \D escape sequence.
-n	Turns off the GNU groff extensions to the troff drawing commands.
-t	Enables TEX mode.
-T *dev*	Specifies the output device.
-v	Displays version number.
-z	Draws dots as zero-length lines in TEX mode.

Table P.6: Options Available with pic

pico

A popular text editor often used in conjunction with the Pine mailer.

■ *See also* **emacs, ex, jove, vi.**

PID

An acronym that is formed from process ID and is normally followed by a unique number. This number is assigned to the process by Unix when the process first starts running and lets you refer to that process at a later time. PID numbers are usually within the range of 0 to 30,000; all systems have a limit to the number of processes that can be active on the system at any given time, as well as a limit to how many processes any specific user can have. These limits vary from system to system and are set in the Unix kernel.

■ *See also* **kill, managing processes, ps.**

Pine

A popular e-mail program with a menu-driven graphical user interface (GUI) that includes easy-to-use text processing features in the pico editor, a spelling checker, as well as mail management options. You can also use pico as a text editor independently from Pine if you wish.

Pine is an excellent choice for beginning or occasional e-mail users but may not be powerful enough for more experienced users. Pine also supports MIME so you can attach nontext files, such as graphics or a spreadsheet, to a mail message.

■ *See also* **elm, mail, Mail, mailx, MH, mush.**

ping

Acronym formed from packet internet groper. A command used to test for network connectivity by transmitting a special diagnostic packet to a specific node on the network, forcing the node to acknowledge that the packet reached the correct destination. If the system responds, the link is operational; if not, something is wrong. The word ping is often used as a verb, as in "ping that workstation to see if it is awake."

ping is designed for network testing, troubleshooting, and measurement, and because of the large load it can impose on a busy, working network, it should not be used during normal operations, unless the system administrator is tracing a specific problem on the network.

The syntax for this command is usually:

```
ping hostname
```

Here's an example of the command and a typical response:

```
ping elvis
elvis is alive
```

Most Unix systems (as well as other operating systems, such as Novell NetWare or Microsoft Windows NT) implement their own options for this command, so see the man pages on your system if you want to learn more about ping.

pipe

A mechanism used by one command to pass information to a second command for processing; a pipe connects the standard output of one command to the standard input of the next, without creating an intermediate file.

A pipe is symbolized by the vertical bar (|) character, and if you want to pause output from a long directory listing, you could type the following at the command prompt:

```
ls -l | more
```

This sequence creates the long directory listing and then pipes the output from `ls` to the `more` command, which displays the results on the standard output, usually the screen, one page at a time.

A pipe is a one-way conduit for information, but a special form of pipe, known as a *named pipe*, allows two processes to exchange information; this concept has been extended in several network operating systems as a method of interprocess communications, allowing data to be exchanged between applications running on networked computers.

■ *See also* **FIFO file.**

pipeline

A group of commands connected by a pipe. Commands in a pipeline are executed simultaneously, with the output of one command serving as the input for the next.

pipelining

- In microprocessor architecture, a method of fetching and decoding instructions that ensures that the processor never needs to wait; as soon as an instruction is executed, another is waiting.
- In parallel processing, the method used to pass instructions from one processing unit to another.

.plan

A file in your home directory, originally intended to contain information about your location and immediate plans, but is normally used for humorous purposes. The `finger` command displays the contents of your `.plan` file to the person using `finger`.

■ *See also* **`finger`, `.profile`.**

platform

- An operating system environment, such as a Unix platform or a Novell NetWare platform.
- A computer system based on a specific microprocessor, such as an Intel-based platform or a PowerPC-based platform.

plot

A BSD command used to plot data contained in a file, or input from the standard input, onto a terminal screen.

plus symbol

The + character. A metacharacter used by `awk` and `grep` to locate one or more characters placed before the symbol when searching a regular expression. The plus symbol matches one or more occurrences of the previous character, whereas the question mark matches zero or one occurrence.

■ *See also* **asterisk.**

polymorphism

In object-oriented programming, an object's ability to choose the correct internal procedure (known as a method), based on the type of data received in a message. For example, a print object might receive a message containing a binary floating point number or a text file. With polymorphism, the object should take the appropriate action, even if the message contents were unknown at the time the program was written; at the very least, the object should fail gracefully.

■ *See also* **encapsulation, inheritance.**

P

popd

A built-in C shell command that removes the current entry from the directory stack. The C shell stores a list of directories you are using, and you manipulate the stack using `popd` and `pushd`; the `dirs` command lists the contents of the directory stack.

■ *See also* **`dirs`, `pushd`.**

port

- To move a program or operating system from one hardware platform to another. For example, Unix portability refers to the fact that the same operating system can run on both Intel and reduced instruction set computing (RISC) architectures, as well as many other hardware platforms.
- The point at which a communications circuit terminates at a network, serial, or parallel interface card; usually identified by a specific port number or name.
- A number used to identify a specific Internet application.

portability

The ability to transfer an application or operating system from one vendor's hardware to another, quickly and easily, without affecting its performance.

There are several ways that this can be achieved:

- Write the program in a portable language such as C.
- Use only standard programming language features.
- Use standard libraries.
- Don't make assumptions about word size or byte ordering.
- Use layers of software to distance the application from hardware dependencies.
- Don't write the application so that it relies upon specific aspects of the hardware.

■ *See also* **POSIX.**

portable

Describes a program that can be used on more than one version of Unix with a minimum number of changes.

■ *See also* **port.**

POSIX

Acronym for portable operating system interface. An Institute of Electrical and Electronics Engineers (IEEE) standard that defines a set of portable operating system services similar to those found in Unix. The seven adopted POSIX standards are listed in Table P.7; at least 20 more standards are still in the draft stage.

Each of the standards defines a specific aspect of an operating system, and the additional standards still under development will cover areas such as system administration, system security, networking, the user interface, and other topics.

When a program meets or exceeds the appropriate POSIX standard, it is said to be "POSIX-compliant."

post

An individual article or e-mail message sent to a USENET newsgroup or a mailing list, rather than a message sent to a specific individual.

■ *See also* **cross posting, posting.**

posting

The process of sending an individual article or e-mail message to a USENET newsgroup or mailing list.

■ *See also* **cross posting, post.**

postmark

An item in the header of an e-mail message that tells you who sent you the message and when it was delivered to your system.

Table P.7: Adopted POSIX Standards	
STANDARD	DESCRIPTION
POSIX.1	The original POSIX standard describes the basic system-level interfaces for C programs. Adopted in 1988 and revised in 1990, it was adopted as an international standard by the ISO and the International Electrotechnical Commission (IEC) and is available as ISO/IEC IS 9945-1:1990.
POSIX.2	The shell and utilities standard, based on the Korn shell, describes the way that the shell and utilities work with different character sets and with location-specific information, such as time and date formats. Adopted in 1992.
POSIX.3	The test suite standard, adopted in 1991, defines the tests used to determine POSIX compliance. For POSIX.1, the test suite POSIX.3.1 specifies over 2400 individual test elements, and the draft test suite for POSIX.2 details over 10,000 individual items for testing.
POSIX.4	The standard that defines C language interfaces for real-time applications, in which real-time is defined as "the ability of the operating system to provide a required level of service in a bounded response time." Adopted in 1993.
POSIX.5	The version of POSIX.1 for the Ada programming language, adopted in 1992.
POSIX.9	The version of POSIX.1 for the Fortran 77 programming language, adopted in 1992.

PostScript

A page description language developed by Adobe Systems, used when printing high-quality text and graphics. Programs that create PostScript output can print on any PostScript printer or imagesetter because PostScript is hardware-independent. An interpreter in the printer translates the PostScript commands into commands that the printer can understand. This means that you can create your document and print it on any PostScript printer to produce the final printed output.

PostScript uses English-like commands to scale outline fonts and control the page layout; because of this, users have a great deal of flexibility when it comes to font and color specification.

pound sign

The # character, sometimes called a *hash symbol*. Some British keyboards also have a pound sterling currency symbol (£).

The pound sign (#) is used as the shell prompt for the superuser as a reminder of the superuser's special powers.

You can also start a comment line in a shell script or `awk` script with a pound sign, and the shell ignores everything that follows on that same line.

In the `.cshrc` file, a pound sign indicates that the rest of that line is a comment and should be ignored.

■ *See also* **Bourne shell.**

PPID

An environment variable that contains the process ID number of the parent shell.

■ *See also* **`kill`, `ps`, `who`.**

PPP

Abbreviation for Point-to-Point Protocol. A TCP/IP protocol used to transmit IP packets over serial lines and modem/telephone connections.

PPP establishes a temporary but direct connection to an Internet host, eliminating the need for connecting to an interim system. PPP also provides a method of automatically assigning an IP address, so that remote or mobile systems can connect to the network at any point.

See also **SLIP.**

pr

A command used to format text files according to certain specified options.

▶ Syntax

The syntax to use is:

```
pr [options]filename...
```

If you don't specify any options for `pr`, each printed page consists of a five-line header, a 66-line page, and a five-line footer. The header contains the page number, filename, and the file's date and time. Output is to the standard output and is usually redirected by pipe to a printer.

▶ Options and Arguments

The `pr` command formats *`filename`*, which can be a single file or a list of filenames. If you omit *`filename`*, or use `–`, the `pr` command reads from the standard input. Table P.8 lists the options you can use with `pr`.

▶ Examples

To print two files side-by-side on the default printer, use:

```
pr -m results.jan
➥ results.feb | lp
```

To print a file containing C language source code with line numbers, use:

```
pr -n program.c | lp
```

See also **cat, grep, lp, paste, more, nl, pg.**

precedence

The order in which a program performs arithmetic operations; usually multiplication, division, addition, and subtraction. By placing parentheses around an expression, you can control the order in which expressions are calculated.

Programming languages also follow a strict precedence in their execution of mathematical operations.

preemptive multitasking

A form of multitasking, in which the operating system executes an application for a specific period of time, according to its assigned priority. At that time, it is preempted, and another task is given access to the CPU for its allocated time. Although an application can give up control before its time is up, such as during input/output waits, no task is ever allowed to execute for longer than its allotted time period.

preprocessor

A software development tool that manipulates source code before it is passed to the compiler or assembler. The preprocessor can delete comments, expand macros, and import special files such as header or include files. The preprocessor is invoked automatically by the C compiler.

See also **cc, ccp, compiling a C program.**

presentation layer

The sixth of seven layers of the ISO/OSI model for computer-to-computer communications. The presentation layer defines the way in which data is formatted, presented, converted, and encoded.

Pretty Good Privacy

Abbreviated PGP. A popular public-key encryption program, written by Phil Zimmermann, available at no charge from certain Internet sites.

primary mailbox

The mailbox where e-mail software first places your e-mail messages before you look at them; also known as the *system mailbox.*

See also **secondary mailbox.**

Table P.8: Options to Use with pr	
OPTION	DESCRIPTION
+*page*	Starts formatted output at *page*; the default is page 1.
-*n*	Formats output with *n* columns; the default is 1 column.
-a	Displays the file in multicolumn format; long lines that don't fit are truncated.
-d	Double-spaces the output.
-e*cn*	Expands spaces into tabs every *n*th position, with *c* as the tab character.
-f	Separates pages using a formfeed rather than a series of blank lines.
-F	Folds input lines to avoid truncation by -a or -m.
-h *string*	Uses *string* as the page header text; ignored when -t is used or when the -l option sets the page length to ten or fewer lines.
-i*cn*	Converts spaces to the *c* character at every *n*th position; the default is a tab set at every eighth position.
-l*n*	Sets the page length to *n* lines; the default is 66 lines.
-m	Merges up to eight files, displaying them all, one in each column. Long lines are truncated; this option cannot be used with -n or -a.
-n*cn*	Provides *n* digit line numbers followed by the field separator specified by *c*.
-o*n*	Offsets each line by *n* spaces; the default is 0 spaces.
-p	Pauses before displaying each page on a terminal.
-r	Suppresses error messages.
-s*c*	Uses *c* as a column separator.
-t	Omits header and footer lines at the top and bottom of each page.
-w*n*	Sets the line length to *n* characters; the default is 72 characters.

print

A built-in Korn shell command used to display text. The syntax to use with `print` is:

`print [options][string]`

The `print` command displays *string* on the standard output, and you can use the options shown in Table P.9 with this command.

■ *See also* **echo.**

printable character

Any character that can be printed or has a graphical representation.

■ *See also* **nonprinting character.**

printenv

A command that prints the names and values of the variables in the environment. If you specify a *name*, only that value is printed.

■ *See also* **env.**

printf

A command used to print formatted output. `printf` is based on the C library function of the same name and works in the same sort of way. The syntax looks like this:

`printf format [string...]`

and *string* is printed on the standard output according to *format*, which can be text characters, C language escape characters, or a set of conversion arguments. See the `man` pages on your system for more details.

■ *See also* **echo, print.**

priority

A number that the kernel's scheduler uses to decide how often to run a process. A higher priority process runs more frequently, and so terminates faster than an equivalent process that is running at a lower priority.

Table P.9: Options for use with print

OPTION	DESCRIPTION
- or --	Ignores all following options.
-n	Suppresses the final newline character.
-p	Sends *string* to the process created by |& rather than to the standard output.
-r	Ignores any echo escape sequences.
-R	Ignores any echo escape sequences, and ignores subsequent options except -n.
-s	Sends *string* to the history file.
-u*n*	Sends *string* to file descriptor *n*; the default is file descriptor 1.

Ordinary users can only lower the priority of their own processes; the superuser can both raise and lower priorities.

■ *See also* **nice.**

Privacy Enhanced Mail

■ *See* **PEM.**

privileged account

Another name for the superuser or root account on a Unix system.

/proc

An SVR4 directory that contains a list of all the processes running on the system.

■ *See also* **ps.**

procedural language

Any programming language in which the fundamental programming element is the procedure, also known as a *subroutine* or a *function*. Most of the popular high-level languages, such as C, Pascal, Ada, and Fortran are procedural languages.

process

In Unix, the strict definition of a process is a single thread of execution with its own PID, but most people refer to any program running on the system as a process. One of the places where this less-precise definition falls down, for example, is when several people simultaneously use a program like **`emacs`**; several processes are executing, one for each user, but only one program is running. Also, a command line that uses a pipe always starts two or more processes.

A process may start or spawn a new process as a part of its operation; the original process is called the *parent process,* and the new process is known as a *child process.* On a Unix system with job control, you can run a process in the background or foreground.

■ *See also* **`kill`**, **managing processes**, **`nice`**, **program**, **`ps`**.

process ID

■ *See* **PID.**

process status

The status of a process. Unix has eight different process states: running in user mode, running in kernel mode, waiting, sleeping, idle, swapping, stopped, and dead or zombie.

prof

A command that displays an object file's profile data.

■ *See also* **`gprof`**, **`ldd`**, **`lorder`**, **`lprof`**.

.profile

A startup file located in your home directory, which is executed by the Bourne and Korn shells when you first log in to the system. You can use the **`.profile`** file to set variables, define functions, and run commands.

■ *See also* **`.cshrc`**, **`.login`**.

program

A collection of machine-readable, executable instructions contained in a file. The Unix utilities, shell scripts, and applications are all programs.

Many people use the terms *program* and *process* as though they were interchangeable, but we can make an important distinction; a program is a file on disk or tape, and when it begins to execute under Unix, it becomes a process.

Project Athena

An MIT project that ran from 1983 to 1991, sponsored by MIT, DEC, and IBM, which developed the X Window system and the Kerberos user authentication system, as well as several other important relational database and network-related systems.

prompt

A C shell environment variable that contains the prompt string. You can use `set prompt ="`*`string`*`"` in your `.cshrc` file to customize your prompt.

■ *See also* **`PS1`**, **`PS2`**, **`PS3`**, **`PS4`**.

prompt string

A character or short message that a program displays on the screen to indicate that it is waiting for input from you.

The default prompt for the Bourne shell and Korn shell is the dollar sign (`$`), and for the C shell, the percent sign (`%`). You can change the default prompt to something else if you wish. Other programs also display prompts; for example, the `ftp` command interpreter displays `ftp>`.

■ *See also* **`prompt`**, **`PS1`**, **`PS2`**, **`PS3`**, **`PS4`**.

P

protocol

In networking and communications, the formal specification that defines the procedures to follow when transmitting and receiving data. Protocols define the format, timing, sequence, and error checking used on the network.

See also **communications protocol, ISO/OSI model, protocol stack.**

protocol stack

The several layers of software that define the computer-to-computer or computer-to-network protocol. The protocol stack on a Unix system using TCP/IP is different from that used on a Novell NetWare network or on a Banyan VINES system.

See also **ISO/OSI model.**

ps

A command that displays information about active processes.

▶ Syntax

The syntax to use with `ps` is as follows:

```
ps [options]
```

The `ps` command provides a snapshot of system activity; if you re-execute the command later, you may see completely different information.

If you use `ps` without options, you will see the status of all the processes controlled by your terminal arranged in the four columns described in Table P.10.

If you use the -l option to produce a long listing, you will see information arranged in the columns described in Table P.11.

▶ Options and Arguments

For the SVR4 version of `ps`, the options you can use are listed in Table P.12. Any arguments contained in *`list`* should be either enclosed in double quotes or separated by commas.

In the BSD version, options work differently, as shown in Table P.13.

▶ Examples

To display information about active processes, use:

```
ps
```

```
  PID     TTY     TIME   COMD
24559   tty12    0:07    sh
25668   tty12    0:12    ps
```

The first process is the shell, and the second is the process executing the `ps` command. If you run the long version of `ps`, use the `more` filter to stop the extensive output from scrolling off the screen:

```
ps -el | more
```

See also **`kill`, `nice`, process status, `pstat`, `whodo`.**

Table P.10: ps Output Without Options

COLUMN	DESCRIPTION
PID	The process ID number of the process.
TTY	The number of the terminal that controls this process.
TIME	The length of CPU time, in minutes and seconds, that this process has been running.
COMD	The command name with which this process was called; if you use the `-f` option, you will see the whole command line.

Table P.11: Long Listing of ps Output

COLUMN	DESCRIPTION
F	Lists the status flags.
S	Shows the state of the process as a single character; B and W indicate the process is waiting, I indicates idle, O indicates it is running, R means that it is loaded into a queue as a runnable process, S shows the process is sleeping, T means it is being traced, X indicates it is waiting for more memory, and Z indicates that the process is a zombie, meaning it has terminated.
UID	User ID of the owner of the process.
PID	The process ID number of the process.
PPID	The process ID of the parent process.
C	Processor utilization; this number is used for scheduling.
STIME	The starting time of the process (Solaris only).
PRI	The priority of the process; the higher the number, the lower the priority.
NI	The `nice` value for priority.
ADDR	The memory or disk address of the process.
SZ	The size, in blocks, of the core image of the process.
WCHAN	If the process is waiting or sleeping, this indicates the event it is waiting for.
TTY	The number of the terminal that controls this process.
TIME	The length of CPU time, in minutes and seconds, that this process has been running.
COMD	The command name with which this process was called; if you also use the `-f` option, you will see the whole command line.

P

Table P.12: SVR4 ps Options

OPTION	DESCRIPTION
`-a`	Displays information about all processes except group leaders and those processes that are not associated with a terminal.
`-c`	Displays scheduler data set by `prioctrl`.
`-d`	Displays information about all processes except group leaders.
`-e`	Displays information about all processes.
`-f`	Creates a full listing.
`-g` *`list`*	Displays output for the specified process groups.
`-j`	Displays the process group ID and session ID.
`-n` *`list`*	Displays information for processes running on *`list`*.
`-p` *`list`*	Displays information for the specified process IDs.
`-s` *`list`*	Displays information for the specified session leader IDs.
`-t` *`list`*	Displays information for the specified terminals.
`-u` *`list`*	Displays information for the specified users.

Table P.13: BSD ps Options

OPTION	DESCRIPTION
`-a`	Displays information about all processes.
`-C`	Uses an alternative CPU time calculation.
`-e`	Displays the environment as well as the command.
`-h`	Repeats the display header to give one header per page.
`-j`	Creates a full report.
`-l`	Creates a long report.
`-L`	Lists all the keywords.
`-m`	Sorts by memory usage rather than by process ID.
`-M` *`name`*	List information for *`name`*.
`-N` *`name`*	Extracts the name list from *`name`*.
`-o` *`keywords`*	Displays information in space- or comma-separated lists of *`keywords`*.

Table P.13: BSD ps Options (continued)

OPTION	DESCRIPTION
`-O keywords`	Adds the information specified by space- or comma-separated lists of *keywords* to the default display.
`-p list`	Displays information on the specified process ID.
`-r`	Sorts by CPU usage rather than by process ID.
`-S`	Uses an alternative process time calculation.
`-t list`	Displays information for the specified terminals.
`-T`	Displays information for the process associated with the standard input.
`-u`	Specifies a different set of information for the full display.
`-v`	Specifies a different set of information for the long display.
`-w`	Uses 132-column display.
`-W filename`	Specifies *filename* as the source of swap information rather than `/dev/swap`.
`-x`	Displays information for processes not associated with terminals.

PS1

A Bourne shell and Korn shell variable that contains the primary prompt string that, by default, is a dollar sign ($). You can customize your prompt if you wish.

■ *See also* **PS2, PS3, PS4.**

PS2

A Bourne shell and Korn shell variable that contains the secondary prompt string that, by default, is a greater than sign (>). This secondary prompt is used to indicate that the shell is expecting more input and is not often customized by the user.

■ *See also* **PS1, PS3, PS4.**

PS3

A Korn shell variable that contains the prompt string used inside a shell `select` loop to read replies from the standard input.

■ *See also* **PS1, PS2, PS4.**

PS4

A Korn shell variable that contains the prompt string used when in debug mode, a plus sign (+). Use the `-x` option to the shell, which you can use with `set`, to turn on this debug mode.

■ *See also* **PS1, PS2, PS3.**

pstat

An SCO command that displays system information for the process table, i-node table, and open file table.

▶ Syntax

The syntax for `pstat` is as follows:

```
pstat [options][filename]
```

`pstat` displays information from *filename*, if specified; otherwise, it displays information from `/dev/mem` and `/dev/kmem`.

Information in the open file table display is arranged in the columns described in Table P.14.

P

Table P.14: Open File Information in pstat

COLUMN	DESCRIPTION
LOC	Location of this table entry
FLAGS	Assorted stream state variables
CNT	Number of processes related to this open file
INO	Location of the i-node table entry for this file
OFFS	File offset

Information in the i-node table display is arranged in the columns described in Table P.15.

Information in the process table display is arranged in the same columns as shown for the long (`-l`) form of the SVR4 `ps` command provided earlier in this chapter.

▶ Options and Arguments

The options you can use with `pstat` are shown in Table P.16.

■ *See also* **kill**, **nice**, **process status**, **ps**.

ptx

A BSD command used to create a permuted index.

▶ Syntax

The syntax for this command is:

```
ptx [options][infile[outfile]]
```

If you don't specify an *infile* or an *outfile*, standard input and standard output are used instead.

▶ Options and Arguments

The options listed in Table P.17 are available with `ptx`.

Table P.15: I-Node Table Information in pstat

COLUMN	DESCRIPTION
LOC	Location of this table entry
FLAGS	Assorted state variables
CNT	Number of open file table entries for this i-node
DEVICE	Major and minor device numbers for the filesystem
INO	I-number
FS	Filesystem type
MODE	Mode bits
NLK	Number of links to this i-node
UID	User ID of the owner
SIZE/DEV	Number of bytes in an ordinary file, or the major and minor device numbers of a special file

Table P.16: Options Available with pstat

OPTION	DESCRIPTION
-a	Displays information for all processes.
-f	Displays the open file table.
-i	Displays the i-node table.
-n *list*	Displays information for the system specified in *list*.
-p	Displays the process table.
-s *filename*	Displays swap information from *filename* rather than from /dev/swap.
-u	Displays information for a specific process.

Table P.17: Options to Use with ptx

OPTION	DESCRIPTION
`-b` *filename*	Use the characters specified in *filename* as word separators.
`-f`	Ignores case when sorting keywords.
`-g` *n*	Specifies *n* characters as the gap between columns.
`-i` *filename*	Ignores the keywords listed in *filename*; opposite of `-o`.
`-o` *filename*	Uses only the keywords specified in *filename*; opposite of `-i`.
`-r`	Uses the first field in *infile* as a page or chapter reference identifier separate from the rest of the line text.
`-t`	Prepares the output for phototypesetting; maximum line length is 100 characters.
`-w` *n*	Sets the line length; the default is 72 characters.

pushd

A built-in C shell command that swaps the top two directories in your directory stack. The C shell stores a list of directories you are using, and you manipulate the stack using **popd** and **pushd**; the **dirs** command lists the contents of the directory stack. If you use a numeric argument to **pushd**, that directory is placed at the top of the stack; directories are listed in numerical order starting with 0 at the top of the stack.

■ *See also* **dirs**, **popd**.

push pin

A feature of Open Look that forces a pop-up menu to stay open after you have made your selection. The push pin lets you "pin" a menu or dialog box onto the screen so that you can use the menu several times without it closing after each selection.

■ *See also* **X Window.**

pwd

A command that displays the full pathname of the current working directory. The Bourne shell and Korn shell both have built-in commands of the same name, and the C shell has the **dirs** command. These shell commands are often faster than the Unix utility.

■ *See also* **cd.**

THE unix DESK REFERENCE

Q

QIC

■ *See* **quarter-inch cartridge.**

QNX

A Unix-like operating system, based on microkernel technology, from Quantum Software Systems.

■ *See also* **Mach.**

quarter-inch cartridge

Abbreviated QIC. A set of tape standards defined by the Quarter-Inch Cartridge Drive Standards, a trade association established in 1987.

Several standards are in use today, and Table Q.1 lists the most common capacities and densities of the DC-2000 series of minicartridges.

Other QIC data cartridge formats allow for higher capacities: QIC-1350 for up to 1.35 GB of tape storage, QIC-2100 for up to 2.6 GB, and QIC-5010 for up to 13 GB.

query language

In a database management system, a programming language that allows a user to extract and display specific information from a database. Structured Query Language (SQL, pronounced "sequel") is an international database query language that allows the user to issue high-level English-like commands or statements, such as SELECT or INSERT, to create or modify data or the database structure.

Comprehensive SQL-based products from Sybase, Oracle, Ingres, or Informix are available for most mainstream Unix platforms. Object Query Languages (OQLs) have evolved to provide better support for nontext multimedia data types and to solve some of the performance limitations of the relational database model; a variant known as Object Relational, which overlays object-oriented concepts on top of a relational schema, has also gained some popularity.

Table Q.1: QIC Minicartridge Standards

STANDARD	CAPACITY (UNCOMPRESSED)	BITS PER INCH
QIC-40	60 MB	10,000
QIC-80	125 MB	14,700
QIC-100	40 MB	10,000
QIC-128	128 MB	16,000
QIC-3010	255 MB	22,125
QIC-3020	500 MB	44,250
QIC-3030	580 MB	40,600
QIC-3040	840 MB	40,600
QIC-3080	1.6 GB	60,000
QIC-3090	2 GB	93,333
QIC-3070	4 GB	67,773

question mark

The **?** character, used as a metacharacter representing a single character in a filename or in a regular expression.

■ *See also* **asterisk.**

queue

Pronounced "q." A temporary list of items waiting for a particular service. An example is the print queue of documents waiting to be printed; the first document received in the queue is usually the first to be printed, although priorities can be attached to place certain print jobs ahead or behind others.

quota

A BSD command used to display a user's disk usage and limits.

▶ Syntax

The syntax for `quota` is as follows:

```
quota [options] username
```

▶ Options and Arguments

With no options, `quota` displays information on all the filesystems detailed in `/etc/fstab`. Only the superuser can use the `-u` option with a *`username`* to inspect information for other users. The other options are listed in Table Q.2.

quote

To remove any special meaning a character might have for the shell by preceding the character with a backslash (\). You can also quote several characters by placing single quotes around them.

■ *See also* **C shell, escaped character.**

Table Q.2: Options for Use with `quota`

OPTION	DESCRIPTION
`-g`	Displays group quotas.
`-q`	Displays information only on filesystems that are over quota.
`-v`	Displays quotas for filesystems on which no storage is allocated.

quoting

- To place a backslash (\) before a single metacharacter or to surround a group of characters with single quotes so that any special meaning the metacharacter had is removed.
- To include a relevant portion of someone else's article when posting a followup to a USENET newsgroup. It is considered to be poor netiquette to quote more of the original post than is absolutely necessary to make your point.

■ *See also* **escaped character.**

THE unix DESK REFERENCE

R

r

A built-in Korn shell command that re-executes the last command. The `r` command is an alias of `fc -e -` and is predefined by the shell. To run the last command in the background, use `r &`, and to repeat the second last command, use `r -2`. You can also repeat a command if you can remember how the command line started; for example, to repeat the last command that used `grep`, type **`r grep`**.

See also **fc, history.**

RAID

Acronym for redundant array of inexpensive disks. In networking and mission critical applications, a method of using several hard disk drives—often SCSI or Integrated Drive Electronics (IDE) drives—in an array to provide fault tolerance in the event that one or more drives fail.

Each of the different levels of RAID is designed for a specific use:

- **RAID 0:** Data is striped over one or more drives, but there is no redundant drive. RAID 0 provides no fault tolerance because the loss of a hard disk means a complete loss of data. Some classification schemes omit RAID 0 for this reason.
- **RAID 1:** Two hard disks of equal capacity duplicate or mirror each other's contents. One disk continuously and automatically backs up the other disk. This method is also known as *disk mirroring* or *disk duplexing*, depending on whether one or two independent hard disk controllers are used.
- **RAID 2:** Bit-interleaved data is written across several drives, and then parity and error-correction information is written to additional separate drives. The specific number of error-correction drives depends on the allocation algorithm in use.
- **RAID 3:** Bit-interleaved data is written across several drives, but only one parity drive is used. If an error is detected, the data is reread to resolve the problem. The fact that data is reread in the event of an error may add a small performance penalty.

- **RAID 4:** Data is written across drives by sectors rather than at the bit level, and a separate drive is used as a parity drive for error detection. Reads and writes occur independently.
- **RAID 5:** Data is written across drives in sectors, and parity information is added as another sector, just as if it were ordinary data.

The appropriate level of RAID for any particular installation depends on network usage. RAID levels 1, 3, and 5 are available commercially, and levels 3 and 5 are proving popular for networks.

■ *See also* **disk striping, disk striping with parity, SLED.**

`random`

An SCO command that generates a random number between 0 and ***`scale`*** on the standard output and returns this value as the exit value. The syntax is:

```
random [option][scale]
```

If you don't specify ***`scale`***, the number will be either 0 or 1. The single option available with this command, `-s`, just prevents the number from being printed on the standard output.

RANDOM

A Korn shell environment variable that stores a random number between 0 and 32,767. A new random number is generated each time this variable is referenced.

`ranlib`

A BSD command that makes a table of contents for archive libraries used by the loader `ld`.

■ *See also* **`ar`, `ld`, `lorder`, `nm`.**

raw

Jargon for anything that has not completed processing to produce a final product. Unprocessed data is often called *raw data.*

raw device

Any device that is written to or read from directly, without any intermediate buffering; sometimes called an *unbuffered device.*

raw mode

A mode that bypasses the usual Unix input/output system and writes characters directly to the device, usually a terminal. Raw mode is fast but is device-dependent, and so removes some of the portability benefits that Unix provides.

■ *See also* **`cbreak` mode, cooked mode.**

`rbash`

The command used to start the restricted Bourne Again shell (`bash`) from the FSF. `rbash` limits users to read-only access to files and directories and does not let them change to another shell or use a different pathname.

■ *See also* **Bash, Unix shell.**

`rc`

A small elegant shell that replaces the Bourne shell, developed by Tom Duff and extended by Byron Rakitzis. `rc` eliminates many of the technical shortcomings of the Bourne shell but does not have some of the advanced features that you find in some of the other shells, including job control or command-line editing. Its programming language is based on the C language.

■ *See also* **Unix shell.**

`.rc` file

A file containing commands that establish custom values for environment variables for individual users.

■ *See also* **dot file, `.exrc`, `.kshrc`, `.mailrc`, `.netrc`, `.newsrc`.**

rcp

A TCP/IP command used to copy files between two different computer systems that can communicate over a network.

▶ Syntax

The syntax for `rcp` is as follows:

```
rcp [options] source-file
➥ destination-file
```

or

```
rcp [options] source-file-list
➥ destination-directory
```

Like the `cp` utility, `rcp` has two modes; the first mode copies one file to another, while the second mode copies one or more files to a directory.

▶ Options and Arguments

source-file is the pathname of the file to copy. If you want to copy a file from a remote computer to your own, you must precede the pathname with the name of the remote computer followed by a colon (**:**). The *destination-file* is the pathname that `rcp` assigns to the resulting copy of the file, and to copy a file to a remote computer, add the name of the system followed by a colon.

The *source-file-list* contains a list of the files you want to copy, and if you use the `-r` option, this can include directories, too. The *destination-directory* is the name of the directory where `rcp` places the copied files; again, add the name of the remote computer to the beginning of this path, separated by a colon.

The options you can use with `rcp` are listed in Table R.1.

▶ Examples

To copy a file called `memo` from the `/home/jenny` directory on the `fullerton` computer into your home directory, use:

```
rcp fullerton:/home/jenny/
➥memo .
```

To copy two files, `memo` and `file.log`, to the `/pub` directory on the system called `fullerton`, use:

```
rcp memo file.log
➥ fullerton:/pub
```

▶ Notes

The 4.4BSD version of `rcp` has several options that deal with Kerberos authentication; see your system documentation for more details.

You must have a login account on the remote system before you can use `rcp` to copy files.

■ *See also* **cp, ftp, rlogin, rsh, telnet.**

Table R.1: Options to Use with rcp

OPTION	DESCRIPTION
`-p`	Preserves the modification times and file-access permissions from the original files.
`-r`	Used when working with directories; causes `rcp` to copy the contents of a directory and all subdirectories within that directory.

RCS

Abbreviation for Revision Control System; a set of programs designed to keep track of multiple revisions to files, usually in a software development environment, and to minimize the amount of hard disk space needed to store the revisions. The RCS system is not usually a standard part of SVR4; you can get RCS from the Free Software Foundation.

Using RCS, you can automatically store and then retrieve revisions, compare and merge revisions, keep a complete change log, and specifically identify particular revisions. Table R.2 lists the major programs in the RCS suite and describes their use.

Table R.2: RCS Programs

PROGRAM	DESCRIPTION
`ci`	Stores the contents of the working files into their corresponding RCS files, and deletes the original.
`co`	Retrieves a previously checked-in revision.
`ident`	Extracts keyword or value symbols.
`merge`	Performs a three-way merge of files using the `diff` utility.
`rcs`	Lets you set up the RCS system and specify certain default attributes of RCS files.
`rcsclean`	Tidies up the RCS files by comparing checked-out files against the appropriate revision and, if there is no difference, by deleting the working file.
`rcsdiff`	Compares revisions using `diff`.
`rcsfreeze`	A shell script that assigns a name to a set of RCS files to mark them as a single unit.
`rcsmerge`	Performs a three-way merge of revisions, merging two different versions and incorporating the differences into a third working file.
`rlog`	Displays log messages associated with each revision, the number of lines added or removed, date of last check in, and so on.

On many systems, you find a **`man`** page called `rcsintro` included with the RCS programs. To look at the page that includes basic RCS information as well as examples of how to use the programs, enter the following:

```
man rcsintro
```

■ *See also* **SCCS, version number.**

rcsclean

■ *See* **RCS.**

rcsdiff

■ *See* **RCS.**

rcsfreeze

■ *See* **RCS.**

rcsmerge

■ *See* **RCS.**

rdist

A BSD and SCO TCP/IP command that makes sure that files are consistent on different computer systems.

▶ Syntax

The syntax for this command is:

`rdist [`*`options`*`][`*`name...`*`]`

The `rdist` command runs commands contained in a file called `distfile`, located in the current directory and specified using the `-f` or `-c` options; if you use `-`, the standard input is used instead. On most systems, `cron` runs `rdist` automatically.

▶ Options and Arguments

The options for use with `rdist` are detailed in Table R.3.

R

Table R.3: Options to Use with `rdist`

OPTION	DESCRIPTION
`-b`	Performs a binary comparison and updates files if they are different.
`-c` *`name[login@]`* ➥*`host[:dest]`*	Makes `rdist` interpret *`name[login@]host[:dest]`* as a *`distfile`*.
`-d` *`variable=value`*	Sets *`variable`* equal to *`value`*; this option overrides definitions contained in the *`distfile`*.
`-f` *`distfile`*	Uses the specified *`distfile`*.
`-h`	Follows symbolic links.
`-i`	Ignores unresolved links.
`-m` *`host`*	Specifies a host computer to receive the update.
`-n`	Prints the commands without executing them; used for debugging a *`distfile`*.
`-q`	Turns off the printing of modified filenames on the standard output.
`-R`	Deletes any extra files found on the remote system that do not exist in the original master directory.
`-v`	Verifies that all files on the remote systems are up-to-date. The names of out-of-date files are displayed, but no changes are made.
`-w`	Preserves the directory structure of the files being copied.
`-y`	Does not update files that are younger than the master copies; prevents newer files from being overwritten.

▶ Notes

On some systems, you find that the system administrator does not allow use of `rdist`; this is usually for security reasons.

■ *See also* **`rcp`**.

read

A built-in Bourne shell and Korn shell command that reads the standard input and assigns each word read to the corresponding variable. All leftover words are assigned to the final variable; if you only specify one variable, all input is assigned to that variable. For example:

```
read first last address
Peter Dyson 2021 7th Avenue
echo "$first $last\n$address"
Peter Dyson
2021 7th Avenue
```

In the Korn shell, you can use the options detailed in Table R.4, as well as use a **?** syntax for prompting. When you follow a variable name with `?`*`string`*, *`string`* is displayed as a prompt for the user and the input stored in the variable.

Table R.4: Korn Shell `read` Options

OPTION	DESCRIPTION
`-p`	Reads from the output of a |& coprocess.
`-r`	Ignores \ as the line-continuation character.
`-s`	Saves the input into the history file.
`-u[n]`	Reads input from the file descriptor specified by *n*.

read ahead

The Unix capability of processing current input while simultaneously processing earlier input.

`readnews`

An older and mostly obsolete newsreader used to access posts to USENET newsgroups.

■ *See also* **`nn`, `rn`, `tin`, `trn`.**

read only

Describes a file or other collection of information that may only be read; it may not be updated in any way or deleted.

In Unix, a file has three different sets of permissions—read (`r`), write (`w`), and execute (`x`)—for three different classes of user, the owner of the file, the group that the owner belongs to, and all other users.

You can designate certain important files as read-only to prevent you from deleting them by accident.

■ *See also* **file permissions, read-only filesystem.**

`readonly`

A built-in Bourne shell and Korn shell command that prevents you from changing a variable value; variables can be read but not overwritten.

read-only filesystem

A filesystem set up by the system administrator as read-only so that no one can make changes to the files it contains. Most filesystems are mounted to allow write access for those users with the appropriate permissions.

real-time system

An operating system capable of responding to an external event in a predictable and appropriate way every time the external event occurs.

Systems used in airplane automatic pilots, patient monitoring, process control, or traffic control are all real-time systems; computers that perform batch-processing operations are not.

rebuilding the kernel

The Unix kernel usually looks after itself and does not normally need much in the way of attention or maintenance; however, from time to time, the system administrator may have to rebuild the kernel for one or more of the following reasons:

- You receive a new version of the kernel.
- You want to reduce the size of the kernel by removing unused device drivers.
- You are experiencing problems automatically sensing certain hardware.
- You are upgrading certain hardware elements on your system.

The amount of effort needed to rebuild the kernel varies tremendously from system to system; some require long manual procedures while others automate as much of the process as they can. On other systems, you may need to recompile all or part of the kernel. A partial recompilation is needed if your kernel is in two parts: a set of configuration files you can change and a group of object files that you cannot change. A full recompilation occurs when you recompile the whole kernel.

As an example, here are the steps you follow on a Linux system to rebuild the kernel. All these steps are carried out from `/usr/src`:

1. Run **`make config`**, which asks you questions about which device drivers you want to include in the new kernel.
2. Run **`make depend`** to collect the appropriate dependencies for each source file and add them to the makefiles.
3. If you have built a kernel from this source tree in the past, run **`make clean`** to throw away all the old object files and make sure that the kernel is rebuilt from scratch.
4. Run **`make`** (with no arguments) to rebuild the kernel.
5. When the recompilation is complete, you will find a file called `zImage` in `/usr/src/linux`, an executable image of the kernel compressed by `gzip`; when the kernel boots, it will uncompress itself into memory.
6. Place the kernel image file on a boot floppy, or configure LILO to boot the new kernel from the hard disk.

record locking

A method of controlling file access in a multiuser environment in which there is always a possibility that two users will attempt to update the same file at the same time but with different information.

The initial attempt at solving this problem was to use file locking in which the first user to access the file locks out all the other users and prevents them from opening the file. After the file is updated and closed again, the next user can gain access. File locking is a simple way to prevent simultaneous updates but can seriously degrade system performance if many users attempt to access the same files time after time. To prevent this slowdown, many database management systems use record locking, which limits access to individual records within the database. Record locking is a much more precise solution to the problem than is file locking.

recursive

- In programming, the ability of a program or subroutine to call itself. Recursion is often used when solving problems that repeat the same processing steps over and over. Some limiting factor or terminating condition must be present; otherwise, the program would never stop running.
- In Unix file-manipulating commands, an option that processes the entire directory tree.

recursive editing

An **`emacs`** feature that lets you stop a search and replace operation temporarily so that you can complete an editing task.

red

A command used to access a restricted version of the **`ed`** text editor. Using **`red`**, you can only change text files located in the current directory, and you cannot use **`!`** shell commands.

redirection

A mechanism in the shell that causes the standard input for a program to come from a file rather than from the terminal. It also causes the standard output and standard error to go to a file rather than to the terminal. Table R.5 shows the most common redirection operations in the C shell, Bourne shell, and Korn shell.

Because Unix is a file-based operating system, and terminals and other devices are treated as files, a program doesn't care or even know if its output is going to your terminal or to a file.

■ *See also* **pipe, `tee`.**

reduced instruction set computing

■ *See* **RISC.**

R

Table R.5: Common Redirection Operations		
FUNCTION	C SHELL	BOURNE & KORN SHELLS
Sends standard output to *file*.	*command* > *file*	*command* > *file*
Sends standard error to *file*.		*command* 2> *file*
Sends standard output and standard error to *file*.	*command* >& *file*	*command* > *file* 2>&1
Reads standard input from *file*.	*command* < *file*	*command* < *file*
Appends standard output to end of *file*.	*command* >> *file*	*command* >> *file*
Appends standard error to end of *file*.		*command* 2>> *file*
Appends standard output and standard error to end of *file*.	*command* >>& *file*	*command* >> *file* 2>&1

reentrant

Describes a programming technique that allows one copy of a program to be loaded into memory and shared.

When one program is executing reentrant code, a different program can interrupt and then start or continue execution of that same code. Many operating system service routines are written to be reentrant so that only one copy of the code is needed. The technique is also used in multithreaded applications, in which different events are taking place concurrently in the same computer.

refer

A GNU `groff` command that reads in a bibliography file and creates `troff` formatted output. `groff` is the Free Software Foundation's implementation of the Unix text processing commands `nroff` and `troff`. `groff` is distributed with many systems, including BSD and Linux.

■ *See also* **indxbib, lkbib, lookbib.**

regcmp

An SVR4 command that compiles the regular expressions in one or more files into C language source code. The default source code file is called *filename*.i; but if you use the – option, the file is called *filename*.c instead.

register

A BSD command used to register a new user with the Kerberos authentication system. You are prompted to enter your current password and then to enter a new password for use only with Kerberos. You can register with Kerberos only once.

■ *See also* **kdestroy, kinit, klist.**

regular character

A character that always represents itself in an ambiguous file reference or regular expression and has no special meaning.

■ *See also* **metacharacter.**

regular expressions

A sequence of characters that can match a set of fixed-text strings used in searching for and replacing text. Many Unix programs, including **ed**, **vi**, **emacs**, **grep**, **awk**, and **sed** use regular expressions.

A regular expression is just a series of characters, most of which represent themselves; for example, the regular expression **moth** matches any string containing these letters in this sequence, including **moth**, **mothball**, **mother**, and **behemoth**. Several special characters have a much more general meaning, as Table R.6 shows.

You can use these symbols together. For example, the regular expression **moth** matches the string **moth**, **^moth** matches **moth** at the beginning of a line, **moth$** matches **moth** at the end of a line, and **^moth$** matches **moth** when it is the only word on a line. Obviously, these symbols can be combined to create some very complex and powerful regular expressions. Regular expressions form the basis of text processing in Unix, and you should take the time to learn how to use them properly.

Table R.6: Symbols Used in Regular Expressions

<table>
<tr><th>SYMBOL</th><th>DESCRIPTION</th></tr>
<tr><td>.</td><td>Matches any single non-null character except a newline.</td></tr>
<tr><td>*</td><td>Matches zero or more of the preceding character.</td></tr>
<tr><td>^</td><td>Matches the following regular expression at the beginning of a line.</td></tr>
<tr><td>$</td><td>Matches the following regular expression at the end of a line.</td></tr>
<tr><td>\<</td><td>Matches characters at the beginning of a word.</td></tr>
<tr><td>\></td><td>Matches characters at the end of a word.</td></tr>
<tr><td>[ ]</td><td>Matches any one of the enclosed characters. A hyphen indicates a range of consecutive characters.</td></tr>
<tr><td>[^]</td><td>Matches any character that is not enclosed.</td></tr>
<tr><td>\</td><td>Takes the following symbol or character literally and turns off any special meaning.</td></tr>
<tr><td>\(\)</td><td>Saves the pattern enclosed between \(and \). Up to 9 patterns can be saved on a single line, and they can be repeated in substitutions by the escape sequences \1 to \9.</td></tr>
<tr><td>+</td><td>Matches one or more instances of the preceding regular expression.</td></tr>
<tr><td>?</td><td>Matches zero or one instances of the preceding regular expression.</td></tr>
<tr><td>|</td><td>Matches the regular expression specified before or after; the | acts as an OR.</td></tr>
<tr><td>( )</td><td>Applies a match to the enclosed group of regular expressions.</td></tr>
</table>

rehash

A built-in C shell command that rebuilds the hash table used in the path variable. You may have to use **rehash** as you add new commands from time to time to make sure that your path is up-to-date.

■ *See also* **unhash.**

relational operators

An operator that allows for the comparison of two or more expressions.

The six relational operators are: equal to (==), not equal to (!=), less than (<), less than or equal to (<=), greater than (>), and greater than or equal to (>=).

■ *See also* **Boolean, conditional statement.**

R

relative pathname

A pathname that begins in your current directory. A relative pathname does not begin with /.

■ *See also* **absolute pathname, parent directory.**

relogin

An SVR4 command that changes the login entry to reflect the current window running under `layers` to ensure that commands such as `who` or `write` use the latest login information. One option is available, `-s` to suppress error messages.

remote

An SCO command that runs commands on a remote system.

▶ Syntax

The syntax for this command is:

```
remote [options]hostname
➥ command [options]
```

▶ Options and Arguments

In the syntax above, *`hostname`* is the name of the remote computer, and *`command [options]`* represents the command and the command options that you want to run on that remote computer; if you use – instead of *`command [options]`*, then input comes from the standard input on the local computer, not from the remote host. The options available with `remote` are listed in Table R.7.

▶ Examples

To run the `ls` command on the `/pub` directory on a remote computer called `sybex`, use:

```
remote sybex ls /pub
```

Remote File System

■ *See* **RFS.**

Table R.7: Options to Use with `remote`

OPTION	DESCRIPTION
`-f` *`filename`*	Uses the specified local *`filename`* as the standard input for the *`command`* on the local computer.
`-m`	Mails the user to report the completion of *`command`*; normally, only errors are mailed.
`-u` *`user`*	Sends any mail to *`user`*.

remote filesystem

Any filesystem on a remote computer that has been set up so that you can access the files and directories it contains as though they were stored on your own computer's hard disk. This is usually done over a network with NFS.

■ *See also* **mounting a filesystem, RFS.**

remote login

The action of logging in to a remote computer to access files and directories just as a local user would.

■ *See also* **`rcp`, `remote`, `rlogin`, `rsh`, `rusers`, `rwho`, `telnet`.**

remote mapping

A security mechanism under RFS for controlling access by remote users to shared files and directories. Remote mapping can create groups and group permissions.

Remote Procedure Call

■ *See* **RPC.**

removing a user

■ *See* **deleting a user.**

repeat

A built-in C shell command that repeats a command a specified number of times. The syntax for `repeat` is:

```
repeat n command
```

where *n* specifies the number of times you want to repeat *command*.

reset

An SVR4 command used to reset a hung or confused terminal. `reset` uses the value of the `TERM` environment variable to reset the terminal.

■ *See also* **tset**.

reset string

A string that your system administrator can send to your terminal to reset it when your terminal is hung or in an indeterminate state.

■ *See also* **reset**.

resolver

A library of programs used by host systems with DNS to resolve host names into IP addresses.

resource

Any separately identifiable hardware element found on a network, including memory, hard disks, printers, tape drives, and CD-ROMs.

resource sharing

The ability of an operating system to share separate resources between different processes at the same time, without causing any interference.

■ *See also* **deadlock, deadly embrace.**

restore

The act of reloading files from a backup to replace files that have become corrupted or have been accidentally deleted.

restoring a backup

To restore corrupted or accidentally deleted files from a backup, you use the same programs you used to create the backup originally; `tar` is probably the most popular choice.

With `tar`, check that the file is on the archive first with:

```
tar t | lp
```

This option creates a listing of all the files in the archive and sends it to the standard output; you can use a pipe to send the list to a printer instead, as in this example. This action not only confirms that the file you want is on the tape, but it also lets you see the full pathname that the file has been stored under; you'll need this information when you try to restore the file with:

```
tar -x /home/pmd
```

If the archive was compressed, you must use the appropriate decompression program before you can recover the file or files you are seeking.

restricted account

An account purposely created with fewer permissions than normal to increase security by limiting the user's access to the system. A restricted account is often used when the account is accessed by modem.

■ *See also* **restricted shell.**

restricted shell

A special version of the shell that provides the user with limited access to the system; for example, when using a restricted shell, the user may not be able to leave the current directory, change the `PATH` or `SHELL` variables, or start a program.

■ *See also* **restricted account, rsh, rksh.**

return

A built-in Bourne shell and Korn shell command that is used inside a function definition.

■ *See also* **exit.**

return code

■ *See* **exit status.**

return value

■ *See* **exit status.**

`rev`

A BSD command that reverses lines in a file. The syntax is:

```
rev filename...
```

`rev` copies the specified *`filename`* to the standard output, reversing the order of the characters in each line; if you don't specify a *`filename`*, then `rev` reads from the standard input.

reverse video

On a terminal screen, reversed foreground and background colors or attributes, often used to highlight an area or identify selected text.

Revision Control System

■ *See* **RCS.**

RFC

Abbreviation for Request for Comments. A document or set of documents in which proposed Internet standards are described or defined. Well over a thousand RFCs are in existence, and they represent a major method of online publication for Internet technical standards.

■ *See also* **IAB, RFD.**

RFD

Abbreviation for Request for Discussion. In USENET, a post sent to `news.announce.newsgroups` proposing the formation of a new newsgroup. Followup postings to this newsgroup will contain for and against opinions, and if most opinions are positive, the original proposer will issue a Call for Votes.

RFS

Abbreviation for Remote File System. A distributed file system network protocol that allows programs running on a computer to use network resources as though they were local. Originally developed by AT&T, RFS has been incorporated as a part of Unix System V Interface Definition.

■ *See also* **NFS.**

`.rhosts`

A file in your home directory on a remote system that contains a list of the computers that you are allowed to log on to without using a password.

■ *See also* **`rlogin`.**

RISC

Acronym for reduced instruction set computer, pronounced "risk." A processor that recognizes only a limited number of assembly-language instructions.

RISC chips are relatively cheap to produce and debug, as they usually contain fewer than 128 different instructions. CISC processors use a richer set of instructions, typically somewhere between 200 to 300. RISC processors are commonly used in workstations and can be designed to run as much as 70 percent faster than CISC processors.

`rksh`

A restricted version of the Korn shell used on certain systems. This version prevents you from leaving your home directory, changing the `PATH` variable, and redirecting output. On some systems this program is called `krsh`.

■ *See also* **`rsh`.**

`rlog`

■ *See* **RCS.**

Table R.8: Options to Use with rlogin

OPTION	DESCRIPTION
`-8`	Allows 8-bit data (instead of 7-bit data) to pass across the network.
`-e` *c*	Sets the escape character to *c*; the default is a tilde (~). The escape character can be specified as a literal character or as an octal number in the form `\`*nnn*.
`-l` *username*	Logs in to the remote computer with *username* rather than the current user's name.

R

rlogin

A command used to log in to a remote computer.

▶ Syntax

The syntax to use with `rlogin` is:

rlogin [*options*]*hostname*

You will be prompted to enter a password unless the `.rhosts` file in your home directory on the remote machine contains the host name and your username. *hostname* is a computer system you can access over a network.

▶ Options and Arguments

The options you can use with `rlogin` are listed in Table R.8.

■ *See also* **ftp**, **rcp**, **.rhosts**, **telnet**.

rm

A command used to remove files.

▶ Syntax

The syntax for the `rm` command is as follows:

rm [*options*] *filename*

You must have write permission for the directory that holds the file or files you want to remove, but you do not have to have write permission for the file; the permissions are displayed and you are prompted to confirm that you want to delete the file.

▶ Options and Arguments

The options available with `rm` are detailed in Table R.9.

▶ Examples

To remove one of your own files even though the file is write-protected, use:

```
rm -f myfile.doc
```

and to ask for confirmation before deleting every file in the current directory, use:

```
rm -i *
```

▶ Notes

New users should use the `-i` option until they are comfortable with this command, because `rm` normally runs without displaying any output at all, and this can result in files being deleted by accident.

■ *See also* **rmdir**.

rmail

The mail facility built into some versions of `emacs`.

rmb

An SCO filter command that removes blank lines from a text file; any series of more than two blank lines is reduced to two lines.

rmdel

■ *See* **SCCS.**

Table R.9: Options to Use with rm	
OPTION	DESCRIPTION
-f	Forces the removal, even if the permissions do not allow it.
-i	When used with the -r option, asks whether to delete each file or to examine each directory.
-P	A BSD option that overwrites each file three times before it is deleted.
-r	Recursively deletes the files and subdirectories associated with a directory as well as the directory itself; be careful—this can be a dangerous option if used without care.

rmdir

A command used to remove empty directories.

▶ Syntax

Here's the syntax for `rmdir`:

```
rmdir [options] directories
```

The directory must be empty before you can use `rmdir`.

▶ Options and Arguments

This command deletes the named *directories* but not their contents; use `rm -r` for this task if a directory is not empty. Some versions of `rmdir` (4.4BSD and Solaris, for example) do not have any options; other versions have the options listed in Table R.10.

Table R.10: Options to Use with rmdir	
OPTION	DESCRIPTION
-p	Removes the specified *directories* as well as any subdirectories that become empty as a result.
-s	Turns off any error messages generated by the -p option.

▶ Examples

To remove the empty `elvis` directory, use:

`rm elvis`

To remove the directory `documents` using an absolute pathname:

`rm /home/brenda/documents`

▪ *See also* **mkdir**, **rm**.

rn

A widely available and popular newsreader, used to subscribe to USENET newsgroups, written by Larry Wall and Stan Barber. `rn` is not a threaded newsreader and so cannot organize posts into threads, but it does have very powerful pattern-matching features used when searching through the text of posts.

Table R.11 lists the `rn` commands you can use while selecting a newsgroup or executing a shell command. Table R.12 lists the commands used when selecting an article within a newsgroup.

▪ *See also* **.newsrc**, **nn**, **tin**, **trn**.

roffs

Jargon for the Unix text-processing commands `nroff`, `roff`, and `troff`.

root

- The name of the directory at the top of the directory tree from which all other directories are descended.
- The name of the superuser, user number 0.

▪ *See also* **avatar**.

R

Table R.11: `rn` Commands Used When Selecting a Newsgroup

COMMAND	DESCRIPTION
Basic Commands	
`h`	Displays help information.
`q`	Quits `rn`.
`v`	Displays the `rn` version number.
`x`	Quits `rn` and abandons all updates to your `.newsrc` file.
Reading Articles	
`space`	Performs the default operation.
`y`	Starts displaying the current newsgroup for reading.
Working with Newsgroups	
`^`	Goes to the first newsgroup that contains unread articles.
`$`	Goes to the end of the list of newsgroups.
`c`	Marks all the articles in the newsgroup as having been read; catch up mode.
`g` *`newsgroup`*	Goes to the specified *`newsgroup`*.
`l` *`pattern`*	Lists the unsubscribed newsgroup names that contain *`pattern`*.
`L`	Lists the current state of newsgroups in `.newsrc`.
`n`	Goes to the next newsgroup that contains unread articles.
`p`	Goes to the previous newsgroup that contains unread articles.
/`pattern`	Searches forward for a newsgroup name containing *`pattern`*.
?`pattern`	Searches backward for a newsgroup name containing *`pattern`*.
`/`	Searches forward for previous *`pattern`*.
`?`	Searches backward for previous *`pattern`*.
Executing Unix Commands	
`!` *`command`*	Executes the specified *`command`*.
`!`	Pauses `rn` and starts a shell.

Table R.12: `rn` Commands Used When Selecting an Article

COMMAND	DESCRIPTION
Basic Commands	
`c`	Marks all articles in the newsgroup as read.
`h`	Displays help information.
`k`	Marks as read all articles with the same subject; effectively kills unread articles.
`n`	Goes to the next unread article.
`q`	Quits this newsgroup.
`u`	Unsubscribes from the current newsgroup.
`Ctrl-N`	Goes to the next unread article on the same subject.
Redisplaying the Current Article	
`b`	Goes back one page.
`v`	Redisplays the current article with its header.
`X`	Decodes the current page using rot13.
`Ctrl-L`	Redisplays the current page.
`Ctrl-R`	Redisplays the current article.
`Ctrl-X`	Decodes the current article using rot13.
Selecting Another Article	
`-`	Redisplays the last article displayed.
`N`	Goes forward to the next article.
`$`	Goes forward to the end of the last article.
`p`	Goes backward to the previous article.
`Ctrl-P`	Goes backward to the previous article with the same subject.
`P`	Goes backward to the next article, read or unread.
`^`	Goes backward to the next unread article.

Table R.12: `rn` Commands Used When Selecting an Article (continued)	
COMMAND	**DESCRIPTION**
Using Article Numbers	
=	Displays a list of all the unread articles.
number	Goes to the article with the specified *number*.
#	Displays the number of the last article.
Searching for an Article	
/*pattern*	Searches forward for a subject containing *pattern*.
?*pattern*	Searches backward for a subject containing *pattern*.
/	Searches forward for previous *pattern*.
?	Searches backward for previous *pattern*.
Responding to an Article	
f	Starts the **Pnews** program to create a followup post.
F	Starts the **Pnews** program to create a followup post and includes a copy of the original message.
r	Sends a mail message to the author of the article.
R	Sends a mail message to the author of the article and includes a copy of the original message.
Saving an Article	
s *filename*	Saves the article in the specified *filename*.
w *filename*	Saves the article without the header in the specified *filename*.
Executing Unix Commands	
! *command*	Executes the specified *command*.
!	Pauses `rn` and starts a shell.

rootdev

A kernel variable used to set the major and minor device numbers for the root filesystem.

root directory

The common ancestor for all directories in the Unix filesystem and the start of all absolute pathnames. The name of the root directory is `/`.

root filesystem

The filesystem available when Unix is brought up in single-user mode. The root filesystem is called `/` and cannot be mounted or unmounted. Only the programs and files in the root directory are available until the user mounts other filesystems.

root login

The login name of the superuser.

rot13

Pronounced "rote-13." A simple encryption scheme often used to scramble posts to USENET newsgroups. rot13 works by swapping each alphabetic character with one of 13 characters from its location in the alphabet, so that `a` becomes `n`; numbers and punctuation symbols are unaffected.

rot13 makes the article unreadable until the text is decoded and is often used when the subject matter might be considered offensive. Many newsreaders have a built-in command to unscramble rot13 text, and if you use it, don't be surprised by what you read; if you think you might be offended, don't decrypt the post.

You will also find other, unoffensive material encoded by rot13, including spoilers that give away the ending of a book or film and answers to puzzles or riddles.

■ *See also* **tr**.

RPC

Abbreviation for Remote Procedure Call, a set of procedures used to implement client/server architecture in distributed programming. RPC describes how an application initiates a process on another network node and how it retrieves the appropriate result.

rpcgen

A BSD software development tool that generates C language source code to implement a Remote Procedure Call (RPC) protocol.

■ *See also* **cc, cpp**.

rsh

A command used to start a shell on a remote system and execute a single command. When the command terminates, `rsh` also terminates.

▶ Syntax

The syntax for this command is:

rsh [*options*] *hostname*
➥ [*command*]

The commands that you can use on the remote system are determined by the system administrator for that system.

▶ Options and Arguments

The `rsh` command attempts to connect to the remote computer *hostname* and execute the specified *command*. If you don't specify *command*, you can use `rlogin` to log in to the system. The options you can use with this command are shown in Table R.13.

▶ Examples

To list the contents of your home directory on the remote computer system called `bigone`, use:

```
rsh bigone ls
```

This command:

```
rsh bigone ls > dirfile
```

makes a directory listing on the remote system called

bigone, and redirects the output from the **ls** command to a file called **dirfile** on your local system. To create **dirfile** on the remote system instead, you must quote the redirection symbol like this:

```
rsh bigone ls ">" dirfile
```

You can also use the append symbol (>>) in the same way.

▶ Notes

On some systems the **rsh** command is known as **remsh**.

Remember that shell metacharacters are interpreted on the local computer but not on the remote computer, unless you quote them.

■ *See also* **rcp, rlogin, telnet.**

Table R.13: Options to Use with rsh

OPTION	DESCRIPTION
-l *user*	Logs in as *user* rather than under your own login name.
-n	Allows you to run **rsh** in the background without expecting any input.
-x	Turns on DES encryption for all data exchange; using this option causes a significant delay in response times (BSD only).

rsh

A command used to start the restricted version of the Bourne shell. This version of the shell won't let you change directories, change **PATH** or **SHELL** variables, or specify a command or path that contains a /. Also, you may not use redirection.

■ *See also* **rksh, Rsh.**

Rsh

Another name for the restricted Bourne shell, which is usually called **rsh**. The advantage of using **Rsh** is that there is no confusion with the **rsh** remote shell command.

■ *See also* **sh.**

rstat

A BSD command that displays a summary of the system status of a specified host computer. The syntax is:

```
rstat host
```

Output from this command details how long the computer system has been running, and the one-, five-, and 15-minute load averages.

■ *See also* **ruptime, uptime.**

run

To execute a program.

runnable process

A process that has been started but is waiting until the system has sufficient resources to execute it.

runtime library

A group of library routines that perform specific, commonly used functions that a programmer can incorporate into a program. These routines are then called as the program runs. A runtime library saves the programmer time and effort, as they don't have to write (or debug) these routines.

rup

A Solaris command that shows host status of local systems.

▶ Syntax

Here's the syntax for **rup**:

```
run [options] hostname
```

▶ **Options and Arguments**

The options you can use with `rup` are listed in Table R.14.

See also **ping, ruptime, who.**

ruptime

An SVR4 command that displays the status of all systems on the local area network.

▶ **Syntax**

The syntax to use with `ruptime` is:

`ruptime [`*`options`*`]`

This command displays each system name, how long each host has been running, the number of users on each host, and the load average of each host.

▶ **Options and Arguments**

When used without options, this command displays the status information sorted by host name. Available options are listed in Table R.15.

See also **finger, rup, rusers, rwho, uptime.**

rusers

A command that displays information about who is logged on to the local area network.

▶ **Syntax**

Here's the syntax:

`rusers [`*`options`*`]`*`hostname...`*

▶ **Options and Arguments**

When used with a *hostname* argument, `rusers` queries only the specified remote computer, and to respond, the remote computer must be running the `rusers` daemon. Options for `rusers` are given in Table R.16.

See also **finger, rup, ruptime, rwho, uptime, who.**

Table R.14: Options to Use with `rup`

OPTION	DESCRIPTION
`-h`	Sorts the listing alphabetically by host name.
`-l`	Sorts the listing by load average.
`-t`	Sorts the listing by up time.

Table R.15: Options to Use with `ruptime`

OPTION	DESCRIPTION
`-a`	Includes information on users who have been inactive for longer than one hour; these users are normally not counted.
`-l`	Sorts the list of systems by load average.
`-r`	Reverses the sort order.
`-t`	Sorts the list of systems by the amount of time each system has been up and running.
`-u`	Sorts the list of systems by the number of users on each system.

Table R.16: Options to Use with `rusers`

OPTION	DESCRIPTION
`-a`	Displays a report even if no users are currently logged on.
`-h`	Sorts alphabetically by host name.
`-i`	Sorts by idle time.
`-l`	Creates a long listing, similar to that provided by `who`.
`-u`	Sorts by the number of users.

Table R.17: Options to Use with rwall	
OPTION	DESCRIPTION
-n *netgroup*	Sends the message to those users defined by *netgroup*, rather than to all users logged in to *hostname*.
-h *hostname*	Sends the message to the specified *hostname*. This option is used when both a *netgroup* and a *hostname* are specified.

rwall

A command that broadcasts a message to all users on the network.

▶ Syntax

The syntax to use with `rwall` is as follows:

```
rwall [options] hostname
```

▶ Options and Arguments

The `rwall` command reads a message from the standard input and, when it sees an end-of-file character, it then broadcasts the message to all the users who are logged in to *hostname*. The text, `Broadcast Message`, appears before the text of the message. Options are listed in Table R.17.

■ *See also* **talk**, **wall**, **write**.

rwho

A TCP/IP command that displays who is logged on for all machines on the local area network. You can use the `-a` option with `rwho` to list all users, even if they have been inactive for more than an hour.

■ *See also* **finger**, **rup**, **ruptime**, **rusers**, **users**, **who**.

RZSZ

A package of tools used to implement the Zmodem file-transfer protocol. You will find these utilities in the package:

- `rz` Receives files using the Zmodem protocol; if the sending program does not initiate a transfer within 50 seconds, rz changes to rb mode.
- `rb` Receives files using the Ymodem protocol.
- `rx` Receives files using the Xmodem protocol.
- `sz` Sends files using the Zmodem protocol.
- `sb` Sends files using the Ymodem protocol.
- `sx` Sends files using the Xmodem protocol.

Table R.18 lists the most useful `rz` options, while Table R.19 lists the most useful `sz` options.

You can get RZSZ from `ftp.cs.pdx.edu` in the directory `/pub/zmodem`, as well as from other sites that archive the standard Unix source files, including `ftp.cs.unm.edu` and `plaza.aarnet.edu.au`.

Because most of the popular PC terminal emulation and communications programs support Zmodem, this package makes it easy to swap files between Unix systems, PCs, and Macintosh computers.

■ *See also* **C-Kermit, Kermit, Xmodem, Ymodem, Zmodem.**

Table R.18: Useful Options to Use with `rz`	
OPTION	**DESCRIPTION**
`-+`	Appends rather than overwrites existing files.
`-a`	Receives ASCII text files.
`-b`	Receives binary files.
`-D`	Sends output to `/dev/null`; a useful test mode.
`-e`	Makes the sending program escape control characters.
`-p`	Skips a transfer if a file of the same name already exists; this can prevent the completion of an interrupted file transfer.
`-q`	Turns off messages.
`-t` *n*	Sets the timeout to *n* in tenths of a second.
`-v`	Adds a list of transferred filenames to a log file `/tmp/rzlog`.

Table R.19: Useful Options to Use with `sz`	
OPTION	**DESCRIPTION**
`-+`	Makes the receiving program append transmitted data to an existing file.
`-a`	Sends ASCII text.
`-b`	Sends binary files.
`-d`	Tries to reconcile filename differences between systems.
`-e`	Escapes control characters.
`-f`	Forces the full pathname to be sent in the transmitted filename.
`-l` *n*	Sets the packet length to *n* bytes.
`-L` *n*	Sets the Zmodem subpacket length to *n* bytes.
`-n`	Overwrites a file if the source file is newer than the destination file.
`-N`	Overwrites a file if the source filename is longer than the destination filename.
`-p`	Doesn't transfer the file if the destination file exists.
`-q`	Turns off messages.
`-r`	Resumes an interrupted transfer.
`-t` *n*	Sets the timeout to *n* tenths of a second.
`-v`	Adds the names of transferred files to the log file `/tmp/szlog`.
`-y`	Overwrites existing files with the same name.
`-Y`	Overwrites existing files with the same name, but does not send files with the same pathname on the destination system.

SA

▪ *See* **system administrator.**

sact

▪ *See* **SCCS.**

SAGE

Acronym for System Administrator's Guild, a special interest group formed by the USENIX Association in 1993. The main aims of the guild are to set guidelines for education and qualifications to ensure a career path for system managers and administrators, to recognize technical excellence, and to communicate with users, management, and vendors with a single, unified voice.

sane flag

An option used with the `stty` command that restores a terminal to its normal standard operating state.

sash

Acronym for standalone shell, a program started during the boot process as the system initializes and begins running.

SATAN

Acronym for Security Administrator Tool for Analyzing Networks. A software package written by Dan Farmer, available free over the Internet, that allows system administrators to identify gaps in their security systems. Critics of the program argue that SATAN lets hackers exploit the information contained in the program on how to infiltrate these security systems, but so far, the program seems to have acted as a wake-up call for system administrators.

You can get SATAN from several sites, including `ftp.win.tue.nl` in the directory

pub/security/admin-guide-to-cracking.Z, ftp.demon.co.uk in the directory pub/mirrors/satan, and ftp.lerc.nasa.gov in the directory security.

See also **intruder, security.**

save

To write a new file or to overwrite an existing file after you have made modifications to it.

savehist

A C shell environment variable that displays the number of commands saved in the /home/.history history file at the end of a session.

/sbin

An SVR4 directory that contains programs for starting the system and for system recovery.

scalability

The ability of a system to match its size and throughput to the needs of the applications software that it runs. Such a system may be freely expanded to meet changing requirements.

SCCS

Abbreviation for Source Code Control System; a set of programs designed to keep track of multiple revisions to files, usually in a software development environment, and to minimize the amount of hard disk space needed to store the revisions.

Using SCCS, you can automatically store and then retrieve revisions, compare and merge revisions, keep a complete change log, and specifically identify particular revisions. Table S.1 lists the major programs in the SCCS suite and describes their use.

In SCCS, each set of changes is known as a "delta" and is assigned a SCCS ID (sometimes abbreviated sid) consisting of either two components (a release and a level number in the form of *a.b*) or four components (release, level, branch, and sequence numbers in the form of *a.b.c.d*).

Table S.1: SCCS Programs

PROGRAM	DESCRIPTION
admin	Creates and configures a new SCCS file.
cdc	Changes the comments associated with a particular delta.
comb	Combines consecutive deltas into a single delta.
delta	Creates a new delta.
get	Retrieves a text file from the SCCS archive.
help	Opens the SCCS help system; at the prompt you can enter a command name or an error code and read a brief explanation.
prs	Prints a portion of the specified SCCS file.
rmdel	Removes an accidental delta from the SCCS file.
sact	Reports which files are being edited but that have yet to be updated using delta.
sccsdiff	Reports the differences between two SCCS files.
unget	Cancels a get operation without creating a new delta.
val	Validates an SCCS file.
what	Searches SCCS files for a specified pattern and then prints out the following text.

Each time a delta is entered into SCCS, the system notes which lines have been changed or deleted since the most recent version, and from this information,

SCCS can re-create the file on demand. This means that each change depends on all previous changes.

See also **RCS, version number.**

sccsdiff

See **SCCS.**

scheduler

That part of the Unix kernel that schedules processes for execution and determines the order in which they will be run, at what time, and for how long.

SCO

Abbreviation for Santa Cruz Operation, the developers of several important strains of Unix, including XENIX, SCO UNIX, and the SCO OpenServer series of Unix products. SCO began shipping Unix products based on Intel computers in 1982, and now their Unix systems account for approximately 40 percent of the Unix market, with over 8,000 different applications available from various vendors.

In 1995, SCO bought the rights to Unix from Novell and expects to combine the features found in SCO's OpenServer with those in Novell's UnixWare over the next two years.

SCO's World Wide Web site is `http://www.sco.com`, and SCO also maintains several USENET newsgroups, including `biz.sco.announce`, `biz.sco.general`, `biz.sco.magazine`, `biz.sco.opendesktop`, `biz.sco.sources`, and `biz.sco.wserver`.

See also **Open Desktop.**

SCOadmin

A set of graphical system administrator tools provided with SCO OpenServer. SCOadmin lets you add or remove users, manage printers and filesystems, and check your network configuration quickly and easily. You can also run SCOadmin in text mode if you wish.

See also **`sysadmsh`.**

SCO OpenServer

A set of Unix products from SCO; OpenServer Desktop, OpenServer Host, and OpenServer Enterprise.

OpenServer includes a journaling filesystem, integrated symmetrical multiprocessing, and a set of graphical system administration tools, as well as Merge, which allows you to run your DOS applications, and WABI, which lets you run selected Microsoft Windows 3.1 applications in an X Window.

See also **SCO UNIX, XENIX.**

SCO UNIX

A popular version of Unix from SCO, based on System V Release 3.2 with many SVR4 enhancements. SCO UNIX includes the Korn shell, X Window, Level C2 security, multiprocessor support, and full network support, as well as the ability to run DOS programs and read and write DOS files on a floppy disk.

See also **XENIX.**

screen editor

A text editor that lets you enter, edit, and display text anywhere on the screen; `vi` and `emacs` are both popular screen editors. Sometimes called a *visual editor*.

See also **line editor.**

script

A list of commands in a text file to be executed by an interpreter. The terms "script" and "shell program" are often used interchangeably, with the vague suggestion that a script is usually simpler; for example, a login script may execute the same specific set of instructions every time a user logs in to the system.

See also **shell script.**

script

A command that saves a copy of everything you type during your current session into a file that is called `typescript`. The syntax to use is:

```
script [option][filename]
```

You can also specify the *`filename`* you want to use, and the single option, **`-a`**, lets you append the current session to the end of *`filename`* rather than overwrite its contents. This command is useful for occasional users who might want to document their sessions or for when the system administrator performs some particularly grueling task and wants to collect all the output from a time-consuming command for later reuse or as a record.

When you press Ctrl-D or type **`exit`**, you see the message:

```
Script is done,
➥ file is typescript
```

(unless you specified a different name), before you are returned to the system prompt.

`script` places everything that appears on your screen during your session into the file, including commands such as backspace and form feed. So be careful when you print out the file; you may get more than you bargained for.

scroll

To move the lines on a terminal screen, either up or down, to make room for new lines to be displayed. In a graphical user interface, you can scroll the display to the left and to the right, as well as up and down.

SCSI

Acronym for small computer system interface, pronounced "scuzzy." A high-speed parallel interface defined by the ANSI X3T9.2 committee. SCSI is used to connect a computer to peripheral devices using just one port. Devices connected in this way are said to be "daisy-chained" together, and each device must have a unique identifier or priority number.

Today, SCSI is often used to connect hard disks, tape drives, CD-ROM drives, and other mass storage media, as well as scanners and printers.

There are several SCSI interface definitions:

- **SCSI-1:** A 1986 definition of an 8-bit parallel interface with a maximum data transfer rate of 5 megabytes per second (Mbps).
- **SCSI-2:** This 1994 definition broadened the 8-bit data bus to 16 or 32 bits (also known as *Wide SCSI*), doubling the data transfer rate to 10 or 20 Mbps (also known as *Fast SCSI*). Wide SCSI and Fast SCSI can be combined to give Fast-Wide SCSI with a 16-bit data bus and a maximum data-transfer rate of 20 Mbps. SCSI-2 is backward compatible with SCSI-1, but for maximum benefit, you should use SCSI-2 devices with a SCSI-2 controller.
- **SCSI-3:** This definition increased the number of connected peripherals from seven to sixteen, increased cable lengths, and added support for a serial interface and for a fiber optic interface. Data transfer rates depend on the hardware implementation, but data rates in excess of 100 Mbps are possible.

SCSI bus

Another name for the SCSI interface and communications protocol.

SCSI terminator

The SCSI interface must be correctly terminated at both ends to prevent signals echoing on the bus. Many SCSI devices have built-in terminators that engage when they are needed. With some older SCSI devices, you must add an external SCSI terminator that plugs into the device's SCSI connector.

scuzzy

■ *See* **SCSI.**

sdb

A symbolic debugger for C, for assembly language, and for Fortran. **sdb** is used to check programs and to examine core files from aborted programs.

See also **adb, dbx, gdb.**

sdiff

A command that creates a side-by-side comparison of two files.

▶ Syntax

Here's the syntax:

sdiff [*options*] *filename1* ➥ *filename2*

This command is very useful for comparing two versions of a file because the output is much easier to read than that created by the regular version of **diff**.

▶ Options and Arguments

You can use the options listed in Table S.2 with **sdiff**.

▶ Examples

The output from **sdiff** has two columns. The text on the left is from *filename1*, the text on the right is from *filename2*, and you may also see the following:

text text	Indicates that the two lines are identical.
text <	Indicates that **text** only occurs in **filename1**.
> *text*	Indicates that **text** only occurs in **filename2**.
text | *text*	Indicates that the two lines are different.

S

Table S.2: Options to Use with sdiff

OPTION	DESCRIPTION
-l	Lists only the lines from *filename1* that are identical.
-o *outfile*	Sends identical lines from *filename1* and *filename2* to *outfile*. You can then enter one of the following commands to edit *outfile*: l — Adds left column to output file. r — Adds right column to output file. s — Suppresses printing of matching lines. v — Turns off the **s** option. e l — Invokes **ed** to work on the left column. e r — Invokes **ed** to work on the right column. e b — Invokes **ed** to work on both columns. e — Invokes **ed**. q — Quits **ed** and **sdiff**.
-s	Does not print matching lines.
-w *n*	Sets the line length to *n*; the default is 130.

To list the lines from `sales.95` on the left side of the screen that match lines in `sales.96`, use:

```
sdiff -l sales.95 sales.96
```

See also **bdiff, diff, diff3, ed.**

SDK

Abbreviation for software development kit. A software development package from an operating system vendor that contains useful software development tools, libraries, and technical information.

search

In text processing, a program feature that locates a specific word or words. Also, to find the location of a file in a filesystem.

See also **regular expressions, search and replace.**

search and replace

In text processing, a program feature that locates a specific word or words and then replaces them with text that you specify. You can also use it to search for and then delete a set of characters.

See also **awk, grep, regular expressions, search.**

search path

That list of directories that the shell searches to locate the program file you want to execute. Your search path usually includes your home directory, the `/bin` directory, and the `/usr/bin` directory, although it may include others too. You can add directories to your search path by changing the `path` or `PATH` environment variables.

See also **path, PATH, pathname.**

search pattern

See **search string.**

search string

One or more characters to be matched in a search operation. You might specify a search string using a text editor or a utility that will search through several files to try to match the characters in the search string. Sometimes called *search pattern.*

See also **awk, grep, regular expressions.**

secondary mailbox

The mailbox used to hold your e-mail messages once you have read them.

See also **mailbox, primary mailbox.**

secondary prompt

A prompt displayed by the shell to indicate that the command you are entering is incomplete and more information is needed. The default secondary prompt is the greater than symbol (>).

See also **PS2.**

SECONDS

A Korn shell environment variable that contains the number of seconds since the shell was started.

security

Any safeguards employed to protect the integrity of the system and the privacy of the data maintained on that system.

The basic Unix security system of passwords and directory and file permissions protects the users from one another, but when the system is connected to an external network, or the Internet, then other broader security concerns come into play to protect against external intruders.

See also **firewall, Kerberos, SATAN, Trojan Horse.**

sed

The Unix stream or batch editor. `sed` is more like a filter command than the traditional Unix text editors `vi` or **emacs**. It takes data from the standard input or from a file, applies a transformation to the data, and sends the changed data to the standard output. If you want to capture this output to a file, you must redirect standard output to the file.

▶ Syntax

The syntax for **sed** is:

```
sed [options][files]
```

Here's how **sed** operates:

- Each line of input is copied into a buffer called the *pattern space.*
- All the editing commands in the **sed** script are applied to the data in the order in which they are specified. This can sometimes have unexpected results because **sed** applies every editing command to the first input line before reading the second input line, rather than, as some people imagine, applying the first editing command to all lines in the file before applying the second editing command.
- Editing commands are applied to all lines globally, unless they are restricted by line addressing.
- If a command changes the input, all subsequent commands will act on the current, changed line, rather than the original text. A pattern that once matched the original text may no longer match if that text has been changed.
- Output is written to the standard output, but you can redirect it to a file.

▶ Options and Arguments

The options listed in Table S.3 are available with **sed**.

Table S.3: Options to Use with sed

OPTION	DESCRIPTION
-e *command*	Applies the editing *command* to the file.
-f *script*	Applies the editing instructions contained in *script*.
-n	Turns off echoing of lines to the standard output once all commands have been applied.

▶ sed Scripts

The general form of a **sed** script is:

```
[address[,address]]function
➥[arguments]
```

where the addresses are optional. If you leave them out, **sed** applies the *function* to all input lines; otherwise, they are restricted to the specified address or range of addresses. The *function* is a **sed** editing command, and the *arguments* depend on which *function* you use. An *address* can be zero, one, or two line numbers; an *address* can also be a regular expression. Table S.4 lists the main **sed** editing commands.

You can also use **!** as a NOT, and you can enclose a group of commands in braces so that they all act upon a single address.

See also **awk, ed, grep.**

select

A Korn shell programming construct that displays a numbered list of items and lets a user select one of them. A **select** statement might look like this:

```
select element [in list]
do
        commands
done
```

If no *list* is specified, items are read from the standard input. After the items in *list* are displayed, **select** displays the **PS3** prompt string to receive the user's selection; if the user makes a valid selection, *commands* are executed.

Table S.4: Major sed Editing Commands

COMMAND	DESCRIPTION
`d`	Deletes a line
`n`	Processes the next line of input with the next function, rather than resuming at the beginning of the `sed` script.
`a`	Appends one or more lines to the currently selected line.
`i`	Inserts one or more lines before the currently selected line.
`c`	Changes the selected line.
`s`	Substitutes a replacement pattern with a new pattern for each addressed line.
`p`	Writes selected lines to the standard output.
`w` *`filename`*	Writes selected lines to the specified *`filename`*.
`r` *`filename`*	Reads the contents of the specified *`filename`* and appends it to the selected line.
`q`	Stops `sed` processing.

semaphore

An interprocess communications signal that indicates the status of a shared system resource, such as shared memory.

Event semaphores allow a process to tell other processes that an event has occurred and that it is safe for them to resume execution. Mutual exclusion (sometimes abbreviated mutex) semaphores protect system resources such as files, data, and peripherals from simultaneous access by several processes. Multiple wait (abbreviated muxwait) semaphores allow threads to wait for multiple events to take place or for multiple resources to become free.

semicolon

- The `;` character. Used as a command separator in C programming and shell scripts.
- A special character used to separate multiple commands on the command line.

In speech, the semicolon is often referred to as simply "semi," as in "semi-semi-star" meaning `;;*`.

sendbug

A BSD command that sends a bug report, written in a standard format, to `4bsd-bugs@Berkeley.edu`.

sendmail

A Unix program that acts as a mail transport agent in an e-mail system, receiving messages from a user's e-mail program such as Pine or `elm`, and then routing the mail to the correct destination. Normal Unix users rarely come into direct contact with `sendmail`.

See also **`elm`, Pine, `smail`, SMTP.**

sentence

In the `vi` text editor, any string of characters ending in a period, comma, question mark, or exclamation mark, which is followed by at least two spaces or a newline character.

server

A program or a computer that offers a service or a resource on request over a network. A server computer typically has more memory and a larger hard disk than a single-user workstation and may have more than one processor. A program that requests services from a server is known as a *client*.

See also **client/server.**

session

The period of time during which you are using the system between login and logout. One person can actually use several sessions at the same time by using multiple terminals or by using several windows on the same terminal.

In communications, a session is also the name for the active connection between two computers; many different transactions may take place during a single session.

session layer

The fifth of seven layers of the ISO/OSI model for computer-to-computer communications. The session layer coordinates communications and maintains the session for as long as it is needed, performing security, logging, and administrative functions.

set

A built-in shell command used to set variable values. When used without arguments, `set` lists the values of all variables known to the current shell.

See also **Bourne shell, C shell, Korn shell, `setenv`.**

set uid bit

A file permission that gives the file the permissions of its owner rather than the permissions of the user who called it. This is often done so that a person running a program can access files that he or she would normally not be allowed to access. For example, a multiuser database system might use a process validation program with superuser privileges to allow it to gain access to system process information every time a user (who does not have superuser privileges) logs on to the system.

setenv

A built-in C shell command that assigns a value to a named environment variable; by convention, the name must be in uppercase. The syntax is:

```
setenv [name[value]]
```

`value` can be either a single word or a quoted string; if no *`value`* is specified, the null value is used. If you don't specify any arguments, `setenv` lists the names and values of all environment variables.

See also **`set`.**

SGML

Abbreviation for Standard Generalized Markup Language. An ISO standard (ISO 8879) for defining the structure and managing the contents of any digital document.

The standard specifies a definition for formatting a digital document so it may be modified, viewed, or output on any computer system. Each SGML document consists of two parts: the DTD (Document Type Definition) defines the structure of the document, while the Document Instance describes the data, or text, of the document.

HTML, used in many World Wide Web documents on the Internet, is a part of SGML.

sh

Command used to invoke the Bourne shell, the original Unix command processor.

▶ Syntax

Here's the syntax:

```
sh [options][arguments]
```

▶ Options and Arguments

Table S.5 lists the command-line options you can use with `sh`.

You may find that different implementations of `sh` vary somewhat; it is available in some form on almost all Unix systems because it is the preferred shell for running shell scripts.

▶ Examples

To run `sh` in a mode to debug shell scripts, use:

```
sh -vx
```

The `-x` option echoes each command you enter, and `-v` echoes any data replacement in the shell script.

See also **Bash, `csh`, `ksh`, `rksh`, `rsh`, Tcsh, Zsh.**

Table S.5: Options to Use with sh

OPTION	DESCRIPTION
-a	Automatically exports variables after they have been defined or changed.
-c *string*	Reads commands from the specified *string*.
-e	Exits if a command returns a non-zero exit status.
-f	Ignores the filename metacharacters * ? [ ].
-h	Locates commands as they are defined.
-i	Starts an interactive shell.
-k	Assignment of a value to a variable can take place anywhere on the command line.
-m	Enables job control.
-n	Reads commands but does not execute them.
-p	Starts up without processing commands contained in .profile.
-r	Starts a restricted shell; same as rsh.
-s	Reads commands from the standard input, sends output from built-in commands to file descriptor 1, and all other shell output goes to file descriptor 2.
-t	Executes one command and then exits.
-u	Treats unset variables as errors rather than null.
-v	Displays the shell command line.
-x	Turns on shell-script debugging.

shar

A widely used archiver, written by Bill Davidsen, that allows you to create an archive in text form that you can then include in an e-mail message.

▶ Syntax

The syntax for this command is:

shar [*options*]*file*...

▶ Options and Arguments

Table S.6 lists the command-line options available with shar; use redirection to send output from this command to a file.

▶ Examples

To place a group of files in a shar archive and put this archive into a file called document.shar, use:

```
shar memo.one memo.two
➥ memo.three > document.shar
```

To unpack and extract these files, use the sh command. This runs the file as a shell script to unpack the archive automatically:

```
sh document.shar
```

Table S.6: Options to Use with shar	
OPTION	DESCRIPTION
-b	Assumes all files are binary and converts them to text using **uuencode**.
-c	Adds a "cut here" line at the beginning of each output file.
-d*delim*	Uses *delim* as the delimiter character between files in the archive.
-D	Includes the date, user, and name of the current directory when the archive was created.
-f	Uses just the filename part of each pathname for the output file in the archive; this lets you unpack each file from the archive into the current directory.
-l*size*	Limits the archive to *size* kilobytes.
-M	Assumes files are both text and binary; binary files are converted to text using uuencode.
-o*filename*	Sends output to the specified *filename*.
-s	Checks files for damage using the **sum** command.
-v	Displays all messages; verbose mode.
-x	Prevents overwriting of existing files when unpacking an archive.

▶ **Notes**

A file created by this utility will have the filename extension .shar.

■ *See also* **compress, mail, tar, uuencode.**

shared memory

An interprocess communications technique in which the same area of memory is accessed by more than one program running in the same system. Semaphores and other management elements prevent the applications from colliding or trying to update the same information at the same time.

shareware

A form of software distribution that makes copyrighted programs freely available, often on a trial basis; if you like the product and use it, you are expected to register your copy and send a small fee to the original creator. Once your copy is registered, you might receive a more complete manual, technical support, or information about upgrades.

■ *See also* **FSF, GNU.**

shell

The Unix system command processor. The shell accepts commands from the user, interprets them, and passes them on to the operating system for processing. Most shells also include a programming language interpreter so that users can write small programs without having to invoke a complete language compiler.

The three major shells are the Bourne shell (the original Unix shell from AT&T), the C shell (developed as part of the BSD Unix efforts), and the Korn shell (also developed by AT&T). In recent years several public-domain shells have become very popular, including Bash (the Bourne-again shell) often used on Linux, Tcsh, and Zsh.

■ *See also* **Unix shell.**

SHELL

An environment variable that contains the name of the user's preferred shell.

shell escape

The **!** character, when used from within a program to indicate that the next command should be passed to the shell for processing, rather than acted upon locally inside the program. Once the command executes, you exit from the shell and automatically return to your previous state within the program.

■ *See also* **shell out.**

shell file

■ *See* **shell script.**

shell function

A series of commands stored by the shell for execution at some later time. Shell functions are similar to shell scripts but they run faster because they are stored in memory rather than in files on disk. Also, a shell function is run in the same environment as the shell that calls it, whereas a shell script is usually run in a subshell.

shell option

In the Korn shell, a variable that acts like a toggle or an on/off switch. In the C shell, such a variable is known as a *shell variable*.

shell out

Jargon for creating a new shell while you are still in an existing program such as an editor or mailer.

■ *See also* **shell escape.**

shell program

Any program written in the shell programming language and interpreted by a shell process; also known as a *shell script*. The shell programming languages are all very similar, with the most important differences appearing in the flow-control structures, including `if`...`then` and `while` loops.

Shell programs are usually written to automate complex or infrequently used tasks. When the shell program gets too large and cumbersome, you are often better off translating the program into C, particularly if speed of execution is important.

■ *See also* **Bash, Bourne shell, C shell, shell programming language.**

shell programming language

A programming language provided by the Unix shell. A shell program is often developed quickly to speed up a mundane task or automate a little-used procedure.

The shell programming languages are interpreted and provide flow control, the ability to execute Unix utilities, input/output redirection, and simple variable manipulation. The shell programming languages are best suited to those tasks that can take advantage of existing Unix utilities and are not good at tasks that perform extensive arithmetic or require high performance.

■ *See also* **Bash, Bourne shell, C shell, `perl`, shell script, Tcl, Tk.**

shell prompt

An indication from the shell that it is ready to receive the next command from the command line. By default, the percent sign (`%`) is the C shell prompt, and the dollar sign (`$`) is the Bourne shell prompt.

■ *See also* **`PS1`, `PS2`, `PS3`, `PS4`, secondary prompt.**

shell script

Any program written in the shell programming language and interpreted by a shell process; also known as a *shell program*. The shell programming languages are all very similar, with the most important differences appearing in the flow-control structures, including `if`...`then` and `while` loops.

Shell programs are usually written to automate complex or infrequently used tasks. When the shell program gets too large and cumbersome, you are often better off translating the program into C, particularly if speed of execution is important.

See also **Bash, Bourne shell, C shell, shell programming language.**

shell variable

In the C shell, a variable that represents a value. Some shell variables act as on/off switches, while others contain a string of characters.

In the Korn shell, a shell variable is the same as a global variable.

See also **environment variables, shell option.**

shielded cable

Cable protected against electromagnetic and radio-frequency interference (RFI) by metal-backed mylar foil and plastic or PVC.

See also **unshielded cable.**

shielded twisted pair cable

Abbreviated STP. Cable with a foil shield and copper braid surrounding the pairs of wires.

The wires have a minimum number of twists per foot of cable length; the greater the number of twists, the lower the interference or crosstalk. STP offers high-speed transmission for useful distances, and it is often associated with Token Ring networks, but its bulk quickly fills up wiring conduits.

See also **shielded cable, unshielded twisted pair cable.**

shift

- A C shell programming keyword used to shift the words in a specified wordlist variable. The syntax is:

  `shift [`*`variable`*`]`

  If no *`variable`* is specified, this command shifts the command-line arguments; `$2` becomes `$1`, `$3` becomes `$2`, and so on. `shift` is typically used in a `while` loop.
- A Bourne shell and Korn shell programming keyword used to shift the command-line arguments; `$2` becomes `$1`, `$3` becomes `$2`, and so on. If you specify an integer value, the command-line arguments are shifted the specified number of places to the left. In the Korn shell, this value can be an integer expression.

shl

An SVR4 command used to run more than one shell from a single terminal.

See also **`layers`.**

shutdown

- A shell script used by the system administrator to shut down the system in a logical and orderly manner.
- Turning off the power to the system.

See also **`shutdown`, shutting down the system.**

shutdown

An SVR4 command used by the system administrator or superuser to perform an orderly system shutdown.

▶ Syntax

The syntax to use with `shutdown` is:

`shutdown [`*`options`*`]`

On SVR4 systems you find `shutdown` in `/usr/sbin`, on BSD systems in `/usr/etc`, and on SCO systems in `/etc`.

▶ Options and Arguments

The options you can use with `shutdown` do vary somewhat between different Unix systems; Table S.7 lists the options available on SVR4.

The `shutdown` command goes through an orderly sequence of events to ensure a safe and complete system halt. First, it terminates all user processes and goes from a multiuser state to a single-user state. `shutdown` then posts a warning message, waits for 60 seconds, posts a final message, and then prompts for confirmation that you still want to take the system down.

■ *See also* **`init`, shutting down the system, state.**

Table S.7: Options to Use with `shutdown`

OPTION	DESCRIPTION
`-g`*n*	Uses a grace period of *n* seconds rather than the default 60 seconds.
`-i`*k*	Tells the `init` command to place the system in the state specified by *k*.
`-y`	Suppresses the default confirmation prompt.

shutting down the system

A procedure performed by the system administrator to stop the operating system in an orderly way so that users do not lose work. The system may be shut down for a variety of reasons, including preventative maintenance, troubleshooting hardware problems, or the installation or upgrade of new or existing hardware.

The system administrator usually runs a shell script named `/usr/sbin/shutdown` on SVR4, `/usr/etc` on Solaris, or `/etc` on SCO; refer to your system manual for more details. This script brings the system down gracefully by killing existing processes and synchronizing disks by writing the contents of the cache out to disk.

■ *See also* **booting, `init`.**

signal

A short message that the Unix kernel or the user can send to a process, usually indicating some sort of abnormal condition.

When a process receives a signal, one of three things may happen: the process may follow the default action of the signal if there is such a default; the process may be forced to terminate; or the process may execute special code to handle the signal.

■ *See also* **kill.**

signature

A short text file that is automatically added to the end of any e-mail message or USENET post.

Your signature file usually contains your name (or alias) and e-mail address, and some people like to add pithy quotes. Netiquette dictates that a signature file should always be short, between one and five lines long; anything longer will invite a flame.

single quote symbol

The `'` character. You can use single quotes around a part of the command line where you want the shell to override the meaning of any metacharacters in your commands. For example, the asterisk (`*`) is often used as a wild card, but becomes merely an asterisk when enclosed in single quotes.

■ *See also* **backquote, double quote, quoting.**

single-user state

A Unix state in which only the system administrator has access to the system, and only the root filesystem is mounted. No multiuser processes can run, and the system can be accessed only through the console. Single-user state is most often used when the system administrator is troubleshooting the system or making repairs to the filesystem. Single-user state is also used just after the system boots and just before it shuts down.

■ *See also* **`init`.**

single-user system

A computer operating system designed for use by one person at a time, often on a personal computer. DOS, the Macintosh System 7, OS/2, and Microsoft Windows are examples of single-user operating systems. Unix and most network operating systems are multiuser systems, although Unix does have a single-user state that is used just after the system boots and just before it shuts down.

■ *See also* **multiuser system.**

site license

A method of licensing a software package or operating system to a company or other organization so that the software can be used by anyone belonging to that company. The alternative to a site license is to buy individual licenses (in other words, individual copies of the software) for each person who wants to use the package. Some network applications can use application metering, in which a specific number of people can use the application at the same time.

■ *See also* **source license.**

`size`

A software development command used to display the data and text segment sizes of an object or binary file.

■ *See also* **`gprof`, `lprof`, `nm`, `prof`.**

Slackware Linux

■ *See* **Linux.**

slash

The / character. The slash is used to separate elements (file and directory names) in a pathname and is also the name of the root filesystem.

■ *See also* **absolute pathname, relative pathname, root.**

SLED

Acronym for single large expensive disk. The traditional alternative to RAID (redundant array of inexpensive disks), used by most networks.

sleep

To suspend execution of a process. Processes in Unix sleep when waiting for input/output to complete, when waiting for the death of a child process, or when suspended by a user. When a process wakes up again, it continues execution from the point at which it was suspended.

■ *See also* **`sleep`, wakeup.**

`sleep`

A command that suspends animation for a specified time.

The syntax is:

```
sleep seconds
```

where *`seconds`* represents the length of time that you want to delay the process. This command is often used in shell scripts.

■ *See also* **`at`, sleep, wakeup.**

SLIP

Acronym for Serial Line Internet Protocol. A protocol used to run TCP/IP over serial lines or telephone connections using dial-up modems.

SLIP establishes a temporary direct connection to the Internet via modem and appears to the host system as a port somewhere on the host's network.

SLIP is slowly being replaced by PPP (Point-to-Point Protocol).

`smail`

A Unix program that acts as a mail transport agent in an e-mail system, receiving messages from a user's e-mail program, such as Pine or `elm`, and then routing the mail to the correct destination. Most users of Unix will never come into contact with `smail`.

■ *See also* **`elm`, Pine, `sendmail`.**

S

smart terminal

A terminal with local processing power used to perform functions independently from the main host computer; also known as an *intelligent terminal.*

See also **dumb terminal.**

smiley

A group of text characters used in e-mail and USENET posts to indicate humor or other emotions. You must turn a smiley on its side to read it. There are hundreds of different smileys in common use, and new ones appear all the time. Two favorites are :-) for smiling and ;-) to indicate winking or flirting.

See also **emoticon.**

`smit`

The system administration program on IBM's AIX. `smit` has both X Window and ASCII terminal user interfaces, as well as extensive online help. You can use `smit` to configure networking options and devices, install and upgrade software, manage and tune the system operating parameters, and look at and change print job priorities. There are also troubleshooting and diagnostic routines available.

See also **`sysadmsh`.**

SMP

See **symmetrical multiprocessing**

SMTP

Abbreviation for simple mail transport protocol. The TCP/IP protocol for exchanging e-mail. Many third-party vendors sell host software for Unix capable of exchanging SMTP e-mail with proprietary e-mail systems such as IBM's PROFS.

SMTP provides a direct end-to-end mail delivery, which is rather unusual; most mail systems use store-and-forward protocols.

See also **MIME, TCP/IP.**

snail mail

A rude reference to the relatively slow speed of the conventional postal system when compared with the speed of online e-mail systems.

sneakernet

An informal method of file sharing in which a user copies a file onto a floppy disk and then carries the disk to the office of a co-worker.

sniffer

A small program loaded onto a system by an intruder, designed to monitor specific traffic on the network. The sniffer program watches for the first part of any remote login session (`telnet`, `ftp`, or `rlogin`, for example) that includes the login ID, password, and host name of a person logging in to another machine. Once this information is in the hands of the intruder, they can log in to that system at will. One weakly secured network can therefore expose not only other local systems but also any remote systems to which the local users connect.

See also **cracker, firewall, Trojan Horse, SATAN.**

socket

An interprocess communications mechanism used in networking. Sockets allow processes that are not running at the same time or on the same system and that are not children of the same parent to exchange information; pairs of cooperating sockets manage communications between the processes on your computer and those on the remote system in a networked environment.

You can read data from, or write data to, a socket just as you can to a file. Socket pairs are bidirectional; either process can send data to the other. Sockets allow the utilities `telnet`, `rlogin` (remote login), and `rcp` (remote copy) to work.

Sockets were first implemented in the BSD-based versions of Unix and are identified by the letter `s` in the file type character of a long format `ls` file listing.

See also **FIFO file, pipe.**

soelim

A Unix text processing command that reads an `nroff/troff` input file and strips out all of the `.so` commands, replacing them with the contents of the specified file. The `.so` (switch out) command reads the contents of another file into the current input file.

soft link

To reference one file to another by using a pathname rather than by a specific i-node address. By using an absolute pathname, soft links can cross filesystems.

See also **hard link, link, symbolic link.**

Solaris

A version of Unix from SunSoft that runs on Intel-based PCs and Sun workstations; SunSoft is a subsidiary of Sun Microsystems.

Solaris is based on Unix System V Release 4, and includes networking support, the OpenWindows graphical user interface, and DeskSet, an integrated desktop that includes almost 20 productivity tools.

See also **SunOS.**

sort

To arrange a set of individual elements into some kind of logical sequence, usually into alphabetical, numerical, or ASCII order, although files can be sorted by some other criteria such as time and or date. Additionally, a sort may be ascending or descending.

sort

A command that sorts the contents of text files.

▶ Syntax

Here's the syntax to use:

sort [*options*][*files*]

The `sort` command sorts lines within a text file and then writes the output to the standard output or to a specified file. Output lines are sorted character by character, left to right; if you specify more than one file as input, the files are sorted and collated.

▶ Options and Arguments

If you don't specify an option, `sort` orders the file in the machine collating sequence, which is usually ASCII. The options for use with `sort` are detailed in Table S.8.

`sort` is often used in conjunction with `uniq` to remove duplicate or partially duplicate lines from a text file.

▶ Examples

To sort the file `names` and write the output to the sorted file `names.sort`, use:

```
sort -o names.sort names
```

You can sort the contents of several files, combining the output into a single file:

```
sort section[a-d]
➥ -o section.sorted
```

This command sorts four files, `sectiona` through `sectiond` and stores the output in the file called `section.sorted`.

See also **`comm`, `join`, `uniq`.**

source

A built-in C shell command used to read and execute commands from a C shell script file. If you use:

```
source ~/.cshrc
```

you can re-execute the contents of the `.cshrc` startup file without logging out and immediately logging back in again.

In the Bourne and Korn shells, the dot, or period, command (`.`) performs the same function.

Table S.8: Options to Use with `sort`	
OPTION	DESCRIPTION
`-b`	Ignores leading blanks (tabs or spaces), making `sort` treat blanks as field delimiters with no value.
`-c`	Checks to see if the file is already sorted and, if it is, performs no action.
`-d`	Sorts in dictionary order, ignoring all punctuation and control characters.
`-f`	Considers all lowercase letters to be in uppercase; used when sorting files that contain both uppercase and lowercase text.
`-i`	Ignores nonprinting characters (those outside the range of decimal 32 to 126) when performing a non-numeric sort.
`-m`	Assumes multiple input files are already in sorted order and merges them without checking.
`-M`	Selects the first three nonblank characters, shifts them to uppercase, and sorts them into month order from `JAN` to `DEC`; invalid entries are placed at the beginning of the list.
`-n`	Performs a numeric sort, observing minus signs and decimal points; blanks are ignored.
`-o`*`filename`*	Stores the output from `sort` in the specified file rather than sending it to the standard output.
`-r`	Reverses the direction of the sort.
`-t`*`c`*	Specifies *`c`* as the separator character in the input file.
`-u`	Identical lines from the input file are output only once.
`-y`*`memory`*	Reduces the amount of memory available to `sort`; without this option, `sort` uses all available space. Specify *`memory`* in kilobytes; use 0 to make `sort` run in the smallest possible space.
`-z`*`rec`*	Specifies *`rec`* as the maximum line length when merging files and prevents `sort` from abnormally terminating if it reads an extremely long line; do not use this option if you are sorting files.

source code

The original, human-readable version of a program, written in a particular programming language, before the program is compiled or interpreted into machine-readable form.

■ *See also* **compiler, interpreter.**

source file

- A file that contains the uncompiled source code to a program or part of a program.
- The original file from which data is obtained to perform a specific function.

source license

A software license that includes the right to a copy of the source code. At one time, all Unix licenses were source licenses, but as the operating system grew more commercial, source licenses became very expensive and were often limited to research institutions or universities. Nowadays, very few, if any, Unix source licenses are available.

■ *See also* **binary license, site license.**

space character

A printable character represented by ASCII 32 (decimal), considered to be a blank, or white, space.

spamming

To flood someone's mailbox with unwanted e-mail.

spawn

■ *See* **fork.**

SPEC benchmarks

Acronym for Systems Performance Evaluation Cooperative benchmarks. A series of ten standardized tests designed to measure workstation performance. Six of the tests evaluate floating point performance, while four tests concentrate on integer performance. Results are reported as SPECmarks, a geometric mean of all ten scores.

■ *See also* **Dhrystones, Whetstones.**

special character

A character that has a special meaning for the operating system. The special characters most commonly used in the Unix shell are the asterisk (`*`) and the question mark (`?`).

■ *See also* **metacharacter, wildcard.**

special file

A file that is neither a regular file nor a directory and is used as an interface to a device. Also known as a *device file* and usually located in the `/dev` directory.

There are two types of special files: character special files and block special files. You will find at least one special file for every hardware device attached to your system, including terminals, hard disk partitions, and tape drives.

■ *See also* **FIFO file, major device number, minor device number.**

spell

A command that compares the contents of a file to the system dictionary and reports all the misspelled words.

▶ Syntax

Here's the syntax to use with `spell`:

```
spell [options][files]
```

The output from `spell` is a list of words that cannot be found in the dictionary. The list is arranged in alphabetical order and is sent to the standard output. If you specify more than one file, `spell` generates one list of words for all the files.

▶ Options and Arguments

Table S.9 details the options you can use with `spell`.

The `spell` command is by no means a foolproof way of finding errors; in English, so much depends on context. `spell` does not identify correctly spelled but misused words.

▶ Examples

To check the file `chapter.one` for errors and write any words not in the system dictionary to a file called `corrections`, use:

```
spell chapter.one
➥ > corrections
```

■ *See also* **`sort`, `uniq`.**

Table S.9: Options to Use with spell

OPTION	DESCRIPTION
-b	Accepts British spelling of words such as *colour*, *honour*, *centre*, and *travelled*.
-l	Follows all nroff and troff include files (all files referenced in .so and .nx requests).
-v	Displays all words not literally in the system dictionary; words that can be derived from the dictionary are displayed, showing a possible derivation.
-x	Displays every possible stem for each word on the standard error.
+*wordlist*	Specifies *wordlist* as an additional dictionary file; *wordlist* should be a sorted file containing one word per line. This option is very useful for adding proper names and technical terms.

splat

Jargon for the asterisk character (*) that you can yell across a crowded, noisy room without fear of being misunderstood.

■ *See also* **bang.**

spline

A BSD and SCO command that interpolates a smooth curve between data points.

▶ Syntax

The syntax for the spline command is:

```
spline [options]
```

The spline command takes pairs of numbers from the standard input as abscissa and ordinates of a function and plots them on the standard output; there is a limit of 1,000 input points.

▶ Options and Arguments

The options available for use with this command are listed in Table S.10.

■ *See also* **graph, plot.**

split

A command that divides a text file into a number of smaller pieces. The syntax is:

```
split
➥ [option][infile][outfile]
```

infile is the name of the input file, and this file remains untouched during the processing. It is divided into files called *outfile*aa, *outfile*ab, and so on. If you don't specify an *infile*, the standard input is used instead.

The single option, -*n*, lets you specify the number of lines each *outfile* should contain; the default is 1000 lines.

■ *See also* **cat, csplit, cut, sed.**

spoof

■ *See* **sniffer.**

spool

Acronym formed from simultaneous peripheral operation online. Software designed to manage one or more peripheral devices, particularly printers, by temporarily storing the output on disk until the printer is available.

■ *See also* **queue, /spool.**

Table S.10: Options Available with spline	
OPTION	DESCRIPTION
-a*n*	Automatically provides the abscissa with spacing of *n* or 1 if *n* is not a number.
-k*n*	Specifies the constant *n* used in the boundary value calculation.
-n*n*	Specifies the spacing *n* between x-axis values; the default is 100.
-p	Makes the output periodic.
-x*lu*	Sets the *l* lower and *u* upper x-axis limits.

/spool

A directory that contains any print jobs waiting to be printed by the spooler.

spooler

The software that manages print jobs sent to a shared or network printer when that printer is busy. Each print job is stored on disk in a separate file and is printed in turn when the printer becomes available. Sometimes called a *print spooler.*

■ *See also* **queue, spool, /spool.**

SPX

Abbreviation for Sequenced Packet Exchange. A set of Novell NetWare protocols implemented on top of IPX to form a transport layer.

SPX provides additional capabilities over IPX. For example, it guarantees packet delivery by having the destination device verify that the data was received correctly; if no response is received within a specific time, SPX retransmits the packet. If several retransmissions fail to return an acknowledgment, SPX assumes that the connection has failed and informs the operator. All packets in the transmission are sent in sequence, and they all take the same path to their destination.

■ *See also* **IPX.**

square brackets

The characters [ ]. Special characters that enclose character sets in regular expressions. In the C shell, square brackets enclose array indices.

■ *See also* **braces, brackets.**

srchtxt

A command used to search message files for a regular expression.

■ *See also* **exstr, gettxt, mkmsgs.**

stack

A reserved area of memory used to keep track of a program's internal operations, including functions' return addresses, passed parameters, and so on. A stack is usually maintained as a "last in, first out" (LIFO) data structure, so that the last item added to the structure is the first item used.

standard directories

The basic layout of the Unix filesystem is fairly constant with some variations occurring between systems from different vendors. Table S.11 lists the main directories you will encounter in SVR4; your own system will undoubtedly add many more directories.

standard error

A file to which a program can send output, usually of error messages. Standard error is associated with file descriptor 2. Unless you use redirection, standard error output goes to the terminal. Also called stderr.

■ *See also* **Bourne shell, C shell, Korn shell.**

Table S.11: Unix Standard Directories

DIRECTORY	DESCRIPTION
/	The root directory, which is always present, and the ancestor of all files in the filesystem.
`/dev`	Contains device files, including terminals, printers, and hard disks.
`/etc`	Contains system administration and configuration files, the most important of which is `/etc/passwd`.
`/home`	The directory containing the home directories of all users on the system.
`/opt`	The root directory for filesystems used by add-on applications.
`/sbin`	Contains programs used when booting the system and in system recovery.
`/spool`	Contains the directories for spooling files.
`/spool/lp`	Contains spooling files for the printer.
`/spool/uucp`	Contains files queued for UUCP.
`/spool/uucppublic`	Contains files placed here by UUCP.
`/stand`	Contains the standard programs and configuration files used when booting the system.
`/tmp`	Contains temporary files created by Unix.
`/usr`	Contains user-accessible programs.
`/usr/bin`	Contains executable programs and utilities.
`/usr/ucb`	Contains the BSD compatability package.
`/usr/sbin`	Contains executable programs for system administration.
`/usr/games`	Contains Unix games.
`/usr/lib`	Contains libraries for programs and for programming languages.
`/var`	Contains files whose contents vary as the system runs.
`/var/admin`	Contains system logging and accounting files.
`/var/mail`	Contains user mail files.
`/var/news`	Contains messages for users.
`/var/opt`	The root of a subtree of files for add-on applications.
`/var/tmp`	Contains temporary files.
`/var/uucp`	Contains UUCP files.

standard input

A file from which a program can receive input. Standard input is associated with file descriptor 0. Unless you use redirection, standard input comes from the keyboard.

Also called *standard in* or `stdin`.

See also **Bourne shell, C shell, Korn shell.**

standard output

A file to which a program can send output. Standard output is associated with file descriptor 1. Unless you use redirection, standard output goes to the terminal. Also called *standard out* or `stdout`.

See also **Bourne shell, C shell, Korn shell.**

start bit

In asynchronous communications, a start bit is transmitted to indicate the beginning of a new data word.

See also **data bits, parity, stop bit.**

startup file

A file that the login shell executes when you first log in to the system. Both the Bourne shell and Korn shell run a file called `.profile`; the C shell runs a file called `.login`; and `bash` runs `.bash_profile`. The C shell also runs a file called `.cshrc` when you invoke a new C shell; the Korn shell runs a file called `.kshrc`; and `bash` runs a file called `.bashrc`.

Startup files are used to customize shell functions and to store aliases.

See also **dot files.**

state

The level of access granted to a user. The two fundamental Unix states are the single-user state, which limits access to the system administrator, and the more usual multiuser state, which gives access to many users.

Both of these states can be divided into further states by the system administrator; the most important states are shown in Table S.12.

Table S.12: Unix System States

SYSTEM STATE	DESCRIPTION
state 0	Shutdown state
state 1	Administrative state
state 2	Multiuser state
state 3	Remote file sharing state
state 4	User-defined state
state 5	Firmware state
state 6	Stop and reboot state

status

In the C shell, an environment variable used to indicate the status of the last command you executed; 0 represents a successful completion, while 1 represents failure.

status line

The last line on the terminal; used by `vi` and other editors to display information about the current editing session as well as error messages.

stderr

See **standard error.**

stdin

See **standard input.**

stdout

See **standard output.**

S

sticky bit

An access permission bit associated with an executable file that allows the program to stay in memory when it has finished executing. This makes the program load faster for the next user. Modern virtual memory designs have made the sticky bit obsolete, but you still hear it mentioned occasionally.

`stop`

A built-in Bourne shell command used to suspend a background job specified by its job identifier. The syntax is:

`stop` *`jobID`*

stop bit

In asynchronous communications, stop bits are transmitted to indicate the end of the current data word. Depending on the convention in use, either one or two stop bits are used.

■ *See also* **parity, start bit.**

store-and-forward

A method that temporarily stores messages at intermediate sites before forwarding them to their final destination. This technique allows messages to be sent over networks that are not available at all times and lets you take advantage of off-peak rates when traffic and tariffs might both be lower.

stream

A sequence of similar items. The Unix filter commands often allow you to treat their input as a stream, which means that they can process input of unlimited length.

stream editor

A text editor that operates on a continuous input stream. Unlike more conventional text editors, a stream editor can process the input only once; it cannot back up or jump forward. `sed` is the Unix stream editor.

streaming tape

A high-speed tape system designed to optimize throughput; the tape is never stopped during operation. To use a streaming tape, the computer and tape software must be fast enough to keep up with the tape drive at all times.

■ *See also* **QIC, tape cartridge.**

string

A sequence of zero or more letters, numbers, or special characters.

`strings`

A command that extracts printable ASCII strings from a binary file.

▶ Syntax

The syntax to use is:

`strings [`*`options`*`]` *`files`*

▶ Options and Arguments

The `strings` command defines a printable string as being four or more characters in length, terminated by a newline or a null. The options you can use with `strings` are detailed in Table S.13.

■ *See also* **`hexdump`, `od`.**

string search

A command available in most text editors that allows you to search for a specific set of characters within the text file or document.

■ *See also* **search and replace.**

Table S.13: Options for Use with `strings`

OPTION	DESCRIPTION
`-a`	Searches the whole file; you can also specify this option as `-`.
`-nn`	Specifies the minimum length of a string as *n* characters; the default is 4.
`-o`	Displays the string's offset position before the string.

strip

A command that removes unnecessary information from executable files, reducing their size to save disk space. `strip` deletes information used by debuggers, assemblers, and some loaders. This is a one-way process, so make sure that you no longer need the information before you run `strip`.

■ *See also* **`ld`**.

struct

A BSD software development command used to translate a specified Fortran program into Ratfor.

stty

A command used by the superuser to display or set terminal parameters.

▶ Syntax

Here's the syntax:

```
stty [options][modes]
```

▶ Options and Arguments

Using `stty` you can control many terminal settings, including baud rate and parity, character size, and the type of handshaking. The *`modes`* are chosen from an extremely long list of terminal attributes; see your system documentation for more details. The options you can use with `stty` are listed in Table S.14.

Table S.14: Options to Use with `stty`

OPTION	DESCRIPTION
`-a`	Lists all settings.
`-g`	Lists the current settings in a way that can be used as input to `stty`.

▶ Notes

Both the physical settings on the terminal and the system setup must match; otherwise, communications will stop.

The `stty` command changes the way in which the system's `tty` driver works.

■ *See also* **sane flag, `tput`, `tset`, `tty`**.

style

A BSD command that reports on the writing style used in a document.

▶ Syntax

The syntax for `style` is as follows:

```
style [options]filename...
```

▶ Options and Arguments

The options you can use with `style` are listed in Table S.15. `style` displays a readability index and reports on sentence length and construction, word length, word usage, verb type, and expletives.

■ *See also* **`diction`**.

su

A command that temporarily substitutes another user ID for your own.

▶ Syntax

The syntax to use with `su` is as follows:

```
su username arguments
```

The `su` command is often used by the system administrator when changing to the superuser account.

Table S.15: Options to Use with `style`

OPTION	DESCRIPTION
`-a`	Calculates sentence length and readability index.
`-e`	Displays all sentences starting with an expletive.
`-l`*n*	Displays all sentences longer than *n* words.
`-ml`	Skips lists contained in the document.
`-mm`	Skips macros contained in the document.
`-p`	Displays all sentences containing a passive verb.
`-P`	Labels text in the document according to word type.
`-r`*n*	Displays all sentences with a readability index of more than *n*.

▶ **Options and Arguments**

The `su` command temporarily switches your user ID to that specified by *`username`*. `su` prompts you to enter a password, just as if you were logging in, and the contents of your shell configuration file are executed. Any *`arguments`* specified on the command line are passed to the shell.

On many systems, specifying a dash tells `su` to execute a full login to the user's environment. The command:

```
su -name
```

runs the `.login` file in the C shell or the `.profile` file in the Bourne and Korn shells for the specified *`name`*. If you don't use the – option, your current environment is transferred to the new login.

■ *See also* **env, login, passwd.**

subdirectory

A directory that is located within another directory. In Unix, all directories except the root directory are subdirectories. In day-to-day conversation subdirectory is often abbreviated to directory.

subscribe

To identify a USENET newsgroup you want to access with your newsreader, or to join a mailing list. This is not a subscription in the normal sense of a magazine subscription; no money ever changes hands.

subshell

A shell, forked as a duplicate of the parent shell, that executes a specified command or list of commands within that shell. Also, when you surround commands with parentheses, they are run in a subshell.

■ *See also* **parentheses.**

sum

A command that calculates and prints a checksum for a file and displays the number of 512-byte blocks the file occupies. The syntax is:

```
sum [option]filename
```

The single option, `-r`, calculates an alternative checksum used by BSD systems.

■ *See also* **wc.**

Sun Microsystems

A manufacturer of high-powered workstations that run SunOS or Solaris, and one of the major technical forces in the Unix world. SunSoft is the software subsidiary of Sun Microsystems.

■ *See also* **Java, NFS.**

SunOS

A Unix operating system from SunSoft, the software subsidiary of Sun Microsystems. SunOS 4.1 (also known as *Solaris 1*) is based on BSD Unix, while SunOS 5 (also known as *Solaris 2*) is based on SVR4. Interactive Unix, also from SunSoft, is based on the System V Release 3.2 kernel.

■ *See also* **Java, NFS.**

superblock

A block that contains the control information for a filesystem, including the filesystem size, number of i-nodes in the filesystem, and the location of free blocks. Each time a filesystem is mounted, the kernel sets aside space to hold the superblock. Sometimes written as *super block.*

supercomputer

The most powerful class of computer. The term was first applied to the Cray-1 series. Supercomputers can cost over $50 million each. The Cray T3E has a top speed of more than one trillion operations per second, or one teraflop. They are used by large government agencies and major companies for tasks such as weather forecasting and complex three-dimensional modeling.

■ *See also* **parallel processing.**

superpipelining

A preprocessing technique used in some microprocessors in which two or more execution stages (such as fetch, decode, execute, or write back) are divided into two or more pipelined stages giving considerably higher performance.

■ *See also* **RISC.**

superscalar

A microprocessor architecture that contains more than one execution unit, or pipeline, allowing the processor to execute more than one instruction per clock cycle.

For example, the Pentium processor is superscalar and has two side-by-side pipelines for integer instructions. The processor determines whether an instruction can be executed in parallel with the next instruction in line. If it doesn't detect any dependencies, then the two instructions are executed.

superserver

A Unix-based multiprocessor computer acting as a file server for a network of workstations or PCs. A 20-processor Symmetry 5000 cluster from Sequent Computer Systems, running Dynix/ptx, a proprietary version of SVR4 with symmetrical multiprocessing extensions, can cost up to $1.4 million, while a Nile 150 From Pyramid Technology Corporation, running CD/OSx, a proprietary version of SVR4 with symmetrical multiprocessing extensions, can cost up to $750,000. IBM sells systems based on the RS/6000 running AIX for $125,900.

superuser

A specially privileged user who has access to anything that a normal user has access to and more. The system administrator must become the superuser to create new accounts, change passwords, and perform other administrative tasks that ordinary users are not allowed to carry out for security reasons. The superuser's login name is usually root with a user ID of 0.

■ *See also* **avatar.**

surfing

To browse your way through various Internet resources, exploring tangents whenever you feel like it; sometimes called *net surfing.*

suspend

To temporarily stop a process that can then be either restarted later (in the foreground or in the background) or killed.

SVID

Abbreviation for System V Interface Definition. A set of documents released by AT&T that defined the Unix System V interfaces and operating system calls. The last version of SVID was published in 1989 and revised in 1990.

■ *See also* **POSIX.**

swap

To temporarily move a process from memory to disk, so that another process can use that memory space. When the space becomes available, the process is swapped back into memory again. This allows more processes to be loaded than there is physical memory space to run them simultaneously.

swap space

On a hard disk, an area used to store parts of running programs that have been temporarily swapped out of memory to make room for other running processes. Also called *swap area* or *swap file.*

■ *See also* **swap.**

swapping

The temporary storage of an active process on hard disk. When more processes are running than will simultaneously fit into main memory, certain processes may temporarily be moved into a special area on the hard disk known as the *swap area.* When space in memory becomes available, they are swapped back into memory again, so they can continue execution. On a heavily loaded system, swapping can seriously degrade performance and slow down response time.

swconfig

An SCO command used to display software configuration information.

▶ Syntax

The syntax for this command is:

swconfig [*options*]

▶ Options and Arguments

`swconfig` lists information located in `/usr/lib/custom/history`. You can use the options listed in Table S.16 with this command.

■ *See also* **hwconfig.**

Table S.16: Options to Use with swconfig

OPTION	DESCRIPTION
-a	Lists all information sorted in reverse chronological order.
-p	Lists software package information.

switch

A C shell programming construct used to execute commands based on the value of a variable. `switch` is often used when a shell script must manage more than the three choices handled by an `if-then-else` statement. If the value of the variable matches the first pattern, the first set of commands are executed; if it matches the second pattern, then the second set of commands are executed, and so on. If the variable does not match any of the patterns, then the commands under the `default` case are executed. A `breaksw` statement exits from the `switch` after the commands are executed.

■ *See also* **breaksw, case, default, endsw, esac.**

symbolic debugger

A software development program used to find bugs in another program. A symbolic debugger lets the programmer trace program execution, set breakpoints, and examine and change variables and data values. The Unix symbolic debugger is called `sdb`.

symbolic disassembler

A software development program used to deconstruct an executable program into a format that looks like an assembly-language listing. Disassemblers are used to re-create lost source code, or when reverse engineering a program.

symbolic links

A link within the Unix filesystem that is actually the pathname of another file; sometimes abbreviated as symlink. A symbolic link is sometimes called a *soft link* to distinguish it from a hard link and can be used in the same ways that a hard link can. Symbolic links have one major advantage in that they can span filesystems and computer systems (if you are using NFS or RFS) and can connect to a directory or to a file.

When a program opens a symbolic link for reading or writing, the kernel checks the symbolic link for the name of the referenced file and actually opens the referenced file. The short `ls` file listing displays the referenced file, while the long format (`ls -l`) displays the contents of the symbolic link. All BSD and System V Release 4 systems support symbolic links.

symmetrical multiprocessing

A multiprocessing design that assigns a task to a processor in response to system load as the application starts running. This design makes for a much more flexible system than does asymmetrical multiprocessing, in which the programmer matches a specific task to a certain processor while writing the program.

In symmetrical multiprocessing, the overall workload is shared by all the processors in the system; system performance increases as more processors are added into the system. The drawback is that symmetrical multiprocessing operating systems are much harder to design than asymmetrical multiprocessing operating systems.

sync

A command that is either run automatically or is initiated by the system administrator when preparing to shutdown the system. The `sync` command ends all input/output operations, updates changes made in memory, and writes all these changes out to disk, flushing the disk cache buffers so that the information on the hard disk is absolutely up-to-date.

syntax

The formal rules of grammar as they apply to a specific programming language or operating system command; in particular, the exact sequence and spelling of command elements required for the command to be correctly interpreted.

syntax error

An error in the use of a programming language or operating system command syntax—for example, misspelling a keyword or omitting a required space.

/sys

A BSD root directory that is reserved for utilities used for working with the kernel.

sysadmsh

A menu-driven system administration package from SCO, which can be started from the command line or from the Open Desktop. Using `sysadmsh` you can add and remove users; perform backups; manage the print system, files, and directories; prepare disks and tapes; configure system resources; and prepare reports on system status.

■ *See also* **SCOadmin.**

system administration

Those day-to-day administration and management tasks performed by the system administrator, including:

- Starting up and shutting down the system.
- Setting the system date and time.
- Assigning and changing passwords.
- Adding and removing users and groups.
- Monitoring system security.
- Installing, updating, and removing software packages and installing operating system upgrades.
- Backing up the system, storing archives off-location, and restoring files when necessary.
- Installing and configuring hardware such as printers, terminals, and modems.
- Mounting and unmounting filesystems as required.
- Monitoring system performance and making tuning adjustments as needed.
- Running system diagnostics as needed to track down hardware problems.

See also **superuser.**

system administration commands

Those commands that have to do with administration and management of the operating system.

On most commercial Unix systems, the system-administration program is menu driven and relatively easy to use without detailed background knowledge. On SVR4 systems (including UnixWare), you find `sysadm`, on Solaris `admintool`, on AIX `SMIT`, on SCO systems `sysadmsh` or, more recently, `SCOadmin`, and on HP-UX `SAM`.

system administrator

The person charged with the responsibility of managing the system; often abbreviated to SA. On a very large installation, the system administrator may in fact be several people or even a small department; if you are running Linux on your PC at home, then you have to be your own system administrator.

See also **SAGE, superuser.**

system call

The lowest level of access to the Unix operating system, a system call tells the kernel to carry out a certain operation. Programmers access system calls directly by writing programs or indirectly by using a library routine. Most versions of Unix have approximately 100 system calls used to control processes, to manage the filesystem, and to control input/output to peripheral devices.

System V

The latest version of Unix, pronounced "system five." The most recent release is known as System V Release 4.2, often abbreviated as SVR4 or SVR4.2.

See also **SVID, System III, Unix history.**

system state

See **state.**

System III

The release of Unix from AT&T prior to System V. System III was the first Unix to be ported to the Intel series of microprocessors and formed the basis for SCO's release of XENIX. System IV Unix was never released outside AT&T to avoid any confusion with the 4.*x*BSD series of products.

See also **Unix history.**

T

T

■ *See* **tera-**.

tabs

A command used to set tab stops on your terminal. The default Unix tabs are set eight spaces apart across the screen, but you can use `tabs` to set them wherever you like. Input is a comma-separated list of numbers or a filename containing this information. Your terminal must support host-set tab stops for this command to work correctly.

■ *See also* **newform**.

tail

A command that displays the last ten lines of a text file.

▶ Syntax

The syntax to use with `tail` is as follows:

```
tail [options][filename]
```

▶ Options and Arguments

The `tail` command used without options displays the last ten lines of *filename*; if no *filename* is specified, `tail` reads from the standard input.

If a plus sign precedes an option, `tail` displays characters, lines, or blocks counting from the beginning of the file; if a hyphen precedes the option, `tail` counts from the end of the file. The options you can use with `tail` are detailed in Table T.1.

▶ Examples

To display the last three lines of the file `phonelist`, use:

```
tail -3l phonelist
```

■ *See also* **head, less, more, pg**.

Table T.1: Options to Use with `tail`

OPTION	DESCRIPTION
`+n`	Displays the number of characters, lines, or blocks specified by *n*, counting from the beginning of the input.
`-n`	Displays the number of characters, lines, or blocks specified by *n*, counting from the end of the input.
`-b`	Specifies blocks when used after `+n` or `-n`.
`-c`	Specifies characters when used after `+n` or `-n`.
`-f`	Enters an endless loop after displaying the last part of the file and waits for additional input. This can be useful for monitoring a background process which is sending its output to the file; use the `kill` command to terminate `tail`.
`-l`	Specifies lines when used after `+n` or `-n`.
`-r`	Reverses the specified order.

talk

A command that opens a two-way, terminal-to-terminal communications path. Here is the syntax you need to use with `talk`:

```
talk [username][tty]
```

where *`username`* is the name of the other person you want to talk to. If the person uses the same computer that you do, you can use his or her login name; otherwise, you have to add the name of his or her system in the form *`user@hostname`*. Once the connection is established, you send messages back and forth just by typing them in. If the user you want to contact is logged in more than once, use the *`tty`* argument to specify which terminal you want to talk to. Type Ctrl-L to redraw your screen, and type Ctrl-D when you are ready to exit. The `talk` command has no options.

See also **`mail`, `mailx`, `mesg`, `who`, `write`.**

tape cartridge

A self-contained tape storage module, containing tape much like that in a video cassette. Tape cartridges are primarily used as backup systems.

See also **QIC, streaming tape.**

tape drive

A peripheral that reads and writes to and from magnetic tape. The tape drive may use an open reel or one of the smaller, enclosed tape cartridges. Because tape-management software has to search from the beginning of the tape every time you ask it to find a file, tape is too slow to use as a primary storage system, but tapes are often used to back up hard disks.

See also **QIC, streaming tape.**

tar

A command that can create, list, add to, and retrieve files from an archive file, which is usually stored on tape.

▶ Syntax

The syntax for `tar` is:

```
tar option[modifiers]
➥[file-list]
```

The *`options`* and *`modifiers`* for `tar` vary considerably from Unix system to system, even among SVR4- or BSD-style systems. In the discussion that follows, only the most common arguments are covered;

see the `tar man` pages for specific information on your own system.

▶ Options and Arguments

You tell `tar` what you want it to do by specifying one *`option`* from Table T.2 and then adding one or more *`modifiers`* from Table T.3 to fine-tune the *`option`*. The modifiers do not require a leading hyphen.

Following these arguments is the *`file-list`* that lists the filenames of the files you want to read in or write out. If you use a directory name in *`file-list`*, `tar` references all files and subdirectories within that directory.

▶ Examples

To store all the files in your home directory and all files and subdirectories in that directory in an archive on the default tape drive, use:

```
tar -cv /home/pd
a /home/pd/ch.one 51 blocks
a /home/pd/ch.two 41 blocks
a /home/pd/ch.three 47 blocks
a /home/pd/ch.four 67 blocks
```

The `v` modifier makes `tar` list all the files as it writes them to tape, erasing anything that was previously on the tape.

▶ Notes

You can use ambiguous file references or wildcards when you write files but not when you read them; this is because `tar` does not perform filename expansion. Filename expansion is done by the shell, and the results are passed to `tar`. This can be a problem when you have deleted a file by accident and want to extract the file from an archive. Because the file doesn't exist as part of the filesystem, the shell cannot complete the filename expansion to match these nonexistent files.

Files are extracted from an archive in the same way that they were originally created. If you write a file using a relative pathname, it will appear with that same relative pathname, starting from the current directory, when you read it back. If you use an absolute pathname, `tar` uses the same absolute pathname when it reads the file back.

■ *See also* **cpio**, **ls**.

tar archive

A tape or file in `tar` format. A `tar` archive has the filename extension `.tar`.

■ *See also* **tar**.

Table T.2: Options to Use with tar

OPTION	DESCRIPTION
`c`	Creates a new archive file, overwriting any previous archive on the tape or disk.
`r`	Appends the *`file-list`* to an existing archive; existing files are unchanged.
`t`	Lists the contents of the archive.
`u`	Performs an update, appending files to the archive if they are not already present or if they have been modified since they were originally written to the archive. This option can run very slowly due to all the checking it must do, so use it with care.
`x`	Extracts *`file-list`* from an archive; if *`file-list`* is not specified, this option extracts all the files from the archive.

Table T.3: Modifiers to Use with tar

MODIFIER	DESCRIPTION
b*n*	Specifies a blocking factor of *n*; the default is 1, and the maximum is 20.
f *device*	Uses the specified archive *device*. If *device* is specified as -, tar uses the standard input, and this lets you use tar in a pipeline.
l	Displays error messages if links to archived files cannot be resolved.
m	Updates file modification times to the time of extraction from the archive.
o	Disregards ownership information when extracting a file from an archive.
v	Displays the name of each file as it is archived or extracted.
w	Waits for user confirmation before taking any action.
z	Compresses and expands the archive using gzip and gunzip.
Z	Compresses and expands the archive using compress and uncompress.

task

Any individual element of a running program and the resources that it uses. A task may be an operating system process or may be part of an application.

task switching

To switch from one running program to another so that the computer can better utilize system resources.

See also **symmetrical multiprocessing.**

TB

See **terabyte.**

tbl

A preprocessor for the nroff/troff text-processing system capable of formatting tables.

▶ Syntax

The syntax to use with tbl is:

```
tbl [options][filename]
```

tbl reads a troff file that contains pairs of special codes. The beginning of a table is always marked by the .TS macro, and the end of a table by the .TE macro, while the internal structure of the table is defined by other macro commands that can:

- Left or right justify or center data in a column
- Align numbers on their decimal points
- Add horizontal or vertical lines to a table
- Allow entries to span several rows
- Transform a block of text into table entries

The output from tbl is a troff input file that includes troff instructions for creating the table on the printed page.

▶ Options and Arguments

The options available with tbl are listed in Table T.4.

▶ Examples

When you use the Unix text-processing commands in a pipeline, make sure you specify that tbl precedes eqn; this makes processing more efficient:

```
tbl textfile | troff | lp
```

Table T.4: Options to Use with `tbl`

OPTION	DESCRIPTION
-me	Prepends the me macro package to the beginning of the specified *filename*.
-mm	Prepends the mm macro package to the beginning of the specified *filename*.
-ms	Prepends the ms macro package to the beginning of the specified *filename*.
-TX	Creates output using only full linefeeds and not partial linefeeds.

This sequence formats `textfile` first with `tbl` and then with `troff`, sending the formatted output to the printer.

See also **eqn, groff, LATEX, me macros, mm macros, ms macros, nroff, pic, TEX.**

/tcb

A directory found on certain SCO systems that contains program files for the Trusted Computing Base (TCB), which give the system a C-2 level security.

Tcl

Acronym for Tool Command Language, pronounced "tickle." Developed by John Ousterhout while at the University of California at Berkeley, Tcl is a general purpose, extensible scripting language supplied as a C library. Tcl is also available on DOS, Microsoft Windows, and the Macintosh. To find out more, check out the USENET newsgroup `comp.lang.tcl` or *Tcl and the Tk Toolkit*, by John Ousterhout; you can also anonymous `ftp` to `ftp.aud.alcatel.com`, where you will find the main Tcl archive.

See also **C, perl, Tk.**

tcopy

A BSD command used to make or verify magnetic tapes.

▶ Syntax

The syntax for this command is:

```
tcopy [options]
➥[source[destination]]
```

▶ Options and Arguments

If you specify only a *source*, `tcopy` displays record and file information for the contents of that tape. If you also specify *destination*, `tcopy` makes an exact copy of the *source*. The options you can use with `tcopy` are listed in Table T.5.

▶ Examples

To copy the tape on `/dev/rmt0` to the tape on `/dev/rmt1`, use:

```
tcopy /dev/rmt0 /dev/rmt1
```

▶ Notes

The `tcopy` command assumes that there are always two end-of-tape markers at the end of the tape.

See also **cp, cpio, tar.**

Table T.5: Options to Use with `tcopy`

OPTION	DESCRIPTION
-c	Copies *source* to *destination*, and then verifies that the two tapes are identical.
-s*n*	Sets the maximum block size to *n*.
-v	Verifies that the two tapes are identical.
-x	Sends all messages to the standard error.

T

TCP

Abbreviation for Transmission Control Protocol. The connection-oriented, transport-level protocol used in the TCP/IP suite of protocols.

■ *See also* **IP, UDP.**

TCP/IP

Abbreviation for Transmission Control Protocol/Internet Protocol. A set of communications protocols first developed by the Defense Advanced Research Projects Agency (DARPA) in the late 1970s. The set of TCP/IP protocols encompasses media access, packet transport, session communications, file transfer, e-mail, and terminal emulation:

- Address Resolution Protocol (ARP), which translates between Internet and Ethernet addresses
- Internet Control Message Protocol (ICMP), an error-message and control protocol
- Point-to-Point Protocol (PPP), which provides synchronous and asynchronous network connections
- Reverse Address Resolution Protocol (RARP), which translates between Ethernet and Internet addresses
- Serial Line Internet Protocol (SLIP), which implements IP over serial lines
- Simple Mail Transport Protocol (SMTP), used for mail over TCP/IP
- Simple Network Management Protocol (SNMP), which performs distributed network management functions
- User Datagram Protocol (UDP), which provides data transfer but without the reliability of TCP

TCP/IP is supported by a large number of hardware and software vendors and is available on many different computers, from PCs to mainframes. Many corporations, universities, and government agencies use TCP/IP, and it is also the basis of the Internet. To find out more, consult one of the excellent books that have been written on TCP/IP for readers of all technical levels.

■ *See also* **`ftp`, IP, TCP, `telnet`, `tn3270`.**

TCP/IP architecture

The TCP/IP set of protocols exist as four layers of software built on top of the fifth layer—the network hardware itself. The four layers are:

- Application layer, consisting of applications that use the network
- Host-to-host Transport layer, providing end-to-end data delivery services
- Internet layer, defining the datagram and managing the routing
- Network Access layer, consisting of routines to access the network hardware

Below these theoretical layers, you find the network hardware. When data is received from the network, it travels up through these layers, and when it is sent to the network, it travels down.

■ *See also* **ISO/OSI model.**

Tcsh

An upward-compatible replacement for the C shell; pronounced "tee-see-shell."

Development of Tcsh was started in the late 1970s by Ken Greer at Carnegie Mellon University and was continued in the 1980s by Paul Placeway at Ohio State. Since then, many people have contributed to Tcsh, and it is now maintained by a group at Cornell University. Tcsh is public-domain software.

Tcsh adds the following to the C shell:

- Easy retrieval of previously executed commands, which can then be edited and re-executed
- Interactive editing of the command line
- Interactive filename and command name completion
- Immediate documentation access as you type a command
- Addition of timestamps to the history list
- Ability to schedule a command for periodic execution

tee

A program, used within a pipe, that saves data in a specified file and at the same time sends the data to another program. Typically used when you want to review a program's standard output on the screen, while storing it in a file at the same time.

tee

A command that reproduces the standard input to its standard output and to one or more specified files.

▶ Syntax

The syntax for this command is:

```
tee [options]filename ...
```

`tee` lets you capture in a file the information going to the standard output, while still allowing that information to flow through standard output.

▶ Options and Arguments

The options available with `tee` are listed in Table T.6.

▶ Examples

To print a report file called `draft.final` and also save a formatted copy of this report in a file called `printed.report`, use:

```
pr draft.final | tee printed.
➥report | lp
```

■ *See also* **cat, echo, script.**

Table T.6: Options to Use with tee

OPTION	DESCRIPTION
-a	Appends the output to the specified *filename* instead of overwriting the existing contents.
-i	Ignores interrupts.

telecommuting

Working at home on a computer connected to the office by modems and telephone lines instead of commuting to the office. Telecommuting saves time, cuts down on automobile use and pollution, and decreases stress. Some local and state governments encourage telecommuting to keep the number of commuters as low as possible.

A recent survey showed that 33 million people in the United States did some form of telecommuting, compared with 10 million in 1985. Most studies indicate that home workers are happier and more productive. However, some jobs by their very nature do not lend themselves to telecommuting; welding and brain surgery are very difficult to do over the phone.

teleconferencing

The use of audio, video, or computer systems, linked by a communications channel, to allow geographically separated individuals to take part in a discussion or meeting all at the same time. Desktop video and chalkboard programs are becoming more and more common, and groupware applications such as Lotus Notes are helping people work together.

teletype

An obsolete electro-mechanical device with a keyboard that displayed its output on a small printer; abbreviated tty. The teletype is the ancestor of all Unix terminals, and that is the reason why you see so many references to tty connections and devices.

telnet

A command that lets you communicate with a remote computer using the Telnet protocol. The resulting session behaves as if you had a standard terminal connected directly to the remote host.

▶ Syntax

The usual `telnet` syntax is:

```
telnet [hostname[port]]
```

where *hostname* is a domain address or IP address, and *port* specifies the port number on that system you want to log into. Once the connection is established, anything you type on your keyboard is passed to the remote computer, and anything displayed by the remote computer appears on your screen.

▶ Using Command Mode

You can also start the program in command mode if you do not specify a *hostname* on the command line. When you type:

telnet

command mode starts, and you see the prompt:

telnet>

on your terminal, which indicates that the program is ready to accept one of the common telnet commands listed in Table T.7. If you started telnet with a *hostname*, you can also enter command mode by typing Ctrl-].

▶ Examples

To connect to NASA Spacelink to review information about the history, current status, and future plans for space flight, use:

telnet spacelink.msfc.nasa.gov

using newuser for both the login and the password. Many other sites are accessible using telnet; consult one of the many books on the Internet for more information.

▶ Notes

telnet does not have a built-in file-transfer mode. To copy a file from the remote system, you must use ftp instead.

Many non-Unix systems also support the Telnet protocol, allowing you to use telnet to connect to many different types of systems. Once you use telnet to log in, you can often access other services, such as specific applications or special databases.

■ *See also* **cu, ftp, rlogin, rsh, tn3270.**

Table T.7: Common telnet Commands

COMMAND	DESCRIPTION
?	Displays a list of telnet commands.
close	Closes the connection to the remote system but continues to run telnet.
display	Lists the current telnet operating parameters.
open *hostname*	Opens a connection to *hostname*.
quit	Closes the connection to the remote system and exits from telnet.
set *value*	Sets the telnet operating parameters.
status	Displays the current status of telnet, including the name of the remote system you are connected to.
unset	Unsets the telnet operating parameters.
z	Suspends the session with the remote computer and returns to the login shell on your local system; to resume your telnet session, use fg at a shell prompt.

temporary directories

Directories used to hold temporary files or data, including `/tmp` and `/lost+found`.

10/100

A term used to indicate that a device can support both Ethernet (at a data rate of 10 megabits per second) and Fast Ethernet or 100VG-AnyLAN (at a data rate of 100 megabits per second).

tera-

Abbreviated T. A prefix meaning 10^{12} in the metric system, 1,000,000,000,000; commonly referred to as 1 trillion in the American numbering system, and one million million in the British numbering system.

terabyte

Abbreviated TB. In computing, usually 2^{40}, or 1,099,511,627,776 bytes. A terabyte is equivalent to 1,000 gigabytes and usually refers to extremely large hard-disk capacities.

term

- A C shell variable that holds the name of the terminal type you are using.
- A client/server application that lets you open several login sessions over the same modem and dial-up connection. This utility is often included with Linux, and other freely available Unix systems.

■ *See also* **PPP, SLIP.**

termcap

Acronym formed from terminal capability. On BSD systems, the `termcap` file contains a list of terminals and their visual attributes. In SVR4, this function is found in `terminfo` instead.

■ *See also* **`terminfo`.**

terminal

A combination of keyboard and screen, used to send information to, and receive and display information from, the Unix operating system. In some Unix installations, the terminal will actually be a PC or a workstation connected to a network. You will also hear a terminal called several other names, including CRT (cathode ray tube), VDU (visual display unit), monitor, or tube.

■ *See also* **dumb terminal, smart terminal, terminal emulation, tty.**

terminal emulation

A program that makes a PC or workstation work like a terminal connected to a large computer system. Many terminal emulation programs can emulate DEC terminals, including the VT52, VT100, and VT200 series terminals.

■ *See also* **dumb terminal, smart terminal, terminal emulation, tty.**

terminfo

Acronym formed from terminal information. On SVR4 systems, the `terminfo` directory contains many subdirectories, each containing many files. Each of these files is named for, and contains information on, a specific terminal. In BSD systems, this function is found in `termcap` instead.

■ *See also* **`termcap`.**

test

A built-in Bourne shell and Korn shell command used to evaluate a condition, and, if the condition is true, return a zero exit status. Otherwise, it returns a non-zero exit status. You can use `test` from the command line, but it is most often used within a shell script.

▶ Syntax

You can use the `test` command in three different ways:

```
test condition
```

or you can use square brackets rather than the word `test`:

`[condition]`

and in some versions of the Korn shell, you can use an additional form with two sets of square brackets:

`[[condition]]`

In these examples, you must type the square brackets.

▶ Options and Arguments

The *`condition`* contains one or more criteria for `test` to evaluate; see Table T.8 for a list.

Because each element within *`condition`* is a separate argument, you must separate one from another with a space. You can use `-a` as a logical AND between two criteria—both must be true for `test` to return a zero exit status—and `-o` as a logical OR. You can negate any criterion by placing an exclamation mark (`!`) before it, and you can group criteria using parentheses.

▶ Examples

To test whether a file exists, use:

```
test -r /home/pmd/chapter.one
```

▶ Notes

You must quote any special characters you use within the *`condition`* so that the shell does not interpret them but passes them on to `test`.

See also **`if`**.

TEX

A typesetting language developed by Donald E. Knuth of Stanford University, capable of professional quality typeset text, particularly of mathematical equations and scientific, Japanese, Chinese, Cyrillic, and Arabic text.

The input file to TEX is an ordinary text file that contains control sequences to add the special formatting instructions. Each control sequence starts with a backslash and may appear anywhere, not just at the beginning of the line. Output from TEX does not go to the standard output but goes instead to a file. TEX is not easy for the casual user to master, and there are several TEX macro packages available containing macros designed to solve specific typesetting problems.

TEX is available for DOS, OS/2, Microsoft Windows NT, and the Macintosh, as well as for Unix systems. You can access a very large collection of public-domain tools and documents with anonymous `ftp` at `ftp.shsu.edu`, at `ftp.tex.ac.uk`, or at `ftp.dante.de`. Several commercially supported TEX packages are also available.

See also **`eqn`, LATEX, `nroff`, `pic`, `tbl`, text processing, `troff`**.

Texinfo

A text processing system used by the GNU Project to create both online documentation and printed manuals using TEX. If the GNU Info pages are installed on your system, you will find that they contain complete `Texinfo` documentation.

text editor

A program used to prepare an ordinary text file. Some text editors, called *line editors*, work on a file line-by-line, while others, called *screen editors,* let you enter, edit, and display text anywhere on the screen.

See also **`ed`, `emacs`, `ex`, `jove`, `pico`, `vi`**.

text file

A file that consists of text characters without any embedded formatting information. Also known as an *ASCII file*, a text file can be read by any editor or word processor.

text formatter

A Unix utility that provides standard formats for preparing documents. The programs `nroff` and `troff` and their associated preprocessors `eqn`, `pic`, and `tbl`, all fall into this category as do the TEX and LATEX packages.

See also **me macros, mm macros, ms macros.**

Table T.8: `test` Expressions	
EXPRESSION	DESCRIPTION
File Tests	
-b*filename*	True if *filename* exists and is a block special file.
-c*filename*	True if *filename* exists and is a character special file.
-d*filename*	True if *filename* exists and is a directory.
-f*filename*	True if *filename* exists and is an ordinary file.
-g*filename*	True if *filename* exists and its set group ID bit is set.
-G*filename*	True if *filename* exists and its group is the effective group ID.
-k*filename*	True if *filename* exists and its sticky bit is set.
-L*filename*	True if *filename* exists and is a symbolic link.
-O*filename*	True if *filename* exists and its owner is the effective owner.
-p*filename*	True if *filename* exists and is a FIFO special file or named pipe.
-r*filename*	True if *filename* exists and you have read access permission to it.
-s*filename*	True if *filename* exists and its size is greater than zero bytes.
-S*filename*	True if *filename* exists and is a socket special file.
-t*n*	True if the file associated with file descriptor *n* is a terminal.
-u*filename*	True if *filename* exists and its set user ID bit is set.
-w*filename*	True if *filename* exists and you have write access permission to it.
-x*filename*	True if *filename* exists and you have execute access permission to it.
filename1 -ef ➥ *filename2*	True if *filename1* is another name for *filename2*; the files are linked or point to the same i-node.
filename1 -nt ➥ *filename2*	True if *filename1* is newer than *filename2*.
filename1 -ot ➥ *filename2*	True if *filename1* is older than *filename2*.
Integer Comparisons	
n1 -eq *n2*	True if *n1* equals *n2*.
n1 -ge *n2*	True if *n1* is greater than or equal to *n2*.

Table T.8: test Expressions (continued)

EXPRESSION	DESCRIPTION
n1 -gt *n2*	True if *n1* is greater than *n2*.
n1 -le *n2*	True if *n1* is less than or equal to *n2*.
n1 -lt *n2*	True if *n1* is less than *n2*.
n1 -ne *n2*	True if *n1* is not equal to *n2*.
String Comparisons	
string	True if string is not null.
string1=*string2*	True if *string1* is identical to *string2*.
string1!=*string2*	True if *string1* is not identical to *string2*.
-n*string*	True if *string* is not empty.
-z*string*	True if *string* has zero length.
Combined Comparisons	
!*condition*	True if *condition* is false.
(*condition*)	True if *condition* is true.
condition1 ➥ -a *condition2*	True if *condition1* and *condition2* are both true.
condition1 ➥ -o *condition2*	True if either *condition1* or *condition2* is true.
Option Test	
-o*option*	True if *option* is turned on.

text processing

The preparation of text for printing or typesetting. In the Unix world, text processing systems such as TEX or `troff` are extremely flexible, but they are much more like programming languages than the word processors found in the PC world. When you use a Unix text processing system, you insert the formatting commands in the text, and you don't see what the output looks like until you print it or display it on your screen using an appropriate viewer.

On the other hand, the big advantage to the Unix text processing approach is that all the files are simple text files prepared using `vi` or `emacs`, and you can use any of the Unix utilities and text preprocessors on them; nowhere will you find the binary and proprietary formats used by commercial word processors.

■ *See also* **eqn**, **LATEX**, **nroff**, **pic**, **tbl**, **troff**.

`tfmtodit`

A command that creates font files for use with **`groff`**. This topic is beyond the scope of this book; see the **`man`** pages on your system for more details.

`tftp`

An interactive command, often called *trivial ftp,* used to transfer files between remote systems. Because it has no security associated with it, many system administrators do not support its use and recommend the **`ftp`** utility instead.

the Net

Jargon used to refer to two different, but related, networks: the Internet and USENET. You often hear people say, "I got it on the Net," or "I read that in a post on the Net."

`then`

A shell programming construct that is normally part of an **`if`** statement; **`then`** begins the execution of subsequent commands. A typical statement might look like this:

```
if condition1 then
    statement1
else
    statement2
fi
```

See also **`elif`, `else`, `fi`, `if`.**

thick Ethernet

Connecting coaxial cable used on an Ethernet network. The cable is 1 centimeter (0.4 inch) thick—almost as thick as your thumb—and can be used to connect network nodes up to a distance of approximately 1006 meters (3300 feet). Thick Ethernet is used primarily for facility-wide installations.

See also **thin Ethernet.**

thicknet

See **thick Ethernet.**

thin Ethernet

Connecting coaxial cable used on an Ethernet network. The cable is 5 millimeters (0.2 inch) thick—about as thick as your little finger—and can be used to connect network nodes up to a distance of approximately 165 meters (500 feet). Thin Ethernet is used primarily for office installations.

See also **thick Ethernet.**

thinnet

See **thin Ethernet.**

thrashing

An excessive amount of disk activity that causes a virtual memory system to spend all its time swapping programs in and out of memory and no time executing the application.

Thrashing can be caused when poor system configuration creates a swap area that is too small or when insufficient memory is installed in the computer. Increasing the size of the swap area or adding memory are often the best ways to reduce thrashing.

thread

- A concurrent process that is part of a larger process or program. In a multitasking operating system, a single program may contain several threads, all running at the same time. For example, one part of a program can be making a calculation while another part is drawing a graph or chart.
- A connected set of postings to a USENET newsgroup. Many newsreaders present postings as threads rather than in strict chronological sequence.

See also **multiprocessing, session.**

threaded newsreader

An application used to read the articles posted to USENET newsgroups. A threaded newsreader groups the newsgroup posts into threads of related articles, but unthreaded newsreaders present the articles in their original order of posting. Of the two types, threaded newsreaders are much more convenient to use. Examples of threaded newsreaders in the Unix world include `nn`, `tin`, and `trn`; `rn` is not a threaded newsreader.

ticket

A token used within the Kerberos authentication system that contains the user's name and address, as well as the service the user requested, security information, a time deadline, and authorization information so that he or she can use the system.

tilde escape commands

A command used within the Unix `mail` program that is always preceded by a tilde (~). Tilde escape commands can be issued while you are entering a message; the tilde must always be the first character on a line, and each tilde escape command must be on a line by itself. Table T.9 summarizes the tilde escape commands.

tilde symbol

The ~ symbol. Used to represent the name of the user's home directory in the Korn shell, the C shell, `bash`, `tcsh`, and Zsh, but not in the Bourne shell. In the Korn shell, you can also use `~+` as a shortcut for the name of the current directory and `~-` as the name of the previous directory. In the C shell, you can use `~`*`name`* to represent the home directory of the user specified by *`name`*.

Also used to separate a command from normal text entry in the `mail` and `mailx` programs.

In the `vi` editor, a tilde in the first character position on a line shows that the line is empty.

■ *See also* **tilde escape commands.**

time

A command that displays (in seconds) the total elapsed time, execution time, and system time taken by a specified command. The syntax looks like this:

```
time command
```

You can also specify any appropriate arguments for *`command`*.

The Bourne shell also has a similar `time` command, with the difference that you can use the built-in command to time other built-in commands as well as all the commands in a pipeline.

This command has no options.

■ *See also* **`nice`, `ps`, `times`.**

timeout

Many procedures require a device to respond or reply to an inquiry within a certain period of time; if the device does not respond, a timeout condition occurs, thus preventing the procedure from hanging up the computer.

Timeouts are also used in communications to detect transmission failures. Some timeouts are fixed, such as the amount of time during which an operating system will attempt to access a modem or printer; others can be specified by the user.

■ *See also* **`TIMEOUT`.**

TIMEOUT

A Bourne shell variable containing the time limit on entering commands at the prompt; if this interval elapses before you enter a command, the shell automatically logs you out.

■ *See also* **`TMOUT`.**

times

A built-in Bourne shell command that displays the accumulated times for user and system. The user time is the amount of time that a command takes to execute, and

Table T.9: Summary of Tilde Escape Commands

COMMAND	DESCRIPTION
`~?`	Help. Displays a list of tilde escape commands.
`~b` *`address`*	Add the specified *`address`* to the Blind Copy line.
`~c` *`address`*	Add the specified *`address`* to the Copy line.
`~d`	Reads in the contents of the `dead.letter` file.
`~e`	Starts the preselected text editor.
`~f` *`messages`*	Reads in the text of the specified old messages.
`~h`	Opens a prompt for the header information, including the Copy and Blind Copy information.
`~m` *`messages`*	Reads in the text of the specified old messages and shifts right one tab.
`~p`	Prints the current message with no header.
`~q`	Quits the `mail` program and cancels the current message.
`~r` *`filename`*	Reads in the contents of the specified *`filename`*.
`~s` *`subject`*	Changes the Subject line to that specified by *`subject`*.
`~t` *`address`*	Adds the specified *`address`* to the Address line.
`~v`	Starts the preselected text editor; same as `~e`.
`~w` *`filename`*	Writes the current message to the specified *`filename`*.
`~!` *`command`*	Executes the specified shell *`command`*, then returns to the message.
`~|` *`filter`*	Pipes the current message through the specified *`filter`*.
`~~`	Ignores the tilde escape and places a tilde in the text of the message.

the system time reflects the time used by Unix to execute the `times` command.

See also **`nice`**, **`ps`**, **`time`**.

timestamp

- The time when a file was last modified or accessed or had a change made to its i-node.
- A specific time attached to a Kerberos ticket, after which access to the requested service will be denied.

tin

A threaded newsreader for reading posts and subscribing to USENET newsgroups, originally developed by Ian Lea. Start the newsreader by typing:

`tin`

at the command prompt; you can also include the name of a newsgroup you want to access. `tin` reads the contents of your `.newsrc` file and compares it to the master list of newsgroups. If there are new newsgroups,

`tin` asks if you want to subscribe. `tin` then presents you with a newsgroup selection list, and when you make a choice, `tin` shows you a list of all the threads currently active in the newsgroup. You can choose a thread to read, and as you read you can save an article to a file on your computer, mail a copy of an article to someone else, kill all the posts with the same subject, decode an article using rot13, or respond to an article by posting a followup post or mailing directly to the original author.

Table T.10 lists the main `tin` commands, Table T.11 details the command you use when selecting a newsgroup, Table T.12 lists the commands you use when selecting a thread, and Table T.13 shows the commands used when reading articles.

For all single-letter commands, you do not have to press the Return or Enter key; just press the command letter and `tin` will immediately do as you ask.

Sometimes `tin` will display a list of possible choices and suggest one of the options as the most likely choice; just press the Return key to accept this default.

See also **.newsrc, nn, rn, trn.**

Table T.10: Main `tin` Commands

COMMAND	DESCRIPTION
Quitting	
`q`	Returns to the previous level.
`Q`	Exits `tin`.
Getting Help	
`h`	Displays a list of commands.
`H`	Toggles the help line at the bottom of the screen on and off.
`M`	Displays a menu of configurable options.
Displaying Information	
PgDn or space	Displays the next page.
Ctrl-D or Ctrl-F	Displays the next page.
PgUp or `b`	Displays the previous page.
Ctrl-U or Ctrl-B	Displays the previous page.
Posting an Article	
`w`	Posts an article to the current newsgroup.
`W`	Displays a list of all the articles you have posted.
Entering Unix Commands	
`!`	Pauses `tin` and starts a new shell.
`!`*`command`*	Executes the specified Unix *`command`*.

Table T.11: Commands for Selecting a Newsgroup in `tin`

COMMAND	DESCRIPTION
Displaying the Selection List	
↓ or `j`	Moves down one line.
↑ or `k`	Moves up one line.
n Return	Goes to the newsgroup number *n*.
`$`	Goes to the last newsgroup in the list.
`N`	Goes to the next newsgroup containing articles you have not yet read.
`g` *name*	Goes directly to the specified newsgroup.
`/`*name*	Searches forward for the specified newsgroup.
`?`*name*	Searches backward for the specified newsgroup.
Controlling the Display	
`d`	Toggles between showing the newsgroup name and showing the newsgroup name and description.
`r`	Toggles between showing all newsgroups and showing the newsgroups with unread articles.
Controlling Newsgroups	
`m`	Moves the newsgroup.
`s`	Subscribes to the current newsgroup.
`S`	Subscribes to all newsgroups that match a specified pattern.
`u`	Unsubscribes from the current newsgroup.
`U`	Unsubscribes from all newsgroups that match a specified pattern.
Reading Newsgroups	
→ or Return	Starts displaying the articles in the current newsgroup.
Tab or `n`	Goes to the next newsgroup containing articles you have not yet read.

Table T.12: Commands for Selecting a Thread in `tin`	
COMMAND	DESCRIPTION
Selecting a Thread	
n Return	Goes to thread number *n*.
`$`	Goes to the last thread.
/	Searches forward for a subject containing a specified pattern.
`?`	Searches backward for a subject containing a specified pattern.
`K`	Marks a thread as read and then opens the next unread thread.
`N`	Goes to the next unread thread.
`P`	Goes to the previous unread thread.
Reading an Article	
→	Opens the current thread for reading.
Tab	Opens the next unread thread for reading.
-	Returns to the last thread you were reading.
Controlling the Display	
`d`	Toggles between showing the subject and showing the subject and author.
`r`	Toggles between showing all threads and showing unread threads only.
Changing Newsgroups	
`n`	Goes to the next newsgroup.
`p`	Goes to the previous newsgroup.
Working with Threads	
`m`	Mails the thread.
`o`	Prints the thread.
`s`	Saves the thread in a file.

T

Table T.13: Commands for Reading an Article in `tin`

COMMAND	DESCRIPTION
Displaying an Article	
↓	Displays the next page.
↑	Displays the previous page.
`d`	Decodes the current article using rot13.
`g` or Ctrl-R	Goes to the first page of the article.
`G` or `$`	Goes to the last page of the article.
Ctrl-H	Redisplays the article showing the header.
Selecting Another Article	
→ or Tab or `N`	Goes to the next unread article.
Return	Goes to the next thread.
`k`	Marks the thread as read, goes to the next unread article.
`K`	Marks the entire thread as read, and goes to the next unread article.
`n`	Goes to the next article.
`p`	Goes to the previous article.
`P`	Goes to the previous unread article.
`-`	Returns to the last article you read.
Responding to an Article	
`f`	Posts a followup including the original post.
`F`	Posts a followup without including the original post.
`r`	Replies to the original author by mail, and includes the original post.
`R`	Replies to the original author by mail without including the original post.

tip

A Solaris and BSD command used to log in to a remote computer using a dial-up connection and a modem.

▶ Syntax

The syntax for `tip` is as follows:

`tip [`*`phonenumber`*`]`

Once the connection is established, a remote session behaves just like any other interactive session on your terminal, and you can copy files between the two systems. `tip` does not support Xmodem protocols and cannot transfer binary files. The appropriate hardware to support the connection must be installed on both local and remote computers, and you must have an account on the remote system.

▶ Commands

Once you have connected to the remote computer, you must use tilde commands to perform tasks on your local system; Table T.14 lists some of the most common tilde commands.

▶ Examples

To connect to a system at the telephone number 444-1212, use:

`tip 4441212`

`tip` displays the message `dialing...` then places the call using your system's modem. When the remote system answers, you see `connected`, and you can log on to the system.

■ *See also* **`cu`**, **`rlogin`**, **`rsh`**.

Tk

The extensions to Tcl that allow programmers to create and manipulate X Window widgets such as buttons, scrollbars, menus, and so on.

TMOUT

A Korn shell variable containing the time limit on entering commands at the prompt; if this interval elapses before you enter a command, the shell automatically logs you out.

■ *See also* **`TIMEOUT`**.

/tmp

A directory used to hold temporary files or data.

■ *See also* **`/lost+found`**.

Table T.14: `tip` Tilde Commands

COMMAND	DESCRIPTION
`~?`	Displays a summary of all the tilde commands.
`~!`	Escapes to a new shell so you can access your local system and remain connected to the remote system. When you exit from this shell, you return to `tip`.
`~.`	Disconnects from the remote system; you may still be logged on to the remote system.
`~c`*`directory`*	Changes the directory on your local system.
`~p`	Puts a file on (or sends a file to) the remote system.
`~t`	Takes (or receives) a file from the remote system.

tn3270

A variation of the telnet program designed to give access to an IBM 3270 series computer with 3278 page-mode terminals. Most of the computers on the Internet use Unix, but if you ever encounter an IBM mainframe, you will definitely need tn3270.

So how do you know when to use tn3270 rather than telnet? If you try to connect to an Internet host using telnet and one of the following happens, it's time to load up tn3270:

- The on-screen messages are all in uppercase letters rather than the usual Unix mix of uppercase and lowercase letters.
- You see "VM" or "VMS" anywhere in the login message. These are both names of IBM operating systems.
- Your session is aborted before it really gets started.

For information on starting and using tn3270, see the telnet entry; in command mode, tn3270 accepts and executes all the telnet commands.

toggle

A command or selection that is alternately turned on and off again each time you select it.

toolkit

A collection of software development tools used to assist in the creation of application programs.

See **SDK.**

touch

A command used to change the file access and modification times.

▶ Syntax

The syntax for touch is as follows:

```
touch [options][time]file-list
```

The touch command sets the modification and access time to the current time or to a time that you specify. If the file doesn't exist, it is created with default permissions and the specified or current times. You cannot change the file creation time.

▶ Options and Arguments

The *file-list* contains the pathname of the files that you want to update. The *time* argument specifies the new date and time, using this format:

```
MMddhhmm[yy]
```

where *MM* is the month number (01-12), *dd* is the day of the month (01-31), *hh* is the hour (00-23), *mm* is the minutes (00-59), and *yy* is an optional two-digit year number. On some systems, you can use this form for the time:

```
[[CC]yy]MMddhhmm[.ss]
```

where *CC* and *yy* specify the century and the year, and *ss* the number of seconds (0 to 61). If you don't specify a year, touch uses the current year, and if you don't specify a *time*, touch uses the current system time.

Table T.15 lists the options available with touch.

If you don't use the -a or the -m options, touch updates both the access and modification times.

▶ Examples

Certain commands such as make and find use a file's access and modification time, and so touch can be very useful in forcing these commands to treat files in a certain way.

To set the access and modification times of all files in the current directory to the current time, use:

```
touch *
```

See also **date, time.**

t protocol

A UUCP protocol originally used with TCP/IP networks; no longer in common use.

See also **e protocol, f protocol, t protocol, x protocol.**

Table T.15: Options to Use with touch	
OPTION	DESCRIPTION
`-a`	Changes the file's access time, leaving the modification time unchanged.
`-c`	Does not create a file if the specified file does not exist.
`-f`	Attempts to force the update even if the file permissions do not allow it.
`-m`	Changes the file's modification time, leaving the access time unchanged.
`-r`*`filename`*	Changes the access and modification times to those of the specified *`filename`* rather than the current time.
`-t`*`time`*	Changes the access and modification times to the specified *`time`*.

tput

A command that displays information from the `terminfo` database or sends setup instructions to your terminal. The `tput` syntax is:

`tput [`*`option`*`]`*`attribute`*

The `-T`*`terminal`* option specifies your terminal type, and the attribute can be one of the ones listed in Table T.16.

■ *See also* **stty**, **termcap**, **terminfo**, **tset**.

tr

A command that translates characters in a file from one form to another. A common use of `tr` is to convert the text in a file from lowercase to uppercase or to change all the tabs into spaces.

Table T.16: Attributes to Use with the -T*terminal* Option to tput	
ATTRIBUTE	DESCRIPTION
`clear` *`parameter`*	Sends the string that clears the screen.
`init` *`parameter`*	Sends the terminal initialization string.
`longname`	Displays the complete name of the terminal.
`reset` *`parameter`*	Sends the terminal reset string.

▶ Syntax

Here's the syntax:

`tr [`*`options`*`][`*`string1`*`][`*`string2`*`]`

`tr` copies the standard input to the standard output, translating occurrences from *`string1`* into corresponding characters in *`string2`*.

▶ Options and Arguments

By using one argument, *`string1`*, and an option from Table T.17, you can use `tr` to delete the characters specified in *`string1`*. Used with no arguments, `tr` just copies its standard input to its standard output. Table T.17 lists the options you can use with `tr`.

You can also specify a range of characters by hyphenating them and enclosing them in square brackets.

▶ Examples

To translate all the uppercase and lowercase letters in the file `chapter.one` into lowercase and store the result into a file called `chapter.lower`, use:

```
cat chapter.one | tr "[A-Z]"
➥ "[a-z]" > chapter.lower
```

■ *See also* **comm**, **cut**, **dd**, **expand**, **fold**, **paste**, **translate**, **unexpand**, **uniq**.

Table T.17: Options to Use with `tr`

OPTION	DESCRIPTION
`-c`	Complements the set of characters in *`string1`*; the complement consists of all non-null characters that are not in *`string1`*, taken in their machine collating order.
`-d`	Deletes characters that match those specified in *`string1`*.
`-s`	Reduces any sequence of several identical characters in *`string2`* to a single occurrence.

trackball

An input device used for pointing, designed as an alternative to the mouse.

A trackball is almost an upside-down mouse; it stays still and contains a movable ball that you rotate using your fingers to move the cursor on the screen. Because a trackball does not need the area of flat space that the mouse needs, trackballs are popular with users of portable computers.

translate

An SCO command that translates files from one format to another.

▶ Syntax

The syntax to use with `translate` is:

```
translate [options]
➥[input-file][output-file]
```

▶ Options and Arguments

`translate` used without arguments reads from the standard input and writes to the standard output. The options you can use are listed in Table T.18.

■ *See also* **`comm`**, **`cut`**, **`dd`**, **`expand`**, **`fold`**, **`paste`**, **`tr`**, **`unexpand`**, **`uniq`**.

Table T.18: Options to Use with `translate`

OPTION	DESCRIPTION
`-ae`	Translates from ASCII to EBCDIC.
`-af`*`format`*	Translates from ASCII to a user-defined *`format`*.
`-bm`	Translates from binary to `uuencode` ASCII.
`-ea`	Translates from EBCDIC to ASCII.
`-ef`*`format`*	Translates from EBCDIC to a user-defined *`format`*.
`-fa`*`format`*	Translates from a user-defined *`format`* to ASCII.
`-fe`*`format`*	Translates from a user-defined *`format`* to EBCDIC.
`-mb`	Translates from `uuencode` ASCII to binary.

transport layer

The fourth of seven layers of the ISO/OSI model for computer-to-computer communications. The transport layer defines protocols for message structure and supervises the validity of the transmission by performing some error checking.

trap

An instruction that is used as an interface between an application program and the kernel. When the application executes the trap instruction, the kernel takes over, performs the appropriate service or system call, and then resumes the application.

■ *See also* **`exec`**, **`kill`**, **signal**, **system call**, **`trap`**.

trap

A built-in Bourne shell and Korn shell command that executes a specified command if one or more signals are received. `trap` can be used from the command line but is most often used in shell scripts.

The syntax looks like this:

```
trap [[commands]signals]
```

`trap` executes the *commands* when any of the *signals* is received; multiple commands should be quoted as a group and separated by semicolons.

If you use a null string as *commands*, then `trap` ignores the specified *signals*; for example:

```
trap "" 1 2 3 15
```

ignores the hangup, interrupt, quit, and software termination signals.

If both *commands* and *signals* are omitted, `trap` lists the current `trap` assignments.

See also **exec, kill, signal, trap.**

trn

A public-domain threaded newsreader for reading posts and subscribing to USENET newsgroups, originally developed by Wayne Davison and based on the `rn` newsreader. Most, if not all, the standard `rn` commands are available in `trn`, and the online help in `trn` assumes a working knowledge of `rn` and focuses almost entirely on the `trn`-specific features of the program.

Table T.19 lists the `trn` commands you can use while selecting a newsgroup or executing a shell command. Table T.20 lists the commands used when selecting an article within a newsgroup.

See also **.newsrc, nn, rn, tin.**

Table T.19: Commands for Selecting a Newsgroup in trn

COMMAND	DESCRIPTION
Basic Commands	
h	Displays help information.
q	Quits `trn`.
v	Displays the `trn` version number.
x	Quits `rn` and abandons all updates to your `.newsrc` file.
Reading Articles	
Space	Performs the default operation.
+	Invokes the thread selector to read the current newsgroup.
=	Displays a list of subjects in the current newsgroup.
y	Starts displaying the current newsgroup for reading.
Working with Newsgroups	
^	Goes to the first newsgroup that contains unread articles.
$	Goes to the end of the list of newsgroups.

Table T.19: Commands for Selecting a Newsgroup in `trn` (continued)

COMMAND	DESCRIPTION
`A`	Abandons all read and unread changes to this newsgroup.
`c`	Catchup mode: marks all the articles in the newsgroup as having been read.
`g` *`newsgroup`*	Goes to the specified *`newsgroup`*.
`l` *`pattern`*	Lists the unsubscribed newsgroup names that contain *`pattern`*.
`L`	Lists the current state of newsgroups in `.newsrc`.
`n`	Goes to the next newsgroup that contains unread articles.
`p`	Goes to the previous newsgroup that contains unread articles.
`u`	Unsubscribes from the current newsgroup.
`/pattern`	Searches forward for a newsgroup name containing *`pattern`*.
`?`*`pattern`*	Searches backward for a newsgroup name containing *`pattern`*.
`/`	Searches forward for previous *`pattern`*.
`?`	Searches backward for previous *`pattern`*.
Executing Unix Commands	
`!` *`command`*	Executes the specified *`command`*.
`!`	Pauses `trn` and starts a shell.

Table T.20: Commands for Selecting an Article in `trn`

COMMAND	DESCRIPTION
Basic Commands	
`+`	Invokes thread selection mode.
`c`	Marks all articles in the newsgroup as read.
`h`	Displays help information.
`k`	Marks all articles with the same subject as read; effectively kills unread articles.
`n`	Goes to the next unread article.
`q`	Quits this newsgroup.
`Ctrl-N`	Goes to the next unread article on the same subject.

Table T.20: Commands for Selecting an Article in `trn` (continued)	
COMMAND	DESCRIPTION
Redisplaying the Current Article	
`b`	Goes back one page.
`v`	Redisplays the current article with its header.
`X`	Decodes the current page using rot13.
`Ctrl-L`	Redisplays the current page.
`Crtl-R`	Redisplays the current article.
`Ctrl-X`	Decodes the current article using rot13.
Selecting Another Article	
`-`	Redisplays the last article displayed.
`N`	Moves forward to the next article.
`$`	Moves forward to the end of the last article.
`p`	Moves backward to the previous article.
`Ctrl-P`	Moves backward to the previous article with the same subject.
`P`	Moves backward to the next article, read or unread.
`^`	Moves backward to the next unread article.
Using Article Numbers	
`=`	Displays a list of all the unread articles.
`number`	Goes to the article with the specified *`number`*.
`#`	Displays the number of the last article.
Searching for an Article	
`/pattern`	Searches forward for a subject containing *`pattern`*.
`?pattern`	Searches backward for a subject containing *`pattern`*.
`/`	Searches forward for previous *`pattern`*.
`?`	Searches backward for previous *`pattern`*.

Table T.20: Commands for Selecting an Article in `trn` (continued)	
COMMAND	DESCRIPTION
Responding to an Article	
`f`	Starts the `Pnews` program to create a followup post.
`F`	Starts the `Pnews` program to create a followup post, and includes a copy of the original message.
`r`	Sends a mail message to the author of the article.
`R`	Sends a mail message to the author of the article, and includes a copy of the original message.
Saving an Article	
`s` *`filename`*	Saves the article in the specified *`filename`*.
`w` *`filename`*	Saves the article without the header in the specified *`filename`*.
Executing Unix Commands	
`!` *`command`*	Executes the specified *`command`*.
`!`	Pauses `trn` and starts a shell.

troff

A text-processing command used to format a text file for output to a typesetter; pronounced "tee-rof" for "typesetter runoff."

Unix often includes two programs for text processing, `nroff` and `troff`. The `nroff` program is used when you want to output formatted text to a line printer or to a line-oriented display, and `troff` is used when you want to send text to a laser printer, bitmapped display, or to a typesetter. `troff` supports proportionally spaced fonts, while `nroff` supports only monospaced fonts.

An input file for `troff` contains lines of text interspersed with lines that begin with a period and contain one- or two-letter commands. `troff` also allows you to define a macro as a series of input lines, and three major macro packages are available that automate complex formatting functions.

The main benefit to using `nroff` and `troff` rather than a commercial word processor is that their input files are simple text files. This allows you to use many other Unix utilities (`grep`, `diff`, and so on) with your files, which is something you can't do with the proprietary formats used by word processors. These files also tend to be smaller than equivalent files from commercial packages, and they can be copied from machine to machine quickly and easily.

See also **eqn, LATEX, `groff`, me macros, mm macros, ms macros, `nroff`, `pic`, `soelim`, `tbl`, TEX, `Texinfo`.**

troff macros

A macro designed to manage a standard formatting function and create a standard document such as a letter, report, memo, manual, or book. Several important macro packages are available, including:

- **me** macros. A set of over 80 `nroff` and `troff` macros distributed with BSD systems, originally created by Eric Allman while at Berkeley. The **me** macro package is equivalent to the **ms**

and mm macro packages on SVR4 systems and supports all common preprocessors such as `eqn`, `tbl`, and `refer`.

- mm macros. A set of almost 100 `nroff` and `troff` macros distributed with SVR4 systems. The mm macro package is equivalent to the `me` macro package on BSD systems.
- `ms` macros. The original set of approximately 50 `nroff` and `troff` macros. The `ms` macro package is no longer supported but is often found on many systems.
- `man` macros. A macro package used to format Unix `man` pages
- `mview` macros. A package of macros used to create overhead transparencies.

Trojan Horse

A type of computer virus that pretends to be a useful program, such as a game or a utility program (the name `ls` is a common choice, as it can be virtually guaranteed that you will use it sooner rather than later), when in reality it contains special code that will intentionally damage any system onto which it is loaded.

See also **sniffer.**

true

A shell command used in shell scripts to test whether a task has been completed. `true` is often used in a `while` loop; as long as a successful response (a value of zero) is received, the loop continues to run. If any other value is returned, the loop terminates.

See also **false, if, test, while.**

truncate

To shorten a file or a number by cutting off and abandoning a series of lines or digits.

truss

A troubleshooting command used to trace system calls and signals and to display information on the standard output. Only used by the system administrator.

tset

A command for setting the system interface to terminals and dial-up modems, designed for use with `termcap`.

▶ Syntax

The syntax to use is:

```
tset [options][type]
```

`tset` is most often used in shell scripts; it is not often used from the command line.

▶ Options and Arguments

In the syntax above, *`type`* is your terminal type; the options are listed in Table T.21.

Used without options, `tset` displays the settings for the erase, kill, and interrupt keys:

```
tset
Erase set to Delete
Kill set to Ctrl-U
Interrupt set to Ctrl-C
```

See also **stty, termcap, terminfo, tput, tty.**

tty

Abbreviation for teletype, pronounced "tee-tee-why." Refers to a terminal or a serial port.

tty

A command that displays the pathname of your terminal's device file.

▶ Syntax

The syntax for this command is:

```
tty [options]
```

▶ Options and Arguments

You can use the options listed in Table T.22 with `tty`; the command takes no arguments.

See also **stty, tput, tset, tty.**

Table T.21: Options to Use with tset	
OPTION	DESCRIPTION
-	Displays the terminal name without initializing the terminal.
-e*c*	Sets the erase character to *c*; the default is Ctrl-H, backspace.
-i*c*	Sets the interrupt character to *c*; the default is Ctrl-C.
-I	Suppresses the terminal initialization setting.
-k*c*	Sets the kill-line character to *c*; the default is Ctrl-U.
-m[*port*[*baud*]:*tty*]	Maps the specified parameters from a port type to a terminal. *port* is the port type (often **dialup**), *baud* is the baud rate of the port, *tty* is the terminal type.
-Q	Suppresses the display of the erase, interrupt, and kill-line information.
-r	Displays the terminal type on the standard error.
-s	Displays the commands used to set TERM.
-S	Displays the terminal type and termcap entry.

Table T.22: Options to Use with tty	
OPTION	DESCRIPTION
-l	Prints the synchronous line number.
-s	Causes tty not to print any output but still to set the exit status to 0 if the standard input file is a terminal, and to 1 if it is not.

tunneling

The encapsulation of one protocol within another, often used to transport a local-area network (LAN) protocol across an intermediate network that does not support that particular protocol.

twinaxial cable

A cable with two coaxial cables inside a single insulating shield. Twinaxial cable is most often used with IBM AS/400 minicomputers.

twisted pair cabling

Abbreviated TP. Cable that comprises two or more pairs of insulated wires twisted together at six twists per inch. In twisted pair cable, one wire carries the signal and the other is grounded. The cable may be shielded or unshielded. Telephone wire installed in modern buildings is often twisted pair wiring.

twm

The name of the Tab Window Manager included with the X Window system. twm has served as the model for many window managers, including the Motif and the Open Look window managers.

- *See also* **mwm, olwm.**

type

A command used to show whether a name is a Unix command, a built-in shell command, or a defined shell function.

In the Korn shell, this is an alias for whence -v.

- *See also* **whence.**

typeahead

Input entered from the keyboard before the system prompt indicates that the system is ready to accept keyboard input.

■ *See also* **typeahead buffer.**

typeahead buffer

A small amount of system memory used to store the most recently typed keys, also known as a *keyboard buffer.*

`typeset`

A built-in Korn shell command used for several different purposes in shell scripts.

▶ Syntax

The syntax to use is:

```
typeset [options]
➥[variable[=value...]]
```

▶ Options and Arguments

The `typeset` command assigns a type to each *`variable`*, as well as an optional initial *`value`*. When you specify a *`variable`*, *`+option`* enables it, while *`-option`* disables it. With no *`variable`*, *`+option`* prints the names, and *`-option`* prints the names and the values of all the set variables. You can use the options listed in Table T.23.

Table T.23: Options to Use with `typeset`

OPTION	DESCRIPTION
`-f`	Defines the current *`variable`* as a function; if no *`variable`* is given, lists the current function names.
`-H`	Maps Unix filenames to host filenames on non-Unix systems.
`-i`*`n`*	Defines *`variable`* as an integer of base *`n`*.
`-L`*`n`*	Defines *`variable`* as a flush-left string *`n`* characters in length.
`-l`	Converts uppercase to lowercase.
`-r`	Marks *`variable`* as read-only.
`-R`*`n`*	Defines *`variable`* as a flush-right string *`n`* characters in length.
`-t`	Marks *`variable`* with a user-defined tag.
`-u`	Converts lowercase to uppercase.
`-x`	Marks *`variable`* for automatic export.
`-Z`*`n`*	When used with `-L`, strips leading zeros.

▶ Examples

To list the names, values, and types of all set shell variables, use:

```
typeset
```

To list the names, values, and types of all exported shell variables, use:

```
typeset -x
```

■ *See also* **`autoload`**, **`integer`**, **`readonly`**.

U

UDP

Abbreviation for User Datagram Protocol. The connectionless, transport-level protocol used in the TCP/IP suite of protocols, usually bundled with IP layer software. Because UDP does not add overhead, as does connection-oriented TCP, UDP is often used with SNMP (Simple Network Management Protocol) applications.

ul

A BSD command that translates underlining in a text file into characters that your current terminal can display.

▶ Syntax

The syntax for `ul` is as follows:

```
ul [options]filename...
```

▶ Options and Arguments

The `ul` command reads from the specified *`filename`* or the standard input if no filename is given and translates any underlining into characters understood by your terminal. If the terminal cannot display any form of underlining, underlining is ignored. The options you can use with `ul` are listed in Table U.1.

▶ Examples

To display the contents of the file `chapter.txt` with underlining support for a VT100 ASCII terminal, use:

```
ul -t vt100 chapter.txt
```

■ *See also* **colcrt**, **man**, **nroff**, **pg**, **term**.

Table U.1: Options to Use with `ul`

OPTIONS	DESCRIPTION
`-i`	Indicates that underlining is contained in a separate line containing dashes.
`-t` *`terminal`*	Overrides your current terminal type with *`terminal`*.

ulimit

A built-in Korn shell command used to limit system resources.

▶ Syntax

Here's the `ulimit` syntax:

`ulimit [options][number]`

`ulimit` displays the value of one or more resource limits or, if *number* is specified, sets the resource limit to that value.

▶ Options and Arguments

Resource limits can be either hard or soft limits; only the superuser can increase a hard limit, although anyone can lower one. Soft limits must be lower that the hard limit. Using `ulimit`, you can set either type of limit and display the value of the soft limits. Table U.2 lists the options available with `ulimit`.

See also **env, printenv, set.**

Table U.2: Options to Use with ulimit

OPTION	DESCRIPTION
-H	Sets a hard limit.
-S	Sets a soft limit.
-a	Displays all limits.
-c	Sets the maximum block size of core files.
-d	Sets the maximum size of the data segment or heap in kilobytes.
-f	Sets the maximum block size of files; this is the default option.
-n	Sets the maximum file descriptor plus 1.
-s	Sets the maximum stack segment in kilobytes.
-t	Sets the maximum number of CPU seconds.
-v	Sets the maximum amount of virtual memory in kilobytes.

Ultrix

A version of Unix from Digital Equipment Corporation that looks and works like BSD Unix.

umask

A built-in Unix command and shell command that lets you display or change the current file creation mask that determines the default permissions when you create a new file.

▶ Syntax

Here's the syntax:

`umask [number]`

▶ Options and Arguments

Using `umask` without arguments displays the current file creation mask, and if you specify an octal *number*, you can set the file creation mask. This mask is a three-digit octal number, where each digit corresponds to permissions for the owner of the file, members of the group the file is associated with, and everyone else. When you create a new file, Unix subtracts these numbers from the numbers corresponding to the default access permissions that the system usually grants and so arrives at an appropriate set of permissions. Table U.3 illustrates how these octal numbers work. The `umask` command has no options.

By default, new files are given the permission mode 666 (`rw-rw-rw-`), which gives everyone read and write access, while directories are given the permission mode 777 (`rwxrwxrwx`), which gives everyone read, write, and search permission.

The `umask` command is available in almost all the popular shells, including the C shell, Bourne shell, and Korn shell, and is often used in one of the shell startup files such as `.profile` or `.login`.

Table U.3: umask Permissions

NUMBER	FILE PERMISSION	DIRECTORY PERMISSION	DESCRIPTION
0	`rw-`	`rwx`	Grants read and write permission for files, and read, write, and search permission for directories.
1	`rw-`	`rw-`	Grants read and write permission for files and directories.
2	`r—`	`r-x`	Grants read permission for files and read and search permission for directories.
3	`r--`	`r--`	Grants only read permission for files and directories.
4	`-w-`	`-wx`	Grants write permission for files and write and search permission for directories.
5	`-w-`	`-w-`	Grants only write permission for files and directories.
6	`---`	`--x`	Grants no permissions for files and only search permission for directories.
7	`---`	`---`	Denies all permissions for files and directories.

▶ **Examples**

To set the file creation mask so that the owner and group have all permissions but the rest of the world only has read permission (equivalent to —`r`—), use:

`umask 002`

You can omit the leading zeros if you wish.

■ *See also* **chmod, chown, ls.**

umask value

An octal number that specifies the file permissions to be masked out when a file is created.

■ *See also* **chown, chmod, ls, umask.**

unalias

A built-in command found in the Korn shell and the C shell that removes an alias created by the `alias` command. The syntax is:

`unalias` *`name`*

where *`name`* is the name of a previously created alias. For once, the C shell and Korn shell versions of this command are identical. `unalias` has no options.

■ *See also* **alias.**

uname

A command that reports system information to the standard output.

▶ Syntax

The syntax for **uname** is as follows:

```
uname [options]
```

▶ Options and Arguments

The options you can use with this command are detailed in Table U.4.

See also **hostid**, **hostname**.

Table U.4: Options to Use with uname

OPTION	DESCRIPTION
-a	Displays a complete report as though all the remaining options were specified.
-m	Displays the name of the system hardware.
-n	Displays the name of the network node.
-r	Displays the operating system's current release level.
-s	Displays the name of the operating system.
-v	Displays the operating system version level.

unbuffered device

See **raw device.**

uncompact

A BSD command that restores an original file from a file compressed by **compact**. The syntax is:

```
uncompact [option]filename
```

The single option, **-v**, displays the names of the files as they are processed. If no *filename* is specified, the standard input is uncompressed to the standard output.

See also **ccat**, **compact**.

uncompress

A command that uncompresses compressed files. The syntax is:

```
uncompress [option]file-list
```

where *file-list* contains the names of the files you want to expand; the filename extension **.Z** is assumed so you don't have to specify it on the command line. **uncompress** has one option, **-c**, which writes the compressed file to the standard output but does not change any files. This is the same as using the **zcat** command.

See also **compact**, **compress**, **gzip**, **pack**, **uncompact**, **zcat**.

unexpand

A Solaris command that copies a file (or the standard input) to the standard output, replacing leading whitespace by a sequence of tabs and spaces. This command reverses the effects of the **expand** command.

The syntax is:

```
unexpand [option]filename
```

The single option, **-a**, inserts tab characters when replacing a run of two or more space characters and creates a smaller output file.

See also **expand.**

unget

See **SCCS.**

unhash

A built-in C shell command that removes the internal hash table. After you invoke **unhash**, the C shell stops using hashed values to locate a command and spends more time searching directory pathnames.

■ *See also* **hash, rehash.**

unicode

A 16-bit character code, defined by the Unicode Consortium and the International Organization for Standardization (ISO 10646), that supports up to 65,536 different characters, rather than the 256 characters available in the current ASCII character set. Unicode allows all the characters and symbols in a language to be represented by a single code; for example, the Chinese language defines almost 10,000 basic ideographs. When universally adopted, Unicode will make multilingual software must easier to write and maintain.

unifdef

A BSD software development command that removes `ifdef` directives used to control conditional compilation. `unifdef` removes `#ifdef`, `#ifndef`, `#else`, and `#endif` lines and understands the C language well enough to know when one of these directives is contained inside a comment or within single or double quotes.

Uniform Resource Locator

■ *See* **URL.**

UniForum

A nonprofit organization formed in 1980 dedicated to improve Unix through the open exchange of ideas and information between users and developers. Previously known as `/usr/group`, UniForum has several hundred thousand members in many countries throughout the world.

■ *See also* **SAGE, UniNews, USENIX.**

UniNews

The biweekly publication for UniForum members, with information on trade shows, conferences, and product announcements.

Uninterruptible Power Supply

■ *See* **UPS.**

uniq

A command used to remove or report adjacent duplicate lines in a sorted text file.

▶ Syntax

Here's the syntax to use:

```
uniq [options]
➥[inputfile[outputfile]]
```

Repeated lines in the input to `uniq` are not detected unless they are adjacent, so it may be wise to sort the file before using `uniq`.

▶ Options and Arguments

`uniq` removes the adjacent duplicate lines from the sorted *`inputfile`* sending one copy of each line to the standard output or to *`outputfile`*. Table U.5 lists the options you can use with `uniq`.

▶ Examples

The `uniq` command is often used as a filter and is good at combining two files to produce one output file with all duplicates removed. To combine two lists of names into one that contains no duplicates, use:

```
cat mylist yourlist | sort |
➥ uniq > ourlist
```

which combines `mylist` and `yourlist` using the `cat` command, sorts the result, removes any duplicates, and stores the result into the file `ourlist`.

■ *See also* **comm, sort.**

Table U.5: Options to Use with uniq

OPTION	DESCRIPTION
-c	Precedes each line by a count of the number of times it occurred in the input.
-d	Displays all duplicate lines once, but does not display unique lines.
-f *n*	Ignores the first *n* fields in a file and any spaces preceding them; not available in all versions of uniq.
-s *n*	Ignores the first *n* characters and any spaces preceding them; not available in all versions of uniq.
-u	Displays only unique lines; does not display repeated lines.
-*n*	Ignores the first *n* fields in a file; this option is obsolete in some versions of uniq.
+*n*	Ignores the first *n* characters in a field; this option is obsolete in some versions of uniq.

units

An interactive program used to convert between different units of measure. The units program can only do multiplicative conversions, so while it can convert temperatures from Kelvin to Rankine, it cannot convert from Fahrenheit to centigrade. In addition, many of the currency conversion rates fluctuate and may not be up-to-date. Here's a short example of how it works:

```
units
You have:   inch
You want: cm
        *2.54000e+00
        / 3.93701e-01
```

British units that differ from their U.S. counterparts are prefixed with br as in:

```
brgallon
```

and currency as:

```
germanmark
```

or

```
britainpound
```

Most familiar units are recognized, including metric prefixes and abbreviations. For a complete list of the 500 or so units recognized, look in /usr/share/units on BSD and SunOS systems, /usr/lib/units on SVR4, /usr/lib/unittab on SCO, and /usr/share/lib/unittab on Solaris and AIX.

See also **bc, dc.**

Unix

Pronounced "yoo-nixs." An operating system designed and developed in 1969 at AT&T's Bell Labs by Ken Thompson and Dennis Ritchie. Since the initial development, the Unix environment has been enriched with a large number of utilities and other programs. The real turning point was the period between 1972 and 1974 when Unix was rewritten in the C language with portability as a major design goal. Unix has gone on to become the most widely used general-purpose operating system in the world. Table U.6 lists the names and developers of Unix and Unix-like operating systems.

Of the approximately 500 USENET newsgroups in the comp category, about 30 deal with Unix or Unix-related topics, while the others deal with hardware, software, or commercial applications, as well as the distribution of public domain software and shareware. Alternative

Table U.6: Unix Systems and Their Developers

UNIX SYSTEM	DEVELOPER
386BSD	Free from the Internet and other sources
AIX	IBM
A/UX	Apple
BSD	University of California, Berkeley
BSD-Lite	University of California, Berkeley
BSD/386	Berkeley Software Design
Coherent	Mark Williams Company
DC/OS	Pyramid Technology
Dynix	Sequent Computer Systems
FreeBSD	Free from the Internet and other sources
HP-UX	Hewlett-Packard
Hurd (GNU)	Free Software Foundation
Interactive Unix	Sun Microsystems
Irix	Silicon Graphics
Linux	Linus Torvalds; free from the Internet and other sources
Mach	Carnegie Mellon University
Minix	Andrew Tannenbaum
MKS Toolkit	Mortice Kern Systems
NetBSD	Free from the Internet and other sources
NeXTStep	NeXT
OSF/1	Digital Equipment Corporation (DEC)
SCO OpenServer	Santa Cruz Operation
SCO UNIX	Santa Cruz Operation
Solaris	Sun Microsystems
SunOS	Sun Microsystems
Ultrix	Digital Equipment Corporation (DEC)
Unicos	Cray Research
UnixWare	Novell/Santa Cruz Operation

groups include `gnu`, devoted to the Free Software Foundation's GNU Project, with about 30 more discussion groups; `alt.bbs.unixbbs`, which lists Unix bulletin boards; and `info.unix-sw`, which lists Unix software available by anonymous `ftp`.

■ *See also* **BSD, K&R, Unix history.**

Unix games

It is sometimes said that Ken Thompson and Dennis Ritchie developed Unix so that they could play Space Travel on a scavenged PDP-7. (Space Travel was said to be a serious astronomical simulation program, not just a game.)

Be that as it may, plenty of games are available on most Unix systems, ranging from the Dungeons of Doom to computerized card and board games, such as blackjack and backgammon, and word games like boggle and hangman. You can find them in `/usr/games`.

Unix history

Over the last 25 years, there have been three major strands of Unix development:

- Original AT&T Unix from Versions 1–7, and Systems III–V
- Microsoft/SCO XENIX
- Berkeley releases from 1BSD to 4.4BSD

Figure U.1 shows a simplified version of the Unix family tree.

Figure U.1 is an oversimplification, of course, since a large number of Unix-related systems have been released by a large number of commercial vendors. Unix is available on a range of computational hardware, ranging from PCs to huge Cray supercomputers, and is also available in other related forms.

The first version of Unix, written in 1969, ran on a DEC PDP-7 computer, and in 1970 Ken Thompson and Dennis Ritchie moved it to the DEC PDP-11/20. Ritchie also designed and created the first C language compiler so that he could write a portable version of the system. In 1973, Thompson and Ritchie rewrote the Unix kernel in C.

The so-called Fifth Edition (not to be confused with System V) was the first Unix licensed to universities for educational purposes; the Sixth Edition, released in 1976, was also widely distributed. The Seventh Edition, released in 1978, was the first Unix to have ease of portability as a major design goal and was made available on several hardware platforms. The two most influential results of the Seventh Edition release were System V from AT&T and the various Berkeley Software Distribution (BSD) systems.

System V, released in 1983, was billed as the industry standard and subsequent releases were System V Release 2.0 (1984), System V Release 3.0 (1986), and System V Release 4.0 (1989). The latest release is System V Release 4.2, which you often see abbreviated as SVR4.

The role of the computer science department of the University of California at Berkeley in the evolution of Unix has been enormous, including the development of the C shell, `vi`, `termcap`, and support for the TCP/IP series of protocols. Because Berkeley was strictly interested in research, BSD Unix was not supported in any modern sense, and bug fixes were certainly not guaranteed. (See the "BSD" entry earlier in this book for detailed information on BSD releases.) Finally, in June 1993, Berkeley released 4.4BSD and disbanded the Computer Science Research Group (CSRG) at the same time, thus ending Berkeley's contribution to the development of Unix.

XENIX was jointly developed by Microsoft and SCO between 1979 and 1981 as a Version 7 release intended for Intel-based PCs. XENIX added several important features to Unix, including record locking and semaphores for signal synchronization. Microsoft sold its interest in XENIX to SCO in 1987.

In 1990, that part of AT&T maintaining System V was turned into a subsidiary called UNIX System Laboratories (USL), and Novell became a major shareholder in this new company. In 1991, USL and Novell formed a joint venture called Univel, and in the fall of 1992 released UnixWare 1.0 (based on System V Release 4.2) to run on 32-bit Intel-based hardware. At about the same time, Novell agreed to purchase USL from AT&T, and the deal was completed in 1993. At the end of 1993, Novell turned the Unix trademark and the certification process over to X/Open. In 1995, Novell sold its Unix rights to SCO, and SCO expects to combine the features found in SCO's OpenServer with those in Novell's UnixWare with new releases over the next two years.

Several free (or almost free) versions of Unix are available for the Intel platform, including Linux, FreeBSD, and NetBSD. These systems provide excellent performance and a full range of Unix utilities and other features. Since they contain no proprietary code, they are not affected by any licensing restrictions other than the GNU General Public License.

Unix now is a very different animal from the Unix of the 1970s and 1980s. A typical system then consisted of a single processor serving a set of dumb terminals. Unix today is more likely to be a workstation running X Window, acting as a part of a large complex network of systems. Unix in the early days was a small, not very commercial product aimed at a small, specific set of users, most of whom were professional programmers. Unix today is a large and complicated commercial

Figure U.1: A Simplified Unix Family Tree

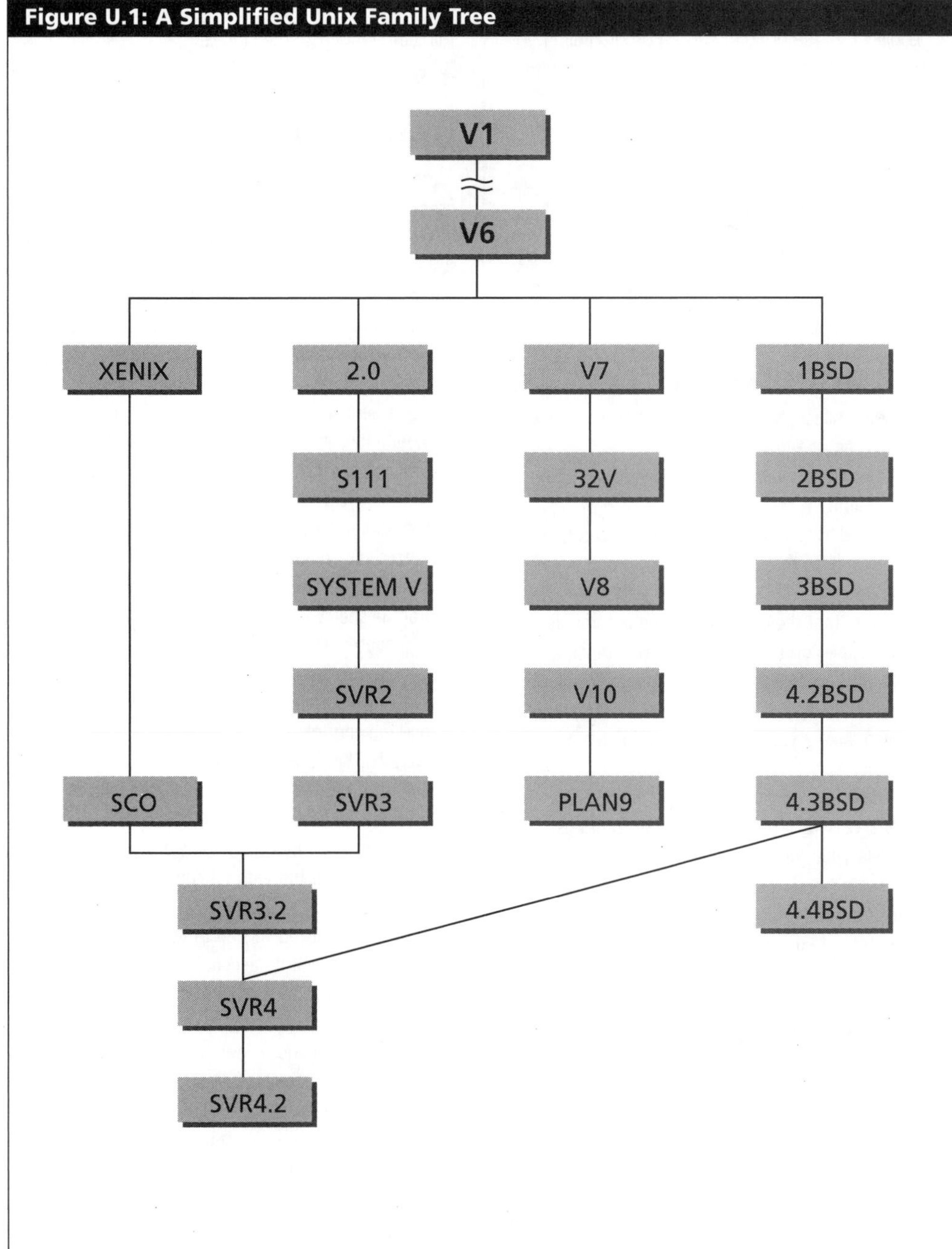

offering, used in a wide range of applications and often by people with little or no interest in programming.

For more information about the sometimes confusing and always intricate history of Unix, I recommend an excellent book by Peter Salus called *A Quarter Century of Unix*.

Unix lookalike

An operating system that looks and works like Unix but does not contain any proprietary AT&T code and so is not restricted by the terms of the AT&T licenses.

Unix philosophy

The original philosophy behind the design of Unix can be summarized in a few simple rules:

- A program or command should only do one thing but should do it very well.
- If you need a new program, it is better to combine existing utilities than to write a new program from scratch.
- Make sure that the output from one program is in a form suitable for use as the input to another; in other words, create a new Unix filter if possible.
- Place portability above efficiency. Write the program in as portable a way as possible, and make no assumptions.
- Store data in an ordinary ASCII file so that it can be easily accessed by other Unix utilities; don't use a proprietary file format.
- No news is good news. If the command completes without encountering any problems, don't create any output; if an error occurs, then post a message to that effect.

Unix Programmer's Manual

A set of reference materials that describe all the features of the Unix operating system. The traditional documentation was organized into eight sections. As systems have grown in complexity, however, the old numbering scheme has largely been abandoned, and the manual has been split up into separate volumes. Most manuals still feature the permuted index.

■ *See also* **`man` pages.**

Unix shell

A program found on every Unix system that acts as the user interface, interpreting the commands that you type at the keyboard and passing them on to the operating system below for execution. Also called a *command interpreter*, the shell sets up standard input, standard output, and standard error, lets you customize your Unix session environment, and gives access to a shell programming language for creating shell scripts.

Some versions of Unix provide only one shell, others provide many, and you choose which one you like best. Common shells include:

- Bourne shell: Very compact and simple to use, the Bourne shell is the original Unix shell.
- Korn shell: Perhaps the most popular shell, the Korn shell is an upward compatible extension to the Bourne shell with a history file, command-line editing, aliases, and job control.
- C shell: The first BSD shell, the C shell uses C-like syntax and offers a history mechanism, aliasing, and job control.
- `bash`: The Bourne-again shell from the Free Software Foundation extends the capabilities of the Bourne shell in a way similar to the Korn shell.
- `rc`: A small, compact, and elegant shell with a strong C flavor but without command-line editing or job control.
- Tcsh: An enhanced version of the C shell.
- Zsh: A large shell that seems to offer all the features present in all the other shells.

Restricted versions of many of these shells are also available, which do not allow the user the same flexibility that the normal shells offer; for example, when using a restricted shell, you may not be allowed to change to another directory, and you may be limited to read-only access to files and directories. This might be used when restricting access for guest accounts or for systems accessed by modem.

■ *See also* **Bash, `csh`, `ksh`, `rc`, `sh`, Tcsh, Zsh.**

UnixWare

A version of the Unix operating system, based on Unix System V Release 4.2, originally available from Novell and now available from SCO.

UnixWare is available in two versions:

- Personal Edition: A two-user system for applications that supports up to two processors.
- Application Server: A multiuser, server system that can scale up to twelve processors.

UnixWare supports multiple threads and offers extensive network support. A separate software development kit, which includes a C/C++ compiler, debugger, and other development tools, is also available.

Unix wars

A term that describes the differences of opinion expressed by adherents of different versions of Unix.

See also **holy wars.**

`unlimit`

A built-in C shell command that removes a resource limit. It is used to undo any `limit` commands, and the syntax is:

```
unlimit [resources]
```

where *`resources`* is one of the elements listed in Table U.7.

If you don't specify *`resources`*, all limits are removed.

See also **`limit`.**

unmoderated newsgroups

A USENET newsgroup or mailing list in which posts are not subject to review before distribution. You will find the discussions in unmoderated newsgroups to be wildly spontaneous, but they will also contain more than their fair share of flames and flame wars.

See also **alt newsgroups, moderated newsgroups.**

unnamed pipe

A special file used to pass the standard output of one program to the standard input of another. Unnamed pipes can only be used between processes that share the same parent process.

See also **named pipe, pipe.**

`unpack`

A command that expands a file compressed with `pack`. The syntax is:

```
unpack file-list
```

where *`file-list`* contains the names of the packed files you want to uncompress. All such files have the filename extension `.z`; this is assumed so you don't have to type it on the command line.

See also **`compact`, `compress`, `gzip`, `pack`, `pcat`, `uncompact`, `uncompress`, `zcat`.**

Table U.7: Resource Names Used with `unlimit`

RESOURCE	DESCRIPTION
`cputime`	Maximum number of processor seconds
`filesize`	Maximum size of any file
`datasize`	Maximum size of data, including the stack
`stacksize`	Maximum size of the stack
`coredumpsize`	Maximum size of a core dump file

unset

A built-in command that removes one or more variables. The Bourne shell syntax is:

```
unset names
```

where *names* specifies the variable or variables you want to remove.

In the Korn shell, functions must be explicitly stated using the `-f` option, as in:

```
unset -f names
```

if you want to turn off a shell option.

And in the C shell, you can specify variable names using filename metacharacters. You can also unset C shell variables by setting them to their opposite value.

■ *See also* **set, setenv, unsetenv.**

unsetenv

A built-in C shell command that removes an environment variable. The syntax is:

```
unsetenv name
```

where *name* represents the variable you want to remove. You cannot specify environment variable names using filename metacharacters.

■ *See also* **set, setenv, unset.**

unshielded cable

Any cable not protected from electromagnetic interference or radio frequency interference (BFI) by an outer foil shield.

unshielded twisted pair cable

Abbreviated UTP. Cable that contains two or more pairs of twisted copper wires. The greater the number of twists, the lower the crosstalk or interference between the pairs. UTP is offered in both voice grade and data grade. The advantages of UTP include ease of installation and low cost of materials. Its drawbacks are limited signaling speeds and shorter maximum cable-segment lengths.

■ *See also* **shielded twisted pair cable.**

unsubscribe

To remove the name of a USENET newsgroup from the list of newsgroups maintained by your newsreader. If you change your mind, you can subscribe to that same newsgroup again in the future.

until

A Bourne shell and Korn shell programming construct often used with `test` to set up a loop. The loop continues to run as long as the results are false (returns a non-zero value). When a true value is returned, the loop terminates. An example might look like this:

```
until condition
do
    commands
done
```

■ *See also* **do, done, fi, for, if, then, until, while.**

unvis

A BSD command that reverses the effect of the `vis` command, and converts nonprinting characters back into their original forms.

■ *See also* **vis.**

UPS

Abbreviation for uninterruptible power supply, pronounced "you-pea-ess." An alternative power source, usually consisting of a set of batteries, used to power a computer system when the normal power service is interrupted or falls below acceptable levels. An online UPS continuously monitors and modifies the power flowing through the unit. If an outage occurs, the UPS continues to provide regulated power.

An offline UPS monitors the AC level but only switches in when the power drops below a preset level, so a slight time lag is possible. Because a UPS system is expensive, it is usually applied only to the most critical devices on the network, such as servers, routers, gateways, and independent hard disks.

`uptime`

A command that shows how long the system has been up by displaying the current time, how long the system has been running, the number of users currently logged in, and the system load averages for the last one, five, and fifteen minutes.

See also **`ruptime`, `w`, `who`.**

URL

Acronym for Uniform Resource Locator, pronounced "earl." A method of accessing Internet resources.

URLs contain information about both the access method to use and also about the resource itself. They are used by Web browsers to connect you directly to a specific document or page on the World Wide Web, without your having to know where that resource is located physically. A sample URL might look like this:

```
http://www.austin.ibm.com
```

The first part of the URL, before the colon, specifies the access method. On the Web, this is usually `http` (for Hypertext Transfer Protocol), but you might also see file, `ftp`, or gopher instead. The second part of the URL, after the colon, specifies the resource. The text after the two slashes usually indicates a server name, and the text after the single slash defines the directory or individual file you will connect to. If you are linking to a document, it will usually have the filename extension `.html`, the abbreviation for Hypertext Markup Language.

URLs are always case-sensitive, so pay particular attention to uppercase and lowercase letters and to symbols as well.

usage message

A message displayed when you try to use a command with incorrect command-line arguments.

USENET

Acronym for User Network. An international, noncommercial network, linking many thousands of Unix sites.

Although there is a very close relationship between the Internet and USENET, they are not the same thing by any means. USENET predates the Internet; in the early days, information was distributed by dial-up connections. Not every Internet computer is part of USENET, and not every USENET system can be reached from the Internet.

Like the Internet, USENET has no central governing body; USENET is run by the people who use it. With well over 10,000 different newsgroups, USENET is accessed by millions of people every day, in more than 100 countries.

See also **alt newsgroups, moderated newsgroups, USENET newsgroups, UUCP.**

USENET articles

An individual message sent to one of the USENET newsgroups. A USENET article has three parts: a header, followed by the body text, and the signature.

The header contains technical information about the article and can contain up to 20 lines; indeed, sometimes the header is longer than the actual article text. Some newsreaders show all header information, others do not, and some can be configured either way.

The body text is the actual text of the article; the part that you want to read.

The signature is optional and is added to the end of an article. It is a good idea to keep your signature short.

USENET newsgroups

The individual discussion groups within USENET.

USENET newsgroups contain articles posted by Internet and USENET subscribers; very few of them contain actual hard news.

Most newsgroups are concerned with a single subject; the range of subjects available through USENET is phenomenal—you can choose from over 10,000 different newsgroups. If people are interested in a subject, you are sure to find a newsgroup for it somewhere; you can post your own articles and browse through similar items posted by others. When you reply to a post, you can reply to the newsgroup so that other subscribers can read your reply, or you can respond directly to the originator in a private e-mail message.

The newsgroups that specialize in pictures contain the word `binary` somewhere in the newsgroup name. The picture files are first converted to text with the `uuencode` utility; you use `uudecode` to turn this text back into a graphical image you can view.

■ *See also* **netiquette, newbie.**

USENIX

A nonprofit organization founded in 1975 for individuals and institutions interested in Unix.

USENIX fosters communication of technical developments, provides a forum for discussion of technical issues, and sponsors two large technical conferences every year, as well as other smaller symposia.

USENIX publishes transactions from these technical meetings, a bimonthly newsletter called `;login`, and a technical quarterly called *Computing Systems.*

You can contact USENIX at:

The USENIX Association
2560 Ninth Street
Suite 215
Berkeley, CA 94710 U.S.A.

You can also contact them by e-mail at `office@usenix.org`.

■ *See also* **SAGE.**

user

A person, known to the system, who is allowed to log on and use the system. Sometimes abbreviated usr.

user identifier

A number kept in the `/etc/passwd` file, which identifies a specific user of the system and, along with the group identifier, defines the user's access permissions to the system. Sometimes abbreviated user ID or even UID.

■ *See* **username.**

username

The name of a specific user; also called *login ID.*

■ *See also* **user identifier.**

users

A command that displays the currently logged-in users as a space-separated sorted list. `users` has no options.

■ *See also* **`finger`, `last`, `rusers`, `rwho`, `w`, `who`.**

/usr

A general-purpose directory that contains the subdirectories and files that make up most of the Unix system software and documentation. In SVR4, `/usr` has a number of important subdirectories, as shown in Table U.8.

If you are working on a proprietary Unix or an earlier release of System V, you may find the contents of `/usr` are slightly different.

■ *See also* **`/bin`, `/etc`, `/home`, `/lost+found`, root directory, `/tmp`, `/var`.**

utility

A program included as part of the standard Unix package. You can use a utility by entering its name at the command prompt, or you can include it in shell scripts. Utilities are often referred to as commands in casual conversation, but they should not be confused with built-in shell commands.

Table U.8: /usr Subdirectories	
DIRECTORY	DESCRIPTION
/usr/bin	Contains executable versions of Unix commands and utilities.
/usr/include	Contains header files for C programs.
/usr/games	Contains Unix games.
/usr/lib	Contains compiled C program library files, daemons, and the like.
/usr/local	Contains programs specific to your installation.
/usr/sbin	Contains executable programs used when the system first starts running (on older systems these programs may be in /bin or /etc) and system administration programs.
/usr/share	Contains platform-independent documentation, including man pages and source files if they are available.
/usr/src	Contains Unix source files if they are available.
/usr/ucb	Contains BSD-specific versions of certain programs, and you may also find the BSD compatability package in this directory.

uucp

A command used to copy files from one Unix system to another using a dial-up line and a modem.

▶ Syntax

The syntax to use for uucp is:

```
uucp [options][source!]file
➥[destination!]file
```

▶ Options and Arguments

The uucp command copies one or more files from the *source* to the *destination*, where *destination* is usually a remote Unix system; sometimes *destination* specifies a directory. *source* and *destination* can also be preceded by an optional host name followed by a bang or exclamation point in the form:

hostname!*filename*

and any wildcards used are expanded on the appropriate machine. See Table U.9 for a description of the options you can use with uucp.

▶ Examples

To copy all the prog files from /home/jenny on the remote manor system to /home/pmd, use:

```
uucp manor\!/home/jenny/
➥prog.\* /home/pmd/
```

In this example, note that the exclamation point (!) and the wildcard (*) must be escaped with a backslash (\); these metacharacters must be protected from expansion on the local computer.

▶ Notes

If the file being transferred is an executable file, the file permissions are preserved after the transfer.

uucp cannot connect to just any Unix system; certain files on the remote machine must be configured properly first; see your system administrator for more details.

Table U.9: Options to Use with uucp

OPTION	DESCRIPTION
`-c`	Uses the original source file, rather than copying the file to the spool directory first; this is the default mode on most systems.
`-C`	Copies the original file to the spool directory and transmits this copy.
`-d`	Creates all the necessary directories if they do not already exist.
`-f`	Does not create intermediate directories if they do not already exist.
`-g`*`n`*	Sets a priority of *`n`*; use `uuglist` to display the values available for *`n`*.
`-j`	Displays the `uucp` job number; you can then use `uustat` to check the status of the job.
`-m`	Sends an e-mail message to the person requesting the transfer when the job is complete.
`-n` *`user`*	Notifies *`user`* on the remote system by e-mail that the transfer is complete.
`-r`	Queues the job without starting the transfer.
`-s` *`filename`*	Sends a status report to *`filename`*.
`-x` *`n`*	Sets the debug level to *`n`*, where *`n`* is between 0 and 9 with the higher numbers giving more detailed output.

`uucp` is a spooled process; it takes your requests and executes them for you so you do not have to interact with or watch the program work.

See also **uudecode, uuencode, uuglist, uulog, uuname, uupick, uuq, uusend, uustat, uuto, uux.**

UUCP configuration

UUCP is a Unix-to-Unix communications package, developed at Bell Laboratories by Mike Lesk in the mid-1970s for serial communications between in-house Unix systems. It was revised in 1978, and in the early 1980s, a package known as BNU (basic networking utilities) was developed by P. Honeyman, D.A. Nowitz, and B.E. Redman. This version became known as HoneyDanBer UUCP. An even newer version, known as Taylor UUCP, is also available on some systems, particularly Linux.

UUCP provides:

- File transfer between two hosts
- A communications protocol for e-mail and USENET newsgroups
- Control of communications devices
- A set of utilities for managing the UUCP package

UUCP is usually set up by a system administrator, and configuration consists of:

- Telling your system what kind of modems you have on your computer and where they are located
- Describing how to talk to these modems
- Listing all the other systems that you would like to connect with, along with their phone numbers and passwords

The directory structure on System V Release 4 HoneyDanBer uses four major directories and subdirectories within these directories: `/etc/uucp` contains control files, `/usr/lib/uucp` contains `uucp` utilities, `/var/uucp` contains temporary files, and /var/spool/uucp contains public files. Other systems may be different: SCO stores control files in /etc, utilities and data files in /usr/lib/uucp, and temporary files and log files in /usr/spool/uucp.

UUCP is a set of utilities just like other Unix utilities. Table U.10 summarizes the various utilities in the UUCP system.

Because UUCP was designed for in-house use, it has some features that are less than secure in these days of crackers, viruses, and worms; talk to your system administrator about security. UUCP networks are found throughout the world and continue to perform important functions, connecting users who cannot access the Internet directly. Because UUCP is available on all sorts of systems, many other applications have been made compatible with it. UUCP is a big subject, and several very good books are available, covering system administration issues, security, and using **uucp** with USENET.

See also **uucp, uudecode, uuencode, uuglist, uulog, uuname, uupick, uuq, uusend, uustat, uuto, uux.**

uucp network address

See **bang path.**

uudecode

A command that reads a file encoded by **uuencode** and recreates the original file. The syntax is:

```
uudecode filename
```

See also **uucp, uuencode, uuglist, uulog, uuname, uupick, uuq, uusend, uustat, uuto, uux.**

uuencode

A command that reads a binary file and converts it into an ASCII text file that can be sent over communications links that do not support binary transfers. This technique is often used to send binary files to a USENET newsgroup as e-mail. The recipient of the encoded file must use **uudecode** to restore the file back into binary form before the file can be used.

The syntax for **uuencode** is as follows:

```
uuencode filename pathname
```

Table U.10: UUCP Utilities

UTILITY	DESCRIPTION
uucico	Manages file transport for the UUCP system.
uucp	Sends files between Unix systems, and lets you request files from other systems.
uuglist	Lists options available for uux and uucp.
uuname	Lists names of UUCP hosts.
uupick	Obtains files from a remote system.
uuq	Manages the UUCP queue (BSD systems only).
uusend	Sends a file to a remote host (BSD systems only).
uustat	Displays the status of the UUCP queue for both local and remote systems.
uuto	Sends a file from one Unix system to another.
uux	Executes commands on the remote system.

U

where *filename* is the name of the binary file and *pathname* specifies where the decoded file should be stored.

When you encode a binary file with `uuencode`, the file grows by approximately 35 percent, so you often find that a particularly large file is divided into several smaller sections labeled, if the file is divided into four parts, for example, 1/4, 2/4, 3/4, and 4/4. You must find all the parts before you can decode and use the file. A large file may also be compressed before being encoded.

Due to the current popularity of the Internet and USENET, `uuencode` and `uudecode` programs are available on many different operating systems, including DOS, OS/2, and Microsoft Windows.

See also **uucp, uudecode, uuglist, uulog, uuname, uupick, uuq, uusend, uustat, uuto, uux.**

uuglist

A command that lists the priority levels available for use with the `-g` option of `uucp` or `uux`. A single option, `-u` lists the priorities available to the current user.

See also **uucp, uudecode, uuencode, uulog, uuname, uupick, uuq, uusend, uustat, uuto, uux.**

uulog

A command that displays the contents of the `uucp` and `uux` log files using the `tail` command.

See also **tail, uucp, uudecode, uuencode, uuglist, uuname, uupick, uuq, uusend, uustat, uuto, uux.**

uuname

A command that lists the names of known remote UUCP hosts. The syntax is:

```
uuname [options]
```

Two options are available; `-c` lists the names of the systems known to the `cu` command, and `-l` displays the name of your own system.

See also **uucp, uudecode, uuencode, uuglist, uulog, uupick, uuq, uusend, uustat, uuto, uux.**

uupick

An SVR4 command used to retrieve files sent to you by a user on a remote system using the `uucp` command. When files arrive from a remote system, they are stored in a special directory, usually `/usr/spool/uucppublic/receive/`*user*`/`*system*, where *user* is your username and *system* is the name of the computer from which the files were transferred. You can use `uupick` to move the files to a more appropriate location. `uupick` has one option, `-s` *system*, which limits it to locating files transferred from that remote *system*.

The program is interactive and presents you with the names of the files sent to you one-by-one. You can use the interactive options listed in Table U.11 to tell `uupick` what to do with them.

See also **uucp, uudecode, uuencode, uuglist, uulog, uuname, uuq, uusend, uustat, uuto, uux.**

uuq

A BSD command that displays the entries in the `uucp` queue.

▶ Syntax

The syntax for this command is as follows:

```
uuq [options]
```

▶ Options and Arguments

The options available for use with `uuq` are listed in Table U.12; the default display only shows each job's number.

See also **uucp, uudecode, uuencode, uuglist, uulog, uuname, uupick, uusend, uustat, uuto, uux.**

Table U.11: Options to Use with uupick

OPTION	DESCRIPTION
`?` or `*`	Displays a summary of commands.
Enter or Return	Goes to the next item.
`a` *`directory`*	Moves all the files to the specified *`directory`*; if *`directory`* is not specified, the current directory is assumed.
`d`	Deletes the current entry.
`m` *`directory`*	Moves the current entry to the specified *`directory`*; if the current item is a directory, all its subdirectories are also moved.
`p`	Sends the current file to the standard output; does not apply to directories.
`q`	Quits `uupick`.
`!`*`command`*	Executes *`command`* in a subshell.

Table U.12: Options to Use with uuq

OPTIONS	DESCRIPTION
`-b`*`baud`*	Uses the specified *`baud`* when calculating transfer times; the default is 1200.
`-d`*`jobnumber`*	Deletes the specified *`jobnumber`*.
`-h`	Displays summary information for each file, including system name, number of jobs, and total number of bytes to send.
`-l`	Displays complete information for each file, including job number and username, number of files waiting for transmission, number of bytes to send, and the type of command (`S` for sending files, `R` for receiving files, and `X` for remote `uucp`).
`-r`*`sdir`*	Uses the specified *`sdir`* directory as the spool directory, rather than the default directory.
`-s`*`system`*	Displays information for the specified *`system`*.
`-u`*`user`*	Displays information for the specified *`user`*.

uusend

A BSD command used to send a file to a remote host. This remote host does not have to be directly connected to your system, but a chain of `uucp` links must exist between the two systems so that the file can be transmitted.

The syntax is:

```
uusend [option]source
➥ hostname!...!destination
```

where *`source`* is the name of the file you wish to transmit, *`hostname`* is a `uucp` network address or bang path to the remote computer, and *`destination`* is the name for the file once it reaches the remote system.

A single option, `-m` *`number`*, sets the file mode to the specified octal number. If you don't use this option, the original mode of the source file is used.

■ *See also* **uucp, uudecode, uuencode, uuglist, uulog, uuname, uupick, uuq, uustat, uuto, uux.**

uustat

An SVR4 command that shows you the status of jobs waiting transmission by `uucp` and the status of `uucp` communications with remote systems. You can also use `uustat` to cancel `uucp` requests.

▶ Syntax

Here's the syntax:

```
uustat [options]
```

▶ Options and Arguments

You will find that the `uustat` options vary from system to system; check the `man` pages on your system before using this command. Table U.13 lists the most common command-line options; others are available but only to the superuser.

The `-s` and `-u` options can be used together; all other options must be used by themselves.

■ *See also* **uucp, uudecode, uuencode, uuglist, uulog, uuname, uupick, uuq, uusend, uuto, uux.**

Table U.13: Common Options to Use with uustat

OPTION	DESCRIPTION
`-a`	Displays the names of all jobs waiting to be transmitted.
`-k` *`id`*	Kills the job with the identifier of *`id`*; you must be the owner to execute this option.
`-s` *`system`*	Reports the status of jobs destined for *`system`*.
`-u` *`user`*	Reports the status of jobs originated by *`user`*.

uuto

An SVR4 command that sends a set of files or directories to a remote system, where a user can retrieve the file using `uupick`. The syntax is:

```
uuto [options] files
➥ destination
```

where *`files`* represents the files or directories you want to transmit, and *`destination`* is in the form of:

```
system!user
```

Two command-line options are available, as shown in Table U.14.

■ *See also* **bang path, uucp, uudecode, uuencode, uuglist, uulog, uuname, uupick, uuq, uusend, uustat, uux.**

uux

A command that lets you transfer files to a remote system and then execute a command on the specified system.

▶ Syntax

The syntax to use with `uux` is as follows:

```
uux [options]
➥[[system]!command]
```

Table U.14: Options to Use with uuto	
OPTION	**DESCRIPTION**
`-p`	Copies each file to be transmitted into a spool directory; any subsequent changes to the original are not reflected in the transmitted file.
`-m`	Sends an e-mail message to the sender when the transmission is complete.

▶ Options and Arguments

The options you can use with **uux** are listed in Table U.15.

▶ Notes

Some system administrators will not let you use this command on their systems for security reasons.

■ *See also* **bang path, uucp, uudecode, uuencode, uuglist, uulog, uuname, uupick, uuq, uusend, uustat, uuto, uux.**

Table U.15: Options to Use with uux	
OPTION	**DESCRIPTION**
`-`	Makes the standard input to **uux** the standard input to *command*; same as `-p`.
`-a`*name*	Uses *name* instead of original username.
`-c`	Uses the original source file, rather than copying the file to the spool directory first; this is the default mode on most systems.
`-C`	Copies the original file to the spool directory and transmits this copy.
`-g`*n*	Sets a priority of *n*; use **uuglist** to display the values available for *n*.
`-j`	Displays the **uux** job number.
`-n`	Does not send e-mail if the job fails.
`-p`	Makes the standard input to **uux** the standard input to *command*; same as `-`.
`-r`	Queues the job without starting the transfer.
`-s` *filename*	Sends a status report to *filename*.
`-x` *n*	Sets the debug level to *n*, where *n* is between 0 and 9 with the higher numbers giving more detailed output.
`-z`	Notifies user on successful completion.

U

V

vacation

A command that tells anyone who sends you e-mail that you are on vacation.

▶ Syntax

The syntax for this command is:

```
vacation [options]
```

▶ Options and Arguments

You can use the options listed in Table V.1 with the `vacation` command.

▶ Examples

Once you return from vacation, you can disable this command by entering:

```
mail -F " "
```

■ *See also* **`mail`**, **`mailx`**.

val

■ *See* **SCCS.**

vanilla

A term used to describe something that is considered to be ordinary and lacks additional features.

■ *See also* **canonical.**

/var

An SVR4 directory that contains system files that often change, such as files waiting to be printed, log files, and mail files. On older Unix systems, these files are scattered through several subdirectories of `/usr`.

Subdirectories include `/var/admin`, which contains accounting information and other files used by the system administrator, and `/var/spool`, which holds spool files, temporary files waiting for processing. You can also find the subdirectories `/var/adm`, `/var/cron`, `/var/lp`, `/var/mail`, `/var/news`, and `/var/uucp` on most systems.

■ *See also* **`/dev`**, **`/etc`**, **`/sbin`**, **`/home`**, **`/lost+found`**, **`/tmp`**, **`/usr`**.

Table V.1: Options to Use with vacation	
OPTION	DESCRIPTION
-a*alias*	Handles messages for *alias* in the same way as those received for your normal login name.
-i	A BSD option that initializes the vacation database file.
-I*username*	A Solaris option that forwards your mail to *username*, and sends back a message that you are on vacation.
-r*days*	A BSD option that sets the reply interval to *days*; the default is seven days.
-t*n*	A Solaris option used to set the time interval between repeat replies to the same sender to the value *n*; the default is one week.

variable

A data item name and its associated value. The shell inherits several variables when it is invoked, and it maintains these and other variables as it runs. You can also create your own variables and use them in your shell scripts.

■ *See also* **global variable, local variable.**

vedit

A command that is an alias for the `vi` editor specially configured for beginning users. Using `vedit` is just like using `vi`, except that certain internal `vi` variables are set so that the user easily avoids problem areas.

■ *See also* **`vi`, `view`.**

Veronica

A search service built into the Gopher Internet application. When you use Veronica to search a series of Gopher menus (files, directories, and other items), the results of the search are presented as another Gopher menu, which you can use to access the resources your search has located. Veronica supposedly stands for very easy rodent-oriented net-wide index to computer archives.

■ *See also* **Archie, Gopherspace, Jughead.**

Version 4

AT&T's 1974 release of Unix. This version was not widely distributed outside AT&T.

■ *See also* **BSD, Unix history.**

Version 5

AT&T's 1977 release of Unix. This version was distributed to colleges and universities.

■ *See also* **BSD, Unix history.**

Version 6

AT&T's first official release of Unix, made in 1977. This version was distributed commercially, and although primitive by today's standards, it marked the beginning of widespread interest in Unix.

■ *See also* **BSD, Unix history.**

Version 7

AT&T's second official release of Unix, made in 1979. This version was distributed commercially and is considered by many to be the first viable Unix system. Version 7 introduced many features considered standard today, including the Bourne shell and the `troff` typesetting system.

■ *See also* **BSD, Unix history.**

version number

A method of identifying a particular software or hardware release.

The version number is assigned by the software developer and often includes numbers before and after a decimal point; the higher the number, the more recent the release. The number before the decimal point indicates the major revision levels, while the part after the decimal indicates a minor revision level, which in some cases can actually produce a significant difference in performance.

Many people steer clear of any release labeled 1.0, because this number implies the first release of a product that may not have had extensive real-world use. Microsoft has recently avoided this issue in several innovative ways. The first release of Windows NT was called version 3.1 (instead of 1.0) to associate it in the minds of buyers with the incredibly successful Windows 3.1, and then the replacement for Windows 3.1 was called Windows 95 (again, instead of 1.0), so as to avoid associations with the version numbering scheme entirely.

vertical application

An application program specifically created for a very narrow and specialized market or profession. Software that manages a veterinary hospital is an example of a vertical application.

vertical bar symbol

The | symbol. Used on the command line to pipe the output of one program into the input of another. For example:

```
ls -l | more
```

pipes the long format listing created by the `ls` command into the `more` filter so you can look at the output page by page. In the C shell, you can use |& to pipe both standard output and standard error.

Two vertical bars together on the command line:

`command1` || *`command2`*

means to execute *`command2`* if *`command1`* fails.

A vertical bar is also used in `awk` and `grep` to separate two regular expressions by an OR.

vgrind

A BSD command used to format program listings using `troff`. Any comments in the source code are printed in italic, keywords are printed in bold, and the name of the current function is listed in the margin.

vi

A popular Unix screen editor based on `ex`, originally written by Bill Joy as part of the BSD Unix systems. Pronounced "vee-eye," an acronym for visual editor.

▶ Syntax

The syntax used to start `vi` is as follows:

`vi [`*`options`*`][`*`filenames`*`]`

Here are some of the most common ways you can start `vi`:

`vi` *`filename`*

opens the editor on the specified file starting at line one. If you don't include a *`filename`*, `vi` opens an empty buffer.

To open the specified file starting at line *n*:

`vi +`*`n filename`*

To open the file at the last line:

`vi +` *`filename`*

To open the specified file at the first line containing *`pattern`*:

`vi +/`*`pattern filename`*

If you are using `vi` to recover files after a system failure, the following command displays the names of files that you can recover:

```
vi -r
```

To start `vi` and recover the specified file:

`vi -r` *`filename`*

▶ Options and Arguments

The command-line options you can use with `vi` are similar to those used with `ex` and are listed in Table V.2.

▶ Command Mode and Input Mode

Unlike some of the other editors you encounter in the Unix world, `vi` operates in two quite different modes: input mode and command mode. When `vi` is in input mode, everything you type is inserted as text into the current editing buffer. When `vi` is in command mode, all the characters you type are interpreted as commands.

`vi` starts an editing session in command mode, and you can:

- Use the `vi` editing commands.
- Move the cursor to a new location in the editing buffer.
- Invoke a Unix shell, and use Unix utilities or commands.
- Change to insert mode.
- Save the current version of the editing buffer into a file.

Several commands put `vi` into input mode, including Append, Change, Insert, Open, and Replace. Table V.3 briefly describes these commands.

When you are in input mode, everything you type is treated as text and is added to the edit buffer; you can press the Escape key to return to command mode. To enter a control character, use Ctrl-V followed by the control character you want to use.

Table V.2: Options to Use with vi

OPTION	DESCRIPTION
`-c`*`command`*	Starts an editing session by executing the specified `vi` command.
`-C`	Same as `-x` but assumes that *`filename`* is in encrypted form.
`-l`	Runs in LISP mode.
`-L`	Lists filenames saved due to an editor or system crash.
`-r`*`filename`*	Recovers and opens the specified *`filename`*.
`-R`	Opens `vi` in read-only mode; files cannot be changed.
`-t` *`tag`*	Edits the file containing *`tag`*.
`-w`*`n`*	Sets the window size to *`n`*.
`-x`	Requires a key to encrypt or decrypt *`filename`*.
`+`	Starts `vi` on the last line of the file.
`+`*`n`*	Starts `vi` on the line of the file specified by *`n`*.
`+/`*`pattern`*	Starts `vi` on the line of the file that contains *`pattern`*.

▶ Moving Around in vi

There are many `vi` commands for moving the cursor to a new location, and for moving through the edit buffer. These commands are listed in Table V.4.

▶ Editing Commands

In `vi`, editing commands look like this:

```
[n] operator [m] item
```

where the *`operator`* might be `c` to begin a change, `d` to begin a deletion, or `y` to begin a yank (copy) operation, and *`n`* and *`m`* are multipliers indicating how many times the operation is to be performed. The *`item`* can be a word, sentence, paragraph, or whole section of text. `vi` uses a large number of editing commands, and some of the most useful are listed in Table V.5.

The editing commands in Table V.5 that start with a colon (`:`) are actually `ex` commands invoked from inside `vi`.

▶ Searching for Patterns

Searching for a specific pattern of characters is an excellent way to navigate through the edit buffer. If you type `/`, `vi` displays a `/` on the command line at the bottom

Table V.3: Commands That Invoke Input Mode in `vi`	
COMMAND	DESCRIPTION
`a`	Initiates input mode, and appends new text after the current cursor position.
`A`	Initiates input mode, and appends new text at the end of the current line.
`c`	Initiates input mode, and starts a change operation.
`C`	Initiates input mode, and starts a change to the end of the line.
`i`	Initiates input mode, and lets you insert new text before the cursor position.
`I`	Initiates input mode, and allows you to insert new text at the beginning of the current line.
`o`	Initiates input mode, and opens a new line before the current line; the cursor moves to the start of this new blank line.
`O`	Initiates input mode, and opens a new line after the current line; the cursor moves to the start of this new blank line.
`R`	Initiates input mode, and begins overwriting text with as many new characters as you specify until you press the Escape key. `vi` then returns to command mode.

V

Table V.4: `vi` Cursor Movement Commands	
COMMAND	DESCRIPTION
Moving the Cursor	
`h` or ← or `backspace`	Moves the cursor one position to the left, without moving past the beginning of the current line. If you precede this command with a count *n*, the cursor moves *n* characters.
`j` or ↓	Moves the cursor one position down.
`k` or ↑	Moves the cursor one position up.
`l` or → or `space`	Moves the cursor one position to the right, without moving past the end of the current line. If you precede this command with a count *n*, the cursor moves *n* characters.
-	Moves the cursor to the beginning of the previous line.
+ or `Return`.	Moves the cursor to the beginning of the next line.
0	Moves the cursor to the beginning of the current line.
$	Moves the cursor to the end of the current line.
^	Moves the cursor to the first nonspace or tab in the current line.

Table V.4: `vi` Cursor Movement Commands (continued)

COMMAND	DESCRIPTION
`b`	Moves the cursor backward to the first character of the previous word. If you precede this command with a count *n*, the cursor moves back *n* words.
`e`	Moves the cursor forward to the last character of the next word.
`w`	Moves the cursor forward to the first character of the next word. If you precede this command with a count *n*, the cursor moves forward *n* words.
`B`	Same as `b` ignoring punctuation. If you precede this command with a count *n*, the cursor moves back *n* words.
`E`	Same as `e`, ignoring punctuation.
`W`	Same as `w`, ignoring punctuation. If you precede this command with a count *n*, the cursor moves forward *n* words.
`)`	Moves the cursor forward to the beginning of the next sentence.
`(`	Moves the cursor backward to the beginning of the previous sentence.
`}`	Moves the cursor forward to the beginning of the next paragraph.
`{`	Moves the cursor backward to the beginning of the previous paragraph.
`]]`	Moves the cursor forward to the next section boundary.
`[[`	Moves the cursor backward to the previous section boundary.
`H`	Moves the cursor to the first line of the editing buffer.
`L`	Moves the cursor to the last line of the editing buffer.
`M`	Moves the cursor to the middle line of the editing buffer.
Moving through the Editing Buffer	
`Ctrl-B`	Moves up one screenful.
`Ctrl-D`	Moves down half a screenful.
`Ctrl-F`	Moves down one screenful.
`Ctrl-U`	Moves up half a screenful.
Going to a Line Number	
n`G`	Goes to line number *n*.
`1G`	Goes to the first line in the buffer.
`G`	Goes to the last line in the buffer.

Table V.5: `vi` Editing Commands

COMMAND	DESCRIPTION
Making Changes	
`~`	Changes the case of a letter.
`c`*`move`*	Replaces from the cursor location to *`move`* by inserting new text.
`cc`	Replaces the entire contents of the line by inserting new text.
`C`	Replaces from the position of the cursor to the end of the line by insertion.
`ddp`	Transposes two lines.
`deep`	Transposes two words.
`r`	Replaces one character but does not enter input mode.
`R`	Replaces by overstrike.
`s`	Replaces the current line by insertion.
`xp`	Transposes two characters.
Undoing and Repeating Changes	
`.`	Repeats the last command to modify the editing buffer.
`u`	Undoes the last command that modified the editing buffer. To undo the undo, use `uu`, which leaves the line in its original state.
`U`	Restores the current line.
`Ctrl-l`	Refreshes the screen.
Deleting Text	
`d`*`move`*	Deletes from the cursor to *`move`*.
`dd`	Deletes the current line.
`dG`	Deletes from the current line to the end of the buffer.
`:`*`line`*	Goes to the start of the specified *`line`*.
`:`*`line`*`d`	Deletes the specified line.
`:`*`line`*`,`*`line`*`d`	Deletes the specified range of lines.

Table V.5: vi Editing Commands (continued)

COMMAND	DESCRIPTION
D	Deletes from the cursor to the end of the line.
x	Deletes the character at the position of the cursor.
X	Deletes the character to the left of the cursor.
Inserting Text	
:*line*r *filename*	Inserts contents of *filename* after the specified *line*.
:r *filename*	Inserts contents of *filename* after the current line.
:*line*r !*command*	Inserts the output of *command* after the specified *line*.
:r !*command*	Inserts the output of *command* after the current *line*.
:r !look*pattern*	Inserts words that begin with the specified *pattern*.
Copying and Moving Lines	
:*line*co*target*	Copies the specified line, and inserts it after *target*.
:*line*,*line*co*target*	Copies the specified range, and inserts it after *target*.
:*line*m*target*	Moves the specified line, and inserts it after *target*.
:*line*,*line*m*target*	Moves the specified range, and inserts it after *target*.
Executing Shell Commands	
:!*command*	Pauses vi, and executes the specified shell *command*.
:!!	Pauses vi, and executes the previous shell *command*.
:sh	Pauses vi, and starts a shell.
:!csh	Pauses vi, and starts the C shell.
Saving Your Work	
:w	Writes data out to the original file without quitting vi.
:w *filename*	Writes data out to the specified *filename*.
:w> *filename*	Appends data to the end of the specified filename.
Quitting vi	
:q	Quits vi without saving data.
ZZ	Saves data, and quits vi.

of the screen. Enter a pattern, press Return, and `vi` searches for the next occurrence of that pattern. Press / followed by Return to repeat the same search. Table V.6 lists the commands you can use when searching for and replacing a pattern, as well as the characters you can use in regular expressions.

▶ Notes

When `vi` first starts up, it looks for a file called `.exrc` in your home directory and executes any `ex` commands that it contains.

■ *See also* **`emacs`, `ex`, `vedit`, `view`, `vi` local variables.**

`vi` local variables

The `vi` editor has approximately 40 local variables you can set to customize your `vi` editing sessions. You can look at or change their values using the `vi :set` command. Some of these variables are either enabled or disabled, while others have a number or a string as their value. You can include commands for setting these variables in the `.exrc` file in your home directory.

■ *See also* **`vedit`, `vi`.**

`view`

A command that starts the `vi` text editor in read-only mode, which is the same as using `vi -R`.

■ *See also* **`vedit`, `vi`.**

view mode

In `emacs`, a read-only mode where you can look at but not change the contents of a file.

virtual console

A feature found in Linux, UnixWare, and certain other systems that allows you to log on as though you were different users. To open a new virtual console, press and hold the Alt key as you press one of the function keys F1 through F8. As you press each function key, you see a new screen complete with its own login prompt. Each virtual console displays its own output on its own virtual screen.

■ *See also* **virtual terminal.**

virtual memory

A memory management technique that allows information in physical memory to be swapped out to a hard disk. This technique provides application programs with more memory space than is actually available in the computer.

True virtual memory management requires specialized hardware in the processor for the operating system to use; it is not just a question of writing information out to a swap area on the hard disk at the application level.

In a virtual memory system, programs and their data are divided into smaller pieces called *pages*. At the point at which more memory is needed, the operating system decides which pages are least likely to be needed soon (using an algorithm based on frequency of use, most recent use, and program priority), and it writes these pages out to disk. The memory space that they used is then available to the rest of the system for other application programs. When these pages are needed again, they are loaded back into real memory, displacing other pages.

■ *See also* **paging, swapping.**

virtual terminal

A simulated terminal that behaves as though it is an independent connection to the computer but actually shares the same keyboard and screen. Linux, UnixWare, and several other systems that run on Intel-based hardware support virtual terminals.

■ *See also* **virtual console.**

`vis`

A BSD filter command that displays non-printing characters.

■ *See also* **`unvis`.**

Table V.6: Search and Replace Commands in `vi`	
COMMAND	DESCRIPTION
Searching for a Pattern	
/*expression*	Searches forward for the next occurrence of the specified regular expression.
/	Repeats the forward search for the same regular expression.
?*expression*	Searches backward for the previous occurrence of the specified regular expression.
?	Repeats the backward search for the same regular expression.
n	Repeats the last / or ? command in the same direction.
N	Repeats the last / or ? command in the opposite direction.
Replacing a Pattern	
:s/*pattern*/*replace*/	Substitutes *replace* for *pattern* in the current line.
:*lines*/*pattern*/*replace*/	Substitutes *replace* for *pattern* in the specified *lines*.
:*line*,*lines*/*pattern*/ ➥*replace*/	Substitutes *replace* for *pattern* in the specified range of lines.
:%s/*pattern*/*replace*/	Substitutes *replace* for *pattern* in all lines.
Special Characters Used in Regular Expressions	
.	Matches any single character except newline.
*	Matches zero or more of the preceding characters.
^	Matches the beginning of a line.
$	Matches the end of a line.
\<	Matches the beginning of a word.
\>	Matches the end of a word.
[ ]	Matches any of the enclosed characters.
[^]	Matches any of the characters not enclosed.
\	Interprets the following character literally, removing any special meaning the character may have had.

VISUAL

A Korn shell environment variable that invokes the visual command-line editing option in `emacs`, `gmacs`, or `vi`.

■ *See also* **emacs**, **vi**.

VMS

A popular operating system from the Digital Equipment Corporation (DEC) that runs on their popular line of VAX computers.

vmstat

A command that reports statistics on virtual memory and how it is being used. It shows the number of processes, the amount of RAM and swap area available, paging information, and disk statistics.

volume

- A named hard disk partition
- A magnetic tape on to which a filesystem has been written

VP/ix

A DOS emulation package from Sun Microsystems that allows you to access programs and data files normally under the DOS partition and use them in the Unix environment, as a task under Unix. To the user, the sessions look exactly as they would if you had changed partitions and booted DOS.

■ *See also* **Merge.**

w

A command that reports on system usage, logged on users and what they are doing, and the load average. The load average is the average number of processes in the last 1, 5, and 15 minutes.

▶ Syntax

Here's the syntax to use:

```
w [options]username
```

▶ Options and Arguments

Normally, `w` reports on all users, but if you specify *`username`* as a comma-separated list of names, the report is restricted to information on just these names. The options available with this command are listed in Table W.1.

■ *See also* **finger**, **ps**, **uptime**, **who**, **whodo**.

WABI

Abbreviation for Windows Application Binary Interface. A specification developed by Sun Microsystems that defines how Microsoft Windows and DOS applications run on Unix workstations. The WABI interface translates the system calls made by the application into system calls that the underlying Unix system can process.

WAIS

Acronym for Wide Area Information Service, pronounced "ways." A service used to access text databases or libraries on the Internet.

WAIS uses simple natural language queries and takes advantage of index searches for fast retrieval. Unlike Gopher, which only searches through the names of Gopher resources, WAIS can search the content of all documents retrievable from WAIS databases. WAIS is particularly adept at searching through collections of articles, USENET newsgroups, electronic texts, and newspaper archives.

Table W.1: Options to Use with w		
OPTION	DESCRIPTION	
`-h`	Turns off the report header line.	
`-l`	Creates a long listing, including the following columns:	
	`User`	The name of the logged on user
	`Tty`	The number of the terminal
	`Login@`	Time the user logged in
	`Idle`	Number of minutes since the user typed anything at the terminal
	`JCPU`	CPU minutes accumulated by all jobs run during this login session
	`PCPU`	Minutes accumulated by the current process
	`What`	Name of the current process and its arguments
`-q`	Creates a quick listing that consists of `User`, `Tty`, `Idle`, and `What`.	
`-t`	Displays only the heading line; equivalent to the output from `uptime`.	

wait

A command used in shell scripts that waits for all background processes to complete. If you specify a process ID, this command waits for that process to complete.

wakeup

To resume execution after sleeping for a period of time.

■ *See also* **sleep**, **`sleep`**.

wall

A command that broadcasts a message to all logged on users. The syntax is:

`wall` *`message`*

where ***`message`*** is read from the standard input and is terminated with Ctrl-D. When you receive such a *`message`*, you see:

`Broadcast Message:`

on your terminal, followed by the text of the message.

This command is often used by the system administrator to tell everyone that the system will shut down shortly. There are no options for this command.

■ *See also* **`mesg`**, **`write`**.

wc

A command that counts all the characters, words, and lines in a file.

▶ Syntax

The syntax for **`wc`** is as follows:

`wc [`*`options`*`][`*`filename`*`]`

▶ Options and Arguments

If you don't specify *`filename`*, **`wc`** reads from the standard input instead. If you specify more than one file, **`wc`** displays totals for each file and a grand total from all the files in the group. The options for **`wc`** are listed in Table W.2. The default report is equivalent to specifying all the options at once.

Table W.2: Options to Use with wc

OPTION	DESCRIPTION
`-c`	Counts the bytes in the specified *`filename`*.
`-C`	Counts the characters in the specified *`filename`*.
`-l`	Counts the lines in the specified *`filename`*.
`-w`	Counts the words in the specified *`filename`*.

▶ **Examples**

The `wc` command is very useful in pipelines, as in the following sequence, which combines the `ls` command with `wc` to count the number of lines in the `ls` output—that is, the number of files in a directory:

```
ls | wc -l
```

▶ **Notes**

The `wc` command defines a word as any sequence of characters bounded by space, tab, or newline, or any combination of these elements.

Web browser

A World Wide Web client application that lets you look at hypertext documents and follow links to other HTML documents on the Web. When you find something that interests you as you browse through a hypertext document, you can click on that object, and the system automatically takes care of accessing the Internet host that holds the document you requested; you don't need to know the IP address, the name of the host system, or any other details.

The Mosaic program, often referred to as NCSA Mosaic, created by the National Center for Supercomputing Applications (NCSA), is an example of a popular Web browser.

■ *See also* **Lynx, Mosaic, URL.**

wedged

A slang expression for a frozen or hung terminal. Normal interaction with the terminal stops and can often be resumed only by killing and restarting the program.

what

■ *See* **SCCS.**

whatis

A command that gives a quick, one-line description of a Unix keyword summarizing the header line of the appropriate `man` page entry. The syntax is:

```
whatis command
```

where *`command`* represents the keyword you are interested in. The result is the same as using `man -f`.

■ *See also* **`apropos`.**

whence

A built-in Korn shell command that shows whether a command is a Unix command, a built-in shell command, a defined shell function name, or an alias. The syntax is:

```
whence [options] command
```

where *`command`* represents the keyword you are interested in. `whence` has two options, as shown in Table W.3.

■ *See also* **`type`, `which`.**

Table W.3: Options to Use with whence

OPTION	DESCRIPTION
`-p`	Searches for the pathname of *`command`*.
`-v`	Displays a long report; same as `type -v`.

W

whereis

A BSD command used to locate a program; when a copy of the program is found, **whereis** displays the complete pathname. Here's the syntax:

```
whereis program...
```

On some systems, the **-m** option displays the locations of the manual page files corresponding to the specified program name.

■ *See also* **find, whence, which.**

Whetstones

Pronounced "wet-stones." A benchmark program used to quantify and compare the performance of different computers when performing arithmetic or floating point operations. The program reports system performance in units called whetstones.

■ *See also* **Dhrystones, SPEC benchmarks.**

which

A command that locates a Unix command and displays its pathname; **which** cannot locate built-in shell commands. The syntax to use is:

```
which command
```

which returns the name of the file that would be executed if you ran *command* by searching your shell configuration file **.cshrc** for aliases and searching the **path** variable. This command has no options.

■ *See also* **type.**

while

A C shell programming construct used to set up a loop. The loop continues to run as long as the results are true (returns a zero value). When a false value is returned, the loop terminates. An example might look like this:

```
while condition
        commands
end
```

You can use **break** and **continue** to terminate or continue the loop.

■ *See also* **do, done, fi, for, if, shift, then, until.**

whitespace

A collective name used for groups of spaces, tabs, and newlines, those printable characters that only produce blank spaces.

who

A command used to list the names of all users currently logged in to the system.

▶ Syntax

The syntax for this command is:

```
who [option]filename
```

▶ Options and Arguments

With no options, **who** lists the names of the users currently logged on to the system. Some versions of **who**, including those from Solaris and the BSD, have no options, while versions from other sources have the options listed in Table W.4.

You can use an optional argument ***filename*** to supply additional information; the default is **/var/adm/utmp**.

▶ Examples

The **who** report on most systems includes the following fields:

- **NAME**: login name of the user
- **STATE**: state of the terminal (see **-T** in Table W.4)
- **LINE**: the device number
- **TIME**: date and time the user logged in
- **IDLE**: length of time since the terminal was last used. A period indicates it was used within the last

minute, and the word `old` indicates it has not been used for at least 24 hours.

- `PID`: process ID
- `COMMENTS`: any optional comments

See also **finger, ps, rwho, users, w, whoami, whodo.**

Table W.4: Options to Use with who

OPTION	DESCRIPTION
-a	Turns on all options except -T.
-b	Indicates when the system was last booted.
-d	Lists dead processes that have not been respawned by init.
-H	Adds the heading line to the report.
-l	Lists just the unused terminals where no one is logged in.
-p	Lists the active processes started by init.
-r	Displays the current run level of init.
-q	Displays only a space-separated list of usernames and a count of users.
-s	Displays only the name, terminal, and login time for each user.
-t	Indicates when the system clock was last changed.
-T	Displays the terminal state as writable (+), not writable (–), or unknown (?).
-u	Lists only the current users.
am i	Displays the username of the person invoking who.

whoami

A command that displays your login name.

See also **finger, ps, rwho, users, w, who.**

whodo

An SCO command that formats `who` and `ps` command output to show you who is doing what, where.

See also **finger, ps, rwho, users, w, who, whoami.**

whois

A TCP/IP command that searches an Internet directory for the person, login, or organization specified on the command line. The syntax is:

```
whois [option]name
```

The single option, `-h` *`host name`*, limits the search to the specified *`host name`*.

See also **finger, who.**

widget

A high-level programming element that is in the X Window system and is used by programmers to create the windows, buttons, scrollbars, and pull-down menus that form the user interface.

widget library

A library of programming elements in the X Window environment, used by programmers to create larger pieces of the user interface, including windows, buttons, scrollbars, and pull-down menus.

wildcard

A character appearing in a filename that stands for a set of possible characters. Sometimes it is written as *wild card* and is also known as a *metacharacter*. In filenames, a question mark (?) stands for any single character, while an asterisk (*) stands for any sequence of zero or more characters. You can also use square brackets to

match any characters listed in the brackets; for example, `a[ab]` matches `aa` or `ab`.

Wildcards do not match files whose names begin with a dot to prevent you from deleting these important files by accident.

See also **filename completion, filename substitution, globbing.**

window

In a graphical user interface, a rectangular portion of the screen that acts as a viewing area for an application program.

Windows can be tiled (arranged side-by-side) or cascaded (overlapping, with each title bar visible) and can be individually moved and sized on the screen. Some programs can open multiple document windows inside their application window to display several different data files at the same time.

`window`

A BSD command that implements a windowed environment on an ASCII terminal. When `window` starts running, it executes the commands contained in the `.windowrc` file in your home directory. If this file doesn't exist, two equally sized windows are created by default. `window` supports up to nine different windows, but only one window at a time can receive input from the keyboard.

See also **X Window.**

window manager

An X Window program that controls how windows appear on the screen and how you interact with them, including mechanisms for creating and destroying windows, moving windows around the screen, and changing their appearance. Several different window managers are in common use, including `twm`, `mwm`, and `olwm`. Check the USENET newsgroup `comp.windows.x` for more on window managers.

See also **Motif, Open Look.**

`wksh`

A special version of the Korn shell that includes X Window system extensions and is used to provide an X Window interface for applications developed for the Korn shell.

workflow software

Software that allows users to move and manage information among themselves, combining the functions of e-mail, imaging, and document management.

A document moves through various stages of processing as it is edited, signed, or validated by the various members of the workgroup. Each stage is orchestrated and validated by the workflow software.

See also **groupware.**

workgroup

A group of individuals who work together and share the same files and databases over a local area network (LAN). Special software, such as Lotus Notes, coordinates the workgroup and allows users to edit and exchange files and update databases as a group.

See also **workflow software.**

working directory

Jargon for the current working directory, also known as the *current directory.*

workstation

A small, high-performance computer optimized for graphics applications, such as computer aided design (CAD), computer aided engineering (CAE), or scientific applications. A workstation is typically designed to fit on a desk and be used by one person.

World Wide Web

Abbreviated WWW, W3, or simply the Web. A huge collection of hypertext pages on the Internet.

World Wide Web concepts were developed in Switzerland by the European Laboratory for Particle Physics (known as CERN), but the Web is not just a tool for scientists; it is one of the most flexible and exciting tools in existence for surfing the Internet.

Hypertext links connect pieces of information (text, graphics, audio, or video) in separate HTML pages located at the same or different Internet sites, and you explore these pages and links using a Web browser such as NCSA Mosaic.

You can also access a WWW resource directly if you specify the appropriate URL (Uniform Resource Locator). World Wide Web traffic is growing faster than most other Internet services, and the reason for this becomes obvious once you try a capable Web browser; it is very easy to access World Wide Web information.

■ *See also* **home page.**

`write`

A command that opens an interactive communications session with another user. The syntax for the `write` command is as follows:

```
write user tty
```

where *`user`* is the login name of the person you want to talk to and *`tty`* is an optional argument to resolve any ambiguity if the person is logged in to more than one terminal.

When you use `write`, a message appears on the specified *`user`* terminal, telling the user that you are about to send a message. Type the text of your message, and then press Ctrl-D when you are finished to terminate the `write` command. You can use an exclamation mark (`!`) followed by a command in the middle of a `write` session to execute a shell command; the other user does not see the exclamation mark, the command, or the output from the command.

■ *See also* **`mail`, `mailx`, `mesg`, `talk`, `wall`.**

write permission

Permission for your programs to write data to a certain file or to create files in a directory.

■ *See also* **execute permission, file permissions.**

WWB

Abbreviation for Writer's Workbench, a set of writers' tools capable of reviewing documents and suggesting grammatical, spelling, and other changes, created by Lorinda Cherry and released by AT&T.

WWW

■ *See* **World Wide Web.**

xargs

A command that lets you pass a long list of arguments to a command, often a list of filenames passed by a pipe.

▶ Syntax

The syntax to use with **xargs** is as follows:

```
xargs [options][command]
```

▶ Options and Arguments

xargs repeatedly invokes *command* using arguments read from the standard input as command-line arguments until the standard input is exhausted. The *command* must not read from the standard input, and if no *command* is specified, it defaults to the **echo** command. The options you can use with **xargs** are listed in Table X.1.

xbench

A public domain X Window benchmark program that runs approximately 40 individual tests consisting of different X operations. The results of these tests are combined into a single measurement of the performance of your system called an *Xstone*; the higher the number, the faster your system. As with many benchmark programs, the tests may not give an accurate representation of actual performance when running your mix of applications.

■ *See also* **Dhrystones, Whetstones, x11perf.**

xbiff

An X Window version of the **biff** program; **xbiff** lets you know when the mail has arrived. **xbiff** is a picture of a mailbox in a small window on your screen; when the flag on the mailbox is up, you have mail. When the flag is down, you are up-to-date on reading your mail.

■ *See also* **biff, mail, mailx, X client, xmh.**

X

Table X.1: Options to Use with xargs

OPTION	DESCRIPTION
-e*string*	Stops passing arguments when *string* is encountered; the default is the underscore character(_).
-i	Passes arguments to *command*, replacing any curly braces on the command line with the current line of input.
-l*n*	Executes *command* for *n* lines of input.
-n*n*	Calls *command* with up to *n* arguments.
-s*size*	Calls *command*, limiting the length of the command line to *size* characters.
-t	Enables trace mode, and echoes each *command* before it is executed.
-x	Terminates if the argument list is longer than the -s option allows.

xcalc

An X Window version of a scientific calculator operated by using a mouse. xcalc can emulate a Texas Instruments TI-30 or a Hewlett-Packard 10C. To run the TI calculator in the background, enter:

```
xcalc &
```

To use the HP 10C, enter:

```
xcalc -rpn &
```

■ *See also* **bc, dc, X client.**

X client

An X Window program, an application such as a spreadsheet or graphics program, that uses an X server to act as its interface with a terminal.

X is not limited to one server and one client, and many combinations are possible. Several clients may interact with a single server when several different applications display on the same terminal, or a single client can communicate with several servers and display the same information on several different terminals.

The command-line options for an X client can be long and complex. A – usually turns an option on, while a + turns an option off—just the opposite of what you might expect. You can also abbreviate an option to its shortest unambiguous form, so you can use -bg rather than -background or -fn rather than -font. Table X.2 lists the most commonly used X client command-line options; most of these options define characteristics of the window in which the application runs and can be used with most X programs. Other options may be available on your system; see your documentation for details.

Many common Unix programs are available in X versions; there are X-based troff and TEX viewers, X-based editors and debuggers, X-based Internet-access programs, including xgopher, xarchie, and xmosaic, and even X-based plotting and display programs. See the FAQ in the USENET newsgroup comp.windows.x for more details.

■ *See also* **X server.**

xclock

An X program that displays a clock on your terminal. You can use the command-line options detailed in Table X.3 to configure the clock display to your liking.

A variation of xclock, called oclock, displays a round clock face instead of the rectangular face used by xclock.

■ *See also* **X client.**

Table X.2: Common X Client Command-Line Options	
OPTION	DESCRIPTION
-bd *color*	Specifies *color* as the window border color.
-bg *color*	Specifies *color* as the window background color.
-bw *width*	Specifies a window border of *width* pixels.
-e *program*	Executes *program*, and uses *program* as the window title, unless you also use the -title option.
-fg *color*	Specifies *color* as the window foreground color.
-fn *font*	Specifies the name of the fixed-width font to use.
-help	Displays a list of command options.
-rv	Simulates reverse video by swapping the foreground and background colors. Use +rv to prevent this swapping when reverse video is set as the default.
-title *string*	Specifies *string* as the title of the window if the window manager requests a title.

Table X.3: Options to Use with xclock	
OPTION	DESCRIPTION
-analog	Displays an ordinary 12-hour clock face, the default.
-chime	Chimes once on the half hour and twice on the hour; a good way to annoy your coworkers.
-digital	Displays a 24-hour digital clock.
-hd *color*	Specifies *color* as the color of the hands.
-hl *color*	Specifies *color* as the color of the edges of the hands.
-padding *n*	Specifies *n* pixels of space around the clock; the defaults are 8 for an analog clock and 10 for a digital clock.
-update *n*	Specifies that the clock be updated every *n* seconds; the default is 60. Any value of less than 60 adds a second hand to the analog clock, and the clock is updated every second.

X

xcolors

A X program that displays a color chart so you can see what the different named colors actually look like.

■ *See also* **X client.**

X Consortium

A group of vendors that develops and maintains products based on the X Window specifications. The consortium was originally formed in 1988 at MIT by Apple, AT&T, DEC, Hewlett-Packard, and Sun. In 1993, the X Consortium became an independent, nonprofit organization.

.Xdefaults

An X Window configuration file in your home directory that sets window-related values for all X clients.

`.Xdefaults` is a text file, and the syntax used to set a resource requires the name of a general resource such as `background` or a program name and a resource such as `xclock*background`. To establish a blue background for all instances of `xclock`, include the following in your `.Xdefaults` file:

```
xclock*background: blue
```

You can enter statements in any order, but it makes good sense to group like statements together; use an exclamation point to begin a comment line, and X Window ignores anything else on that same line. Use the `xrdb` program to display or edit the values in `.Xdefaults`.

■ *See also* **`X client`, `xinit`, `.xinitrc`, `xrdb`.**

xdm

The X Window display manager. A program that starts your X server and opens a window that you can use to log in to the system. `xdm` then starts `xterm`, a shell script, or an application that you specify. When you finish and log out, `xdm` resets the server and displays the login window once again, ready for the next user.

■ *See also* **X client, `xterm`.**

xdos

A version of the `dosemu` DOS emulation package specifically designed to be run in an X window. Although still under development, `xdos` is available as a part of the Linux package, and you can get it by anonymous `ftp` to `unix.hensa.ac.uk` in `/pub/tggdrasil/usr/X386/bin/xdos`.

■ *See also* **Linux.**

xdpr

An X Window program that captures and prints a standard screen dump.

■ *See also* **X client, xwd.**

x11perf

An MIT X Window benchmark program that tests over 150 different aspects of an X server operation. The results of these tests are not combined into a single measurement of system performance but are listed so you can make your own judgment for your own particular application mix. The `x11perfcomp` program takes output from `x11perf` and presents it in tabular form.

■ *See also* **Dhrystones, Whetstones, `xbench`.**

X11R3

Abbreviation for the X 11 Release 3 specification for the X Window system.

X11R4

Abbreviation for the X 11 Release 4 specification for the X Window system.

X11R5

Abbreviation for the 1991 X 11 Release 5 specification for the X Window system. This release of the specification added the ability to support scalable fonts, certain international symbols, as well as 2D and 3D graphics.

X11R6

Abbreviation for the 1994 X 11 Release 6 specification for the X Window system, which added an object-oriented interface, improved 3D graphics, servers capable of performing multiple tasks, screen savers, and improved performance over a dial-up modem.

XENIX

A version of Unix developed from Unix Version 7 as a joint venture between Microsoft and SCO and released in 1980. XENIX was intended to support commercial applications on the IBM PC (versions were also developed for the Motorola 68000 and Zilog Z8000), and for a while XENIX was the most successful Unix in terms of sheer numbers sold. Microsoft sold its interest in XENIX to SCO in 1987.

■ *See also* **Unix history.**

`xfd`

An X Window program that displays the characters in a specified font in their own window. The syntax is:

```
xfd -font font-name
```

where *`font-name`* indicates the name of the font you want to look at. The window contains the name of the font being displayed, a grid containing one character per cell, and three buttons: `Prev Page`, `Next Page`, and `quit`. The characters are displayed in increasing ASCII order from left to right and from top to bottom.

■ *See also* **X client, `xfontsel`, `xlsfonts`.**

X.500

A recommended standard, first released in 1988 and revised in 1992, for a global directory system for locating e-mail users, to be used with the X.400 e-mail services. X.500 is similar to a worldwide telephone book.

`xfontsel`

An X Window program that lists and displays the fonts available to the X server.

■ *See also* **X client, `xfd`, `xlsfonts`.**

X.400

A recommended standard, released in 1984 and revised in 1988, for public or private international e-mail distribution systems, defining how messages will be transferred across the network or between two or more connected heterogeneous networks. X.400 defines the components of an electronic address, as well as the details of the envelope surrounding the message and the rules to follow when converting between message types, such as text or fax.

■ *See also* **X.500.**

XFree86

A version of the X11R6 X Window system freely available for Intel-based Unix systems such as Linux and FreeBSD. You can get XFree86 using anonymous `ftp` to `sunsite.unc.edu` in the `/pub/Linux/X11` directory.

`xinit`

An X Window program used to manually start the X server and an initial X client program; if your system does not start X Window automatically, you can use `xinit`. `xinit` executes the configuration commands in the `.xinitrc` file; if this file does not exist, `xinit` opens an `xterm` window.

■ *See also* **X client, `.xinitrc`, X server.**

`.xinitrc`

An X Window initialization file executed by `xinit` when starting X. On SCO's Open Desktop, this file is called `.startxrc` instead.

xkill

An X Window program that forces the X server to close its connection to an X client. You can use `xkill` to get rid of a hung window, but the clients that it kills may not always terminate cleanly.

■ *See also* **kill, signals, X client, X server.**

xlax

An X Window program used by system administrators to execute the same commands on many different host computers, where each host has its own `xterm` window.

■ *See also* **X client, xterm.**

xlib

A library of over 300 C language routines that provide the basics of the X Window system. The library includes groups of functions for:

- Opening connections to servers
- Issuing X requests
- Receiving events and information from the server
- Performing X-related tasks
- Improving X performance

■ *See also* **library.**

xlock

An X Window program that locks your terminal and displays a screen saver to prevent anyone from using your system if you leave your office for a few moments and would rather not log off the system. The screen saver also prevents anyone from looking at your work while you are out of the office.

To regain control of your system, press a key or click the mouse; you will be prompted to enter your login password.

■ *See also* **X client, xset.**

xlsfonts

An X Window program that lists the available fonts. Specify the font you are interested in with:

```
xlsfonts font-name
```

where *`font-name`* is the name of the font you are interested in; if you omit *`font-name`*, information is displayed for all the fonts. You can also use the wildcard characters **?** and ***** to match characters.

■ *See also* **X client, xfd, xfontsel.**

xman

An X Window program that provides an X interface to the Unix `man` pages. When `xman` starts, the initial `Manual Browser` window displays three buttons: `Help`, `Quit`, and `Manual Page`. Click on the `Manual Page` or `Help` buttons to see a set of instructions on how to use `xman`. At the top of the window you see two menus: `Options` and `Sections`. `Options` determines what you do next, and `Sections` lets you choose between the major sections of the Unix online documentation. See the help screen for more details.

■ *See also* **apropos, cat, man, man pages, X client.**

xmh

An X Window program that offers an X interface to the public domain **MH** mail system. To use **xmh**, you must have **MH** installed on your system already.

Several other X-based mail programs are available, including **MMH**, a Motif interface to **MH**, `MuMail`, an X-based `elm`-like mailer, and Z-Mail, a commercially available product.

■ *See also* **MH, X client.**

Xmodem

A popular file transfer protocol available in many off-the-shelf and shareware communications packages. Xmodem was originally developed by Ward Christiansen for early PCs using the CP/M operating system. Xmodem divides the data for a transmission into blocks. Each block consists of the start-of-header character, a block number, 128 bytes of data, and a checksum. An acknowledgment byte is returned to the sender if the checksum calculation is identical to the sender's checksum; however, this requirement to acknowledge every transmitted block can lead to poor performance.

An extension to Xmodem, called Xmodem-CRC, adds a more stringent error-checking method by using a cyclical redundancy check (CRC) to detect transmission errors rather than Xmodem's simple additive checksum.

Another variation is Xmodem-1K, which transfers data in 1,024-byte blocks.

See also **Kermit, RZSZ, Ymodem, Zmodem.**

X/Open

An organization of European computer vendors formed in 1984 to formulate standards for open systems not bound by any specific computer architecture.

x protocol

A UUCP protocol, designed for use over X.25 connections. The `x` protocol is similar to the `g` protocol, except that there is no per-packet checksum and the packet size is larger at 512 rather than 64.

See also **`e` protocol, `f` protocol, `t` protocol.**

xrdb

An X Window program used to create and display the collection of global X resources available to all X clients using your X server. The syntax for `xrdb` is:

```
xrdb [options]filename
```

where *`filename`* specifies a file containing a set of resources that you want to load and use rather than the existing resources. The normal filename is `.Xdefaults`. The most important options for `xrdb` are listed in Table X.4; you can also use those options listed with the X client entry earlier in this book.

See also **`.Xdefaults`, `xinit`, `.xinitrc`, `xset`, `xsetroot`.**

Table X.4: Options to Use with `xrdb`

OPTION	DESCRIPTION
`-load`	Loads the global resource database from the standard input.
`-merge`	Merges the standard input into the global resource database.
`-query`	Displays the current contents of the global resource database on the standard output.
`-remove`	Empties the global resource database.

xrn

An X Window interface to the `rn` newsreader used to access USENET newsgroups.

See also **`rn`, X client.**

xsend

A set of BSD utilities that implements an encrypted e-mail system on top of the normal `mail` program. There are three parts to the system:

- `enroll` asks you to specify a password. You must use this password to access the other two parts of the system.
- `xsend` works just like `mail`, except that it does not send copies of your message to cc recipients.
- `xget` is used to read encrypted e-mail.

See also **Pretty Good Privacy.**

X server

An X Window display server. X is not limited to one server and one client, and many combinations are possible. Several clients may interact with a single server when several different applications display on the same terminal, or a single client can communicate with several servers and display the same information on several different terminals.

■ *See also* **X client.**

xset

An X Window program used to configure several user-selected items, including the pathname for font directories, keyboard adjustments, screen-saver parameters, and mouse speed settings. The command:

```
xset q
```

lists the current settings; note that the option is **q** and not **-q** as you might expect.

Any X settings that you change are lost or reset to their default values when you log off unless you add them to the **.xinitrc** file in your home directory.

■ *See also* **set, X client, .xinitrc, xsetroot.**

xsetroot

An X Window program used to change the appearance of the root window, the background behind all the other windows. See your system manual for information on the options available with this command.

■ *See also* **X client, xset.**

xstr

A BSD software development command that removes text strings from a program and replaces them with references to a strings database.

xterm

An X Window command that opens a text-based terminal emulation window on a graphics terminal. **xterm** emulates a VT100 and a Tektronics 4015 graphics terminal; you are unlikely to have either of these terminals, but the purpose of these emulations is to provide a consistent interface.

The name of the X terminal emulator may vary depending on the version of Unix you use. In the SCO Open Desktop, **xterm** is known as **scoterm**, and in Hewlett-Packard systems as **hpterm**; in Sun systems, you find **cmdterm** and **shelltool** in addition to **xterm**, and in UnixWare, you find a **Terminal** window.

Because **xterm** acts just like a real terminal running your shell, you can still run all the old familiar character-based commands and utilities, such as **ls**, **pwd**, even **vi**, all without leaving X. Running these character-based applications with **xterm** gives you several other advantages too, including:

- You can cut and paste between **xterm** and other X windows, giving a degree of communications between the older programs and your X clients.
- You can customize your keyboard and map function keys separately for each window.
- You can scroll text output or log your session to a file.
- You can connect each **xterm** window to a different host computer so you can perform work on several different computers, all from the same physical terminal.
- You can open multiple terminals in different windows and run several simultaneous copies of the same program.
- By using **telnet** from an **xterm** window, you can run applications on computers that do not have X Window support.

You can activate the **xterm** menus by holding down the Ctrl key and using the mouse as follows:

- Ctrl and clicking the left mouse button opens the **xterm** menu, which contains selections you can use to start logging and to send signals of various kinds to the current foreground process.

- Ctrl and clicking the middle mouse button opens a menu containing options to set the various terminal modes. On some systems with a two-button mouse, you have to press both buttons simultaneously to simulate this option.
- Ctrl and clicking the right mouse button may open a menu containing font selections; on some systems, this combination does nothing.

The main command-line options you can use with `xterm` are listed in Table X.5. You can also use those options listed in Table X.2.

See also **virtual terminal, X client, `xlax`.**

X terminal

A high-quality graphics terminal with a large amount of memory, designed for use with the X Window system. X terminals usually contain X server software in read-only memory (ROM).

xtod

A command that converts Unix text files into DOS format. The syntax is:

```
xtod filename > outputfile
```

where *`filename`* is the name of the Unix file you want to convert, and *`outputfile`* is the name you want to give to the DOS file after the conversion.

Unix uses the newline character to indicate the end of a line, while DOS uses two characters: a carriage return and a linefeed. DOS also uses Ctrl-Z as an end-of-file marker. `xtod` adds an extra carriage return to the end of each line, and Ctrl-Z to the end of the file. You cannot use `xtod` on binary files.

See also **DOS commands, `dtox`.**

xtract

An SCO command that extracts one file from a `cpio` archive. The syntax is:

```
xtract options filename
➥ archive
```

where *`options`* are `cpio` options, and *`filename`* defines the name of the file that you want to extract from the *`archive`*. The extraction is actually done using `cpio -iv`.

See also **`cpio`.**

xwd

An X Window program that writes a copy of the screen to a file and then uses the `xwud` program to display or print the image.

See also **X client, `xdpr`.**

Table X.5: Options to Use with `xterm`

OPTION	DESCRIPTION
`-j or +j`	Turns jump scrolling on or off, which makes `xterm` much faster when scanning long files; also called *speed scrolling.*
`-l`	Sends `xterm` input and output to the default log file `XtermLog.`*`n`*, where *`n`* is a five-digit number that represents the process ID number.
`-sb` or `+sb`	Turns the scroll bars on or off, and saves text that rolls off the top of the screen in a buffer so you can look at it later.
`-sl` *`n`*	Specifies the number of lines in the text buffer.

X Window

A windowing system originally developed at MIT and now jointly owned and distributed by the nonprofit X Consortium.

X is a windowing system that allows multiple resizable windows so that you can have many applications displayed on your screen at the same time. Unlike most windowing systems that have a specific built-in user interface, X is a foundation upon which you can construct almost any style of user interface. The unique feature of X is that it is based on a network protocol rather than the more usual programming procedure calls.

The X system consists of three main parts:

- The X server software, which controls your display, keyboard, and mouse. It accepts requests sent across the communications link from client application programs to open a window on the screen, change the size or position of a window, and display text and draw graphics in these windows. The server sends back events to the clients, telling them about keyboard or mouse input.
- The X client software or application programs, which are completely separate from the server. X is not limited to one server and one client; many combinations are possible.
- A communications link that connects the client and the server. This link can be implemented in one of two ways, either as an interprocess communications mechanism such as shared memory, when both client and server are running on the same computer, or over a network, when client and server are running on different computers.

This definition separates the X client software from the X server to the extent that they can run on hardware from different vendors

The protocol is the real definition of X Window, and it defines four types of messages that can be transferred over the communications link. Requests are sent from the client to the server, and replies, events, and error messages are sent from the server to the client. The X Window system is complex enough so that whole books are devoted to it; one publisher in particular, O'Reilly & Associates, has produced a library of about twenty technical books in its X Window System series. Check out `http://www.ora.com` with your World Wide Web browser for details.

X Window versions of many popular programs are available; what usually happens is that the programmer indicates the X Window version by prefacing the old program name with an **`x`**, so **`biff`** becomes **`xbiff`**, **`man`** becomes **`xman`**, **`gopher`** becomes **`xgopher`**, and so on.

See also **Motif, Open Look, widgets, `window`, window manager, `.Xdefaults`, X client, X server, `xterm`.**

yacc

A program used to create a parser (a program that converts text files into something else) from a simple set of rules contained in a file. `yacc` reads in the set of rules or the language syntax from the file and outputs a C or Ratfor (a version of Fortran originally called rational Fortran) program to recognize that language. The name `yacc` is an acronym formed from yet another compiler compiler.

■ *See also* **`lex`**.

yellow pages

The original name for the Network Information Service (NIS).

yes

A BSD and SCO command that prints either the `y` character or a specified string, continuously. The syntax is:

```
yes [string]
```

This command is used in pipes to commands that prompt for input and require a `y` response. The `yes` command terminates when the command it pipes to itself terminates.

Ymodem

A popular file transfer protocol available in many off-the-shelf and shareware communications packages.

Ymodem, a variation of the Xmodem protocol, divides the data for the transmission into blocks; each block consists of the start-of-header character, a block number, 1 KB of data, and a checksum. Ymodem's larger data block means less overhead for error control when compared with Xmodem, but if the block has to be retransmitted because the protocol detects an error, there is more data to resend. Ymodem also incorporates the ability to send multiple files in the same session and to abort file transfer during the transmission.

■ *See also* **Kermit, Zmodem.**

Y

yppasswd

An NIS command used to change your NIS password. When you type this command, you are prompted first for your current NIS password, then for your new NIS password.

See also **passwd**.

yyfix

A BSD command used to extract tables from **yacc**-generated files.

See also **yacc**.

zcat

A command that uncompresses one or more compressed files to the standard output leaving the compressed files unchanged. The syntax is:

```
zcat filename...
```

The `zcat` command has no options.

■ *See also* **compact, compress, pack, pcat, uncompact, uncompress, unpack.**

zcmp

A BSD command that invokes the **cmp** command on a compressed file. The syntax is:

```
zcmp [cmp-options]filename1
➥ [filename2]
```

where *cmp-options* are passed directly to the **cmp** command. See the **cmp** entry earlier in this book for details.

■ *See also* **cmp, diff, gzip, zmore, znew.**

zdiff

A BSD command that invokes the **diff** command on a compressed file. The syntax is:

```
zdiff [diff-options]filename1
➥ [filename2]
```

where *diff-options* are passed directly to the **diff** command. See the **diff** entry earlier in this book for details.

■ *See also* **cmp, diff, gzip, zmore, znew.**

zero-length file

A file that has no contents but exists as a standard file in the filesystem.

zero or more

A term that indicates you can use one or more of a specific item, or you can use none and omit the item entirely.

zforce

A BSD command that forces a `.gz` filename extension on all `gzip` files so that `gzip` will not compress them twice. On systems with a 14-character limitation on filenames, you may find that a long filename is truncated to make room for the `.gz` suffix.

■ *See also* **gzip, zcmp, zdiff, zgrep, zmore, znew.**

zgrep

A BSD version of `grep` for use on compressed files. Any command-line options you specify are passed directly to `grep`, and files you specify are automatically uncompressed and then passed to `grep`.

■ *See also* **gzip, zcmp, zdiff, zmore, znew.**

'zine

Also written as zine or e-zine. An underground electronic magazine or fanzine available on the Internet, distributed by e-mail, Gopher, or the World Wide Web.

Most 'zines are pretty ephemeral, and most are really not produced with profit in mind.

Zmodem

A popular file transfer protocol available in many off-the-shelf and shareware communications packages.

Zmodem is similar to Xmodem and Ymodem but is designed to handle larger data transfers with fewer errors. Zmodem also includes a feature called *checkpoint restart* that allows an interrupted transmission to resume at the point of interruption, rather than starting again at the beginning of the transmission. If you have a choice between several protocols, choose Zmodem if you can; it is fast as well as convenient.

■ *See also* **Kermit, RZSZ.**

zmore

A BSD filter command used to view compressed files. `zmore` works on files compressed by `gzip`, `pack`, or `compress`, as well as files that have not been compressed.

`zmore` works just like `more`, and displays:

```
– More –
```

at the bottom of the screen; press Return to display the next line, or press Space to display the next screenful.

■ *See also* **gzip, more.**

znew

A BSD command that recompresses files from `compress` format (with a `.Z` filename extension) to files in `gzip` format (with a `.gz` filename extension).

▶ Syntax

Here's the syntax:

```
znew [options]filename.Z...
```

▶ Options and Arguments

The options you can use with `znew` are listed in Table Z.1.

■ *See also* **compress, gzip, zforce.**

zombie

A dead process that has not yet been deleted from the process table. Most zombies disappear almost immediately, although from time to time you may find one that is impossible to delete without rebooting the system. Zombies do not consume any system resources, aside from their slot in the process table.

■ *See also* **orphan process, ps.**

Table Z.1: Options to Use with `znew`

OPTIONS	DESCRIPTION
`-9`	Uses the slowest compression method for the greatest degree of compression.
`-f`	Forces a recompression from `.Z` format to `.gz` format even if a file in `.gz` format already exists.
`-K`	Keeps the `.Z` format file when it is smaller than the `.gz` format file.
`-P`	Uses pipes during the conversion to conserve disk space.
`-t`	Tests the new files before deleting the originals.
`-v`	Displays the filename and percentage compression as each file is processed.

Zsh

A replacement for the Bourne shell and C shell developed by Paul Falstad; pronounced "zee-shell." Zsh is a relatively new shell, first released in 1990, and offers command-line editing among other advanced features. Zsh has developed something of a cult following among C programmers and advanced Unix users.

- *See also* **Bourne shell family, Unix shell.**

Appendix 1

THE unix DESK REFERENCE

Unix and DOS Command Comparison

If you have a background in working with DOS-based Intel computer systems, you know that there is quite a lot of similarity between DOS and Unix, and the reason for this is that many of DOS's best features came from Unix in the first place.

However, there are some major differences between DOS and Unix:

- In DOS, you can use your computer as soon as the operating system is loaded; in Unix, system security requires that you log on and provide an appropriate password before you can use the system.
- In DOS, usually just one shell, `COMMAND.COM`, is available, whereas in Unix, you may be able to choose between several shells and use the one you like best.
- Directory names in a DOS path are separated by `\`, while those in a Unix path are separated by `/`.
- Filenames in DOS are case insensitive, whereas in Unix they are always case sensitive.
- In a DOS filename, a period separates the name from the extension; the name can be up to eight characters and the extension can be up to three. Some DOS applications even require a filename to have a specific filename extension before the file can be loaded. In Unix, the period acts just like any other character in a filename and has no special meaning. So a Unix filename may contain no periods or it may contain several. A Unix filename can have as many characters as the system allows, up to 14 on some versions, and up to 256 on others.
- In DOS, each filesystem is located on its own separate hard disk, or hard disk partition, and is accessed using a pathname that includes a drive letter. In Unix, all filesystems are part of a single hierarchical structure that starts at the root (/) directory.
- DOS file attributes (archive, read-only, hidden, and system) are much simpler than the Unix file permissions (read, write, and execute for user, group, and everyone else).
- In a DOS text file, the end of a line is indicated by the two-character sequence of carriage return and

linefeed, while in Unix, the end of the line is indicated by the single newline character.

- DOS is a single-threaded operating system, while Unix is multithreaded.
- DOS is a single user system, and Unix is most often configured as a multiuser system.
- Certain versions of Unix are promoted as open systems with source code freely available; DOS is a proprietary system, and source code is never available.

Many systems, such as SCO, UnixWare, and Solaris, include a DOS emulator; a very good emulator called `dosemu` is available for Linux. Sometimes though, it may just be easier to reboot to DOS and use DOS commands and applications than to use the emulator running under Unix. Table 1.1 presents a list of DOS commands and their Unix equivalents.

Table 1.1: DOS Commands and Their Unix Equivalents

DOS COMMAND	UNIX COMMAND	DESCRIPTION
`attrib`	`chmod, ls -l`	Displays or changes file attributes or permissions.
`backup`	`cpio`, `tar`	Creates an archive.
`cd`	`cd, pwd`	Sets or displays the current directory.
`command`	`sh, csh, ksh, bash`	Starts a shell.
`comp`	`cmp`	Compares files byte-by-byte.
`copy`	`cp`, `cat`	Copies files.
`date`	`date`	Displays or sets the date.
`del`	`rm`	Deletes a file.
`dir`	`ls`	Lists the contents of a directory.
`edlin`	`ed`	Edits text files.
`exit`	`exit`	Exits from the command processor.
`fc`	`cmp`, `diff`	Compares files.
`find`	`grep`	Searches a set of files for a specific text string.
`md`	`mkdir`	Creates a new directory.
`more`	`more, less`	Displays a file screen-by-screen.
`path`	`set PATH`	Sets the search path for commands.
`print`	`lp, lpr`	Prints files.

Table 1.1: DOS Commands and Their Unix Equivalents (continued)		
DOS COMMAND	UNIX COMMAND	DESCRIPTION
`prompt`	`set prompt, set PS1`	Sets the command prompt.
`rem`	`echo`	Displays a comment.
`ren`	`mv`	Renames files.
`rd`	`rmdir, rm -r`	Deletes directories.
`set`	`set, setenv`	Sets or displays the contents of environment variables.
`sort`	`sort`	Sorts data in files.
`time`	`time`	Displays or sets the time.
`type`	`cat`	Displays the contents of a file.
`xcopy`	`cp, cpio -p`	Copies files and subdirectories.

ASCII Tables

This appendix presents the standard and extended ASCII character sets in decimal, hexadecimal, and octal. Table 2.1 shows the first 32 ASCII characters (0–31), also known as the *control characters*.

Table 2.2 shows the 7-bit standard ASCII character set (comprising characters 0–127), which is implemented on all computers that use ASCII.

Table 2.3 shows characters 128–255 of the 8-bit IBM extended ASCII character set, which is usually implemented as the default DOS character set.

Table 2.1: ASCII Control Characters				
DECIMAL	HEXADECIMAL	OCTAL	CHARACTER	CONTROL CHARACTER
0	00	000	NUL (Null)	Ctrl-@
1	01	001	SOH (Start of heading)	Ctrl-A
2	02	002	STX (Start of text)	Ctrl-B
3	03	003	ETX (End of text)	Ctrl-C
4	04	004	EOT (End of transmission)	Ctrl-D
5	05	005	ENQ (Enquire)	Ctrl-E
6	06	006	ACK (Acknowledge)	Ctrl-F
7	07	007	BEL (Bell)	Ctrl-G
8	08	010	BS (Backspace)	Ctrl-H
9	09	011	HT (Horizontal tab)	Ctrl-I
10	0A	012	LF (Linefeed)	Ctrl-J
11	0B	013	VT (Vertical tab)	Ctrl-K
12	0C	014	FF (Form feed)	Ctrl-L
13	0D	015	CR (Carriage return)	Ctrl-M
14	0E	016	SO (Shift out)	Ctrl-N
15	0F	017	SI (Shift in)	Ctrl-O
16	10	020	DLE (Data link escape)	Ctrl-P
17	11	021	DC1 (Device control 1)	Ctrl-Q
18	12	022	DC2 (Device control 2)	Ctrl-R
19	13	023	DC3 (Device control 3)	Ctrl-S
20	14	024	DC4 (Device control 4)	Ctrl-T
21	15	025	NAK (Negative acknowledgment)	Ctrl-U
22	16	026	SYN (Synchronous idle)	Ctrl-V
23	17	027	ETB (End transmission block)	Ctrl-W
24	18	030	CAN (Cancel)	Ctrl-X
25	19	031	EM (End of medium)	Ctrl-Y

Table 2.1: ASCII Control Characters (continued)				
DECIMAL	HEXADECIMAL	OCTAL	CHARACTER	CONTROL CHARACTER
26	1A	032	SUB (Substitute)	Ctrl-Z
27	1B	033	ESC (Escape)	Ctrl-[
28	1C	034	FS (File separator)	Ctrl-/
29	1D	035	GS (Group separator)	Ctrl-]
30	1E	036	RS (Record separator)	Ctrl-^
31	1F	037	US (Unit separator)	Ctrl-_

Table 2.2: Standard Seven-Bit ASCII Character Set			
DECIMAL	HEXADECIMAL	OCTAL	CHARACTER
32	20	040	space
33	21	041	!
34	22	042	"
35	23	043	#
36	24	044	$
37	25	045	%
38	26	046	&
39	27	047	'
40	28	050	(
41	29	051	)
42	2A	052	*
43	2B	053	+
44	2C	054	,
45	2D	055	-
46	2E	056	.
47	2F	057	/
48	30	060	0

Table 2.2: Standard Seven-Bit ASCII Character Set (continued)

DECIMAL	HEXADECIMAL	OCTAL	CHARACTER
49	31	061	1
50	32	062	2
51	33	063	3
52	34	064	4
53	35	065	5
54	36	066	6
55	37	067	7
56	38	070	8
57	39	071	9
58	3A	072	:
59	3B	073	;
60	3C	074	<
61	3D	075	=
62	3E	076	>
63	3F	077	?
64	40	100	@
65	41	101	A
66	42	102	B
67	43	103	C
68	44	104	D
69	45	105	E
70	46	106	F
71	47	107	G
72	48	110	H
73	49	111	I
74	4A	112	J
75	4B	113	K

Table 2.2: Standard Seven-Bit ASCII Character Set (continued)			
DECIMAL	HEXADECIMAL	OCTAL	CHARACTER
76	4C	114	L
77	4D	115	M
78	4E	116	N
79	4F	117	O
80	50	120	P
81	51	121	Q
82	52	122	R
83	53	123	S
84	54	124	T
85	55	125	U
86	56	126	V
87	57	127	W
88	58	130	X
89	59	131	Y
90	5A	132	Z
91	5B	133	[
92	5C	134	\
93	5D	135	]
94	5E	136	^
95	5F	137	_
96	60	140	`
97	61	141	a
98	62	142	b
99	63	143	c
100	64	144	d
101	65	145	e
102	66	146	f

Table 2.2: Standard Seven-Bit ASCII Character Set (continued)			
DECIMAL	HEXADECIMAL	OCTAL	CHARACTER
103	67	147	g
104	68	150	h
105	69	151	i
106	6A	152	j
107	6B	153	k
108	6C	154	l
109	6D	155	m
110	6E	156	n
111	6F	157	o
112	70	160	p
113	71	161	q
114	72	162	r
115	73	163	s
116	74	164	t
117	75	165	u
118	76	166	v
119	77	167	w
120	78	170	x
121	79	171	y
122	7A	172	z
123	7B	173	{
124	7C	174	|
125	7D	175	}
126	7E	176	~
127	7F	177	DEL

Table 2.3: IBM Extended ASCII Character Set			
DECIMAL	HEXADECIMAL	OCTAL	CHARACTER
128	80	200	Ç
129	81	201	ü
130	82	202	é
131	83	203	â
132	84	204	ä
133	85	205	à
134	86	206	å
135	87	207	ç
136	88	210	ê
137	89	211	ë
138	8A	212	è
139	8B	213	ï
140	8C	214	î
141	8D	215	ì
142	8E	216	Ä
143	8F	217	Å
144	90	220	É
145	91	221	æ
146	92	222	Æ
147	93	223	ô
148	94	224	ö
149	95	225	ò
150	96	226	û
151	97	227	ù
152	98	230	ÿ
153	99	231	Ö
154	9A	232	Ü

Table 2.3: IBM Extended ASCII Character Set (continued)			
DECIMAL	HEXADECIMAL	OCTAL	CHARACTER
155	9B	233	¢
156	9C	234	£
157	9D	235	¥
158	9E	236	₧
159	9F	237	ƒ
160	A0	240	á
161	A1	241	í
162	A2	242	ó
163	A3	243	ú
164	A4	244	ñ
165	A5	245	Ñ
166	A6	246	ª
167	A7	247	º
168	A8	250	¿
169	A9	251	⌐
170	AA	252	¬
171	AB	253	½
172	AC	254	¼
173	AD	255	¡
174	AE	256	«
175	AF	257	»
176	B0	260	░
177	B1	261	▒
178	B2	262	▓
179	B3	263	│
180	B4	264	┤
181	B5	265	╡

Table 2.3: IBM Extended ASCII Character Set (continued)			
DECIMAL	HEXADECIMAL	OCTAL	CHARACTER
182	B6	266	╢
183	B7	267	╖
184	B8	270	╕
185	B9	271	╣
186	BA	272	║
187	BB	273	╗
188	BC	274	╝
189	BD	275	╜
190	BE	276	╛
191	BF	277	┐
192	C0	300	└
193	C1	301	┴
194	C2	302	┬
195	C3	303	├
196	C4	304	─
197	C5	305	┼
198	C6	306	╞
199	C7	307	╟
200	C8	310	╚
201	C9	311	╔
202	CA	312	╩
203	CB	313	╦
204	CC	314	╠
205	CD	315	═
206	CE	316	╬
207	CF	317	╧
208	D0	320	╨

Table 2.3: IBM Extended ASCII Character Set (continued)

DECIMAL	HEXADECIMAL	OCTAL	CHARACTER
209	D1	321	╤
210	D2	322	╥
211	D3	323	╙
212	D4	324	╘
213	D5	325	╒
214	D6	326	╓
215	D7	327	╫
216	D8	330	╪
217	D9	331	┘
218	DA	332	┌
219	DB	333	█
220	DC	334	▄
221	DD	335	▌
222	DE	336	▐
223	DF	337	▀
224	E0	340	∝
225	E1	341	β
226	E2	342	Γ
227	E3	343	π
228	E4	344	Σ
229	E5	345	σ
230	E6	346	μ
231	E7	347	τ
232	E8	350	Φ
233	E9	351	Θ
234	EA	352	Ω
235	EB	353	δ

Table 2.3: IBM Extended ASCII Character Set (continued)			
DECIMAL	HEXADECIMAL	OCTAL	CHARACTER
236	EC	354	∞
237	ED	355	ϕ
238	EE	356	ε
239	EF	357	∩
240	F0	360	≡
241	F1	361	±
242	F2	362	≥
243	F3	363	≤
244	F4	364	⌠
245	F5	365	⌡
246	F6	366	÷
247	F7	367	≈
248	F8	370	°
249	F9	371	•
250	FA	372	•
251	FB	373	√
252	FC	374	η
253	FD	375	²
254	FE	376	■
255	FF	377	

The newest version of the all-time classic.
Second Edition
Stan Kelly-Bootle
Understanding
UNIX
An Updated and Comprehensive Edition Covering All Versions, Including System V Version 4.2
Written by an Internationally Renowned UNIX Expert
SYBEX

New 4th Edition—Over 150,000 in Print!

NOW AVAILABLE WHEREVER COMPUTER BOOKS ARE SOLD.

GURU MARK MINASI WILL BRING YOUR PC BACK FROM THE DEAD.

Whatever your PC's age, this comprehensive book will help you decide how and when to upgrade, how to keep your computer trouble-free, and how to improve its performance. The book's CD contains hard disk utilities and more than 600 megabytes of hands-on, step-by-step instructional video from Mark Minasi's renowned seminars!

1,296 pages
ISBN 1660-4

SYBEX Inc. • 2021 Challenger Drive • Alameda, CA 94501 • 800-227-2346 • 510-523-8233

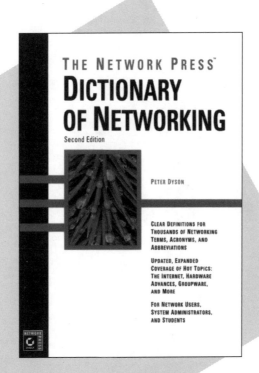